NANKING

Anatomy of an Atrocity

MASAHIRO YAMAMOTO

Westport, Connecticut
London

Library of Congress Cataloging-in-Publication Data

Yamamoto, Masahiro, 1959–
    Nanking : anatomy of an atrocity / Masahiro Yamamoto.
      p. cm.
    Includes bibliographical references and index.
    ISBN 0–275–96904–5 (alk. paper)
    1. Nanking Massacre, Nanjing, Jiangsu Sheng, China, 1937. 2. Nanjing (Jiangsu
Sheng, China)—History. I. Title.
DS796.N2.Y35   2000
951'.136—dc21   99–059655

British Library Cataloguing in Publication Data is available.

Library of Congress Catalog Card Number: 99–059655
ISBN: 0–275–96904–5

First published in 2000

Praeger Publishers, 88 Post Road West, Westport, CT 06881
An imprint of Greenwood Publishing Group, Inc.
www.praeger.com

Printed in the United States of America

The paper used in this book complies with the
Permanent Paper Standard issued by the National
Information Standards Organization (Z39.48–1984).

10 9 8 7 6 5 4 3 2 1

Contents

Contents vii

Illustrations

Acknowledgments

I am indebted to many people who have helped me complete this book in various ways.

Researchers and staff members of the National Archives and Records Administration in College Park, Maryland, were always very helpful in locating valuable primary source materials. I am especially grateful to Mr. John E. Taylor, who provided me with useful guidance in exploring the archival materials. I cannot exaggerate how the meeting with him during my first visit to the National Archives facilitated my subsequent research there. Although I am not one of the Japanese researchers who gave him an award recently for his outstanding assistance to Japanese scholars, I am no less indebted to him than they are.

My gratitude also goes to the archivists of the Japanese Defense Agency's Military History Division as well as the staff of the Japanese Diplomatic Archives. Among these archivists, Mr. Hara Takeshi of the Military History Division not only personally talked with me about some critical issues but also sent me some important materials.

I would also like to thank Mr. Hata Ikuhiko, a leading Japanese scholar in the field of Japan's modern history. Mr. Hata, an author of a book dealing with the same subject as this book, kindly sat with me to discuss some touchy topics related to the Rape of Nanking.

I must mention a whole community at Randolph-Macon College in Ashland, Virginia, where I now teach. The staff members of the library always handled my requests for interlibrary loans promptly. Although almost all the materials I could obtain through the interlibrary loan were secondary sources, their assistance undoubtedly helped me pave the way for further research. Staff members of the Information and Technology Service were also a valuable group of people in completing the last phase of this project. Without them, many computer-related problems might have ruined everything I had accumulated.

Although not academically, Mr. Noro Ichiro, who is now a part-time instructor in multiple Japanese institutions, supported me considerably both materially and psychologically. His generous offer to allow me to stay in his apartment room during my two-week research trip to Tokyo in 1996 alleviated my financial situation considerably. Also, my parents, Yamamoto Kazuo and Yamamoto Tsuyako, and my sister Yamamoto Sanae have always been continuous supporters.

I cannot exaggerate valuable suggestions, advice, and criticisms provided by faculty members of the University of Alabama, where I completed a basic framework of this book as my Ph.D. dissertation. Among them are dissertation committee members: Dr. Howard Jones, Dr. John F. Beeler, and Dr. George S. Williamson of the History Department as well as Dr. Donald M. Snow of the Political Science Department. Also, it was a pleasant surprise that occasionally some professors who were not dissertation committee members gave me relevant information. I am grateful to Dr. Maarten Ultee and Dr. Hugh Ragsdale for their occasional communications with me. Above all, what helped me most was the careful and thoughtful advising by Dr. Harold E. Selesky, who kindly supervised my research and writing as a chief adviser amid his busy schedule. I believe that his perspective in military history was one of the crucial elements that refined this book.

Although he did not advise me directly on the actual content of this book, Dr. John P. Mertz of North Carolina State University gave me useful suggestions and advice to familiarize me with the publication business in the United States. Dr. Mertz, whose specialty is Japanese literature and language, has been in touch with me since I came to the United States in 1988.

Last, but not least, I would like to thank the editing staff members of Praeger Publishers of the Greenwood Publishing Group, who painstakingly read my manuscript and made various suggestions to make it a publishable work. Above all, I truly appreciate the patience, kindness, and scholarly insight of Dr. Heather R. Staines and the careful editing work of Mr. Frank Saunders.

Without the assistance of all these people and others who asked me not to mention their names here for a certain reason, I could not have completed this work.

Abbreviations

CCAA	Central China Area Army
CDN	*Chicago Daily News*
CE	Court exhibit
DD	Defense document
DNSZ	*Documents of the Nanking Safety Zone* (Shanghai, China)
DSKS	Dai-10-gun Sakusen-shido ni Kansuru Sanko-shiryo [Reference Materials Concerning the Tenth Army's Operations]
GS	Gaiko Shiryokan [Diplomatic Record Office, Japan]
HP	*Jih-pen Ti-kuo Chu-i Ch'in-hua Tang-an Hsuan-pian* [Selected Archival Documents Relating to Japan's Imperialistic Aggression against China] (Peking, China)
ICNSZ	International Committee for the Nanking Safety Zone
IMTFE	International Military Tribunal for the Far East (in text) International Military Tribunal for the Far East: Proceedings 1946–1948 (in notes)
IPS	International Prosecution Section
KS	*Nankin Jiken: Kyoto Shidan Kankei Shiryoshu* [Rape of Nanking: Materials Relating to the Kyoto Division] (Tokyo, Japan)
KCCC	*K'ang-jih Chan-cheng Cheng-mian Chan-ch'ang* [Resistance War against Japan: Regular Warfare Front] (Chiangsu Province, China)
LC	Library of Congress
M976	Records of the Department of State Relating to Political Relations between China and Japan, 1930–1944, Record Group 49, M976
M1444	Correspondence of the Military Intelligence Division Relating to General, Political, Economic and Military Conditions in China 1918–1941, Record Group 164, M1444

M1513   The Military Intelligence Division Regional File Relating to China 1929–1944, Record Group, 165, M1513

M1613   Numerical Case Files Relating to Particular Incidents and Suspected War Criminals, International Prosecution Section, 1945–1947, Record Group 331, M1683

M1690   Numerical Evidentiary Documents Assembled as Evidence by the Prosecution for Use before the International Military Tribunal for the Far East 1945–1947, Record Group 331, M1690

MHD   Military History Division, Defense Agency, Japan

NA1   National Archives and Record Administration in Washington, D.C.

NA2   National Archives and Record Administration in College Park, MD

n.d.   No date

NDG   *Nankin Daigyakusatsu no Genba e* [Visit to Rape-of-Nanking Locations] (Tokyo, Japan)

NDK   *Nankin Daigyakusatsu no Kenkyu* [Study of the Rape of Nanking] (Tokyo, Japan)

NDKK   *Nankin Daigyakusatsu o Kirokushita Kogun Heishitachi* [Imperial Japanese Army's Soldiers Who Recorded the Rape of Nanking] (Tokyo, Japan)

NEM   *Nankin e no Michi* [Road to Nanking] (Tokyo, Japan)

NJK   *Nankin Jiken o Kangaeru* [Analyses of the Nanking Incident] (Tokyo, Japan)

n.p.   No place, no publisher

NP   *Yuan Kuo-min-tang Chiang-ling Chan-cheng K'ang-jih Chan- chen Ch'in-li-shih: Nanking Pao-wei-chan* [Personal Experiences of Former Nationalist Party Generals in Resistance War against Japan: Defense of Nanking] (Peking, China)

NS   *Nankin Senshi* [Nanking Campaign Chronology] (Tokyo, Japan)

NSS1   *Nankin Senshi Shiryo-shu* [Nanking Campaign Chronology Primary Source Collection], vol. 1 (Tokyo, Japan)

NSS2   *Nankin Senshi Shiryo-shu* [Nanking Campaign Chronology Primary Source Collection], vol. 2 (Tokyo, Japan)

NYT   *New York Times*

PNTJ   Papers of Nelson Trusler Johnson

POW   Prisoner of war

RG   Record Group

RMD   Rikushi Mitsu Dainikki [Army's Secret Diary about the China Campaign]

RNFH   *The Rape of Nanking: The Forgotten Holocaust of World War II* (New York)

SEF   Shanghai Expeditionary Force

SL   *Ch'in-hua Jih-chun Nanking Ta-t'u-sha Shih-liao* [Source Materials Re-
        lating to the Massacre Committed by the Japanese Troops in Nanking]
        (Chiangsu Province, China)

"SNS"   "Shogen ni yoru Nankin Senshi" [Nanking Campaign Chronology Based
        on Eyewitness Accounts], *Kaiko* April 1984–March 1985 (Tokyo, Japan)

TA   *Ch'in-hua Jih-chun Nanking Ta-t'u-sha Tang-an* [Archival Documents
        Relating to the Massacre Committed by the Japanese Troops in Nanking]
        (Chiangsu Province, China)

TWCT   *The Tokyo War Crimes Trial: The Complete Transcripts of the Proceed-
        ings of the International Military Tribunal for the Far East in Twenty-
        Two Volumes* (New York)

Introduction

The history of almost every country records some dishonorable events that peoples of other countries continue to condemn and the people of that country would like to forget or at least to justify. In particular, the 20th-century world has witnessed many atrocious incidents such as the mass murder of Armenians by the Turks during World War I, the Nazi persecution and attempted extermination of European Jewry prior to and during World War II, and the ethnic cleansing conducted by the Serbs and other ethnic groups of former Yugoslavia in the Balkans in the 1990s. Among these notorious historical events, the Rape of Nanking is exceptional because of the unusual degree of attention paid to it for an extraordinarily long time. Despite the time and energy of many people who have discussed this subject, however, there appears to be no consensus over such crucial questions as how and why the Rape of Nanking happened and how extensive the loss of human life was.

In the wake of the sixtieth anniversary of the incident in 1997, Princeton University hosted a commemorative event concerning the Rape of Nanking. In a document that described the event, one could find the following passage, which represents an orthodox view of the Rape of Nanking today: "Most experts agree that at least 300,000 Chinese died, and 20,000 women were raped. Some estimate the numbers to be much higher—340,000 and 80,000, respectively."[1] The reality is, however, that there is no agreement on these numbers. In the proposal of the same event, its organizers admit the existence of various opinions: "On one hand conservative Japanese histories de-emphasize or deny the atrocities of the Nanking Massacre, while on the other Chinese histories exaggerate Japanese excesses."[2] The second unique aspect is the high degree of emotion that has complicated the Rape of Nanking controversy. Princeton University defined the purpose of the commemorative events as "a much needed step in the long-stalled healing process," an apparent reference to the highly agitated words those with opposing views on the incident often exchange with each other. The healing process is, however, not an easy task because emotion inhibits the search for historical truth by creating a vicious cycle: attempts to investigate the subject by one group precipitate emotional counterarguments from other groups, resulting in more emotion and little additional clarity. Typically, despite what might seem to be a slightly pro-Chinese tone in Princeton University's events—notably a reference to the massacre of 300,000 Chinese as an opinion shared by "most experts"—one of the event organizers said that they had received many hostile reactions from people "unhappy with our [their] apparent 'pro-Japanese' slant."[3]

A glimpse into the way Japanese intellectuals and journalists have discussed the Rape of Nanking since the early 1970s also shows how difficult the "healing process" will be. Honda Katsuichi, a newspaper correspondent, and Hora Tomio, a university professor, were notable among those who represented the orthodox or traditionalist view, which a majority of scholars in the West shares today. Representing more or less the politically liberal side, they have argued for Japan's responsibility for the incident. Among those who have refuted the orthodox thesis and represented the revisionist opinion were Suzuki Akira, a journalist, and Tanaka Masaaki, who had been a secretary of Matsui Iwane, the Japanese army commander in Nanking. Speaking for the politically conservative side, they have questioned the traditionalist interpretations, especially the number of victims—300,000 people killed in six weeks. In the heated exchange of words over more than a decade, neither side showed the slightest sign of giving in to the other. Yet there was a positive aspect in this debate in Japan. Although each side has criticized the other in emotional and agitated ways, the recurring debates in Japan about the Rape of Nanking have at least stimulated the search for primary sources and refined the quality of scholars' publications. While the traditionalists no longer persist in asserting the figure of 300,000 dead, the revisionists have by now admitted that the Japanese did indeed commit atrocities in Nanking. Some Japanese writers today assume a middle position by adopting a part of both positions: they admit to the occurrence of atrocities by accepting the traditionalist position but refute the scale and nature of the atrocities in agreement with the revisionists.

This brief survey of the wide range of Japanese opinions about the Rape of Nanking actually serves to summarize how I have approached this issue throughout my life. My first experience with this topic was during elementary school in Japan. As a sensitive child, I was horrified to listen to the atrocity stories narrated by my sixth-grade teacher. For many years, I hardly doubted the accuracy of every detail: that the Japanese slaughtered innocent civilians indiscriminately; that two Japanese officers engaged in a killing competition for fun; and that the death toll reached almost or more than 300,000. I was thus a believer in the traditionalist theory until about twenty-two or twenty-three years of age.

When a controversy erupted in the early 1980s over the textbook description about the Rape of Nanking, initially I had nothing but contempt for the revisionist view. Then, I had a chance to read a book published about that time—the Japanese translation of *Japanese Terror in China* by H. J. Timperly, a British journalist who personally witnessed the atrocities. Before opening the book cover, I thought that I had another publication supporting the traditionalist view and expected to read many accounts of mass murder and other brutal acts. It was a book written by a national of a third country and seemed to be a credible primary source. By the time I finished reading it, however, I was stunned. Timperly, mostly by quoting from another source entitled *Documents of the Nanking Safety Zone*, enumerated over 400 cases of Japanese soldiers' misconduct in Nanking. I had, and still have today, a feeling that almost every one of these cases really happened and was truly revolting. Yet, I was also struck by a totally different picture of the Rape of Nanking that implicitly emerged from the descriptions in that book compared with what I had been taught in elementary school. Instead of ruthless and indiscriminate killing of civilians, Timperly told about Japanese soldiers wandering around the city without officers and committing scandalous, but not necessarily lethal, crimes. Instead of a mass slaughter of 300,000, the total death toll I could count in Timperly's book was less than fifty.

Thereafter, I started reading the revisionists' works, and at one point I converted more or less to the revisionist side. After more in-depth research using Japanese and English primary sources as well as some Chinese language materials, I shifted my position a little back toward the traditionalist side. At present, I do accept the savage and fiendish nature of Japanese atrocities in Nanking as a fact, but I reject the prevailing traditionalist interpretation of the incident because of some of its questionable theses as well as negative ramifications that are already obvious today and may become more serious in the future.

At present, those ramifications seem to be more potent outside Japan, notably in the United States. In contrast with the presence of opposing views in Japan, a vast majority in the United States has adopted the traditionalist interpretation of the incident. Recent publications such as Shi Young and James Yin, *The Rape of Nanking: An Undeniable History in Photographs*, and Iris Chang, *The Rape of Nanking: The Forgotten Holocaust of World War II*, strengthened that tendency. So far, an overwhelming majority reacted to these publications favorably, and few people have criticized them. This lack of criticism stands in stark contrast with the American reaction to other allegations of wartime atrocities. A notable case was their reaction to James Bacque's publications such as *Other Losses* and *Crimes and Mercies* in the late 1980s to the 1990s. In response to Bacque's contention in *Other Losses* that from 800,000 to nearly one million German prisoners of war perished in the Allies' camps after World War II, Stephen E. Ambrose and other reviewers questioned not only his theory but also his research methods. Bacque's next controversial work, *Crimes and Mercies*, which accused the Allies of having caused nine million German civilians to die in the aftermath of World War II, met a similar reaction. I share the opinion of these critics, and I do not lend too much credence to Bacque's works. In the same way, I do not give so much credit to recent publications dealing with the Rape of Nanking, unlike a majority of this country. Some may argue that it is ill advised to compare Bacque's monographs with the story of the Rape of Nanking. But one aspect worthy of investigation regarding the Rape of Nanking is the attitude of researchers, that is, whether Westerners who commented positively on these recent Rape of Nanking publications did so after they had subjected these books to the same scrutiny as Ambrose and others had done to Bacque's *Other Losses* and *Crimes and Mercies*. As I will elaborate later, one must answer to this question in the negative.[4]

The ways American researchers have approached the Rape of Nanking are seriously flawed, resulting in an incorrect analysis and conclusion. Consequently, many people in this country accept the conclusion of such a flawed research and analysis and develop their own ideas—some of them problematic—about the incident as well as about the Japanese in general. The most extreme example of how the unconditional acceptance of the traditionalist view unfolds is the following:

consider that the United States, on all fronts, lost 323,000 in the four years of World War II. Or that at Auschwitz the Nazis killed on average 350,000 every two months. The Japanese killed roughly the same number in a few months without the benefit of the technology of mass murder available to the Nazis and without the advantage of concentration camps. . . . What's more, the Japanese troops weren't "specialized": nothing comparable to the *Einsatzgruppen* existed in their military. These were the boys next door. . . . the Rape of Nanking reminds us how recently Japan emerged from its medieval age; a scant 140 years ago, less than 100 at the time of the Rape.[5]

One may argue that this is an opinion of an extremist—as I myself said—and that a majority of the American people does not share it. Yet I must say that this passage, however offensive and outrageous it may sound, is logically constructed. (There is, however, one obvious flaw: to claim that "Japan emerged from its medieval age" very recently does not make sense in explaining what is supposed to be an atrocity of unprecedented scale, which, according to the same reviewer, rivaled or even superseded the Nazi atrocities.) The writer of this passage is at least more realistic than some authors who insist on the death toll of 300,000 and demand that the Japanese government admit its legal responsibility for the atrocities and compensate the victims. If the death toll in Nanking had really been so high as to defy all historical conventional wisdom, one may accept the conclusion implicit in the previously quoted passage: the Japanese people themselves were—and maybe still are—extraordinary by nature. If the Japanese were that extraordinary, the Japanese would probably have to be quarantined internationally for re-education or reformation purposes before being held legally accountable for the atrocities. But few people advocate this. To pressure the Japanese to recognize their legal responsibility for their wartime conduct and to prove that Japan can afford it financially, such authors point to Japan's postwar economic success and prosperity—a fact that one cannot easily reconcile with the extraordinary negative character of the Japanese as an ethnic group.

As the passage suggests, the alleged death toll of the incident had a profound impact on the minds of people in this country. In the course of completing this work, which started as my doctoral dissertation, quite a few people told me that *how many* people were killed does not matter and that the mere fact of atrocities is the significant aspect. They are certainly correct from a humanitarian stand-point, and I have no hesitation in acknowledging the savage and cruel behavior exhibited by many Japanese soldiers in China. Yet the logic implicit in that passage, which is, most regrettably, likely to be influenced by a certain kind of prejudice, clearly demonstrates how essential the investigation into details—the numerical analysis, for example—is, not only historically but also in other ways. Historically, how many lost their lives in what circumstances is a question concerning the nature of the incident—whether it was a genocide-type atrocity or one caused by other factors. This question is closely connected with another: how and to what extent Japanese were responsible. At the same time, one can foresee a possible long-term ramification. Suffice it to say that the logic used in the above quoted article may easily be employed against other nationalities or ethnic minorities in the United States. In the future, the Chinese and Chinese Americans, who today seem to be quite satisfied with such manner of criticism against the Japanese, might face the same form of verbal attack in connection with China's alleged persecution of ethnic minorities, the Tibetans in particular. It is easy to imagine that quite a few Japanese, who have been under attack for the Rape of Nanking issues, will willingly join the ranks of accusers in that eventuality. Such a reciprocal expression and resulting escalation of inter-ethnic hatred will be the most undesirable consequence one may anticipate. Thus, what the Princeton University group defined as "healing process" may leave a serious trauma without sensitive considerations for the future.

Of course, the consideration of future ramifications must not be a justification for covering up the past. One must look at both the past and the future to address the questions and issues today. I hereby propose a guideline for any person who wants to investigate touchy historical issues like the Rape of Nanking. If his-torians start conducting research on such a topic by relying heavily on a sec-ondary source, they possibly follow the same path I followed—a traditionalist being converted to a revisionist, then stepping backward a little to the original stance—or completely the reverse—namely, a revisionist being turned into a traditionalist, and then returning a little to the revisionist side. To avoid such a pendulum-like swing, they have to pursue two tasks at the same time: history and historiography. In case of the Rape of Nanking, historical research should attempt to determine why, how, and to what extent the Japanese committed the alleged atrocities, while historiographical research investigates how accurately historians and journalists have studied the Rape of Nanking issues. Although it is inevitable that each researcher will reach a conclusion that is viewed by others as pro-Japanese or pro-Chinese, historiographical study can weed out the most egregious political and ideological motivation behind some secondary sources so that it does not subconsciously affect the way the researcher investigates what happened in Nanking. This book is an attempt to approach the various issues surrounding the incident commonly called the Rape of Nanking in such a manner. I suspect that a majority of American readers will disagree with the thesis of this book, which more or less contradicts the prevailing interpretation of the incident. Also, some may speculate that this work is analogous to the denial of the Jewish Holocaust, which has long been existent in the Western world. Yet I hope that readers will try first to grasp the logic and reasoning that will unfold in the following chapters, instead of speculating on my motive by looking at my nationality and last name. (One cautionary note: I am *not* related to the planner of the Pearl Harbor attack.) Careful readers will acknowledge that this is certainly "revisionism" but not "denial."

The arrangement of chapters in this book is chronological. Because publications about the Rape of Nanking, Japanese publications in particular, always touch on war crimes trials, the discussion of the war crimes trials must precede the analysis of the literature. In turn, the discussion of the war crimes trial would be impossible without first establishing the known facts about the incident itself. This book thus consists of two major parts: the first four chapters are historical and the remaining three historiographical. The first part will investigate the exact nature of atrocities; the second will analyze the mindsets of the people who have participated in the Rape of Nanking debate.

The historical analysis starts with a study of war atrocities in general to examine what has caused atrocities in the history of warfare. The first chapter places in context some patterns observable in war atrocities not only prior to Nanking but also at Nanking itself. Those readers who are interested only in the Rape of Nanking and who do not want to be bothered by a long prelude to the main topic may skip this chapter, but I would encourage them to read it, because it includes some information to facilitate understanding of the analysis in later chapters. The second chapter traces the events leading to the fall of Nanking in December 1937 to examine what factors helped set the stage for atrocities. The third and fourth chapters, the core of the book, are a qualitative and quantitative analysis of the Rape of Nanking that investigates numerous atrocity cases in minute detail. The third chapter concludes with the quantitative analysis of the estimated number of total victims, a subject that has been most controversial in the debate. The fourth chapter will contain qualitative descriptions of atrocities in comparison with historical cases discussed in the first chapter. The analyses in these four chapters will lead to the conclusion that the traditionalist interpretation of the Rape of Nanking—that the Japanese massacred 300,000 Chinese people deliberately and systematically—does not reflect the truth. Although a massacre on a large scale did happen, it was not a Nazi Holocaust-style indiscriminate slaughter. A close examination of reliable primary materials indicates that a large majority of victims were adult males whom the Japanese troops rounded up and subsequently executed on the pretext of clearing the city of former soldiers disguised in civilian clothes. Apart from such mass executions of soldiers and civilians misidentified as soldiers, individual Japanese soldiers committed numerous criminal acts. Yet, these were violent acts that the soldiers engaged in as individuals outside the supervision of the military command and did not result in a huge number of deaths.

The fifth chapter treats one of the most neglected aspects of the Rape of Nanking, that is, reaction to the event by various parties up to the start of war crimes trials after World War II. This chapter will reveal that the Western eye-witness accounts in the late 1930s described the atrocities in Nanking in the same way as I have done in Chapters 3 and 4, and that wartime propaganda during World War II drastically affected the depiction of the incident and transformed its image into a Nazi-like atrocity in both scale and nature. The war crimes trials, the International Military Tribunal for the Far East in particular, are the topic of the sixth chapter. This chapter discusses different perceptions, interpretations, and definitions of the Nanking atrocities in the minds of trial participants, not only as the crucial determinants of their opinions or judgments but also as the source of subsequent controversy. The last chapter will critically analyze modern interpretations of the Rape of Nanking. This chapter will begin with the survey of the Rape of Nanking controversy in Japan. Although the recent publications and a TV program on the History Channel claimed that there has been a deliberate cover-up of the Rape of Nanking in Japan, a mere glimpse into the Japanese research of this topic, as I will summarize, will be more than enough to prove that there was no cover-up, and that instead Japanese researchers have studied this incident much more intensively than those of any other countries.[6] This chapter will also touch on a recent tendency to establish a parallel between the Rape of Nanking and the Holocaust of European Jewry—a context in which recent popular books on the subject should be analyzed historiographically. Since the word *holocaust* is often used as a generic term to refer to atrocious incident or conduct, some people may claim that the use of this word does not necessarily mean the allusion to the Nazi Holocaust. Yet, the analysis of this last chapter will reveal that there have been obvious efforts to depict the Rape of Nanking as an Asian counterpart to the Nazi Holocaust. Finally a major theme of the last two chapters is an imbalance between the verdict and the sentence given to the Japanese commander in Nanking at the Tokyo War Crimes Trial—an imbalance that originated from the gap between the perception of the Rape of Nanking in the late 1930s and that of 1945 and which still affects the people who discuss the Rape of Nanking today.

The Wade-Giles system—the one in use when the Rape of Nanking happened—is the primary style of Chinese language transcription here, but some words such as Nanking that are more widely used than their Wade-Giles version are written in the Postal Atlas system. Also exempt from the Wade-Giles transcription are the titles of some English-language newspapers, magazines, and books published in mainland China and in the United States today. All Asian names are written in the Asian manner—that is, the surname first and given name next.

NOTES

1. Princeton University, *Nanking: Commemorating the 60th Anniversary of the Nanking Massacre*, main page, http://www.princeton.edu/~nanking/. Internet web page addresses cited in the notes are those at the time of the research and might be obsolete.

2. Ibid., "Proposal."

3. One of the organizers of Princeton University's Rape of Nanking sixtieth anniversary commemorative event to Masahiro Yamamoto, 14 October 1997, re: conference on Nanking Massacre, through e-mail.

4. Among critical commentary of Chang's book are Richard B. Finn, "The Real Numbers Are Bad Enough," *Washington Post*, 5 March 1998, p. A20; David M. Kennedy, "Horror," *Atlantic Monthly*, April 1998, pp. 110–16; Joshua Fogel's review on the *Journal of Asian Studies* (August 1998): pp. 818–20. For critical reviews of James Bacque, *Other Losses: An Investigation into the Mass Deaths of German Prisoners at the Hands of the French and Americans after World War II* (Toronto: Stoddart, 1989), see Jonathan Osmond's review in *International Affairs* (July 1991): p. 597; Michael Howard, "A Million Lost Germans," *Times Literary Supplement*, 14 September 1990, pp. 965–66; Stephen E. Ambrose, "Ike and Disappearing Atrocities," *New York Times Book Review*, 24 February 1991, pp. 1, 35–37; and John Keegan, "James Bacque and the 'Missing Million,' " *Times Literary Supplement*, 23 July 1993, p. 13. Maclean Hunter and David Stafford wrote critical reviews of James Bacque, *Crimes and Mercies: The Fate of German Civilians under Allied Occupation, 1944–1950* (Toronto: Little, Brown, 1997): MacLean Hunter, "Were the Allies Genocidal? Most Historians Dismiss Claims That 9.3 Million Germans Starved to Death," *MacLean's*, 3 November 1997, p. 74; David Stafford, "Case Not Proven," *Times Literary Supplement*, 10 July 1998, p. 29.

5. Russell Jenkins, "The Japanese Holocaust," *National Review*, 10 November 1997, p. 58.

6. "History Undercover: The Rape of Nanking" on the History Channel, 22 August 1999.

1

What Causes War Atrocities: A Historical Analysis

In 1946, the Chinese prosecutor for the International Military Tribunal for the Far East (IMTFE) charged that Japanese troops had committed atrocities at Nanking in 1937 "to crush forever all will to resist on the part of the Chinese people."[1] He thus implied that the Japanese army had sacked the city as part of a deliberate scheme to break the morale of the enemy. One, however, should not conclude that a desire to intimidate the opponent is the sole factor that motivates war atrocities. Attackers in many cases in history wanted to avoid massacre and plunder because they recognized the military necessity of securing supplies and maintaining discipline among soldiers. Moreover, some Westerners, at least initially, did not attribute the incident to a Japanese army policy of intimidation. A *New York Times* editorial, for example, described the news reports of atrocities at Nanking as "the stories of war hundreds of years ago . . . when . . . a conquered city with its helpless inhabitants should be given over for twenty-four hours to the unbridled lust of the victors."[2]

Since this editorial was based on the contemporary news coverage of the time, one may accept this view as a more accurate characterization of the event. Yet, it seems that neither interpretation derives from an in-depth examination of the incident. Although the *New York Times* editorial did make an analogy based on past history, it stopped short of studying the causes of atrocities. To understand the nature of the Nanking atrocities, it is necessary to trace the history of war atrocities and examine other similar cases to establish a range of possible causes that may contribute to their occurrence. Based on such an analysis, one can then better determine whether the incident was (1) truly an ancient- or medieval-type atrocity that happened in modern time, as the *New York Times* editorial indicated; (2) the result of the Japanese military's planned brutality as the Chinese prosecutor argued at the IMTFE; (3) attributable to other factors to be explored in this chapter; or (4) the combination of all or some of these.

The first question I address is what has changed and what has remained unchanged in the history of war atrocities. How and for what purposes have military men treated, or mistreated, combatants and noncombatants at different ages in the world? Here, although the Rape of Nanking happened in Asia, I first focus on Western military history for several reasons. First, Japanese and Chinese troops at the time were Westernized armies that were trained and equipped to fight in Western ways of warfare. Second, the concept of *jus in bello*, or the regulations on military conduct in wartime, developed mainly in the West and ultimately was more or less accepted in other parts of the world. Third, one must understand the Western thinking about the atrocities in view of the strong influence of Western opinions on the controversy about the Rape of Nanking from its very beginning. A special focus is on atrocities related to siege warfare, because the Nanking battle preceding the alleged atrocities was very much like a siege and also because siege warfare, regardless of age, plunged the populations into more immediate danger and thus created environments amenable to atrocities.[3] Then, I shift my attention to some factors and historical contexts unique in Japan and China—the two central players in the incident. A major question to be answered here will be if some cultural characteristics that were likely to affect their conduct on the battlefield existed on either side. This part also summarizes the history of Sino-Japanese relations in the modern era as a prelude to the Second Sino-Japanese War of 1937–45.

HISTORY OF WAR ATROCITIES

From Ancient Time to Napoleonic Wars

Since ancient times, military forces often slaughtered combatants and noncombatants even after the termination of military action, while they plundered conquered areas at will. Such carnage was especially severe when the war was fought against a culturally different group and when a siege ended violently.[4]

People in the premodern age apparently accepted violence against defeated enemy soldiers and the population of a fallen city as the norm, not the exception. One factor that strengthened such a notion was the concept in medieval European siege warfare that a city besieged was "forefeit [*sic*] for the contumacious disregard of a prince's summon to surrender."[5] A prince could carry out the subsequent crushing of a city's resistance as enforcement of justice, not military action. As a result, attackers did not observe the military rules usually valid on an open battlefield. The second factor that promoted rough behavior among soldiers was poor logistics. Since no logistic system at that time could sustain an army operating in enemy territory, plunder was the rule. Further aggravating such a tendency was the ordinary soldier's expectation that he could acquire wealth in war. Especially, those who had besieged a town had an expectation of plunder as a reward for the privation they had suffered during the siege. Military commanders also recognized the need to reward their soldiers for enduring hardship. It seems that the aforementioned *New York Times* editorial on the Nanking atrocities referred to a version of this custom. Although military leaders sometimes tried to restrain the conduct of soldiers by the publication of military ordinances, such measures did not remedy the heart of the problem— the lack of regular pay. Besides murder and plunder, which were distinguishable from military actions, troops sometimes conducted military operations that were targeted at noncombatants for strategic reasons and subsequently caused atrocities. A notable example was the scorched-earth policy adopted by Sir John Fastolf of England during the Hundred Years' War in France.[6]

At the root of such violence was an almost complete disregard for life and the welfare of common soldiers and inhabitants in the ancient and middle ages. Although medieval chivalry and the custom of paying ransom helped develop the idea of protecting prisoners, only the knights enjoyed that privilege, and ordinary enlisted soldiers and noncombatants were totally outside this system. Moreover, ordinary soldiers sometimes became the target of an even harsher form of brutality. Crossbowmen, for example, were often subjected to cruel treatment in the event of their capture for what the mounted knights regarded as an unfair way of fighting, thereby foreshadowing the often cruel treatment of irregulars in modern times. It is premature to assume that these atrocities typical in the premodern time have ceased to occur. Wherever armed men find themselves in conditions similar to these faced by ancient and medieval troops, these atrocities may happen even today.[7]

Early modern times saw what looked like two contradictory trends in war atrocities: the systematic massacre of the enemy, often including civilians, and the expanded protection of disarmed soldiers and civilians. Attackers in siege warfare sometimes conducted a systematic massacre of the defeated population even if that population belonged to the same cultural or ethnic group, or even when siege did not end violently. The Dutch Revolt in the 16th century witnessed many such cases. When the Calvinists in the city of Valencienne surrendered to the Spanish in 1567, the Catholics ignored a promise not to sack the city and subjected the city's population to murder and robbery. Such intentional killing occurred when the besiegers had a strong determination to crush the morale or will of the opposing side: the reason the Chinese prosecutor at the Tokyo War Crimes Trial cited as the Japanese army's motivation for the Nanking atrocities. As in the middle ages, intentional killing typically happened in a religious war in which the victors often justified their killing of the vanquished as a "righteous judgment of God upon these barbarous wretches," as Oliver Cromwell said in his defense of the massacre of Drogheda in 1649. This harsh treatment of opponents reflected the conviction held by the perpetrators of massacre that they indisputably represented the lawful government, and that all who stood against them should be treated as traitorous rebels rather than prisoners of war. The same conviction sometimes contributed to carnage attributable to defenders. The siege of Magdeburg in 1631 during the Thirty Years' War was a case where defenders were more responsible for the carnage following the violent end of siege. According to recent scholars, leaders of the Catholic force that besieged Magdeburg wished to take the city without bloodshed to capture the city's wealth in order to supply their own troops. It was the Protestant officer in charge of the defense of the city who ordered his men to set fire to the city and thus magnified its destruction.[8]

The revolutions and religious strife in the 16th and 17th centuries thus gave rise to intentional and systematic massacres of people and destruction of property, attributable either to the attackers or to the defenders. At the same time, however, there was a gradual movement to restrain the excesses of troops on the battlefield. First, enforcing discipline on soldiers became easier among state-financed troops than in the private mercenary armies of the medieval age. For example, higher military authorities tried to protect POWs and prohibited privately arranged ransom, while punishing soldiers who had committed plundering. Also, the leadership began to punish the unauthorized massacre of POWs. Second, the process of deconfessionalization, especially after the treaty of Westphalia in 1648, worked to mitigate atrocities motivated by religion. Third, the chivalric rule of extending immunity to combatants was gradually extended to all the categories of soldiers. Behind those moderations in the conduct of warfare was a consensus, which became evident in the Enlightenment era, that only legal military measures were those necessary for achieving military purposes. Although strategic devastation and destruction were still accepted customs of war, there was a growing notion that invading troops should conduct such measures with moderation and only when necessary.[9]

The two contradictory trends in the previous era became more evident at the time of the French Revolution and the Napoleonic wars. Mass armies in these wars had to live off the land since their sheer size did not allow the military authorities to provide them with sufficient logistical backup. Regulated requisitioning, however, replaced uncontrolled pillaging when regular troops took the place of mercenaries on the battlefield. The French revolutionary government's concern about its own legitimacy prompted its army to enforce stricter discipline regarding civilian lives and properties in enemy territory. At the same time, noncombatants became a more common target for military operations because revolutionary wars strengthened the notion that all the subjects of one nation are enemies of the subjects of the other. Since any army invading a foreign country had to face a hostile population inflamed by nationalism, it had to deal with opposition in the form of irregular forces such as guerrillas. One could define such fighting as the "inner front" as opposed to the "outer front," meaning the military confrontation with regular forces. The inner front posed a challenging task for the attackers since the belligerents were concealed among the civilians and sometimes undistinguishable from them. It was likely that military action directed against civilians often caused civilians to attack the invading troops, resulting in a spiralling of atrocities, the most prominent example being the Peninsular War.[10]

Summing up how the moderation and escalation of atrocities progressed simultaneously, Geoffrey Best says that " 'circumstances' made observance of the law difficult or impossible, rather than because men's minds had turned against the idea of the law itself." What appeared to be two contradictory trends were in a sense two sides of the same coin. Best also states that "the chances of the law of war's observance were heightened by the intermittent presence within the French armies of representatives of all classes of French society," but that "circumstances" lessened the same chances. The very "circumstances" that contributed to the reduced effectiveness of the law of war originated from the same factor that prompted its fostering—participation in war by all classes of society in the enemy country.[11]

19th Century

The U.S. Civil War was a modern war in which terror was not inflicted on people but on property. General William T. Sherman's march to the sea was a prime example of devastation for strategic purposes, but not for the sake of destroying human lives. A Civil War veteran recalled nearly half a century after the war, "I never knew of an officer being called upon to protect a woman against mistreatment by our soldiers."[12] But the war was not entirely without brutal killing targeted at nonmilitary personnel. As Sherman prophetically said, "There is a class of people, men, women, and children, who must be killed or banished before you can hope for peace and order."[13] The western theater of the U.S. Civil War, Kansas and Missouri in particular, saw the activities of Confederate "bushwhackers" and Union "jayhawkers," who often raided and killed enemy civilians. Their atrocities, such as the sack of Osceola conducted by James H. Lane's jayhawker brigade on September 23, 1861, and the massacre at Lawrence, Kansas, on August 21, 1863, by William Clark Quantrill's bushwhackers, were the results of unique conditions in the West. First, the Union commanders in occupation of part of Missouri tended to regard local residents as secessionists and rebels without distinction and took a harsh attitude toward them. Such an attitude caused bitter resentment among the local population and created the conditions amenable to guerrilla activities. Second, the Union military leadership made it a policy to execute summarily the bushwhackers upon their capture. Finally, such a policy led to a "maelstrom of retaliation and counter-retaliation" and culminated at a point where both sides took few prisoners.[14]

Jayhawkers and bushwhackers had characteristics of both the medieval mercenary and the modern guerrilla. Many of them were not regular soldiers and were more interested in plunder. They thus resembled, and in a sense were descendants of, medieval mercenary soldiers. Their tactics, however, had some elements of modern-day guerrillas. For example, they usually killed only the civilians they had marked in advance. In this respect, they were a precursor of modern-day insurgents like the Viet Cong who assassinated local notables on the government side. The jayhawkers and bushwhackers were thus irregular troops of a transitional stage and conducted both new- and old-type atrocities.[15]

Although the sacking of towns and cities during the U.S. Civil War happened more in sparsely populated areas in the West, one may easily imagine how a similar escalation of violence in urban areas was likely to unfold. Other nations of the world witnessed such examples around the same period. The Paris Commune in 1871, although an incident during a civil war, was one of the first examples of how war might develop if it happened in an urban area in modern times.

Paris was under siege twice in 1870–71—first by the Prussians and then by government forces intent on crushing the Commune. The siege by the Prussians did not cause many casualties. Although the lack of food contributed to numerous deaths from sickness and malnutrition, the bombardment of the city itself killed only ninety-seven people and wounded 278.[16]

The residents of Paris suffered much more severely in the civil war between the Communards and the Versailles-based French government led by Louis-Adolphe Thiers. Thiers ordered the storming of Paris because the Prussians threatened to re-enter Paris if the French government hesitated to suppress further resistance. The Commune leaders appealed to ordinary citizens to take up arms and resist the government forces. They passed a decree to conscript every man, married or unmarried, between the ages of nineteen and fifty-five.[17]

The Commune's plan for defense was, however, far from satisfactory. Its leaders, who were apparently not familiar with tactical planning, anticipated a frontal assault on the city center and were totally taken by surprise when the Versailles force made a series of flanking movements and rendered useless most of the elaborately constructed defense positions. As a result, the Communards fought "piecemeal and *ad lib*." Commune leaders then ordered the firing of "any houses capable of jeopardizing [the] defense."[18]

In the confusion during the final phase of the siege, government troops committed many atrocities. Each time a barricade fell, the defenders were put up against a wall and shot. In some military hospitals set up by the Commune, government troops massacred the patients and staff, claiming that shots had been fired from the hospitals. Ordinary citizens were not spared the carnage. The raging fire created a rumor that *petroleuses*, women carrying incendiary-filled bottles, were setting fires everywhere in the city. Because of this rumor, government troops executed many innocent women. They also summarily executed men who were wearing army boots or had a discoloration on their right shoulders, a mark that might have resulted from carrying a rifle butt.[19]

The leaders at Versailles never instructed their troops to carry out summary executions. Thiers himself told the assembly that civilization had triumphed and that the restoration would take place in the name of the law and by the law. Thiers also claimed in his memoirs that he had issued strict orders to restrain the anger of the soldiers. Thiers was, however, determined to crush the Commune in his proclamation calling for "complete expiation." The French army of 130,000 soldiers faithfully interpreted this phrase and killed 20,000 to 25,000 people.[20]

One may see both a factor consistent through time and a new factor of the modern age as contributing to this massacre. That Paris became like a besieged city stormed by attackers undoubtedly caused a considerable amount of confusion on the one hand. In this aspect, atrocities followed the traditional pattern of siege warfare. On the other hand, the Commune's mobilization of civilians contributed to the government troops' intensification of street battles and mopping-up operation in Paris, resulting in large-scale atrocities. Thus, another cause of atrocities was an increasingly obscure distinction between combatants and noncombatants in modern warfare.

Hague Convention and World War I

Prior to World War I, major powers codified the laws of belligerency, which had so far existed mainly in the form of unwritten custom. The Hague Conventions of 1899 and 1907 were the first international treaties signed by a considerable number of powers for the regulation of the conduct of war.[21]

Regarding the protection of POWs, article 4 of the 1907 Hague Convention Respecting the Laws and Customs of War on Land said, "Prisoners of war are in the power of the hostile government, but not of the individuals or corps who capture them. They must be humanely treated."[22] Article 23 also contained a clause that forbade belligerents to kill or wound an enemy who has surrendered at discretion. Under these provisions, belligerents were prohibited from taking reprisal against POWs or using them to extort ransom.

Article 28 prohibited the pillage of a town or place, even when taken by assault. It is apparent that this article referred to the practice observed traditionally by besieging troops—that victors were entitled to unlimited pillaging in a forcibly captured city for a certain period of time. The military leadership was also required to extend due protection to the inhabitants of occupied areas. Article 43 stated, "The authority of the legitimate power having in fact passed into the hands of the occupants, the latter shall take all the measure in his power to restore, and ensure, as far as possible, public order and safety, while respecting, unless absolutely prevented, the laws in force in the country."[23]

One subject that remained unclear was the status of irregular troops like guerrillas. The only provision relating to this matter was Article 2, which said, "The inhabitants of a territory which has not been occupied, who, on the approach of the enemy, spontaneously take up arms to resist the invading troops . . . shall be regarded as belligerents *if they carry arms openly* and if they respect the laws and customs of war. [Italics added.]"[24]

Apart from this provision, the Hague Convention imposed restrictions on irregular military activities. One of the clauses of Article 23 forbade armed forces "to make improper use of a flag of truce, of the national flag or of the military insignia and uniform of the enemy, as well as the distinctive badges of the Geneva Convention."[25] The drafters of the convention were aware of the existence of many areas not covered by the convention and inserted in the preamble the so-called Martens clause: "Until a more complete code of the laws of war has been issued, the high contracting Parties deem it expedient to declare that, in cases not included in the Regulations adopted by them, the inhabitants and the belligerents remain under the protection and the rule of the principles of the law of nations, as they result from the usages established among civilized peoples, from the laws of humanity, and the dictates of the public conscience."[26]

World War I was the testing ground for the effectiveness of these articles, while it also revealed the existence of these "gray" areas in the laws of war. Two cases of atrocities in World War I are worthy of attention not only as examples of these gray areas but also due to a certain degree of resemblance with the Rape of Nanking and as an illustration of the Western attitude about atrocities in modern-day total war. The two cases are the German atrocities in Belgium, which some Westerners called the "rape of Belgium," and the massacre of Armenians in Turkey, an event some people today call the first case of "genocide"—a term recently used by some people to describe the Rape of Nanking.[27]

The Entente powers in World War I accused Germany of extensive murder, destruction, and plundering in Belgium in the early part of the war. A British commission's report made public in May 1915 had a major impact on people's perception of German atrocities. The report compiled by the Bryce Commission, named after its chairman, Viscount Bryce, concluded that

... there were in many parts of Belgium deliberate and systematic organized massacre of the civil population, accompanied by many isolated murders and other outrages.

... In the conduct of the war generally innocent civilians, both men and women, were murdered in large numbers, women violated, and children murdered.

... Looting, house burning, and the wanton destruction of property were ordered and countenanced by the officers of the German Army.[28]

Among numerous cases of alleged German atrocities, the case of Louvain in August 1914 acquired a particular notoriety since the city was a well-known academic town with an old university. According to the Bryce report, there was an exchange of friendly fire between some German soldiers who had been defeated by Belgian troops in a skirmish nearby and German soldiers in occupation of Louvain. The Germans in the town blamed the firing on civilians in the city and started a systematic destruction of buildings, rounding up residents and executing some of them. Among the buildings burned to ashes were university buildings, including the library. The commission concluded that the Germans had committed these acts, assuming that by exceptional severities at the outset they could cow the spirit of the Belgian nation. The commission distinguished the German atrocities in Belgium from past cases in history: "It was to the discipline rather than the want of discipline in the army that these outrages, which we are obliged to describe as systematic, were due."[29]

Many contemporary writers shared this conclusion that the German atrocities in Belgium were unprecedented in their deliberate and systematic nature:

. . . so far from constituting exceptional crimes and contraventions against an established discipline, these acts are to be attributed to the form of discipline itself and consequently to the system of command.[30]

They were willfully committed as part of a deliberately prepared and scientifically organized policy of terrorism.[31]

The worst crimes committed were committed not by brutes escaping from discipline, but by soldiers obeying orders. They were not accidents of war, but details in a carefully compiled plan of making war. They expressed the conclusion of the German mind that the way to conquer a foe was to terrify him, that the way to rob his arm of strength and his spirits of determination was to burn, to rape, to rob, and to murder, until the spirit broke and the soldier laid down his arms to escape a continuation of horrors wreaked upon his women and children.[32]

To counter such allegations, the German government charged in its "White Book" published shortly following the Bryce Commission's report that the Belgian civilian population had committed various hostilities against Germans, including the shooting of troops, the throwing of boiling water, the maiming of the wounded, and the assassination of officers. The German government justified the destruction in Louvain and other locations in Belgium as measures to suppress these attacks. A notable point here is that the German government did not deny resorting to stern measures and instead tried to justify them as military necessities.[33]

It seems that both sides accused the other of violating the laws of war: while the Bryce Commission blamed the Germans for the mistreatment of the people in the occupied area, the Germans charged the Belgian population with illegal military activities. The case of World War I Belgium thus exemplified one of the gray areas in the Hague Convention.[34]

In 1958, a group of German and Belgian historians concluded that the German White Book had no claim of credibility, since its approach did not meet the standards of historical inquiry. At the same time, instead of simply blaming the Germans, historians began probing into the psychology of the aggressors. According to a recent analysis, the German soldiers in Belgium were infected, at all ranks and levels, with the *"franc-tireur* psychosis." In other words, they firmly believed that Belgian irregulars, comparable to French volunteer fighters called *franc-tireur* during the Franco-Prussian War of 1870–71, were in operation against them and were hiding among the civilian population. The Belgian regular army's tendency to resort to guerrilla tactics such as assaults on supply and communication lines strengthened these German fears. The German actions in Belgium were thus due in part to the German troops' concern for their own safety, and not entirely to a deliberate intent to break the morale of the population of the occupied area.[35]

The German troops in Belgium were in a sense surrounded by a hostile population. The case of the Armenians in Turkey was different: the victims of atrocities were a minority population in a land ruled by the perpetrators. This was yet another blind spot not covered by the Hague Convention.

Armenians have lived in several countries in central Asia. They constitute a Christian minority in Turkey and even before World War I had experienced persecution at the hands of the Muslim central government. The government justified its policy by accusing the Armenian reform or autonomous movement, which was sometimes supported by outside forces such as Russia, as breaching the Muslim common law that allowed the people of different faith to live peacefully as long as they remained subservient to the Muslim authorities. After the Balkan War of 1912 stripped Turkey of a large amount of territory in Europe, the recurrence of the reform movement undertaken by the Armenians convinced the Turkish leaders of the need to solve their "Armenian Question" once and for all. The outbreak of World War I then provided the Turkish authorities with a favorable environment in which to execute their policy against the Armenians and allegedly to initiate a systematic persecution of Armenians on the pretext of relocating them for security reasons.[36] Eyewitnesses reported that

several bands of Turkish horsemen made a concerted rush into the Armenian quarters at Moush, first attacking the shopkeepers in the bazaar, burning, looting and murdering as they went. The massacre went on till far in the night, even the regular police joining. Fully 250 men were killed. The women, if old and ugly, were murdered or beaten; if young and pretty, were taken away. The children generally were spared, but a few were put to death for sheer amusement.[37]

. . . the roads and the Euphrates are strewn with corpses of exiles, and those who survive are doomed to certain death, since they will find neither house, work, nor food in the desert.[38]

The Armenian death toll during World War I, including those who were killed and those who died of privation, amounted to two million people according to Armenians, and 200,000 to 300,000 according to Turkish sources.[39] Although the word genocide had not yet been coined, a notion implicit in the word crept into the thoughts of some contemporaries:

It is a plan to exterminate the whole Armenian people.[40]

The atrocities which filled the first eight months of 1915 were carefully organized, and represented the fulfillment of a long-cherished policy.[41]

. . . the massacres are the result of a deliberate plan of the Turkish Government to "get rid of the Armenian question."[42]

On May 24, 1915, the governments of Russia, France, and Britain jointly issued a public denunciation of Turkish brutality against Armenians. The Turkish government replied that it was merely exercising its sovereign right of self-defense. The German government defended its ally's action in a way reminiscent of its own justification of atrocities in Belgium. The German ambassador to the United States said in September 1915 that the Turkish actions were in response to provocation by the Armenians. Having described the incident as "extreme penalties," the ambassador said that attempts to stir up rebellion and revolt and treasonable activity had made the "Armenian policy" a necessary wartime measure. Scholars sympathetic to the Turkish position still maintain this line of argument and even argue that the Turkish government did everything it could to guarantee the safety of the deportees. Although they do admit that there were some massacres, they also point to revolts, bandit attacks, famine, and disease as causes of deaths.[43]

The truth seems to be close to the interpretation of "genocide," but not so conclusive as in the case of Nazi Holocaust. There has so far been no solid or definitive evidence found to indicate that the Turkish leaders had a deliberate plan to wipe out the entire Armenian population. The Turkish government authorized the high command of the army only to deport non-Muslim elements of the population from points of concentration and from the army's line of communication. Thus, as far as one looks at the ostensible motive of the Turkish government leaders, the deportation of Armenians in World War I Turkey was motivated by security concerns. Unlike the Jews under Nazi rule, conversion from Christianity to Islam did save the lives of some Armenians: an estimated 200,000 did convert from Christianity, although forcibly in many cases. Yet, under the guise of "relocation" as promulgated by the Turkish government, Armenian deportees were openly executed by the military and "special organization" formed by the government and composed mainly of convicted criminals. Survivors usually perished due to starvation because the Turkish authorities were poorly prepared to undertake the Armenian deportation. This lack of preparation was very likely the result of willful negligence. The plight of the Armenians thus bears resemblance to the fate of the Jews under Nazi rule. In terms of cruelty and their intended objective, Turkish policy toward Armenians finds a modern echo in the ethnic cleansing conducted by the Serbs in Bosnia and in Kosovo in the 1990s.[44]

Despite the codification of the laws of war, World War I experiences show that the patterns of atrocities since ancient times have remained constant to a considerable extent. First, belligerents sometimes conducted the systematic massacre of the inhabitants of an occupied area or an ethnic minority within their own territory. They took these measures to eliminate any potential resistance in wars in which the distinction between combatants and noncombatants became increasingly obscure. Second, devastation for strategic purposes happened, sometimes accompanying killing, as it happened in Belgium. Third, lack of military discipline could still be a source of atrocities, especially when supply became difficult. For example, German soldiers' looting often slowed the German offensive in the spring of 1918. Their looting became so rampant that one division created special "booty commands" to prevent the disordering effect of looting.[45]

A notable, and in a sense ironic, characteristic found in the Western reporting of atrocities was a racial or religious bias. Many of the *New York Times* articles reporting the Armenian massacre, for example, referred to Armenians as "Christians," implying a Western concern about the Armenians' plight due to a religious and cultural affinity with the victims.[46] Therefore, this seemingly rightful criticism of racially or ethnically motivated persecution was also based on another racial bias. Westerners brought their racial biases with them in the 19th century when they started extensive contact with the peoples of Asia, especially the Japanese and the Chinese, the aggressors and victims in the Rape of Nanking.

ATROCITIES IN ASIA

Chinese Military Conduct through the 19th Century

Throughout the premodern history of China, one may recognize the same factors that caused war atrocities in the Western world. For example, whether it was a war between Chinese and nomadic invaders or an internal rebellion, it was an accepted custom to slaughter the defenders of a town that had resisted to the bitter end. As happened in European cities, warfare in an urban area was almost always characterized by looting.[47] Yet, with all these similarities in the actual committing of atrocities, there were several peculiar Chinese concepts about warfare that made the nature of atrocities different.

Chinese Confucian tradition regarded war as a result of the failure of a sovereign ruler's duty to maintain social order and thus refrained from glorifying it, unlike the Westerners or the Japanese. Mencius, an ancient Chinese philosopher, described war in which belligerents contest over land or city as the one "leading on the land to devour human flesh" and said, "Death is not enough for such a crime. . . . Therefore, those who are skillful to fight should suffer the highest punishment."[48] Even Sun Tzu, a Chinese military philosopher who wrote *The Art of War* around the 5th century B.C., said in his work, "those who win every battle are not really skillful—those who render other's armies helpless without fighting are the best of all. The best victory is when the opponent surrenders of its own accord before there are actual hostilities. . . . When you do battle, it is necessary to kill people, so it is best to win without fighting."[49]

Chinese intellectuals thus defined war as an abnormal event that interrupts the normal time of peace and thus should be terminated as soon as possible. Because of this attitude, war and peace were not clearly or legally differentiated. Consequently, the Chinese apparently did not develop a firm concept of *jus in bello*. Although Confucian ethics served as a mitigating factor on the overall conduct of war on the political level, disesteem of physical coercion derived from that very Confucian tradition, ironically, resulted in the virtual nonexistence of regulations concerning the restrictions of violence in battle and thus served to aggravate war atrocities. More often than not, in violation of diplomatic immunity, which was recognized in contemporary Europe, they killed diplomatic envoys dispatched by enemies. They paid no attention to the fate of POWs, and it was their accepted practice to hurl the severed heads of captured soldiers into a besieged town to intimidate its defenders. Not only attackers but also defenders adopted a scorched-earth policy: it was a Chinese practice from siege warfare in the middle ages to modern times that the defenders of walled towns burnt everything that might be of use to the enemy before the start of siege to deny supplies to the enemy as well as remove anything that could be useful as obstacles in battle.[50]

The Chinese military tradition characterized by the lack of *jus in bello* apparently continued well into the 19th century when the Western powers began their imperial advance in Asia. The British were sometimes embarrassed to encounter Chinese customs of war completely different from theirs. Although the Chinese captured only a small number of British nationals as POWs during the Opium War in 1840–42, their treatment of captives was identical with, or even worse than, the punishment of common criminals. They confined, for example, captured British soldiers in a small cage in which a person could barely sit and left them in the marketplaces of several towns so that passers-by could see their humiliating posture.[51]

Other than the mistreatment of prisoners, there were no reported cases of atrocities committed against the Westerners. But the Chinese did conduct military operations that made atrocities against their own people likely. British sailors often found colorful boxes, usually used by Chinese women to keep clothing, floating in the river. It turned out that many of them contained explosives, which were detonated upon opening the lid. One may see such a ploy as a precursor to booby traps set by insurgents such as the Viet Cong in later times. At the outset of the Second Opium War in 1857 there was also a reported case of an attempted mass poisoning of British nationals in Hong Kong by injecting a large amount of arsenic into bread. Another gruesome practice witnessed by Westerners during the Second Opium War was mass suicide of Chinese local officials and their families when the British captured towns. In Tinghai, Chapu, and Chinkiang, for example, British soldiers found that all the local magistrates had killed their children and wives by hanging or drowning them and had then cut their own throats. No Western witnesses or scholars have given a rational explanation for this cruel custom, which had not previously been a norm in China. Although the humiliation of allowing what they called "foreign devils" to occupy their towns seems to have been a major reason for their suicide, a Chinese military tradition probably also contributed to this mass suicide. Under the successive Chinese dynasties, the post of military commander was a court appointment. Although success in military campaign brought commanders a reward, failure resulted in severe penalties, often death. This custom made a military commander's defection to the enemy easy, whether it was in a civil war or a war against non-Chinese ethnic groups in the north. In the Opium War, in which the Chinese fought against the Westerners, many local leaders likely concluded that such defection was impossible and found no way but suicide to account for their failure to defend their towns.[52]

One cannot conclude, however, that unique Chinese characteristics alone caused war atrocities in China. An illustrious example was a massacre that took place in China at approximately the same time as the destruction of the Paris Commune in Europe. Incidentally, it happened in Nanking, where the Japanese troops allegedly committed similar kinds of atrocities about seventy years later.

The Taiping Heavenly Kingdom, which started as a popular uprising in 1850, dominated a substantial part of China until the early 1860s. The ruling Ch'ing Dynasty tried to suppress the rebellion. Finally, in December 1863, a Ch'ing army besieged the city of Nanking, where the remnants of the Taiping faithful entrenched themselves. The 80,000 Ch'ing troops started strangling the soldiers and inhabitants of Nanking by denying food supplies to the city. The Ch'ing leaders were determined to exterminate "the whole movement through the death of its core of leaders and followers"—remarks that contain a strikingly similar tone to the "complete expiation" used by Thiers, who ordered the destruction of the Paris Commune.[53]

In an all-out offensive on July 19, Ch'ing troops exploded a part of the city walls and stormed the city. According to a Taiping leader, at the time there were only 30,000 civilians and 10,000 soldiers in the city, of whom only 3,000 to 4,000 were combat-ready. Nevertheless, they fought street by street and ultimately committed suicide en masse by burning or drowning themselves. The Ch'ing troops put to death 7,000 prisoners. Because the Taiping faithful defied the Ch'ing's custom of shaving off most of their long hair, they were distinguishable by their hair. Apparently, people with long hair were executed systematically since one Taiping leader, who left a long memoir during his captivity after the fall of Nanking, testified that the local people sympathetic to him advised him to shave his head to flee from Ch'ing soldiers. Again, the Ch'ing troops' method of searching Taiping rebels was similar to the way the French government troops rounded up Communards: both looked for physical traits such as long hair and discoloration on shoulders.[54]

Overall, the end of the Taiping Kingdom's capital strikingly resembled the last day of the Paris Commune except for the mass suicide of the Taiping leaders, which was similar to the mass suicide of Chinese local political leaders during the Opium War. One may conclude that both universal factors and unique Chinese cultural traits contributed to the atrocities in this case.

Japanese Military Conduct through the 19th Century

Japan's contact with the Western nations came a little later than China's encounter with these powers. Commodore Matthew Perry's visit to Japan in

1853 and the domestic political turmoil that it triggered ended the two-and-a-half century rule of the warrior government of the Tokugawa family in 1868. In the Meiji Restoration, anti-Tokugawa forces, which had overthrown the Tokugawa government, reinstalled the Imperial House as the head of the state. One pressing concern of the new Japanese government was Japan's national security. Prior to the Meiji Restoration, some of these leaders who took a firsthand look at the situation in China and its struggle against the Western powers argued for the strengthening of Japan's defense. In particular, the Meiji government felt an urgent need for a forward base on the continent to preclude outside powers' advance into areas close to Japan or even to the homeland itself. Initially, Japan tried to turn the Korean peninsula into Japan's sphere of influence. Japan's ostensible objective was to maintain the independence of Korea from China, which regarded Korea as one of its vassal states. After a series of incidents involving Japanese and Chinese legation troops in Korea, the two countries finally went to war in 1894. This was the first modern war Japan fought against an outside power and was a conflict in which Westerners wished to see whether the Japanese and Chinese were able to wage war in accordance with Western customs.[55]

A lapse of about half a century after the Opium War or three decades after the Taiping Rebellion was apparently not enough for the Chinese to accept completely Western customs in warfare. In the Sino-Japanese War, some Chinese civilian and military leaders offered prizes for Japanese heads. As a result, Chinese soldiers mutilated the bodies of dead Japanese soldiers even prior to the first major battle of war in mid-September 1894.[56] The Japanese leadership had anticipated the occurrence of such incidents. General Yamagata Aritomo, commander of the Japanese First Army, issued the following directive to his soldiers on September 13, 1894: "The enemy has exhibited an extremely cruel nature from ancient times. If you are captured alive in military engagement, you will surely be subjected to a cruel torture which will make you wish for death."[57]

Some contemporary observers said that savage behavior by Chinese troops was a partial cause of the massacre of Port Arthur in November 1894—an incident in which the Japanese army allegedly committed an indiscriminate massacre of the inhabitants. The Port Arthur campaign during the Sino-Japanese War of 1894–95 offers the most interesting comparison with the Nanking campaign. First, it happened in China and involved the same belligerents. Second, Western journalists initially reported the incident as they did in Nanking in 1937–38. Finally, there was a heated controversy over the incident immediately after it took place. Before delving into the details of the Port Arthur massacre, one must consider Japanese behavior in addition to Chinese military behavior since it was indeed the Japanese who were at center stage in this incident.

Overall, during the Sino-Japanese War of 1894–95, the Japanese troops tried to observe a "civilized" way of warfare by adhering to "Western" rules of belligerency. The Japanese army ministry issued a directive on September 22, 1894, reminding the troops bound for the continent of the principle that military and naval operations should be properly confined to the military and naval forces actually engaged. The directive also said that "the common principles of humanity dictate that succor and rescue should be extended even to those of enemy's forces who are disabled either by wounds or disease." What prompted the military authorities to issue such a statement was apparently their concern about Japan's image in the eyes of Westerners since the directive ended with a sentence: Japanese soldiers "have now an opportunity to afford practical proof of the value they attach to these [humanitarian] principles [governing warfare in the Western world]."[58]

One may reason that Japanese *bushido*, the traditional code of Japanese warriors, also affected the attitudes of Japanese soldiers in this period. Traditionally, Japanese *samurai* warriors often respected opponents of the same social status, like their Western counterparts bound by the code of chivalry. In essence, however, *bushido*, like its Western counterpart, could be the source of both a gentlemanly attitude and a barbaric act, depending on circumstances. Just as the Europeans did in the ancient and middle ages, Japanese warriors sometimes showed ruthless attitudes toward cultural outsiders. When the Mongols attempted to invade Japan in the 13th century, for instance, the Japanese executed the captured Mongol soldiers, whose number ranged from several thousand to 30,000 depending on which record one believes. Lack of compassion toward commoners was also a trait exhibited by Western knights and Japanese *samurai* alike. In the 16th century, the troops led by Akechi Mitsuhide, one of the generals under warlord Oda Nobunaga, were known for their well-disciplined behavior of refraining from any looting or rape. Such a reputation attests to the poor discipline of most other soldiers who often gambled among themselves over the loot they expected to get in the coming battle. Also, removing the slain enemy soldiers' ears as trophies was a long observed custom of Japanese warriors from the war in Korea in the 7th century through Toyotomi Hideyoshi's expedition to Korea in the 16th century.[59]

In view of such historical examples, one may assume that the army ministry's directive was not based on a deep-rooted, law-abiding tradition but was an extension of the Japanese government's diplomatic endeavor to revise the unequal treaties that the Tokugawa Shogunate had concluded with the Western powers in the mid-19th century. The Japanese troops operating in Korea and China during the Sino-Japanese War, for example, took particular care not to damage any buildings bearing the mark of the cross so that they would not tarnish their own image in the eyes of foreign missionaries. In the absence of such eyes, however, some Japanese soldiers took revenge on Chinese prisoners in a brutal manner even before the massacre at Port Arthur. After the battle of Pyongyang on September 15, 1894, there was a reported case of Japanese soldiers who beheaded Chinese POWs on the spot for the purpose of retribution after they found that those Chinese POWs were carrying the severed heads of their commanding officer and fellow soldiers killed in action. Of course, in such circumstances soldiers of any country might react in the same way.[60]

Massacre at Port Arthur

The alleged massacre of Port Arthur happened after the Japanese Second Army commanded by General Oyama Iwao entered the port city on the tip of the Liaotung peninsula on November 21, 1894. By then, the Chinese defenders had fled from their outposts, and the Japanese occupied Port Arthur without severe fighting. Then, the December 12 issue of the *New York World* reported that the Japanese troops had massacred practically the entire population of Port Arthur in cold blood. In a dispatch from Yokohama, Japan, *World* correspondent James Creelman said,

The defenseless and unarmed inhabitants were butchered in their houses, and their bodies were unspeakably mutilated. There was an unrestrained reign of murder, which continued for three days. The whole town was plundered with appalling atrocities.

It was the first stain upon Japanese civilization. The Japanese in this instance relapsed into barbarism.

All pretenses that circumstances justified the atrocities are false. The civilized world will be horrified by the details.

The foreign correspondents, horrified by the spectacle, left the army in a body.[61]

From the beginning, not only other war correspondents such as Frederic Villiers of the London *Standard* and K. Cowan of the *Times* but also Japanese officials admitted to the occurrence of massacre. They, however, presented conflicting opinions regarding its extent and cause. Japanese foreign minister Mutsu Munemitsu immediately cabled a message to the *World*, which was printed in the December 17 issue. Although Mutsu said that the Japanese government was not yet in possession of all the facts about the incident, he admitted that "discipline was unavailing in this single instance." He then presented an explanation, which the Japanese authorities have maintained ever since. According to Mutsu, the Japanese troops, transported with rage at the mutilation of their comrades by the enemy, broke through all restraints. Then, further exasperated by the wholesale attempts of Chinese troops to escape disguised as citizens, they inflicted vengeance without discrimination.[62] On the following day, Kurino Shin'ichiro, Japanese minister to the United States, made public an official statement cabled by foreign minister Mutsu. Mutsu further elaborated on the cause of the alleged massacre in his statement:

Many of the Chinese soldiers at Port Arthur and from the outlying fortifications taken by the Japanese discarded their uniforms, and it is now known that almost all of the Chinese in plain clothes who were killed there were soldiers in disguise. The inhabitants of Port Arthur quitted before the engagement. A few remained, however, having been armed under orders to resist the Japanese by firing on them. This they did, and in the confusion of the fight it was impossible to distinguish them from the Chinese soldiers.[63]

This was virtually the same explanation the Germans would provide two decades later in the wake of their atrocities in Belgium.

The Westerners were not satisfied with this explanation. In the December 20 issue of the *World*, Creelman followed up his initial report by providing a more detailed account of what had happened in Port Arthur immediately after its fall. Creelman contended that all attempts to justify the massacre of the wretched people of Port Arthur and the mutilation of their bodies were mere afterthoughts, and then he described the scenes he had witnessed:

All along the streets I could see the pleading storekeepers shot and sabred. Doors were broken down and windows torn out. Every house was entered and robbed.

. . . I saw a white-haired, toothless merchant disembowelled on the threshold of his own shop, which had been looted.

Another victim had his breast ripped open by a Japanese sword, and a pet dog lay shivering under his arms.

There was a dead woman lying under a heap of slain men in every conceivable attitude of agony and supplication.[64]

He said that the killing continued on the second and third days—when the excitement and frenzy after the battle should have died down. According to him, "at least 2,000 unarmed men were put to death."[65]

Judging from the descriptions some Japanese soldiers entered in their diaries, it is undoubtedly true that the Japanese committed a terrible slaughter in Port Arthur. For example, Private First Class Kubota Chuzo said,

The enemy retreated and we dogged them, attacking from three sides. Unable to escape, some disguised themselves as farmers, others hid in Chinese homes, and others ran from roof to roof like scattering ants. Entering Port Arthur, we found the head of a Japanese prisoner of war on a wooden spike. The mutilation enraged and incensed us, and we wanted to tear any Chinese soldier into pieces. We killed all of them, even those dressed as civilians. So many bodies covered the streets that marching was difficult. We found and killed at least two in every house. The whole town stank of their blood. . . .

Corpses were everywhere and we couldn't sleep. . . . We kept the fires going all night, burning picket fences and doors. The next day, we couldn't find any drinking water; it had all been contaminated by the dead bodies. . . . According to later investigations, we had killed more than forty women. We couldn't differentiate in the dark. We were so enraged by the Chinese barbarism we had seen earlier.[66]

Meanwhile, faced with such horrible reports, some Westerners were shocked and puzzled because the Japanese army had maintained their discipline so far and seemingly followed the civilized, that is Western, ways of warfare. One observer said that such an outburst of "cold-blooded brutality" was the very last thing he had thought possible. Quite a few opinions expressed in the Western press had a racial overtone. Creelman noted, "Japan at heart is a barbarous nation, not yet to be trusted with sovereign power over the lives and property of civilized men." In a letter to the *World*, an anonymous journalist also stated, "Scratch a 'Jap' and you have a savage, notwithstanding his pretensions to civilization." In a speech delivered at the Hanson Place M. E. Church, Brooklyn, Reverend Louis Albert Banks in a more moderate and explanatory tone referred to the massacre in Port Arthur as "not an astonishing thing at all" because "the ruling class in Japan has not accepted Christianity to any great extent."[67]

Yet quite a few Westerners were sympathetic to the Japanese even though they accepted Creelman's account at face value. In a letter to the *World*, Colonel E. F. Gregory, who identified himself as a U.S. Civil War veteran, maintained, "It is sometimes difficult, nay, almost impossible, for officers to restrain their men, in the best disciplined and regulated armies, from committing excesses." *World* reader Samuel T. Robertson also defended the Japanese by saying that "the Japanese killed people who were openly at war with them."[68] It seems that Gregory discussed the traditional human factors in war such as excitement and brutalization among soldiers, while Robertson implied a modern factor—the existence of an "inner front"—as an important reason.

In addition, there were other witnesses and analysts who disputed all or part of the original account by Creelman. On December 17, the *New York Times* called the reports about the Port Arthur atrocities "unfounded" and quoted a dispatch to the Navy Department as saying that nothing was destroyed in Port Arthur. Also, a London *Times* correspondent was quoted as saying that there were regrettable Japanese excesses at Port Arthur, but that the conduct of the Japanese was excusable, being paralleled in the best European armies. According to the special correspondent of Frank Leslie's *Illustrated Weekly*, who claimed to be an eyewitness to the Port Arthur campaign, the Japanese soldiers had encountered the mutilated bodies of their dead comrades on their way to Port Arthur. Moreover, the Chinese had used cartridges with explosive bullets, which caused horrible injuries. After those experiences, "the Japanese soldiers knew no limit. They charged through the city and killed many."[69]

There seem to have been roughly three groups of opinions in the Port Arthur massacre controversy: (1) those who believed the story to be true and blamed the uncivilized nature of the Japanese for its occurrence; (2) those who accepted the account of atrocities but regarded such behavior as a natural consequence of war; and (3) those who discounted all or part of the initial report of the massacre itself. As one of the later chapters will show, almost the same pattern developed in the debates over the Nanking incident.

Japanese newspapers also reported the Port Arthur massacre in Japan, although their coverage was limited. The *Tokyo Nichinichi Shinbun* [Tokyo Nichinichi Newspaper] carried articles containing the following passages:

[Mutilation of Japanese dead and wounded soldiers] was a major factor shaping our attitude toward the enemy in Port Arthur. We put to death mercilessly many of those in Port Arthur if they showed a slight sign of resistance.

[Chinese soldiers] suddenly sniped at us [from a house]. Our [Japanese] soldiers broke into that house, searched a room, and found seven to eight of them instantly. The situation thus did not allow our soldiers to relax. Therefore, they tore down the front and rear doors of every house to look for the soldiers in hiding. They found over thirty straggling soldiers, beheaded them, and displayed their heads on the street. After a further intensive search, other enemy soldiers, being unable to hide themselves, dived into the sea to escape by swimming. Our soldiers aimed shots at them and killed a countless number of them.[70]

That such stories could appear on newspaper pages illustrated the perception of average Japanese people at the time that those stories described brave acts of soldiers in the field rather than atrocities. Yet, it is also probable that these stories represent more or less the normal state of wars at the time, as some U.S. newspaper readers suggested.[71]

It soon became apparent that a diplomatic issue was also affecting the controversy over the Port Arthur massacre. At the time, the U.S. Senate was deliberating, and was soon to vote on, a treaty with Japan. The proposed treaty would abolish the extraterritorial jurisdiction in Japan in 1899 as well as allow the Japanese to impose higher tariffs on imports. The *World* on the one hand contended that official corroboration of the terrible butchery reported was all that was necessary to cause the treaty to be laid aside until Japan could clear herself of an unmistakable relapse into barbarism. The *New York Times* on the other hand suggested in a critical tone that commerce, which was likely to be affected by the proposed new treaty, had something to do with the reporting of the atrocities. Later in the same month, an American journalist who identified himself as the special correspondent of Frank Leslie's *Illustrated Weekly* also charged that the main objective of these statements seemed to be to prevent the new treaty with Japan from passing the Senate. Such a heated exchange of opinions, however, does not seem to have happened in the Senate, which approved the treaty on January 30, 1895.[72]

The controversy was, however, far from over. Frederic Villiers, who identified himself as a special artist for *Black and White* and correspondent of the London *Standard*, emphatically stated that the Port Arthur massacre had really happened. In the March 1895 issue of the *North American Review*, Villiers first described an atrocity he had witnessed. According to Villiers, the Japanese soldiers who saw the mutilated heads of their comrades hanging by the road were maddened by the ghastly sight, lost touch with their officers, and commenced shooting every living thing they met in the street. As for this incident, Villiers said, "It must have been difficult, under the circumstances of the mutilated heads, to keep even the best of disciplined troops from showing temper." But Villiers claimed that the Japanese troops started a "bloody drama" that went on for three whole days after the occupation of Port Arthur and in the end about "thirty-six Chinamen were the only Celestials remaining in the city." He said that he had seen the band of soldier fiends busy shooting old men who were kneeling with their hands behind their back in front of the Japanese rifles.[73]

There was an immediate counterattack against Villiers' contention. In the March 20 issue of the *New York Times*, a Japanese citizen who only identified him- or herself as a Japanese student pointed out some inaccuracies about the Japanese army in Villiers' article and said that Villiers had described the three-day indiscriminate killing of Chinese civilians only "in the most general way."[74] Villiers countered in the *New York Times* on March 24 by saying that he had been in Port Arthur and the Japanese student had not. There is, however, ample reason to doubt some parts of Villiers' story. Villiers, who had previously stated that only thirty-six people remained alive in Port Arthur, said in his March 24 letter to the *New York Times*, "I would never in my dispatches refer, nor have I in my lectures referred to the massacre of women and children. I only saw the dead bodies of one woman and child, and I thoroughly believe that they were accidently killed."[75] The implication is that what Villiers witnessed was the massacre of soldiers and not the indiscriminate slaughter of civilians.

On July 8, 1895, the *New York Times* carried an article about a letter written by a military expert witness. The witness, Lieutenant M. J. O'Brien, was among the military observers with the Japanese army at the time of the Port Arthur campaign. The U.S. Army had just recalled O'Brien from Japan, possibly because, according to the *New York Times*, the Japanese government found the content of his letter to the War Department disagreeable. In the letter, O'Brien admitted that the Japanese troops killed men who not only could have been made prisoners without resistance, but who were plainly unarmed and in a position of most humble surrender. He also mentioned the mutilated bodies of killed Japanese officers as a factor that excited the Japanese, and he then suggested that the Chinese failure to surrender formally was an indirect cause of the killing. He said that "when they [Japanese troops] advanced through the town [Port Arthur], it is my belief that they were momentarily looking for resistance, and, with such an idea, began to clear the way, with the result that the troops soon got out of hand and made unnecessary slaughter. I do not think the excuse sufficient, but it ought to be borne in mind that such occurrences happen in all armies, and it is hardly fair to expect miracles of the Japanese."[76]

One may accept O'Brien's description and analysis as being more or less accurate when considering the Port Arthur campaign a siege. Unlike ordinary siege campaigns that ended violently, the Chinese defenders abandoned their outposts promptly and fled. Nevertheless, the effect on the attackers was very similar. Usually, attackers continued killing the enemy because after long days of siege they could not accept that the battle had actually ended. As for the Japanese troops entering Port Arthur, they did not, or could not, believe the battle was over because they had anticipated a more stubborn Chinese resistance and "expected to die in its capture." Furthermore, the Japanese soldiers, who were appalled to see the mutilated bodies of their comrades, searched the whole city looking for Chinese soldiers who had discarded their uniforms. The Japanese soldiers did so in "elation at survival and also contempt towards the Chinese defenders." Occasionally, they met resistance by not only plain-clothed soldiers but also civilians mobilized by the regular troops. In the process, the Japanese troops killed many unarmed soldiers as well as civilians.[77]

Again, the massacre of Port Arthur was not exceptional if one considers it an example of a siege. It is not appropriate to claim that the incident symbolized the Japanese military's allegedly savage character that became evident later in the Second Sino-Japanese War and World War II.[78] The Japanese army's conduct in the next war corroborates this conclusion. During the Russo-Japanese War, Japanese soldiers treated Russian POWs humanely and with dignity, and there were no reported incidents like the massacre of Port Arthur. Shortly following the Japanese troops' capture of Port Arthur in the Russo-Japanese War in January 1905—after a three-month siege that had claimed 59,000 casualties— a German observer visiting the city noted how healthy looking the Russian POWs in the city were. Quite a few Russian soldiers who had learned about hospitable treatment at Japan's POW camp in Matsuyama, Japan, shouted "Matsuyama!" when they surrendered.[79]

Already during the Russo-Japanese War, however, the Japanese soldiers began to form a notion that becoming a POW was shameful. There were several reported cases of Japanese soldiers who inadvertently fell into the enemy's hands due to injury and committed suicide either by refusing medical treatment or not eating. Also, quite a few former Japanese POWs of the Russo-Japanese War saw themselves socially ostracized in their hometowns after the war, even though military authorities had exonerated them of any wrongdoing or in some cases even decorated them. It is natural that such a harsh attitude toward their own POWs eventually affected the Japanese opinion toward POWs they captured. A story told in the memoir by Lieutenant General Tamon Jiro, who had participated in the Russo-Japanese War, illustrates how easily the Japanese treatment of POWs might have changed. According to Tamon, a Russian private captured by his unit told Tamon that a Russian captain was hiding on a mountain nearby. Hoping to capture that captain as well, Tamon and his unit searched the mountain for two days, but could not find anyone. Out of frustration, Tamon ordered a sergeant of his unit to behead the prisoner. While the sergeant was hesitating, Tamon began to pity the Russian private and changed his mind.[80] This episode shows how easily the Japanese soldiers would have killed POWs despite the overall humanitarian attitude witnessed by many foreign observers.

Moreover, some Japanese military men were apparently critical of overly generous treatment of POWs during the Russo-Japanese War. One Japanese officer said,

The POW camp built in Matsuyama reportedly treats POWs very well. Generosity, however, has gone too far as to be the hotbed of despicable incidents such as beating of Japanese nationals, other acts of physical violence, drinking at brothel, quarrel among themselves, and even attempted rape of Japanese women. . . . We soldiers fighting in battlefield feel our blood up to hear such stories and like to slash all such misbehaving POWs to death whether they number several thousands or several tens of thousands.[81]

The Japanese military authorities could not ignore such a pervasive feeling among the rank and file of the army and the navy as well as in society. Finally, reports about a huge number of POWs during World War I in Europe led a Japanese army general to write an article in which he called for reliance on valor instead of material strength in military conduct and condemned captivity as a disgrace to be cleared only with death.[82] This view ultimately affected Japan's participation in international agreements. Japan, which had signed the 1899 and 1907 Hague Convention, did not ratify the 1929 Geneva Convention on the treatment of POWs.

Patterns of war atrocities have been consistent in the history of warfare: massacre, destruction for strategic purposes, and violence attributable to the lack of discipline. Also, the violent end of a siege has consistently been a situation in which extensive killing and destruction took place. Yet, war atrocities began to assume different appearances in the early 20th century prior to the Rape of Nanking in 1937, reflecting a larger scale of warfare in which the distinction between combatants and noncombatants was becoming increasingly obscure. In particular, massacre took two distinct forms: the extensive killing of enemy combatants or civilian sympathizers in occupied territory, and a large-scale persecution of ethnic groups within a nation. The deliberate devastation of enemy territory for strategic purposes acquired more intensity in total war where the defeat of the opponent required the destruction of not only the enemy's military forces but also of his war-waging capabilities. Although looting due to a lack or lapse of discipline appeared to be less frequent because of greater professionalism in military forces, the breakdown of logistics could easily turn modern troops into undisciplined marauders. The violent end of siege could also result in a larger death toll as the population of cities grew in the modern era.

All these tendencies pointing to greater violence manifested themselves at the same time as the international community embarked on the codification of laws of war. Geoffrey Best's opinion seems to be valid again in the early 20th century: the observance of the law of war became difficult not because men's minds turned against the ideas of the law itself, but because circumstances made the observance difficult or impossible.[83]

In Asia, some cultural contexts were likely to compound these war atrocities. The lack of development in regulations concerning military conduct in China might add another volatile element to modern warfare. Especially, the military's age-old custom of changing into civilian clothes at the time of defeat was likely to prove compatible with modern-day guerrilla warfare where the distinction between combatants and noncombatants is obscure. The Japanese warrior tradition of despising captivity, which began to be reasserted in the early 20th century, was also likely to create a less favorable environment for POWs in Japanese hands at the same time as the expanding scale of warfare tended to produce an even larger number of POWs. These factors were all present in the late 1930s when the Japanese army started fighting a long war in China.

NOTES

1. International Military Tribunal for the Far East. "Record of Proceedings of the International Military Tribunal for the Far East" (Tokyo: Court House of the Tribunal, 1946, henceforth IMTFE), p. 3,887, microfilm. The proceedings of the trial are also available in R. John Pritchard and Sonia Magbanua Zaide, comp. and ed., *The Tokyo War Crimes Trial: The Complete Transcripts of the Proceedings of the International Military Tribunal for the Far East in Twenty-Two Volumes* (New York: Garland Publishing, 1981).

2. *NYT*, 19 December 1937, p. 8.

3. Christopher Duffy, *Siege Warfare: The Fortress in the Early Modern World 1494–1660* (London: Routledge and Kegan Paul, 1979), p. 250.

4. One of the oldest examples of war atrocities was the conduct of Assyrian troops. See A. T. Olmstead, *History of Assyria* (Chicago: University of Chicago Press, 1968), pp. 93, 97, 256. For the discussion of the Greek and Roman military conduct toward cultural outsiders, see Michael Howard, "Constraint on War," in *The Laws of War: Constraints on Warfare in the Western World*, ed. Michael Howard, George J. Andreopopulos, and Mark R. Shulman (New Haven: Yale University Press, 1994), p. 8; and Josiah Ober, "Classical Greek Times," in ibid., p. 18. Notable examples of siege battles ending violently in the ancient and medieval times were the Roman army's capture of Jotapata in 67 A.D., the first Crusade's storming of Jerusalem in 1099, and the fall of Constantinople to the Ottoman Turks in 1453. For detailed descriptions of these incidents, see Graham Webster, *The Roman Imperial Army of the First and Second Centuries A.D.* (Totowa, NJ: Barnes & Noble Books, 1985), p. 254; Rosalind Hill, ed., *Gesta Francorum et aliorum Hierosolimitanorum* [The Deeds of the Franks and the Other Pilgrims to Jerusalem] (New York: Thomas Nelson and Sons, 1962), p. 91; and Steven Runciman, *The Fall of Constantinople* (Cambridge: Cambridge University Press, 1965), pp. 76–145.

5. Maurice H. Keen, *The Laws of War in the Late Middle Ages* (London: Routledge and Kegan Paul, 1965), p. 123.

6. Martin van Creveld, *Supplying War: Logistics from Wallenstein to Patton* (Cambridge: Cambridge University Press, 1977), p. 7. C. T. Allmand, "The War and the Noncombatant," in *The Hundred Years War*, ed. Kenneth Alan Fowler (London: Macmillan, 1971), pp. 167–70, 180–81. Runciman, *A History of the Crusades*, vol. 1, *The First Crusade and the Foundation of the Kingdom of Jerusalem* (Cambridge: Cambridge University Press, 1951), p. 286.

7. Robert C. Stacey, "The Age of Chivalry," in *The Laws of War*, ed. Howard et al., p. 36. Bernard Brodie and Fawn M. Brodie, *From Crossbow to H-Bomb* (Bloomington: Indiana University Press, 1973), p. 56.

8. John Lothrop Motley, *The Rise of the Dutch Republic: A History*, vol. 2 (New York: Harper and Brothers, 1871), pp. 78–79. James Burke, "The New Model Army and the Problems of Siege Warfare, 1648–51," *Irish Historical Studies*, vol. 27, no. 105, May 1990, pp. 12, 21, 26. C. V. Wedgewood, *The Thirty Years War* (New Haven: Yale University Press, 1939), pp. 288–89. Samuel Rawson Gardiner, *The Thirty Years' War, 1618–1648* (London: Longmans, Green & Co., 1912), p. 134.

9. John Adair, "The Court Martial Papers of Sir William Waller's Army, 1644," *Journal of the Society for Army Historical Research* 44 (1966), pp. 218–22. Burke, "The New Model Army," p. 21. Geoffrey Parker, "Early Modern Europe," in *The Laws of War*, ed. Howard et al., pp. 52, 54. Geoffrey Best, *Humanity in Warfare* (New York: Columbia University Press, 1980), pp. 49, 65.

10. Best, *Humanity in Warfare*, pp. 54, 80, 90. Basil Liddel-Hart, *The Revolution in Warfare* (New Haven: Yale University Press, 1947), pp. 51–52. J. F. C. Fuller, *The Conduct of War 1789–1961: A Study of the Impact of the French, Industrial, and Russian Revolutions on War and Its Conduct* (Westport, CT: Greenwood Press, 1961), p. 74. Ian Clark, *Waging War: A Philosophical Introduction* (Oxford: Clarendon Press, 1988), p. 84.

11. Best, *Humanity in Warfare*, pp. 83, 122.

12. George Haven Putman to the editors of the *NYT*, 3 June 1915, *NYT*, 4 June 1915, p. 10.

13. Allan Nevins, *Ordeal of the Union*, vol. 8 (New York: Scribner's, 1971), p. 170, quoted in Thomas Goodrich, *Bloody Dawn: The Story of the Lawrence Massacre* (Kent, OH: Kent State University Press, 1991), p. 23.

14. Gerald F. Linderman, *Embattled Courage: The Experience of Combat in the American Civil War* (New York: Macmillan, 1987), p. 180. Richard S. Brownlee, *Gray Ghosts of the Confederacy: Guerrilla Warfare in the West, 1861–1865* (Baton Rouge: Louisiana State University Press, 1984), pp. 31, 64–65. Robert N. Scott, comp. and ed., *War of the Rebellion: A Compilation of the Official Records of the Union and Confederate Armies*, series 1, vol. 8 (Washington, D.C.: U. S. Government Printing Office, 1883), pp. 463–64, 476–78. Albert Castel, *A Frontier State at War: Kansas, 1861–1865* (Westport, CT: Greenwood Press, 1979), p. 63. A typical example of military commanders' effort to spare civilian lives was an operation order issued by a federal military headquarters under Sherman in 1864. It said that in case there were local hostilities targeted at troops, "the army commanders should order and enforce a devastation more or less relentlessly" and did not mention any reprisal against humans. Special Field Order no. 120, Headquarters, Military Division of the Mississippi, in the Field, Kingston, Georgia, 9 November 1864, in Edgar L. McCormick, Edward G. McGehee, and May Strahl, ed., *Sherman in Georgia: Selected Source Materials for College Research Paper* (Boston: D. C. Heath, 1961), p. 65.

15. Castel, *A Frontier State at War*, pp. 55, 106. Goodrich, *Bloody Dawn*, p. 100.

16. Alistair Horne, *The Fall of Paris: The Siege and the Commune 1870–71* (New York: St. Martin's Press, 1965), p. 217.

17. Ibid., pp. 358, 363.

18. Ibid., pp. 375–76, 385.

19. Ibid., pp. 375–76, 385, 393, 414–15. Steward Edwards, *The Paris Commune 1871* (New York: Quadrangle Books, 1971), p. 330.

20. Edwards, *The Paris Commune*, p. 340. Horne, *The Fall of Paris*, pp. 380, 418.

21. Forty-one countries signed the Hague Convention on October 18, 1907. Among the signatories were Japan and the United States, but not China. The United States ratified it on November 27, 1909. So did Japan on December 13, 1911. Although China was not one of the original signatories, it ratified the convention on May 10, 1917. Adam Roberts and Richard Guelff, ed., *Documents on the Laws of War*, 2nd ed, (Oxford: Clarendon Press, 1989), pp. 58–59.

22. James Brown Scott, ed., *The Hague Conventions and Declarations of 1899 and 1907*, 3rd ed, (New York: Oxford University Press, 1918), p. 108.

23. Ibid., p. 123.

24. Ibid., pp. 107–08.

25. Ibid., p. 116.

26. Ibid., pp. 101–02.

27. The phrase, "the rape of Belgium," appeared in A. J. Carnoy, "The German 'White Book' Rejected: Futile as an Apology for *the Rape of Belgium* and Worthless as a Document of Facts—How the Evidence Was Taken," *NYT*, 4 June 1915, p. 10. [italics added.] For the depiction of the Armenian massacre as the first case of "genocide," see Jay Winter and Blaine Baggett, *The Great War and the Shaping of the 20th Century* (New York: Penguin Studio, 1996), p. 148.

28. Bryce Commission's Report printed in the *NYT*, 13 May 1915, p. 8.

29. Ibid., p. 6.

30. J. Selden Willmore, *The Great Crime and Its Moral* (New York: George H. Doran, 1917), p. 145.

31. Francis A. March, *History of the World War: An Authentic Narrative of the World's Greatest War* (Philadelphia: United Publishers of the United States and Canada, 1919), p. 88, quoting Brant Whitlock, United States Minister to Belgium.

32. Frank H. Simonds, *History of the World War*, vol. 2 (New York: Doubleday Page, 1919), p. 27.

33. *NYT*, 25 May 1915, p. 1.

34. For a legal debate over the alleged German atrocities between the French and German scholars, see John Horne and Alan Kramer, "German 'Atrocities' and Franco-German Opinion, 1914: The Evidence of German Soldiers' Diaries," *Journal of Modern History*, vol. 66, no. 1 (March 1994): pp. 9–11.

35. Mark Derez, "The Flames of Louvain: The War Experience of an Academic Community," in *Facing Armageddon: The First World War Experienced*, ed. Hugh Cecil and Peter H. Liddle (London: Leo Cooper, 1996), pp. 619–20. Horne and Kramer, "German 'Atrocities' and Franco-German Opinion, 1914," pp. 16–23.

36. Massacres of Armenians by the Turkish central government occurred in 1895–94 and in 1909, with the former reportedly resulting in 200,000 to 250,000 deaths while the latter claimed 25,000 lives. Vahakn N. Dadrian, *The History of the Armenian Genocide: Ethnic Conflict from the Balkans to Anatolia to the Caucasus* (Providence, RI: Berghahn Books, 1995), pp. 147, 155, 182, 193–96, 240–43.

37. *NYT*, 1 June 1915, p. 7.

38. Aneurin Williams to the *Daily News*, quoted in the *NYT*, 18 August 1915, p. 5.

39. Stanford J. Shaw and Ezel Kural Shaw, *History of the Ottoman Empire and Modern Turkey*, vol. 2, *Reform, Revolution, and Republic: The Rise of Modern Turkey 1808–1975* (Cambridge: Cambridge University Press, 1977), p. 315, opts for a smaller number, quoting an unidentified source. Armed Emin, *Turkey in the World War* (New Haven: Yale University Press, 1930), p. 221, adopts a higher figure. Dadrian, *The History of the Armenian Genocide*, p. 225, quoting from an official Turkish source, says that those directly killed by the Turkish military and some "special forces" alone numbered 800,000.

40. Aneurin Williams to the *Daily News*, quoted in the *NYT*, 18 August 1915, p. 5.

41. John Buchan, *A History of the Great War*, vol. 2 (Boston: Houghton Mifflin, 1923), p. 395.

42. *NYT*, 15 December 1915, p. 3, quoting a remark by Viscount Bryce.

43. Martin Gilbert, *The First World War: A Complete History* (New York: Henry Holt, 1994), p. 166. *NYT*, 29 September 1915, p. 1. Shaw, *History of the Ottoman Empire and Modern Turkey*, vol. 2, pp. 315–16.

44. Shaw, *History of the Ottoman Empire and Modern Turkey*, vol. 2, p. 316. Winter and Baggett, *The Great War and the Shaping of the 20th Century*, p. 148. Gilbert, *The First World War*, p. 167. Emin, *Turkey in the World War*, pp. 217, 220. Dadrian, *The History of the Armenian Genocide*, p. 236. Emin denied the existence of a deliberate plan to exterminate the Armenians, but acknowledged that there was a very short time allowed for evacuation; that the deported Armenians were not only unprotected from marauders but also deliberately exposed to their attacks; and that the area chosen for the Armenians' resettlement was a desert incapable of supporting a substantial number of people.

45. Hew Strachen, "The Morale of the German Army, 1917–18." in *Facing Armageddon: The First World War Experienced*, ed. Cecil and Liddle, p. 391.

46. For example, see the *NYT* (all in 1915), 28 April, p. 2; 29 April, p. 2; 1 May, p. 1; 15 May, p. 6; 12 July, p. 4.

47. Herbert Franke, "Siege and Defense of Towns in Medieval China," in *Chinese Ways in Warfare*, ed. Frank A. Kierman, Jr. and John K. Fairbank (Cambridge: Harvard University Press, 1974), pp. 151, 176.

48. James Legge, ed., *The Chinese Classics*, vol. 1, *Confucian Analects, The Great Learning, The Doctrine of the Mean* (Taipei: SMC Publishing, 1991), p. 305.

49. Sun Tzu, *The Art of War*, trans. Thomas Cleary (Boston: Shambhala Publications, 1988), p. 67.

50. Kierman and Fairbank, ed., *Chinese Ways in Warfare*, pp. 6–7, 9–10. Frederick W. Mote, "The T'u-mu Incident of 1449," in ibid., p. 266. Franke, "Siege and Defense of Towns in Medieval China," in ibid., pp. 152–53, 186.

51. Edgar Holt, *The Opium War in China* (Chester Spring, PA: Dufour Editions, 1964), pp. 113–14.

52. Ibid., pp. 107, 141, 144, 147, 200. Charles A. Peterson, "Regional Defense against the Central Power: The Huai-hsi Campaign, 815–817," in *Chinese Ways in Warfare*, ed. Kierman and Fairbank, p. 108.

53. Franz Michael, *The Taiping Rebellion: History and Documents*, vol. 1, *History* (Seattle: University of Washington Press, 1966), p. 174.

54. Ibid. "The Confession of Li Hsiu-cheng," in Michael, *The Taiping Rebellion*, vol. 3, *Documents*, ed. Michael, pp. 1,487, 1,504. Flavia Gifford Anderson, *The Rebel Emperor* (London: Victor Gollancz, 1958), pp. 333–34.

55. In the mid-1860s, Sakamoto Ryoma, one of the Meiji Restoration leaders, proposed an eight-point program the future government should undertake. One of these eight proposed policies was to strengthen Japan's naval force. Marius B. Jansen, *Sakamoto Ryoma and the Meiji Restoration* (Stanford: Stanford University Press, 1971), p. 296. Japan's intention at the time of the First Sino-Japanese War was more defensive than expansionistic. The Japanese naval and military leaders planned the homeland defense extensively in the event of Japan's military failure on the continent and Chinese invasion of the Japanese islands. Hara Takeshi, "Nisshin Senso ni okeru Hondo Boei" [Japanese Defense Plans of the Homeland during the Sino-Japanese War], *Gunji Shigaku* [Journal of Military History, Japan] vol. 20, no. 3 (December 1994), pp. 35–46.

56. Trumbull White, *The War in the East: Japan, China, and Corea* [sic] (Philadel-

phia: P.W. Ziegler & Co., 1895), p. 468, quoting a letter from U.S. Minister to China to U.S. Secretary of State, 1 September 1894. Kojima Noboru, *Oyama Iwao* [Biography of Oyama Iwao], vol. 3 (Tokyo: Bungeishunju, 1985), pp. 348–49. Stewart Lone, *Japan's First Modern War: Army and Society in the Conflict with China, 1894–95* (London: St. Martin's Press, 1994), p. 156.

57. Quoted in Hata Ikuhiko, "Nihon-gun ni okeru Horyo Kannen no Keisei" [The Idea of POWs in the Making: The Case of the Imperial Japanese Army], *Gunji Shigaku* [The Journal of Military History, Japan] (September 1992), p. 10. All translation from foreign languages into English is by the author unless otherwise indicated. The English titles of the *Gunji Shigaku* articles are those given by the journal's editing staff.

58. White, *The War in the East*, pp. 514–15.

59. Hasegawa Shin, *Nihon Horyo-shi* [POW History of Japanese People], vol. 1 (Tokyo: Chuo Koron, 1979), pp. 23, 110–11. In and around today's Kyoto, which was Japan's ancient capital, there are many places where those ears were reportedly buried. Ibid., vol. 2, pp. 199–200.

60. Lone, *Japan's First Modern War*, p. 146. Min'yusha, *Nisshin Gunki* [Soldiers' Stories of Sino-Japanese War] vol. 1 (Tokyo: Min'yusha, 1894), pp. 45–48, quoted in Otani Tadashi, "Ryojun Gyakusatsu Jiken no Ichi Kosatsu" [An Analysis of Port Arthur Massacre], *Senshu Hogaku Ronshu* [Journal of the Senshu University Law School], no. 45 (March 1987), pp. 266–67.

61. *New York World*, 12 December 1894, p. 1.

62. Ibid., 17 December 1894, p. 1.

63. *NYT*, 18 December 1894, p. 5.

64. *New York World*, 20 December 1894, p. 1.

65. Ibid.

66. Okabe Makio, comp. "Ichi Heishi no Mita Nisshin Senso: Kubota Chuzo no Jugun Nikki" [Sino-Japanese War Witnessed by A Soldier: Field Diary of Kubota Chuzo] *Sobun*, no. 126 (November 1974), pp. 21–22, quoted in Okamoto Shumpei, *Impressions of the Front: Woodcuts of the Sino-Japanese War, 1894–95* (Philadelphia: Philadelphia Museum of Art, 1983), p. 37.

67. Cowan to an unidentified person, n.d., quoted in White, *The War in the East*, p. 600. *New York World*, 23 December 1894, pp. 3–4.

68. *New York World*, 22 December 1894, p. 4.

69. *NYT*, 17 December 1894, p. 5; 19 December 1894, p. 5.

70. *Tokyo Nichinichi Shinbun* [Tokyo Nichinichi Newspaper], 4 and 7 December 1894, quoted in Otani, "Ryojun Gyakusatsu Jiken no Ichi Kosatsu" [An Analysis of Port Arthur Massacre], pp. 270–71.

71. Otani, "Ryojun Gyakusatsu Jiken no Ichi Kosatsu" [An Analysis of Port Arthur Massacre], pp. 266–67. Lone, *Japan's First Modern War*, pp. 160–61.

72. *New York World*, 13 December 1894, p. 1. *NYT*, 17 December 1894, p. 5; 30 December 1894, p. 9.

73. Frederic Villiers, "The Truth about Port Arthur," *North American Review* (March 1895), pp. 327, 330.

74. *NYT*, 20 March 1895, p. 10.

75. *NYT*, 24 March 1895, p. 13. A Virginia woman named Alice Mabel Bacon, who seemed to be familiar with Japan and the Japanese people, also questioned the credibility of Villiers' account in a letter to the *NYT*. Bacon suggested that Villiers did not have sufficient knowledge of Japanese and pointed out his inaccurate spellings of some Jap-

anese terms such as *samuri* instead of *samurai* [sword-bearing warrior] and *katang*, which one should spell *katana* [sword]. His lack of knowledge of Japanese cast doubt on his account that he saw thirty-six Chinese wearing caps with a slip of white paper carrying an inscription in Japanese "This man is not to be killed." Bacon also mentioned Villiers' misconception that the *samurai* was a peculiar sect in Japanese society and that the Japanese army used the *samurai* as "armed coolies." She said that the *samurai* was a distinctive social class in the premodern age, comparable to English gentry, and that most politicians and military men were of *samurai* origin. But she strenuously denied the presence of mercenary-like soldiers within the Japanese army. *NYT*, 26 March 1895, p. 13. The *NYT* printed the subsequent exchange of opinions by these two people until early April the same year. They debated mainly the identity of the "armed coolies," who reportedly committed atrocities in Port Arthur along with the regular soldiers. It seems, however, that neither of the two realized the presence of *gunzoku* within the Japanese army. *Gunzoku* denotes the civilians hired by the Japanese military organizations and those belonging to this category were most likely identified as "armed coolies."

76. *NYT*, 8 July 1895, p. 2. In his report, Villiers contended that the Japanese could discredit the American and European press reports but could not deny the reports by military observers, among whom he listed Lieutenant O'Brien at the top. Villiers, "The Truth about Port Arthur," p. 326.

77. Lone, *Japan's First Modern War*, p. 159. Some episodes attest to the intensity of the Japanese troops' mopping-up operation. In a theater within Port Arthur, Chinese actors performed the plays free of charge during and after the siege campaign so that the Japanese soldiers would not mistake them as plainclothes soldiers. At a year-end party, a Japanese company that had participated in the campaign selected those who had killed more than ten Chinese soldiers to let them lead the dance in the banquet. It turned out that eleven soldiers chosen had killed a total of 166. Kojima, *Oyama Iwao*, vol. 4, pp. 102–04.

78. A prime example of literature that concludes that the Port Arthur massacre was a precursor of Japanese atrocities in later wars is Fujimura Michio, *Nisshin Senso* [Sino-Japanese War] (Tokyo: Iwanami Shoten, 1973), p. 132.

79. Hasegawa, *Nihon Horyo-shi* [POW History of Japanese People], vol. 1, p. 161. Ibid., vol. 2, p. 125.

80. Ibid., vol. 1, pp. 204–07.

81. Ibid., vol. 2, p. 124.

82. Hata, "Nihon-gun ni okeru Horyo Kannen no Keisei" [The Idea of POWs in the Making: The Case of the Imperial Japanese Army], p. 19, quoting an article by General Nara Takeji, then director of the army ministry's military affairs, in *Kaikosha Kiji* [Kaikosha Magazine] (June 1918).

83. Best, *Humanity in Warfare*, p. 83.

2

The Battle of Shanghai and the Prelude to Nanking

THE OUTBREAK OF THE SECOND SINO-JAPANESE WAR AND THE BATTLE OF SHANGHAI

The victory in the Sino-Japanese War of 1894–95 did not consolidate Japan's dominant position in Korea. Instead, it opened a way to conflict with another major power, Russia, which was pursuing its traditional policy of southward advance. Russia's influence on Korea and Manchuria increased especially after the Boxer Rebellion, a popular anti-foreign movement among the Chinese people, which temporarily besieged the diplomatic residential area in Peking in 1900.[1] To settle the dispute relating to this incident with major powers, the Ch'ing government of China signed an agreement with these powers, including Japan and Russia, to allow them to station their troops in China. The troop unit that Japan maintained thereafter in the Peking–Tientsin area in accordance with this treaty provision was called the Tientsin Garrison.

Japan finally entered a war against Russia in 1904 and would eliminate the Russian presence in Korea and Southern Manchuria by 1905.[2] Japan ultimately annexed Korea in 1910 and held it as a part of Japan until 1945. The peace treaty of the Russo-Japanese War also entitled Japan to some interests in Southern Manchuria. At the same time, Japan was allowed to maintain a military force in Manchuria to protect the Southern Manchurian Railway, one of these acquired interests. This was the beginning of the Kwantung Army, which later became notorious for its active roles in Japan's continental expansion in the late 1920s to the 1930s. Thereafter, Japan viewed Korea and Southern Manchuria as an area of prime importance because "victories in the field [had] created a new pantheon of national heroes and a pervasive sense of nationalism. These accomplishments also sanctified Japanese rights and interests in Korea and Manchuria as matters of national honor."[3]

The Kwantung Army, which was supposed to be subordinate to the Japanese army's high command in Tokyo, began to demonstrate its propensity for independent actions as the Japanese began to see the rise of Chinese nationalism as a threat to Japan's interests in Manchuria.[4] Since the Ch'ing Dynasty's fall in 1912, the Chinese Nationalist Party, founded by Sun Yat-sen, had aimed to unify China, which was then divided by many warlords. Chiang Kai-shek, Sun's successor as the Nationalist Party leader, embarked on a military expedition to unify the country in the mid-1920s and had virtually achieved his objective by 1928 by either defeating the warlords or incorporating them into the Nationalist rule.

As the Nationalists' influence grew, some Kwantung Army staff officers formulated a radical plan to safeguard Japan's presence in Manchuria—to detach Manchuria from the rest of China. Finally, in September 1931 the Kwantung Army had a part of the Southern Manchurian Railway blown up by its own soldiers, blamed the incident on the Chinese, and started a military operation to drive the Chinese Nationalists' presence out of Manchuria. Then, the Japanese troops stationed in Korea crossed the border, entered Manchuria, and swept through Manchuria with the Kwantung Army. Although the Japanese troops on the continent conducted all these operations without any prior approval from the central government in Tokyo, the Japanese political leaders approved these actions *ipso post facto* since an overwhelming majority of the Japanese people, who had been struck hard by economic depression, cheered at the remarkable military success in Manchuria.[5] Under Japan's protection, Manchukuo, or the Manchurian Empire, was established in the following year with Henry Pu Yi, the last emperor of the Ch'ing Dynasty, as its Emperor.

Japan's subsequent policy in China was to safeguard Manchukuo. Although the Japanese did not openly acquire or detach further territory from Chiang Kai-shek thereafter, they attempted to erode the Nationalist government's influence in provinces adjacent to Manchukuo. The Japanese policy in China was certainly aggressive and undeniably had an invasionist character. Yet, the way the Japanese political—and even military—leaders made their decisions shows that the Japanese policy in China was incrementalism. In other words, leaders responded to situations as they arose. Thus, "it would be reckless to view Japanese policy decisions regarding China as predetermined and deliberately planned."[6]

In addition to Japan's encroachment on Chinese sovereignty, Chiang also had to face another opponent, the Chinese Communists. Chiang initially intended to destroy the Communists first because, according to his logic, China could not resist external aggression while having an enemy inside. Then, an incident occurred that changed Chiang's stance and the Nationalist policies toward the Communists and the Japanese. On December 12, 1936, Chang Hsueh-liang, one of Chiang Kai-shek's subordinate military commanders, abducted the generalissimo when Chiang went to Chang's headquarters in Sian to encourage him to pursue the anti-Communist military campaign more vigorously. Chang, a one-time warlord whose father Chang Tso-lin had been murdered in a plot organized by Japanese army officers, undertook this rebellion to urge the generalissimo to challenge the Japanese more aggressively. Many questions still remain unanswered today about this event, known as the Sian Incident, such as how Chiang was ultimately released on December 25 and whether he struck a secret deal with the Communists who reportedly mediated between Chiang and Chang. But there was one distinct result: Chiang Kai-shek vigorously pursued an anti-Japanese policy thereafter.[7]

Anti-Japanese sentiment among the Chinese people was mounting even before the Sian Incident. The virtual rapprochement between the Nationalists and the Communists following the Sian Incident added fuel to that sentiment. In view of the increasing tension between the Japanese and the Chinese in the area, the Japanese reinforced the Tientsin Garrison from 2,000 men to 7,000 men by the summer of 1937. Then, a minor skirmish took place between a part of the Tientsin Garrison and the Chinese 29th Army in the suburb of Peking on the night of July 7, 1937. It soon developed into a large-scale undeclared war between the two countries. Following the Tientsin Garrison's entry into Peking on July 28, the conflict spread to Shanghai, where unidentified assailants assassinated a Japanese navy lieutenant and a sailor on August 9. The Japanese Imperial Navy, which commanded its landing forces in Shanghai—the only available Japanese force in the city—sought to settle the incident peacefully in view of the small number of troops stationed there.[8] Moreover, the Japanese had to take into account the foreign interests in the city, a situation unlike that in northern China, where the Japanese overtly attempted to detach some provinces from the control of Chiang's Nationalists and turn them into a semiautonomous administrative unit.[9] Yet, on August 12 the Japanese government decided to dispatch army units to reinforce the landing forces in Shanghai at the request of the navy, which had grave concerns about the fate of its own units.

Since neither Japan nor China was prepared for this undeclared war, the two countries fought the battle of Shanghai and the subsequent military campaign to Nanking without paying sufficient attention to prospective ends. Even their tactical or strategic objectives were unclear. Such an improvised way of fighting was attributable to the inability of the Japanese leaders to restrain the actions of local military commanders and the mounting anti-Japanese feeling among the Chinese people, which compelled the Chinese leaders to fight. Although some groups on both sides welcomed the conflict, most did not expect it.

The Japanese army formed the Shanghai Expeditionary Force (SEF), composed initially of the 3rd and 11th Divisions, with General Matsui Iwane called out from the reserve as commander. The army leadership apparently made this appointment because of Matsui's association with late Sun Yat-sen, the founder of the Chinese Nationalist Party, and other Chinese Nationalist leaders in the past as well as Matsui's political activities in Asian affairs after his retirement from active service.[10] Matsui formed *Dai Ajia Kyokai* or the Great Asian Society in 1935 as an effort to organize Asian peoples, who were then chaotically divided among themselves, into a league-like entity so as to terminate all struggles among Asian races and resist external interference as well as external attempts to disrupt Asian unity.[11] With the support of the government and the army, Matsui toured China the following year and met with Chiang Kai-shek and his political rivals whose power base was in the Kuangtung and Kuangsi area. Matsui's ostensible purpose was to mediate between Chiang and these political rivals and strengthen their anti-Communist stance.[12] Yet Matsui appeared to be more sympathetic to the Kuangtung–Kuangsi leaders. In one of his meetings with Chiang's rivals, Matsui listened to and fully agreed with the latter's remark that the growing Communist influence was a source of calamity in China. In a meeting with Chiang and other Nationalist leaders in March 1936, Matsui reiterated a need to suppress communism and even proposed an agreement between Japan and China for this purpose.[13] It is easy to imagine that Chiang's move toward a united front with the Communists after the Sian Incident irritated Matsui and convinced him that the only solution to Japan's problems on the Asian mainland was to chastise the Chinese leadership in a determined way.[14] This notion significantly affected the subsequent course of events, in particular, the Japanese army's march to Nanking.

A part of the Expeditionary Force landed on the northern shore of Shanghai on August 23. Later the high command in Tokyo assigned four more divisions (the 9th, the 13th, the 14th, and the 101st) to Matsui's command. As a result, the total strength of the Japanese troops in Shanghai amounted to about 190,000 men by September 20. Initially, however, the military leaders in Tokyo intended to deal a devastating blow to the Chinese army in northern China instead of at Shanghai and thus directed the SEF only to "occupy the important defense perimeters in the north of Shanghai and protect the Japanese nationals." This rather passive stance in the initial phase of the Shanghai campaign derived from the Japanese high command's concern that the Soviet military might capitalize on the ongoing conflict in China by invading Manchuria. Foremost among the proponents of a decisive campaign in northern China and defensive operations in Shanghai was Major General Ishiwara Kanji, chief of the Planning Bureau, the army's General Staff. Some army generals, including General Matsui, were, however, in favor of striking at the heart of the enemy, that is, Shanghai and Nanking—the latter being the capital city of China at the time—to deal a smashing blow to the enemy's morale and bring a swift end to the conflict.[15]

The Chinese Nationalists were by no means ready for a military showdown with the Japanese. Although the German advisers attached to Chiang Kai-shek's army had planned to create sixty modern divisions, there were no more than ten such divisions, or approximately 80,000 men, at the time. In fact, Secretary of the Military Affairs Commission Hsu Yung-ch'ang suggested that the Nationalist government should seek a compromise with the Japanese, if possible, in view of the unpreparedness of the army. Nevertheless, the Chinese Nationalist leaders, Chiang Kai-shek in particular, were determined to fight a major battle in Shanghai.[16]

Observers and historians have given several reasons for Chiang's decision. First, he decided on a showdown with the Japanese apparently to strengthen his own popularity in China. This was clearly one of the effects of the Sian Incident, which made Chiang, whether willingly or reluctantly, adopt a clear anti-Japanese stance. Chiang said in a speech on July 17, "If we allow one inch more of our territory to be lost, or our sovereignty to be again infringed, we shall be guilty of committing an unpardonable offense against our race. There will then be no way left but to throw all the resources of our nation into a grim struggle for ultimate victory."[17] Since Chiang's close contact and association with his military advisers from Germany made him familiar with the idea that domestic and international problems were closely linked, it seems that he aimed to increase his domestic prestige by fighting an external war and casting himself as the defender of China's sovereignty. Second, the generalissimo wished to involve Western powers in the war. Most likely, he reasoned that a military conflict in the presence of foreign interests might provoke foreign sympathy, possibly even intervention. Third, the area around Shanghai was a vital economic center that the Chinese Nationalists had to defend at any cost to secure their power base. Fourth, the prospective battleground looked favorable to the Chinese because they had earned a draw with the Japanese in 1932 in the First Shanghai Incident, a conflict the Japanese and the Chinese settled by mutually withdrawing their forces.[18]

Chiang issued a general mobilization order on August 15 and made himself the commander in chief of both the Chinese army and navy. At the same time, he kept reinforcing the troops in Shanghai at a rate of one or two divisions a day and brought the total strength of the Chinese forces in the area to eighty-three divisions consisting of about 700,000 soldiers by the end of the Shanghai campaign.[19] Against the Japanese, who were believed to possess superior equipment and obviously had control of the air, they offered stubborn resistance. Japanese commanders and soldiers alike admitted to the tenacity of Chinese soldiers. Major General Iinuma Mamoru, SEF staff chief, said, "Since the enemy is not only superior in number but also brave and tenacious, we have a hard time making a steady progress in our campaign." Colonel Uemura Toshimichi, deputy chief of SEF staffs, stated in his diary, "The Chinese stick to the defense positions like ticks, and flock again to the original positions like flies even if they are dispositioned." Even common soldiers noticed a change in the way the Chinese fought. In a discussion back in Japan, one soldier commented, "The era of timid and despicable Chinese is gone. Some of them are quite courageous."[20]

Meanwhile, contrary to the Japanese military's intention to seek a decisive battle in northern China, Chiang Kai-shek tried to avoid such a showdown in that theater so as to concentrate his military effort in Shanghai.[21] Subsequently, the Chinese troop concentration and the Japanese initial strategy of maintaining a defensive posture in the Shanghai area resulted in stalemated positional warfare in that area. Historians and observers generally dwell on the more advanced equipment used by the Japanese as compared with the relatively outdated weapons with which the Chinese equipped themselves at the battle of Shanghai.[22] The Japanese troops, however, had their own problems. Although they had more artillery, they did not have sufficient or reliable ammunition. Foot soldiers often complained that many of their hand grenades did not explode. One company commander referred to such a defective weapon as "the leftover of the Russo-Japanese War." As a result, a ranking officer of the General Staff who inspected the Shanghai front concluded in his report that the Japanese army's equipment for close-range fighting was inferior to that of the Chinese troops in terms of both quality and quantity. One soldier of the 19th Mountain Artillery Regiment also said, "The enemy's machine guns, firing almost without interruption, make our infantry charge nearly impossible." In the static battle of attrition, the Japanese losses amounted to 9,115 killed and 31,257 wounded by the end of the Shanghai campaign in early November 1937. Heavy casualties caused bitter resentment at home. At Shizuoka in central Japan, the wife of Colonel Tanoue Hachiro, who commanded the 34th Regiment of the SEF's 3rd Division, committed suicide apparently because she was distressed at the deaths of so many soldiers hailing from the region.[23]

As time went on, it became apparent to the Japanese military leaders in Tokyo that the Japanese troops could not smash the Chinese forces decisively in northern China, where the Chinese army was resorting to delaying actions and conducting flexible operations.[24] Ishiwara, who had consistently been a proponent of a decisive campaign in northern China, left the General Staff on September 27. Major General Shimomura Sadamu took his place and started considering a more aggressive offensive campaign in the Shanghai area.[25] Subsequently, the army General Staff organized the Tenth Army on October 20 to start a new military operation. The Tenth Army, commanded by Lieutenant General Yanagawa Heisuke, included the 18th and 114th Divisions from Japan as well as the 6th Division and the 9th Brigade from the northern China theater. At the same time, the Japanese high command transferred the 16th Division from north China to Shanghai and assigned it to the SEF.

The Tenth Army landed on the shore of Hangchou Bay to the south of Shanghai on November 5 and began to threaten the right flank of the Chinese defense. Two days later, General Matsui, who had thus far commanded the Shanghai Expeditionary Force, became the commander of the Central China Area Army (CCAA), an umbrella command for both the SEF and the Tenth Army. For the time being, Matsui was the commander of both the CCAA and the SEF. The General Staff directed Matsui to annihilate the enemy in and around Shanghai by cooperating with the navy so that the army could break the enemy's will to continue the war and obtain a chance to bring the war to an end. In a specific guideline regarding the CCAA's military operation, the General Staff allowed the CCAA to operate only to the east of the line connecting Soochow and Changshu—cities about 100 kilometers east of Shanghai and west of Lake T'ai. This directive virtually prohibited the army's march to the Chinese capital of Nanking.[26]

It soon became apparent, however, that the Japanese troops could not achieve their objective—the destruction of the main component of the Chinese Nationalist Army—within the limit imposed by the General Staff because the Chinese began to slip away from the Shanghai area. By the time the Tenth Army landed on the shore of Hangchou Bay, the Chinese had suffered over 150,000 casualties due to constant Japanese air raids and shelling from Japanese warships off-shore.[27] By late October, according to Chinese POWs captured by the Japanese, many divisions were so decimated that their strength had shrunk to only 1,000 soldiers each—one-tenth of full strength. As the Tenth Army started threatening the right flank of the Chinese defenses, the Chinese army finally started retreating from the Shanghai area on November 9. Soon, the retreat turned into a rout. Even Chinese Nationalist sources admitted that complete chaos prevailed as the retreating troops' telephone cables were severed, causing a loss of contact between the superior command and subordinate units. Japanese war planes bombed and strafed the retreating Chinese soldiers and further worsened their predicament.[28]

Although the Chinese troops are often said to have fought by trading space for time, the battle of Shanghai was definitely an exception, and a costly one.[29] General Hsiao Tsun-cheng, Operation Chief of the Chinese Eastern War Zone, argued that a political consideration, or even a mood, dictated the Chinese strategy in Shanghai. He said, "The whole country has been aroused by the stand at Shanghai and many of the political leaders were deluded into thinking that the Chinese could hold out forever between Shanghai and Nanking."[30] On the tactical level, one of the German military advisers attached to Chiang also criticized the campaign and said, "[I]n the face of undeniable superiority in enemy fire-power, the tenacious defense of the fixed positions at Shanghai had been courageous but ill-advised."[31] With their elite troops decimated in the Shanghai area, the Chinese could not form new defensive lines about fifty miles to the west of Shanghai as they had originally planned. As a result, the positional war in Shanghai changed into a war of rapid movement.

When the ranking Chinese Nationalist generals and their German advisers assembled in Nanking in mid-November to discuss the possible defense of the capital, General Li Tsung-jen, commander of the Fifth War Zone, opposed the idea. He reasoned,

Strategically speaking, Nanking was a dead end. The enemy could surround it from three sides, while to the north the Yangtze cut off any possibility of retreat. It was impossible for a newly defeated army to hold an isolated city for very long. In history there was no fortress that could not be taken, and our troops were suffering from the recent defeat and lacking in morale. Moreover, no reinforcements could be brought in to help. The enemy was near its goal and the morale of its army was high. Nanking would surely fall.[32]

Li's argument aptly summed up the nature of the Nanking campaign. Even though Nanking looked defensible by virtue of its natural and man-made defenses—the Yangtze River and the city walls—the terrain to the east is quite flat, and that was the very area where the Japanese were approaching. Therefore, it was highly likely that those defenses themselves could become traps for the defenders and turn the battle in Nanking into a gigantic and, for the Chinese, hopeless, siege campaign.

Most of the other generals and the German advisers concurred with Li.[33] Then, General T'ang Shen-chih, who was executive chief of the military affairs committee at the time, proposed to make another stand in the capital. According to Li, T'ang, who had been physically ill and inactive for a while, apparently wanted to take this opportunity to promote his own position within the military and thus said in a stern tone and "with righteous indignation," "The enemy is approaching the nation's capital, which is also the site of the mausoleum of the National Father [Sun Yat-sen]. If, when the enemy is at our door, Nanking does not sacrifice one or two big generals, how can we account for ourselves before the soul of the National Father in heaven, and how can we discharge our duties before the supreme commander? I advocate defending Nanking to the end and fighting the enemy to the death."[34] This contradicts the statement later made by T'ang, who said, "I agreed to the stand in Nanking to gain some time to reorganize the front troops and give them a rest while concentrating the reserves in the rear so that we could delay the enemy's advance."[35]

Thus, although T'ang did agree to the defense of Nanking, he did so, according to him, for a tactical reason, not out of emotion or personal ambition. Even so, T'ang himself confessed that he had realized the impossibility of a prolonged defense of the capital. Answering a friend who asked how long he could hold, T'ang replied, "Only heaven knows."[36]

Li and T'ang, however, concur on one thing—Chiang Kai-shek's willingness to resist the Japanese army again in Nanking. According to T'ang's testimony, Chiang became increasingly emotional in the course of the Shanghai campaign. T'ang describes how Chiang shouted hysterically over the phone at local commanders in Shanghai from his headquarters in Nanking. T'ang also quotes Chiang as saying, "Nanking must be defended. . . . If nobody wishes to defend it, I will do it." As for Li, he records Chiang's joyous reaction to what Li claims to be T'ang's aggressive statement. Li concludes that Chiang's decision to fight another battle in Nanking was a judgment based on emotion, perhaps even on a desire to match his strength against that of the Japanese militarists.[37]

It seems, however, that Chiang himself also realized how hopeless the military situation was. While directing his generals to defend Nanking, the Nationalist government decided to move its capital from Nanking to Chungch'ing on November 19. On November 30, Chiang sent a directive to General T'ang and two other generals who commanded the Third and Seventh War Zones adjacent to Nanking. That directive seems to have reflected Chiang's confused thinking. While ordering the two generals commanding the war zones merely to "delay the enemy's advance," he commanded T'ang to "defend the established defense lines at any cost and destroy the enemy's besieging force by closely cooperating with the troops of the Third War Zone."[38] Thus, emotionalism fueled by rising anti-Japanese sentiment among the populace as well as inconsistent military planning that reflected the leadership's unpreparedness for war characterized the Chinese defense of Nanking.

Chiang formally appointed General T'ang the commander of the Nanking garrison on November 25. By then, the Chinese forces that had fought in Shanghai had been weakened considerably and were retreating inland. So disorganized was their movement that some commanders had to put posters on the walls of houses to let their soldiers know where they should regroup. The retreating Chinese suffered mainly from airplane bombs and artillery fire. A newspaper article in late November underlined this fact with a report that about 90 percent of the wounded Chinese soldiers suffered injuries from shrapnel and bomb fragments, whereas only a few were hit by machine guns and almost none by rifles. Thus, T'ang's garrison force consisted of considerably weakened units. On paper, he had thirteen infantry divisions and other units including artillery and military police. If those units had maintained their maximum force strength, the total number of Chinese soldiers defending Nanking would have amounted to 180,400. But many divisions were not at full strength.[39]

Since the troop strength of the Nanking garrison in relation to the total number of victims has been one of the controversial topics in the Rape of Nanking debate, this issue will be subject to analysis here. Owing to the lack or shortage of official statistics, estimates vary on the actual number of Chinese defenders. The Chinese 160th Division, for example, had 3,000 men less than its full strength on November 18. This figure represented a loss of about 30 percent, most likely as a result of the Shanghai campaign. The 88th Division had about 6,000 or about 40 percent less than full strength. The 51st Division suffered even more in Shanghai and lost about half of its original strength.[40] If a 30 to 50 percent reduction is applied uniformly to all units, the total force strength of the Nanking garrison would have been 90,000 to 130,000.

Recently, a Chinese scholar, using an equally rough computation method, estimated the total strength at about 150,000.[41] Various contemporary sources, however, suggest that the actual number was smaller. The SEF's staff thought after the battle that they had confronted about 100,000 men. Sublieutenant Maeda Yoshihiko, a Japanese platoon commander who apparently had heard the estimate made by Japanese higher commands, noted in his diary on December 10 that the Chinese had a "garrison of about 60,000 men." F. Tillman Durdin, a *New York Times* correspondent stationed in Nanking at the time, put the number of Chinese within the Nanking walls at 50,000. The U.S. Army's intelligence report estimated the force strength in Nanking as of December 5 at 40,000 to 50,000. The smallest estimate was probably the one found in the intelligence data collected by the Tenth Army headquarters. Its information report on December 3, 1937, said, "The Chinese defenders in Nanking numbered about 35,000."[42] Since Maeda, Durdin, the U.S. military intelligence, and the Tenth Army command discussed the Chinese troops within or in the immediate vicinity of the Nanking walls and excluded those troops engaged in battles in the city's

Chart 2.1

Estimated Strength of Chinese Garrison as Reported by Various Sources

Estimate	Source	Note
150,000	Sun Chai-wei's article, 1988	Extrapolation based on a staff officer of the garrison headquarter; likely an overestimation.
110,000	Sung Hsi-lian, chief of Chinese 36th Div., a figure given in his memoir	Estimate by one of the Chinese military leaders; one of probable figures.
100,000	Japanese SEF Staff's estimate found on staff chief Iinuma's diary entry on 17 Dec. 1937	Iinuma apparently assumed that there were 20 Chinese divisions, each with 5,000 men.
81,000	T'an Tao-p'ing, staff officer of the Chinese Nanking Garrison, quoted in Sun Chai-wei's article	Estimate by one of the Chinese military leaders; one of probable figures.
65,500-70,500	Kaikosha, a Japanese group, 1989	Very minute calculation was done, but some questionable aspects are found.
60,000	Japanese Sub-Lt. Maeda Yoshihiko's diary entry on 10 Dec. 1937	Maeda did not give any information source.
50,000	Durdin, NYT correspondent, in *NYT*, 18 Dec. 1937	Durdin must have had an information source, but it was not identified.
40,000-50,000	U.S. G-2 Report, 10 August 1938	No information source was given.
35,000	Japanese 10th Army's report, 3 Dec. 1937	No information source was given.

outskirts, the actual number of Nanking garrison soldiers must have been higher than their estimates.

Recently, an association of former Japanese army officers provided in its publication an estimate of 65,500 to 70,500, using some Chinese sources (Chart 2.1). Although their computation was very detailed, some of their analyses are questionable. For example, they determined the force strength of the Training Unit, which entrenched itself at the Tzuchin Mountain and its vicinity, to be only 5,500 to 6,000 in three regiments, contradicting some Chinese Nationalist army veterans who said there were more than thirteen regiments of 30,000 men.[43] One may argue that this estimate of more than 30,000 was probably a full strength on paper. In addition, some sources point to a certain degree of erosion of its force strength after the Shanghai battle.[44] Yet, the gap between

5,500 to 6,000 and 30,000 is too large to be overlooked. Accordingly, the estimated total strength of the Nanking garrison was likely to be somewhere between the recent Chinese estimate of 150,000 and the Japanese estimate of around 70,000.

Although not completely reliable, one can use the data available in the U.S. Army intelligence and diplomatic documents as another set of sources to narrow this wide numerical range. According to a G-2 report in August 1937, the total manpower of the thirteen divisions that were later to join the garrison amounted to 97,000. As for the strength of other units, they were roughly equal to three divisions since a U.S. diplomatic telegram on December 4 quoted a Chinese military source as saying that sixteen divisions had been assigned to the defense of Nanking. If they had been fully manned, they would have added 30,000 to 97,000 men to bring the total strength of the garrison to 127,000 men. Suppose each of these three divisions had approximately the same force strength as the other thirteen divisions—about 7,500 each—the three divisions would have added 22,500 men to the garrison, bringing the total to nearly 115,000. By approximating these two figures, one can obtain a range of 110,000 to 130,000. The attrition at Shanghai and in subsequent battles undoubtedly reduced the size of some divisions although some of them might have been reinforced later. In addition, one must also take into account the presence of quite a few civilians that the Chinese military inducted into the garrison as militia-like troops. According to a U.S. diplomatic telegram from Nanking on December 4, 1937, the Chinese garrison apparently armed some civilians in the southern area of the city where the Japanese planned their approach. Thus, the Nanking garrison could have been 150,000 strong, including those auxiliaries. It is, however, questionable whether all those soldiers remained in the city and its immediate outskirts when the Japanese troops made their final assault on Nanking. According to U.S. diplomatic sources, the morale of quite a few troops was poor, while many of them were disorganized. Desertion was quite likely in such troops. Moreover, during the battle some troops apparently left the city before the garrison commander issued a formal order for evacuation. It is appropriate to estimate the size of the Chinese garrison force at between 110,000 and 130,000, although it possibly numbered 150,000 at one point, including militia-type soldiers but possibly decreased to 80,000 to 70,000 toward the end of the battle.[45]

The quality of soldiers was another problem the Chinese military leaders faced. Already at Shanghai, the Chinese troops, whose quality was better than that of the Nanking garrison, exhibited their ineptitude. According to General Hsiao, the Chinese soldiers did not understand the necessity of trenches and rather than dig them were willing to stand up and depend on courage alone. Also, an American observer cited as one of their fatal weaknesses the complete lack of anything even resembling a disposition in depth. Then, heavy losses in Shanghai forced almost all units to replace veteran soldiers with new recruits. The 87th Division, for example, had its ranks replenished four times and had to fill two-thirds of its total with new recruits. One may easily imagine how the Chinese defenders of Nanking, the remnant of such troops already decimated in Shanghai or these newly conscripted soldiers, performed in defense of the capital. In addition, the Nanking garrison was augmented by the troops from Szechuan and Yunnan provinces—the units less reliable than those under Chiang's direct command. So unreliable were these troops that there was a report from "a very reliable source" that Chiang Kai-shek delayed his departure from Nanking to prevent the defection of the commanders of those units. An official record of the Chinese Nationalists analyzed the Nanking campaign and attributed its failure to the shortage of experienced soldiers after heavy losses in previous engagements. As a result, the record continues, new recruits joined the fight without training and could not make effective use of fortifications. Also, the record says, commanders did not have mutual respect and lacked the ability to act independently.[46]

If the Chinese did not prepare the defense of Nanking properly, the Japanese did not plan the advance to Nanking very well, either. In this theater at this point, the Japanese military began to display its notorious tendency: local military commanders took independent and unauthorized actions and thereby forced the central command in Tokyo—and eventually even the government—to endorse the *fait accompli*.[47] After the Chinese defense in and around Shanghai crumbled, the ranking Japanese generals wished to pursue the enemy to Nanking. General Matsui, who had been eager to march to the Chinese capital from the beginning of the Shanghai conflict, tried to persuade two colonels dispatched from the General Staff and the War Ministry to agree to the commencement of the Nanking campaign. Major General Iinuma, SEF chief of staff, also noted in his diary that in view of the progress of the battle "we must pursue the enemy up to Nanking by capitalizing on the recent victory." The Tenth Army, which was still fresh on the battlefield, did more than express its wish to conduct further military operations. Without obtaining the permission of higher command, its commanding general Yanagawa ordered its subordinate units to go after the fleeing enemy to Nanking on November 19. Major General Tada Hayao, deputy chief of the General Staff in Tokyo, was alarmed at this report and tried to restrain the movement of Yanagawa's troops.[48]

By this time, events had begun to escape the control of the leaders in Tokyo. General Matsui urged the General Staff in Tokyo on November 22 to allow his troops to occupy Nanking. Matsui stated by telegraph that the enemy's resistance was waning at every defensive position and that they did not seem to have a strong will to hold Nanking at any cost. Matsui then discussed how military inaction would not only allow the Chinese to regain their strength and thus prolong the war, but would also have an adverse effect on public opinion in Japan. He concluded that it was advisable for the Japanese army to conquer Nanking by utilizing their advantageous position at the time and bring a clear end to the military operation in the central China theater. Matsui estimated the time period needed for the operation at two months.[49]

Besides Matsui, some officers of the General Staff were also eager to extend the military operation to Nanking. Although Deputy Chief of General Staff Tada was against the expansion of the operation area, Major General Shimomura, who had replaced Ishiwara as the chief of the Planning Bureau and was in favor of a more aggressive campaign in central China, repeatedly urged Tada to change his mind.[50] Other young officers were also in favor of commencing the operation to capture the Chinese capital.[51] The General Staff finally acquiesced to the pressure and abolished the operation restriction line on November 24. Tada's wording in his instruction on this day symbolically illustrated the feeble control of the central command over the local troops: "It is now no use to operate within the previously determined operation area in view of the situation of our troops and theirs. In addition, a part of CCAA has already moved beyond the said area and is pursuing the enemy by capitalizing on its confusion. Accordingly, the operation restriction line . . . will be abolished *owing to circumstances beyond our control*." [Italics added.][52] The General Staff gave a formal order on December 1 to the CCAA to capture Nanking.[53]

In the process of reaching the decision to conquer Nanking, one can note somewhat irrational and even contradictory aspects, which reflected the improvised nature of the Japanese military's campaign planning following the sudden and unexpected start of the war. Although the Japanese military leadership apparently deployed the troops to attempt an envelopment, Tenth Army commander Yanagawa stated in his message to General Matsui and the Chief of General Staff, "The main objective of the advance toward Nanking is the occupation of the enemy's capital, which is strategically and politically important, and not the interception or destruction of the Chinese troops. . . . We conclude that the opportunity to intercept and annihilate the enemy's main force had already passed when we missed that chance during the battle in the Shanghai area."[54]

Yanagawa did not present a rational estimate regarding the expected resistance by the Chinese, either. He said, "The overall situation right now will not allow us to call off the Nanking campaign. Also, I have a belief *based upon my sixth sense* that we can capture Nanking easily by pursuing the enemy." [Italics added.][55] It seems that political considerations and optimistic estimates weighed heavily in the Japanese army leaders' decision to march on Nanking. Yanagawa seems to have thought, or hoped, that the Chinese Nationalists would give up the war "because of political and strategic damage resulting from the loss of their capital."[56] Matsui apparently shared the same opinion since he defined the Nanking campaign as the "approach to the enemy's heart" when he urged the General Staff to allow him to occupy Nanking on November 22.[57]

The entire process leading to the decision to capture Nanking shows that "Japanese army policy-making was a 'system of irresponsibilities,' lacking accountability and potentially irrational."[58] Such irrationality—symbolized by Yanagawa's reliance on his sixth sense—and irresponsibility plagued every level of the Japanese army and, as the next chapter will show, became an important factor contributing to the occurrence of atrocities.

Map 2.1
Japanese Army's Troop Disposition at the Start of Its March to Nanking

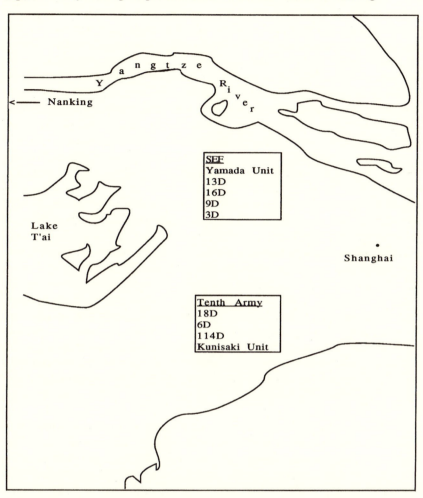

Meanwhile, General Asaka Yasuhiko, army general and uncle-in-law of Emperor Hirohito, was appointed the commander of the SEF on December 2. General Matsui was now the commander of the CCAA only.

JAPANESE ARMY'S MARCH TO NANKING

Under the plan formulated by the CCAA leadership, the SEF was to advance north of Lake T'ai toward Nanking while the Tenth Army was to march in south of the lake (Map 2.1). In the northern theater, the 13th Division and a part of the 11th Division were to cover the northern flank of the three divisions of the 16th, the 9th, and the 3rd advancing eastward to Nanking. A part of the extreme northern flank units formed a detachment force and was under orders to cross the Yangtze in the east of Nanking to cut off the escape route of the Nanking garrison force. Leading this detachment was Major General Yamada Senji, commander of the 103rd Brigade. In the southern theater, the Kunisaki Detachment—the combination of the 41st Regiment and others commanded by Major General Kunisaki Noboru—was to proceed in the extreme south of the area and cross the Yangtze west of Nanking to intercept the Chinese troops expected to retreat from the city. Marching to the north of the Kunisaki Detachment were the 18th, the 6th, and the 114th Divisions. The Tenth Army started its full-scale advance to Nanking on December 3 while the SEF began its drive two days later.

This hastily planned and executed military campaign caused considerable confusion and even contradiction in the conduct of front-line troops. In particular, military headquarters' directives calling for tighter military discipline contradicted the logistical necessities under which the troops had to operate. The SEF headquarters, for example, cautioned its subordinate units to tighten their discipline immediately before they started marching toward Nanking.[59] Lieutenant General Yanagawa, commanding the Tenth Army, also issued the following statement to his soldiers on November 17:

Some reports reaching me suggest that there have been quite a few cases of robbery and rape, which must not happen. I deeply regret the occurrences of such incidents since misconduct like these will not only leave a blot on the military records of the Tenth Army but also tarnish the glorious reputation of the Imperial Japanese Army. I sincerely ask all the officers and soldiers to be mindful of their own conduct and to maintain a strict discipline. At the same time, I hope everyone will do his best to fulfill his respective duties.[60]

One may, however, question how seriously Japanese commanders like Yanagawa expected his soldiers to listen to those warnings when taking into consideration the supply policy of the CCAA. Since the Japanese decided on the Nanking campaign without adequate prior planning or logistical arrangement, they could not supply the advancing troops sufficiently. Apparently, the Japanese depended mainly on water transportation for sending materials forward. Major Kisaki Hisashi, a staff officer of the 16th Division, said in his diary, "Supply columns have not arrived yet. Beyond Tanyang, there is no river route. Moreover, motor vehicles could not run due to the conditions of the road."[61]

When some troops could not obtain necessary food and other materials, these items were sometimes supplied by air drops.[62] In most cases, however, the Japanese army had to live off the land. Even General Matsui apparently hoped to procure a substantial amount of food in the enemy's territory. Although he worried about the supply situation in his diary on November 20, he quickly added, "We need not be concerned about the victuals despite the lack of supply because rice is plentiful in the areas where the troops are operating."[63] Above all, the Japanese military leadership held to a principle that they would sacrifice food supply for effective military campaigning. The operation guideline of the Tenth Army immediately before its landing on November 5 said, "What is expected to be the most difficult problem in the coming campaign will be that of supply. Nevertheless, it is urgently necessary to carry out the operation . . . even by utilizing the logistical facilities almost solely for the transportation of ammunition while depending on the local procuring for food."[64]

The CCAA set forth the same principle in its official guideline for the Nanking campaign, that is, it would give a logistical priority to ammunition, rather than food.[65] A U.S. military attaché's report underlined this supply policy. According to Major Harry I. T. Creswell, acting U.S. Military Attaché to China, the Japanese army used horse-drawn carts as a major means of transportation and loaded most of the carts with ammunition and only a few with "rations for the men and forage for the animals."[66]

The subordinate commanders apparently solved the resulting supply difficulties by living off the land. The 16th Division said in its official report, "The division adopted a policy of feeding soldiers and horses with the materials requisitioned locally to make possible the swift forward movement of the troops. Fortunately, owing to the ample resources available in the region, the food supply situation was generally good."[67] The 9th Division also reported that "the supply columns failed to catch up with the division advancing and pursuing the enemy. As a result, the division conducted its march of over about four hundred kilometers of distance from Shanghai to Nanking almost solely depending on the resources requisitioned locally without receiving food supply."[68]

As for the 114th Division, its report said that "the soldiers walked through the places where clear roads were not found while seeking for food in the enemy's territory."[69] The 6th Division also described its supply situation: "the division received supplies only in Kunshan, Sungchiang, and Chiashan until it reached Nanking and fed itself mainly with the locally procured food during that one month of military actions."[70]

Further complicating the supply situation was the Japanese army's transportation methods, which were not only primitive but also disorderly. Major Creswell of the U.S. Army noted "a curious feature of Japanese march discipline" in his report. According to Creswell, the Japanese infantry put to use almost any kind of vehicle that would roll, such as ordinary baby buggies, rickshas, and low two-handled trucks. An even more unusual practice that showed the straits to which a modern army could be reduced when its logistical infrastructure failed was to force the local Chinese population to transport equipment and supplies. Sublieutenant Miyamoto Shogo of the 65th Regiment's 4th Company said, "So many of our soldiers use the Chinese people as well as their cows and horses that we are sometimes mistaken as Chinese troops."[71]

Since the official policy necessitated that each unit conduct its own requisitioning, the officers and soldiers on the front did not seem to have any remorse about stealing food from the local population. Major Kisaki recorded the requisitioning of 800 bales of rice, 1,000 bales of wheat, 100 bales of sugar, and two motor vehicles in his diary on December 1 with a comment, "It has been fun." Some officers were mindful of discipline problems relating to the requisitioning. Lieutenant Colonel Terada Masao, a Tenth Army staff officer, told about the necessity of clearly distinguishing requisitioning from robbery. The Staff Chief of the 16th Division also maintained that it was necessary for responsible commanders to direct the requisitioning by issuing orders distinctly instead of leaving the matter to the soldiers' licentious acts.[72] In many cases, however, requisitions simply became robbery. This was partly because in numerous instances requisition parties could not find anyone to negotiate with after the civilian population had fled with the approach of the battle. Yet one cannot deny that the Japanese soldiers became like a group of bandits. In a soldier's diary, one could find such passages as "we brought to our unit a big pig we had found at a liquor store" or "the requisition party returned with one hundred chickens." Even a former soldier who strenuously denied the occurrence of the massacre in Nanking admitted that such plundering was the usual practice of the Japanese army operating in China at the time.[73] It is not surprising that some of those who became used to such a practice escalated their misbehavior. A directive issued by the staff chief of the 16th Division enumerated several cases of misconduct: "Some soldiers stole currency owned by Chinese inhabitants, bought and sold among their colleagues the items obtained from the Chinese, and tried to take away the items owned by the [division's] accounting section although they knew where those items belong to. . . . There was a case in which officers neglected to watch their soldiers, who went ashore [from a transport] without any permission and looted the unloaded materials."[74]

The Japanese soldiers seem to have justified their actions by relying on a traditional logic of victor's rights. Private Upper Class Azuma Shiro of the 16th Division quoted some soldiers as saying, "This is not robbery. Instead, it is requisition, which a victorious army is naturally entitled to do."[75] Thus, an age-old conviction that victorious troops could do anything to the conquered further inflamed their urge for robbery, a logic that had justified looting in the aftermath of a siege in medieval warfare. It is undeniable that the Japanese committed large-scale robbery on their march to Nanking in the name of requisition—conduct rather comparable to European troops in the middle ages than to the troops in more recent times such as the Union soldiers in Sherman's army on their way to Savannah during the American Civil War. This comparison is appropriate because the Japanese soldiers in China committed violent crimes not connected with military action much more often than the Union soldiers in the course of robbery. This difference was attributable to a different motive for each: the Japanese robbed the local population for the sole purpose of feeding themselves, whereas the Union troops conducted a strategic destruction and made an effort to spare the lives of common people. Another factor was the more hostile environment the Japanese faced.

The Japanese soldiers sometimes behaved kindly and gentlemanly to local people. For example, Private Upper Class Makihara Nobuo witnessed one Japanese army medic treating a Chinese civilian who had mistakenly exploded firecrackers in his hand. On the following day Makihara paid villagers to purchase some food—instead of simply taking it—after a lengthy negotiation. Makihara described these episodes in his diary on November 4 and 5, 1937—that is, about one month before the start of the Nanking campaign. Private Saito Jiro of the 13th Division's 65th Regiment said that he provided some extra rations to the local people who had lost their houses to fire.[76] It seems, however, that the soldiers soon began to acquire a brutal nature as they fought actual battles. Referring to the overall discipline problem, the SEF's 16th Division said in its official report, "Discipline was generally good, but quite a few soldiers were rough in their behavior immediately after major fighting."[77] Individual soldiers' conduct underlined this statement. When the division was fully engaged in the battle in the Shanghai area, Makihara saw one corporal belonging to another company kick an old Chinese man off a bridge and shoot him to death because the old man refused to carry the corporal's baggage.[78] Corporal Horikoshi Fumio, who served in the radio communications unit of the 65th Regiment, noted on his diary his first experience of slashing an enemy soldier to death with his sword: "I felt so calm in my mind that I could not believe I had killed a man. I was even surprised at the degree of mental tranquility. . . . We used the remnant [of POWs] as laborers or guinea pigs for beheading. I did not feel either anger toward the enemy or excitement. I maintained mental composure even at the sight of bloodshedding."[79]

The Japanese soldiers often burnt houses along their line of march. Private Upper Class Ueba Buichiro said in his diary on December 1, "Many fires broke out due to arson and we were told to put them out. What is supposed to be our mission here?" According to Private Upper Class Kitayama Atau, his unit burned the houses in which they had stayed overnight before their departure on the mornings of December 1, 3, and 7. Sometimes, the Japanese troops had a tactical reason for burning the dwellings, that is, to deny the enemy a place from which to launch an ambush. In other cases, however, the motive for arson was inexplicable. Private Makihara stated in his diary that he felt it "refreshing to set fire to five to six straw-thatched houses and see them burning."[80]

The leadership was apparently concerned about the erosion of discipline and made an effort to restrain the criminal acts committed by the soldiers. In a directive on October 20, 1937, deputy chief of the General Staff Tada hoped that the Tenth Army leadership would "take a due consideration to enforce strict military discipline in view of the [poorly disciplined] troops in charge of supply and other [rear] duties." Tada also warned against incendiarism, referring to a bad habit of destroying and burning housing in the occupied areas in the military campaign currently being undertaken.[81] Again, the effectiveness of such an effort is questionable. In his diary on October 16, Private Kitayama mentioned his platoon commander's order that rape, unauthorized requisition, and other unethical conduct were strictly forbidden, although Kitayama added that he was half-asleep when listening to that commander's instruction. Private Makihara witnessed a battalion commander scolding several soldiers making a bonfire to warm themselves, apparently out of concern that their fire might spread accidentally. Such a warning, however, usually fell on deaf ears. According to Private Upper Class Inoie Mataichi of the 7th Regiment under the SEF's 9th Division, commanders issued a stern order not to make any bonfire in order not to draw the enemy's fire. Nevertheless, he and his comrades defied that instruction to warm themselves on the night of December 12, when the final battle near the Nanking walls was still progressing.[82]

Private diaries and even official records reveal that many cases of murder or executions also took place even before the Japanese reached Nanking. When they burned villages where Chinese soldiers were suspected to be hiding, such operations sometimes resulted in the killing of innocent civilians. Private Makihara said,

As we advanced, young Chinese men fled. We do not know why they ran away. Anyway, we shot one such person after another since they made themselves suspicious-looking by running away. We set fire to twelve to thirteen houses of a village. Soon, an entire village was engulfed by fire. I felt a pity toward a few old men remaining in the village. But I could not do anything else because it was an order. We burned three villages successively. We also shot five or six men.

We mopped up the villages on our way while we shot to death two straggling soldiers trying to escape in a boat. In other occasion, we burnt down an entire village.[83]

The diary of Corporal Meguro Tomiharu of the 19th Mountain Artillery Regiment recorded that his unit went out for requisitioning, burned seventeen houses of Chinese inhabitants, and shot to death local inhabitants on December 5. Meguro attached a brief comment: "How miserable the people of a defeated nation are!"[84] The remarks of these two soldiers epitomize two major ways Japanese fighting men tried to come to grips with the atrocities they witnessed and in which some of them participated. Although Makihara most likely did not consider the legal responsibility of such actions, he seems to have mentioned the "order" from above out of a moral responsibility and an emotional pity he had toward the victims. As for Meguro, he blamed the atrocities on the nature of war itself.

The Japanese soldiers often killed Chinese soldiers upon capture instead of taking them prisoner. Immediately after Private Makihara's unit occupied one village on November 23, they captured and killed two straggling soldiers. Three days later, they used shovels and hoes to kill two Chinese soldiers while taking another to headquarters for interrogation. That one remaining soldier was also shot to death afterward. On December 7, Makihara's unit caught twelve Chinese soldiers. His diary simply says, "We shot them to death immediately." He also witnessed another company killing five to six Chinese with a hand grenade on November 24.[85]

Although these incidents of killing were brutal and not justifiable from either an ethical or legal standpoint, the Japanese did not conduct an indiscriminate massacre comparable to Nazi-type genocidal atrocities. Close examination of each case shows that the victims were usually POWs, soldiers out of uniform, or those suspected to be such. As for civilian victims, they were killed almost accidentally as part of operations to hunt down straggling Chinese soldiers.

Four factors contributed to a rather extensive killing of these groups of Chinese. First, Japanese military men, officers and soldiers alike, cared little about the treatment of POWs due in part to the severity of the fighting, which often did not allow them the latitude, or luxury, of taking prisoners. During the Shanghai battle, General Iinuma of the SEF recorded in his diary of September 6, "About 600 enemy soldiers entrenched in their barracks surrendered, but we killed them after we had observed some hostile acts among them." Iinuma mentioned a similar incident on the following day. Such massacres apparently drew the attention of the foreign press. Iinuma said, "To answer to the foreign news correspondents who suspect that the Japanese army is killing all the POWs, the military attaché is asking us to send some prisoners to the rear. I replied to the attaché that it is almost impossible for the front troops to meet such a request. The matters concerning the prisoners should be left to the troops in the front."[86]

The second reason contributing to the ruthless killing of the prisoners was the stronger anti-Japanese attitude among the population in central China than in northern China. Referring to the degree of the population's hostile attitude in central China, an anonymous soldier of the 16th Division's 20th Regiment, which fought both in the northern and central China theaters, said, "Local population was willing to help us in the north, but they were hostile in central China." Another soldier who had fought in northern China and had been transferred to Shanghai–Nanking thereafter was impressed by anti-Japanese slogans painted on building walls almost everywhere in central China. At the sight of such hostile words, according to one diary, those Japanese soldiers vowed to kill anyone who was hostile to Japanese.[87] The advancing Japanese thought that they were fighting against not only the regular Chinese army but also the ordinary people in the "inner front," or an enemy who is undistinguishable from innocent civilians.

Third, the six Japanese divisions and other detachments participating in the Nanking campaign advanced very rapidly, causing confusion on the battlefield. It was apparent to Japanese military leaders that further delay in the commencement of the Nanking campaign would give the Chinese an opportunity to strengthen their defenses in the capital city. Accordingly, on November 30, the Tenth Army headquarters adopted an operation plan calling for a swift advance to Nanking before the enemy could recover from psychological damage and confusion in their command structure following the Shanghai battle, and also prior to the completion of the defense arrangements in Nanking.[88] They also accelerated their marching speed because they expected only feeble Chinese resistance. They reasoned that the Chinese Nationalist government leaders had already fled from the city and their military leaders, who seemed in the eyes of the Japanese military leaders to be mindful mainly of their own self-preservation, would not earnestly defend Nanking.[89] Although General Matsui wanted to co-ordinate the movement of each division, front-line troops, ranking officers and soldiers alike, felt as if they were competing with each other in a marathon-like race toward the enemy's capital.[90]

Amid the confusion resulting from the fast Japanese advance and the disor-ganized retreat by the Chinese, there were many unplanned encounters between the two armies. The Japanese were not always victorious in such engagements. According to Major Yamazaki Masao, a staff officer of the Tenth Army, a group of straggling Chinese soldiers suddenly attacked an artillery unit trying to catch up with the advancing infantry on December 7. He also noted an incident in which a logistical column consisting of twenty-three vehicles was annihilated by several hundred straggling Chinese soldiers. According to a soldier of the 2nd Independent Light-Armored Vehicle Company, when his scout unit was about to enter a house, some Chinese soldiers hiding inside started shooting and throwing hand grenades at them. Such reports and stories naturally made Jap-anese soldiers watchful. An anonymous soldier of the 7th Regiment under the command of the SEF's 9th Division said, "Since straggling Chinese soldiers might still be around us, smoking was strictly prohibited. We were also told not to speak out unless it was necessary [while marching at night]." A company commander of the 16th Division's 20th Regiment recounted the same situation in his report on December 4: "Since we are in the midst of the enemy's land, we could not light either flashlight or a match." As the Chinese resistance in-tensified, the Japanese soldiers were alerted to possible ambush. Private Maki-hara recorded, "Many straggling soldiers are reported to be in the village below the hill. We are not sure when they will attack us." At the same time, the Japanese soldiers nurtured a strong hatred toward the enemy. Private Ueba, seeing the dead bodies of Chinese and the Japanese bombers flying overhead, described in his diary his frustration at prolonged Chinese resistance: "How can the Chinese keep fighting even with all those damages! I hate them!" One could easily assume that during the rapid advance, troops with such feelings in their minds killed POWs both out of fear or for tactical necessity.[91]

Finally, the Chinese actively used plainclothes units. In reality, some plain-clothes soldiers were not stragglers separated from their original unit after its defeat, but rather troops dispatched to the front line to conduct military activities side by side with uniformed regular troops. The Chinese 160th Division said in its official report describing its activities on November 24, 1937, that it sent out a sizable group of plainclothes soldiers to scout the enemy's strength and activ-ities. The same division also positioned plainclothes soldiers in the town of Chuyou on December 5.[92] It seems that the Chinese soldiers discarded their uniforms not only in the course of a desperate retreat to escape capture but also during some ordinary military actions conducted by regular troops. Such a policy inevitably expanded what the Japanese considered to be the "inner front" in

China, where distinctions between enemy military forces and ordinary civilians were not clear. The instructions the Tenth Army command gave to its subordinate units had a section relevant to this point:

... especially in the Shanghai area, even ordinary Chinese inhabitants including the aged, women, and children sometimes work as spies to inform the enemy of our location and help the enemy troops attack us. Occasionally, they themselves attack our soldiers operating individually in small number. Since there have been many of such instances, we must be alert at any time. Rear units must especially be careful. If such [hostile] acts are committed [against you], you are advised to take a stern measure against the perpetrator without hesitation.[93]

Soldiers about to go to the battlefield received a similar caution. Private Azuma mentioned an instruction given before boarding a transport bound for China:

You are about to go to a battlefield where you must expect to confront the enemy. Plainclothes soldiers are operating even in the area occupied by our troops. Starting tomorrow, lagging behind from your unit will instantly result in a meaningless death. This is because you can find neither hospitals nor POW camps there. It is the place filled only with local population and plainclothes regular troops, who are hostile to us. Remember, once you are separated from your unit, you will certainly die.[94]

Once on the battlefield, they knew the true meaning of these warnings through their actual experiences. Some Japanese soldiers recorded an instance of being sniped at by Chinese soldiers.[95] They also expressed their fear and frustration toward an enemy exceedingly difficult to find and defeat:

[A]lthough they [Chinese civilians] attach a square cloth reading "Welcome Imperial Japanese Army Soldiers" on their chest, we can never relax."[96]

[W]e, a group of two soldiers, passed through an unknown location. . . . Having lost all the pride as a soldier of the Japanese Army, I felt very helpless when pondering a possibility of coming across straggling soldiers.[97]

It is undeniable that Japanese soldiers sometimes killed innocent civilians out of excitement or sheer sadistic pleasure. It is equally beyond doubt that summary execution of prisoners frequently took place. Judging from those descriptions in personal diaries, however, one could deduce a compelling reason—or at least what these soldiers thought to be a compelling reason—for burning villages and killing civilians. Faced with the protean problem of Chinese resistance, they had to deny straggling enemy soldiers a place to hide and to put to death soldiers and suspicious-looking civilians so that they could guarantee their own safety. Such a chaotic situation led to loose bonds of command and the greater possibility of atrocities. The Imperial Japanese Army had encountered a similar situation during its Taiwan expedition following the first Sino-Japanese War. Yet the scale of the problem the Japanese faced in mainland China in the 1930s was much greater than what they had encountered in the 1895 island campaign, which ended after only six months.[98]

The Japanese were not responsible for all the plundering in the Shanghai–Nanking area. A U.S. diplomatic telegram in early November said that there were reports of indiscriminate shooting of civilians, rape, looting, and other ill treatment by Japanese forces, but added, "There are also some authenticated cases of looting by Chinese soldiers." Another telegram in December quoted a British source as saying that Chinese troops at Chinkiang were systematically looting and burning the city. According to some Japanese soldiers' diaries, Chinese soldiers quite viciously robbed the local population of food. Private Upper Class Yaginuma Kazuya of the 65th Regiment noted in his diary that he could not find anything to requisition in a town occupied by his unit on December 3. In some villages, residents who had been deprived of food by Chinese soldiers were so starved that they were eating dogs even before the Japanese marched in.[99]

Nor were the Japanese troops accountable for all incendiarism. Judging from the descriptions in Japanese soldiers' diaries, the fires they caused were mostly blamed on arson or carelessness by individual soldiers or at most by platoon-size units. Thus, these fires were likely to be small in scale, although they were likely to happen in many locations. Fires caused by the Chinese appeared larger in scale since the Chinese army set buildings ablaze during its retreat in accordance with its "scorched-earth" policy, thus causing destruction on a massive scale. A Japanese soldier of the 16th Division, for example, recorded that he saw an extensive fire consuming the village across the Yangtze River before his unit's landing. A Western reporter also noted that Chinese soldiers set ablaze the whole city of Ch'enchiang on the southern bank of the Yangtze River and caused the evacuation of the population of 200,000 people. The residents in Nanking on December 6 could see the horizon to the east and south darkened by the smoke from nearby villages and hamlets set aflame by retreating Chinese soldiers.[100]

Other reliable sources also attest to extensive burning conducted by the Chinese troops. General Hsiao of the Chinese army said, "On the night of the 26th and 27th the Chinese started withdraw [*sic*] south of Soochow Creek. During the evacuation . . . they either set fire to or planted delayed incendiary bombs in hundreds of buildings, and with a few hours the district was an inferno."[101] General Matsui noted on December 3: "a part of the 11th Division is on its way to Ch'enchiang. . . . Ch'enchiang was reportedly burning while the enemy is preparing for a retreat." In its official report, the 4th Company of the 20th Regiment said, "The enemy started setting fire everywhere in the village and apparently began their retreat. Then, at 11:30 P.M. [November 25], they ceased their fire all at once." The strategic burning by the Chinese gradually approached all the way to Nanking. A U.S. diplomatic telegram dated December 6 reported that Chinese detachments were setting fire to farm buildings so that nothing would be left for the Japanese in the vicinity of Nanking. Such burning started immediately outside the Nanking walls around the same time and deepened the sense of crisis among the population.[102]

FALL OF NANKING

Japanese soldiers who marched to Nanking, front-line soldiers and troops on rear duties alike, commonly described their route as being strewn with dead Chinese, mostly soldiers.[103] Although some of those corpses were probably soldiers killed or executed by the Japanese, many were probably fatally wounded Chinese soldiers left behind on the retreat. According to an American military observer, the Chinese troops were plagued by the absence of trained personnel, proper equipment, and transportation for the evacuation of the wounded, and the tendency was a preference for those who possessed funds, resulting in those not having the "necessity" to ensure transportation being dumped by the side of the road or into a ditch.[104]

Meanwhile, those lucky wounded soldiers were transported to Nanking. According to a recent Japanese estimate, the number of such wounded carried into Nanking amounted to 1,700 a day on average. This figure seems to be close to reality, judging from a *New York Times* article, which reported the arrival of between 2,000 and 3,000 wounded soldiers daily in late November and added that the figure had been doubled in comparison with before.[105] Although the evacuation of those wounded to Hankow and other inland areas was proceeding, the hospitals in the city were caring for more than 5,000 wounded. Moreover, there were a large number of wounded soldiers who were unable to find space in hospitals since there were no adequate hospital facilities remaining in Nanking other than the Nanking University Hospital.[106] The result was horrible: "Many times more than 2,000 wounded, after spending two to four days lying on straw in close-packed, jolting trucks or jarring freight cars en route to Nanking, were left lying on concrete platforms at the Hsiak'uan railway station here in the bitter cold for two or three days and nights without any dressings or sanitation whatever and often without even drinking water and food."[107]

While those wounded soldiers were either shipped further inland or left dying on the streets of Nanking, the acutely felt approach of war prompted a pathetic exodus of civilians from the city. Actually, the Nanking inhabitants started leaving the city when the Japanese naval air force intensified its bombing in early September. But the pace of the exodus was accelerated when people learned of a report about the central government's planned removal to the interior.[108] *New York Times* correspondent Durdin reported in a dispatch from Nanking on November 22 that many destitute men and women wandered about in the bitterly cold driving rain, seeking an opportunity to board steamers, sampans, junks, and barges. Durdin also said that enormous piles of abandoned furniture and baggage left behind by fleeing families stretched for half a mile along the Bund.[109] By late November, the evacuation of civilians had steadily reduced the population of Nanking from about one million in July to an estimated 300,000 to 400,000 according to a U.S. diplomatic source quoting the mayor of Nanking, and to merely 200,000 according to some news accounts.[110]

Meanwhile, on November 27 General T'ang, who had become the commander in chief of the Chinese garrison in the capital, warned foreigners of the expected disorder caused by retreating Chinese soldiers. The *New York Times* quoted T'ang as saying, "The Chinese army is composed of troops from all provinces and all types. Therefore, disorganization and disaffections appear inevitable. . . . Nanking will be guarded by well-organized and trustworthy soldiers but troubles are certain to arise with the mass of troops retreating from the fronts."[111] At the same time, T'ang commented on some measures to maintain order within the city: "special units had been detailed to maintain discipline inside the walls [of Nanking] and in a zone thirty miles around the city and . . . no Chinese soldiers would be permitted to enter this zone unless they were prepared to die defending the city."[112]

The foreigners remaining in Nanking had another reason to be concerned about security and safety. Chiang Kai-shek, who was planning to leave Nanking soon, told diplomats of Western countries on November 27 that he would turn over the administration of the city to the military and would leave only a small part of the municipal government in the capital. Madame Chiang then declared that the responsibility for whatever happened and for maintenance of order would rest with the Japanese.[113] This meant that few civilian administrators were to remain in the city to maintain law and order. Although some Westerners had already formed a committee late in November to organize a safety zone for the purpose of sheltering the civilians remaining in the city, such statements by top Chinese leaders heightened their sense of urgency and they tried even harder to obtain agreements from both the Chinese and the Japanese to recognize and respect the safety zone they were planning to create.

The proposed safety zone covering about two square miles, or 12.5 percent of the city, was demarcated by four streets—the North Chungshan Road in the east, the Hsikian Road in the west, the Hanchung Road in the south, and the Shansi Road in the north (Map 2.2). John H. D. Rabe, an executive of Siemens Co. of Germany, chaired the International Committee for the Nanking Safety Zone (ICNSZ) and Lewis S. C. Smythe from the United States, a professor at the University of Nanking, served as secretary. Among other members were John G. Magee, a reverend of the American Church Mission, and M. S. Bates, who taught at the University of Nanking. Magee and Bates later testified as prosecution witnesses at the Tokyo war crimes trial. Rabe, who was also the leader of the German Nazi Party in Nanking, personally asked Adolf Hitler to approach the Japanese government to support this humanitarian scheme. Through diplomatic channels some Americans also urged the Japanese to respect the safety zone. The Japanese military command, however, did not fully accept the proposal. In a diplomatic telegram sent out on December 4, the Japanese ambassador to China told the U.S. ambassador to the same country that the

Map 2.2
City of Nanking

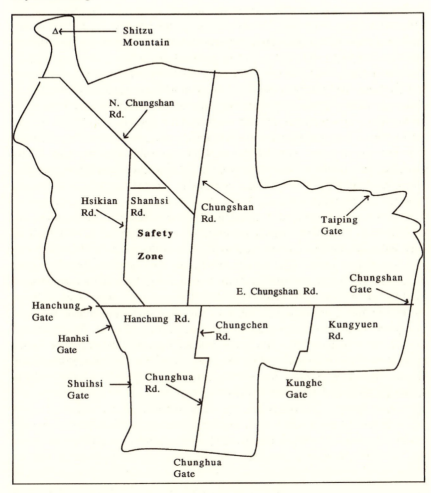

Japanese military authorities were "not in a position to give an undertaking that the said area [safety zone] will not be either bombed or bombarded" because "in and around the said area there exist Chinese military establishments" and there was hardly a guarantee "for entirely preventing Chinese troops from entering into the zone or utilizing it for military purposes." Yet, at the same time, the Japanese also declared that they had no intention whatsoever of attacking such places not utilized by Chinese troops for military purposes or such areas where the Chinese troops had not established their military works and establishment and where there were no Chinese troops stationed.[114]

The bulk of what remained of the Nanking population started moving into the safety zone on December 6, and they were joined by thousands of refugees on the following day. Chiang Kai-shek left Nanking for Hankow on December 7. On the same day, CCAA commander Matsui assigned to the SEF and the Tenth Army the targets they should capture in their attacks on the city walls. He directed the SEF to take three gates in the northeast walls (i.e., the Heping Gate, the Taiping Gate, and the Chungshan Gate), while ordering the Tenth Army to break the defense line connecting the three gates in the southeast: the Kunghe Gate, the Chunghua Gate, and the Shuihsi Gate. Meanwhile, the ICNSZ made one further proposal to both the Japanese and Chinese authorities. According to its new proposal, the two sides would agree to a truce of three days, during which time the Japanese troops would maintain their present positions and the Chinese troops would withdraw from the walled city. By then, T'ang was apparently willing to accept the proposal, contrary to his previous aggressive statement allegedly made in the presence of Chiang, and conveyed his intention to accept this proposal to Chiang Kai-shek in Hankow. The committee members were, however, disappointed at the result. They were informed on December 10 through the U.S. embassy, which had been moved to Hankow, that Chiang Kai-shek had stated he was not in a position to accept that proposal.[115]

Before commencing a final assault on Nanking, on December 9 General Matsui urged the Chinese troops in the city to surrender. A Japanese bomber scattered leaflets printed with Matsui's call for capitulation all over the city. Matsui set the deadline at noon on December 10 and requested a dispatch of envoy to Chungshan Gate, one of the gates in the eastern city walls. Although two Japanese officers of the CCAA and an interpreter waited at the designated place for one hour on the following day, there was no sign of a Chinese delegation. Matsui thus issued an order for the final assault.[116]

The civilians in Nanking now faced the grim prospect of being involved in fighting without a place of shelter. As T'ang had warned, the city of Nanking first experienced misconduct by demoralized Chinese soldiers even before the Japanese arrived. Correspondent Durdin vividly reported their behavior in a dispatch dated November 23 from Nanking:

Poorly-disciplined units now appear to be almost as numerous as civilians. Many squads unceremoniously appropriate civilian properties and even move into occupied homes despite the owners' protests.

The presence within the city of many thousands of wounded who have virtually recovered from their injuries and are permitted to roam through the city unattached to any unit without leadership and without assigned barracks or mess is adding to the atmosphere of deterioration.[117]

Confusion within the city walls intensified as the Japanese troops approached. A company commander belonging to the Japanese 35th Regiment of the SEF's 9th Division saw the sky over Nanking illuminated by fire on December 7. The fires became more frequent as days passed. A U.S. diplomatic telegram reported that the sky over Nanking and surrounding terrain was hazy with smoke from burning houses in the countryside. An extensive fire in the Hsiak'uan area of the city consumed the British Bridge House Hotel on December 10 after it had been subjected to looting. According to Chiang Kung-yi, an army surgeon who was in Nanking at the time, the Transportation Authority building was also burning on the night of December 12. Despite such chaotic conditions, those who were still in the city apparently decided to stay. The remaining population numbered around 200,000—almost unchanged from late November—according to the ICNSZ, which used a phrase "for sake of two hundred thousand civilians" in its December 10 message to a Japanese diplomatic representative.[118]

On December 10, the 16th Division began its final approach to Nanking. The 9th, the 20th, the 35th Regiments, and a part of the 33rd Regiment comprising the division's left wing started attacking the Tzuchin Mountain to the northeast of Nanking while the right wing, consisting of the 30th Brigade—the 33rd and the 38th Regiments—commanded by Major General Sasaki Toichi forced its way to the Hsiak'uan facing the Yangtze to the northwest of the city. The latter's purpose was to cut off the escape route of the Chinese troops that remained inside the city walls. Those advancing to the Tzuchin Mountain had a hard time crushing resistance because they were prohibited from using heavy artillery in a strict observance of orders not to destroy the mausoleum of Sun Yat-sen and the tomb of the Ming Emperor. Their operation was also stalled because defending that mountain was the Training Unit, which was an elite unit among the garrison force and one familiar with the area. It was not until the morning of December 13 that the 20th Regiment breached the fortifications of the Chung-shan Gate and entered the city.[119]

Immediately south of the 16th Division, the 9th Division breached the Chinese defenses outside of Nanking on December 9 (Map 2.3). The 35th Regiment attacked the Tzuchin Mountain on the same day to support the maneuver of the 16th Division operating in the north, while one battalion of the 36th Regiment occupied the Kuanghua Gate in the city walls. The Chinese 87th Division defending the area, however, was soon rushed to the gate and launched a fierce counterattack. Moreover, the 156th Division came to the spot as a reinforcement and did not allow the Japanese to expand their gain for almost three days. But the Chinese defense had already started crumbling. Continuous bombardment by the Japanese prevented the Chinese from sending wounded soldiers to the rear while some Chinese artillery units, for unknown reasons, did not comply with the 87th Division's request for covering fire against the Japanese.[120]

The Tenth Army's 114th Division penetrated the Chinese defensive positions in the Chiangchun Mountain to the south of the city on December 9 and on the following day reached Yuhuatai where the Chinese troops were heavily entrenched. The 6th Division to the immediate south of the 114th coordinated its attack on Yuhuatai to reach the Chunghua Gate. The Japanese soldiers had a tough time not only facing the severe gunfire of the defenders but also crawling over the ground covered with human excrement left by the Chinese. The Chinese

Map 2.3
Japanese Army's Approach to Nanking

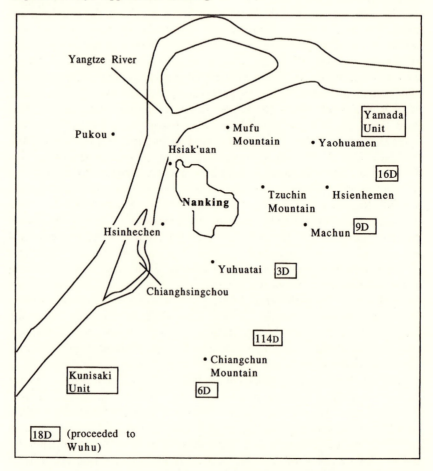

soldiers there were so determined to defend the place that the doors of some pillboxes were locked and chained from the outside. Despite such fierce resistance, the Chinese 88th Division was forced to shrink its defense perimeter on December 11 and retreat to the city walls the next day.[121]

The Kunisaki Detachment crossed the Yangtze on December 11 and marched on the northern bank of the river to the northeast. They reached Pukou, which is across Hsiak'uan, on December 12 and occupied it by the following day.[122]

By December 12, the Chinese defense in Nanking was crumbling while some Japanese units were about to close the escape routes from the city by capturing the key points on the shores of the Yangtze River. On that day, General T'ang ordered the 36th Division to enter the city to prepare for house-to-house fighting. Then, the 87th and 88th Divisions, which had retreated from Yuhuatai, entered the city from the south and moved through Chungshan Street to escape from a gate in the north. Although the 36th Division tried to stop their retreat, the situation became chaotic as the soldiers of those two divisions did not obey the order. T'ang finally issued an order to all the units to break out from the city in the evening of that same day. By then, orderly retreat had become impossible. T'ang divided his troops into six groups and instructed each to take a separate escape route. He instructed most of them to start their escape as late as at 11 P.M., probably in hope that darkness would make the retreat easier for the Chinese. But some other units waited until 6 A.M. the following day to begin their move. Other disorganized troops, however, had already started crossing the Yangtze River to the northern shore even prior to the issuance of that formal order.[123]

The fate of Nanking was sealed. The Chinese soldiers were now desperately trying to escape from the doomed city, where civilians were waiting in fear for what was to come.

The Japanese army's march to Nanking created multiple factors that made the subsequent atrocities in Nanking highly likely. These were the combination of several factors, both old and new. First, the near robbery-like requisitioning by Japanese soldiers caused the breakdown of their discipline. Quite a few cases of murder and rape recorded in private diaries were its natural consequence. In this respect, the Japanese troops degenerated into a premodern army living off the land to support themselves. Lack of logistical preparation for the Nanking campaign due to the typical decision-making process in the Japanese military— local command dragging the central authority—was its major cause. Second, strong anti-Japanese feeling among the Chinese population in the region and the frequent encounters by Japanese troops with straggling and plainclothes soldiers led to the killing of POWs as well as ordinary civilians. Japanese soldiers conducted such ruthless killing because they were highly sensitive to and scared of the plainclothes soldiers. In this respect, the Japanese were fighting a new type of war against the "inner front" as the German soldiers had done in Belgium in World War I. Third, both sides resorted to burning for their own strategic or tactical purposes. The Chinese conducted a "scorched-earth" policy and burned huge areas to deny the advancing Japanese troops any supplies—a campaign of destruction in line with their own tradition. Japanese soldiers frequently burned houses and villages to deprive Chinese irregulars or plainclothes soldiers of their staging bases. Their incendiarism was designed to prevent the enemy's insurgency activities. But other cases were attributable to the breakdown of discipline such as Japanese soldiers' carelessness or the sadistic pleasure they found in seeing houses in flames.

In addition, some factors were unique to this campaign, which resembled siege warfare. First, the Chinese garrison cornered itself in a walled city, which was difficult to defend due to its geographical position. Second, since there was no formal surrender offered by the defenders, the end of battle was quite unclear for the attackers. In these respects Nanking was to become a besieged city taken by storm like Paris in 1871, Nanking under the Taiping rule in 1863, and Port Arthur in 1894. Finally, an effort to organize the safety zone for the protection of civilians obtained only halfhearted support from both the Japanese and the Chinese military authorities. In short, Nanking was about to become a gigantic trap for the helpless Chinese soldiers and civilians.

NOTES

1. For the origins of the Russo-Japanese War, refer to Andrew Malozemoff, *Russian Far Eastern Policy, 1881–1904, with Special Emphasis on the Causes of the Russo-Japanese War* (Berkeley: University of California Press, 1958), pp. 41–176, and Oka-moto Shumpei, *The Japanese Oligarchy and the Russo-Japanese War* (New York: Columbia University Press, 1970), pp. 57–102. J. N. Westwood, *Russia against Japan, 1904–05: A New Look at the Russo-Japanese War* (Albany: State University of New York Press, 1986) is a compactly written book about the military and naval operations of the war.

2. See Raymond A. Esthus, *Double Eagle and Rising Sun: The Russians and Japanese at Portsmouth in 1905* (Durham: Duke University Press, 1988), pp. 207–12, for the content of the Russo-Japanese peace treaty signed in Portsmouth, New Hampshire, in 1905.

3. James B. Crowley, *Japan's Quest for Autonomy: National Security and Foreign Policy, 1930–1938* (Princeton, NJ: Princeton University Press, 1966), p. 4.

4. Mark P. Peattie, *Ishiwara Kanji and Japan's Confrontation with the West* (Princeton: Princeton University Press, 1975), pp. 87–139, compactly summarizes the Kwantung Army's activities through the Manchurian Incident.

5. Ogata N. Sadako, *Defiance in Manchuria: The Making of Japanese Foreign Policy, 1931–1932* (Berkeley: University of California Press, 1964), pp. 105–06.

6. Crowley, *Japan's Quest for Autonomy*, p. 395. In June 1935, Japanese military leaders in China concluded two agreements with local Chinese military leaders to exclude military presence of the Nationalists from two northern provinces of Hopei and Chahar. The agreements were called the Umezu–Ho agreement and the Doihara–Ching agreement after those who signed them: Umezu Yoshijiro, commander of the Tientsin Garrison, Ho Ying-ch'in, chief of the Peking Military Council, Doihara Kenji, chief of the Mukden Special Service of the Japanese Army, and Ching Te-ching, acting governor of Chahar Province. For details of these agreements, see ibid., pp. 216–17.

7. Robert Berkov, *Strong Man of China: The Story of Chiang Kai-shek* (Boston: Houghton Mifflin, 1938), p. 173, said, "To Chiang's way of thinking a China harboring Communist territories could no more resist Japan than a man with a bellyache could battle a tiger." For a summary of the Sian Incident and conflicting interpretations about it, refer to Parks M. Coble, *Facing Japan: Chinese Politics and Japanese Imperialism, 1931–1937* (Cambridge, MA: Council on East Asian Studies, Harvard University, 1991), pp. 342–61.

8. Two Japanese newspaper correspondents, one store owner, one policeman, and one marine soldier were murdered by mobs or unidentified assassins in China in August–September 1936. Also, in September the same year, there was an incident between the Tientsin Garrison and local Chinese troops in the suburb of Peking, although it did not develop into an armed clash. Kojima Noboru, *Nitchu Senso* [Sino-Japanese War], vol. 3

(Tokyo: Bungeishunju, 1988), pp. 218–29. For the origin and the reinforcement of the Tientsin Garrison, see Robert J. C. Butow, *Tojo and the Coming of the War* (Stanford: Stanford University Press, 1961), p. 94; and Dorothy Borg, *The United States and the Far Eastern Crisis of 1933–1938: From the Manchurian Incident through the Initial Stage of the Undeclared Sino-Japan War* (Cambridge, MA: Harvard University Press, 1964), p. 276. Stationed in Shanghai were about 2,300 men of the Shanghai Special Naval Landing Force, 300 of the Hankow Special Naval Landing Force, 539 belonging to the Second Special Naval Landing Force under the command of the Kure Naval Outpost in Japan, the same number of sailors from the Sasebo Naval Outpost, also in Japan, 200 sailors detached from the gunboat *Izumo*, and 200 of the 11th Naval Landing Force. Their total strength amounted to merely about 4,000. Kojima, *Nitchu Senso* [Sino-Japanese War], vol. 4, p. 69.

9. Ch'i Hsi-Sheng, *Nationalist China at War: Military Defeats and Political Collapse, 1937–45* (Ann Arbor: University of Michigan Press, 1982), p. 44.

10. Matsui's career before 1937 is summarized in Tanaka Masaaki, ed., *Matsui Iwane Taisho no Jinchu Nisshi* [Field Diary of General Matsui Iwane] (Tokyo: Fuyo Shobo, 1985), pp. 19–31. One cautionary note is that this author is known for his close association with Matsui as well as his persistent downplaying of the Rape of Nanking.

11. Founding members of the Great Asian Society, "Dai Ajia Kyokai Soritsu Shuisho" [Statement of Purpose for the Founding of the Great Asian Society], in ibid., p. 261.

12. Tanaka, ed., *Matsui Iwane Taisho no Jinchu Nisshi* [Field Diary of General Matsui Iwane], p. 218.

13. Matsui told one of the leaders in the Fukian Province that Chiang should renounce his dictatorship and allow local provinces more autonomy. Matsui, "Seinan Yuki" [Record of Travel to Southwest], 4 March 1936, in ibid., p. 242. Also, see the diary entries of 24 February and 13 March, 1936, in ibid., pp. 230, 249.

14. Matsui Iwane, Diary of Matsui Iwane, 15 August 1937, in Kaikosha, ed., *Nankin Senshi Shiryo-shu* [Nanking Campaign Chronology Primary Source Collection], vol. 2 (Tokyo: Kaikosha, 1993: henceforth *NSS2*), p. 4.

15. The troop strength is from Iinuma Mamoru, Diary of Iinuma Mamoru, 3 October 1937, in Kaikosha, ed., *Nankin Senshi Shiryo-shu* [Nankin Campaign Chronology Primary Source Collection], vol. 1 (Tokyo: Kaikosha, 1989: henceforth *NSS1*), p. 134. The Japanese high command's order is from General Staff, Imperial Japanese Army, "Rin-san-mei" [General Staff Special Order] no. 73, 15 August 1937, in ibid., p. 533. Emperor Hirohito seems to have been puzzled at Ishiwara's rather peaceful stance with respect to the Second Sino-Japanese War in contrast with his aggressive military campaign planning at the time of the Manchurian Incident. See Terasaki Hidenari, ed., "Showa Tenno no Dokuhaku 8-jikan: Taiheiyo Senso no Zenbo o Kataru" [Emperor Hirohito's 8-Hour Monologue about Japan's War in the Pacific], *Bungeishunju* (December 1990): p. 106. Major General Iinuma Mamoru, SEF chief of staff, noted General Matsui's dissatisfaction at the General Staff's policy of seeking a decisive campaign in north China already in the early phase of the battle of Shanghai. Iinuma quoted Matsui as saying that "the attack on Nanking will be effective in the end" and that the Japanese "need to declare war against China." Iinuma Diary, 17–18 August 1937, in *NSS1*, pp. 65, 67–68. Also, Matsui himself told the prosecutor at the Tokyo War Crimes Trial that he had a "desire to push on to Nanking" and made that desire clear to other people. IMTFE, p. 33,843.

16. Ch'i, *Nationalist China at War*, p. 37. Frederick Fu Liu, *A Military History of*

Modern China 1929–1949 (Westport, CT: Greenwood Press, 1981, originally Princeton, NJ: Princeton University Press, 1956), p. 112. Youli Sun, *China and the Origins of the Pacific War, 1931–1941* (New York: St. Martin's Press, 1993), p. 88, quoting the Records of Meetings of the [Chinese Nationalist] High Military Staff, 12 July 1937.

17. Chiang Kai-shek, *Resistance and Reconstruction: Messages during China's Six Years of War 1937–1943* (New York: Harper & Brothers, 1943), p. 5.

18. James C. Hsiung and Steven I. Levine, ed., *China's Bitter Victory: The War with Japan* (New York: M. E. Sharpe, 1992), p. 7. Rodney Gilbert, "The War in China Continues," *Foreign Affairs* 17–2, January 1939, p. 325. Barbara W. Tuchman, "Japan Strikes: 1937" *American Heritage* 12, December 1970, p. 10. Ch'i, *Nationalist China at War*, pp. 45–46. In a directive issued on August 20, Chiang defined the Shanghai area as "the vital political economic center" the Nationalist troops must hold. General Headquarters, Chinese Armed Forces, "Kuo-chun Tso-chan Chih-tao Chi-hua" [Directive for National Army's Operation Planning], 20 August 1937, quoted in Chung-kuo Ti-2 Li-shih T'ang-an Kuan [The Second Historical Archives of China], ed., *K'ang-jih Chan-cheng Cheng-mian Chan-ch'ang* [Resistance War against Japan: Regular Warfare Front, henceforth *KCCC*] (Chiangsu Province: Chiangsu Kuchi Ch'u-pan-she [Chiangsu Classics Publisher], 1987), p. 5. The first Shanghai Incident lasted from January 28 through April 28, 1932. About 40,000 soldiers of the Chinese 19th Route Army and Fifth Army fought against the Japanese Naval Landing Force as well as the Japanese Army's 9th Division and a part of 12th Division. The Chinese casualties amounted to 14,326 including 4,086 killed; the Japanese force, which had slightly more than 20,000 men, had 769 killed and 2,322 wounded. Kojima, *Nitchu Senso* [Sino-Japanese War] vol. 2, pp. 222, 273–74.

19. Kaikosha, ed., *Nankin Senshi* [Nanking Campaign Chronology] (Tokyo: Kaiko-sha, 1989, henceforth *NS*), p. 4. One Chinese division at the time consisted of slightly more than 10,000 men at its full strength. Sun Chai-wei, a Chinese scholar, said its full strength was 10,923 soldiers. Sun Chai-wei, "Nanking Pao-wei-chan Shuang-fang Ping-li De Yen-chiu" [Estimated Force Strength of Two Sides in the Nanking Battle] in *K'ang-jih Chan-cheng-shih Shih-so* [Essays on Resistance War against Japan], ed. Chiangsu Sheng Li-shih Hsueh-hui [Chiangsu Province Historical Society] (Shanghai: Shanghai Ke-hsueh-yuen Ch'u-pan-she [Shanghai Science Academy Publisher], 1988), p. 121. The figure was approximately commensurate with the data provided by General Hsiao Tsun-cheng, Chief of Operation Section under General Staff for Ku Chu-tung, commander of China's Eastern War Zone. Hsiao said that Chinese divisions "were composed of about 8,000 infantry each, with engineers, cavalry, and signal corps, numbered from 12,000 to 14,000 men apiece." Hsiao Tsun-cheng, "The War at Shanghai," in G-2 Report, 25 April 1939, p. 2, Record Group (RG) 165, M1513, The Military Intelligence Division Regional File Relating to China 1922–1944, Reel 40 (henceforth M1513-reel number), National Archives and Record Administration in College Park, Maryland (henceforth NA2).

20. Iinuma Diary, 31 August 1937, in *NSS*1, p. 86. Uemura Toshimichi, Diary of Uemura Toshimichi, 6 September 1937, in *NSS*2, p. 235. "Ichu Kikan ni Saishi Jugo ni Kotau" [Response to Home Front on the Occasion of Transfer and Homecoming], 1 July 1939, comp. The Inoue Unit (the 12th Company, the 3rd Battalion under the 20th Regiment), in Iguchi Waki, Kisaka Jun-ichiro, and Shimosato Masaki, ed., *Nankin Jiken: Kyoto Shidan Kankei Shiryoshu* [Rape of Nanking: Materials Related to the Kyoto Division] (Tokyo: Aoki Shoten, 1989: henceforth, *KS*), p. 424.

21. General Headquarters, Chinese Nationalist Forces, "Kuo-chun Tso-chan Chih-tao Chi-hua" [Directive for National Army's Operation Planning], 20 August 1937, in *KCCC*, p. 4.

22. For example, see Edgar Snow, *The Battle for Asia* (New York: Random House, 1941), p. 42; Furuya Kenji, *Chiang Kai-shek: His Life and Times*, abridged English edition ed. Chun-ming Chang (New York: St. John's University, 1981), p. 552; Li Tsung-jen and Te-kong Tong, *The Memoirs of Li Tsung-jen* (Boulder, CO: Westview Press, 1979), p. 325; and Chiang Wei-kuo, *Kuo-min Ke-ming Chan-shih Ti-3-pu K'ang-jih Yu-wu* [History of the Chinese Revolutionary War, part 3, War of Resistance against Japan], vol. 4 (Taipei: Li Ming Culture Enterprise, 1978), p. 73.

23. Complaint about outdated Japanese weapons is on *NS*, p. 6, quoting an interview with Tsuchiya Masaharu, then a company commander of the 9th Division's 19th Regiment. The soldier who was amazed at Chinese machine guns was Kurosu Tadanobu, who wrote his diary: Diary of Kurosu Tadanobu, 18 October 1937, in *Nankin Daigya-kusatsu o Kirokushita Kogun Heishitachi* [Imperial Japanese Army's Soldiers Who Recorded the Rape of Nanking, henceforth *NDKK*], ed. Ono Kenji, Fujiwara Akira and Honda Katsuichi (Tokyo: Otsukishoten, 1996), p. 340. Casualty figures are from MHD, ed., *Senshi Sosho: Shina-jihen Rikugun Sakusen* [Military History Series: Army's Plannings and Campaigns in Sino-Japanese War], vol. 1, p. 391. Tanoue Chiyoko, the wife of the 34th Regiment chief, poisoned herself in May 1938. Previously, some people reportedly stoned Tanoue's house, and military police were assigned to guard the house. Sankei Shinbun Shizuoka Shikyoku [Sankei Newspaper Shizuoka Branch], ed., *Aa Shi-zuoka 34-rentai: Fusa dake no Gunki to Tomoni* [34th Regiment in Shizuoka: with Regimental Color of Only Tassel] (Shizuoka: Fuji Pr Pro, 1963), pp. 153, 195.

24. General Headquarters, China, "Chan-cheng Chih-tao Fang-an" [Directive for National Army's Operation Planning], 20 August 1937, in *KCCC*, p. 12. The origin of this strategy was apparently German military adviser Alexander von Falkenhausen's situation report in August 1935. Jerry Bernard Seps, "German Military Advisers and Chiang Kai-Shek, 1927–1938" (Ph.D. Diss., University of California, Berkeley, 1972), p. 469.

25. Imoto Kumao, *Sakusen Nisshi de Tsuzuru Shina-Jihen* [Sino-Japanese War Chronology Chronicled by Operation Diaries] (Tokyo: Fuyo Shobo, 1978), p. 158.

26. General Staff, Japan, "Rin-san-mei" [General Staff Special Order] no. 138, 7 November 1937; "Rin-mei" [Army Special Order] no. 600, 7 November 1937, in *NSS1*, pp. 533–34. Japanese equivalent of to "annihilate" is either *gekimetsu* or *senmetsu*, which the military leadership frequently used in operation orders.

27. No official Chinese source provides an exact casualty figure at the Shanghai battle. The figure of 150,000 is found in Edgar Snow, *The Battle for Asia* (New York: Random House, 1941), p. 51. Evans Fordyce Carlson puts it as "over 100,000" in *The Chinese Army: Its Organization and Military Efficiency* (New York: Institute of Pacific Relations, 1940), p. 70.

28. Iinuma Diary, 30 October 1937, in *NSS1*, p. 168. Chiang Wei-kuo, *Kuo-min Ke-ming Chan-shih* [History of the Chinese Revolutionary War], part 3, vol. 5, pp. 69, 76. Hsiao, "The War at Shanghai," p. 17, in G-2 Report, 25 April 1939, M1513-40.

29. For the traditional interpretation of the Shanghai battle, see Lloyd E. Eastman, *Seeds of Destruction: Nationalist China in War and Revolution 1937–1949* (Stanford: Stanford University Press, 1984), p. 133; idem, "Nationalist China during the Sino-Japanese War 1937–1945," in John K. Fairbank and Albert Feuerwerker, ed., *The Cam-*

bridge History of China, vol. 13, *Republican China 1912–1949*, part 2 (New York: Cambridge University Press, 1986), p. 553.

30. Hsiao, "The War at Shanghai," p. 17, M1513-40.

31. Liu, *A Military History of Modern China*, p. 163.

32. Li, *Memoirs of Li Tsung-jen*, p. 327. It is not clear when this conference took place. According to Li, this meeting happened on November 11 since he specifically cited November 12 as "the day after the meeting." Ibid., p. 328. A recent Japanese publication says the Chinese Nationalist military leaders had three conferences: the first on November 12 or 13, the second on November 14 or 15, and the third on November 16 or 17. *NS*, p. 49. T'ang did not indicate any date in his article, T'ang Sheng-chih, "Wei-shu Nanking Chih Ching-wei" [How Nanking was Defended], in T'ang Te-hsin, ed., *Yuan Kuo-min-tang Chiang-ling Chan-cheng K'ang-jih Chan-chen Ch'in-li-shih: Nanking Pao-wei-chan* [Personal Experiences of Former Nationalist Party Generals in Resistance War against Japan: Defense of Nanking, henceforth *NP*] (Peking: Chung-kuo Wen-hsueh Ch'u-pan-she [China Historical Publishing], 1987), pp. 1–5. Liu Fei, then chief of the Planning Bureau of the Nationalist Army's General Staff, said it took place "around November 15–16." Liu Fei, "K'ang-chan Ch'u-ch'i Te Nanking Pao-wei-chan" [Defense of Nanking in the Early Phase of Resistance of War], in ibid., p. 9.

33. George Atcheson, the Second Secretary of the U.S. Embassy in Nanking, to the Secretary of State, Washington, D.C., 23 November 1937, Records of the Department of State Relating to Political Relations between China and Japan, 1930–1944, 793.94/11247, RG49, M976, Reel 45, NA2 (henceforth M976-reel number followed by document number).

34. Li, *Memoirs*, pp. 325–26. Liu Fei obviously agreed with Li regarding T'ang's statement. Liu Fei, "K'ang-chan Ch'u-ch'i Te Nanking Pao-wei-chan" [Defense of Nanking in the Early Phase of Resistance of War], in *NP*, pp. 9–10.

35. T'ang, "Wei-shu Nanking Chih Ching-wei" [How Nanking Was Defended], in *NP*, p. 3.

36. Ibid.

37. Ibid., p. 2. Li, *Memoirs*, pp. 327, 329.

38. Chiang Kai-shek to Ku Chu-tung, Liu Hsiang, and T'ang Sheng-chih, 30 November 1937, in *KCCC*, p. 400.

39. Hsiao, "The War at Shanghai," p. 18, M1513-40. *NYT*, 27 November 1937, p. 6. Sun Chai-wei, "Nanking Pao-wei-chan Shuang-fang Ping-li Te Yen-chiu" [Estimated Force Strength of Two Sides in the Nanking Battle], p. 121.

40. Yue Chen-chung, "Lu-chun Ti-160-shih Hsi-ch'eng Nanking Liang-yi Chan-tou Hsiang-pao" [160th Division's Report on the Battles in Hsich'eng and Nanking], in *KCCC*, p. 436. Lu Wei-san, "Ti-88-shih E-shou Yu-hua-tai Chung-hua-men P'ian-tuan" [An Episode in the 88th Division's Defense in Yu-hua-tai and Chung-hua-men] in *NP*, p. 165n, quoting "Lu-chun Ti-88-shih Nanking Chih Gi Chan-tou Hsiang-pao" [Battle Report of the 88th Division Regarding the Battle of Nanking], Chung-kuo Ti-2 Li-shih Tang-an Kuan [Second Historical Archives of China]. Chinese 51st Division, "Ti-51-shih Chan-tou Hsiang-pao" [Battle Report of the 51st Division], in *KCCC*, p. 426.

41. Sun Chai-wei, "Nanking Pao-wei-chan Shuang-fang Ping-li Te Yen-chiu" [Estimated Force Strength of Two Sides in the Nanking Battle], pp. 118–20. Sun compares the troops strength estimate provided by T'an Tao-p'ing, who was a staff officer of General T'ang at the time, with the data found in official divisional records or those based on the memories of local commanders. T'an's estimate covering the entire garrison

force presents a figure of 81,000. The data belonging to the latter category are available only for seven divisions and another two units, the total force strength of which amounted to 96,458. Sun then calculates the sum total of the strength of the same units recorded in Tan's writing and obtains the number of 52,000. This means a differential of 1.85 times. Apparently on the premise that the figure deriving from official records and local commanders' memories are more reliable, Sun estimates that the total number of remaining troops—29,000—computed by T'an should be 1.85 times larger than that. The resulting figure is 150,108.

42. Iinuma Diary, 17 December 1937, in *NSS*1, p. 217. Major General Sasaki Toichi, commanding the 30th Brigade of the SEF's 16th Division, made the same estimate as Iinuma. Sasaki Toichi, Diary of Sasaki Toichi, 5 January 1938, in ibid., p. 382. Maeda Yoshihiko, Diary of Lieutenant Maeda Yoshihiko, platoon commander, 7th Company, 45th Infantry Regiment, 10 December 1937, in ibid., p. 454. *NYT*, 18 December 1937, p. 10. G-2 Report, 10 August 1938, Appendix A-8. Correspondence of the Military Intelligence Division Relating to General Political, Economic and Military Conditions in China 1918–1941, RG165, M1444, Reel 17 (henceforth M1444-reel number), National Archives and Records Administration, Washington, D.C. (henceforth NA1). Tenth Army Command, "Tei-shudan Shireibu Joho Kiroku" [Tenth Army Information Record] no. 30, 3 December 1937, Gokuhi, Shimitsu 5037-7 [Top Secret, Secret Report from China no. 5037-7], Rikushi Mitsu Dainikki [Army's Secret Diary about China Campaign, henceforth RMD], 1938, vol. 29, no. 4, MHD.

43. *NS*, pp. 59–63. Chinese sources that mention the figure of 30,000 or more are Li Hsi-k'ai, "Tzuchin-shan Chan-tou" [Battle of Tzuchin Mountain] in *NP*, p. 170; P'eng Yueh-hsiang, "Ts'ung Chian-shou Chen-ti tao Pei-ch'e Ch'ang-chiang" [From Defense of Fort till Retreat to North across Yangtze] in ibid., p. 176; and Sun Chai-wei, "Nanking Pao-wei-chan Shuang-fang Ping-li Te Yen-chiu" [Estimated Force Strength of Two Sides in the Nanking Battle], pp. 117, 120. For a criticism of *NS*'s estimate, see Kasahara Tokushi, "Nankin Boeisen to Chugokugun" [Nanking Siege and Chinese Force], in *Nankin Daigyakusatsu no Kenkyu* [Study of the Rape of Nanking], ed. Hora Tomio, Fujiwara Akira, and Honda Katsuichi (Tokyo: Bansuisha, 1992, henceforth *NDK*), pp. 309–10.

44. Kui Yung-ch'ing, commander of the Training Unit, said he had lost one-third of the original strength by the beginning of the Nanking campaign. Chou Erh-fu, *Nanking Te Hsian-lo* [Fall of Nanking] (Peking: Jen-min Pan-hsueh-she, 1987), p. 647, quoting Kui's remark. Liu Yung-ch'eng, then a staff officer of the Training Unit, said that the average size of companies of the unit was 15 percent short of full strength. Liu Yung-ch'eng, "Nanking K'ang-chan Chi-yao" [Summary of Nanking Battle] in *NP*, p. 180. On the Japanese side, Kobayashi Masao, ed., *Sakigake: Kyodo Butai Senki* [Harbingers: Records of Hometown Units] (Ise: Ise Shinbunsha, 1984) says the Tzuchin Mountain, where a substantial portion of the Training Unit was entrenched, "had a ridge shaped like a horse back running from the east to the west, and the deployment of large troops was difficult." The same source also notes that the estimated size of Chinese troops was "about one brigade." pp. 414–15.

45. G-2 Report, no. 9582, 5 August 1937, compiled by Joseph W. Stilwell, pp. 9–12, M1444–17. The divisions whose strength was known at the time were 41st Div. (8,000), 48th Div. (10,000), 159th Div. (6,000), 160th Div. (6,000), 87th Div. (8,000), 88th Div. (9,000), 51st Div. (8,000), 58th Div. (10,000), 36th Div. (8,000), 154th Div. (6,000), 156th Div. (6,000), 103rd Div. (6,000), and 112th Div. (6,000). Diplomatic telegrams that reported the condition of the Chinese army are: Atcheson to the Secretary

of State, 4 December 1937, no serial number; 4 December 1937, 793.94/11465, M976-46; Commander in Chief of Asian Fleet (CINCAF), Information to the U.S. Embassy in China, 7 December 1937, 793.94/11515, M976-46; and CINCAF to the U.S. Embassy in Nanking et al., 12 December 1937, 793.94/11587, M976-45. The figure range between 110,000 and 130,000 is close to an estimate given by Sung Hsi-lian, one of the Chinese divisional commanders. Sung said that the Nanking garrison totaled "over 110,000." Sung Hsi-lian, "Nanking Shou-ch'eng-chan" [Siege Defense of Nanking], in *NP*, p. 233.

46. Hsiao, "The War at Shanghai," p. 12, M1513-40. Harry I. T. Creswell, "Observations in Shanghai Area," in G-2 Report, 17 December 1937, p. 15, M1513-39. Wei Shih-ch'en, "Hu-wei T'uan-ch'i T'ui-ch'u Nanking" [Retreat from Nanking with Regimental Color] in *NP*, p. 159. Atcheson to the Secretary of State, 23 November 1937, 793.94/11247, M976-45; 29 November 1937, 793.94/11358, M976-46. Nanking Garrison Command, "Nanking Pao-wei-chan Chan-tou Hsiang-pao," [Battle Report of the Defense of Nanking], n.d., in *KCCC*, p. 414.

47. Inada Masazumi, then a colonel attached to the Army Ministry's personnel affairs bureau, said in his memoir, "The predominance of staff over commander, the former's manipulation of the latter, and the weakening control of the central command over the local command became especially conspicuous after the Manchurian Incident. Those middle-ranked officers of colonels and lieutenant-colonels seized the initiative in the high command [in Tokyo], and such a group of officers, not content with the stagnated political leadership within Japan, began to exhibit a lamentable tendency of trying to drag the authorities in Japan into a situation of their liking by instigating incidents overseas." Inada Masazumi, "Shina Jihen Senso Shido Kankei Shiryo" [Reflection on Strategic Planning during the China Incident], July 1937–December 1938 pp. 1–2, MHD. Although Inada said such a tendency of young officers manipulating the army leadership had been eminent since the Manchurian Incident, the real beginning was the assassination of Chang Tso-lin in 1928 planned and conducted by then Colonel Komoto Daisaku, a Kwantung Army staff officer. When the army leadership almost court-martialed Komoto, Komoto threatened to disclose all the plot he had carried out to the world and preempted the court-martial. Terasaki, "Emperor Hirohito's Monologue," p. 101. As for the English sources dealing with this subject, see, for example, Hugh Borton, *Japan's Modern Century* (New York: Ronald Press, 1955), p. 350; and Hata Ikuhiko, "Continental Expansion, 1905–1941," trans. Alvin D. Coox, in Peter Duus, ed., *The Cambridge History of Japan*, vol. 6, *The Twentieth Century* (Cambridge: Cambridge University Press, 1988), p. 305.

48. Matsui Diary, 15 November 1937, in *NSS*1, p. 7. Iinuma Diary, 14 November 1937, in ibid., pp. 188–89. Tenth Army Command, Tei-shu-saku-mei [Tenth Army Operation Order], no. 31, 19 November 1937, 7 A.M., in ibid., p. 552. Tada Hayao, Deputy Chief of General Staff, to Matsui, 20 November 1937, Dai-10-gun Sakusen-shido ni Kansuru Sanko-shiryo [Reference Materials Concerning Tenth Army's Operations, henceforth DSKS], vol. 2, MHD. Tada's superior as the Chief of General Staff was Prince Kan'in, an imperial family member. Like the emperor himself, imperial family members assuming high positions in the armed services were likely to be figure heads. Tada was reluctant to endorse further military actions in view of the ongoing peace talks with Chiang Kai-shek through the mediation of Oskar Trautmann, German ambassador to China. Inada, "Shina Jihen Senso Shido Kankei Shiryo" [Reflection on Strategic Planning during the China Incident], p. 22.

49. CCAA Command, Chu-ho-san-den [CCAA to General Staff] no. 167, "Chu-shina

Homen Kongo no Sakusen ni Kansuru Iken Gushin" [Proposal Regarding Future Military Campaign in Central China], 22 November 1937, in *NSS*1, p. 537.

50. Kawabe Torashiro, "Kawabe Torashiro Shosho Otoroku" [Interview with Major General Kawabe Torashiro], interview by Prince Takeda Tsunenori, in Kobayashi Tatsuo, ed., *Gendaishi Shiryo* [Source Materials of Modern History], vol. 12, *Nitchu Senso* [Sino-Japanese War], part 4 (Tokyo: Misuzu-shobo, 1965), p. 437. Kawabe himself was the chief of the General Staff's Second Division and a sympathizer of Shimomura within the General Staff.

51. Even Lieutenant Colonel Inada, who was resentful of local commander's independent action, criticized Tada's effort to restrain the troop movements, arguing that the period of the Japanese army's inaction had provided the Chinese Nationalists with an opportunity to regroup and replenish themselves in the Nanking area. Inada, "Shina Jihen Senso Shido Kankei Shiryo" [Reflection on Strategic Planning during the China Incident], pp. 22–23, 35–37.

52. General Staff, Imperial Japanese Army, Dai-riku-den [Army's Telegraph] no. 19, 24 November 1937, in DSKS, vol. 2. Original Japanese term is *yamu o ezu*, which literally means "being unable to stop."

53. General Staff, Japan, Dai-riku-mei [Army Order] no. 8, 1 December 1937, in *NSS*1, pp. 534–35. It seems that Kawabe, who served under Tada at the time, wanted to conceal the reality of the central command having approved the *fait accompli* created by the local commanders although it was a widely known fact and thus an accepted norm in the Japanese army. The following is an excerpt from an interview with Kawabe conducted by an imperial family member serving the army as an officer:

INTERVIEWER: "Was the operation restriction line [previously imposed by the General Staff to prohibit the advance to Nanking] removed after the local troops had crossed that line?"

KAWABE: "I think the General Staff abolished the restriction line before the actual troop movement took place."

INTERVIEWER: "It appears that the troop movement preceded the removal of restriction."

KAWABE: "Is that true? Maybe, it was because the decision to capture Nanking came very late."

Kawabe, "Interview with Kawabe," *Gendaishi Shiryo* [Source Materials of Modern History], vol. 12, p. 436.

54. Tenth Army Command to Chief of General Staff and CCAA commander, "Nankin Tsuigeki Mondai" [Regarding the Advance toward Nanking], 22 November 1937, in *NSS*1, p. 651.

55. Ibid.

56. Ibid.

57. CCAA Command, Chu-ho-san-den [CCAA to General Staff] no. 167, 22 November 1937, in *NSS*1, p. 536.

58. Meirion Harries and Susie Harries, *Soldiers of the Sun: The Rise and Fall of the Imperial Japanese Army* (New York: Random House, 1991), p. 219.

59. Iinuma Diary, 29 November 1937, in *NSS*1, p. 202.

60. Tenth Army Command, "Kunji" [Directive (to Tenth Army Soldiers)] by Yanagawa, 17 November 1937, in DSKS, vol. 2.

61. Kisaki Hisashi, Diary of Kisaki Hisashi, 3 December 1937, in *NSS*1, p. 415.

62. Matsui Diary, 22 November 1937, in *NSS*1, p. 8. Iinuma Diary, 20 November 1937, in ibid., p. 195.

63. Matsui Diary, 20 November 1937, in *NSS*1, p. 8.

64. Tenth Army Command, "Dai-2-ki Sakusen Shido Yoryo" [Operation Guideline for the 2nd Phase of Campaign], 2 November 1937, in DSKS, vol. 2. Touching on the logistics, Terada Masao, Tenth Army operation staff officer, said, "Logistical problems should not constrain military operations, and this fundamental principle must be understood clearly." Terada Masao, "Dai-10-gun Sakusen Shido ni Kansuru Kosatsu" [Commentary on Tenth Army's Campaign Planning], p. 18, MHD.

65. CCAA Command, "Chu-shina Homen-gun Dai-2-ki Sakusen no Taiko" [Guideline of CCAA's 2nd Phase of Operation], 24 November 1937, DSKS, vol. 2, and in *NSS*1, p. 538.

66. Creswell, "Observations in Shanghai Area," p. 10, M1513–39.

67. Japanese 16th Division, "Jokyo Hokoku" [Report of Situation], 24 December 1937 in, *NSS*1, p. 577.

68. 9th Division, "Dai-9-Shidan Sento Keika no Gaiyo: Shanhai-fukin no Sento yori Nankin Koryaku ni Itaru" [Outline of 9th Division's Military Operation: From Battles in Shanghai Area to Attack on Nanking], MHD.

69. 114th Division, "Dai-114-shidan Sakusen Keika no Gaiyo" [Outline of 114th Division's Operation], 7 November–14 December 1937, in *NSS*1, p. 653.

70. 6th Division, "Senji Junpo" [Wartime Report] no. 15, appendix, in ibid., p. 696.

71. Creswell, "Observations in Shanghai Area," p. 6, M1513–39. Miyamoto Shogo, Diary of Miyamoto Shogo, 9 December 1937, in *NDKK*, p. 132.

72. Kisaki Diary, 1 December 1937, in *NSS*1, p. 415. Terada, "Dai-10-gun Sakusen Shido ni Kansuru Kosatsu" [Commentary on the Tenth Army's Operation Planning], p. 18. Nakasawa Mitsuo, 16th Division chief of staff, "Sanbo-cho no Shiji" [Directive by (Divisional) Chief of Staff], n.d., in Dai-16-shidan Kankei Shiryo Tsuzuri [Collection of Source Materials Relating to 16th Division], MHD.

73. Kitayama Atau, Diary of Kitayama Atau, 20 and 22 November 1937, in *KS*, pp. 61–62. Miyabe Kazumi, *Fuu-un Nankinjo* [Battle of Nanking Walls] (Tokyo: Sobunsha, 1983), p. 92.

74. Nakasawa, "Sanbo-cho no Shiji" [Directive by (Divisional) Chief of Staff], n.d., in Dai-16-shidan Kankei Shiryo Tsuzuri [Collection of Source Materials Related to 16th Division], MHD.

75. Azuma Shiro, Azuma Memoir, n.d., in *KS*, p. 213. As a later chapter will discuss, some scholars and researchers have been debating whether this memoir really describes the truth. Therefore, this quoted portion may not be the description of actual event. But I believe that the story does depict the feeling shared by many Japanese soldiers.

76. Makihara Nobuo, Diary of Makihara Nobuo, 4–5, 18 November 1937, in *KS*, pp. 117–18, 127. Saito Jiro, Diary of Saito Jiro, 15 November 1937, in *NDKK*, p. 23.

77. 16th Division, "Jokyo Hokoku" [Situation Report], 24 December 1937, in *NSS*1, p. 577.

78. Makihara Diary, 18 November 1937, in *KS*, p. 237.

79. Horikoshi Fumio, Diary of Horikoshi Fumio, 20 November 1937, in *NDKK*, pp. 73–74.

80. Ueba Buichiro, Diary of Ueba Buichiro, 1 December 1937, in *KS*, p. 27. Kitayama Diary, 1, 3, 7 December 1937, in ibid., pp. 65–67. Makihara Diary, 27 November 1937, in ibid., p. 134. The Japanese troops burned houses extensively also during the Shanghai campaign, in which the Chinese often "attacked from unoccupied dwellings, which made it necessary for use [*sic*] to set fire to these dwellings." Hirota Koki, Foreign

Minister of Japan, to Saito Hiroshi, Japanese Ambassador to the United States in Washington, D.C., 14 August 1937, RG457, Red Machine: Translation of Japanese Diplomatic Messages, 1934–1938 (henceforth Red Machine), no. 570A, NA2.

81. Tada to Tanabe Moritake, Tenth Army chief of staff, "Dai-10-gun Sanbo-cho ni Atauru Heitan ni Kansuru Chui-jiko" [Directive to Tenth Army Chief of Staff Concerning Logistics], 20 October 1937, in DSKS, vol. 1. The original Japanese version uses a word *soshitsu*, which means "quality," in an apparent reference to poor discipline of these soldiers. The Tenth Army leadership also warned its subordinate units "not to burn houses and villages . . . unless necessary" in view of the situation in Shanghai area, where "there are almost no buildings the army can use as hospital, accommodation, and other facilities because the [front-line] troops burnt almost all the buildings." Tenth Army Command, "Gun Sanbo-cho Chui-jiko" [Directive by (Tenth) Army's Chief of Staff], n.d., in DSKS, vol. 1.

82. Kitayama Diary, 16 October 1937, in *KS*, p. 55. Makihara Diary, 4 December 1937, in ibid., p. 139. Inoie Mataichi, Diary of Inoie Mataichi, 12 December 1937, in *NSS*1, pp. 473–74.

83. Makihara Diary, 28 November 1937, in *KS*, pp. 134–35, 137. Makihara, a soldier of the 16th Division, which used to be in northern China, wondered why villagers were running probably by comparing their reaction to the behavior of the Chinese population in the north. In the north, the Chinese local population was so receptive to the Japanese army that they sometimes put up handmade Japanese flags with a sign reading "Welcome Japanese army" and entertained the soldiers with Chinese liquor. Seki Hiroshi, Diary of Seki Hiroshi, 27 November 1937, a diary written by a soldier of the Independent 9th machine-gun battalion's 3rd company, and currently owned by his son Seki Naohiro in Nagano, Japan.

84. Meguro Tomiharu, Diary of Meguro Tomiharu, 5 December 1937, in *NDKK*, p. 372.

85. Makihara Diary, 24, 26, 29 November, 7 December 1937, in *KS*, pp. 131, 133, 135, 141.

86. Iinuma Diary, 6 September 1937, in *NSS*1, p. 100.

87. Inoue Unit (the 12th Company, the 3rd Battalion under the 20th Regiment), comp., "Ichu ni Saishi Jugo ni Kotau" [Response to Home Front on the Occasion of Transfer and Homecoming], 1 July 1939, in *KS*, p. 425. Azuma Memoir, 24 November 1937, ibid., p. 254.

88. Tenth Army Command, "Nankin Koryaku ni Kansuru Iken" [Proposal for Capturing of Nanking], 30 November 1937, in DSKS, vol. 2.

89. Ibid. Although some Japanese military leaders were stunned at the stiff Chinese resistance in Shanghai, many apparently continued to have their contempt toward the Chinese troops. Tenth Army staff Terada justified the swift advance to Nanking in disregard of logistical difficulty and went on to say, "If we had run out of ammunition, we would have resorted to bayonet charge. *Remember, we faced merely Chinese soldiers*." [italics added.] Terada, "Dai-10-gun Sakusen Shido ni Kansuru Kosatsu" [Commentary on the Tenth Army's Operation Planning].

90. Matsui Diary, 4 December 1937, in *NSS*1, p. 4. Sasaki Diary, 9 December 1937, in ibid., p. 372. Kanemaru Yoshio, Memoir of Sergeant Kanemaru Yoshio, in ibid., p. 361. Miyabe, *Fuu-un Nankinjo* [Battle of Nanking Walls], p. 99.

91. Yamazaki Masao, Diary of Yamazaki Masao, 7 December 1937, in *NSS*1, p. 399. Private N.Y., 7th Infantry Regiment, First Infantry Artillery Platoon, "Shonenhei no

Shuki: Shoen no Aima nite" [Memoirs of First-Year Soldier: In the Interval of Gun Smokes], 8 December 1937, in *NSS*1, p. 485. 4th Company of the 20th Infantry Regiment, "Jinchu Nisshi" [Field Diary] no. 5: December 1–31, 1937, in *KS*, p. 377. Makihara Diary, 10 December 1937, in *KS*, p. 145. Ueba Diary, 26–27 November 1937, in *KS*, p. 27. In yet another instance of Chinese troops' sudden attack, about 400 Chinese soldiers ambushed one platoon of the 2nd Independent Light-armored Vehicle Company on December 1 and killed ten Japanese including a platoon commander. Testimony of Okuaki Kunizo in Unemoto Masami, ed., "Shogen ni yoru Nankin Senshi" [Nanking Campaign Chronology Based on Eyewitness Accounts, henceforth "SNS"] (1), *Kaiko*, April 1984, p. 30.

92. Yue Chen-chung, "Lu-chun Ti-160-shih Hsich'eng Nanking Liang-yi Chan-tou Hsiang-pao" [160th Division's Report on the Battles in Hsich'eng and Nanking], April 1938, in *KCCC*, pp. 437, 440.

93. Tenth Army Command, "Gun Sanbo-cho Chui Jiko" [Directive by (Tenth) Army's Chief of Staff], in DSKS, vol. 1.

94. Azuma Memoir, in *KS*, p. 185.

95. Makihara Diary, 27, 30 November 1937, in *KS*, pp. 134, 136. Meguro Diary, 13 November 1937, 3 December 1937, in *NDKK*, p. 367.

96. Saito Diary, 19 November 1937, in *NDKK*, p. 25.

97. Meguro Diary, 3 December 1937, in *NDKK*, p. 372.

98. The Japanese troops landed on Taiwan on May 29, 1895, and declared the completion of occupation on November 18 the same year. Fujimura, *Nisshin Senso* [Sino-Japanese War], pp. 197–200.

99. Frank P. Lockhart, Nanking, to the Secretary of State, 8 November 1937, 793.94/11021, M976-43. Atcheson to the Secretary of State, 7 December 1937, 793.94/11504, M976-46. Yaginuma Kazuya, Diary of Yaginuma Kazuya, 3 December 1937, in *NDKK*, p. 165. Makihara Diary, 16 October 1937, in *KS*, p. 108.

100. Kitayama Diary, 16 November 1937, in *KS*, p. 59. *Times* (London), 8 December 1937, p. 16. *NYT*, 7 December 1937, p. 13.

101. Hsiao, "The War at Shanghai," p. 15, M1513-40.

102. Matsui Diary, 3 December 1937, in *NSS*1, p. 13. 4th Company of the 20th Infantry Regiment. "Jinchu Nisshi" [Field Diary] No. 5: 1–31 December 1937, in *KS*, p. 367. Atcheson to the Secretary of State, 6 December 1937, 793.94/11491; 7 December 1937, 793.94/11504, M976-46.

103. For example, see Kitayama Diary, 9 December 1937, in *KS*, p. 68; Makihara Diary, 20 November 1937, in ibid., p. 129; Odera Takashi, Diary of Odera Takashi, 6 December 1937, in *NDKK*, p. 189; Endo Takaaki, Diary of Endo Takaaki, 3 December 1937, in ibid., p. 217; Takahashi Mitsuo, Diary of Takahashi Mitsuo, 6 December 1937, in ibid., p. 287; Kurosu Diary, 7 December 1937, in ibid., p. 349; and Sasaki Motokatsu, *Yasen Yubinki: Nitchu Senso ni Jugun Shita Yubin-cho no Kiroku* [Field Postal Flag: Memoir Written by Postal Chief Who Participated in Sino-Japanese War], vol. 1 (Tokyo: Gendaishi Shiryo Shuppan Sentaa [Modern History Source Material Publishing Center], 1973), pp. 200–01.

104. No author, a U.S. Military intelligence report entitled "Medical Services in the Chinese Army," 28 November 1941, M1513-50.

105. "SNS" (2), *Kaiko*, May 1984, p. 14. *NYT*, 27 November 1937, p. 6.

106. Atcheson to the Secretary of State, 8 December 1937, 793.94/11535, M976-46.

107. *NYT*, 27 November 1937, p. 6.

108. Hirota to Saito, 8 September 1937, quoting a conversation between Charge d'Affaires Hidaka Shinrokuro and a Westerner [presumably H. J. Timperly, correspondent of the *Manchester Guardian*], Red Machine, no. 665C. Commander of the Yangtze Patrol, Information to the U.S. Embassy et al., 17 November 1937, 793.94/11165, M976-45.

109. *NYT*, 22 November 1937, p. 12.

110. Atcheson to the Secretary of State, 27 November 1937, 793.94/11318, M976-45. A recent publication about the Rape of Nanking estimated the size of the city's population at the time of its fall at over half a million. Iris Chang, *The Rape of Nanking: The Forgotten Holocaust of World War II* (New York: BasicBooks, 1997, henceforth *RNFH*), pp. 81, 100. Yet, contemporary estimates given by Westerners almost unanimously point to a more drastic reduction in the number of inhabitants. "The capital, which had a population of more than 1,000,000 last July is now estimated to have only 200,000." *NYT*, 22 November 1937, p. 12. "Deserted by . . . four-fifths of its 1,000,000 inhabitants." *Newsweek*, 6 December 1937, p. 27. "At the time the city fell (December 12–13), its population was between 200,000 and 250,000." Lewis S. C. Smythe, *War Damage in the Nanking Area December, 1937 to March, 1938: Urban and Rural Surveys* (Shanghai: Mercury Press, 1938), p. 4. Above all, the diary of John H.D. Rabe—the principal source Chang relied on—contains a description to substantiate the same fact. John H.D. Rabe, *Nankin no Shinjitsu [The Truth of Nanking]: The Diary of John Rabe*, ed. Erwin Wickert, trans. into Japanese Hirano Kyoko (Tokyo: Kodansha, 1997), p. 85. Its English version is John Rabe, *The Good Man of Nanking: The Diaries of John Rabe*, ed. Erwin Wickert, trans. John E. Woods (New York: Alfred A. Knopf, 1998).

111. *NYT*, 28 November 1937, p. 30. A diplomatic source also summarized T'ang's speech in Atcheson to the Secretary of State, 28 November 1937, 793.94/11330, M976-45.

112. Ibid.

113. Atcheson to the Secretary of State, 28 November 1937. 793.94/11330.

114. The committee's proposal quoted in Atcheson to the Secretary of State, 22 November 1937, 793.94/11231, M976-45. Clarence E. Gauss, Consul General at Shanghai, to the Secretary of State, 4 December 1937, 793.94/11456, in Department of State, *Foreign Relations of the United States: Diplomatic Papers 1937*, vol. 3, *The Far East* (Washington, D.C.: U.S. Government Printing Office, 1954), pp. 757–58.

115. Atcheson to the Secretary of State, 7–8 December 1937, 793.94/11504, 793.94/11535, M976-46. CCAA Command, "Nankinjo Koryaku Yoryo" [Instruction Concerning the Capture of Nanking], 7 December 1937, in *NSS*1, p. 539. Atcheson to the Secretary of State, 9 December 1937, 793.94/11549, in *Foreign Relations of the United States, 1937*, vol. 3, *The Far East*, p. 781. Nelson Trusler Johnson, U.S. Ambassador to China, Hankow, to the Secretary of State, 10 December 1937, 793.94/11556, in ibid., p. 784.

116. Matsui Diary, 8–9 December 1937, in *NSS*1, p. 16.

117. *NYT*, 24 November 1937, p. 14.

118. Testimony of Shimizu Sadanobu, commander of the 2nd Company of the 35th Infantry Regiment, in "SNS" (4), *Kaiko*, July 1984, p. 8. Atcheson to the Secretary of State, 8 December 1937, 793.94/11536; 11 December 1937, 793.94/11582, M976-46. Chiang Kung-yi, "Hsian-ching San-yueh-chi" [Three Months in Fallen capital], in *Ch'in-hua Jih-chun Nanking Ta-t'u-sha Shih-liao* [Source Materials Relating to the Horrible Massacre Committed by the Japanese Troops in Nanking in December 1937], ed. Nanking Ta-t'u-sha Shih-liao Pian-chi Wei-yuan-hui [Rape of Nanking Historical Sources

Compilation Committee] and Nanking T'u-shu-kuan [Nanking Library] (Nanking: Chiangsu Ku-chi Ch'u-pan-she [Chiangsu Classics Publishing], 1985, henceforth *SL*), p. 71. Atcheson to the Secretary of State, 10 December 1937, 793,94/11564, M976-46.

119. 16th Division, "Dai-16-shidan Sakusen Keika no Gaiyo" [Outline of the 16th Division's Operation], 10 January 1938, in *NSS*1, p. 580. *NS*, p. 97, quoting 16th Division staff chief Nakasawa's testimony at the Tokyo War Crimes Trial. IMTFE, pp. 32,622–23. Li Hsi-k'ai, "Tzuchin-shan Chan-tou" [Battle of Tzuchin Mountain], in *NP*, p. 173.

120. 9th Division, "Dai-9-shidan Sakusen Keika no Gaiyo" [Outline of the 9th Division's Operation], January 1938, pp. 21–22. MHD; and in *NSS*1, p. 615. Ch'en I-ting, "Ti-87-shih Ts'ai Nanking Pao-wei-chan Chung" [87th Division in the Defense of Nanking], in *NP*, p. 155. The Chinese claimed they annihilated the battalion that occupied the Kuanghua Gate. Nanking Garrison Command, "Nanking Pao-wei-chan Chan-tou Hsiang-pao" [Battle Report of the Defense of Nanking], in *KCCC*, pp. 11–12; and T'an Tao-p'ing, "Nanking Wei-shu-chan" [Garrison War at Nanking], in *NP*, pp. 23–24. In reality, they were pinned down in the narrow area for three days. Kojima, *Nitchu Senso* [Sino-Japanese War], vol. 4, pp. 196–97.

121. 114th Division, "Dai-114-shidan Sakusen Keika no Gaiyo" [Outline of the 114th Division's Operations], 7 November–14 December, 1937, in *NSS*1, p. 653. 6th Division, "Senji Junpo" [Wartime Report] nos. 13–14, in *NSS*1, pp. 689–90. Kojima, *Nitchu Senso* [Sino-Japanese War], vol. 4, p. 206. Testimony of Sakai Tokutaro, commander of the 6th Division's 11th Brigade, in Kumamoto Heidan Senshi Hensan Iinkai [Compilation Committee of Kumamoto Division's Battle Record], ed., *Kumamoto Heidan Senshi* [History of Kumamoto Division] (Kumamoto: Kumamoto Nichinichi Shinbunsha, 1965) quoted in *NS*, pp. 134–35. Eyewitness account of then sergeant Fujita Kiyoshi, attached to the headquarters of the Independent Second Light-armored Vehicle Unit, "SNS" (3), *Kaiko*, June 1984, p. 12. Nanking Garrison Command, "Nanking Pao-wei-chan Chan-tou Hsiang-pao" [Battle Report about the Defense of Nanking], in *KCCC*, pp. 412–13.

122. Kunisaki Detachment Command, "Kunisaki Shitai Sento Shoho" [Battle Report of Kunisaki Detachment] no. 10: 3–16 December 1937, in *NSS*1, pp. 701–04.

123. Nanking Garrison Command, "Nanking Pao-wei-chan Chan-tou Hsiang-pao" [Battle Report about the Defense of Nanking], in *KCCC*, p. 413. CINCAF to the U.S. Embassy et al., 12 December 1937, 793.94/11587, M976-46.

3

Nanking: Analysis of Military Actions and Number of Victims

Immediately following the fall of Nanking, a sudden news blackout left the outside world wondering what had happened in the Chinese capital. Two American news correspondents broke that silence. Archibald T. Steele of the *Chicago Daily News* and F. Tillman Durdin of the *New York Times* left Nanking on board the U.S.S. *Oahu* as soon as they witnessed the events they were going to report. On their way to Shanghai, Steele persuaded a crewman of the *Oahu* to allow him to use the ship's radio transmitter and succeeded in sending the news. Durdin tried to do the same, but failed. As a result, the *Chicago Daily News* carried Steele's article on December 15 while the *New York Times*, which had to wait for Durdin to arrive in Shanghai, reported the incident in Nanking three days later.[1]

Judging from the records and documents available from various other sources, one may conclude that despite some erroneous assumptions and sensationalism typical in media war coverage these two American journalists basically told almost every essential detail of the atrocities in Nanking. Strangely, however, the historians, writers, or journalists who have written books or articles about the incident have relied on their reports less and less frequently as time has passed. Since these two journalists were eyewitnesses from a neutral country, their coverage deserves more attention and analysis.

According to Steele, he saw indescribable panic and confusion among the entrapped Chinese defenders, followed by a reign of terror by the conquering army. While Steele said, "Japanese brutality at Nanking is costing them a golden opportunity to win the sympathy of the Chinese population," Durdin also criticized the Japanese army for having thrown away a rare opportunity to gain the respect and confidence of the Chinese inhabitants and of foreign opinion there. What actually happened, according to Durdin, was wholesale looting, the violation of women, the murder of civilians, the eviction of Chinese from their homes, mass execution of war prisoners, and the impressing of able-bodied men.

Although Steele said that it was difficult to estimate the number of soldiers trapped and killed, he put the number at anywhere between 5,000 and 20,000. In a follow-up report next January, Durdin estimated the Chinese military casualties in Nanking at 33,000, including 20,000 who were executed by the Japanese. Neither of those two correspondents mentioned the number of civilian victims. Steele, however, observed, "Streets throughout the city were littered with the bodies of civilians" while Durdin claimed that civilians of both sexes and all ages were also shot by the Japanese.[2]

The Western news media at the time tended to see the incident only as an atrocity committed by unrestrained troops, one that was typical in traditional siege warfare in premodern times. Notably, a *New York Times* editorial on December 19, 1937, said,

the account in yesterday's [December 18, 1937] *Times* by F. Tillman Durdin, who was present in Nanking when the Japanese Army marched into that city, read like the stories of war hundreds of years ago . . . when victorious soldiers expected as a matter of course that a conquered city with its helpless inhabitants should be given over for twenty-four hours to the unbridled lust of the victors. It appears that the Japanese military command in this case was either unable to control its subordinates or unfit to act in the name of a civilized people.[3]

The Japanese troops' conduct depicted by Steele and Durdin, however, gives an impression that there was more than a breakdown of discipline or instances of uncivilized behavior. They said,

The Japanese could have completed the occupation of the remainder of the city almost without firing a shot, by offering mercy to the trapped Chinese soldiers, most of whom had discarded their arms and would surrender. However, they chose the course of *systematic extermination*. . . . *How many troops were trapped and killed* it is difficult to estimate. [Italics added.][4]

The *mass executions of war prisoners* added to the horrors the Japanese brought to Nanking. After killing the Chinese soldiers who threw down their arms and surrendered, the Japanese combed the city for men in civilian garb who were suspected of being former soldiers. [Italics added.][5]

Their stories suggest that there were actually two phases of the historical event known as the Rape of Nanking. A large-scale killing of POWs characterized the first phase, whereas murder, rape, and looting were the atrocities in the second phase. One can distinguish the first phase from the second by looking at phrases like "mass execution of war prisoners" as compared with "murder of civilians." Such a distinction, which journalists made wittingly or unwittingly, is worthy of attention. This and the following chapter are organized to reflect that distinction.

CASUALTIES FOR WHICH THE CHINESE FORCES
WERE RESPONSIBLE

Both Steele and Durdin assumed that the "bodies piled five feet high" that they had seen near the shore of the Yangtze River had resulted directly from the Japanese attack.[6] According to some other Western and even Chinese accounts, however, these particular Chinese died either from intentional or unintentional killing among the Chinese themselves when the last remaining Chinese military units were trying to extricate themselves from the doomed walled city following the belated evacuation order of General T'ang. The most horrible of such incidents took place in Hsiak'uan, one of the few escape routes open for the Chinese garrison in the last phase of the battle. An eyewitness gave the following account:

The gate blocked, terror-mad soldiers scaled the wall and let themselves down on the other side with ropes, puttees, and belts tied together, clothing torn to strips. Many fell and were killed. But at the river was perhaps the most appalling scene of all. A fleet of junks was there. It was totally inadequate for the horde that was now in a frenzy to cross to the north side [of the Yangtze]. The overcrowded junks capsized, then sank; thousands drowned. Other thousands tried to make rafts of the lumber on the river front, only to suffer the same fate.[7]

General Li added a grim episode to this story: "A small number of courageous troops, not realizing the extent of the situation, had without orders placed machine guns atop the city walls to strafe the men leaving the city. Heavy casualties resulted from this internal slaughter."[8] A Japanese eyewitness who later saw the dead bodies in the same area corroborated these statements in his account: "I had never seen, and did not see afterward, such a large number of regular soldiers lying dead. Those bodies showed a strange outlook. First, I could not find any external injury. Second, they were all on the foot of the bank near Hsiak'uan as if they had died having reached there with their last remaining energy."[9] This eyewitness assumed that a Japanese poisonous gas attack caused their death. But since examination of official records and private testimonies rules out any possibility of gas attacks by the Japanese army in Nanking, they were most likely pressed or trampled to death amid the confusion.[10]

A Chinese eyewitness provides a story similar to the above accounts. An errand boy working at the garrison headquarters within the city was walking among a big crowd toward the Pachiang Gate located in the southeast of Hsiak'uan at midnight on December 13 hoping to escape from the city. According to his testimony, a badly damaged tank of the Nationalist Army was stranded at the gate. Around it were piles of dead bodies, and the endless and continuous waves of crowds trampled over them. If one person fell, he would be crushed to death. The corpses were accumulated as high as one or two meters like a hill at the gate. He also saw dead bodies over the tank. When Colonel

Yasuyama Hiromichi of the Japanese navy passed through the area by car after the battle, he felt the slowly moving vehicle making a gentle creaking sound as if it were running over fully inflated rubber bags. The car was moving over numerous corpses of Chinese soldiers.[11]

Although on a smaller scale and in a different manner, Chinese troops often killed their own soldiers in other areas. When some Chinese troops tried to escape to the north of the city through the Chungshan Road, the Chinese 36th Division tried to stop them, resulting in an exchange of fire. At the battle in Hsinhechen in the west of Nanking on the morning of December 13, Takahashi Yoshihiko, who was then a lieutenant attached to the command of the Japanese Independent 2nd Mountain Artillery Regiment, saw Chinese soldiers wearing armbands reading "battle encouragement" and shooting their own soldiers from behind to prevent their desertion and force them to charge into the Japanese troops. Takahashi said that as many as 10 percent of the Chinese killed in the battle were the results of such friendly fire.[12]

There was yet another group of Chinese who lost their lives in the city, that is, wounded Chinese soldiers who had been transported from Shanghai and other areas east of Nanking. According to a recent estimate, about 9,000 such soldiers died before the Japanese occupied the city. A report by a German news correspondent substantiated the presence of a huge number of unattended, and subsequently dead, soldiers in the city. That female German correspondent witnessed about 2,000 wounded military men carried into the city one day in December but left unattended at a train station for two days. She also said that most of these wounded were neither bandaged nor had shrapnel or bullets removed, and as a consequence had swollen limbs. Apparently, the Chinese did not have time to bury those wounded soldiers who subsequently had died. A Japanese soldier witnessed 400 to 500 half-charred corpses of Chinese soldiers, apparently disposed of by their fellow Chinese soldiers, outside the city walls in the evening of December 13, that is, immediately after the Japanese entry into the city—the timing of which practically ruled out the possibility of direct Japanese responsibility for their deaths.[13]

It is almost impossible to determine how many soldiers lost their lives in such circumstances. Chinese casualties blamed on their own actions were mostly limited to the Hsiak'uan area and thus probably did not constitute a substantial part of the fatalities in the city. A recent estimate computed the death toll in this category as about 1,000.[14] Adding an estimated 9,000 who died of wounds, one may assume that about 10,000 human bodies left in Nanking at the time were the result of the previously mentioned factors attributable primarily to the Chinese.

COMBAT CASUALTIES

The Japanese formulated two plans for the capture of Nanking, contingent on the extent of Chinese resistance. The first plan called for a quick encirclement of the city on the assumption that the already weakened Chinese troops would soon give up the defense of the capital and retreat. The second plan, which Japanese strategists thought less likely to happen, was for a prolonged siege in case the Chinese entrenched themselves in the city. It proposed the use of poison gas and incendiary bombs over a one-week period to turn the Nanking city area into a ruin.[15] Had the second plan materialized, Chinese and Western observers might have regarded all the devastation and killing in the city, however extensive and savage it might have been, as a result of military action and thus might not have coined the term "Rape of Nanking." In reality, however, the Japanese followed the first plan since the Chinese chose not to offer prolonged resistance inside the city walls.

When the Chinese garrison troops were trying to break the closing Japanese ring to escape, there were naturally many chance encounters between the two sides, hence numerous combat casualties. General Matsui recorded in his diary entry of December 14 and 15 combined, "There has been a report of several thousands of straggling soldiers roaming around everywhere although I have not obtained the details." Colonel Uemura Toshimichi, an SEF staff officer, depicted a rather abrupt engagement between the soldiers assigned to SEF headquarters and about 1,000 Chinese soldiers on the evening of December 13. Also, according to Lieutenant General Nakajima Kesago commanding the 16th Division, he was awakened in the early morning of December 13 when a certain battalion pleaded for urgent help to repulse an assault by Chinese soldiers trying to flee from the doomed capital. Although the scale of the attack seemed to be small, the division headquarters panicked for a while. There was also a rumor that a large group of unorganized Chinese soldiers annihilated a searchlight unit after that unit called for help by radio and then suddenly cut off the communication with a cry of "Long live the Emperor!" It turned out later that the unit had suffered only a few losses.[16]

The threat posed by Chinese soldiers trying to escape was sometimes serious and did result in fierce battles. Nevertheless, many of them eventually developed into one-sided slaughters by the Japanese, which, however atrocious they might have been, one may classify as legitimate military actions. Such battles took place mainly on both wings of the Japanese army advancing toward Nanking since they were marching along the escape routes of most of the Chinese garrison troops.

According to the record of the Tenth Army's 6th Division, a cavalry regiment advancing on its left flank encountered about 10,000 Chinese soldiers retreating from the Hsiak'uan area and defeated them after having killed about 1,000. Private Upper Class Fukumoto Tsuzumi, of the 3rd Battalion in the 6th Division's 45th Regiment described a similar battle in his diary. Fukumoto's company was deployed on the extreme left of the regiment and was advancing northward on the southern shore of the Yangtze to cut off the retreat route of the Chinese army. According to Fukumoto, his unit was suddenly surrounded by about 40,000 Chinese soldiers, but kept firing by picking up ammunition from the enemy dead. In what seems to be an exaggerated account of this engagement, he claims to have killed 400 to 500 enemies single-handedly by using hand grenades and a musket. He described the aftermath as "six thousand enemy corpses covering the ground and leaving no ground to step on." The Chinese force that avoided contact with Fukumoto's company found its way to a tributary of the Yangtze, but soon went through a gauntlet of fire from the 2nd Battalion of the same 45th Regiment. Major Naritomo Fujio, commander of the battalion, said that his unit chased away the enemy after they had shot at each other from about twenty meters away for about twenty minutes, and he then found one of the creeks in the area filled completely with dead bodies for a length of forty to fifty meters. Quite a few Chinese were trying to escape over the river on rafts. Sublieutenant Maeda Yoshihiko, a platoon commander within that battalion, was surprised to see one raft after another moving downstream, each carrying more than 100 soldiers. Maeda and his men thought that they should not let them go unharmed and started firing at them. According to Maeda, there was no missed shot since those rafts were moving slowly right underneath their position and all the ammunition was exhausted after having destroyed about five rafts. Maeda, however, soon had to order his men to withdraw from the river bank because the Chinese troops on the rafts began to land ashore and started a counterattack.[17]

On the SEF's front, one of the two brigades of Lieutenant General Nakajima's 16th Division, the 30th Brigade commanded by Major General Sasaki Toichi, was forced to slow its movement due to engagements with unorganized Chinese soldiers.[18] Sasaki described an event on the morning of December 13 as follows:

I woke up around eight o'clock in the morning at the sound of gun shots in the immediate vicinity and saw even radio transmitter and supply soldiers firing guns.

"What is going on?" I asked my adjutant running outside.

"We have just driven them back. They descended from the Tzuchin Mountain in a mass."

"Were they defeated [Chinese] soldiers?"

"They have been charging toward us over and over in a group of five or six hundred, firing machine guns."

"Disarm them."

"They never surrender. We have to kill them all."

A countless number of enemy soldiers were appearing everywhere. They were the soldiers of the Training Division stationed at the top of the Tzuchin Mountain. They launched a desperate attack against us to open an escape route in our battle line. I could hear their shouting and cursing voices amid gun shots.

Some of them continued their resistance by entrenching themselves in houses, while others were attempting to flee by putting on civilian clothing. Those who were about to surrender were either throwing their arms into ponds or setting fire to the houses nearby.[19]

Sasaki estimated the enemy dead left behind in his theater on this day at more than 10,000. In a nearby area, the SEF's cavalry unit, composed of four cavalry regiments, clashed with about 3,000 soldiers while marching to Hsiak'uan in the early morning of December 13. They beat the enemy and counted about 700 dead bodies left on the field, but suffered seventy casualties themselves and lost 204 horses.[20]

A large number of Chinese soldiers were still in the Hsiak'uan area when the Japanese rapidly approached that section of the city. Those who survived the deadly chaos created by the frenzied crowd of their own men could hardly find ships to cross the river. Major General Sasaki's 30th Brigade kept marching toward Hsiak'uan throughout the morning of December 13 and finally reached the shore of the Yangtze in the early afternoon. Of the two regiments under Sasaki's command, the 38th chased the retreating enemy to the river and, according to one estimate, annihilated 5,000 to 6,000 soldiers trying to reach the northern shore either on the southern river shore or in the river. The regiment pressed the remaining enemies toward Hsiak'uan. According to one of the battalion commanders of the regiment, those who were cornered in the Hsiak'uan area numbered no less than 20,000. The 38th Regiment itself, however, reported that it had swept away at least 500 enemies by the evening of that same day after occupying Hsiak'uan. Another regiment of the same brigade, the 33rd, also encountered and mopped up countless straggling soldiers in the villages on both sides of its marching route. Upon arriving at the river shore, the regiment's vanguard unit found numerous Chinese soldiers crossing the Yangtze toward the northern shore. They were either on board privately owned vessels and rafts or holding onto any floating object. The soldiers of the 33rd opened fire immediately and kept shooting at the Chinese soldiers on the river for two hours. The official regimental report estimates the losses they inflicted on the enemy at no less than 2,000.[21]

The ordeal was not over yet for those Chinese who managed to survive the machine gunning from the shore. They came under the gunfire of the Japanese navy's gunboats in the Yangtze River. It was the Navy's Task Force Eleven, comprising twelve gunboats, that was moving upstream to Nanking. Some of these ships opened fire on the soldiers swimming or sailing in the river before they reached a wharf in Hsiak'uan in the afternoon of December 13. In the river an officer on board the gunboat *Hozu* saw quite a few Chinese soldiers who still remained in the Hsiak'uan area and waved joyfully at the Japanese ships, apparently mistaking them for Chinese warships. They too were soon under the machine gun fire from the gunboat and then joined the corpses filling the river and the shore. When a staff officer of Task Force Eleven visited the SEF headquarters, he said that the task force had annihilated 10,000 enemies retreating on board the rafts. This verbal report probably exaggerated the fact. A Chinese source said that about 3,000 to 4,000 men died in the river.[22]

It is almost impossible to determine how many Chinese soldiers lost their lives in combat. Chinese sources initially gave very low estimates, possibly to cover up the disastrous military defeat in the capital city. This was the exact opposite of postwar accounts that have tended to make higher estimates of the

Chart 3.1

Chinese Military Loss as Reported by Multiple Sources

Estimate	Source	Note
3,000-5,000	Durdin, *NYT*, 15 Dec. 1937	Durdin left Nanking on Dec. 15 and thus did not see the entire "mopping-up operation of the Japanese army.
13,000	Durdin, *NYT*, 9 Jan. 1938	Dispatch from Shanghai.
20,000	U.S. military intelligence report, Dec. 1937	Information source was not specified.
33,000	Ho Ying-Ch'in, early 1938	The number of those killed in action in Shanghai through Nanking; Extremely low and unrealistic.
58,774	The Japanese 65th Regiment's report, n.d.	Extremely minute figure; Information source is unclear.
70,000	Michael R. Gibson's Ph.D. Dissertation, 1985	Most likely, Gibson depended on Chinese sources, which were not identified.
84,000	The Japanese army's official announcement, 29 Dec. 1937	Likely to be a cumulative total of body counts reported from subordinate units, and thus to be inflated.
90,000	Sun Chai-wei,'s article in 1988	Sun depended on some primary Chinese sources, but adopted a questionable calculation method.
100,000	Maj.-Gen. Sasaki's diary entry on 5 Jan. 1938	Most likely a sum total of orally reported body counts, which were almost always exaggerated.

death toll (Chart 3.1). A U.S. intelligence officer quoting an unidentified Chinese source said the Chinese casualties in Nanking totaled 20,000. General Ho Ying-ch'in, who assumed the post equivalent of defense minister under Chiang Kai-shek, reported in early 1938 the war casualties in the Shanghai–Nanking campaign as 33,000 killed and 65,340 wounded. These figures seem to be extremely low, especially Ho's data, in view of the heavy losses suffered by the Nationalists in Shanghai. Initial Japanese estimates were very high, probably to boast of their military victory in Nanking. Again, ironically, this is in stark contrast with some postwar Japanese accounts, which tended to estimate the Chinese death toll lower. Major General Iinuma said that "the SEF's divisions destroyed about fifty thousand while the Navy and the Tenth Army killed about thirty thousand," thus giving his estimate of 80,000. The Japanese official communique issued on December 29 stated that the Chinese losses were 84,000, which was very close to Iinuma's figure. Major General Sasaki later said the Japanese inflicted about 70,000 losses on an enemy force of about 100,000. The 65th Regiment's battle report gives 58,774 as the number of dead enemy left behind in the Nanking campaign.[23]

One may accept those figures of about 60,000 to 84,000 from contemporary sources as an actual total of Chinese combat losses. Yet one may also question the validity of Japanese data as a basis of calculation because it is highly likely that Iinuma and other Japanese military leaders simply accumulated the numbers from subordinate units' preliminary battle reports, which tended to exaggerate body counts.[24] Thus, the Chinese combat casualties should have been smaller than the upper figure of this range. The data contained in the 65th Regiment's battle report, almost 60,000, might be close to the actual Chinese losses, although its source is not clear.

Contemporary Western sources gave only rough estimates. *New York Times* correspondent Durdin, who left Nanking on December 15 and thus did not see the entire mopping-up operations, estimated the Japanese and Chinese battle losses at 1,000 and 3,000 to 5,000, respectively. Although the data are again not complete, actual Japanese killed and wounded in action during the Nanking campaign totaled about 7,000.[25] If one assumes that the Chinese suffered three to five times as many losses as the Japanese, as Durdin reported, the killed and wounded Chinese soldiers combined would have amounted to approximately 21,000 to 35,000. Since the Chinese troops attempted a desperate escape from Nanking, one may expect that a substantial number of the wounded soldiers were left behind to die. Thus, the military dead are estimated roughly at between 20,000 and 30,000 if one relies on these data.

Although the most reliable source should be the battle reports compiled by the Chinese military, the battle reports of only a few units contained numerical data. Accordingly, one must rely on guesswork and extrapolation. Sun Chai-wei, analyzing some documents of the time with his own calculation method, estimated the Chinese military dead at about 90,000 after the fall of the city. This figure seems too high when compared with the Japanese claim, which was itself very likely an exaggeration. The numerical records of Chinese military units, wherever available, are mostly sketchy. Among the Nanking garrison, the Second Army Group, comprising the 41st and 48th Divisions, provided quite specific data about their losses. After their evacuation was complete, the two divisions' battle casualties totaled 3,919 killed and 1,099 wounded. This represents an almost four-to-one death-injury ratio and brings the number of casualties to 5,118. Since the two divisions had a strength of 11,703 after their retreat, they lost about one-third of their pre-battle force strength in Nanking. If one applies this casualty ratio to the entire Nanking garrison estimated to be 110,000 to 130,000 strong, the total combat casualties would be about 36,700 to 43,300, including 29,360 to 34,640 killed. These figures would, however, be too small because the Second Army Group was fighting outside the walls and could retreat more easily than other units that must have suffered heavier casualties by entrenching themselves in the immediate vicinity of the city walls. Judging from its report, the 78th Army Group, which was composed only of the 36th Division and assigned to the area in the immediate north of the walls facing the Yangtze River, is believed to have been near its full divisional strength of about 11,000 before the battle started. As of December 30, following its retreat from Nanking, the army had only 4,000, translating to more than a 60 percent attrition rate. The 74th Army, which, according to one of its two divisional commanders, had 17,000 men at the beginning of the battle, could recover only 5,000 one day after its escape from Nanking. This means that the 74th Army lost 70 percent of its manpower. The 66th Army's 160th Division deployed in the southeast of the city is estimated to have been about 8,000 men strong prior to the battle. In the end, only 1,500 soldiers assembled in a designated location after its breakout from Nanking, with the loss ratio standing at over 80 percent. Other units that were fighting in strategically important places closer to the city walls suffered even more. That two brigade commanders of the Chinese 88th Division and one brigade commander of the 87th Division, both assigned to the positions immediately outside the walls, were killed in action testified to the severity of the fighting. Although one cannot obtain even a rough casualty ratio of these units due to the lack of numerical data, their losses were likely to be heavier since the 88th Division and the Training Units together reported only 2,000 soldiers who successfully escaped on December 12 and 13, while the 87th Division could count only about 300. If one accepts those statistics at face value, they lost more than 90 percent. Thus, the casualty ratio of Chinese units ranges from roughly 35 percent to 90 percent. One could boost the lower limit to 40 percent in view of the higher casualty rates in most units. At the same time, one must take into account a considerable number of soldiers who had already deserted prior to the issuance of evacuation orders and were recorded missing as well as those who later rejoined their original units. Therefore, one could lower the top of the range safely to 80 percent. If one applies this range of casualty ratio to the estimated strength of the Nanking garrison—110,000 to 130,000—one could obtain figures ranging from 44,000 to 104,000. Still, it is too wide a range to be accepted as a final tally. Thus, it is necessary to study other factors and statistics. One should, for example, realize that the official Japanese military records often categorized the enemy's captives executed by their own units after the battle as those killed in action. Moreover, to make the matter more complicated, those reported battle casualties might have included civilians mistaken as plainclothes soldiers.[26]

EXECUTION OF PLAINCLOTHES SOLDIERS, POWS, AND MEN OF CONSCRIPTION AGE

A substantial number of Chinese soldiers neither escaped from the encirclement nor lost their lives in the battle. Those who remained in the city or its vicinity had few or no officers to lead them and no longer formed organized military units.[27] Nevertheless, some of them kept fighting in isolation. In a directive issued to the Japanese 30th Brigade in the early morning of December 14, its commander Major General Sasaki said, "The enemy has been defeated in the entire front, but there are still soldiers willing to fight at any place."[28]

Sasaki's prediction proved correct. In his diary he described an event on that day as follows: "Although they were straggling soldiers, some of them were still hiding in villages or mountains. Accordingly, I had them killed without any mercy if they resisted or did not show an obedient attitude. I heard gun shots everywhere all through the day."[29]

Quite a few incidents or rumors underlined Sasaki's concern. SEF staff chief Iinuma noted his worry about the fate of some leaders of the 3rd Division who had reportedly been ambushed by about 500 enemy soldiers. In addition, 16th Division chief Nakajima derisively talked about some rear units that had a sudden encounter with a sizable group of Chinese soldiers and sought help in a panic by exaggerating the number of enemies. At one point on the night of December 13, SEF headquarters came under attack by a group of straggling soldiers and asked the 9th Division to send a regiment to guard the commander. Nakajima viewed this move as an overreaction and criticized the 9th Division for its intrusion into his own division's operation area. The measure was, however, understandable because the SEF commander was Prince Asaka, an imperial family member. In one of several similar cases, a supply column following the 68th Regiment's 3rd Battalion met a surprise attack by about 200 Chinese soldiers accompanied by Chinese civilians wearing Japanese armbands. Private Upper Class Makihara of the 20th Regiment also told a story of six Japanese supply soldiers ambushed and killed on the night of December 13.[30]

Many Chinese soldiers, however, chose to quit the fight. Accordingly, the Japanese troops captured several thousand Chinese soldiers by accepting their surrender. How many prisoners the Japanese took varies depending on the source, ranging from about 10,000 to 40,000.[31] Very often, frenzied Japanese soldiers killed opponents out of sheer fury even when the latter raised their arms. Major General Sasaki described a scene he witnessed on December 13: "prisoners were surrendering en masse, bringing their sum total to several thousand. Enraged soldiers started killing one prisoner after another, and the superior officers' effort to restrain them was of no avail. Even if they were not enlisted soldiers, reflection upon the deceased comrades and hardship they had endured in the past ten days would make them say, 'Finish them off!' "[32]

Once the battle fury subsided, the Japanese usually took the prisoners into their custody more or less peacefully. But those prisoners met a variety of fates. Some Japanese units treated them generously whereas others brutally massacred them. What was notable about the Japanese military's attitude about POWs was a lack of policy rather than a fixed policy characterized by cruelty. Yet it is undeniable that many Japanese troops in Nanking subjected Chinese prisoners to cruel treatment, which one can include in the category of atrocities.

It is reasonable to assume that the most important factor influencing the conduct of many Japanese soldiers was concern over the security of their leaders. One may point to facts that underline this reasoning. First, as the subsequent discussion will show, the SEF was apparently responsible for a massacre on a larger scale than the Tenth Army, most likely because the SEF leadership was concerned about the safety of its commander, Prince Asaka. Second, almost all the systematic execution-style killing happened prior to the victory parade on December 17. Therefore, although not justifiable in the light of contemporary legal or moral standards, one major cause of the Rape of Nanking was this security concern rather than a malicious intent to terrorize the population.

The Japanese military leadership decided to launch the campaign to hunt down Chinese soldiers in the suburban areas apparently because a substantial number of Chinese soldiers were still hiding in such areas and posing a constant threat to the Japanese. Lieutenant Mori Hideo, commander of the 20th Regiment's 3rd Company under the 16th Division, recorded an incident that likely alerted Japanese troops to the presence of fleeing Chinese soldiers. According to his recollection, he first saw a truck flying a red cross flag pass through the Japanese picket line at full speed. Recognizing the red cross mark, the Japanese held their fire. When they realized that the truck was fully loaded with Chinese military men in uniform, it was too late to react and the Japanese saw it pass without ever shooting at it.[33] In addition to such uniformed soldiers, the Japanese military leadership reasonably suspected that a considerable number of plain-clothes Chinese soldiers remained in the city.

Shortly after the collapse of the Chinese defenses, *New York Times* correspondent Durdin witnessed the wholesale undressing of an army that was almost comic and saw some soldiers who disrobed completely and then robbed civilians of their garments. Then, *Chicago Daily News* correspondent Steele saw fear-crazed troops attempt to force their entry into the headquarters of the international committee. Private First Class Chao Shih-fa of the Chinese 88th Division was apparently among such Chinese soldiers, judging from his statement that "I took off my military uniform and put on clothes of an ordinary civilian so that I would not be shot on the spot by the Japanese troops." Both the Japanese soldiers entering Nanking and the Chinese nationals remaining in the city saw the aftermath of this mass self-stripping. Private Upper Class Inoie Mataichi and Private First Class Mizutani So, both of the 9th Division's 7th Regiment, saw the streets within the Safety Zone "littered" or "filled" with the abandoned Chinese military uniforms. Chiang Kung-yi, a Chinese medic who took refuge at the U.S. embassy building, also described the ground in the city as being "covered with piles of thrown-away military uniforms." The 7th Regiment's official record underlines their statements by listing among captured items large amounts of clothes and footwear, including 6,220 coats and 6,695 pairs of trousers. As for Colonel Yasuyama of the Japanese navy, he witnessed piles of gas masks left behind by the Chinese. The Japanese military leaders estimated the number of Chinese soldiers in hiding in the Safety Zone at 10,000 to 20,000.[34]

In the operations to hunt down the Chinese soldiers, the SEF was in charge of half of the city to the north of the demarcation line running from the Kunghe Gate in the south through the Kungyuen Road, Chungcheng Road, the Hanchung Road, and leading to the Hanchung Gate. Within the SEF, the 16th Division used all four of its infantry regiments (9th, 20th, 33rd, and 38th) and covered areas both within and outside the city walls. As I will discuss later, the division's commander, Lieutenant General Nakajima Kesago, was a controversial and notorious figure for his behavior in Nanking and his attitude toward POWs. Of the four regiments Nakajima had, the 33rd Regiment was assigned the Hsiak'uan area near the Yangtze River while two battalions of the 38th Regiment were to operate in the immediate east of the 33rd, and the 20th in the southeast of the 38th, both within the walls. Thus, Nakajima's units were in charge of the areas where a large number of Chinese soldiers tried to escape and were likely to be found. Other units were ordered to clear separate areas in the eastern suburb, one of which included the tomb of Sun Yat-sen. The 9th Division directed its 7th and 35th Regiments to operate to the south of the 16th Division. This division, the 9th, had fought costly battles in Shanghai and thus was likely to have a strong sense of hostility toward the Chinese soldiers. Of them, the 7th Regiment was responsible for most of the Safety Zone, where quite a few Chinese soldiers were believed to be in hiding. The Tenth Army, in charge of the southern area, ordered the 114th Division and the 6th Division to "annihilate the enemies by using any means including the bombardment" and "burn the city proper within the walls if necessary." Compared with SEF units, these divisions of the Tenth Army had limited battlefield experience since their landing at Shanghai early in November. In contrast with 16th Division chief Nakajima, Lieutenant General Tani Hisao, commander of the 6th Division, was known for his gentlemanly behavior as well as his intellectual quality exemplified by his well-known work about the Russo-Japanese War. Most likely, such a difference in these commanders' personal character as well as their units' military records in China profoundly affected how they behaved in their mopping-up operations.[35]

Cases of the SEF: Mass Surrenders and Mass Executions

The SEF's 16th Division is reputed by the Chinese and some historians to have been the most savage killing machine among the Japanese military units in Nanking. This reputation was true to a certain extent. The commander of the division, Lieutenant General Nakajima, bluntly stated how he intended to treat prisoners in his diary entry of December 13: "Since our policy is not to take prisoners, we made a point of executing them as soon as we had captured them. But when they grew into a crowd of one thousand, five thousand or ten thousand, we were unable even to disarm them. We were safe as long as they followed us without any will to fight, but once they started disturbing us, we would be in trouble."[36] Nakajima's diary also describes what appears to be his gruesome personal habit. He had a sword master who happened to visit his headquarters behead seven Chinese POWs using both his own and Nakajima's swords. It seems that some Japanese military men did not have any remorse as long as they killed only a small number of POWs, probably because their forced march to Nanking did not allow them to take prisoners and made them numb to such killing. It appeared to be a common practice for Japanese military and naval personnel to behead prisoners for the sake of testing their swordsmanship.[37]

There was, however, more than the commander's personality or policy affecting the 16th Division's treatment of prisoners. Nakajima complained about the presence of too many prisoners in his diary entry of the same day: "The 16th Division happened to be in the area where an extreme effort is needed to take care of these straggling soldiers. Accordingly, my division is too busy running around to organize a victory march in the city or to find accommodations."[38] Actually, his division was assigned to the Hsiak'uan and adjacent areas where a majority of Chinese soldiers in Nanking were cornered in a desperate and unsuccessful effort to escape in the last phase of the siege. According to Durdin, the Chinese left inside were completely hemmed in and the troops caught in the Hsiak'uan district were systematically wiped out. In view of the presence of many Chinese soldiers in the 16th Division's operation theater, Lieutenant Colonel Cho Isamu of the SEF suggested to SEF staff chief Iinuma on December 16 the deployment of the 3rd Division in the same area to help the 16th quicken the mopping-up operations. Regarding the actual number of enemies, Nakajima said that one of his brigades, led by Major General Sasaki, alone took care of about 15,000 while a company guarding the Taiping Gate also dealt with about 1,300. He added that another 7,000 to 8,000 were gathering around Hsienhemen and that this crowd of prisoners was growing further. Also, Colonel Nakasawa Mitsuo, 16th Division's staff chief, entered on his operation map several figures, which apparently look like the number of captured war prisoners, although these figures were likely to be merely the preliminary tallies reported by the division's subordinate units. According to the map, the 16th Division caught a total of 22,550 at eight different locations, among them 20,000 being the largest group.[39] As for the means to dispose of those prisoners, Nakajima said, "We would need quite a large ditch to take care of them, but we cannot find a large one easily. One solution might be to divide them into groups of hundred or two hundred and lead them to some other places to execute each group one by one."[40]

Nakajima's subordinate commanders implemented his policy in varying degrees. Prior to the mopping-up operation both inside and outside the Nanking walls, Major General Sasaki commanding the 30th Brigade of the division issued a directive saying, "No unit will be allowed to accept prisoners until the divisional command issues a further notice."[41] Some units followed this order faithfully whereas others did not due to some pressing circumstances such as the presence of too many POWs surrendering all at once.

According to a report compiled by the 33rd Regiment under Sasaki's command, the enemy's death toll in its theater of operation totaled 6,830, including 3,096 prisoners. These 3,096 Chinese officers and soldiers surrendered to the regiment on December 10 to 14. Regarding their fate, the report simply said, "The regiment executed the prisoners."[42] There are few source materials that tell how the regiment killed them. SEF staff chief Iinuma referred to the Taiping Gate in the northeastern section of the city walls as the place "where one company of the 33rd Infantry Regiment captured one thousand and several hundred prisoners and executed them." Sergeant Kanemaru Yoshio working for the 16th Division's accounting section noted a rumor told by the soldiers of the 33rd that ten railway carriages loaded fully with Chinese soldiers were rolled into the Yangtze River.[43] Captain Shimada Katsumi, who commanded a machine gun company within the 33rd, also describes a scene that might or might not depict one such execution: "We found 140–50 straggling soldiers in the vicinity of the Shitzu Mountain during the mopping-up operation and killed all of them in an all-out attack. A considerable number of them turned out to conceal hand grenade or pistol in their uniforms. In a chaotic battlefield, we acted on a principle that 'unless we kill them, we will be killed in the next moment.' "[44] Although the 30th Brigade's directive of "accept no POWs" undoubtedly caused the ruthless killing of POWs, this example shows that some of these executions were very close to, and possibly justifiable as, military actions.

The 38th Regiment operated in an area adjacent to the 33rd's as well as in the suburb northeast of the city walls. This regiment took a large number of prisoners around Yaohuamen in the morning of December 14. This huge group had continued to attack the Japanese on the previous day, but had finally given up its fight when faced with superior Japanese forces nearby. According to the regimental report of the 38th, the regiment's 10th Company in charge of the suburban area saw several thousand enemies advancing toward them waving white flags, finished disarming them at one o'clock in the afternoon, and escorted them to the city. Although the acceptance of prisoners was a clear violation of the order mentioned previously, they probably had no choice but to take them prisoners due to their sheer numbers. It is hard to determine the actual number of prisoners since several sources give a wide range of numbers. Sumita Masao, a platoon commander of the 38th Regiment, said the group was composed of about 2,000 soldiers, while Field Postal Chief Sasaki Motokatsu said that he saw about 4,000 disarmed Chinese soldiers in the area. Official reports at the time, however, described the group as about 7,000 or 7,200 prisoners, while Lieutenant Sawada Masahisa, who was on the scene, said the prisoners numbered about 10,000, or at least 8,000. The 16th Division's staff chief provided the largest estimate of 20,000 on his map. Again, there is no way to determine which figure was closest to the real number, although one may dismiss the figure on Nakasawa's map as the one based on preliminary data collected orally from subordinate units. When Lieutenant Sawada reported the capture of these prisoners to the SEF, an unidentified SEF staff officer first told him to shoot them to death, but later instructed him to bring them to one of the city gates after the lieutenant objected to that instruction, either for humanitarian reasons or because the number of POWs was so large. The 38th's report mentions nothing about the fate of those Chinese prisoners. A private memoir suggests that the Japanese massacred them. SEF staff Major Sakakibara Kazue, however, said that the SEF interned about 4,000 to 5,000 prisoners in the prisons in Nanking around the time of the victory march, that is, December 17.[45]

In addition to these operations, the 33rd and the 38th also searched the area in the north of the Tzuchin Mountain on December 16 and, according to Brigadier Commander Sasaki's diary, disposed of several hundred straggling soldiers each.[46]

Each of 16th Division's other two regiments (the 20th and 9th Regiments) used two battalions, composed of eight companies, to clean up the assigned city areas within the walls and had another remaining battalion operate in the suburb. There is, however, no regimental report available to show how many prisoners the two regiments captured or executed. Only the records of subordinate units and private diaries or testimonies tell what happened. These sources suggest that the units in charge of part of the International Safety Zone conducted a relentless hunt for soldiers and executed them. The 4th Company of the 20th Regiment shot to death and buried 328 straggling enemy soldiers, according to its company diary on December 14. Private Upper Class Masuda Rokusuke of that company said in his diary, "The body count of our unit alone amounted to no less than five hundred and other units seem to obtain similar results." Although there is no source material that explains the gap between 328 and 500, one possible explanation is that the latter figure included those killed in action, since the memoir of Corporal Hayashi Masaaki, who led a squad within the 20th Regiment's 3rd Company, suggested that there were still exchanges of fire in the city. Hayashi said that he had captured dozens of unorganized fleeing soldiers in front of the supreme court building, braving the bullets flying toward them from the west. Unlike the 4th Company, however, the 3rd Company of the same regiment apparently did not commit any large-scale killing, contradicting Private Masuda's assumption. The 3rd Company's Private Upper Class Azuma, who wrote a detailed memoir describing his experiences in Nanking, did not mention any atrocious activities undertaken by his unit during the same time period. He only noted that his unit arrested and nearly executed seven suspicious-looking Chinese in a later search of the Safety Zone, but ultimately set them free after a Japanese-speaking Chinese pleaded for their lives.[47]

One may suspect that the 20th Regiment carried out many other cases of execution-style killing of prisoners within the city walls, but their scale was probably small. Maeda Yuji, a correspondent of Domei News Agency, witnessed a noncommissioned officer and several soldiers shooting Chinese prisoners on the shore of a pond behind the Chiaotung Yinhang [communications bank] that was included in the 20th Regiment's operation area. Maeda also saw Japanese soldiers stabbing prisoners and pushing them into a trench under the supervision of a noncommissioned officer at the yard of the military school—another building located in the operation area of the 20th Regiment. When Maeda interviewed that noncommissioned officer, the latter simply said, "This is to educate new recruits."[48]

The 20th ordered its one other battalion to mop up the area around Machun, about three miles east of the city walls. According to the diary of Private Upper Class Makihara, who was a member of a machine gun company operating with this battalion, his unit shot to death all of about 310 soldiers who had already been disarmed. Makihara also witnessed a squad-size group of Japanese soldiers escorting about 1,800 Chinese troops.[49]

If one relies only on the data in the official records, the sum total of Chinese prisoners executed by the 16th Division numbered 3,724—3,096 by the 33rd Regiment, 328 by the 4th Company of the 20th Regiment, and 310 by a battalion of the 20th—which one could round up to 4,000. This might serve as the lower limit, although these figures might have included combat casualties or might have been inflated since these units reported them as battle results. One could obtain the upper limit only by extrapolation of available data. Suppose all of the 20th Regiment's eight companies operating within the walls killed the same number of prisoners as the regiment's 4th Company, that is, 328—although it is unlikely judging from the account given by Azuma—the combined total for them would amount to 2,624. Incidentally, if one adds 310 executed by another battalion of the same regiment that operated in the suburb, the combined total of Chinese soldiers executed by the 20th Regiment would be 2,934 and would come very close to 3,096, that is, the sum total of prisoners executed by the 33rd, one of the fellow regiments of the same division. Although materials are too scarce, one could obtain the figure of 12,000 on the premise that all regiments of the 16th Division killed an average of 3,000 each during their mopping-up operations. Thus, the estimated number of Chinese prisoners executed by the 16th Division ranges from 4,000 to 12,000.

Except for the 20th Regiment, the 16th Division executed those prisoners mainly outside the city walls judging from this statement by Nakajima: "I could not see any enemy soldiers within the city walls. But there is a refugee sector in the area assigned to the 9th Division. Although the population included many children, old people, and women, it is not hard to imagine that there are many straggling soldiers among them."[50] It was the 9th Division that conducted its operation in the Safety Zone and attracted the attention of the foreigners.

The 9th Division claimed to have annihilated about 7,000 straggling soldiers during its mopping-up operation within the city walls.[51] Prior to the start of this operation, one of its two brigades, the 6th Brigade, consisting of the 7th and 35th Infantry Regiments, cautioned its subordinate units of the presence of plainclothes Chinese soldiers in a directive issued in the evening of December 13 that read, "Since the defeated enemy soldiers are believed to be plainclothes, you must arrest any person who is suspected of being so and detain him at an appropriate location. . . . You should regard every adult man up to middle age as straggling or plainclothes soldier, thus arrest and detain him."[52]

The brigade leadership issued such instructions because its regiments, especially the 7th, were ordered to sweep the area where such plainclothes soldiers were believed to be hiding in large numbers, that is, the International Safety

Zone. It seems, however, that the 7th Regiment, at least initially, did not intend to kill all the former soldiers it was to capture. A regimental order issued in the afternoon of December 14 contains an instruction that each unit must detain its prisoners in one place within its operation area and request for provisions to feed them from the divisional command.[53] The regiment, nevertheless, was responsible for the conduct witnessed and reported by the Westerners.

In its letter of December 14 to the Japanese commander in Nanking, the International Committee for Nanking Safety Zone (ICNSZ) admitted that an influx of Chinese soldiers into the zone had occurred. The committee apparently had difficulty in dealing with those soldiers. Its letter on the following day to Fukuda Tokuyasu, attaché to the Japanese Embassy, said that "in the confusion and haste of that [December 13] evening, the Committee was unable to keep the disarmed soldiers separate from civilians, particularly because some of the soldiers had abandoned their military clothing. . . . the Committee further hopes that the Japanese Army will in accordance with the recognized laws of war regarding prisoners and for reasons of humanity exercise mercy toward these former soldiers."[54]

The Japanese troops apparently ignored this plea because they suspected that the Chinese soldiers taking refuge in the Safety Zone were not entirely "former" soldiers. That the 7th Regiment captured a considerable amount of weapons and ammunition justified their concern to a certain extent. The list reveals that the regiment seized four tanks and 39,000 rounds of ammunition; two anti-tank guns; two 15-centimeter and eight 20-centimeter cannons with 600 and 1,000 shells for each; ten mortars and 57,218 shells for their use; forty-five machine guns; 960 rifles and 103 pistols as well as 390,000 and 261,350 rounds of ammunition for each; 55,122 hand grenades; and 2,020 Chinese swords.[55] To eliminate any possible threat from those who might still be in hiding, the 7th Regiment searched for former soldiers relentlessly. Correspondent Durdin reported that "Thousands of prisoners were executed by the Japanese. Most of the Chinese soldiers who had been interned in the Safety Zone were shot en masse. The city was combed in a systematic house-to-house search for men having knapsack marks or other signs of having been soldiers. They were herded together and executed."[56]

Documents about the Safety Zone as well as private records corroborate this report. According to the ICNSZ's complaint filed with the Japanese authorities, on December 14 the Japanese took 200 to 300 men from the Ministry of Justice building, insisting that they had been soldiers. A relentless search for former soldiers apparently led to the arrest of nonmilitary men, that is, civilian officials in uniform such as policemen and firemen. The ICNSZ reported on December 17 that the Japanese had returned to the Justice Ministry building on the previous day and marched off fifty policemen stationed there and forty-six members of the voluntary police, which the committee had organized, probably for execution. In addition, the report on December 18 said that another forty policemen at the Supreme Court had been taken away. The Japanese troops also forced out

200 men from the Military College building on December 16, twenty-six more on December 17, and another thirty on December 18. A Japanese officer belonging to the 19th Regiment, a fellow regiment of the 7th under the same 9th Division, apparently saw some of those soldiers arrested in the Safety Zone being carried away in trucks. He concluded, "We must admit that some of them were shot to death on the shore of the Yangtze." Sasaki Motokatsu, a field post master, also witnessed a considerable number of prisoners who had been caught in plainclothes being marched away somewhere, and later Sasaki heard gunshots, apparently executions, in the direction of Hsiak'uan, on the night of December 15. Also, a Japanese artist who went to Nanking on board a Navy gunboat encountered about 1,000 Chinese prisoners being taken to the Hsiak'uan area. Of all the atrocities of the Rape of Nanking, the extensive effort to search for and arrest plainclothes soldiers in the Safety Zone was probably the case Westerners witnessed and reported on most extensively at this stage.[57] Ordinary civilians also became victims. According to Durdin, "Any person who ran because of fear or excitement was likely to be killed on the spot as was any one caught by roving patrols in streets or alleys after dusk. Many slayings were witnessed by foreigners."[58] Among the victims especially targeted were not only uniformed government officials such as policemen but also uniformed civilians engaging in nongovernmental activities. The ICNSZ reported the killing of six street sweepers employed by the Sanitary Commission of the Safety Zone on December 15.[59]

In its final tally, the 7th counted 6,670 straggling soldiers shot or stabbed to death within the Nanking walls from December 13 through 24. It is obvious that most of the activities to hunt down soldiers occurred in the initial few days, since Colonel Isa Kazuo, who commanded the regiment, said in his diary on December 16 that the three-day mopping-up operation resulted in the stern execution of 6,500 enemies. In addition to the 7th Regiment, the 1st Company of the SEF's 1st Tank Battalion supported the operation on December 14 and rounded up 250 prisoners while killing about seventy to eighty straggling soldiers who showed a rebellious attitude. One may doubt the truthfulness of these figures, especially the 6,670 counted by the 7th Regiment since this is very close to 7,000, which happened to be the number of rifle and machine gun bullets the regiment reported to have spent for the same period. Because of a lack of materials that might dispute this data, however, this research will use these figures found on official records for analytical purposes.[60]

Private records corroborate those official statements and Western news reports to a certain extent, although they also show that each subordinate unit treated prisoners in different ways. The 7th regiment's 1st Company entered the city and rounded up many young men on December 13. According to Mizutani So, first class private of the company, however, they let all of the captured POWs go except for twenty-one persons who looked like military men after various investigations. Private Upper Class Inoie Mataichi of the 2nd Company witnessed about 600 Chinese soldiers taking refuge in a foreign-owned building on

December 14. Judging from his diary, however, Inoie's unit did not kill them. Instead, they asked the Japanese embassy to take care of them. It seems that the executions started on December 14. Private Mizutani's unit continued arresting young men on this day and selected out those who had shoe sores, callouses on the face, extremely good posture, and/or sharp-looking eyes after a close investigation. Japanese soldiers seemingly used these physical characteristics as criteria to distinguish plainclothes former soldiers from ordinary civilians. Then, Mizutani's company shot them all to death along with the twenty-one who had been captured on the previous day. Inoie's 2nd Company bayonetted to death some forty soldiers on December 15 and rounded up 335 young men who looked like straggling soldiers. Inoie added that the soldiers of other units took them to the shore of the Yangtze to shoot them. A Chinese policeman, Wu Chang-te, was apparently one of those arrested by the 7th Regiment's operation. According to Wu, he was arrested on December 15 and was marched to the Hanchung Gate with about 2,000 others for a shooting execution. He survived the execution and later testified at the Tokyo War Crimes Trial. Shen Hsi-en, who took refuge in the Safety Zone, was another witness to the soldier search. While he was in the Ginling College campus, the Japanese troops came on December 17 and forced out about 1,000 young males, including Shen, from the college buildings. In an effort to separate soldiers from civilians, the Japanese soldiers removed the hat worn by any Chinese man apparently to see if he had a sunburn on his forehead. They selected out more than 300, although some of them were allowed to stay after their kin begged frantically for them. The fate of those taken away from the college campus is unknown.[61]

It seems that most of the executions of those plainclothes soldiers took place on the river bank. Kajiya Takeo, cavalry sergeant of the 2nd Port Authorities Headquarters in Nanking, said he saw in Hsiak'uan about 2,000 soldiers being killed by machine guns on each day of December 16 and 17. Matsukawa Sei-saku, then private upper class of the 1st Railway Regiment directly under the CCAA command, also witnessed several hundred but not more than 1,000 soldiers either being stabbed by bayonet or shot at a wharf of Hsiak'uan either on December 15 or 16. One soldier of the 13th Division's 65th Regiment, which was operating in the northeast of the Nanking walls, witnessed the killing of thirty to forty Chinese prisoners at one time, presumably by the 7th Regiment, on December 15.[62]

According to Colonel Nakasawa Mitsuo, staff chief of the 16th Division, the separation of soldiers from refugees was more or less over after the initial mopping-up operation, but was not yet complete. Underlining the further need to seek out Chinese soldiers, Nakasawa said that his unit had captured a battalion commander of the Chinese 88th Division hiding in the city. Moreover, some Chinese soldiers in civilian clothing still posed a threat to the Japanese. Private Upper Class Makihara of the 16th Division's 20th Regiment recorded cases of arson caused by the Chinese soldiers every night as well as a rumor of a Japanese medic sniped at by Chinese. Subsequently, on December 21, Major General Sasaki commanding the 16th Division's 30th Brigade assumed the responsibility for policing the entire Nanking area, including the Safety Zone. Doubling as chairman of a committee in charge of pacification activities, Sasaki defined his objective as the arrest of straggling soldiers mingling with the local population lest any plots by disturbing elements should happen and, at the same time, the placating of the minds of the people by tightening the discipline among his own soldiers for the ultimate purpose of restoring order and tranquility as soon as possible. Accordingly, Sasaki declared that all refugees and civilians must report to the Japanese military authorities to get "civilian passports."[63]

This was the virtual resumption of operations to sift out plainclothes soldiers. The actual procedure was to amass men and instruct all who had been soldiers or who had performed "compulsory labor" to step out from the group. This instruction came with a warning that the Japanese military would kill those who hid their true identity upon the inspection. At the Ginling College campus in early January 1938, what had occurred in the previous month was repeated. A Chinese refugee Shen witnessed the Japanese soldiers' inspection of young men looking for sunburn on the forehead as well as a knapsack mark or discoloration on the shoulder made by a rifle butt. It was true that there were some military men hiding among the civilians. SEF staff chief Iinuma said that the chief of a Chinese security unit and the deputy commander of the 88th Division were among those arrested in early January 1938. Also, *New York Times* correspondent Hallett Edward Abend quoted a Japanese record released late in January, in which the Japanese authority claimed to have captured twenty-three officers, fifty-four noncommissioned, officers, and 1,498 privates. Moreover, a Chinese medic taking refuge at the U.S. embassy noted a rumor that some Chinese soldiers hiding underground had planned an uprising, but were caught. According to a Westerner who was at one such registration, however, "a fair number of them [who stepped forward] had never been soldiers" partly because some Chinese men misunderstood the term "compulsory labor": they thought that it included some jobs not related to the military.[64]

By January 5, Sasaki's soldiers rounded up about 2,000 and interned them in the foreign ministry building while they also took custody of wounded Chinese soldiers thus far hospitalized by foreign missionaries. He added, "We also captured those soldiers who were still rebelling against us continuously. The number of those executed at Hsiak'uan amounted to several thousand."[65]

Some records show what happened to those taken away at the time of registration. A Westerner noted the arrival at the University of Nanking hospital of a Chinese man with five bayonet wounds, who had survived an execution of 500 men separated from refugees at the time of registration. Private Upper Class Inoie described a mass execution that possibly took place in the course of this second round of large-scale operations to catch former soldiers, although Inoie's 7th Regiment was not under Sasaki's command. Inoie and other men escorted 161 soldiers assembled in the battalion headquarters to the suburb on December 22 and forced them into a house beside a pond. The Japanese soldiers took five

Chinese out of the house at a time and stabbed them. When some Chinese refused to come out, the Japanese set fire to the house. Corporal Hayashi Masaaki of the 20th Regiment also said, "Poor Chinese soldiers will be eaten by the fish in the Yangtze River" and noted the figure of 7,000 dead as a final tally, although one cannot determine whether this figure is based on official statistics or mere rumor. This figure is, however, highly questionable since a record filed by the Japanese army's special service in Nanking provides a smaller figure, that is, 4,000 rounded up from December 22, 1937, to January 5, 1938, and an additional 500 between January 6 and February 25. Thus, the number of victims during this second phase of searching ranges from 1,500 to 4,500.[66]

These actions, which the Japanese army undertook more than one week after the occupation of the city, may be categorized as an atrocity much less justifiable than the executions that happened immediately after the fall of the city.

The Yamada Detachment, whose main component was the 103rd Infantry Brigade commanded by Major General Yamada Senji, was responsible for a controversial incident, in which the unit killed an unknown number of Chinese soldiers. The detachment, whose only infantry unit was the 65th Regiment commanded by Colonel Morozumi Gyosaku, advanced on the extreme right of the SEF and was ordered to occupy the Mufu Mountain about four miles north of the city walls at midnight of December 14. The regimental command estimated the strength of the enemy in the area at about 20,000, but met only feeble resistance.[67] According to Yamada, his unit captured 14,777 prisoners at the mountain and detained them at school buildings nearby.[68] Additionally, several hundred Chinese soldiers surrendered on the following day and joined this huge group.[69] In the end, the group swelled to about 15,300 or more.[70] Those captives included not only militia soldiers ranging in age from twelve- or thirteen-year-old boys to middle-aged soldiers in their fifties but also some women. Colonel Morozumi said in his brief memoir he wrote after the war, "We released noncombatants among the soldiers and interned the remainder numbering about eight thousand in several buildings" although diaries of lower ranking soldiers did not note such a release. Morozumi's regiment apparently had a hard time guarding them since the regiment was well under its full strength, with only 1,867 men as of December 6. Another problem was feeding them since the Japanese soldiers did not have enough provisions even for themselves. There were so many prisoners that Yamada said, "Whether we should kill them or let them live, I do not know what to do." When Yamada sent a messenger to the SEF headquarters to obtain an appropriate instruction, the SEF ordered Yamada to "kill them all." According to Morozumi, Yamada did not want to undertake it by himself and asked the SEF to assume the responsibility. Nevertheless, Yamada finally replied to the SEF that he would find some solution to the prisoner problem.[71]

What happened thereafter is unclear since available records contradict each other. What certainly happened first was that a fire erupted among the barracks housing the prisoners when they were cooking their meals on December 16.

According to Morozumi, about half of the remaining prisoners fled amid the confusion of the fire, although no private diaries referred to such an escape. Records written by commanders such as Yamada and Morozumi did not mention the subsequent event, but judging from the diaries of soldiers, the 65th Regiment apparently executed a number of prisoners on the same day on the shore of the Yangtze River. Although the number of Chinese POWs killed on that day ranged from 2,500 to 7,000, it most likely represented about one-third of the entire group. Since the victory parade was scheduled for the following day, one may conclude that the regiment conducted this execution in response to the request of the SEF, which was very much concerned about the safety of leaders, including the SEF chief who was an imperial family member.[72]

What happened to the remaining POWs on the following day, December 17, is even more unclear. According to Morozumi, Yamada and Morozumi secretly instructed one of the battalion commanders to release those prisoners by ferrying them across the Yangtze River at night. After spending all morning of December 17 tying the hands of the prisoners, the 65th's 1st Battalion led by Major Tayama Yoshio escorted them that night. The Japanese soldiers guarded both sides at fifty-meter intervals as the prisoners marched in four columns, and occasionally shot those straying from the columns apparently to drink water in a stream. When they started transporting the prisoners across the river, some boats carrying them were suddenly under fire, either by the Chinese or Japanese soldiers on the northern shore. Frightened by the gunshots, about 2,000 POWs, assembled on the river shore, panicked and began to flee, killing one Japanese officer and eight soldiers who were escorting them. Machine gunners attached to the battalion in case of emergency opened fire on the prisoners, resulting in a considerable number of fatalities.[73]

Whether Morozumi's story tells the truth remains undetermined. Several military leaders described events that apparently referred to this incident in their diaries or memoirs, either contradicting or corroborating Morozumi. Judging from his diary entry, SEF staff chief Iinuma obviously thought that Yamada and Morozumi killed all the POWs in accordance with their plan. Iinuma said,

During the Yamada Detachment's phased execution of more than ten thousand prisoners with the use of bayonets, they were taking a considerable number of prisoners at one time to a certain place one day. I was told of a rumor that the captives, becoming uneasy, caused troubles, and our troops opened fire at them with machine guns, resulting in the death of some of our officers and soldiers as well while allowing quite a few of the prisoners to escape. This is why SEF staff officer Sakakibara, who was instructed to make an arrangement to use these prisoners as a labor force in Shanghai, returned (yesterday) without any consequence.[74]

Colonel Uemura recorded a similar story: "Colonel N told me that the Yamada Detachment erred in its disposal of prisoners. It seems that a large group of them rebelled and our men had to shoot both the enemies and our own men with machine guns, causing the prisoners to run away. It is truly regrettable that they did such a poor job."[75]

Private diaries of soldiers simply said they "disposed of" or "executed" those captives, although the number again ranges from 7,000 to 20,000. Where it happened is also unclear. Most likely, the incident again took place on the river shore, but one Japanese soldier's diary says in its entry of December 17, "we have to dispose of prisoners also today. A total of 15,000, today *in the mountain*. There were casualties and some were killed within the battalion." [italics added.][76]

On the Chinese side, a Chinese official report released shortly after World War II charged that the Japanese interned Chinese civilians of both sexes and of all ages, as well as retreating soldiers, totaling 57,418 in the Mufu Mountain area, leaving them frozen or starving to death, and that they machine gunned or bayoneted to death the survivors of the group on December 16 at a location nearby.[77] This description of the event differs sharply from what the Japanese sources say in terms of both the nature and scale of the atrocity, but partially concurs with the Japanese sources regarding the dates and location of massacre.

Testimony provided by a Chinese eyewitness in the 1980s gives an account that is very close to the Japanese version of the story. According to T'ang Kung-pu, then a soldier attached to the Training Unit's 3rd Brigade headquarters, the Japanese herded and interned about 20,000 people, most of whom were POWs. T'ang said that the Japanese shot to death about 1,000 of them when quite a few prisoners were trying to escape and, finally, executed the remainder on December 18.[78] This testimony on the one hand underlines Morozumi's contention that some Chinese soldiers escaped—the story no private diaries on the Japanese side described—although Tang did not mention the fire that reportedly happened within the makeshift prisoner camp. On the other hand, Tang claimed that the main event took place on December 18, one day after December 17, which most Japanese eyewitnesses recorded as the date of the incident.

Some scholars conclude that the incident was not a pure accident, contrary to Morozumi's explanation, and, instead, was a deliberate massacre because it was highly unusual that Morozumi's unit chose to release prisoners at night. They also point to those diaries of ordinary soldiers to support this theory of planned massacre in a large scale.[79] Some points, however, do not readily support this conclusion. First, why did the Yamada Detachment's leadership divide the prisoners and execute only one-third of the group on December 16? If they had complied with the SEF's order, they should have killed the entire group on that day prior to the victory parade. A possible answer is that they sorted out those who apparently looked like soldiers and executed only that group. Morozumi said in his memoir that his unit screened out those who were apparently civilians—those who were not to be executed.[80] Although the regiment might not have screened out civilians who were to be released, it might have done the opposite—select those who apparently looked like soldiers and were subsequently executed on the night of December 16. Second, why did Morozumi entrust the execution of so many prisoners to only a single battalion, instead of the entire regiment? This question is also relevant to the actual number of prisoners killed. Was it possible for such a small number of Japanese soldiers to handle the large number of prisoners as recorded in diaries? One may thus question the veracity of these figures entered in private records. The wide range of figures suggests that the soldiers did not obtain those data from official sources. Instead, it is likely that they relied on rumors originating from several sources. It is also likely that they did not learn about the release and escape, which, according to Morozumi's account, happened on December 15 and 16 and reduced the number of prisoners in their custody. Third, although the soldiers noted the event on December 17 simply as an "execution," is it not possible that they were not aware of the true intent of the commanders and reached their own conclusion only by looking at the result? One could accept Morozumi's explanation about the event on that day since it was not necessary any more to kill POWs because the victory parade was over. Of course, in view of many of these unanswered questions, there is still much room for discussion of this incident.

The entire picture of the incident involving the 65th Regiment thus still remains obscure. So does the total number of victims. Postwar publications, which do not mention the execution on December 16, define the event on December 17 as an accident and estimate the number of victims at slightly more than 1,000.[81] If one depends solely on private diaries, the victims on December 16 amounted to 2,500 to 7,000 and those who were executed on the following day ranged from 7,000 to 20,000. Some of these figures, apparently derived from rumors and not based on official data, are likely inflated. The combined total again has a wide range—between 3,500 and 27,000. In view of the occurrence of some small-scale executions conducted individually in addition to the reported mass executions, 3,500 is too small while 27,000 is too large compared with the initial number of POWs, even if one takes into consideration some additions later. Among the diaries of 65th Regiment personnel, Sublieutenant Endo Takaaki entered a figure of 17,025 prisoners of war in his record. Although he did not mention any source for this information, this figure could be close to the maximum number of prisoners held by the unit and thus the maximum number killed by the Yamada Detachment. Since the fire on December 16 and the confusion during the incident on December 17 allowed some POWs to escape, the number of victims should be smaller than this figure. Such factors could allow one to narrow the range to between 4,000 and 15,000.

Within the 3rd Division, only the 68th Regiment participated in the storming of the city walls between the SEF's 9th Division and the Tenth Army's 114th Division. They captured the Wuting and Tungchi Gates on December 13. Since the battle report of the 2nd Battalion, which engaged in the battle most actively, is not available—presumably having been destroyed at the end of World War II—it is impossible to determine the extent of damage inflicted on the Chinese defenders by this unit. Judging from other battalions' reports, the heavy engagement on the walls resulted in a considerable number of casualties on the Chinese side. But the subsequent mopping-up operation conducted by the 68th Regiment did not look severe since both the 1st and 3rd battalions completed their operations within the walls by 7 and 6 P.M., respectively. The 1st and 3rd battalions suffered only one killed in action and three wounded and took thirty-three prisoners. The 68th Regiment as a whole was unlikely to have conducted any large-scale executions since its mopping-up operation ended very quickly. One may suspect, however, that its soldiers did kill some prisoners if one examines the 3rd battalion's order issued on December 16: "Heretofore, each unit is required to investigate prisoners as a formality and execute them sternly." The number, however, seems to have been marginal, judging from their brief description of the battle engagements and subsequent actions.[82]

The total number of prisoners, plainclothes soldiers, or men of conscription age the SEF executed is estimated to have been 15,000 to 34,000, if one combines the estimated 4,000 to 12,000 victims of the 16th Division, the officially recorded 7,000 by the 9th Division, and estimated 4,000 to 15,000 victims to the Yamada Detachment's actions. Added to this initial tally were the 1,500 to 4,500 Chinese killed in the second phase of the search for Chinese soldiers. Incorporation of these last figures boost the numerical range to 16,500 to 38,500.

Cases of Tenth Army: Sporadic Killings

Although not on such a large scale as in the SEF theater, quite a few units of the Tenth Army also engaged in similar execution-style killings.

The 6th Division reported 17,100 enemy dead left behind in its theater of operations as well as 5,500 POWs. Overall, this division fought severe battles outside the walls, but did not engage in extensive mopping-up operations within the city. Although a part of the division did enter the city and search the area, the divisional commander, Lieutenant General Tani Hisao, stated in a directive issued on the morning of December 14, "It seems that most of the area inside the walls has been cleaned up." Its activity contrasted starkly with the prolonged and extensive search of the Safety Zone by some SEF units.[83]

On the morning of December 13, the division's 45th Regiment encountered a huge group of enemy soldiers waving white flags outside the walls. Unlike some SEF leaders who either detained or killed prisoners, a Japanese company commander announced on the spot that they were free to go home. Since he could not find any vessels to transport them across the Yangtze River, he handed those prisoners to other units. Testimony of Private Second Class Liu Szu-hai of the Chinese 87th Division suggests that Liu was among these Chinese soldiers. According to Liu, they were told to make white flags so that they could ensure a safe passage to their hometown. Later, however, another Japanese unit took Liu and forty to fifty others without any interrogation or investigation and stabbed them. Liu somehow survived this massacre.[84] Sublieutenant Maeda recorded the fate of another group in his diary of December 15. According to

Maeda, when some new recruits were escorting about 100 prisoners, the following incident occurred:

Since the road was very narrow, one of our soldiers carrying a rifle with a fixed bayonet was pushed to a pool. He probably cursed at or slapped the prisoners out of anger, and the frightened prisoners rushed to the other side of the road, pushing in turn a Japanese soldier on the other side. Soldiers are themselves murderous weapons. Being already scared, they started stabbing or clubbing the prisoners while crying out cursing words. The prisoners began to flee as the panic spread. "Oh, No!" They started firing at the prisoners. "Do not let them go!" "Kill them if they are running away!" Such must have been what happened. . . . Third Battalion Commander Lieutenant Colonel Obara [Shigetaka] became furious to learn about this, but the incident had already happened. There was no excuse for the violence inflicted upon the unarmed soldiers who had surrendered peacefully. Such an incident will surely tarnish the image of His Majesty's army. To cover up that carnage, those new recruits were ordered to bury the victims and spent all the night to finish the job by the morning.[85]

The impression is that the 6th Division conducted smaller-scale executions undertaken independently by its subordinate units, in contrast with the large-scale executions carried out by some SEF units. Although one cannot find a satisfactory explanation for this difference, a possible reason was that the Tenth Army did not have an imperial family member as its commander and was less concerned about POWs or plainclothes soldiers. Also, in contrast with the negative image accompanying some SEF commanders such as Nakajima and one of his brigade commanders Sasaki, one can see an amicable image in the personality of some Tenth Army leaders. This is especially true of Tani commanding the 6th Division and one of his brigade commanders, Major General Ushijima Mitsuru.[86] According to some soldiers' recollections, four straggling Chinese soldiers still carrying arms somehow surrendered to Ushijima, who was completely unarmed, on December 9, 1937, when Ushijima accidentally came across with them during his morning walk. The brigade headquarters used these prisoners as servants and set them free one year later.[87]

Sublieutenant Oda Mamoru of the same division's 23rd Regiment, however, recorded a rumor that a Japanese unit, which he did not identify, captured about 1,000 prisoners who had been hiding in basements of buildings and executed them outside the Hanchung Gate.[88] Since the gate is between the operation areas of the 9th Division's 7th Regiment and the 6th Division's 23rd Regiment, one cannot identify the unit responsible for this reported mass execution by reading the Japanese documents alone. Judging from the previously quoted testimony given by Wu Chang-te, a Chinese policeman at the time, however, it seems that this was an execution conducted by the 7th Regiment.

The 114th Division combed the city's southern section sandwiched between the operation areas of the SEF's 9th and the Tenth Army's 6th Divisions. Apparently, there was little Chinese resistance in this section, since the divisional report stated that the two brigades in charge of mopping-up operations completed their missions more or less by the evening of December 13. The divisional command entered the city on the following day. This division counted about 5,000 enemies killed in its theater of operations from Shanghai through Nanking.[89] Among the units under the 114th Division, the 66th Infantry Regiment recorded a horrible execution. The regiment's 1st Battalion said that it alone had killed 700 enemies and captured 1,657 prisoners in a battle on December 12. The battalion command instructed the 4th Company to guard the prisoners. The company interned them in a building until the following day. Then, according to the battalion's report, the regiment issued this order at 2 P.M. on that day: "Execute all the prisoners in accordance with the brigade's order. Regarding the method for execution, what about making groups of dozens each, tying them up, and shooting them one by one?"[90]

The battalion carried out the order. Its report said,

I met with company commanders at 3:30 P.M. and discussed how to execute prisoners. As a result, we agreed to assign the equal number of prisoners to each of 1st, 3rd, and 4th Companies. We decided to have each company take about fifty of them at one time from the prison and stab them to death. . . . As a precaution, we posted guards around the prison so that the prisoners would never realize what was awaiting them. Each unit started the execution upon the completion of preparation at 5 P.M. and finished killing them by around 7:30 P.M. I reported the result to the regiment. The 1st Company changed their original plan and tried to lock them up in one place to burn them, but failed. Some prisoners who were prepared for death presented their head toward the sword without showing any fear or stood quietly facing a bayonet. Others, however, cried out and begged for life. Such cries became even louder especially when I [battalion commander] was inspecting these executions.[91]

Suppose all the other battalions had killed about 1,500 in the same manner, the 66th would have executed 4,500, and the entire 114th Division 18,000. But this looks like an exorbitant figure in view of the short time period those units spent clearing the assigned area within the city walls. Moreover, although the 114th Division does not give the number of prisoners it took in its report, it is unreasonable to assume that the division operating in the section next to the 6th Division captured more than three times as many prisoners as the 6th Division did. Underlining this assumption is the performance of the same division's 150th Regiment. The 150th Regiment broke the Chinese defense at Yuhuatai after a fierce shootout on December 13 and suffered fifty-five killed and 148 wounded while counting 850 enemy dead soldiers. The regimental report does not say anything about Chinese prisoners taken by the regiment, leaving the section of POWs blank. Although one may assume that the regimental reporter neglected to enter the data or deliberately made no record, the impression remains that the 150th did not take many prisoners since it finished cleaning the assigned city area of the remaining enemy by 5 P.M. that same day.[92]

The Kunisaki Detachment, whose main component was the 41st Infantry Regiment, occupied the city of Pukou on the shore of the Yangtze River opposite Nanking on December 13. It counted about 1,430 dead Chinese soldiers left in the area and took 120 prisoners. The detachment captured only a small number of prisoners probably because the Chinese soldiers, once on the northern shore, could easily find escape routes. The 12th Company of the regiment, however, found 2,350 soldiers on the sands called Chianghsingchou in the Yangtze on the following day. The company forced them to surrender after a minor skirmish that killed one Japanese soldier. Major General Kunisaki instructed the company to disarm and let the prisoners live by themselves on the mid-river island, pending later orders. No official document mentions the fate of those prisoners, but one may assume that the Kunisaki Detachment let them go free since the Chinese map, which indicates the locations of massacres, however small the scale of massacre was presumed to be, does not mark the spot where the Japanese held those prisoners.[93]

Again, the numerical data are very sketchy and make it hard to compute the number of prisoners executed by the Tenth Army. The only known execution on the records was that of the 66th Regiment, a total of 1,657. By taking into consideration other small-scale executions, 2,000 would be the minimum figure. One could obtain the uppermost limit if one assumes that all the prisoners captured by the Tenth Army were killed, although it was highly unlikely in view of the case of mass release by the 45th Regiment. Suppose the 114th Division captured the same number of Chinese prisoners as the 6th, the total would be 11,000. Combined with about 2,500 prisoners taken by the Kunisaki Detachment, the sum total would reach 13,500. Thus, the numerical range is again wide, from 2,000 to 13,500.

TOTAL NUMBER OF VICTIMS

Adding the estimated 16,500 to 38,500 killed by the SEF to the estimated range for the Tenth Army, one obtains figures ranging from 18,500 to 52,000 killed, which could represent the number of POWs, plainclothes soldiers, and civilians misidentified as former soldiers executed by the entire CCAA (Chart 3.2). This numerical range constituted a part of the estimated total of military-related casualties of 44,000 to 104,000, which was computed previously. Narrowing these ranges is not easy. One might be inclined to take the higher estimate adopted by some Chinese sources. A Chinese Central News Agency dispatch from Hong Kong on December 23, 1937, said that during the four-day period after the fall of Nanking those slaughtered by the Japanese amounted to about 50,000. Central News also reported in February that the Japanese had massacred 60,000 to 70,000 military personnel.[94]

One could, however, opt for the lower- or middle-range estimate for several reasons. First, the ranges of figures are the results of computations based in part on Japanese battle reports and rumors at the time, which tended to exaggerate

Chart 3.2
Estimated Number of Executed Chinese POWs

Unit	Minimum no. of POWs Japanese army units executed (figures found in records, and estimates based on them)	Maximum no. of POWs Japanese army units executed (as obtained from extrapolation and other calculation)
20th Reg.(16D)	328	3,000
33rd Reg.(16D)	3,096	3,096
38th Reg.(16D)	no data	3,000
9th Reg.(16D)	no data	3,000
Total for 16th Div.	4,000	12,000
Maj. Gen. Sasaki's operation in Jan. 1938	1,500	4,500
7th Reg.(9D)	6,670	7,000
Total for 9th Div.	7,000	7,000
65th Reg.(Yamada Unit)	4,000	15,000
Total for the SEF	16,500	38,500
66th Reg. (114D)	1,657	1,657
Total for 114th Div.	no data	5,500
6th Div.	no data	5,500
Kunisaki Detachment	no data	2,500
Total for the 10th Army	2,000	13,500
Grand Total	18,500	52,000

the battle results. Second, the 50,000 to 70,000 deaths reported by the Chinese media may well have represented the total estimated Chinese losses in the Nanking campaign instead of the number of those who had been executed. Third and most important, burial records compiled at the time corroborate the lower estimate. The Nanking office of Hung-wan-tzu-hui or the Chinese Red Swastika Society buried 43,071 bodies in and around Nanking from December 1937 through October 1938 (see Appendix B).[95] These figures, however, can only be a basis of calculation; they cannot be the number of victims itself for various reasons. Since many scholars have used the Red Swastika data in the Rape of Nanking controversy, some information about this material is worth noting here.

Although the Red Swastika data were made public for the first time after the war, one could verify their authenticity from some reports compiled by the Japanese military's special service in Nanking in 1938. One such report in February mentioned the Red Swastika Society as being in charge of burial. This

Japanese report, however, contained numerical data seriously contradicting the Red Swastika statistics. Although the Red Swastika's table showed that it disposed of more than 30,000 corpses by the end of February, the Japanese report said that the same organization buried about 5,000 by the end of the same month. Then, the Japanese military again reported in March that by March 15 the Red Swastika had collected 1,793 bodies within the walls while it also had disposed of 29,998 corpses outside the walls. Although the former figure is exactly the same as appeared in the Red Swastika table, the latter is 5,101 fewer than the table shows.[96] Such discrepancies possibly occurred because the Red Swastika Society initially counted only the result of its own burial work, but later included the tallies from other organizations. Although this reasoning is pure speculation, one may note the following points in support of this theory. First, since the Japanese reports mentioned only the Red Swastika Society in its section engaged in the burial, it probably played a dominant or supervisory role in this project. Second, the occasional appearance of an unnaturally large figure in the Red Swastika table might have resulted from the process of inserting the data from other sources later.[97] Third, one can infer the participation by multiple organizations in the burial project from this passage contained in Nanking University professor M. S. Bate's letter in March 1938: "Putting together information from organizations [not "an organization"] interested in burying the dead and other observations, it is estimated that 10,000 persons were killed inside the walls of Nanking and about 30,000 outside the walls. . . . These people estimate that of this total about 30 per cent were civilians." [Underline added.][98]

Since the cumulative total of buried bodies recorded in the Red Swastika data surpassed 38,000 by mid-March, the total of 40,000 mentioned in this letter most likely refers to the same source. Fourth, a recently uncovered document compiled by the Nanking branch of the Chinese Red Cross—the Chinese chapter of the World Red Cross—contains its own burial statistics, which might constitute a part of the Red Swastika data. According to the Red Cross document, it buried 17,907 bodies up to the end of February—a figure that might explain a part of the previously discussed gap between the end-of-February tally of the Red Swastika statistics and that of the Japanese military's report.[99] One may assume that by early April, the Red Swastika had somehow begun to compile the data of all burial activities conducted by several organizations.

It is thus doubtful that the Red Swastika statistics contain only its own data. Yet its numerical information is believed to be credible, judging from other evidence. A letter sent by the Red Swastika to the Nanking Self-Government Committee on April 4, 1938, said that the organization had buried "thirty thousand plus several thousand" and the burial work was still in progress. If one subtracts a total of 4,345, which the organization dealt with after the letter's date according to the table, from the sum total of 43,071, one can obtain the figure of 38,726—a number that fits the description of "thirty thousand plus several thousand." In another letter in October the same year, the Red Swastika mentioned what looked like the final tally of buried corpses, which amounted to more than 40,000.[100]

Based on these analyses, one may conclude that the Red Swastika Society's document describes the bulk of the burial activities in Nanking. It also reveals that the vast majority of victims were men, and that women and children accounted for only 129 of over 40,000 corpses. The predominance of men suggests that the majority of the victims in Nanking died in military-related situations, that is, either in combat or by execution.[101]

Yet another organization, Ch'ung-shan-t'ang, reportedly participated in the burial activities and produced a similar record (see Appendix C). There was no doubt that Ch'ung-shan-t'ang was involved in the burial judging from its letter addressed to a government official asking for a relief fund for its activities, including the organizing of burial parties. Also a report filed by another organization with the Nanking Municipal Government in early 1939 clearly mentions Ch'ung-shan-t'ang as a group responsible for the burial along with the Red Swastika. Yet some historians have disputed the authenticity of this document by pointing to exorbitantly large numbers of corpses reportedly buried in April–May 1938.[102] I share their opinion and exclude its numerical data from the basis of calculation for the following reasons.

First, according to research conducted by a Japanese journalist in the 1980s, materials produced by the Nanking municipal government under the Japanese occupation revealed that the Ch'ung-shan-t'ang was a small charity organization whose activities had almost ceased at the time of the Sino-Japanese War. The journalist, Ara Ken'ichi, concluded that such a small organization was not capable of undertaking the extensive burial activities indicated by its statistics. Although Ara is known for his active reporting leading to a downplaying of the Rape of Nanking, his analysis was quite persuasive. Besides the official document of the Nanking municipal government, Ara referred to an account by two Japanese nationals who made a trip to Nanking in April 1938. According to Ara, these two people, who wrote a detailed journal of their trip, did not mention any conspicuous burial activities in the Nanking area, even though one day they apparently passed through one of the locations where Ch'ung-shan-t'ang was supposedly burying a large number of corpses at that time.[103]

Second, a piece of foreign evidence contradicts the reported activities of this organization. A U.S. military attaché report from China in June 1938 quoted "a reliable foreign investigator" as having computed the number of Chinese civilians killed in Nanking at 41,000 at the end of his investigation in May. This investigator apparently looked at the Red Swastika data, which likely listed military casualties as well, since the number of corpses buried by that organization by the end of May came very close to that figure. Turning on the Ch'ung-shan-t'ang data, one can find that that organization supposedly buried over 100,000 bodies in April 1938—well before the military attaché's report was compiled. If the Ch'ung-shan-t'ang had really conducted burial activities of that gigantic scale, it would have been unlikely that the same careful investigator would have overlooked this extensive project, which, according to its document, in a matter of less than a month had dealt with over twice as many corpses as the Red Swastika had done over six months.[104] For these reasons, the Ch'ung-shan-t'ang data should be dismissed as an unreliable source, which was most likely fabricated.

Therefore, about 43,000 bodies buried by the Red Swastika Society is the starting figure. Here, one must take into consideration several factors in analyzing this figure. First, one cannot assume that these 43,000 were the only people who died of military-related causes. Judging from the various sources, the 7th Regiment, which is believed to have been responsible for the fate of Chinese soldiers and others rounded up in the Safety Zone, and the 65th Regiment, which either intentionally or accidentally killed prisoners it had caught on the Mufu Mountain, threw the bodies into the Yangtze River instead of burying them. Moreover, there must have been quite a few bodies disposed of by the Japanese before the Red Swastika started its activities. Second, one cannot conclude that all those 43,000 lost their lives either in combat or by execution in Nanking. Quite a few wounded Chinese soldiers were left behind in the city and many of them died because of inadequate medical attention. Also, some Chinese soldiers were killed by their fellow countrymen as happened in the Hsiak'uan area. Third, it is highly likely that these dead bodies included the civilians misidentified as plainclothes soldiers and the victims of individually committed crimes—atrocities to be discussed in the next chapter.

If one offsets the number of those buried in the water of the Yangtze—7,000 by the 7th Regiment and 4,000 to 15,000 by the 65th—by the estimated 1,000 who were killed by their own men and the estimated 9,000 who died of wounds, one may roughly estimate that the actual fatalities in Nanking totalled about 1,000 to 11,000 more than the 43,000 indicated by the Red Swastika, that is, 44,000 to 54,000.

Only a few sources give information on the ratio of executed persons to the total military-related casualties. The Japanese 33rd regiment said it counted 6,830 bodies, including 3,096 prisoners, or roughly 45 percent of the total figure. Durdin estimated the total Chinese dead at 33,000, of whom the executed soldiers accounted for 20,000, or about 61 percent.[105] If this percentage ratio range of 45 to 61 percent is applied to the numerical range of 44,000 to 54,000, one can obtain figures between 19,800 and 32,940. Rounding those figures and taking into account the rough calculation method and basis, one may expand this estimated range to between 20,000 and 35,000. Although this is still a wide numerical range, one may accept it as the number of victims who died in the execution-style killing in a part of events known as the Rape of Nanking since any further narrowing of the range without a firm basis for calculation would be quite arbitrary.

The next question is how many civilians were misidentified as former soldiers and executed and how many other civilians were killed for other reasons. Regarding the number of civilian dead, Lewis S. C. Smythe, professor of Ginling

College at the time, conducted a survey and compiled a report entitled *War Damage in Nanking Area: December 1937–March 1938* (see Appendix D). It mentions an estimate of "12,000 civilians killed by violence," probably a sum total of those mistaken as plainclothes soldiers and those who became victims of Japanese soldiers' misconduct. Smythe estimated the number of male civilians taken away from their homes and recorded as missing—presumably because they were misidentified as plainclothes soldiers—at 4,200. This figure could serve as the lower limit of the number of civilians mistakenly executed by the Japanese. In addition, Smythe's analysis concluded that 2,400 male civilians lost their lives within the city walls due to the violence committed by soldiers. Of these 2,400, 47 percent or about 1,100 were within the age range of fifteen and forty-four years old and thus were likely to become victims during the Japanese troops' soldier search. If one adds this figure to the 4,200 who were taken away, one could obtain 5,300—the upper range of victims in this category within city walls. Smythe's research also counted 9,160 dead—7,170 males and 1,990 females—owing to violent causes in the suburban area of Kiangning Hsien, in which Nanking was located. If one limits one's discussion and analysis strictly to the event known as the Rape of Nanking, the inclusion of these data might be inappropriate. Nevertheless, I use these figures as well to make this numerical analysis as flexible as possible. Besides this possible problem concerning the geographical framework, another problem in the use of this rural survey is that Smythe, for unknown reasons, did not calculate the number or percentage of those killed in military operations and established only the category of deaths owing to "soldiers' violence" in addition to "deaths by sickness." Here, however, one should accept Smythe's observation that "practically all of the violence against civilians . . . was done by the Japanese forces" and regard those victims of conscription ages as victims of POW and plainclothes soldier execution. According to one of Smythe's tables, those fifteen to forty-four years old constituted 59 percent of the male victims in the rural area. If one applies this ratio to the 7,170 male victims in the Kiangning Hsien, one obtains a figure of 4,230, a number probably not included in the statistics of burial, which took place in Nanking and its immediate vicinity. Assuming that this figure represents the number of fatalities as a result of unlawful military activities, one may combine it with 5,300 of the city area to obtain the figure of 9,530—the maximum estimate of civilians killed in military executions, both in Nanking and its adjacent area. One could round the range of between 4,200 and 9,530 to between 4,000 and 10,000.[106]

Besides these, there were victims of violence other than execution. Of the 2,400 civilian male victims who died due to soldiers' violence in the city area, those less than fourteen or more than forty-four years of age—or the remainder of 2,400 minus 1,100 presumed to have been executed—account for 53 percent or about 1,300 persons. Adding them to the 650 female victims of soldiers' violence, one may conclude that about 2,000 people lost their lives through atrocities committed by individual Japanese soldiers in the city area. The same method of calculation projects the number of male deaths in this category at about 3,000 in the suburb of Kiangning Hsien plus 1,990 female fatalities, bringing the total to about 5,000. Thus, it is possible to conclude that a total of 7,000 deaths resulted from soldiers' misconduct. Of these, 5,000 fatalities in the suburb were unlikely to have appeared in the earlier statistics, which covered only burials in the city of Nanking and its immediate vicinity.[107]

The civilian deaths in Nanking and its suburbs thus totaled 4,000 to 10,000 due to unlawful military activities, namely executions, and 2,000 to 7,000 from other forms of violence. The combined total ranges from 6,000 to 17,000, which one can round to 5,000 to 20,000. Of this, from zero to about 4,000 in the execution category and zero to 5,000 due to other atrocities are presumed to be outside the burial statistics, its total being zero to 9,000. Together with the 44,000 to 54,000 based on the burial data, the sum total of fatalities in Nanking and its suburbs for all causes amounted to 44,000 to 63,000, which one can approximate into 45,000 to 65,000. Deaths as a result of atrocities amounted to 20,000 to 44,000—a sum total of estimated 20,000 to 35,000 deaths based on burial data and zero to 9,000 presumed to be outside such statistics. By taking into account the rough computation methods, one can widen the range into 15,000 to 50,000 victims.

To sum up, the total human losses in Nanking and its vicinity in 1937–38 amounted to anywhere between 45,000 to 65,000, of which 15,000 to 50,000 were killed in unlawful ways—as a result of execution by the Japanese troops and other atrocities—including about 5,000 to as many as 20,000 civilians.

Provided these numerical ranges more or less correctly describe the atrocities in Nanking in terms of human losses, their meaning will be different depending on one's perspective. First, from the humanitarian standpoint, they still illustrate the magnitude of atrocities that were unjustifiable both legally and morally. Second, for activists and journalists who persist on the Nazi-type genocidal nature of the Rape of Nanking by presenting their own numerical analysis, the data should be compelling enough to reconsider their opinion. Third, professional historians who are interested in this incident purely academically will find the data a useful analytical tool for their further research.

NOTES

1. *NYT*, 15 December 1937, p. 16. Komori Yoshihisa, "Nankin Jiken o Sekai ni Shiraseta Otoko" [A Man Who Reported the Nanking Atrocities to the World], *Bungeishunju*, October 1989, p. 182.

2. *CDN*, 15 December 1937, p. 1. *NYT*, 18 December 1937, p. 1; 9 January 1938, p. 38.

3. *NYT*, 19 December 1937, p. 8.

4. *CDN*, 15 December 1937, p. 1.

5. *NYT*, 18 December 1937, p. 10.

6. *CDN*, 15 December 1937, p. 1. *NYT*, 18 December 1937, p. 10.

7. H. J. Timperly, ed., *Japanese Terror in China* (New York: Modern Age Books, 1938), p. 26, quoting an unidentified eyewitness. One can identify this witness as George A. Fitch, then secretary of the Nanking chapter of the Young Men's Christian Association

(YMCA), by comparing this section to his diary entry on December 12, 1937. Fitch's diary enclosed with Frank W. Price to Maxwell M. Hamilton, Chief, Division of Far Eastern Affairs, Department of State, 17 February 1938, 793.94/12548, p. 7, M976-51.

8. Li, *Memoirs*, p. 328. One could read almost the same story of Hsiak'uan in no. 78 of George Maull, "The Horrors of War: 240 True Stories of Modern Warfare," 1938, a picture-card series accompanied with chewing gum, issued by Gum Inc., Philadelphia, original in the National Museum of American History, Washington, D. C. Also, see A Long, *Nanking Tung-k'u* [Nanking Wails], trans. Sekine Ken into Japanese (Tokyo: Sat-suki Shobo, 1994), p. 176.

9. Fujiwara Shin'ya, ed., *Minna ga Shitteiru: Hyakuman Shina Hakengun ni yoru Chugoku Fujoshi no Junan* [Everybody Knows: Ordeals Suffered by Chinese Women and Children by One-Million Expedition Force to China] (Tokyo: Shun'yodo, 1957), pp. 31–32; quoted in Honda Katsuichi, *Nankin e no Michi* [Road to Nanking] (Tokyo: Asahi Shinbunsha [Asahi Newspaper], 1989, henceforth *NEM*), p. 232.

10. *NEM*, p. 232, Honda, quoting the passage, also attributes their death to a Japanese gas attack. It was, however, highly unlikely that the Japanese troops used poison gas when they were trying to close in upon the opponent in a rapid movement in close engagements. Actually, the Japanese military was so reluctant to use the gas weapon that newly appointed SEF chief Prince Asaka asked his staffs on December 7 why the SEF had not used any gas weapons so far. Uemura Diary, 7 December 1937, in *NSS*1, p. 267. That the Japanese did not use any deadly poison gas at this point is more apparent if one examines an official report in early 1938 that said, "Our [Japanese] Army had achieved its military objectives without using any chemical weapons." Third Field Chem-ical Weapon Experimenting Unit, Ho-gun 3-ya-ka-ho dai-14-go: "Kagaku-sen ni Kansuru Chosa Hokoku" [Area Army's Field Chemical Unit's Report no. 14: "Investigation on Report on Chemical Warfare"], 25 February 1938, RMD, 1938, no. 15. Although Private Miyabe of the 19th Regiment under the SEF's 9th Division admitted to the use of gas by the Japanese military in China by referring to his own experience of wearing a gas mask, he saw only one instance of gas weapons being used in the following year and that weapon was a tear gas shell. Miyabe, *Fuu-un Nankinjo* [Battle of Nanking Walls], p. 218.

11. Testimony of T'ang Kung-pu in *NEM*, p. 284. Yasuyama Hiromichi, "Shanhaisen Jugun Nisshi" [Diary of the Shanghai Battle], vol. 9, 16 December 1937, in *NSS*1, p. 528.

12. Wang Yao-wu, "Ti-74-chun Ts'an-chia Nanking Pao-wei-chan Ching-kuo" [Story of the 74th Army in the Defense of Nanking], in *NP*, p. 146. Testimony of Takahashi Yoshihiko quoted in "SNS" (6), *Kaiko*, September 1984, p. 10.

13. "SNS" (2), *Kaiko*, May 1984, p. 14. Lilie Abegg, "Wie aus Nanking Fluechteten" [How We Fled from Nanking], *Frankfurter Zeitung und Handelsblatt*, 19 December 1937, pp. 1–2. Its Japanese version is idem, "Nankin Dasshutsu-ki: Shuto Nankin Saigo no Hi" [Escape from Nanking: Last Day of Capital City Nanking], trans. Suga Hiroo from ibid., *Bungeishunju*, February 1938, pp. 252–53. Testimony of Fujita Kiyoshi, then sergeant of the Independent Second Light Armored Vehicle Company, "SNS" (2), *Kaiko*, May 1984, p. 14.

14. *NS*, p. 352.

15. Tenth Army Command, "Nankin Koryaku ni Kansuru Iken" [Proposal for the Capturing of Nanking], 30 November 1937, in DSKS, vol. 2.

16. Matsui Diary, 14–15 December 1937, in *NSS*1, p. 17. Uemura Diary, 13 Decem-

ber 1937, in ibid., pp. 270–71. Yamamoto Isamu, *Nankin, Joshu, Bukan-sanchin: Omoide no Shingun* [Nanking, Hsuchou, Wuhan-san-chen: March in My Memory] (Gifu: San-9 Sen'yukai Jimusho, [Ninth Artillery Regiment Veteran's Association] 1973), p. 100. Nakajima Kesago, Diary of Nakajima Kesago 12 December 1937, in *NSS*1, p. 322. Kisaki Hisashi, Diary of Kisaki Hisashi, 13 December 1937, ibid., p. 421. Iinuma Diary, 13–14 December 1937, in ibid., p. 214.

17. 6th Division, "Senji Junpo" [Wartime Report], nos. 13–14, 1–20 December 1937, in *NSS*1, p. 691. Fukumoto Tsuzumi, Diary of Fukumoto Tsuzumi, 13 December 1937, in *NSS*2, pp. 385–86. About a week later, Fukumoto and several others counted 2,377 corpses still remaining on the field. Testimony of Naritomo Fujio quoted in "SNS" (6), *Kaiko*, September 1984, p. 8. Maeda Yoshihiko, Diary of Maeda Yoshihiko, 13 December 1937, in *NSS*1, p. 462.

18. Nakajima Diary, 13 December 1937, in *NSS*1, p. 322.

19. Sasaki Diary, 13 December 1937, in *NSS*1, pp. 376–77.

20. Iinuma Diary, 13 December 1937, in *NSS*1, p. 214.

21. 38th Infantry Regiment, "Hohei Dai-38-Rentai Sento Shoho" [Battle Report of the 38th Infantry Regiment] no. 11: 12–13 December 1937, MHD. 33rd Infantry Regiment, "Nankin-fukin no Sento Shoho" [Report of Battles in the Nanking Area] 10–14 December 1937, MHD. Wang Yao-wu, "Ti-74-chun Ts'an-chia Nanking Pao-wei-chan Ching-kuo" [Story of the 74th Army in the Defense of Nanking], in *NP*, p. 146. Ordinary soldiers tended to inflate battle results and sometimes enter the exaggerated body counts even in their memoirs. Noguchi Toshio, *Nara Rentai Senki* [Battle Stories of Nara (38th) Regiment] (Nara: Yamato Times, 1963), p. 208, says the regiment "swept away nearly 40,000 enemies" and "their bodies covered two to three miles downstream."

22. Testimony of then Lieutenant Hashimoto Mochiyuki of the Imperial Japanese Navy quoted in "SNS" (10), *Kaiko*, January 1985, p. 30. Iinuma Diary, 17 December 1937, in *NSS*1, p. 217. Chou Chen-ch'ien, "Chiao-tao Chung-tui tsai Nanking Pao-wei-chan Chung" [Training Unit in the Defense of Nanking], in *NP*, p. 169. Hashimoto mentioned here later became the captain of Japanese submarine I-58, which sank the U.S.S. *Indianapolis* on her way back from Tinian after it had delivered a part of an atomic bomb to that island.

23. Headquarters, United States Army Troops in China, Office of the Intelligence Officer, "Intelligence Summary 15–31 December 1937," no. 26, p. 5, M1513-39. Ho Ying-ch'in, *Chung-kuo Hsian-tai-shih Tzu-liao Ts'ung-shu: Tui-jih K'ang-chan* [China's Modern Historical Materials Series: War against Japan] (Taipei: Wenhsing Shutien, 1948), quoted in Tanaka Masaaki, *Nankin-jiken no Sokatsu* [Nanking Incident Summed Up] (Tokyo: Kenkosha, 1987), p. 205. Iinuma Diary, 17 December 1937, in *NSS*1, p. 217. Sasaki Diary, 5 January 1938, in ibid., p. 382. 65th Infantry Regiment, "Hohei Dai-65-Rentai Sento Shoho" [Battle Report of the 65th Infantry Regiment], quoted in a memoir by Sugano Yoshio, private first class of the 65th Regiment's Artillery Company, in *NDKK*, p. 305. Among few Western scholars dealing with this subject, Michael R. Gibson used the figure of 70,000 in his dissertation, probably by relying on Chinese sources. Michael Richard Gibson, "Chiang Kai-shek's Central Army, 1924–1938" (Ph.D. Diss.: George Washington University, 1985), p. 388.

24. A Japanese general, who commanded an army in China, said in his diary, "We tripled the body counts in accordance with our custom." A part of the diary of Anami Korechika quoted in Katogawa Kotaro, "Shogen ni yoru Nankin Senshi: Sono Sokatsu-

teki Kosatsu" [Nanking Campaign Chronology Based on Eyewitness Accounts: Concluding Remark], *Kaiko*, March 1985, p. 13.

25. *NYT*, 9 January 1938, p. 38. *NS*, p. 306, accumulates the data of each unit and computes the killed in action at 1,558 and the wounded at 4,619, bringing the overall casualties to 6,177. Terada Masao, then chief planning staff of the Tenth Army, gave the figures of 1,953 killed and 4,994 wounded, totalling 6,947 casualties. Terada Masao, "Dai-10-Gun Sakusen Shido ni Kansuru Kosatsu" [Commentary on Tenth Army's Operation Planning], p. 39. *NS*'s tally is incomplete since it leaves the losses of Yamada Detachment as "unknown" due to the unavailability of data. The margin between *NS*'s figure and Terada's information might represent the killed and wounded of the Yamada Detachment.

26. Sun Chai-wei, "Nanking Pao-wei-chan Shuang-fang Ping-li Te Yen-chiu" [Estimated Force Strength of Two Sides in the Nanking Battle], p. 124. Hsu Yuan-chuan to Chiang Kai-shek, 23 December 1937, in *KCCC*, p. 418. Sung Hsi-lien, "Lu-chun Ti-78-chun Nanking Chih Yi Chan-tou Hsiang-pao" [Chinese 78th Army's Report on Battle of Nanking], January 1938, in *KCCC*, pp. 419–20, 425. Wang Yao-wu, "Ti-74-chun Ts'an-chia Nanking Pao-wei-chan Ching-kuo" [Story of the 74th Army in the Defense of Nanking], in *NP*, pp. 141, 147. According to the 160th Division's report, "The number of the whole division's combat-capable soldiers was 3,000 below its full strength" as of November 18. Yue Chen-chung, "Lu-chun Ti-160-Shih Hsi-ch'eng Nanking Liang-yi Chan-tou Hsiang-pao" [160th Division's Report on the Battles in Hsich'eng and Nanking], April 1938, in *KCCC*, p. 436. Yue Chao, "Lu-chun Ti-66-chun Nanking T'u-wei Chan-tou Hsiang-pao" [66th Army's Battle Report on Its Escape from Nanking], 4 July 1938, in *KCCC*, p. 436. Kuo-fang-pu Shih-cheng Chu [History Section, Defense Department, Republic of China], ed., *K'ang-chan Chien-shih* [Short History of Resistance War] (Taipei: Defense Department's History Section, 1952), p. 52. Kuo-min Cheng-fu Chun-shih Wei-yuan-hui Chan-shih Pien-tsuan Wei-yuan-hui [Military History Compilation Committee, Nationalist Government's Military Affairs Committee], ed., *Sung-hu K'ang-chan* [Resistance War in Sunghu] (n.p., 1938), in Chung-yung Tang-an Kuan [Central Archives], Chung-kuo Ti-2 Li-shih Tang-an Kuan [The Second Historical Archives of China], Chilin-sheng She-hui Ke-hsueh-yuen [Chilin Province Social Science Academy], ed. *Jih-pen Ti-kuo Chui Ch'in-hua Tang-an Hsuan-pien*, vol. 12, *Nanking Ta-t'u-sha* [Selected Archival Documents Relating to Japan's Imperialistic Aggression of China, vol. 12, The Rape of Nanking]. (Peking: Chung-hua Shu-chu [China Publishing], 1995, henceforth *HP*), p. 59. A Chinese newspaper reported about 2,370 Chinese soldiers who had broken the Japanese army's closing ring in the Nanking area and entered the Nationalist-controlled area late in January in early 1938. *Hsin-hua Jih-pao* [New China Daily], 25 January 1938, p. 2.

27. Colonel Uemura rather sentimentally said in his diary, "It seems there are many prisoners of war. There are no officers among them. How pitiful those soldiers are!" Uemura Diary, 15 December 1937, in *NSS*1, p. 271. Also, the 7th Regiment under the command of the SEF's 9th Division stated in its official report, "The investigation of prisoners of war captured until today [December 15] reveals that almost all of them are soldiers or non-commissioned officers and it seems there are no officers among them." 7th Infantry Regiment, Ho-7 Sakumei Kou [7th Infantry Regiment's Operation Order] no. 111, 8:30 P.M., 15 December 1937, in *NSS*1, p. 622.

28. 38th Infantry Regiment, "Hohei Dai-38-Rentai Sento Shoho" [Battle Report of the 38th Infantry Regiment], MHD.

29. Sasaki Diary, 14 December 1937, in *NSS*1, p. 379.

30. Iinuma Diary, 15 December 1937, in *NSS*1, p. 216. Nakajima Diary, 12, 14 December 1937, in ibid., pp. 322, 327. 3rd Battalion of the 68th Infantry Regiment, "Sento Shoho" [Battle Report] 27 November–13 December 1937, in ibid., p. 644. Makihara Diary, 14 December 1937, in *KS*, p. 149.

31. As usual, estimates vary regarding the number of prisoners the Japanese captured. General Matsui said, "The number of prisoners has exceeded ten thousand" in his diary on December 16. Matsui Diary, 16 December 1937, in *NSS*1, p. 18. Colonel Uemura of the SEF headquarters noted the figure of 40,000 as an unconfirmed report. Uemura Diary, 16 December 1937, in ibid., p. 272. Private Upper Class Azuma noted a rumor that "there are about twenty thousand prisoners." Azuma Memoir, in *KS*, p. 303. The biggest figure, which is far from realistic, is 100,000 in the diary of Odera Takashi, private upper class of the 65th Regiment's 7th Company. Odera Takashi, Diary of Odera Takashi, 17 December 1937, in *NDKK*, p. 196.

32. Sasaki Diary, 13 December 1937, in *NSS*1, p. 378.

33. Testimony of Mori Hideo in "SNS" (8), *Kaiko*, November 1984, p. 5.

34. *NYT*, 18 December 1937, p. 10. *CDN*, 17 December 1937, p. 1. Testimony of Chao Shih-fa in *NEM*, p. 224. Inoie Mataichi, Diary of Inoie Mataichi, 15 December 1937, in *NSS*1, p. 475. Mizutani Diary, 15 December 1937, in ibid., p. 502. Chiang Kung-yi, "Hsian-ching San-yueh-chi" [Three Months in Fallen Capital], in *SL*, p. 72. 7th Infantry Regiment, "Hohei Dai-7-Rentai Sento Shoho" [Battle Report], 7–24 December 1937, in *NSS*1, p. 630. Yasuyama, Shanhai-sen Jugun Nisshi [Diary of the Shanghai Battle], 14 December 1937, in ibid., p. 526. Hirota to Saito, 26 December 1937, Red Machine, no. 1171. One recent estimate says, "ninety thousand Chinese troops were trapped" in the city. Iris Chang, "Exposing the Rape of Nanking," *Newsweek*, 1 December 1997, p. 56. This seems far from the truth, judging from the numerical data of the time.

35. 9th Division, 9-Shi Sakumei [9th Division's Operation Order] no. 131, noon, 13 December 1937, in *NSS*1, p. 547. 30th Infantry Brigade, "Hohei Dai-30-Ryodan Meirei" [30th Infantry Brigade Order], 4:50 A.M., 14 December 1937, in ibid., p. 545. Tenth Army Command, Tei-shu Sakumei Kou Gogai: Tei-Shudan Meirei [Tenth Army Operation Order Extra: Tenth Army Order], 13 December 1937, in ibid., pp. 554–55. The 9th Division's loss by early November amounted to 3,833 killed and 8,527 wounded. 9th Division, "Dai-9-Shidan Sento Keika no Gaiyo" [Outline of the 9th Division's Military Operation], MHD.

36. Nakajima Diary, 13 December 1937, in *NSS*1, p. 326.

37. Nakajima Diary, 13 December 1937, in *NSS*1, p. 324. A Japanese artist who went to Nanking on board the navy's gunboat saw a lieutenant of the navy get off the boat on the night immediately after the capture of the city, saying, "I want to try my sword. I have never done it." Sumitani Iwane's memoir originally printed in *Togo*, December 1983, quoted in "SNS" (10), *Kaiko*, January 1985, p. 32. Also, then Lieutenant Colonel Miyamoto Shiro, adjutant of the 16th Division, said a *kendo* [Japanese fencing] instructor of the navy one day visited the divisional headquarters to obtain some Chinese prisoners as guinea pigs for sword practice. Testimony of Miyamoto Shiro in "SNS" (8), *Kaiko*, November 1984, p. 8. Saito Jiro, then private second class of the 65th Regiment, said he killed a Chinese soldier who ran away while an officer tried to behead him "to try the sharpness of his own sword." Saito Jiro, Diary of Saito Jiro, 13 December 1937, in *NDKK*, p. 36.

38. Nakajima Diary, 13 December, 1937, in *NSS*1, p. 324.

39. *NYT*, 9 January 1938, p. 38. Iinuma Diary, 16 December 1937, in *NSS*1, p. 217. Nakajima Diary, 13 December, 1937, in *NSS*1, p. 326. Nakasawa Mitsuo, "Nankin Kogeki-ji no Dai-16-Shidan Taisei" [16th Division's Deployment at the Time of Nanking Operation], a map prepared by Colonel Nakasawa Mitsuo, then staff chief of the 16th Division, MHD. It is not clear whether those figures entered by Nakasawa represent the number of prisoners executed or include those who were killed in action. SEF staff chief Iinuma recorded a rumor that one company of Sasaki's brigade captured 20,000. He also recorded a report that a plane pilot saw four files of prisoners extending as long as eight kilometers and moving toward the north of the Nanking Walls. Iinuma Diary, 14 December 1937, *NSS*1, p. 215.

40. Nakajima Diary, 13 December 1937, in *NSS*1, p. 326.

41. 38th Infantry Regiment, "Hohei 38-Rentai Sento Shoho" [38th Regiment's Battle Report], no. 11: 12–13 December 1937, MHD.

42. 33rd Infantry Regiment, "Nankin-fukin Sento Shoho" [Report on Battles in the Nanking Area], chart no. 3, MHD. Idem, "33-Rentai Sento Shoho" [33rd Regiment's Battle Report], n.d., MHD. The report uses a word *shodan*, which should mean "execution" in this context. Some participants testified after the war that those figures were likely to be the sum total of the numbers reported by subordinate units and presumed to be exaggerated. Testimonies of Hirai Akio, then radio chief of 33rd Regimental Command, and Tsutsumi Chisato, then adjutant of 33rd Regiment's 2nd Battalion, in "SNS" (9), *Kaiko*, December 1984, p. 6.

43. Iinuma Diary, 26 December 1937, in *NSS*1, p. 227. Kanemaru Yoshio, Memoir of Kanemaru Yoshio, in *NSS*1, p. 363. According to Kanemaru, he also encountered a battalion-size group of Chinese prisoners escorted by Japanese soldiers. When Kanemaru asked one of the Japanese about their destination, the answer was, "We are going to dispose of them." He later learned that those prisoners were executed near the Hanhsi Gate and were burned with kerosene, although he himself apparently did not witness the scene of execution. Judging from the location of massacre, the unit responsible for it was unlikely to be a part of the 16th Division. Kanemaru estimated the number killed in such a manner at 500 to 600 per night and 3,000 to 4,000 in all. Ibid.

44. Testimony of Shimada Katsumi in "SNS" (9) *Kaiko*, December 1984, p. 5.

45. 38th Infantry Regiment, "Nankin Jonai Sento Shoho" [Report of Battle within the Nanking Walls], chart no. 3, 14 December 1937, MHD. Testimony of Sumita Masao, then platoon commander of the 38th Regiment's 11th Company, in "SNS" (5), *Kaiko*, August 1984, p. 6. Sasaki, *Yasen Yubinki* [Field Postal Flag], vol. 1, p. 215. 2nd Independent Siege Heavy Artillery Battalion, "Sento Shoho" [Battle Report] no. 9 appendix, in *NSS*1, p. 650. Testimony of Lieutenant Sawada Masahisa, then observation unit chief of the Independent 2nd Siege Heavy Artillery Battalion's 1st Company, in "SNS" (5), *Kaiko*, August 1984, p. 7. Nakasawa, "Nankin Kogeki-ji no Dai-16-Shidan Taisei" [16th Division's Deployment at the Time of Nanking Operation], MHD. Testimony of Sakakibara Kazue in "SNS" (11) *Kaiko*, February 1985, p. 8. Regarding the fate of this group of POWs, Private Upper Class Azuma Shiro, a member of the 20th Regiment's 3rd Company that reportedly helped the 38th escort those prisoners, noted a rumor that "they were herded into groups of two to three hundred each and were killed." Azuma Memoir, *KS*, p. 305. Historian Hata Ikuhiko suggests that these interned prisoners were later killed. According to Hata, Inada Masazumi of the General Staff quoted Sakakibara as having said, "I planned to use the interned prisoners as labor force in Shanghai, but they were killed while I was away on an official trip." Hata, *Nankin Jiken* [Nanking In-

cident], p. 125. It is highly likely that either Inada or Sakakibara confused the fate of those interned prisoners with what happened to the prisoners held by the 13th Division's 65th Regiment—an incident I will discuss later in this chapter. According to SEF staff chief Iinuma, he had sent Sakakibara to the 13th Division on December 20 to have some of the prisoners held by that division transported to Shanghai as labor force, but could not do so due to the 65th Regiment's mishandling of prisoners. Iinuma Diary, 21 December 1937, in *NSS*1, p. 222.

46. Sasaki Diary, 16 December 1937, in *NSS*1, p. 16.

47. 4th Company of the 20th Infantry Regiment, "Jinchu Nisshi" [Field Diary] no. 5, 14 December 1937, in *NSS*1, p. 611. Masuda Rokusuke, Diary of Masuda Rokusuke, 14 December 1937, in *KS*, p. 7. Hayashi Masaaki, Memoir of Hayashi Masaaki, in *NSS*1, p. 519. Azuma Memoir, in *KS*, p. 309. According to some participants in the 16th division's mopping-up operation, the city blocks searched by the 9th and the 20th Regiments had buildings in a sporadic manner and were unlikely to provide suitable hiding locations for straggling soldiers. *NS*, p. 167.

48. Maeda Yuji, "Shanhai-sen kara Nankin Koryaku e" [Battle of Shanghai through the Capture of Nanking] in *Showa no Senso: Jaanarisuto no Shogen* [Wars in Showa Era: Accounts by Journalists], ed., Matsumoto Shigeharu, vol. 1, *Nitchu Senso* [Sino-Japanese War] (Tokyo: Kodansha, 1986), p. 123. One can find the same story in Kobayashi, ed., *Sakigake* [Harbingers], p. 574.

49. Makihara Diary, 14 December 1937, in *KS*, pp. 148–49.

50. Nakajima Diary, 13 December 1937, in *NSS*1, p. 325.

51. 9th Division, "Dai-9-Shidan Sento Keika no Gaiyo" [Outline of the 9th Division's Military Operation], MHD.

52. 6th Brigade, 6-Ryo Sakumei Kou [6th Brigade Operation Order] no. 138, 4:30 P.M., 13 December 1937, in *NSS*1, pp. 550–51.

53. 7th Infantry Regiment, Ho-7 Sakumei Kou [7th Infantry Regiment's Operation Order] no. 107, 1:40 P.M., 14 December 1937, in *NSS*1, p. 621.

54. [ICNSZ Chairman] John H. D. Rabe to [Attaché to the Japanese Embassy] Fukuda Tokuyasu, 15 December 1937, in *DNSZ*, no. 4, pp. 4–5.

55. 7th Infantry Regiment, "Hohei Dai-7-Rentai Sento Shoho" [Battle Report of the 7th Infantry Regiment], 7–24 December 1937, in *NSS*1, p. 630.

56. *NYT*, 18 December 1937, p. 10.

57. [ICNSZ Secretary] Lewis S. C. Smythe, "Memorandum on Incident at the Ministry of Justice," 18 December 1938, in *DNSZ*, no. 11, p. 23. *NYT*, 18 December 1937, p. 1. Rabe to Japanese Embassy; 17 December 1937, 18 December 1937, in *DNSZ*, no. 9, p. 14; no. 10, p. 22. Smythe to Japanese Embassy, "Cases of Disorder by Japanese Soldiers in the Safety Zone," filed 19 December 1937, in ibid., no. 15: case 62, p. 35. Testimony of Tsuchiya Masaharu, then commander of the 19th Regiment's 4th Company, in "SNS" (7), *Kaiko*, October 1984, p. 6. Sasaki M., *Yasen Yubinki* [Field Postal Flag], vol. 1, p. 217. Sumitani Iwane, "Memoir of Sumitani" Iwane, originally printed in *Togo* December 1983, quoted in "SNS" (10), *Kaiko*, January 1985, p. 32.

58. *NYT*, 18 December 1937, p. 1.

59. Smythe to Fukuda, "Cases of Disorder by Japanese Soldiers in the Safety Zone," filed, December 16, 1937, in *DNSZ*, no. 8, p. 9.

60. 7th Infantry Regiment, "Hohei Dai-7-Rentai Sento Shoho" [Battle Reports of the 7th Infantry Regiment], in *NSS*1, p. 630. Isa Kazuo, Diary of Isa Kazuo, 16 December

1937, in ibid., p. 440. 1st Company of the 1st Tank Battalion, "Kodo Kiroku" [Campaign Record], 14 December 1937, in *NSS2*, p. 418.

61. Mizutani Diary, 13 December 1937, in *NSS1*, p. 501. Inoie Diary, 14–16 December 1937, in ibid., pp. 475–76. Testimony of Wu Chang-te in *NEM*, p. 277. Testimony of Shen Hsi-en in *NEM*, pp. 325–27. Tanaka Masaaki in his book disputes the credibility of Wu's testimony by pointing out the fact that the Japanese army did not search the Justice Ministry building on December 15. Tanaka Masaaki, *Nankin Jiken no Sokatsu* [Nanking Incident Summed Up], p. 278. The document of the Safety Zone proves Tanaka's point. A memorandum dated December 18 says, "No officer came on the 15th . . ." Lewis S. C. Smythe, "Memorandum on Incident at the Ministry of Justice," in *DNSZ*, no. 11, p. 24. The discrepancy, however, might be attributable to a simple memory error of Wu.

62. Kajiya Takeo, Diary of Kajiya Takeo, 16–17 December 1937, in *NSS2*, p. 435. Testimony of Matsukawa Seisaku in "SNS" (11), *Kaiko*, February 1985, p. 10. Horikoshi Fumio, Diary of Horikoshi Fumio, 15 December 1937, in *NDKK*, p. 79.

63. Nakasawa Mitsuo, "Nankin ni okeru Moshiokuri Yoten" [Important Information Given at the Time of Transfer of Command in Nanking], in *NSS1*, p. 581. Makihara Diary, 17, 21–22 December 1937, in *KS*, pp. 152–53. Sasaki Diary, 26 December 1937, in *NSS1*, p. 382.

64. Nanking Commander of Military Police of the Japanese Army, "Proclamation by Nanking Commander of Military Police of the Japanese Army," 22 December 1937, a translation from Japanese into English, in *DNSZ*, no. 23, p. 53. M. S. Bates, "Memorandum on Aftermath of Registration of Refugees at Nanking University," 25 January 1938, in *DNSZ*, no. 50, p. 100. Testimony of Sheng in *NEM*, pp. 328–29. Iinuma Diary, 4 January 1938, in *NSS1*, p. 233. *NYT*, 25 January 1938, p. 8. Chiang Kung-yi, "Hsian-ching San-yueh-chi" [Three Months in Fallen Capital], in *SL*, pp. 88, 101.

65. Sasaki Diary, 5 January 1938, in *NSS1*, p. 382.

66. Bates, "Memorandum on Aftermath of Registration of Refugees at Nanking University," in *DNSZ*, no. 50, p. 102. The memorandum also enumerates other stories given by the persons who claimed to be survivors of massacres. Size of captives taken by the Japanese ranged from sixty to 500. The execution seemingly took place at canals in the suburb. Ibid., pp. 104–06. Inoie Diary, 22 December 1937, in *NSS1*, p. 479. Hayashi Diary, 24 December 1937, in *NSS1*, p. 519. Nankin Tokumu Kikan [Nanking Special Service], "Nankin-han Dai-2-ji Hokoku (2-gatsu Jokyo)" [Second Report by Nanking Team (Situation in February)], available in Chinese in *HP*, p. 339. *Tokumu kikan* was a Japanese military unit that mostly undertook nonmilitary or covert operations.

67. Only a company of 120 soldiers spearheaded the assault on the Chinese defenders on and around the mountain. Fukushima Min'yu Shinbunsha [Fukushima Min'yu Newspaper], *Kyodo-butai Funsen-ki* [Battle Records of Hometown Unit] (Fukushima: Fukushima Min'yu Newspaper, 1964), pp. 103–05.

68. Yamada Senji, Diary of Yamada Senji, 14 December 1937, in *NSS2*, p. 331. SEF staff chief Iinuma noted in his diary that "one company of the Sasaki Detachment took about 20,000 prisoners in the northeast of Nanking." Iinuma Diary, 14 December 1937, in *NSS1*, p. 215. Corporal Kurihara Toshikazu of the 65th Regiment remembered the size of prisoner group as about 13,500. Kurihara Toshikazu, Kurihara Memoir, in *NSS1*, p. 765. It seems that the rumor about this group of soldiers was widespread. Medic Ueba Buichiro of the 16th Division said, "According to a rumor, there are 15,000 disarmed

enemies in the north of the walls and our fellow soldiers are watching them with machine guns." Ueba Diary, 15 December 1937, in *KS*, p. 30.

69. Private Upper Class Araumi Kiyoe, 65th Regiment's 1st Battalion, said, "I was busy since POWs were coming all throughout today." Araumi Kiyoe, Diary of Araumi Kiyoe, 15 December 1937, in *NSS2*, p. 345. Private Second Class Saito Jiro noted in his diary, "five to six hundred soldiers were captured also today [December 15, 1937]." Saito Diary, 15 December 1937, in *NDKK*, p. 37. So did Private First Class Nakano Masao: "We were alerted by a report that several hundreds of straggling enemy soldiers were surrendering." Nakano Masao, Diary of Nakano Masao, 15 December 1937, in ibid., p. 116. Sublieutenant Endo Takaaki also said that one platoon took 306 Chinese prisoners on the same day. Endo Takaaki, Diary of Endo Takaaki, 15 December 1937, in ibid., p. 219.

70. Private Upper Class Aratsuma Tomio recorded a rumor that his regiment alone had captured 25,000 to 26,000 as of December 15. Aratsuma Tomio, Diary of Aratsuma Tomio, 15 December 1937, in *NDKK*, p. 178. Private First Class Sugano Yoshio said that the total number of POWs amounted to about 20,000 on December 15, up from about 15,000 on the previous day. Sugano Yoshio, Diary of Sugano Yoshio, 15, 16 December 1937, in ibid., p. 309. Sublieutenant Endo entered a minute figure of 17,025 in his diary. Endo Diary, 16 December 1937, in ibid., p. 219. Regimental commander, Colonel Morozumi, gave the smallest figure of 15,300 in his memoir written after the war. Morozumi Gyosaku, Morozumi Memoir, in *NSS2*, p. 339.

71. Meguro Tomiharu, Diary of Meguro Tomiharu, 13 December 1937, in *NDKK*, p. 373. Morozumi Memoir, in *NSS2*, p. 339. Araumi Diary, 6 December 1937, in ibid., p. 344. Yamada Diary, 14–15 December 1937, in ibid., p. 331.

72. Miyamoto Shogo, Diary of Miyamoto Shogo, 16 December 1937, in *NDKK*, p. 134. Endo Diary, 16 December 1937, in ibid., p. 219. Sugano Diary, 16 December 1937, in ibid., p. 309. Kondo Eishiro, Diary of Kondo Eishiro, 16 December 1937, in ibid., p. 326. Araumi Diary, 16 December 1937, in *NSS2*, p. 345. Morozumi Memoir, in ibid., p. 339. Endo Diary, 16 December 1937, in *NDKK*, p. 219, says, "In the evening, in accordance with the order of the higher command, the 1st Battalion took one third of [17,026] POWs to the shore [of the Yangtze] and shot them to death." According to Kondo Diary, 16 December 1937, in ibid., p. 326, "We decided to execute one third of 20,000, about 7,000, by shooting on the shore of the Yangtze . . . and finished the job. We stabbed to death some survivors."

73. Kurihara Memoir, in *NSS1*, p. 766. For the Japanese commanders' plan regarding how to handle POWs, see Morozumi Memoir, in *NSS2*, pp. 339–40 as well as Suzuki Akira's interview with Major General Yamada in 1972, quoted in Suzuki Akira, *"Nankin Daigyakusatsu" no Maboroshi* [Illusion of the "Rape of Nanking"] (Tokyo: Bungeishunju, 1973), p. 195. Morozumi said that those who fired at his unit were Chinese soldiers. Morozumi Memoir, in *NSS2*, p. 340. Historian Kojima, however, said it was another unit of the 13th Division or the Tenth Army's Kunisaki Detachment guarding the Yangtze shore. Kojima, *Nitchu Senso* [Sino-Japanese War], vol. 4, p. 243.

74. Iinuma Diary, 21 December 1937, in *NSS1*, p. 222.

75. Uemura Diary, 21 December 1937, in *NSS1*, pp. 268–69.

76. The following are the sources that mention the execution on this day. The figure in parentheses is the number of killed POWs as entered in each. Ito Kihachi, Diary of Ito Kihachi, 17 December 1937, in *NDKK*, p. 105 (20,000); Yaginuma Diary, 17 December 1937, in ibid., p. 167 (7,000); Endo Diary, 17 December 1937, in ibid., p. 220

(10,000); Honma Masakatsu, Diary of Honma Masakatsu, 17 December 1937, in ibid., p. 240 (15,000); Meguro Diary, 17 December 1937, in ibid., p. 373 (13,000). Nakano Diary, 18 December 1937, in ibid., p. 116 and Meguro Diary, 18 December 1937, in ibid., p. 373, said that an execution of 17,000 or 13,000 took place also on December 18. It is highly likely that these two persons had a memory error about the date of the event judging from the similar numbers entered into two different dates in their diaries. Araumi Diary, 17 December 1937, in *NSS*2, p. 345.

77. IMTFE, p. 4,537. Nanking Shou-tu Ti-fang Fa-yuan [Capital City District Attorneys' Office], "Nanking Shou-tu Ti-fang Fa-yuan Chien-ch'a-ch'u Feng-ling Tiao-ch'a Ti-jen Tsui-hsing Pao-kao-shu" [Report by the Capital City District Attorneys' Office of Nanking about the Enemy's Criminal Acts], February 1946, *HP*, p. 405.

78. Testimony of T'ang Kung-pu, March 1984, in *HP*, pp. 903–04.

79. Some examples of such an interpretation are *NDKK*, p. xvii; Hora Tomio, *Ketteiban: Nankin daigyakusatsu* [Nanking Massacre, Definitive Version] (Tokyo: Tokuma Shoten, 1982), pp. 222–24; Honda Katsuichi and Ono Kenji, "Bakufuyama no Horyo Shudan Gyakusatsu" [Mass Murder of POWs at Mufu Mountain], in *NDK*, pp. 128–49.

80. Morozumi Memoir, in *NSS*2, p. 339.

81. Fukushima Min'yu Shinbunsha [Fukushima Min'yu Newspaper], *Kyodo Butai Funsen-ki* [Battle Records of Hometown Unit], p. 112. Kojima, *Nitchu Senso* [Sino-Japanese War], vol. 4, p. 243. Endo Diary, 16 December 1937, in *NDKK*, p. 219.

82. The 3rd battalion reported, "We saw dead bodies left in scattered manner everywhere, but did not know the exact number." 3rd Battalion of the 68th Regiment, "Sento Shoho" [Battle Report] 27 November–13 December 1937, in *NSS*1, pp. 637–38, 640, 642, 645–46. Idem, "Jinchu Nisshi" [Field Diary] 16 December 1937, in ibid., p. 648. 1st Battalion of the 68th Infantry Regiment, "Sento Shoho" [Battle Report] 28 November–13 December 1937, in ibid., p. 636.

83. 6th Division, "Senji Junpo" [Wartime Report], nos. 13–14, 1–20 December 1937, MHD. Idem, 6-Shi Sakumei Kou [6th Division Operation Order] no. 84, 11:30 A.M., 14 December 1937, in *NSS*1, p. 558.

84. Testimony of Liu Szu-hai in *NEM*, pp. 220–22.

85. Maeda Diary, 14 December 1937, in *NSS*1, pp. 463–64.

86. Tani had overseas experiences in Britain, India, and France. According to Tani's chief of staff, Tani shared hardship on the battlefield with his soldiers when he was a divisional commander. Shimono Ikkaku, *Nankin Sakusen no Shinso: Kumamoto Dai-6-Shidan Senki* [Truth of Nanking Campaign: Battle Records of Kumamoto 6th Division] (Tokyo: Tokyo Johosha, 1966), pp. 98–99. Ushijima was then the commander of the 36th Brigade under Tani's 6th Division. Toward the end of World War II, he became the commander of the 32nd Army in Okinawa. Appointed to his chief of staff then was Cho Isamu, who had been an SEF staff officer in 1937 and had allegedly issued a verbal order to execute Chinese prisoners. For the story of Cho's verbal order, see Hata, *Nankin Jiken* [Nanking Incident], pp. 143–44.

87. Miyakonojo Hohei Dai-23-Rentai Senki Henshu Iinkai [Compilation Committee of Miyakonojo 23rd Infantry Regiment's Battle Record], *Miyakonojo Hohei Dai-23-Rentai Senki* [Battle Record of Miyakonojo 23rd Regiment] (Miyazaki: Miyakonojo Hohei Dai-23-Rentai Senki Henshu Iinkai [Compilation Committee of Miyakonojo 23rd Infantry Regiment's Battle Record], 1978), pp. 230–31.

88. Oda Diary, 16 December 1937, in *NSS*1, p. 448.

89. 114 Division, "Dai-114-Shidan Sakusen Keika no Gaiyo" [Outline of the 114th Division's Operation], 10 November–14 December, 1937, MHD.

90. 1st Battalion of the 66th Infantry Regiment, "Sento Shoho" [Battle Report], 10–13 December, 1937, MHD.

91. Ibid.

92. 150th Infantry Regiment, "Sento Shoho" [Battle Report], no. 6: 10–13 December, 1937, in *NSS*1, pp. 684–87.

93. Kunisaki Detachment Command, "Kunisaki Shitai Sento Shoho" [Battle Report of Kunisaki Detachment], no. 10: 3–16 December 1937, in *NSS*1, pp. 704–07. 12th Company of the 41st Infantry Regiment, "Koyosu Haizanhei Soto ni Kansuru Sento Shoho" [Battle Report of Mopping-up Operation of Straggling Soldiers on Chianghsingchou], 14 December 1937, in ibid., p. 710. As for a map of atrocity sites, see, for example, the map printed on the rear of the back cover of *SL*.

94. *Hankow Chung-hsi-pao* [Hankow Midwestern Times], 23 December 1937, in *HP*, p. 167. *Hsin-hua Jih-pao* [New China Daily], 9 February 1938, p. 2. The Chinese Nationalist Government's intelligence report quotes the same numbers as well. Kuo-min Cheng-fu T'e-kung Jen-yuan [special agent of the Nationalist Government], "Kuo-min Cheng-fu T'e-kung Jen-yuan Chiu Jih-chun Ta-t'u-sha Shih Kei K'ung Ling-k'an Te Chi-lu" [Intelligence Sent by the Special Agent of the National Government to K'ung Ling-k'an Concerning Japanese Aggressor Troops' Massacre], 7 March 1938, in *TA*, p. 51.

95. See Appendix B. Its source is Shih-chieh Hung-wan-tzu-hui Nanking Fen-hui [Red Swastika Society, Nanking chapter], "Shih-chieh Hung-wan-tzu-hui Nanking Fen-hui Chiu-chi-tui Yen-mai-tsu Yen-mai Shih-t'i Chu-shu T'ung-chi-piao" [Statistics Regarding Bodies Buried by the Burying Group of the Nanking Office of the Red Swastika Society, henceforth Red Swastika Burial Statistics], in *TA*, pp. 431–35. The Red Swastika Society was a Chinese charity organization affiliated with a religious society. It was not a branch of the World Red Cross.

96. Nankin Tokumu Kikan [Nanking Special Service], "Nankin-han Dai-2-ji Hokoku (2-gatsu Jokyo)" [Second Report by Nanking Team (Situation in February)]; "Nankin-han Dai-3-ji Hokoku (3-gatsu Jokyo)" [Third Report by Nanking Team (Situation in March)], in *HP*, pp. 340, 353. The cumulative total of the Red Swastika Society in the suburb by the end of March 1938 was 36,985. (Appendix B, Table 3) The Red Swastika buried 1,886 between March 16 and 31. (Ibid., Table 2) Accordingly, the sum total until March 15 is 35,099. The margin between this and 29,998 as entered in the Japanese report is 5,101.

97. For example, burial of 6,468 bodies was reported for December 28, 1937, 4,684 for February 9, 1938, and 5,705 for February 21. The sum total of these three days' work accounts for 39 percent of the fifty-four-day total. Appendix B, Table 2.

98. Bates, "Notes on the Present Situation," 21 March 1997, p. 2, enclosed to W. Reginald Wheeler to Stanley K. Hornbeck, 28 May 1938, 793.94/13177, M976-54. For the names of other organizations or individuals that participated in the corpse disposal, refer, for example, to Inoue Hisashi, "Itai Maiso kara Mita Nankin Jiken Giseishasu" [Computation of Rape of Nanking Victims Based on Burial Records], in *Nankin Dai-gyakusatsu no Genba e* [Visit to Rape of Nanking Locations], ed. Hora, Tomio; Fujiwara Akira, and Honda Katsuichi (Tokyo: Asahi Shinbunsha [Asahi Newspaper], 1988, henceforth *NDG*), pp. 61–69.

99. Chung-kuo Hung-shih-tzu-hui Nanking Fen-hui [Chinese Red Cross, Nanking

Office], "Chung-kuo Hung-shih-tzu-hui Nanking Fen-hui Yen-mai-tui Ti-1-tui An-yueh T'ung-chi-piao" [Monthly Statistics Regarding the Burial Activities Undertaken by the First Burial Team of the Nanking Office of the Chinese Red Cross] January–May 1938, in *TA*, pp. 440–42. Idem, "Chung-kuo Hung-shih-tzu-hui Nanking Fen-hui Yen-mai-tui Ti-2-tui An-yueh T'ung-chi-piao" [Monthly Statistics Regarding the Burial Activities Undertaken by the Second Burial Team of the Nanking Office of the Chinese Red Cross], January–May 1938, in ibid., pp. 446–48. The total corpses disposed of by the Red Cross amounted to 22,371. Ibid., p. 450.

100. Red Swastika Society, "Shih-chieh Hung-wan-tzu-hui Nanking Fen-hui Ch'ing-ch'iu Yuan-k'uan Yuan-ch'e Yun-shih Chih Jih-Nanking-shih Tzu-chih Wei-yuan-hui Han" [Message from the Nanking Office of the World Red Swastika Society to the Nanking Self-Government Committee Requesting Appropriation of Funds and Cars for the Transportation of Bodies], 4 April 1938, in *TA*, p. 436. Idem, "Shih-chieh Hung-wan-tzu-hui Nanking Fen-hui Ch'ing-ch'iu Yuan-chu Chen-k'uan Chih Jih-Hsing-cheng-yuan Ch'eng-wen" [Report of the Nanking Office of the World Red Swastika Society to the Executive Yuan, Nanking Reformed Government, Requesting Appropriation of Relief Funds], 14 October 1938, in *TA*, p. 437. Appendix B, Table 2.

101. Appendix B, Table 2.

102. Chou Yi-yu, "Ch'ung-shan-t'ang Tang-chang Chou Yi-yu Ch'ing-ch'iu Pu-chu Ching-fei Chih Jih-Chiangsu-sheng Chen-wu Wei-yuan-hui Ch'eng-wen Chi-lu" [Chou Yi-yu's Report to the Chiangsu Relief Commission, Reformed Government Requesting Subsidy], 6 December 1938, in *TA*, p. 426. Shu Teng-fu, "Chang-sheng Tz'u-shan-hui Chuh-si Shu Teng-fu Ch'ing-ch'iu Yuan-k'uan Pu-chu Chih Tu-pan Nanking Shih-cheng Kung-shu Ch'eng-wen" [Shu Teng-fu's Report to the Nanking Municipality Administration Requesting Relief Funds], 21 January 1939, in *TA*, p. 457. See Appendix C for the Ch'ung-shan-t'ang statistics. Its source is Ch'ung-shan-t'ang, "Nanking-shih Ch'ung-shan-t'ang Yen-mai Kung-tso Yi-lan-piao" [Working List of the Nanking Ch'ung-shan-t'ang's Burying Team], in *TA*, pp. 423–24.

103. Ara Ken'ichi, "Kaku Datta Nankin Daigyakusatsu no Shoko: Nazo no 'Suzendo' to Sono Jittai" [Proven Fictionality of Rape of Nanking Evidence: Mysterious "Ch'ung-shan-t'ang" and Its True Outlook], *Seiron* [Sound Argument] (October 1985): pp. 166–78, 177–78.

104. Headquarters United States Army Troops in China, Office of the Intelligence Officer, G-2 Report, 13 June 1938, M1513–39. No one has ever tried to answer one question regarding the Ch'ung-shan-t'ang statistics: if the Ch'ung-shan-t'ang document was indeed a fabrication, why did it formulate its data in such an unnatural manner, that is, to concentrate the bulk of the total disposed bodies—104,718 out of 112,266—in the one-month period in April rather than dividing and distributing the number uniformly over the five-month period? The answer might lie in the existence of another document that the Chinese side had in its possession at the time, that is, a report compiled by the Japanese army's special service in Nanking. Its report for March 1938, apparently in reference to the Red Swastika data, noted the disposal of 31,791 corpses by March 15. Although this is pure speculation, the compiler—or writer—of the Ch'ung-shan-t'ang document might have considered it unwise to enter unrealistically large numbers into the section for the said period—by March 15—and chose to concentrate most of the reported burial figures in the later time, but not so much later since it would have been equally unnatural for such burial activities to continue for a long time. Nankin Tokumu Kikan

[Nanking Special Service], "Nankin-han Dai-3-ji Hokoku (3-gatsu Jokyo)" [Third Report by Nanking Team (Situation in March)], n.d., in *HP*, p. 358.

105. 33rd Infantry Regiment, "Nankin-fukin Sento Shoho" [Report on Battles in the Nanking Area], MHD. *NYT*, 9 January 1938, p. 38.

106. Lewis S. C. Smythe, *War Damage in the Nanking Area December 1937 to March 1938: Urban and Rural Surveys* (Shanghai: Mercury Press, 1938), pp. ii, 8n. See Appendix D, Tables 1–3.

107. Appendix D, Tables 1–3.

4

Nanking: Analysis of Individually Committed Crimes and Nature of Atrocities

CRIMES INDIVIDUALLY COMMITTED

The citizens of Nanking had already been victimized by their own troops prior to the arrival of the Japanese forces. Correspondent Steele, for example, said that the behavior of the Chinese before the city's abandonment was deplorable in many ways, although he quickly added, "It was mild compared to the excesses of the invading force." According to 16th Division chief Nakajima's observation, it was no wonder that the Chinese soldiers committed criminal acts. Nakajima apparently found some military documents abandoned in Nanking that indicated that the Chinese military authorities had not paid many soldiers since April or May 1937. As a result, in Nakajima's words, the Chinese soldiers freely robbed households everywhere and left every residence ransacked completely by the time the Japanese came in. Nevertheless, although it is difficult to determine to what extent each side was responsible for the misconduct in Nanking, various records indicate that it was the Japanese who committed more violent crimes.[1]

Murder

Apart from the previously discussed mass execution of POWs, the senseless murder of civilians did take place. Nevertheless, those cases happened on a much smaller scale and under totally different circumstances from the execution of military men and those suspected to have been military men. The ICNSZ reported a total of only twenty-two murder cases resulting in the death of forty-six people. On the one hand, one may suspect there were more unreported cases in view of the considerably larger number of civilian victims reported in Smythe's investigation. On the other hand, one may assume that the number of victims attributable to the Japanese military's disorder could not reach the level of mass execution since most cases reported to the ICNSZ were about the death of one or two persons in each incident. As for Smythe's statistics, some extraordinary patterns in its data would not allow one to conclude that all victims mentioned in his statistics were the result of soldiers' violence. For example, among the female victims, those forty-five years old or older accounted for 54 percent in the city and a staggering 83 percent in the rural area. Smythe reasoned that these old women stayed behind to guard personal properties because they were considered less liable to be attacked. One could, however, wonder whether the Japanese soldiers subjected such feeble women to violence even if soldiers broke into their houses. Although a large number of old women certainly died due to the circumstances created by military actions on both sides, questions remain regarding the nature and effect of such circumstances.[2]

Thus, statistical data at the time of the incident strongly indicate that the large-scale and indiscriminate slaughter of civilians as commonly alleged today did not happen. Moreover, the other criminal activities committed by Japanese soldiers illustrate their lack of discipline—a quality that makes such a historically unprecedented massacre quite unlikely.

Disorder and Looting

There are other indications that the atrocities caused by individual Japanese soldiers were not as lethal as compared with the executions of POWs and plain-clothes soldiers. That Chinese civilians began to return to the city soon after its fall to the Japanese supports this theory. General Matsui wrote in his diary on December 15 that 4,000 to 5,000 refugees were returning to their homes every day although most of them were the poor. Matsui said at the same time that Chinese civilians were still scared of the Japanese soldiers because of their misbehavior. Underlining this fact, the SEF's 16th Division dwelled on its soldiers' discipline in its report on December 24, 1937: "[The soldiers'] discipline is good in general, but quite a few of them exhibited a violent nature which is typical immediately after battle." Matsui instructed his subordinate commanders to tighten the soldiers' discipline in an oral directive at the memorial service for the deceased CCAA soldiers in the Nanking campaign on December 18.[3] Matsui was apparently aware of the presence of some ill-behaving Japanese soldiers, but apparently tolerated their acts to a certain extent because he said in his diary on December 20 that "I was told that our soldiers committed a few cases of robbery (they mainly stole furniture) and rape for a certain time period. It was inevitable for a certain number of those crimes to happen in view of the situation."[4]

In reality, however, the misbehavior of Japanese soldiers in Nanking was beyond any justification premised on the soldiers' post-battle psychology. As early as December 16, Colonel Uemura of the SEF headquarters was told about misconduct committed within the city walls, and its extent was serious enough to make Uemura feel ashamed. Moreover, starting on the same day, the ICNSZ began to ask the Japanese diplomatic authorities to restrain the soldiers. In a letter of December 16 to Fukuda Tokuyasu, attaché to the Japanese embassy, the ICNSZ complained of the "continued disorder" mostly caused by "wandering groups of three to four soldiers without an officer" and asked the Japanese leadership to prevent any stray Japanese soldiers from entering the Safety Zone. The committee enumerated fifteen cases of either murder, rape, or robbery, adding, "Many more have been reported to our worker." The ICNSZ reported an additional fifty-five cases three days later, followed by twenty-six on December 20, seventeen on December 21, and eighteen on December 26. The reports of disorder continued through early 1938 and brought the total number of cases to 445 by February 8, 1938. Even the Japanese Foreign Ministry's message transmitted by diplomatic cable said that in the refugee area up until December 19 cases of looting, rape, and so on were innumerable.[5]

It was the Japanese military leadership's ill-advised decision that created the circumstances in which such disorder took place. Originally, the army commanders intended to allow only selected troops to march into the city and prohibit any entry into historic sites such as the tomb of Sun Yat-sen. The 9th Division's 7th Regiment referred to a similar divisional order and forbade those other than the units in charge of mopping-up operations from moving freely inside the walls. The 66th Regiment's 1st Battalion also strictly prohibited requisitioning inside the walls prior to its attack against the city, while ordering its soldiers not to steal any money even outside the walls. In reality, however, already by December 15 many units of each division and others entered the city and filled the streets. Such an influx of soldiers occurred partly because the CCAA command succumbed to the pressure of subordinate units that wished to participate in the planned victory parade by any means possible. Behind such a demand was a primitive idea transmitted from the premodern era that those who had fought hardest should police the city they had taken. There was, however, another pressing reason. Some units apparently moved inside the walls because there were no accommodations available for soldiers due to the extensive burning of suburban areas.[6]

Major General Sasaki, in command of the 16th Division's 30th Brigade, worried about possible delinquency after the battle. Sasaki was especially concerned about the quality of reserve soldiers who were dressed inappropriately. Sasaki's worry was not unfounded. Major General Yamada, commander of the 13th Division's 103rd Brigade, enumerated the attitude problems of reserve soldiers, including a lack of discipline, arson, rape, random shooting of birds and animals, and robbery. Even Yamada's brigade headquarters was robbed of one horse, and Yamada contemptuously called those soldiers a gang of bandits. Also, a soldier's diary recorded incidents such as theft of meat, random pistol shooting, and assault on superiors. These soldiers started running wild throughout the city. Hunger caused by poor logistical arrangements apparently precipitated the initial robbery, judging from Durdin's statement that food apparently was in first demand. Major General Sasaki said that the CCAA seized about one million bags of rice in Nanking, but that amount of requisitioned rice apparently did not satisfy the soldiers. Major Yamazaki Masao, a Tenth Army staff officer, witnessed soldiers searching every household for booty, taking out liquor and drinking water from liquor stores, and removing food such as pickles from grocery stores. Sublieutenant Maeda was also disgusted to see soldiers carrying away food and clothing by breaking in doors and windows. Maeda apparently shared Major General Sasaki's opinion that reserve soldiers belonging to rear units must have been responsible for the robbery. Official records substantiate this point. Of the 102 soldiers the Tenth Army's legal department convicted by February 18, 1938, ninety-seven were reserve or rear reserve soldiers. Also, the army's official report about delinquent soldiers in April 1938 gave five examples of those who were carrying forbidden items home at the time of quarantine inspection, and of these five three were connected to reserve units.[7]

The ICNSZ's reports narrate the stories of thievery committed by starving soldiers in corroboration of the Japanese official records and private accounts. Among the cases of disorder filed by the committee on December 16 were the following:

2. A carriage loaded with rice was taken on December 15 at 4 p.m. near the gate of Ginling College by Japanese soldiers.

11. Our Ninghai Road rice shop was visited on December 15 in the afternoon by Japanese soldiers who bought three bags of rice (3.75 tan or piculs) and only paid five dollars. The regular price of rice is nine dollars per tan, so the Imperial Japanese Army owes the International Committee 28.75 dollars for this.

13. On December 14, Japanese soldiers entered the home of Miss Grace Bauer, an American missionary, and took a pair of fur-lined gloves, drank up all the milk on the table, and scooped up sugar with their hands.[8]

Private Upper Class Kitayama of the 16th Division's 20th Regiment was apparently one of those looting the city. He found a pile of cider bottles at a store within the Safety Zone during the mopping-up operation on December 16 and had a large amount of them carted away.[9]

The delinquent Japanese soldiers were not satisfied with stealing food. On the morning of December 21, Field Postal Chief Sasaki was stunned to find that one of the trucks he was using for postal businesses had been stolen. Even 16th Division chief Nakajima, who was amazed at the extent of robbery committed by the Chinese, was appalled at the pillage by his own soldiers. After he set up the divisional headquarters within the Chinese Nationalist government building, he was astonished to find almost all the contents of the room, including some antiques, taken away even though he had posted a sign reading "16th Division HQ" on the door. Nakajima said that some soldiers of an artillery brigade had trespassed into the official residence of the Chinese military academy's principal, which was supposed to be occupied by his 9th Regiment, and looted the building. He apparently tolerated the robbery committed by his soldiers within their jurisdictional area to a certain extent. But he condemned crimes committed by other troops in the area under his jurisdiction as being of "extremely mean quality." The extent of robbery so escalated as to make SEF staff Colonel Uemura lament the gradual destruction of academically and culturally important assets in Nanking by ignorant treasure-hunting soldiers. According to the statistics compiled by the Nanking Municipal Autonomous Committee in secret cooperation with some Americans, the Chinese residents in Nanking lost more than eleven million Chinese yuan—worth about 3.26 million U.S. dollars at the time—of property to Japanese looting. This estimated total is almost three times as high as the value of movable properties considered to have been lost to "stealing" by the Chinese.[10]

The lack of discipline among the soldiers finally caused international problems when those soldiers broke into foreigners' residences. A Dutch citizen who was living in Nanking at the time filed a claim with the Japanese government through a diplomatic channel on September 5, 1938. The man named Bourdrez sought compensation for the properties looted by four Japanese soldiers on December 17, 1937, and by five soldiers on the following day. Judging from the stolen items such as two cameras, one bicycle, four pairs of spectacles, one hydraulic glass, two leather handbags, and one motorcar, these Japanese soldiers apparently did not conduct an officially sanctioned requisition.[11] Compared with other instances, however, he was lucky. In an official letter to the Japanese Foreign Ministry, the German Foreign Ministry reported the material losses suffered by a German citizen named Adolf Bautz, who had temporarily left Nanking and later returned to his home in the city. The letter said, that "the residence had been severely plundered and Mr. Bautz's car had disappeared from the garage in the house yard. According to the observations by eyewitnesses, Japanese soldiers emptied the house in question completely and carried away his property by wagon. The premise was occupied for the time being by the Japanese soldiers, who apparently removed the German Embassy's certificate seal of protection."[12] Bautz estimated the damage at $6,939.

The Japanese government initially adopted a policy of not assuming responsibility for the damages suffered by third country nationals in China because the government pronounced Japanese military actions as "defensive measures." At the same time, however, the Japanese leadership also decided to respond to damage claims if the damage was apparently caused by fault on the Japanese side or if a quick solution by compensation was deemed necessary or advantageous to Japan's international relationships. In reality, there seems to have been many cases in the first category attributable to the misbehavior of the Japanese troops in Nanking. A Japanese foreign ministry document shows that the Japanese government paid a total of 41,780 Chinese yuan to British nationals to compensate for eight cases of damage, 180,850.50 yuan to Americans for eight cases, and 115,750 yuan to Germans for 20 cases. Of these officially listed cases, seventeen were classified as looting. These settled cases, however, represented only the tip of the iceberg. When the German counsel at the German embassy in Tokyo visited a ranking Japanese foreign ministry official on January 25, 1938, the counsel said that among the German residents' private houses in Nanking, four were burnt and thirty residencies were looted more or less. In the end, the German diplomatic service reported forty-eight cases of either lost or looted properties and enumerated fifty-five individuals who needed damage compensation. As for the Americans, the U.S. Consulate in Nanking reported twenty-seven cases, of which twenty-three were attributed to Japanese misconduct, one to the Chinese, and three to unidentified nationals.[13]

Ultimately, Japanese soldiers even broke into the offices of the Western diplomatic representatives. U.S. Ambassador Nelson T. Johnson, who had already moved inland to Hankow, informed the State Department on December 25 of a break-in and car theft at the U.S. embassy building in Nanking two days earlier. The U.S. embassy staff filed a protest with the Japanese consulate, which in turn notified the foreign ministry in Tokyo as well as military leaders both in Nanking and Tokyo of the incident. According to a report received by the Japanese Foreign Ministry,

On the evening of [December] the 23rd armed Japanese soldiers entered the Embassy compound at least four times. They helped themselves to three automobiles and at the same time made away with four bicycles, two kerosene lamps and several pocket flashlights. Also, one corps led by an officer searched the persons of the employees and robbed them of about 250 dollars in cash, as well as of watches, rings and other personal effects. Another soldier, attempting to open [second secretary of the embassy Hall] Paxton's office, which was locked, pierced the door with his bayonet. Two other soldiers attempted to rape two Chinese women. . . . At 2 a.m. Japanese soldiers again entered the compound. In departing they took a motor truck and made off also with one sack each of flour and rice, a pocket flashlight and 11.80 dollars in cash from the gate-keepers room.[14]

This incident apparently prompted the Japanese military leadership to take necessary measures to improve the situation. The Japanese Army Minister and Chief of Staff jointly urged the CCAA to be mindful of its own image in the eyes of foreigners. The CCAA in turn sent its staff to the SEF to criticize the SEF soldiers' disgraceful acts against a foreign representative, and the SEF called on the deputy commanders of its subordinate units stationed in the Nanking area on December 30 to issue a stern warning against a lack or lapse of discipline, especially misconduct toward foreign diplomatic offices.[15]

By that time, however, widespread misconduct such as arson and rape had already occurred and continued to take place.

Incendiarism

Some Japanese units were ready to conduct systematic burning before the attack on Nanking. The 114th Division issued the following order prior to the start of mopping-up operations on December 13: "[Units in charge of the in-wall campaign] are required to annihilate the enemy by employing artillery and any other means. To accomplish this objective, the areas within the walls should be burned so that the enemy will not be able to use any tricks against us."[16] The Japanese also intentionally burned houses in the course of the mopping-up operation in the suburb. Private Upper Class Makihara of the 16th Division's 20th Regiment participated in an operation on December 16–17 outside the city walls and saw his unit setting fire to every village they passed through on their way back to the city. The destruction was so extensive that the 9th Division's 7th Regiment, which was ordered to move to the same area later, had a hard time finding accommodations there.[17]

Nevertheless, most of the city area was spared from the fires caused by military engagements. CCAA commander Matsui felt relieved to see most of the government and private buildings unscathed by the battle and maintaining their original appearance at the time of the victory parade on December 17. The survey conducted by the Nanking Municipal Autonomous Committee substantiated Matsui's observation. The survey said that the losses as a result of military operations accounted for only 1 percent of the total losses suffered in the city in terms of monetary value. On December 22, Matsui left for Shanghai and did not return to Nanking until February 6 the following year.[18]

Even before Matsui's departure, the city began to witness destruction by fires due to either arson or negligence. According to the same survey, fires were blamed for over 50 percent of the losses in Nanking. SEF staff chief Iinuma mentioned some specific incidents: "According to a report by the military police, someone set fire to a building in the Sun Yat-sen mound on December 18, and the fire is still burning now. I was also told that a unit led by an officer broke into the refugee zone and committed rape. Rumors about similar crimes have reached me as well."[19]

The CCAA's initial policy to protect the Sun Yat-sen mound proved ineffective. Colonel Nakasawa of the 16th Division said later that so many people had shamefully vandalized the mound that they were limiting the number of visitors. The Japanese army thus did not destroy the mound during the battle under a strict order issued by General Matsui, but disgraced it later through the soldiers' misconduct. But the Japanese military did chain and lock the room where Sun Yat-sen's body was enshrined and posted guards in front of the door, most likely by abiding by the order of Matsui, who had contact with Sun Yat-sen before the latter's death.[20]

Meanwhile, continuous fires caused the further destruction of Nanking. The ICNSZ pleaded with Japanese authorities that the burning of large sections of the city be stopped and what remained of the city be spared from either reckless or systematic burning. Further emphasizing the cause of the fires, in a follow-up report the committee attributed them to the soldiers' bonfires burnt on the floors of houses. The higher command threatened to punish the subordinate units for careless use of fire. Nevertheless, soldiers who broke into empty buildings for robbery sometimes set them ablaze. SEF staff chief Iinuma said late in December, "Discipline has not been tightened enough, but arson has ceased," thus suggesting that the Japanese soldiers were responsible for quite a few fires. Sublieutenant Maeda of the 6th Division's 45th Regiment, for example, saw a three-story Western-style building going up in flames and blamed fellow soldiers. Yet, there were also Chinese arsonists who, most likely, were soldiers hiding in the city. In his diary of January 1, 1938, 16th Division chief Nakajima mentioned arson committed by the Chinese everywhere in the city of Nanking. It is almost impossible to determine how much of the destruction by fire was attributable to the Chinese or the Japanese.[21]

Rape

As the phrase "Rape of Nanking" suggests, sexual assault on women was one of the most infamous crimes committed by Japanese soldiers. Like the cases of arson and looting, the Chinese military men were responsible for some cases. A news report in January 1938 told of a Chinese colonel and six of his subordinates who were found to have been in hiding at Ginling College, one of the refugee camps in the city. According to the *New York Times*, they occasionally left the building at night to loot in the city and one night raped at least one girl, blaming the incident on the Japanese.[22] Still, the Japanese undoubtedly committed most cases of rape in the city. After all, that the arrested Chinese colonel blamed the rape he had committed on the Japanese suggests how numerous the rape cases perpetrated by the Japanese were during these days. According to Smythe's investigation, of 1,300 women who were injured inside the walls, those aged fifteen to twenty-nine accounted for 65 percent.[23] This high ratio suggests that the injuries suffered by the females of this age group were related to sexual assault. Even a Japanese official report confirmed this fact. Tenth Army staff chief Major General Tanabe Moritake said in his official message to subordinate units that cases of sexual assault on women alone totaled more than one hundred in Nanking.[24] Apparently, these more than 100 cases represented merely a fraction of the total. The ICNSZ listed numerous cases, among which are,

5. On the night of December 14, there were many cases of Japanese soldiers entering Chinese houses and raping women or taking them away. This created a panic in the area and hundreds of women moved into the Ginling College campus yesterday. Consequently, three American men spent the night at Ginling College last night to protect the 3,000 women and children in the compound.

18. On the night of December 15 a number of Japanese soldiers entered the University of Nanking buildings at Tao Yuen and raped 30 women on the spot, some by six men.

55. December 18, evening, 450 terrorized women fled for shelter to our office and spent the night in our yard. Many had been raped.

101. On December 20, 3 p.m., three Japanese officers intruded into the office of the Refugee Camp in the Hankow Road Primary School. The staff talked to them with an interpreter, but the officers ordered them out of the office and in broad daylight and in the same office raped two women.

146. December 25, 3 p.m., two Japanese soldiers came to the Hankow Primary School Refugee Camp searching for property and then raped a Miss Hwang of the staff. . . . The same evening, other Japanese soldiers came and raped Mrs. Wang's daughter. About 7 p.m. three other Japanese soldiers raped two young girls, one of whom was only 13 years old.[25]

Even some former Japanese military men, who are proud of their units and their battle records, have admitted to the occurrence of rape. Sergeant Fujita Kiyoshi, who was a member of a mechanized unit at the time of the Nanking campaign, said that two members of his company sneaked out from their accommodation every night, apparently to look for women. Sublieutenant Oda of the 9th Division's 23rd Regiment noted in his diary a rape incident committed by two soldiers of a machine gun company on December 16. Finally, SEF staff officer Onishi Hajime said that he caught a soldier raping a woman and turned him in to that soldier's regiment.[26]

Various sources give a wide range of estimates regarding how many rape cases happened in Nanking. M. S. Bates, ICNSZ member, gave the ICNSZ's official estimate of about 8,000 cases, although he also quoted some German nationals as having estimated the number of rape victims at 20,000. Oskar Trautmann, German ambassador to China, agreed to the latter estimate in his statement that the Japanese had violated about 20,000 women and girls in his report to the German Foreign office on January 14, 1938. Although these data probably copied rumors, one may assume that they were not far from the truth. Smythe's survey shows that rape was committed "to the extent of 8 percent of all females of 16–50 years" and adds that this ratio was an "understatement" due to the reluctance of victims and their relatives to provide information. This ratio would translate into about 4,000 to 5,000 rape victims. This range is the lowest estimate. The actual number of victims could easily be twice or three times as many.[27]

The military leaders were not unaware of these incidents. SEF staff chief Iinuma asked Lieutenant Colonel Cho Isamu, an SEF staff officer, on December 19 to have brothels set up as quickly as possible.[28] For the time being, however, it was imperative for the leadership to maintain discipline by force. The problem was that only a small number of military policemen (MP) were available initially to restrain such soldiers who were commiting licentious crimes. According to Japanese diplomatic correspondence, there were only seventeen MPs, including one officer, until December 19. To rectify this shortage of MPs, Tenth Army commander Yanagawa on December 15 ordered two companies under his command to serve as auxiliary MP units. Then, the CCAA created its own military police unit of 401 men on January 6, 1938, and assigned 119 of them to Nanking. The military police, however, seemed to be powerless. Two days later, quoting a military police report, SEF staff Colonel Uemura complained bitterly about the obscene crimes committed by recently enlisted lieutenants and sublieutenants. The impression is that a major source of the problem was the less disciplined officers and soldiers who filled the ranks of units depleted by the Shanghai and Nanking battles.[29]

Many cases of rape happened even after the creation of the new MP force. In mid-January, Japanese soldiers abducted eight women from Ginling College and took away a piano after making a hole in a building wall. On January 26, Major Hongo Tadao of the SEF headquarters reported to staff chief Iinuma about a rape incident perpetrated by a lieutenant of the 16th Division's 33rd Regiment two days before. That lieutenant, a company commander, with his men broke into a shop run by an American and raped two women they had taken from another place. When two Americans tried to investigate the house, the lieutenant had his men punch the Americans and refused to leave. Lieutenant Colonel Hongo finally arrived at the scene and found the lieutenant still in bed with a woman. On January 29, the SEF leadership decided to have that lieutenant court-martialed. He was later convicted and imprisoned at a military prison in Port Arthur.[30]

The Japanese military police apparently had some serious problems that affected their morale. First, some of the military policemen were not paid well. Although one cannot know the minute details of this problem, a message sent by the CCAA command to the army ministry in early 1938 urged the army leadership to rectify the "extremely unfair payment system for military policemen." The CCAA said that rectifying the system was a pressing matter for the administration of military police affairs and that it was absolutely necessary to maintain the morale and discipline of the military. Second, there was possibly a conflict of jurisdiction between the newly created CCAA military police and the existing military police forces of the SEF and the Tenth Army. For unknown reasons, the regulations concerning the CCAA military police made them subordinate to the SEF and Tenth Army police. Although there is no clear-cut answer as to why the Japanese army's policing in Nanking was so poor, one might trace the problem to the very beginning of the Nanking campaign, that is, when the army leadership decided to capture the capital city of China, where a sizable population was expected to be residing, without enough logistical preparation. If the leaders paid so little attention to supply problems, it is easy to imagine that they also did not fully understand the need for a strong military police presence, either.[31]

NATURE AND CAUSES OF ATROCITIES IN NANKING

Roughly speaking, there were two phases in the historical event known as the Rape of Nanking. Although one cannot draw a clear demarkation time line between these two, the mass execution of prisoners, plainclothes soldiers, and those suspected of being so marked the first phase, whereas the delinquent acts of soldiers, such as individually committed murder, robbery, and rape, characterized the second phase. The first category of atrocities happened in a very short time period, most notably during December 13 to 16 before the victory parade, and claimed the lives of men mainly of conscription age. The latter extended through a considerable length of time and affected the entire population in an almost uniform fashion.

A Chinese report that lists some individual victims in three separate categories of murder, abduction, and rape signifies this point. The table, which was attached to a report submitted to the Nationalist Government's Justice Ministry, enumerated 104 individual victims of murder, 23 rape victims, and 112 abductees who were recorded as missing. A comparison between the 112 abductees and the 104 murder victims reveals some interesting facts. Of the 112 abductees, (1) all but one of those 112 listed as missing were men; (2) of these 111 men, fifty-one were entered with the dates of their abduction and forty-six of them were taken away in December 13–16; (3) of the 111 men, sixty-two were recorded with their ages at the time of their disappearance and fifty-five were between fifteen and forty-five years old. These breakdowns strongly suggest that they were mainly the victims of the Japanese army's operation to hunt down former soldiers—an atrocity in the first category. As for the 104 murder victims, (1) females accounted for sixteen of the total; (2) of the thirty-seven male victims whose ages are known, sixteen—less than half of the total—were within the fifteen- to forty-five-year-old range and the victims were dispersed almost uniformly throughout all age groups; (3) although few cases are supplied with precise dates, twenty-one are reported to have happened on December 13—most likely as a result of combat or semicombat situations—while the occurrence on other dates was almost equally distributed. These findings show that these were the victims of the atrocities that affected the entire population over a long period of time, that is, individually committed crimes in the second category. It is appropriate to analyze separately the nature and cause of these two categories of atrocities.[32]

Execution of Plainclothes Soldiers, POWs, and Men of Conscription Age

One may define the mass executions conducted more or less systematically by each Japanese unit as a "massacre," as many historians and journalists have termed it. This was indeed an atrocity of a monstrous scale, for which the Japanese military leaders were responsible. Yet the number of victims seems to have been far below the oft-claimed 300,000 or more. ICNSZ documents corroborate this point since a series of reports consistently estimated the population of the city as being 200,000—approximately the same as the newspapers had reported before the battle.[33] Another notable fact contradicting a commonly accepted notion about the Rape of Nanking was that the majority of those killed were soldiers, either taken prisoner or plainclothes, despite the inclusion of civilians mistakenly identified as former military men. In other words, the Japanese did not kill Nanking residents indiscriminately, regardless of sex or age, as conducted by the Nazi *Einsatzgruppen*.

The most fundamental question is why the Japanese killed the soldiers who had surrendered. One cannot attribute these unlawful acts entirely to the violent end of the siege—a factor that has tended to promote the occurrence of atrocities regardless of the era—because the Japanese accepted the surrender of Chinese soldiers outside the Nanking walls more or less peacefully, while they caught the plainclothes soldiers in the Safety Zone almost without a fight. A traditional interpretation is that the Japanese wanted "the horrors to remain as long as possible, to impress on the Chinese the terrible results of resisting Japan."[34] The Japanese military's official order, however, does not include any instruction that would encourage the soldiers to be cruel to the enemy. To the contrary, the CCAA ordained before the entry into Nanking that "each unit is required to tighten the discipline further so that the Chinese people, military and civilian alike, will respect the dignified manner of His Majesty's army and become obedient. Accordingly, each unit is expected never to commit any deed that would disgrace our honor."[35] Moreover, General Matsui met with a local Chinese leader as early as December 15 to discuss the establishment of Chinese civilian authorities in the area. Matsui was also concerned about the local population's fear of the Japanese army and discussed it during the talks.[36] Therefore, one cannot compare the atrocities in Nanking to a calculated policy of genocide like the Nazi Final Solution.

One possible explanation is that the Japanese military men's contemptuous attitude toward war prisoners—a view that had been nurtured for decades, as the first chapter discussed—affected the Japanese troops' behavior. Actually, the Japanese army incorporated such an attitude into its operation manual. A booklet compiled by the Japanese army's infantry school contains the following passage: "There will not be so much of a problem even if we execute Chinese soldiers not only because the Chinese census registration is incomplete but also because there are quite a few soldiers of homeless origin whose presence cannot be confirmed easily."[37] At the same time, the Japanese military's tendency to regard captivity as shameful had pervaded the entire nation by that time. Joseph Clark Grew, U.S. ambassador to Japan, recorded an event that showcased the Japanese attitude toward POWs at the time of the Sino-Japanese War. According to Grew, the Chinese government conveyed to the U.S. Embassy in Tokyo the name of a Japanese soldier who had been captured by Chinese Nationalist troops. That soldier apparently tried to contact the Japanese government to inform his family that he was still alive. The Japanese government, however, replied to Grew that it was not interested in receiving such information and that, as far as his own family was concerned, that man was officially dead. The Japanese authorities added that "Were he to be recognized as a prisoner of war, shame would be brought upon not only his own family, but also his Government and his nation."[38] Also, Japanese military leaders at the time seemingly considered the execution of POWs as an extension of military activity instead of a war atrocity. That some official military records openly described POW executions substantiates this view.

The killing was, however, not always the Japanese way of solving the prisoner problem. If the Japanese army had a predetermined policy of executing Chinese prisoners, massacres would have happened continuously. To the contrary, however, when the city of Hangchou fell to the Japanese on December 24 in the same year, a Western news source reported no wholesale executions in Hangchou as marked the Japanese capture of Nanking. The Japanese policy toward war prisoners was inconsistent even on an individual level. Although 16th Division chief Nakajima bluntly stated his policy of "not taking prisoners" in his diary, he did not necessarily adhere to these words. When Nakajima inspected a Nanking flour milling factory administered by his division's accounting section on December 23, he encountered about 300 Chinese prisoners working under the supervision of the division's accountant sergeant. Nakajima was surprised to find that the sergeant was completely unarmed while directing those prisoners. Then, he was stunned to see a more incredible scene: the weapons confiscated from these prisoners were not stored in another space but were left within their easy reach. Nakajima scolded the accountant sergeant furiously for such carelessness, but left the factory without ever ordering the execution of the prisoners. Moreover, in his conversations with other ranking SEF generals he later spoke proudly of that "brave unarmed sergeant using a large number of prisoners." This was another example of the lack of POW policy in the Japanese army, as one can see in the varied treatment of Chinese POWs in Nanking in the preceding chapter. In the end, the Japanese military's attitude to POWs alone does not explain sufficiently why Japanese troops in Nanking killed so many POWs.[39]

Although researchers have tended to focus on long-term causes such as the character of the Japanese people in general, one must also take into consideration some immediate causes.

The outcome at Nanking was attributable in part to decisions on the Chinese side. The first was the poor judgment of the Chinese commanders. Almost entirely out of emotion, Chiang Kai-shek decided to make another stand in the capital city, which was a walled city located on the river shore and thus likely to be a trap for defenders, after the Shanghai campaign had depleted his crack military troops. Garrison commander T'ang's eleventh-hour evacuation order further added confusion to the retreat conducted by the defeated Chinese troops. Second, Chinese leaders failed to endorse the Safety Zone in advance, although the Japanese did not recognize it fully, either. The considerable amount of weapons and ammunition that the Japanese troops seized in the Safety Zone convinced them of a pressing need to search for plainclothes soldiers. Finally, one must point to a custom peculiar among the Chinese soldiers who had not developed the clear idea of *jus in bello*, that is, their traditional practice of changing into civilian clothes in times of defeat. It seems that most Chinese soldiers did so in an attempt to save their own lives, but the result was to endanger not only their lives but also those of innocent civilians. The Japanese soldiers, who had been alert to small-scale guerrilla-style activities conducted by plainclothes soldiers on their march to Nanking, seemingly possessed a mentality similar to the "*franc-tireur* psychosis"—a notion prevalent among German soldiers operating in World War I Belgium that they were under a constant threat of volunteer troops engaging in guerrilla activities. The Japanese soldiers started a relentless search for such soldiers. Subsequently, the Safety Zone was turned into a "danger zone."

Despite these possible factors attributable to the Chinese decisions and actions, the Japanese military leadership was responsible for its own problems. First, for a reason still unknown, CCAA commander Matsui was eager to hold the victory parade and ceremony at the earliest possible date. Actually, he decided as early as December 14, which was a mere one day after the capture of Nanking, to hold it on December 17. Unlike Matsui, SEF leaders were not prepared for such an early celebration of victory. To the phone call from the CCAA notifying the SEF of the date for the victory parade, SEF staff chief Iinuma replied that December 17 would be unacceptable because the mopping-up operation was still progressing. The SEF's 16th Division also wished to postpone the parade until after December 20, and its staff chief went on to say that the division could not assume the full security responsibility. Even SEF commander Prince Asaka himself expressed concern about the hasty scheduling of the parade.[40] Probably being irritated at such reluctant attitudes, Matsui said on December 16, "Although the holding of victory ceremony tomorrow looks like a hasty scheduling, I do not like to postpone it further. Therefore, I decided to carry it out tomorrow by all means."[41] It was possible that Matsui was under political pressure from Tokyo, since the Japanese news media prematurely reported the fall of Nanking on December 12, one day earlier than the actual date of occupation.

Yet the major reason for his insistence on holding the victory parade at the earliest possible time was possibly a trivial one. Already on December 15, 16th Division commander Nakajima had organized a victory parade for his own division. Although Matsui did not make any comment about it, Matsui was likely to be displeased to learn about this event, which Nakajima had conducted without obtaining any consent from Matsui. It is possible that Matsui wanted to hold the victory as soon as possible after learning about the 16th Division's parade organized by Nakajima, who was not on good terms with Matsui. For whatever reason, Matsui's decision to hold the victory parade in such a hasty manner quickened the pace of mopping-up operations in the Nanking area and contributed to the mass execution of prisoners. What escalated the scale of killing was the concern about the safety of the SEF commander who happened to be an imperial family member. When General Matsui transferred the command of the SEF to Prince Asaka on December 4, 1937, Matsui instructed all troops to study and implement as many precautionary measures as possible to guarantee the prince's personal safety. It is quite likely that, faced with an almost overwhelming number of POWs and plainclothes soldiers, the Japanese military leaders, SEF staff officers in particular, concluded that the easiest way to achieve that objective was to execute the captives.[42]

The second immediate cause attributable to the Japanese side was the food problem. The forced march from Shanghai to Nanking made the Japanese dependent on robbery-like requisition for their food provisions and caused a constant food shortage. One can easily imagine how difficult it might be for troops, who had trouble feeding themselves, to allot food to POWs. According to Major Sakakibara Kazue, an SEF staff officer, the SEF made available one food ration for POWs out of every five rations given to the Japanese soldiers.[43] Provisions were so scarce that the prisoners interned within the city walls suffered from hunger. Hanekura Shoro, who was a squad commander of the 16th Division's engineer regiment, noted a rumor that the hunger was so acute that some prisoners had even committed suicide by hanging themselves. Hanekura also witnessed a dismal scene: "One day I saw some prisoners carrying rice (about three tons) transported by a cargo truck up to the gate of a POW camp. Some punched holes on hemp bags and put some grains into their mouth on the spot while others scattered rice on the ground on purpose to scoop it up with sand. The prisoners hit each other to take away the rice. The scene was like a living hell."[44] This was the situation in the POW internment facilities inside the city walls, where food was relatively easy to find. It was beyond imagination how those captured by the Japanese outside the walls fared. Major General Sasaki of the 16th Division's 30th Brigade said in his diary entry of December 13, "We do not have even a grain of rice. Although we can probably find some within the city walls, we cannot spare any food to prisoners." A soldier of the 65th Regiment, which reportedly took about 17,000 prisoners, said that some prisoners who had been without food for a few days even prior to their capture by the Japanese ate grass and that the Japanese guarding the prisoners seemed to be at a loss how to provide food and water for them.[45] As the previous discussion shows, when local commanders who encountered this difficulty reported the situation to the higher command, they often received an order either to kill the captives or take care of them appropriately. Faced with such an order, the local commanders had three choices: (1) to carry out the order and kill them; (2) to ignore the order and keep the prisoners under their strict supervision; or (3) to ignore the order and release them. Of these choices, the second one was difficult to implement due to the shortage of food, while the third was risky since those prisoners, once released, might disturb the victory parade in which an imperial family member was scheduled to participate. Thus, one can assume that to the Japanese military leaders, a resort to executions was often the only available course of action they could think of. Of course, however reluctantly they carried out the execution, such actions were not justifiable either morally or legally.

Another question is who issued the actual order for the executions. The only explicitly written official order commanding subordinate units to kill prisoners is found in the record of the 66th Regiment, which referred to a brigade order as the responsible authority. Some orders disallowed the capture of prisoners, but others instructed subordinate units to herd them together in one place. Some scholars suggest that a privately and verbally issued order, notably by Lieutenant Colonel Cho Isamu of the SEF, was the cause of the massacre.[46] It is, however, doubtful that officers of superior ranks in the subordinate units followed such an order without official and written authentication since executing an unwritten order would place all responsibility on them. According to the memoir of 65th Regiment chief Colonel Morozumi, his superior, Major General Yamada, and the SEF headquarters had a series of talks to decide whether Yamada and Morozumi should execute the prisoners in their hands or the SEF should take care of them.[47] Had the SEF issued a written order to shoot them in the name of its commander, Prince Asaka, Yamada could not have resisted it. Judging from Yamada's resistance as described by Morozumi, however, the SEF probably did not give a written order and, instead, told Yamada only orally to dispose of them. Thus, the two commands tried to shift the responsibility to each other regarding the handling of prisoners.

The 30th Brigade chief's instruction disallowing his units to accept prisoners pending the divisional command's further notice is another example of dodging responsibility by leaving the final decision about prisoners to the division.[48] The 66th Regiment chief's instruction to one of his battalion commanders about the execution of prisoners was along the same lines in its specific mention of "brigade order." Another noticeable tendency was the ambiguous wording of such orders. A private record says that one battalion command instructed a subordinate unit to dispose of prisoners *in some way or the other*.[49] Then, responsibility dodging or diffusing happened even among those units actually in charge of the killing. The 66th Regiment's 1st Battalion, for example, divided the prisoners to be executed equally among its subordinate companies. Thus, an overall tendency seems to have been that the higher command vaguely ordered the local commander to execute the prisoners but allowed a certain degree of latitude with respect to the actual method of disposal. Because of this downward transmission of the execution order, relatively small units—companies or battalions—actually undertook the executions in the end. This explains why most of the Japanese accounts of how the troops massacred the Chinese prisoners describe the execution of relatively small numbers, that is, dozens to several hundreds, except for the one conducted by Morozumi's 65th Regiment near the Mufu Mountain. Although many people mentioned the mass killing of several thousands in their memoirs and diaries, they recorded it only as hearsay, probably after having heard about the cumulative figure of those small-scale executions.[50]

Such a method of dodging or transferring responsibility, which one may call "command irresponsibility," reflected the Japanese military's tendency seen from the beginning of the Sino-Japanese War. While the high command in Tokyo allowed the local commanders to start the Nanking campaign without enough preparations or provisions, those local commanders in turn entrusted to still lower commands the disposal of prisoners without providing them with sufficient provisions to deal with that problem. Therefore, despite what looked like systematic execution in some instances, the Japanese executed the Chinese prisoners in an ad hoc manner rather than in accordance with shrewd or deliberate planning. Without deliberate and systematic planning, what many Chinese and American scholars and journalists call a historically unparalleled massacre of 300,000 people over a two-month period could not have happened.

Crimes Individually Committed

The criminal acts committed individually in Nanking had multiple characteristics. Except for the fires for which Chinese soldiers hiding in the city were reportedly also responsible, it was the Japanese military that should be held accountable for these incidents. According to Maruyama Masao, a Japanese political scientist, these atrocities, which continued to happen in World War II, were attributable to the nature of Japanese society in which the people transferred the oppression from the upper social class to those in the lower level of the social strata. Maruyama said that "the masses" who constituted the bulk of the rank-and-file soldiers had no object to which they could transfer oppression, and thus they turned their frustration toward the people in the conquered areas.[51] This analysis, however, does not explain the well-disciplined behavior of the Japanese soldiers in the first Sino-Japanese and Russo-Japanese Wars when Japan's level of modernization was far less advanced than in the 1930s. One should again focus on more immediate causes.

Lieutenant Colonel Inada Masazumi, then an officer of the Army Ministry's Military Affairs Division, summarized what made the soldiers so violent:

The unexpectedly costly battle in Shanghai fostered a sense of vengeance while the complication of the military situation caused the loss of morale and ethic among the troops. These tendencies led to numerous cases of arson, robbery, and physical abuse even during the Shanghai campaign, resulting in the tarnishing of the honorable image of His Majesty's armed services in the eyes of the world. . . . It is a thousand pity that [the Japanese troops] had turned themselves into an oppressive armed horde.[52]

Local requisition of food further accelerated the Japanese troops' degeneration into an army that conducted itself like a premodern horde. By the time they reached Nanking, the soldiers had become like bandits indulging in theft and other criminal activities. The soldiers who entered the enemy's capital, either consciously or unconsciously, demanded plunder to make up for the pains they had suffered and started a rampage throughout the city. These were the atrocities blamed on a lack or loss of discipline, and they were markedly different from the mass execution of POWs and plainclothes soldiers.

One can see the contrast between the two categories of atrocities in the soldiers' attitudes. Because delinquent soldiers committed these crimes as individuals, their behavior was less atrocious—sometimes timid, manageable, and even friendly—in contrast with the image of the ranks of savage killers massacring Chinese prisoners. Those who support a theory that the Japanese army slaughtered civilians indiscriminately regardless of age and gender may have to consider the Japanese soldiers' actual behavior in this second phase of the Rape of Nanking. For example, when some Japanese soldiers intruded into the U.S. embassy compound looking for valuables on December 23, they were scared at a phone bell and ran away after severing the phone line. According to an ICNSZ report, two Japanese soldiers tried to rape a woman in a schoolroom on December 19, but her husband saved her because he could speak Japanese. Another ICNSZ report also said that a Japanese soldier who found a Chinese woman badly molested and wounded by other soldiers took her to a hospital on January 2. The Japanese troops' conduct was indeed criminal and by no means justifiable, but it shows little resemblance to the systematic pattern of mass killing as seen in the Nazi *Einsatzgruppen*. The stark contrast in the behavior of soldiers engaging in the two different kinds of atrocities is also reflected in the number of victims. The total number of executed former soldiers and civilians misidentified as ex-military men totaled tens of thousands, even according to the contemporary Japanese records, whereas the number of civilians murdered by delinquent soldiers, as revealed by the ICNSZ reports, was about fifty.[53]

Ultimately, one could trace the causes of the criminal acts committed by individual Japanese soldiers to the same "command irresponsibility" that motivated the prisoner executions. The hastily planned Nanking campaign, which local military leaders had initiated without explicit advance authorization from the central command, forced the leadership to make its troops live off the land and fostered criminal behavior among the soldiers that caused their degeneration into mercenary-like plunderers. It is no wonder that the behavior of Japanese soldiers described in Western newspaper articles and the ICNSZ reports was reminiscent of hungry medieval troops sacking towns.

There is no clear-cut explanation regarding the origin of "command irresponsibility." Anthropologists and sociologists might be tempted to point to the way the Japanese people perceive responsibility in their society. A recent study suggests that Japanese tend to emphasize an individual's responsibility within a group or context whereas Americans tend to emphasize an individual's concrete deeds.[54] Such a social trait could be one of the factors that shaped the Japanese military men's minds in Nanking. But such a cultural element alone cannot explain this "command irresponsibility" because not all Japanese organizations or individuals behaved in such a manner. One possible explanation lies in the attitude change in the rank and file of the Japanese military with respect to how military men should assume responsibility. Ultimately, that attitude change was attributable to the transformation of the Japanese army.

The Japanese army was initially dominated by the leaders of Choshu, one of several semiautonomous units in Western Japan during the era of the Tokugawa Shogunate. Although the Choshu people's strong influence not only in the army but also in the government drew criticism from other groups, it had merit: the personal bonds among them contributed to consistency in government policy as well as good coordination between military strategy and politics in a strict adherence to the Clausewitzian dictum. At the time of the first Sino-Japanese War (1894–95) and the Russo-Japanese War ten years later, the central command had a tight rein over the local military commanders so that military operations would serve their political objectives well. A notable example was the case of General Yamagata Aritomo, who was dismissed from his post as commander of the First Army during the first Sino-Japanese War after he had attempted to conduct an independent and unauthorized military operation. Erosion of the central authorities' control over local military commanders started with events in Manchuria in the late 1920s and early 1930s. This was the period when the army began to be divided within itself and officers formed cliques after the ex-Choshu men's dominance had disappeared. The effect of this division was that loyalty to individuals or ideologies became more important than obedience to legitimate orders—and from time to time, the High Command lost control of whole sections of the army. That the central command often approved unauthorized operations *post facto* rather than reprimanding subordinate commanders paralyzed the military's sense of responsibility and led to the loss of central control. Ultimately, Matsui joined the ranks of those local military leaders who ignored or defied the central command. That Matsui was a general senior to almost all army leaders in Tokyo undoubtedly contributed to the erosion of control from Tokyo in the case of the Nanking campaign. Yet even Matsui himself could not escape the same problem in his relationships with subordinates, most notably 16th Division commander Nakajima.[55]

Another factor was a changing attitude of these military men toward Westerners. They became less and less concerned about their own image in the eyes of Westerners than they had been at the time of the first Sino-Japanese and Russo-Japanese Wars. After the Manchurian Incident and the establishment of Manchukuo, not only the Japanese military personnel but also the Japanese people in general began to feel that they were now completely equal to Westerners. Typically, one contemporary Japanese writer said, "For the first time in history a non-white race has undertaken to carry the white man's burden."[56] Once they felt themselves to be equal to Westerners, instead of continuing to observe Western traditions, Japanese people in general started emphasizing their unique Asian characteristics as opposed to the Occident. In 1935, for example, the foreign office in Tokyo announced that the name "Nippon" was to be preferred to "Japan" as the official name of the country, and "Eastern Asia" to "Far East" as the name of the geographical region where Japan is located.[57] As a consequence, Japanese military men in general began to be more arrogant toward Westerners. Further strengthening such an attitude was the Japanese officers' lack of education in the international field. The Japanese army's cadet school in Tokyo, the Japanese counterpart to West Point, for example, did not provide any course in international relations or international law.[58] The result was the Japanese solders' frequent intrusion into foreign property and their commanding officers' tolerance of such behavior in Nanking.

It was symbolic that General Matsui Iwane was the leader of the Great Asian Society and an advocate of "Asia for the Asiatics." Although Matsui himself, who had participated in the Russo-Japanese War, was concerned about the Japanese army's reputation among Westerners, not all his subordinates shared his concern. Thus, at the heart of the Japanese troops' lack of discipline in Nanking was their lack or loss of incentive to enforce discipline. This happened after they had ceased to be mindful about their own image in the eyes of Westerners and before they would have been able to find or create new incentives. Judging from numerous cases of atrocities committed against allied military and civilian personnel in the Pacific War, one may conclude that they were unable to find a new incentive and that this lack of incentive to enforce discipline plagued the Japanese military through the end of World War II.

Historical Analysis

Many battles on and after December 13 were mostly one-sided, resulting in a near-slaughter by the Japanese. The descriptions of the events in Chapter 3 do not include these military engagements in the category of atrocities since they were the results of lawful military activities. Yet this phase of the Nanking battle is worth examining as a near-atrocity case.

It is possible to attribute these one-sided slaughters to the savage or primitive nature of the Japanese military. One should, however, take into account the circumstances that precipitated such engagements. Since some of the Chinese defenders trying to break the encirclement kept fighting, the final phase of the Nanking campaign became like a siege coming to a violent end. One factor transcending time and place was present: there was no apparent end to the battle for soldiers participating in it. Major General Sasaki's story, in which his soldiers had to kill enemy soldiers due to their sheer number, describes the confusion that marked the end of Nanking's defense as had happened in Port Arthur in 1894. Accounts of the engagements fought by the cavalry of both the SEF and the Tenth Army as well as by the 45th Regiment also support this conclusion. Unlike some siege battles in the past, notably Paris in 1871, however, the Chinese soldiers' attempt to escape from the city spared the civilians remaining in the city from direct military engagement. As for the shooting of fleeing soldiers in the river by some units of the 30th Brigade and the navy, some scholars call it a brutal and inhumane atrocity.[59] For the soldiers who had been pursuing the enemy in a series of fierce battles, however, it was difficult both emotionally and because of operational necessity to cease firing at the enemy even though their opponents were powerless and on the run. Had those killed in such a manner been unarmed civilians clearly distinguishable from military personnel in the eyes of attacking soldiers, it would be easy to classify this action as an atrocity. But this was not the case. For military forces, reduction of the strength of an enemy force that could potentially regroup and turn against them was a justifiable military operation. If one looks for a comparable case, the U.S. and its allies' air campaign against retreating Iraqi forces at the end of the Gulf War may stand as a similar instance. Although the one-sided air attack left the column of Iraqi army's vehicles and soldiers in charred ruins, practically no one has called it an atrocity. Thus, although the Japanese army's military action was a one-sided slaughter, one should regard it as a continuation of military action instead of an atrocity.

Of the three types of atrocities observed over time—massacre, destruction for strategic purposes, and violence attributable to lack of discipline—the Japanese conducted mainly the first and third of these while the Chinese chiefly pursued the second in Nanking. The execution of POWs and plainclothes soldiers belonged in the category of massacre, while numerous criminal acts committed by individual soldiers stemmed from lack of discipline. Fires at the time of the fall of the city were attributable to the scorched-earth strategy of retreating Chinese troops. Although the Japanese had burned villages and houses for strategic or tactical purposes on their way to Nanking, there were few recorded cases of this in the Nanking city proper.

The mass execution of POWs in Nanking was in a sense a unique case in the history of war atrocities. Unlike Paris in 1871 or World War I German atrocities in Belgium, the Japanese military leaders did not have a clear intention to punish or retaliate against the victims. Nor did any ideology or religion contribute to the massacre, unlike other cases in premodern to early modern times. In terms of motive, the closest example might be the Turkish government's persecution of Armenians in a sense that both of them happened due to security or safety concerns—domestic security for the Turks and the safety of military leaders, Prince Asaka in particular, for the Japanese.

Although the Japanese motive was unique, the actual process of catching and executing POWs in Nanking bore a striking resemblance to cases of past history. These previous examples include the rounding up of Communards in Paris in 1871, the Ch'ing troops' hunt for Taiping rebels in 1863, and the German troops' execution of Belgians during World War I. Notably, the Japanese troops tried to identify the plainclothes soldiers in simple and crude ways as the French government force had done in Paris, that is, to look for face and body marks unique to soldiers. The massacre phase of the Rape of Nanking thus exhibited a tendency common in modern war against an "inner front" and was an atrocity attributable "to the discipline rather than the want of discipline." Another episode that attests to the modern counterinsurgency nature of the Japanese military conduct was observable during their search for plainclothes Chinese military men. The Japanese employed a technique that looked very much like a modern-day counterinsurgency operation. The arrest of a Chinese colonel hiding in a refugee camp late in December 1937, for example, was the result of a covert operation conducted by a Chinese officer whom the Japanese had converted into their own spy.[60]

The methods of execution, however, revealed the Japanese military's inefficiency, which is ascribable to its somewhat premodern quality. According to a witness, a group of thirty to forty prisoners, with their hands tied behind their backs, was assembled on the river shore. The Japanese soldiers forced one soldier at a time to walk to the edge of the pier, where a Japanese soldier was waiting to kill him either by shooting or bayoneting. A British observer noted that Japanese soldiers sometimes formed a circle, forced captured Chinese soldiers into that circle, and then bayoneted them all at once. The Japanese troops thus conducted a massacre replete with modern characteristics without the means to carry it out quickly or on a huge scale.[61]

The premodern quality was more evident in the various crimes such as murder, rape, arson, and looting. It was mostly the lack of discipline, a timeless phenomenon, that contributed to the occurrence of individual crimes. Apart from some fires by the Chinese immediately before the fall of Nanking, what actually caused the destruction of the city was mostly carelessness on the part of the conquerors. The Japanese troops were so accustomed to living off the land that even the leadership, which was supposed to tighten discipline among soldiers, turned a blind eye on or even encouraged their robbery-like requisition as medieval military leaders had done. A typical example was the following instruction issued by the 66th Regiment's command on December 13, 1937, prior to its attack on Nanking: "[Each unit] must be especially careful in the maintenance of military discipline and ethics to prevent the arson and robbery. [Soldiers are] never allowed to break into houses *except for those owned by the Chinese.*" [Italics added.][62] Although this wording did not explicitly condone the intrusion into private dwellings, one could interpret it as implicit permission for soldiers to enter the residences inhabited by the Chinese for whatever purposes.

The leadership, which frequently issued directives or warnings concerning discipline, was mindful of the soldiers' conduct to a certain extent. But very often they were not able to enforce discipline due to logistical necessity and subsequently turned a blind eye toward the soldiers' misdeeds. Although the lack of discipline is a timeless factor in the history of war atrocities, at the root of the problem facing the Japanese military leadership was one of the aspects of modern-day total war, that is, the necessity of mobilizing a larger and larger number of men, which resulted in the inclusion of less disciplined men in the ranks. This was especially true among the soldiers assigned to rear duties after the costly Shanghai battle forced the military authorities to fill the depleted ranks with less experienced and disciplined soldiers. The Tenth Army's legal department, which was apparently aware of their presence, held a spiritual education session for these soldiers every morning on board transports bound for China. The result of the education was more or less a disappointment since the legal department's report about two weeks later said, "The discipline of soldiers behind the front is not good."[63] Thus, a dilemma facing almost all modern military leaders also existed among the Japanese leaders, namely that " 'circumstances' made observance of the law difficult or impossible, rather than because men's minds had turned against the idea of the law itself."[64] Yet, some of the "circumstances" the Japanese leaders faced originated from their own decisions, such as the initiation of campaigns without enough preparation. They were at least responsible for these decisions.

NOTES

1. *CDN*, 15 December 1937, p. 1. Nakajima Diary, 19 December 1937, in *NSS*1, p. 332. Lieutenant Colonel Yamazaki of the Tenth Army headquarters mentioned the "aftermath of the looting by the Chinese" in his diary. Yamazaki Diary, 14 December 1937, in ibid., p. 401.

2. Cases of disorder that describe or imply murder in the ICNSZ reports are; no. 1 [6 killed] (*DNSZ*, p. 9); 15 [2] (p. 11); 16 [5] (p. 28); 19 [1] (pp. 18–19); 36 [1], 37 [1] (p. 31); 41 [1], 46 [5] (p. 32); 51 [1] (p. 33); 62 [2] (p. 35); 63 [2] (p. 36); 66 [1] (p. 37); 69 [1] (p. 38); 176 [1] (pp. 64–65); 180 [1]; 181 [3], 182 [1] (p. 77); 185 [1] (p. 78); 188 [1] (pp. 80–81); 195 [1] (p. 94); 215 [1] (p. 120); and 425 [4] (pp. 161–62). In addition, the ICNSZ reported three killed on January 15, 1938. Tsitsa-shan Temple, "Memorandum by Tsitsa-shan Temple," *DNSZ*, no. 60, p. 136. These figures exclude those who were apparently taken away in the course of mopping-up operation. See Appendix D, Tables 1 and 3 for Smythe's data relevant to this paragraph. See Smythe, *War Damage in the Nanking Area*, p. 23, for his reasoning regarding the high death ratio of older women. Yamamoto Shichihei, *Watashi no Naka no Nihongun* [Japanese Military within Myself], vol. 2, (Tokyo: Bungeishunju, 1983), p. 11, tells the following story that might or might not have happened in Nanking. When an old woman crouching on the street of Nanking saw three Japanese soldiers approaching her, probably out of instinct or fear she threw a hand grenade that she had picked up somewhere. The grenade turned out to be a dud and the soldiers were about to stab the woman with their bayonets. At that moment one of them, noticing that she was an old woman, shouted, "Stop it. She is an old lady." Although this is a novel, A Long, *Nanking Tung-k'u* [Nanking Wails], p. 206, also describes a Japanese soldier kneeling in front of a Chinese woman, saying that she was like his mother.

3. Matsui Diary, 15 and 18 December 1937, in *NSS*1, pp. 18, 20. 16th Division, "Jokyo Hokoku" [Situation Report], 24 December 1937, in ibid., p. 577. In his diary of December 27, 16th Division commander Nakajima admitted that his soldiers' behavior was not exemplary: "especially the 33rd Regiment suffered more losses reflecting its aggressiveness on the field and tends to show rough behavior. It seems that [regimental commander] Colonel Noda [Kengo] cannot deal with this problem immediately." Nakajima Diary, 27–31 December 1937, in ibid., p. 339. For the Japanese military leaders' concern about the soldiers' discipline, see also Iinuma Diary, 18 December 1937, in ibid., p. 218; and Uemura Diary, 18 December 1937, in ibid., p. 274.

4. Matsui Diary, 20 December 1937, in *NSS*1, p. 22.

5. Uemura Diary, 16 December 1937, in *NSS*1, p. 272. A similar description regarding soldiers' misbehavior is in the diary entry of December 19. Ibid., p. 275. Smythe to Fukuda, 16 December 1937, in *DNSZ*, no. 7, pp. 7–8. Smythe to Fukuda, "Cases of Disorder by Japanese Soldiers in the Safety Zone," filed, December 16, 1937, in ibid., no. 8, pp. 9–11. Of the 445 cases, *DNSZ* does not list cases nos. 114 through 143, 155 through 164, and 204 through 209. Hirota to Saito, 23 December 1937, Red Machine, no. 1185.

6. CCAA Command, "Nankinjo no Koryaku oyobi Nyujo ni Kansuru Chui Jiko" [Directive Concerning the Military Operation in and Entry to Nanking], in DSKS, vol. 3. 7th Infantry Regiment, "Ho-7 Sakumei Kou" [7th Infantry Regiment's Operation Order] no. 109, 10 P.M., 14 December 1937, quoted in "Hohei Dai-7-Rentai Sento Shoho" [Battle Report of the 7th Infantry Regiment], in *NSS*1, p. 621. 1st Battalion of the 66th Regiment, "Daitai Meirei" [Battalion Order], 2:30 P.M., 12 December 1937, quoted in the battalion's "Sento Shoho" [Battle Report], 10–13 December 1937, in ibid., p. 666. Sasaki Diary, 15 December 1937, in ibid., p. 380. Yamazaki Diary, 16 December 1937, in ibid., p. 405. Oda Diary, 15 December 1937, in ibid., p. 448. An illustration of the soldiers' wish to be rewarded for hard fighting: according to an anonymous private of the 9th Division's 7th Regiment, the soldiers of the 7th Regiment took it for granted that the soldiers of their division would be assigned to police Nanking because they had fought hardest along with the SEF's 16th Division and had broken the Chinese defense first among the Japanese units. They apparently based their expectation on a previous example, that is, that the 3rd Division—the most heavily engaged unit in Shanghai—had assumed the guard duty in Shanghai after the battle. N.Y., "Shonenhei no Shuki: Shoen no Aima nite" [Memoir of First-year Private: Amid Battle Dust], in ibid., p. 494.

7. Sasaki Diary, 15 December 1937, in *NSS*1, p. 380. Kitayama Diary, 13–16 January 1938, in *KS*, p. 76. *NYT*, 18 December 1937, p. 1. Yamazaki Diary, 14 December 1937, in *NSS*1, p. 401. Maeda Diary, 16 December 1937, in *NSS*1, p. 467. Tenth Army's Legal Department, "Dai-10-gun (Yanagawa Heidan) Homubu Jinchu Nisshi" [10th Army (Yanagawa Army Group) Legal Department Record], in *Zoku Gendaishi Shiryo* [Source Materials of Modern History: Second Series], vol. 6, *Gunji Keisatsu* [Military Police]. (Tokyo: Misuzu Shobo, 1982), pp. 112–17. Deputy Minister of the Army to CCAA et al., "Shina Jihen yori Kikansuru Guntai oyobi Gunjin no Gunki Fuki oyobi Keiko Bukken no Shido Torishimari ni Kansuru Ken" [Report about the Morale/Discipline of Troops and Soldiers Returning from China and about the Supervision of Items They Are Carrying to Homeland], 8 April 1938, RMD, 1939, vol. 90, no. 267, MHD. Touching on the specific examples of how reserve soldiers behaved inappropriately, Major General Yamada said, "[reserve soldiers] do not salute; they wear ring, muffler, and weird foot wear around their legs; they neglect to take care of their weapons and uniforms, leaving them rusted or muddy; during march, they stray from marching column without any permission to break into civilian houses and had their bags carried by Chinese civilians, oxen, or carriages while occasionally sitting asleep (almost none of them cross their rifles on the ground); they use their rifle as a balancing pole [to carry things]." Yamada Diary, 24 December 1937, in *NSS*2, p. 334.

8. Smythe to Fukuda, "Cases of Disorder by Japanese Soldiers in the Safety Zone," filed, December 16, 1937, in *DNSZ*, no. 8, pp. 9–11.

9. Kitayama Diary, 16 December 1937, in *KS*, p. 72. Kitayama said that his fellow soldiers also stole beds, other furniture, liquor, sugar, candies, and record players.

10. Sasaki M., *Yasen Yubinki* [Field Postal Flag], p. 224. Nakajima Diary, 19 December 1937, in *NSS*1, pp. 332–33. Uemura Diary, 27 December 1937, in ibid., p. 280. Theft within a unit seems to have been a common practice among the Japanese soldiers. Private Upper Class Makihara of the 16th Division's 20th Regiment said he stole beef and sugar from other company's mess and cooked *sukiyaki*. Makihara Diary, 17 January 1938, in *KS*, p. 158. There was a rumor that the Japanese looted the ancient Chinese cultural treasure left behind in Nanking. *NYT*, 7 January 1938, p. 11. In reality, however, the treasure was undamaged. According to Na Chih-liang, who worked for the Nationalist Government's agency to preserve such cultural assets, he returned to Nanking after the war and found that all the treasure remained intact. Kojima, *Nitchu Senso* [Sino-Japanese War], vol. 5, p. 394. The statistics concerning the damaged and lost properties are from John M. Allison, Third Secretary of the U.S. Embassy in Nanking, to the Secretary of State, "Preliminary Summary of Losses of Families Living in Nanking Now" (henceforth "Preliminary Summary of Losses") in "Losses Suffered in Nanking by Chinese as a Result of Present Hostilities," 28 April 1938, M1513-42. The same survey said that looting by the Japanese accounted for 32 percent while stealing by the Chinese comprised 10 percent of the total. The value of properties stolen by the Chinese was estimated at about 3.6 million yuan, translating into about one million U.S. dollars at the time.

11. The list of items stolen from Bourdrez's residence on the following day includes thirteen bottles of red wine, eight bottles of white wine, four bottles of whisky, and two spring overcoats. The total value he claimed to have lost over the two-day period was $1,052.2. Consul General for the Netherlands in Shanghai to the Japanese Foreign Ministry, "Value of Losses: House Mr. Bourdrez, Shanghai Road 86, Nanking, 24 February 1938," accompanied with Dutch Ministry in Tokyo to Japanese Foreign Minister Ugaki Kazushige, "Nankin Zaiju Orandajin Tonan Jiken ni kansuru 9-gatsu Itsuka zuke Zaikyo Oranda Koshi Hatsu Ugaki Daijin ate Shokan" [A Letter Addressed to (Foreign) Minister Ugaki from the Dutch Ministry in Tokyo Dated September 5 Regarding the Looting Committed against a Dutch Man Living in Nanking], 5 September 1938, in "Shina Jihen: Dai-san-koku-jin Kankei Jiko oyobi Higai Kankei (Hakengun Kodo ni yoru Jiko o Fukumu)" [China Incident: Materials Relating to Incidents Involving Third Countries' Nationals and Damages Suffered by Them (including the incidents caused by the actions of Expeditionary Forces)] (henceforth "Higai Kiroku" [Damage Records]), "Gaimusho Kiroku" [Foreign Ministry Record] (henceforth GK) A110-30-11, Gaiko Shiryokan [Japanese Diplomatic Record office] (henceforth GS).

12. Deutsche Botschaft nach das Kaiserlich Japanische Ministerium der Auswaertigen Angelegenheiten [German Embassy to the Imperial Japanese Ministry of Foreign Affairs], "Verbalnote" [verbal note], 22 June 1938, p. 2, in "Higai Kiroku" [Damage Records] Doitsujin Kankei (2) [Cases Concerning German Nationals (2)], GK A110-30-11, GS.

13. Japanese Foreign Ministry, "A Guideline Regarding the Damage Claim Filed by Third-Country Nationals in the Course of the Sino-Japanese War," 22 November 1937, quoted in "Zai-shi Doitsu-jin Higai Baisho Seikyu ni taisuru Oshu-furi ni Kansuru Ken" [Regarding the Response toward the Compensation Demand for Damages by German Nationals in China], 7 September 1938, in "Higai Kiroku" [Damage Records] Doitsujin Kankei (1) [Cases Concerning German Nationals (1)], GK A110-30-11, GS. Higai Chosashitsu [damage assessment team], "Shina Jihen ni yoru Daisankokujin Higai Anken Kaiketsuhyo" [Charts regarding Solutions to Damages Suffered by Third Countries' Nationals during the Sino-Japanese War], July 1941, in "Higai Kiroku" [Damage Reports],

pp. 22–77, GK A110-30-11, GS. Inoue, chief of the Japanese Foreign Ministry's European and Asian Affairs Department, "Nankin Dokujin Kaoku Higai Mondai tou ni kanshi Zaikyo Doku Taishikan 'Neeberu' Sanjikan Inoue O-a Kyokucho Raidan Yoshi" [Summary of Conversations between Counsel Nebel of the German Embassy in Tokyo and European and Asian Department Chief Inoue about the German Residents' Houses Damaged in Nanking], 25 January 1938, in "Higai Kiroku" [Damage Records] Doitsujin Kankei (1) [Cases Concerning German Nationals (1)], GK A110-30-11, GS. Japanese Foreign Ministry, "Zaikyo Doitsu Taishikan nite Sakusei-seru Zaishi Doitsujin Higaihyo: Nankin ni okeru Higai Jiken" [Table compiled by the German Embassy in Tokyo to list the German individuals who suffered damages in China: Data Concerning Nanking], ibid. Yamashita Tomoyuki, Staff Chief of Hoku Shina Homen-gun [North China Area Army], to Yamawaki Masataka, Deputy Minister of the Army, "Nankin ni okeru Beikokujin no Songai Ichiranhyo Sofu no Ken" [Concerning the sending of the list showing material losses suffered by Americans in Nanking], 21 June 1939, quoting an unidentified source. RMD, 1939, vol. 65, no. 104, MHD. *Ryakudatsu jiken*, meaning "robbery case," is the term used to describe the instances of looting. *Chohatsu jiken* refers to "requisition case" and *higai jiken* can be translated into "damage case."

14. N. T. Johnson, Hankow, to the Secretary of State, 25 December 1937, 793.94/ 11804, in *Foreign Relations of the United States, 1937*, vol. 4, *The Far East*, pp. 414– 15. Also quoted in Hirota to Saito, 26 December 1937, Red Machine, no. 1162. The Japanese version of this report about the Japanese soldiers' intrusion to the U.S. embassy compound is within Gunmuka [Military Affairs Division of the Ministry of Army] to CCAA staff chief, "Nihonhei no Nankin Beikoku Taishikan Shinnyu ni Kansuru Ken" [Concerning Japanese Soldiers' Intrusion into the U.S. Embassy in Nanking] in Rikushi Mitsuden [Army's Secret Telegram to China] no. 753, 28 December 1937, RMD, 1938, vol. 7, no. 114, MHD. The army's report quoted Hidaka Shinrokuro, counsel at the Japanese Consulate in Shanghai, as reporting that the Japanese law enforcement confirmed all the cases except the attempted rape.

15. Colonel Uemura of SEF noted a report, possibly filed by military police, about the Japanese soldiers' theft of nine automobiles belonging to the British embassy, six owned by the U.S. Embassy, and one used by Nanking's self-administrative commission. Uemura Diary, 26 December 1937, in *NSS*1, p. 279. Timperly quoted a Westerner as telling of "three cars stolen from the [embassy] compound and two more this [December 24] morning." Timperly, *Japanese Terror in China*, p. 40. Iinuma Diary, 30 December 1937, in *NSS*1, p. 229.

16. 114th Division, "114-Sakumei Kou" [114th Division's Operation Order] no. 62, 9:30 A.M., 13 December 1937, in *NSS*1, p. 556.

17. Makihara Diary, 17 December 1937, in *KS*, p. 150. Isa Diary, 26 December 1937, in ibid., p. 441.

18. Matsui Diary, 17, 22 December 1937, *NSS*2, pp. 142, 145. Allison to the Secretary of State, "Preliminary Summary of Losses," M1513-42. According to this survey, of the 2,828 buildings damaged in the city's main business streets, those destroyed by military action accounted for only 3 percent, arson 33 percent, and the fire originating from looting 54 percent. Also, see Smythe, *War Damage in Nanking Area*, Table 15.

19. Iinuma Diary, 19 December 1937, in *NSS*1, p. 220.

20. Nakasawa, "Nankin ni okeru Moshiokuri Yoten" [Important Information Given at the Time of Transfer of Command in Nanking], in ibid., p. 581. Yasuyama, Shanhaisen Jugun Nisshi [Diary of the Shanghai Battle], 18 December 1937, in ibid., pp. 531–32.

21. The ICNSZ's plea is in: Foreign Community of Nanking to Japanese Embassy, signed by twenty-two foreigners, 21 December 1937, in *DNSZ*, no. 20, p. 48. Its follow-up report is Fitch et al., "Finding Regarding Burning of Nanking City," 21 December 1937, in ibid., no. 22, p. 52. The Japanese effort to restrain arson is found in CCAA Command, "Nankinjo no Koryaku oyobi Nyujo ni Kansuru Chui Jiko" [Directive Concerning the Military Operation in and Entry to Nanking], in DSKS, vol. 3, in *NSS1*, p. 540. The 9th Division's 6th Brigade repeated the same warning against arson in its order issued on December 13 and obligated its subordinate units to extinguish any fire. "Soto Jisshi ni Kansuru Chui" [Instructions Regarding Mopping-up Operation] in 6th Brigade, "6-Ryo Sakumei Kou" [6th Brigade operation order] no. 138, 4:30 P.M., 13 December 1937, in *NSS1*, p. 551. Iinuma Diary, 24 December 1937, in ibid., p. 225. Maeda Diary, 19 December 1937, in ibid., p. 468. For the descriptions about Chinese arsonists, see Makihara Diary, 17, 21, 26 December 1937, in *KS*, pp. 152–53; Kitayama Diary, 22 December 1937, in ibid., p. 73; and Nakajima Diary, 1 January 1938, in *NSS1*, p. 344. Since Nakajima did not specify any sources of information to substantiate the Chinese responsibility for fire, one may doubt his account. Nakajima, however, frankly recounted his own soldiers' robbery in the previous diary entries. Therefore, if there had been any information suggesting the Japanese soldiers' responsibility for those fires, he would likely have said so. See ibid., 19 December 1937, in *NSS1*, pp. 332–33.

22. *NYT*, 4 January 1938, p. 2. The colonel assumed the post of assistant intendant of the Ginling campus refugee camp. He and other gang members were arrested on December 30, 1938. Tokyo (Hirota) to Washington, 3 January 1938, Red Machine no. 1193B. Also, Smythe, "Memorandum of Interview Regarding Wang Hsing-lung Case," 31 December 1937, in *DNSZ*, no. 28, p. 59, might have dwelt upon a similar incident, judging from its content.

23. Smythe, *War Damages in Nanking Area*, Table 5. Smythe did not provide any data about injuries in the suburban area. The female fatalities in the same age group in the said area, however, represented only 11 percent of the total. He reasoned that "more of the younger women migrated in search of safety or were kept out of harm's way in times of obvious danger." Ibid., p. 23 and Table. 24.

24. Tanabe to 18th and 101 Division Chiefs, et. al, "Koshu Senryo ni Tomonau Chitsujo Iji oyobi Haishuku tou ni Kansuru Ken" [About the Maintenance of Order and Arranging of Accommodation Following the Occupation of Hangchou], 20 December 1937, DSKS, vol. 3.

25. Smythe to Fukuda, "Cases of Disorder by Japanese Soldiers in the Safety Zone," filed 16 December 1937, in *DNSZ*, no. 8, p. 10; "Cases of Disorder by Japanese Soldiers in the Safety Zone," filed 19 December 1937, in ibid., no. 15, pp. 28, 33. Smythe to Japanese Embassy, "Cases of Disorder by Japanese Soldiers in the Safety Zone," filed 21 December 1937, in ibid., no. 19, p. 46; "Cases of Disorder by Japanese soldiers in the Safety Zone," filed 26 December 1937, in ibid., no. 25, p. 54.

26. Testimony of Fujita Kiyoshi in "SNS" (6), *Kaiko*, September 1984, p. 6. Oda Diary, 17 December 1937, in *NSS1*, p. 448. Testimony of Onishi Hajime in "SNS" (8), *Kaiko*, November 1984, p. 9.

27. Bates to unidentified addressees, 10 January 1938, enclosed to N. T. Johnson to the Secretary of State, 11 February 1938, p. 2,793.94/12728, M976–52. Also, IMTFE, pp. 2,634, 4,594. International Prosecution Document (IPS) 4039; Court Exhibit (CE) 329. Smythe, *War Damage in Nanking Area*, p. 7. Smythe estimates the population in Nanking at 200,000 to 250,000, of which female population accounted for 102,000 to

127,500 based on the sex ratio of 103.4 (females per 100 males). The females between fifteen and forty-nine years old constituted 49.8 percent of the total and thus numbered 55,080 to 68,850. Eight percent of this numerical range will be 4,063.68 to 5,079.6, which can be rounded into 4,000 to 5,000. Ibid., p. 4 and Table 2.

28. Iinuma Diary, 19 December 1937, in *NSS*1, p. 220. The military authority did not open the brothel until January 1938. A soldier of the 16th Division's medical unit noted the inauguration of a brothel in which seventy prostitutes welcomed 500 soldiers on January 1. Ueba Diary, 1 January 1938, *KS*, p. 32. According to another private diary, Japanese soldiers in Nanking cheered wildly at a parade of prostitutes on board five trucks running on the city's streets in mid-January. Several days later, there was an announcement that the entertaining facilities were ready. Azuma Memoir, in *KS*, p. 310.

29. Hirota to Saito, 23 December 1937, Red Machine, no. 1185. Tenth Army Command, Tei-shu Sakumei Gogai [Tenth Army Operation Order extra], 9 A.M., 15 December 1937, DSKS, vol. 3. Iinuma Diary, 6 January 1938, in *NSS*1, p. 234. Tsukada Osamu, CCAA Staff Chief, to Umezu Yoshijiro, Deputy Army Minister, "Chu-Shina Haken Kenpeitai no Hensei Haichi oyobi Fukumu ni Kansuru Ken Hokoku" [Report Concerning the Formation, Deployment, and Jurisdiction of CCAA Military Police], 12 January 1938, RMD, 1938, vol. 2, no. 97. Uemura Diary, 8 January 1938, in *NSS*1, p. 287.

30. Iinuma Diary, 21, 26 January 1938, in *NSS*1, pp. 240, 242. Smythe, "Notes on Present Situation," 22 January 1938, in *DNSZ*, no. 48, p. 95. Uemura Diary, 29 January 1938, in *NSS*1, p. 295. Hata, *Nankin Jiken* [Nanking Incident], p. 178.

31. Tsukada, CCAA Staff Chief, to Deputy Army Minister and Deputy Chief of General Staff, "Shoshu Kenpei Kashikanhei no Kyuyo ni Kansuru Ken" [Regarding the Payment to Noncommissioned Military Police Officers], 31 January 1938, RMD, 1938, vol. 11, no. 33. CCAA command, "Chu Shina Hakengun Kenpeitai Fukumukitei" [CCAA Military Police Regulations], in "Chu-Shina Haken Kenpeitai no Hensei Haichi oyobi Fukumu ni Kansuru Ken Hokoku" [Report Concerning the Formation, Deployment, and Jurisdiction of CCAA Military Police], 12 January 1938, RMD, 1938, vol. 2 no. 97.

32. Kuo-min Cheng-fu [Nationalist Government], "Nanking Ta-t'u-sha Shi-chien Pei-hai Jen-min Hsiang-piao" [Table of Rape of Nanking Individual Victims] in "Kuo-min Cheng-fu Chu-hsi Hsiang-yuan Mi-shu-ch'u Chih Szu-fa Hsing-cheng-pu Han" [Correspondence from the Secretary's Office of the National Government's General Secretary to the Ministry of Justice], 17 January 1946, in *HP*, pp. 485–507.

33. In the first reference to the size of the population in the city, the ICNSZ said, "It is hard to see how starvation may be prevented among many of the 200,000 Chinese civilians if order is not restored at once among the Japanese soldiers in the city." Rabe to Japanese Embassy, December 17, 1937, in *DNSZ*, no. 9, p. 17. Another letter to Japanese Embassy, December 18, 1937, also cited the same figure. Rabe to Japanese Embassy, in ibid., no. 10, p. 18. So did Rabe to Japanese Embassy, 27 December 1937, in ibid., no. 26, p. 57. The committee revised the figure to "250,000 to 300,000" in Rabe to Fukuda, 14 January 1938, in ibid., no. 41, p. 84. The number stood at 250,000 in the next letter on January 17 (Rabe to Japanese Embassy, 17 January 1938, in ibid., no. 43, p. 86) and remained at that level through Smythe, "Memorandum on Relief Problems," 10 February 1938, which made the final reference to the city's population as being numbered 250,000. Ibid., no. 68, p. 164.

34. *NYT*, 18 December 1937, p. 10.

35. CCAA Command, "Nankinjo no Koryaku oyobi Nyujo ni Kansuru Chui Jiko"

[Directive Concerning the Operation in and Entry to Nanking], DSKS, vol. 3, in *NSS*1, p. 540.

36. Matsui Diary, 15 December 1937, in ibid., p. 18.

37. Rikugun Hohei Gakko [Army's Infantry School], "Tai-Shina-Gun Sento-ho no Kenkyu" [How to Fight the Chinese Military], 1933, quoted in Yoshida, *Tenno no Guntai to Nankin Jiken* [Emperor's Military and the Nanking Incident], p. 45.

38. Joseph Clark Grew, *Report from Tokyo: A Message to the American People* (New York: Simon and Schuster, 1942), pp. 29–30.

39. *NYT*, 6 January 1938, p. 6. Kobayashi, ed., *Sakigake* [Harbingers], pp. 577–80.

40. Iinuma Diary, 14–15 December 1937, in *NSS*1, pp. 215–16. Uemura Diary, 16 December 1937, in ibid., p. 272.

41. Matsui Diary, 16 December 1937, in *NSS*1, pp. 18–19.

42. Nakajima Diary, 15 December 1937, in *NSS*1, p. 328. Matsui Diary, 4 December 1937, in ibid., p. 14.

43. Testimony of Sakakibara Kazue in "SNS" (11), *Kaiko*, February 1985, p. 8.

44. Hanekura Shoro, "Watashi no Mita Nankin Kanraku Zengo" [My Observation of Nanking Before and After Its Fall], *Kaiko*, June 1983, p. 19.

45. Sasaki Diary, 13 December 1937, in *NSS*1, p. 378. Miyamoto Diary, 14 December 1937, in *NDKK*, p. 133.

46. Hata, *Nankin Jiken* [Nanking Incident], pp. 143–44, and Hora, *Ketteiban: Nankin Daigyakusatsu* [Nanking Massacre: Definitive Version], p. 34, are examples of those that strongly suspect Colonel Cho's active involvement in the massacre.

47. Morozumi Memoir, in *NSS*2, p. 339.

48. 30th Infantry Brigade "Hohei Dai-30-Ryodan Meirei" [30th Brigade order], 4:50 a.m., 14 December 1937, in *NSS*1, p. 545.

49. Unidentified source quoted in *NEM*, p. 273. The original Japanese phrase corresponding to "in some way or the other" is *tekito ni*.

50. In his book, historian Hata Ikuhiko enumerated seventeen cases of prisoner execution, quoting from eyewitness accounts, while discussing other major cases, such as the massacre near the Mufu Mountain, in other parts of the book. Among those seventeen, thirteen were about the killing of less than 200. Hata, *Nankin Jiken* [Nanking Incident], p. 139.

51. Maruyama Masao, *Thought and Behavior in Modern Japanese Politics*, ed. Ivan Morris (New York: Oxford University Press, 1969), p. 19.

52. Inada Masazumi, "Shina Jihen Senso Shido Kankei Shiryo" [Reflection on Strategic Planning during the China Incident], pp. 38–39.

53. Chiang Kung-yi, "Hsian-ching San-yueh-chi" [Three Months in Fallen Capital] in *SL*, p. 77. Rabe to Japanese Embassy, "Cases of Disorder by Japanese Soldiers in Safety Zone," filed 20 December 1937, in *DNSZ*, no. 17, p. 43. Rabe to Japanese Embassy, "Cases of Disorder by Japanese Soldiers in the Safety Zone," filed 4 January 1938, in ibid., no. 32, p. 65.

54. V. Lee Hamilton and Joseph Sanders, *Everyday Justice: Responsibility and the Individual in Japan and the United States* (New Haven: Yale University Press, 1992), pp. 130, 134.

55. For a brief description of Choshu's dominance of the army, see Hillis Lory, *Japan's Military Masters: The Army in Japanese Life* (Westport, CT: Greenwood Press, 1943), pp. 153–56. See ibid., pp. 156–59, 173–98, for a summary of factional strife within the Japanese army. At the time of the First Sino-Japanese War, Yamagata Aritomo

was the commander of the First Army, which was advancing to Manchuria through the Korean peninsula. Although the central command in Tokyo decided not to launch a winter campaign in the First Army's operation theater in late 1894, Yamagata was eager to march to Peking and ordered his troops to advance without any authorization from Tokyo late in November. The central high command did not dismiss Yamagata outright to save his face. Instead, Emperor Meiji issued an edict to summon Yamagata on the pretext of the latter's illness. Fujimura, *Nisshin Senso* [Sino-Japanese War], pp. 129–31.

56. K. K. Kawakami, *Manchoukuo* [sic]: *Child of Conflict* (New York: Macmillan, 1933), p. vi.

57. Arthur Morgan Young, *Imperial Japan, 1926–1938* (Westport, CT: Greenwood Press, 1974), p. 250. Some Western sources called this idea an "Asiatic Monroe Doctrine." For example, see Crowley, *Japan's Quest for Autonomy*, p. 188.

58. Lory, *Japan's Military Master*, p. 99.

59. Some of the examples of such interpretations are Yoshida, *Tenno no Guntai to Nankin Jiken* [Emperor's Military and the Nanking Incident], pp. 107–10. Idem, "15-nen Sensoshi Kenkyu to Senso Sekinin Mondai: Nankin Jiken o Chushin ni" [Academic and War Responsibility Issues Concerning the 15-Year War, the Nanking Incident in Particular], in *Nankin Jiken o Kangaeru* [Analyses of Nanking Incident], ed. Fujiwara Akira, Honda Katsuichi, and Hora Tomio (Tokyo: Otsuki Shoten, 1987, henceforth *NJK*), p. 84. Kasahara Tokushi, "Nankin Boeigun no Hokai kara Gyakusatsu made" [From the Collapse of Nanking Garrison to Massacre], in *NDG*, p. 104. Yoshida, "Nankin Jiken to Kokusaiho" [Nanking Incident and International Law], in *NDK*, p. 114.

60. Hirota to Saito, 3 January 1938, Red Machine, no. 1193B.

61. Testimony of Ishimatsu Masatoshi, adjutant of the 2nd Field Anti-Aircraft Artillery Unit in "SNS" (11) *Kaiko*, February 1985, pp. 9–10. K. G. Kagan, Major, U.S. Marine Corps, Assistant Naval Attaché, "Resume of the Political-Military Situation: Shanghai-Nanking-Hangchou Area," 11–20 January 1938, pp. 5–6, M976–52, quoting a British Embassy source.

62. 1st Battalion of the 66th Infantry Regiment, "Sento Shoho" [Battle Report], MHD.

63. Tenth Army's Legal Department, "Dai-10-gun (Yanagawa Heidan) Homubu Jinchu Nisshi" [10th Army (Yanagawa Army Group) Legal Department Record], pp. 16, 36.

64. Best, *Humanity in Warfare*, p. 83.

5

Aftermath and Reaction
until 1945

JAPAN

Some researchers claim that Japanese military leaders deliberately allowed their soldiers to misbehave in Nanking.[1] In their diaries, however, the ranking military personnel of the CCAA, the SEF, and the Tenth Army lamented the crimes committed by their soldiers. Among these leaders, SEF deputy staff chief Uemura noted in his diary that the soldiers' correspondence contained exaggerated accounts of what happened and sometimes included altogether erroneous information about events that did not occur.[2] The Japanese army's report about the soldiers returning from China gave some examples of such stories found in soldiers' letters:

Several [Japanese] soldiers have been killed by the Chinese when they attempted to rape Chinese women.

Japanese military men are pardoned even if they commit robbery, rape, or arson.

Soldiers can obtain Chinese golden or silver coins and make purchases using them because their superiors usually overlook such transactions.

Soldiers do not have trouble in finding food since they are allowed to requisition food freely when they are not in military action.[3]

Although one could discount the truthfulness of these remarks as Uemura suggested, a glimpse at a table of items confiscated from these returnees from China compels one to accept at least some of these stories at face value, especially those about theft. According to the table, the military police seized a total of 23,720 items from returning soldiers from December 28, 1937, to March 15,

1938. They included 2,082 items of jewelry, 2,816 pieces of art and furniture, 3,186 items of clothing, and 7,416 pornographic photos.[4]

The stories of disorder in Nanking, symbolized by these data, reached the high command in Tokyo and prompted the chief of the army's General Staff to issue a directive calling for the enforcement of tighter discipline among the troops. In the directive addressed to the CCAA commander on January 4, General Prince Kan'in Kotohito said, "It is beyond doubt that there were many cases of shameful misconduct due to the lack of discipline and morale." Prince Kan'in then advised the local military commanders to restrain the licentious acts committed by soldiers so that the Japanese army could impress the enemy and third countries alike and acquire the confidence of the local population.[5]

Actually, the lack of discipline was evident not only among ordinary soldiers but also within the military leadership. Lieutenant General Nakajima, the 16th Division chief, apparently had some art pieces he had found in Nanking shipped out to the homeland when his division was ordered to move out from Nanking. CCAA chief Matsui expressed his disgust at Nakajima and instructed the checking of soldiers' personal belongings, and possibly of Nakajima himself, so that they could not carry out any items stolen in Nanking.[6] Nakajima, however, retorted, "Why does the stealing of art pieces matter so much when we are stealing a country and human lives? Who would benefit from these items even if we left them behind?"[7]

Matsui, who was apparently ashamed of these disgraceful acts perpetrated by a person in a leadership position, rebuked the subordinate commanders at the memorial service held for the deceased soldiers in Nanking on February 7. In what *New York Times* correspondent Hallett Edward Abend called an "extraordinary address" in a cold, windswept parade ground, Matsui said that "It was absolutely necessary . . . to put an immediate end to adverse reports about the discipline and conduct of Japanese troops toward Chinese people and Chinese property, and exemplary discipline was particularly necessary in view of the fact that the Japanese Army was facing the prospect of prolonged hostilities before successfully achieving Japan's mission in East Asia."[8] According to Matsui's recollection after the war, however, many commanders did not take his words seriously and one divisional commander, probably Nakajima, even said, "What's wrong about it?"[9]

Strained personal relations among these leaders aggravated the discipline problem. Although it is not unusual for ranking generals to have a certain degree of animosity among themselves, the relationships among the Japanese military leaders in Nanking were somewhat extraordinary. Prior to the Nanking campaign, there was already a rumor about discord between Matsui and Yanagawa. The victory in Nanking did not improve the situation. Colonel Uemura, for example, recorded a heated argument between two ranking SEF generals at a party table in the presence of SEF chief Prince Asaka. Although Uemura kept their identities anonymous, judging from the diary's contents and the last name initials Uemura used, one can identify these two as Nakajima and one of his brigade commanders Sasaki. Uemura added that Sasaki "went so excessively" in his conversation with Nakajima, Sasaki's superior, that Prince Asaka scolded him in the end. The relations between Matsui and Nakajima had already been strained before they came to China. They had nurtured a strong animosity toward each other since they had exchanged harsh words over the phone in Tokyo earlier that same year over a political issue. Nakajima on the one hand referred to Matsui in his diary as a "person concerned with trivial things" when Matsui rebuked him over the stealing of art pieces. Matsui on the other hand said in his own diary, "His [Nakajima's] remarks were insulting *just as usual*." [italics added.] Prince Asaka also expressed to Matsui his disgust at Nakajima's behavior as a "source of discipline problems." Such strained personal relations among the Japanese military leaders were rumored so widely that even the Westerners obtained information pertinent to these problems as early as the end of December 1937.[10]

The General Staff in Tokyo also sensed something extraordinary and sent an envoy led by Major General Honma Masaharu, then chief of the General Staff's Second Bureau, to central China late in January. The envoy visited CCAA and SEF headquarters ostensibly only for liaison purposes, but in reality Honma intended to investigate some incidents committed against Westerners in the Nanking area. Naturally, Honma and his entourage learned about what had happened in Nanking through their own investigation. Lieutenant Colonel Inada Masazumi, who accompanied Honma, noted in his personal report that the Japanese troops committed not only a slaughter of mass scale on the pretext of lack of supply or for the purpose of preventing the enemy's "guerrilla" activities but also robbery and arson incessantly immediately following the occupation. It is not clear whether Honma reported such an observation to Tokyo or whether the envoy's opinion influenced the army high command's subsequent decisions. Even before Honma's return to Tokyo, General Hata Shunroku, the Army's Superintendent of Education, suggested to General Sugiyama Hajime, Minister of the Army, that Matsui be recalled to Japan along with the reserve and rear reserve soldiers of his units in view of "quite a few disgusting cases deriving from a lack of discipline, robbery, and rape." The army leadership accepted his proposal and named Hata as the successor to Matsui and on February 15 ordered Matsui to return to Japan. The high command relieved not only Matsui but also SEF chief Prince Asaka and Tenth Army commander Yanagawa at the same time.[11]

One may conclude that one of the reasons why the high command decided to replace Matsui was the slack discipline of his soldiers. But there is no indication that the high command or any other Japanese leaders censured CCAA generals, including Matsui, for their soldiers' discipline problems. In describing the occasion when Matsui, Yanagawa, and Prince Asaka had an audience with Emperor Hirohito on February 26, Matsui only noted, "We received gracious words from His Majesty."[12] The major reason for the reshuffling of local commands was apparently the lack of harmony among these leaders. General Hata quoted Army Minister Sugiyama as saying,

Three army commands in central China are expressing their own opinions contradicting each other at their own will: Matsui . . . recently said he would better serve as an administrator in the occupied area and proposed to establish a provisional government in central China, which should take over the administration in the north . . . Yanagawa's command, without ever thinking about the provisional government, wanted to shift main troops to the north by leaving behind only about three divisions in central China; the headquarters of the Prince [Asaka] was of the opinion that the army should continue the on-going operation in the Yangtze area.[13]

Another reason for the reshuffling was Matsui's keen interest in political affairs, especially in the Shanghai area. After the Japanese troops drove the Chinese forces from Shanghai, Matsui declared himself "the master of all of Shanghai" and said that he would not refrain from taking complete control of the International Settlement in the city. In an interview with a Japanese magazine, Matsui went so far as to say that he did not recognize the neutrality of foreign settlements, and he would like to see China's sovereignty exercised over them. That "he made no attempt to conceal his anti-foreign views" angered the Westerners and gave them the impression that Matsui was "a law unto himself." Probably aware of such foreign sentiments, the Japanese vice foreign minister, commenting on the reshuffling of military leadership, said that Hata, who was Matsui's successor as CCAA commander, was a good soldier and less interested in politics than Matsui.[14] Another possible concern for the Japanese leadership in Tokyo was Matsui's propensity for independent military action. Matsui apparently proposed to the General Staff another military campaign to solidify the CCAA's gain, but the General Staff rejected his proposal. According to his diary, Matsui was extremely frustrated and lamented the "lack of guts among the military planners who were not familiar with the overall situation." When he spoke to his staff members prior to his departure for Japan, Matsui said, "Depending on the situation, we cannot rule out the possibility that the army has to conduct operations by overriding the instruction to be given by the high command in Tokyo."[15] Thus, one may compare the recall of Matsui from China in 1938 to that of Douglas MacArthur from Korea in 1951.

The Japanese diplomatic service was more alarmed than the military leaders at the reports of atrocities because the diplomats had to receive and respond to the complaints filed by other countries about the Japanese soldiers' violation of foreign interests in Nanking. Initially, the Japanese foreign office, most likely having consulted with the military command, justified such violations by emphasizing the illegal methods of warfare employed by the Chinese army such as the misuse of foreign flags.[16] Some diplomats were, however, deeply ashamed of the behavior of their own countrymen in China. Ishii Itaro, Director of the

Japanese Foreign Ministry's East Asian Affairs Bureau, said in his diary on January 6, 1938: "I received a message from Shanghai reporting about the violent behavior of our own troops. The message said that the extent of robbery and rape was too intense to keep looking at. Alas! Is this what His Majesty's army is? This is a serious social problem since it shows the degradation of the Japanese people's moral standard."[17]

On January 15, Ishii was visited by Eugene H. Dooman, Counselor of the U.S. Embassy in Tokyo, who wanted to discuss how Japanese soldiers had gained forcible entry to American property in Nanking. According to a U.S. document, Ishii heard Dooman's representation "with repeated exclamations of dismay." Ishii had a lasting negative image about his own country's military. At the Tokyo War Crimes Trial, he provided testimony more beneficial to the prosecution than to the defense, although he testified as a defense witness. Apart from Ishii, however, most Japanese diplomats who received the reports of the Japanese army's disorder in Nanking dismissed them as exaggerated. Yet Japanese Foreign Ministry officials apparently felt the need to launch a propaganda campaign to counter Japan's negative image in the wake of such incidents. They hired an American cameraman in the spring of 1938 to help the Japanese foreign office initiate a propaganda program to foster a better image of Japan in the United States.[18]

Meanwhile, the discipline of Japanese soldiers in Nanking had apparently improved by early February. The Associated Press (AP), in a dispatch from Shanghai on February 10, quoted a Japanese diplomat as saying that more than ten Japanese soldiers had been court-martialed and punished for breaches of military discipline at Nanking. One cannot ascertain, however, to what extent the court-martialing of offenders contributed to the improvement of military discipline in Nanking because the SEF court-martial record, which ought to contain most of criminal cases in Nanking, is still missing—most likely having been destroyed at the end of World War II. Judging from the available legal documents of the Tenth Army and the CCAA, however, the punishment offenders received must have been lukewarm at best. In the criminal cases committed and tried either before or after the occupation of Nanking, for example, the Tenth Army's legal department sentenced three reserve soldiers of a supply unit to one year in prison for arson; a private of a rear reserve unit to one and a half years for the murder of a Chinese woman; and a rear reserve private to four years for the murder of a Chinese man and the rape of his wife. These sentences were obviously milder compared with the sentences handed down in the cases of soldiers who committed infractions of internal army discipline, such as the five and a half years' imprisonment given a private who threatened his superior and injured a horse; and the four years plus fifteen-yen fine to a reserve private for gambling and displaying a rebellious attitude toward his superior. Moreover, military judges often acquitted defendants or reduced their prison terms in consideration of certain circumstances. A CCAA court-martial record, which contains verdicts and sentences handed down after the occupation of Nanking, shows that a civilian employed by the CCAA's special service unit was acquitted of a robbery charge because his crime was motivated merely by a momentous ill will; he repented his conduct deeply and most of the items he stole were worthless because they had already been damaged or too dirty. In a rape case the CCAA court tried, a defendant was given a suspended sentence of two years in prison due to the "purely accidental" nature of the crime and also because the victim did not resist the attack. Judges also gave lighter penalties when other factors were involved, such as drunkenness—a behavior Japanese society in general was, and still is, tolerant of—and a defendant's low education level.[19]

Whatever the reason, the improvement of discipline prompted the ICNSZ to rename itself the Nanking International Relief Committee on February 18. ICNSZ members said that new name should be more in conformity with the committee's purposes and suggested that the committee's activities were now shifting from the maintenance of the safety and security of the Chinese citizens or refugees to providing food and other daily necessities to them. Still, criminal activities did not cease entirely. Prior to his return to Japan, Matsui told his successor Hata that the troops should be camped in a way to reduce their contact with the ordinary Chinese people and maintain their discipline. Possibly because of this measure, a U.S. military intelligence report said that Chinese civilians were returning to their homes from the Safety Zone by mid-March 1938. The same report, however, sarcastically described the degree of improvement in discipline by observing that the number of rapes and assaults on civilians had been reduced to only two or three each daily. It was, however, possible that some of these crimes were committed by the Chinese since Smythe said that, beginning early in January, looting and robbery by Chinese civilians gradually developed.[20]

One of the few Japanese military men who criticized the incident openly at the time was Major General Ishiwara, chief of the Planning Bureau of the Japanese army's General Staff prior to the commencement of the Nanking campaign and later vice chief of staff of the Kwantung Army. In an interview with *Chicago Daily News* correspondent Steele in early 1938, Ishiwara said that Matsui was completely responsible for the troops' behavior and added that the morale of the Japanese had never been at a lower level.[21] Yet such an opinion was a lone voice among most other Japanese military men, who regarded the POW executions as an extension of lawful military activity and overlooked the soldiers' misbehavior to a certain extent.

Censorship was one of the reasons why ordinary Japanese people could not obtain information about the atrocities in Nanking. Ishikawa Tatsuzo, a writer, accompanied the Japanese troops to Nanking and later wrote a novel based on his experiences and interviews with soldiers. The novel was full of what looked like soldiers' atrocious deeds in battles leading to the occupation of Nanking. When he published a part of the novel in a magazine under the title of *Ikiteiru Heitai* [Living Soldiers] in February 1938, the government censored his work and put him on trial. He was convicted and sentenced to four months in prison with a three-year suspension. As for the information originating from foreign sources, a British woman arranged to have motion picture films taken in Nanking by a U.S. Episcopal Church mission shown to some Japanese Christians sometime in 1938–39. She, however, did not pursue that project further because of concerns about what might happen to those who viewed the film.[22]

The Japanese military leadership tried to prevent the recurrence of similar incidents, but their efforts were not effective enough. When Japanese troops marched into the city of Hsuchou, Kiangsu Province, in May 1938, they entered the city in an orderly manner, according to an eyewitness. Japanese soldiers, however, immediately started engaging in disorderly acts. A U.S. diplomatic report, quoting a missionary's account, described their activities as a duplication of the "orgy of looting, raping, drinking and murder which marked the entry of the Japanese forces into Nanking." The atrocities in Hsuchou were apparently not as extensive as those in Nanking since another report said that discipline and order were rigorously maintained after the first day. Still, this instance illustrates the Japanese way of military occupation: they could not complete the occupation without misbehavior.[23]

Japanese military leaders did tighten discipline when they were about to capture bigger cities where a substantial number of foreigners were living. When the Japanese army was about to march into the tri-cities of Wuchang, Wuhu, and Hankow—the last of which was a Nationalist government stronghold at the time—in October 1938, the staff chief of the Eleventh Army in charge of the operation issued a directive to prevent the occurrence of soldiers' misdeeds "in view of the bitter experience in Nanking, where the lawlessness following its capture caused many cases of disgraceful acts." The directive cautioned that soldiers were likely to commit robbery, arson, and rape a few days after the occupation of a city rather than immediately following the capture, and ordered the subordinate commanders to punish severely and without mercy those who would dare to commit these crimes in order to preserve the honor of the Japanese army.[24] That effort apparently paid off because third-party reports described the Japanese occupation of these cities as mostly "orderly."[25] One report specifically stated that "no reports have been received to indicate that the Japanese taking Hankow behaved in anything like the scandalous manner which brought such odium upon them after their entry into Nanking."[26]

The leadership's effort to discipline the soldiers, however, did not affect all troops all the time because even the relatively peaceful occupation of these cities was not without incident. A missionary in Hankow counted one case of murder and several instances of rape, while Wuchang witnessed the looting of buildings, including the American church mission. A similar pattern repeated itself in Canton, which fell into Japanese hands in the same month. Overall, the Japanese behavior in Canton was as good as could be expected, according to a U.S. observer. Nevertheless, the Japanese troops looted houses in a part of the city, using Chinese coolies to carry away the loot, although they did not violate properly marked foreign properties.[27]

Statistics reveal that the number of criminal acts committed and reported to the CCAA command declined from 776 in 1938 to 452 in 1939, and to 335 in 1940. It is likely, however, that these figures represented merely a fraction of the whole. One impression is that in 1938 and thereafter, Japanese atrocities became more rampant in rural areas than in big cities. A report from the American Consulate General in Hankow under the Japanese occupation, for example, suggests that the people living in the countryside suffered greatly, probably because the leadership's disciplinary measures were effective only in the urban area. The report quoted an anonymous American as saying that Japanese soldiers often held up farmers on their way back from market to rob them of money, while killing farm animals for food and for unknown reasons. It also told the story of 300 to 400 women taking refuge in a missionary compound when the Japanese troops passed through the area. There was a report about many cases of rape by Japanese soldiers in the southern suburb of Canton while the relatively orderly occupation of the city itself was progressing. Yet another report describing the situation in Shantung quoted an unidentified American as saying that "the continuing atrocities there [Shantung] are on a par with those committed in Nanking in the early days of Japanese occupation."[28]

The increase in atrocities in rural areas reflected not only the declining morale or discipline of Japanese soldiers but also the nature of the war being fought after the fall of Nanking. Although they were witnessing similar kinds of atrocities, contemporary observers apparently detected a change in the nature of the Japanese military's conduct. One military analyst in early 1938, for example, attributed the cause of the Rape of Nanking to Japanese frustration at Chinese resistance. An implication was that this analyst saw no deliberate planning in the execution of atrocities in Nanking. As the war went on, a different analysis of Japanese atrocities committed thereafter in China emerged. A U.S. diplomat in North China in July 1938 described the Japanese military's conduct in the countryside as "a definite policy of destruction," whose purpose was to deny local support to irregular troops. The difference between the two analyses reflected the reality. In the course of fighting guerrilla warfare, there was a mutual escalation of cruelty. A U.S. military intelligence report late in 1938 touched on this mutual escalation and said in a general comment about the Sino-Japanese War that "neither side takes prisoners." Japanese troops repeatedly executed regular and irregular soldiers as well as many able-bodied males, although in many cases on a much smaller scale than in Nanking. Unlike the Japanese military commanders in Nanking, who seemingly had a certain degree of hesitation in executing Chinese POWs, the Japanese military operating in China thereafter was determined to carry out a policy of terror to suppress Chinese resistance. Thus, Japanese conduct after the Nanking incident resembled German atrocities in Belgium during World War I in terms of both the motive and nature of the conduct. The Japanese, for example, rounded up eighty-two men in Hsuchou and apparently executed them; only one survived, who was hospitalized for the treatment of his bayonet wound and severe burns. In the course of such counterinsurgency warfare, civilians became military targets as well. In early 1939 a local Japanese military commander in Shantung issued a notice threatening to burn entire villages and kill all able-bodied men if these villages harbored Nationalist or communist guerrillas. The most extensive of such campaigns targeted at civilians took place in the spring of 1942 when the Japanese troops marched into the Chinese-controlled Kiangsi Province in search of the crewmen of James H. Doolittle's squadron, which had bombed Tokyo and several other Japanese cities and landed on Chinese soil in April the same year. Based on a population census, an American eyewitness estimated that the Japanese killed about 10,000 out of one million residents in the area.[29]

CHINA

An immediate effect of the Nanking battle on Chinese Nationalist military forces was the disintegration of their troops and their loss of cohesion.[30] Chiang Kai-shek, who had decided on the almost hopeless defense of Nanking, apparently learned a bitter lesson and became determined not to repeat his mistake. As the Japanese were expected to advance to the Wuhan area, Chiang issued the following directive regarding the anticipated battle in Wuhan: "it would be a mistake to risk the loss of the whole of, or the great part of, the Chinese Army in a defense which might end in defeat; but he [Chiang] must withdraw his best troops and equipment before the Japanese can succeed in endangering their safety."[31]

When the Japanese troops were closing in on the Wuhan area, especially Hankow, its garrison commander Kuo Ch'an ordered the complete withdrawal of the Chinese troops from the city in compliance with Chiang's warning. The reason was to prevent the recurrence of the Nanking atrocities, which the Japanese committed in the name of hunting down plainclothes former soldiers. This shows that the Chinese side also understood, at least initially, that one of the causes of the atrocities was the nature of the war in China—that is, that civilians and military men were often indistinguishable from each other.[32]

The Chinese reaction to the Rape of Nanking was generally slow, partly because after their retreat inland they could obtain information about the atrocities only through Western sources. Chinese Vice Minister of Information Tung Hsien-kuang, known as Hollington K. Tong to Westerners, said in his memoir written after the war that the Chinese authorities did not report the incident, not only because foreign correspondents and other foreigners in Nanking would give firsthand accounts, but also because what the Chinese government would say might be discounted as coming from a biased source. The reality was, however, that the Chinese did have their own information channels and began their media reporting about the incident at an early date. On December 23, 1937, the *Hankow Chung-hsi-pao*, or the *Hankow Midwestern Times*, quoted a Central News Agency dispatch as saying that the Japanese had killed 50,000 men in four days. The same article also mentioned the Japanese troops' rounding up and executing of adult males in the Safety Zone in the course of catching former soldiers. Underlining this reporting, a Chinese Nationalist government source later said that the Japanese massacred as many as 60,000 to 70,000 men when the Chinese garrison retreated. These figures apparently referred to military-related casualties since the same report noted separately that "civilian victims amounted to several thousand in the initial few days." Mayling Soong Chiang, or Madame Chiang Kai-shek, also shared this view. In her letter to an American friend on January 5, 1938, she described "the slaughter" in Nanking as the "shooting [of] all able-bodied men, singly and in batches." Therefore, the initial Chinese reports told mainly about the massacre of military men, the first phase of the Rape of Nanking, as did Western news correspondents such as Durdin and Steele.[33]

Thereafter, their coverage began to touch on numerous criminal activities— the atrocities in the second phase—apparently based on information from Western sources since their initial reports were about the Westerners in Nanking. The *Hsin-hua Jih-pao* or the *New China Daily*, for example, quoted a Central News Agency dispatch on January 22, 1938, as saying that the Japanese army in Nanking insulted the American flag as many as fifteen times and intruded into American church missions. Regarding the damage done to the Chinese people, the same article reported only on the fires consuming the city area. Afterward, in mid-February to early March, the Chinese news media provided more detailed accounts of atrocities committed against the Chinese population such as the "murdering of no less than ten thousand civilians . . . more than twenty thousand cases of rape," "seven or eight cases of arson every day," and the "searching of every house seven or eight times" for the purpose of stealing.[34]

The initial Chinese media coverage of the incident was thus quite consistent with the Western news reports. A notable feature is that while they did touch on the death toll in the city, they did not view the incident as an unprecedented atrocity as many of today's researchers and journalists claim. Typically, one contemporary English-language magazine printed in Shanghai focused more on the material damage than the loss of human life. The headline of a *China Weekly Review* article, which commented on Smythe's *War Damages in the Nanking Area*, read "Nanking War Toll Set at $246,000,000." Nevertheless, as time passed, a notable tendency began to manifest itself, and possibly has continued ever since, that is, what looked like an inflated estimate of the number of victims. The March 5 issue of the *New China Daily* said that the enemy killed about one hundred of Chinese men a day. This figure sharply contradicts the information provided around the same period by U.S. military intelligence, that is, about two to three cases of rape or assault a day. The *Daily* also reported in May that the total number of murder victims amounted to no less than 100,000 between December 13, 1937, and late March 1938. Most of the Chinese Nationalist sources later accepted this figure as the total number of Rape of Nanking victims.[35]

Prior to the appearance of this article, there was yet another estimate that projected the death toll much higher. The January 24 issue of the *New China*

Daily quoted what was said to be a Japanese diplomatic telegram cited by H. J. Timperly, a correspondent of the *Manchester Guardian* of Britain: "Since return (to) Shanghai (a) few days ago I investigated reported atrocities committed by Japanese Army in Nanking and elsewhere. Verbal accounts (of) reliable eye-witnesses and letters from individuals whose credibility (is) beyond question afford convincing proof (that) Japanese Army behaved and (is) continuing (to) behave in (a) fashion reminiscent (of) Attila (and) his Huns. (Not) less than three hundred thousand Chinese civilians slaughtered, many cases (in) cold blood."[36]

The Japanese diplomatic representative in Shanghai indeed sent this message to the Foreign Ministry, which in turn conveyed it to the Japanese embassy in Washington in view of the possible repercussions this message might have caused in Western news media. The fact was, however, that this was an article Timperly himself had written and was about to send to Britain, when the Japanese military authorities in Shanghai censored it. The *Manchester Guardian* criticized this censoring as "discrimination" on the grounds that other messages on the same subject had been allowed to pass. In reality, however, no other Western newspapers carried an article with similar content. Although the reason why Timperly wrote this article is still unclear, Japanese diplomatic correspondence complained about Timperly's attitude of planning "to make trouble over the matter" and mentioned a rumor that he was paid to do propaganda work for Chiang Kai-shek. Whatever the article's source, it is probably one origin of the widely accepted 300,000-victim theory today. Apparently, a majority of people at the time, including the Chinese, did not take this figure seriously. Even the *New China Daily*, which had printed Timperly's article, at a later date estimated the number of victims in Nanking at 100,000.[37] As for the reliability of this figure itself, it is doubtful. First, even Timperly himself provided a different account later in his publication—the book he wrote in the safety of his home country without any concern about the Japanese censorship. He said, "According to a careful estimate made by a foreign observer who had visited these regions on several occasions, *both before and after the Japanese occupation*, at least 300,000 Chinese civilians have lost their lives *as a result of the Sino-Japanese hostilities in the Yangtze Delta*. A considerable portion of these people were slaughtered in cold blood." [Italics added.][38]

Second, anonymous observers quoted in a G-2 report in June 1938 estimated the Chinese civilian dead in the eleven-month period from the beginning of the war throughout all of China at 200,000.[39]

After the outbreak of World War II, the official account of the Nanking atrocities began to take a different shape, most likely because it was affected by the reports of Japanese atrocities in other areas. A Nationalist publication in 1943, for example, described the events in Nanking as "a systematic murdering of Chinese civilians, raping of women, looting and burning of properties which lasted for about five months" without mentioning the execution of war prisoners. It thus gave readers the impression that the Japanese subjected only civilians to atrocities. Still, judging from their exclusion of the fall of Nanking and subsequent atrocities from the list of "national holidays, anniversaries, and memorial days" in the same book, the Chinese did not yet treat the Rape of Nanking as a monumental event that they should remember. They simply mentioned it as one of the numerous atrocious incidents perpetrated by Japanese troops.[40]

After the inauguration of the United Nations Commission for Investigation of War Crimes in 1943, the Chinese Nationalist government sent envoys to the United States and collected some materials from eyewitnesses such as Smythe and Fitch. Then, in October 1944, the Chinese War Damage Investigation Commission began to assess human and material losses of the war. Still, a full-scale investigation of the Rape of Nanking did not start until after the end of World War II due to the Chinese authorities' inaccessibility to the area where the actual atrocities had taken place. With the perpetrators and victims being inactive in the discussion of the incident, it was the Westerners, Americans in particular, who shaped the image of the Rape of Nanking.[41]

THE WEST (ESPECIALLY THE UNITED STATES)

One American said early in 1938 that "the sympathy of 99 and a half percent of the American people is with China."[42] Although the figure might have been an exaggeration, this statement at least reflected the prevailing mood in the United States. The atrocities against the Chinese certainly shocked Americans and consolidated this anti-Japanese and pro-Chinese attitude to a certain extent. Nevertheless, initial U.S. reaction to the incident was passive in general. A primary reason was isolationist sentiment—a desire to avoid involvement in a war overseas. Even when some incidents affected the lives or interests of their own countrymen in China, Americans still hoped that the United States could be kept out of the Far Eastern conflict.

The first Japanese military activity that drew hostile reaction from the West was the aerial bombing of China's big cities such as Nanking and Canton. The Japanese navy, which was actually in charge of the bombing campaign, issued a statement on September 20, 1937, that the Japanese would start a bombing campaign against Nanking. At the same time, the navy warned third country nationals of the anticipated danger. The U.S. government made a protest to Tokyo through the U.S. ambassador to Japan, Joseph Clark Grew. The statement issued by the U.S. government urged cancellation of the bombing because these operations would almost inevitably result in extensive destruction of noncombatant life and nonmilitary establishments. The memorandum went on to express Washington's concern over the safety of Americans: "the American Government strongly objects to the creation of a situation in consequence of which the American Ambassador and other agencies of this government are confronted with the alternatives of abandoning their establishments or being exposed to grave hazards."[43] Meanwhile, the British government independently filed a similar protest through Sir Robert Craigie, ambassador to Japan, in an attempt to draw attention to the fact that such attacks would endanger the lives of civilians, including a number of British nationals.[44]

The Americans criticized the Japanese aerial bombing as a clear policy of *Schrecklichkeit* [frightfulness] in disregard of civilized ways of warfare that were supposed to make a distinction between combatants and noncombatants. Although there was certainly concern over the fate of the Chinese civilian population, clearly the Americans and the British protested to Japan chiefly out of their concern for the lives of their own nationals. In a meeting with Japanese Foreign Minister Hirota Koki, for example, Ambassador Grew expressed his thanks to the Japanese for their decision not to bomb the Hankow–Canton railway during the evacuation of Americans on September 22 before he made some representations that the bombing itself might pose a serious danger to "foreign diplomatic establishments and personnel, as well as other noncombatants." The Western reaction to the bombing of Nanking thus repeated a pattern the Western democracies had followed in April of the same year when they only mildly criticized the bombing of Guernica during the Spanish Civil War.[45]

There was another form of reaction to the bombing, a racist-oriented reaction that was a prototype of anti-Japanese propaganda in World War II. For example, a *New York Times* editorial of September 17, 1937, analyzed the Japanese bombing operations by quoting Pearl Buck's words: "The Orient, she [Pearl Buck] points out, has not had in its civilization a humanitarian development. Individual life is worthless. . . . there is no 'such thing as fair play in war or distress,' and the lives of non-combatants or prisoners are 'of no more value than any other,' "[46] Those tendencies—a strong concern over their own countrymen and occasional criticisms with racial tones—became more evident when Japanese military activities actually did harm to Americans and British in the course of the battle of Nanking.

During the battle of Nanking, a U.S. river gunboat, the *Panay*, was sailing upstream on the Yangtze River with three river tankers belonging to the Standard Oil Co. The *Panay* was protecting American citizens and embassy personnel by carrying them through the war zone. H.M.S. *Ladybird* was also near Wuhu on the same mission for British citizens. Japanese naval airplanes bombed and sank the *Panay*, killing two people on board, and destroyed the three tankers. A Japanese army unit shelled and strafed the *Ladybird* from the river shore and killed one person.

People involved in the incidents, as well as scholars ever since, have debated whether the Japanese followed a deliberate plan in their attacks on those ships or whether they merely assumed that the *Panay* and *Ladybird* were Chinese vessels disguised as Western ships. Judging from the subsequent reaction of the Japanese government, it is appropriate to conclude that at least no military or political leaders in Tokyo instructed the Japanese military or naval personnel in China to attack the ships of third countries.[47] The Japanese government quickly admitted the responsibility of its armed forces and avoided a diplomatic crisis. According to Ambassador Grew, then Japanese Foreign Minister Hirota Koki made no effort to pretend that it might have been caused by Chinese planes and expressed the profound apologies and regrets of the Japanese government. Although the settlement was quick on the diplomatic level, the apology of the Japanese government was not enough to soothe American public opinion. The attack on the U.S. ship caused almost the same sensation in some American news media as did the explosion of the battleship *Maine* in the Spanish-American War or the sinking of the *Lusitania* during World War I. The *Chicago Daily News* in a dispatch from Shanghai on December 13 charged that the sinking of the *Panay* was the eleventh incident involving either British or American lives since hostilities had broken out in China and said that the *Panay* sinking capped the climax of a long and disgraceful array of complete breaches of faith on the part of the Japanese high army and navy commands.[48]

The news reports of the Nanking atrocities reached the United States when the outrage of American citizens over the attack on their own vessel was still at its peak. As a consequence, the anti-Japanese sentiment, which had so far been politically oriented, began to acquire emotional elements. The *New York Times*, in an editorial on December 19, criticized the Japanese conduct in Nanking as an expression of "the unbridled lust of the victors" typical in premodern war "before Grotius laid the basis of the international law of war and peace."[49] The *Chicago Daily News* then made even a harsher criticism against Japan by linking the massacre in Nanking with the *Panay* incident: "It is not our gunboats, our guards and our citizens who should now leave China but Japan's armies. They have no right there whatsoever, not even the blustering sanction of a declaration of war. Their legal status is precisely that of international bandits, engaged on a vast scale in acts of wholesale massacre, pillage and destructions."[50]

Except for these two papers, however, U.S. newspaper coverage of Nanking atrocities was slow to appear, due probably to both the lack of interest and the scarcity of information. Although they reported the executions of POWs at early dates, most papers seemingly treated these moves as an extension of military actions instead of atrocities—a view similar to the one held by the Japanese military personnel at the time. Arthur Menken, Paramount newsreel cameraman, for example, did write for the AP, "All males found with any signs of having served in the army were . . . executed," but then followed with a story that the Japanese kept the Sun Yat-sen mound intact. AP reporter C. Yates McDaniel also emphasized the Japanese troops' sparing of the Safety Zone from military operations in his initial report from Nanking. A part of McDaniel's diary printed in several papers on the following day did tell about the Japanese executions of about 500 civilians and disarmed soldiers as well as about a Chinese man with his hands tied in his back frantically seeking McDaniel's help to save his life. This article by McDaniel in the *Chicago Daily Tribune* was, however, unlikely to catch readers' attention since it appeared on the eighth page of the paper.[51]

Meanwhile, John M. Allison, formerly consul in Tsinan, arrived in Nanking on December 31 to take charge of the embassy building. Allison was appalled at the destruction wrought upon the embassy facilities and the city's business district, but was also impressed with the courteous attitude of Japanese civil and military officials he met, a scene that contradicted prior reports about the Japanese soldiers' violent behavior. Allison, however, soon found out the reality. Many newspapers, although not on their front page, carried AP dispatches reporting Allison's protest to the Japanese authorities regarding the continuing trespassing into American property and institutions in mid-January. There were a series of negotiations between the Japanese and U.S. diplomatic representatives in Tokyo to settle the dispute. Counselor Dooman of the U.S. embassy in Tokyo met with Ishii Itaro, chief of the Japanese Foreign Ministry's East Asian Affairs Bureau, and Yoshizawa Kenkichi, American Affairs Bureau chief, on January 15 and 19, respectively. As for Ambassador Grew, he visited Japanese Foreign Minister Hirota on January 17.[52]

While the two countries were debating this issue, a news report appeared by *New York Times* correspondent Hallett E. Abend about the "reign of disorder" and "lawless and scandalous" conditions in Nanking under the Japanese occupation. Commenting on this report, an editorial of the *Los Angeles Times* condemned the Japanese military leadership and insisted that "a continuing reign of terror and bestiality cannot be tolerated."[53] Then, another incident happened on January 26. When Allison and another American citizen forced their entry into the Japanese troops' compound to investigate the abduction and rape of a Chinese female employee of the U.S. embassy, a Japanese sentry blocked their path and slapped their faces. The reaction of the U.S. government to this insult inflicted on one of its overseas representatives was immediate. The State Department instructed Ambassador Grew to make "appropriate representations" to the Japanese government on January 28, and Grew did so on the following day. At the same time, public attention on the events in Nanking peaked as almost every newspaper reported this incident on its front page, a kind of treatment not accorded the news of atrocities against Chinese civilians.[54] The *Los Angeles Times*, again, commented on the incident in strident language. Referring to the Japanese official explanation about Allison's disobeying of the sentry's order, it asked, "Will the military authorities please explain what rights Japanese sentries have on Chinese territory, when Japan and China are formally at peace?"[55]

The Japanese and U.S. governments, however, reached a quick settlement when the Japanese Vice Minister for Foreign Affairs expressed profound regret to the U.S. ambassador in Tokyo on January 30, while Allison was informed of the impending court-martial of responsible military personnel in Nanking on the same day.[56] The effect of this incident on U.S. public opinion did not last long, judging from the lack of subsequent news coverage of the incident.

In general, the Americans maintained a passive stance toward the *Panay* incident and the Nanking atrocities, especially toward the latter since the Japanese did not mean to kill Americans. Quite a few newspapers and their readers voiced isolationist sentiment. A letter to the editor of the *New York Times* said, "It is my hope that the United States will not be provoked into war and that it will not be enticed into proposing any international intervention or conference for the settlement of this conflict. Japan started this thing and let her finish it. In my judgment, she can't finish it; bankruptcy will come first."[57] One letter addressed to the Secretary of State had a more passive and even self-incriminating tone. The letter expressed concern about government policies that might carry the United States into "a senseless war" and questioned whether the *Panay*'s mission was really a peaceful one.[58] There were even appeasers. An anonymous reader wrote to the *New York Times*:

if we undertake to cultivate friendship with Japan, we can obtain at once and at almost no cost great advantages for ourselves and for the world. Underwriting her [Japanese] new empire in the East, we give Japan great prestige and a new position and make it possible for her to support her political gains. We should stabilize the East and establish peace upon a basis not inacceptable [sic] to the Chinese themselves. We should increase our own prestige, strengthen the hands of the free powers, quench fascism, spread the gospel of peace and productivity.[59]

A majority of Americans at the time, about 70 percent according to one poll, preferred the withdrawal of the U.S. presence from China.[60] Since the safety of American citizens was a major concern of U.S. public opinion, news articles about Japanese terror against the Chinese people seemingly caught American attention only insofar as they reinforced the stance that Americans in China should not remain in danger. Thus, the atrocities in Nanking were overshadowed by the *Panay* incident, which took place at almost the same time, or at best were mentioned in connection with their concern over the physical security of their own countrymen. In essence, "the absence of an immediate threat to United States interests justified a policy of acquiescence which ignored the immorality of Japan's action in China."[61]

Many Westerners at the time interpreted and analyzed the Rape of Nanking in similar ways as they had done at the time of the Port Arthur Massacre during the Sino-Japanese War of 1894–95. The massacre of Port Arthur, which some Western media reported as an indiscriminate massacre of civilians, was a result of the Japanese troops' military action to search for Chinese soldiers in the city, although some civilians also became victims in the process. There were three different interpretations of this event among Americans: (1) it was an example of Japan's uncivilized behavior; (2) the story was untrue, exaggerated, or distorted; and (3) the Japanese behaved in the same way Westerners did. The same pattern of reactions resurfaced in the wake of the Rape of Nanking. First, quite a few used racist expressions such as "a terror which has been truly Asiatic in its disregard of humanities and decencies"; "characteristics [inherited] from a Mongol ancestry"; "no better than untutored oriental savages"; and "oriental brutality aggravated by the deadliness of mechanized weapons." Second, one person, apparently a former missionary in Japan, discounted the truthfulness of the atrocity stories by pointing to the *New York Times* report about the arrest of former Chinese military men who committed rape at a Nanking refugee camp and blamed it on the Japanese. This line of argument, which disputed the atrocity stories in the defense of the Japanese, was, however, much more rare than at the time of the Port Arthur massacre largely because Japan's stance and military conduct were much less justifiable in the eyes of Westerners. There was a third opinion, which regarded Japanese ways of warfare as no different from what Westerners had done. A reader of the *Washington Post* referred to a passage in the Bible and hinted that the Japanese way of aggression was nothing new in history. Some argued that the Japanese in the course of their aggression in China were merely imitating Britain's economic exploitation of its colonies, Italy's invasion of Ethiopia, and the brutality on both sides of the Spanish Civil War. Along a similar line, one reader of the *Chicago Daily Tribune* even defended the Japanese sentry who slapped Allison, saying that "there is one time when a private is higher than the highest ranking general."[62]

Regarding the more immediate cause of atrocities, Westerners proposed several theories. The first was that the Japanese wrought their anger and frustration on the inhabitants of Nanking when they realized that the occupation of Nanking would not allow them to dictate peace to Chiang Kai-shek. Some even guessed that the Japanese military leadership deliberately turned the soldiers loose in the city as a punitive measure. The second explanation was that the Japanese tried to impress the Chinese with the powerlessness of the Westerners so that the Chinese would no longer expect foreign intervention in the Sino-Japanese conflict. Third, there was speculation about mutiny among Japanese soldiers who defied the orders of their commanders. But by far the most commonly accepted—and correct, judging from other primary sources—interpretation was that the Japanese military leadership lost control over its soldiers and subsequently caused situations characterized by expressions like the "lack of discipline," "irregularities in the discipline," "misbehavior," "military unruliness" and "lawlessness."[63]

Some people analyzed the nature of atrocities in an historical context. Westerners analyzed and criticized the Japanese air raid on Nanking as a military conduct "unparalleled in history" because it was deliberately targeted at noncombatants. Contemporary Western observers, however, detected in Japanese conduct in Nanking something reminiscent of past historical events rather than a new type of atrocity. Nelson Trusler Johnson, then U.S. ambassador to China, for example, told an acquaintance that the Japanese military campaign was "anachronistic," and compared the Japanese soldiers to the Mongols led by Genghis Khan. Johnson thus referred to the premodern and primitive elements that had led to atrocities, typically an advancing army's way of supplying itself by living off the land. One scholar drew on a much more recent historical example. M. S. Bates, then a University of Nanking professor of history and member of ICNSZ, briefly analyzed the World War I German atrocities in Belgium, where the Germans massacred a considerable number of civilians in retaliation for alleged sniping. Bates established a parallel between the Japanese conduct in Nanking and that of the Germans in Belgium, but suggested that the former was more extensive in its scale and more cruel in its nature. It seems that the analysis of Bates was primarily concerned with the execution of POWs and plain-clothed soldiers, that is, an atrocity more typical in modern times. In whichever case, contemporary Western observers apparently regarded, again correctly, the Japanese atrocities in Nanking as an event they could explain based on their knowledge of past history rather than as a new phenomenon. It is noteworthy that, for the purpose of comparison, the Westerners at the time did not mention the persecution of Armenians during World War I, an event some modern writers refer to as the first case of attempted genocide. Also, the Westerners in the 1930s more or less correctly blamed the Japanese army's conduct in Nanking on the local military leadership and did not see any deliberate intention of the central government behind it.[64]

Although almost all commentators and analysts blamed the Japanese alone, a few people attributed the occurrence of atrocities, at least partially, to the Chinese as well. U.S. ambassador to China Johnson, after reading *New York Times* correspondent Durdin's article, said that the flight of Chinese garrison commander T'ang Sheng-chih was criminal and that it was a crime that the Chinese ever tried to hold Nanking because the trapping of the Chinese soldiers inside the Nanking walls was a foregone conclusion. United States ambassador to Japan Grew, alluding most likely to the extensive use of plainclothes soldiers by the Chinese troops, said that the atrocities were partially inspired by Chinese disregard for the usual rules of conduct for noncombatants and for combatants as respectively distinguished. In an editorial, the *Chicago Daily Tribune* also referred to the "Chinese bent for irregular warfare" as a factor contributing to the horrible incidents in Nanking.[65]

As the year 1938 went on, quite a few reports by missionaries who had spent time under Japanese occupation trickled back to the United States. Most of these reports found their way to the State Department through relatives or friends with a condition attached, that the department would not make them public lest those who compiled these reports be subjected to persecution by the Japanese military authorities in Nanking.[66] Nevertheless, at least one of these missionaries went public once he was back in the United States. George A. Fitch, general secretary of the YMCA in Nanking and the ICNSZ director, told of his experiences in Nanking to State Department officials in March. Thereafter, Fitch told his stories to the Office of War Information and the House Foreign Affairs Committee as well as to many private organizations until he left for China late in the same year. Apparently, he used films taken by John G. Magee, Episcopal missionary in Nanking, in his lecture entitled "What I Saw in Nanking." Fitch, however, later decided not to show the films frequently because he thought them "too ghastly, and sometimes they made people ill." According to one private source, Fitch estimated the civilian death toll alone in Nanking at 60,000, which was much higher than other contemporary estimates. One, however, cannot find any numerical data to support this contention. Nor did Fitch repeat this information in his later work, *My Eighty Years in China*.[67]

It was pictorial journalism that brought some visual images of the Nanking atrocities to the general public. *Life* magazine in its section named "The Camera Overseas" in its January 10, 1938, issue showed four pictures taken in Nanking under a headline "The Japanese conqueror brings 'a week of hell' to China's national capital of Nanking." In essence, the magazine gave almost the same account of the situation in Nanking as the newspapers and other sources had reported. It said,

About 150,000 Nanking civilians . . . cowered throughout the siege in a "safety zone" unofficially organized by some 27 white men who stayed in Nanking. . . . Soldiers and civilians were tied in groups of fifty and executed by the Japanese Army. . . . the Japanese Army commissariat needs food more than prestige. In the "indescribable confusion" Japanese shot down everyone seen running or caught in a dark alley. . . . A few uninvestigated cases of rape were reported. . . . The Japanese Army in Nanking permitted organized looting by its men, presumably because its supplies are getting low.[68]

What distinguished the *Life* magazine article from previous newspaper correspondents' reports were the sensational pictures, which for the first time conveyed dramatic visual scenes of the Nanking atrocities to people in the West. One photo showed some dead Chinese soldiers and civilians on the street where Japanese soldiers were busy looking for food. Another caught a cold-blooded scene of a Chinese man's head wedged into a barbed-wire barricade. Those photographs surrounded a close shot of General Matsui sitting calmly in a chair, giving the readers an impression that Matsui orchestrated the brutal massacre or turned a blind eye to the incident. Later in the same year, *Look* magazine published much more shocking photos in its November 22 issue. The four pictures, according to the accompanying explanation, showed the Japanese soldiers bayoneting or burying alive Chinese prisoners and civilians in Nanking and Soochow. Regarding how these pictures became available to Westerners, the magazine quoted an American citizen living in Hankow, China, as stating that the Japanese soldiers took the pictures and sent them to a Shanghai film developing store, where some Chinese employees produced more reprints than they were supposed to. Actually, the U.S. diplomatic office in Shanghai first obtained these photos plus eight others, and sent them to the State Department three months before with a comment that "they have been obtained from a reliable source." Therefore, there is no doubt that these pictures originated from Shanghai.[69] The authenticity of these photos has been debated ever since. It is worth noting that *Look* magazine's readers, despite a rising tide of anti-Japanese sentiment in American public opinion, regarded these photos with skepticism. One reader used the word "propaganda" to describe the reaction of almost everyone who had seen these photos, while another reader, though he said he was only guessing, noted, "It is convenient that every face is in shadow and that the man who "has just received the death thrust" should have turned so that the bayonet could not be seen entering. . . . Why do these Japanese soldiers, unlike other Japanese soldiers, not have their heads shaved?"[70]

Another reader living in Hong Kong narrated his own personal experience: he witnessed Chinese men dressed in Japanese uniforms having a picture taken while pretending to beat a Chinese child in front of a helpless-looking mother. Judging from these accounts, one cannot say that these alleged atrocity photos, which have been widely used by various sources, captured real scenes of atrocities. Another notable fact is that *Look* magazine did not treat these photographs as ones taken during the Rape of Nanking. An American who had first obtained the photographs said in his letter to the magazine editors that the Japanese soldiers in the photos were wearing summer uniforms and that "the killings happened at least six months after the occupation of these cities [Nanking and Soochow]."[71]

After the initial sensation caused by those newspapers and magazines began to subside, some journalists reminded people of the events in Nanking by frequently referring to what had happened in the Chinese capital as the "rape of Nanking." One can find one of the earliest uses of this phrase in a letter sent by Fitch to Frank W. Price, a resident of Richmond, Virginia, in early 1938. Yet it took quite a while before this phrase became a permanent fixture in the American mind. Some people initially used several different phrases such as "sack of Nanking." It was, most probably, Hallett Edward Abend, a *New York Times* correspondent, who made the phrase "rape of Nanking" familiar to ordinary readers and was largely responsible for keeping it alive even today. He used the phrase frequently in his book *Chaos in Asia.* He first called the event "the sack and rape of Nanking," and then in a later page referred to it as "the rape of that city," and finally used the phrase "the rape of Nanking." After his book went into print in 1939, many people started using this phrase, although quite a few people still said "sack" in place of "rape."[72]

Still, in the eyes of Westerners the carnage in Nanking was merely one of many ordeals the Chinese and other peoples endured in the ongoing military conflicts throughout the globe. In 1938 Gum, Inc. of Philadelphia produced a card series in 1938 entitled "The Horrors of War" as an accompaniment to its chewing gum. Some of the 240 cards described the atrocity stories in Nanking, but many others also told about other events in China as well as Nazi aggression and wars in different regions in the 1930s. A magazine titled *International Golden Rule Fellowship*, which summarized the American relief activities to war-torn nations worldwide, carried a world map in its October 1940 issue to indicate the cities devastated by the ongoing wars in Europe and in Asia. Although the map shows Nanking as a city destroyed by the war, it also depicts other cities including Shanghai, Hankow, and Chungch'ing in the same way and does not give special attention to Nanking.[73]

Meanwhile, Edgar Snow, who was not in Nanking at the time, produced his own account of the tragedy in Nanking in *The Battle for Asia* printed in 1941. Snow not only said that the number of victims in Nanking amounted to 42,000, but also added a new story that "300,000 civilians were murdered by the Japanese in their march between Shanghai and Nanking." Although Snow did not provide any sources of information, the most likely sources were an account by Bates for the 42,000 and Timperly's story for the 300,000.[74]

Overall, the Sino-Japanese War, of which the Rape of Nanking was a part, deepened anti-Japanese sentiment in the United States. The American League against War and Fascism organized a small-scale demonstration in front of the Japanese Embassy building in Washington, D.C., as early as August 1937 and staged another early in October the same year. The Japanese Consulate in Chicago saw a great increase in threatening letters after the *Panay* Incident and the *Chicago Daily News'* reporting of the atrocities in Nanking. Even when a U.S. diplomat had lunch with a Japanese diplomat, he later privately expressed "distaste for the society of almost any Japanese." Despite such an overwhelmingly negative view about Japan, the Western media did not take a hostile attitude toward General Matsui, at least not before Pearl Harbor. Western newspapers dismissed the possibility of the direct role played by Matsui and other leaders of Japanese armed forces in the Nanking atrocities. They rated Matsui as a general of high moral standard representing the fine tradition of the Japanese armed forces, most likely in reference to positive images of the Japanese armed forces in the late 19th to the early 20th centuries, especially in the Russo-Japanese War in which Matsui had served. Such a view was consistent even after the West later obtained more detailed information about the atrocities. When General Matsui retired from active service in 1939 and decided to spend the rest of his life in prayers for the dead, a *New York Times* editorial implicitly praised Matsui's attitude, noting that "few Western generals have ever devoted their declining years to the memory of the men who died in their battles." The editorial also analyzed the incident in Nanking as having been caused "due rather to his neglect than to his deliberate intention."[75]

One may conclude that the American criticism of the Rape of Nanking in the late 1930s was very mild since most people viewed the incident, more or less correctly, as an incident attributable to the lack of discipline rather than to the deliberate plan formulated by military leadership.

It was during World War II that Americans started talking about the Nanking atrocities from a different perspective. Nanking became the symbol of Japan's aggression in China just as Pearl Harbor stood as a symbol of Japan's aggression against the United States. The Nanking atrocities also became a propaganda tool to advertise America's unity with its wartime ally China. A typical example was a booklet titled *China—America's Ally*. Published during the war, it referred to the incident as the "Rape of Nanking" by capitalizing the initial letter—one of the first such examples—and made the incident look like a symbolic and unique event to be marked in history books thereafter.[76]

For Americans, the Rape of Nanking was also a precursor of the Japanese military's savage acts against their own countrymen during World War II such as the Bataan Death March. The September 1942 issue of *Coronet* carried an article about the Japanese army's cruelties against the allies' military and civilian personnel. That article started with the following paragraph: "Five years ago at Nanking occurred a tragedy so barbaric that even in an era when tragedy has become almost commonplace the name of Nanking still causes us to shudder."[77] The article then painted a slightly different picture of the atrocities in Nanking from the earlier reporting. Contrary to the initial ICNSZ and newspaper accounts recounting many cases of rape committed by "wandering soldiers," the article referred to such an act as "the orgy of Japanese troops who sated themselves by the platoon, by the company, by the battalion upon any Chinese woman they could find." It thus implied that the Japanese committed such criminal activities under official sanction.[78]

At the same time, anti-Japanese propaganda began to acquire emotional and racial elements, this time with a momentum lasting through the end of the war, and, to a certain extent, even today. *New York Times* correspondent Abend commented on the atrocities in Nanking and discussed the quality of the Japanese people in general in his book *Ramparts of the Pacific*:

It is not only their aggressive brutality, their greed, their lust, and their blood lust which makes the Japanese unfit to fill their self-appointed role as the leaders of East Asia. . . . They do not know how to treat subject peoples like self-respecting human beings. . . . If they could invade this country [the United States] that's the way the Japanese would treat us. If they made prisoners of any Americans when they captured defenseless Guam, that is the way they treated them no doubt.

Not in the next thousand years must they be permitted to become strong enough to do these things again.[79]

Abend also pointed to a specific personality whom he thought was responsible for the atrocities in Nanking, although Abend never mentioned any information source. In another work entitled *My Life in China*, he openly said that "Prince Asaka was the man who permitted the shocking rape of Nanking, but since he is related to the imperial family his name was never mentioned in connection with that ghastly three-day reign of savagery."[80]

Meanwhile, the estimate of the number of victims began to grow. Agnes Smedley said in her *Battle Hymn of China* that the Japanese army put to the sword some 200,000 civilians and unarmed soldiers in Nanking.[81] One cannot find any source for her information, but it was likely a distorted version of Timperly's story.

Newspapers made references to Nanking almost every time there was a report of Japanese atrocities against American military personnel. In particular, three news reports contributed profoundly to impressing the American people with what they described as Japanese brutality. These three events were (1) the execution of the airmen who participated in Doolittle's air raid of Tokyo and other major Japanese cities in April 1942; (2) the discovery of a Japanese soldier's diary telling about the beheading of an American pilot captured by the Japanese; and (3) the disclosure of detailed accounts of the Bataan Death March by survivors who escaped from a Japanese prison camp.[82]

Almost all U.S. newspapers reported the execution of the Doolittle airmen on the front page on April 22, 1943. Among the editorials that appeared on the following days, the *Washington Post* made a clear reference to Nanking as a previous example of "Japanese barbarity" and condemned Matsui for having "allowed his incoming troops complete license for a full month." It seems that this news coverage started two other trends. First, U.S. opinion displayed its racial bias more strongly than before, as the *Washington Post* editorial's use of the phrase "this evil nature of our Japanese enemy" shows, and Americans began to see the whole nature of atrocities as a problem deeply rooted in the Japanese people's minds. Second, the Americans and the Chinese further deepened their mutual empathy not only as wartime allies but also as victims of what they described as Japanese cruelty. Immediately after Americans learned about the execution of the Doolittle airmen, there were reports about Japanese atrocities committed against the Chinese who allegedly shielded some Doolittle airmen.[83]

The same pattern of reactions repeated itself following the October 5, 1943, report about a Japanese soldier describing in his diary the beheading of an American pilot. The *Chicago Tribune* in an editorial entitled "Hirohito Must Hang" enumerated the past records of Japanese atrocities, including the massacre in Nanking. It called the Japanese "blood lusting savages in long pants" and defined the nature of their conduct not only as "brutality" but also as "bestiality."[84] The *Tribune* continued its attack on the Japanese on the following day in another editorial and presented its own interpretation of the Japanese atrocities in anticipation of war crimes trials: "From the emperor down to the subordinate military officers who have been guilty of indescribable crimes against humanity, there must be a punishment which will leave no trace of the barbarism and cruelty *deliberately fostered by the government itself.*" [Italics added.][85] Then, although probably by pure coincidence, the *Seattle Post Intelligence* carried an atrocity story provided by a Christian bishop returning from China on October 17 the same year.[86]

When the survivors' accounts of the Bataan Death March occupied the front pages of U.S. papers, the *Washington Post* again referred to Nanking and analyzed the Japanese atrocities as being "planned, deliberate, sanctioned by high Japanese military authority, an expression of the Japanese military code." On the following day, AP correspondent Morris Harris followed up the previous day's *Post* editorial with a story of thousands of the Chinese Nanking defenders having been burned alive. Then, a *New York Times* article touched on the recent Japanese military conduct in China with a reference to Nanking.[87] This pattern of newspaper coverage, a report concerning Japanese atrocities against Chinese immediately following newspaper coverage of Japanese mistreatment of their own countrymen, most likely had a profound effect in shaping the American people's stance toward the Rape of Nanking even before the start of postwar war crimes trials. The Americans deepened their empathy toward the Chinese people and became ready to accept any atrocity claim the Chinese would make. Its effect remains potent even today in view of the unconditional acceptance by an overwhelming majority of Americans of the Chinese position with respect to the Rape of Nanking issues.

By the end of the war, the image of the Rape of Nanking had undergone a substantial transformation in the minds of Westerners, especially Americans. The initial interpretation characterized by phrases like "lack of discipline," "irregularities," and "misbehavior" in the late 1930s—individually committed criminal acts reminiscent of medieval warfare—was completely replaced by one based on the idea of "planned and deliberate" atrocities orchestrated by government and military leaders—atrocities resembling the Jewish Holocaust. The wartime reporting that identified the Japanese as the Far Eastern counterpart of the European Fascists reinforced this trend. Initially, the Americans saw the Japanese as imitators of German military conduct. Later, they began to perceive the Japanese as a more awful enemy than the Germans. One newspaper article immediately after Germany's surrender said, "The Japanese have exceeded, if that were possible, the German atrocities." As a later chapter shows, this is another trend inherited by some researchers and journalists today.[88]

A *New York Times* editorial shortly after the end of World War II illustrated and summarized this transformation of the image of the Rape of Nanking in the minds of Americans. As its title "Remember Nanking" suggests, the massacre had become a revenge slogan. The editorial capped Matsui's name with an adjective "notorious" in a dramatic turnaround from a favorable image of the general who decided to spend the rest of his life in prayers for the dead in that same paper's editorial six years before. It condemned the Rape of Nanking as "one of the most horrible blood baths in history" and "a pattern of conquest they [the Japanese] have followed faithfully since." The article added that the estimates ran as high as 60,000 to 100,000 regarding the number of victims. Finally, it declared, in an apparent anticipation of upcoming war crimes trials, that "Nanking is only one of many crimes for which the Japanese must answer."[89]

NOTES

1. The most recent example of such analysis is "History Undercover: The Rape of Nanking" on the History Channel, 22 August 1999.

2. The diary entries where one can find references to the soldiers' misconduct are Matsui Diary, 26, 29 December 1937, in *NSS*1, p. 24; Iinuma Diary, 19 December 1937, in ibid., p. 220; Uemura Diary, 16, 19, 27–28 December 1937; 8, 21 January 1938; 7 February 1938, in ibid., pp. 272, 275, 279–80, 287, 292; Nakajima Diary, 19 December 1937, in ibid., pp. 332–33; Yamazaki Diary, 14 December 1937, in ibid., p. 401.

3. The source of soldiers' letters is Deputy Minister of the Army to CCAA et al.,

"Shina Jihen Chi yori Kikansuru Guntai oyobi Gunjin no Gunki Fuki oyobi Keiko Bukken no Torishimari ni Kansuru Ken" [Report about the Morale/Discipline of Troops and Soldiers Returning from China and about the Inspection of Items They Are Carrying to Homeland], 8 April 1938, RMD, 1939, vol. 90, no. 267, p. 7, MHD.

4. Deputy Minister of the Army to CCAA et al., "Senchi Kikan Shohei Fusei Keiko Bukken (Taizoku Kamotsu o Fukumu) Ichiran-hyo" [List of Illegal Items Carried by Soldiers Returning from Battlefield (including those transported as baggage of military units)] 28 December 1937 to 15 March 1938, appendix to ibid.

5. Kan'in Kotohito to CCAA chief, Chu-ho-san Dai-19-go [Telegram no. 19 to CCAA], "Gunki Fuki ni Kansuru Sanbo-socho Yobo" [Directive from Chief of Staff Concerning Military Discipline and Ethics], 4 January 1938, RMD, in NSS1, pp. 564–65.

6. Nakajima Diary, 23 January 1938, in NSS1, pp. 353–54. Matsui Diary, 24 January 1938, in ibid., p. 33.

7. Nakajima Diary, 23 January 1938, in NSS1, p. 353.

8. NYT, 8 February 1938, p. 3. There was a confusion among researchers regarding the date when Matsui scolded his subordinates. Historian Hata in his book says Matsui did so on December 18 immediately after the victory parade. Hata, Nankin Jiken [Nanking Incident], pp. 106, 225. So did Iris Chang, RNFH, p. 51. Both Hata and Chang apparently based their theory on the memoir written by Matsumoto Shigeharu, then chief correspondent of Japanese news service agency Domei's Shanghai branch. Matsumoto Shigeharu, Shanhai Jidai [Shanghai Era], vol. 3 (Tokyo: Chuko Shinsho, 1974), p. 248. Recently, however, one of the editors of NS found a memory error on the part of Matsumoto and concluded that Matsui's disciplining of subordinates took place on February 7, 1938. NS, p. 408.

9. Matsui made a negative remark about his subordinate generals immediately before his execution as a war criminal. Hanayama Shinsho, Eien e no Michi: Waga Hachijunen no Shogai [Path to Eternity: My Eighty-Year Life] (Tokyo: Nihon Kogyo Shinbunsha, 1982), p. 220. Idem, The Way of Deliverance: Three Years with the Condemned Japanese War Criminals, trans. Suzuki Hideo, Noda Eiichi, and James K. Sasaki (New York: Charles Scribner's Sons, 1950), p. 186. Hanayama was a Buddhist chaplain who met with the Japanese war criminals at the Sugamo Prison in Tokyo. He spoke with each of seven defendants sentenced to death immediately before they went to the gallows.

10. Kawabe, "Kawabe Torashiro Shosho Otoroku" [Interview with Major General Kawabe Torashiro], in Gendaishi Shiryo [Source Materials of Modern History], vol. 12, Nitchu Senso [Sino-Japanese War], part 4, p. 435. Uemura Diary, 17 January 1938, in NSS1, p. 291. Nakajima Diary, 23 January 1938, in ibid., pp. 353–54. Matsui Diary, 24 January 1938, 6 February 1938, in ibid., pp. 33, 39. Gauss to the Secretary of State, 20 December 1937, 793.94/11739, M976-47. The issue that brought Matsui and Nakajima into a head-on collision happened when retired army general Ugaki Kazushige tried to become a prime minister in January 1937. Matsui was one of the principal supporters of Ugaki's bid. Nakajima, then chief of the Military Police, tried to block Ugaki's effort by representing a majority of army leaders who hated Ugaki because of his past record—an army minister responsible for the arms reduction in the 1920s. Matsui and Nakajima reportedly had a heated argument over the phone about this issue. Takada Norifumi, "Watashi no Mita Nakajima Kenpei Shireikan" [Military Police Chief Nakajima in My Eyes] quoted in Kimura Kuninori, Koseiha Shogun Nakajima Kesago [Nakajima Kesago: A General of Unique Personality] (Tokyo: Kojinsha, 1987), p. 184. The same book, in

defense of Nakajima, said Nakajima did not own the confiscated items privately; instead he sent them to the army's association of officers. Kimura, ibid., p. 214.

11. Uemura Diary, 1 February 1938, in *NSS*1, p. 296. Inada Masazumi, "Shina Jihen Senso Shido Kankei Shiryo" [Reflection on Strategic Planning during the China Incident], p. 39, MHD. Hata Shunroku, Diary of Hata Shunroku, 29 January 1938, in Ito Takashi, ed., *Zoku Gendaishi-shiryo* [Source Materials of Modern History: Second Series], vol. 4, *Rikugun* [Army] (Tokyo: Misuzu Shobo, 1983), p. 120. Honma, who led the envoy to China, was the same Honma who was later held responsible and executed in connection with the Bataan Death March during World War II.

12. Matsui Diary, 26 February 1938, in *NSS*1, p. 45.

13. Hata Diary, 8 February 1938, in *Zoku-Gendaishi-shiryo* [Source Materials of Modern History: Second Series], vol. 4, p. 121.

14. Yoshida Shigeru, Japanese ambassador to Britain, to Hirota, 11 November 1937, Red Machine no. 889C, quoting the *Evening Standard*, n.d. Headquarters, United States Army Troops in China, Office of the Intelligence Officer, "G-2 Digest of Information: Sino-Japanese Situation, 23–29 January 1938," 793.94/12401, M976-50. *Manchester Guardian*, 25 February 1938, p. 10. Gauss, "Report on Japanese Military Operations during the Month of February 1938," 10 March 1938, 793.94/12832, M976-52. Grew to the Secretary of State, 23 February 1938, 793.94/12496, M976-51.

15. Matsui Diary, 29–30 January 1938, in *NSS*1, p. 36; 16 February 1938, *NSS*2, p. 176.

16. Hirota to Grew, 15 February 1938, quoted in Grew to the Secretary of State, 16 February 1938, 793.94.393.1115, M976-50.

17. Ishii Itaro, *Ishii Itaro Nikki* [Diary of Ishii Itaro], 6 January 1938, ed. Ito Takashi (Tokyo: Chuo Koronsha, 1993), p. 240.

18. Ishii, conversation with E. H. Dooman, Counselor of the U.S. Embassy in Japan, 15 January 1938, enclosure no. 15 to Grew to the Secretary of State, 21 January 1938, 793.94/12345, M976-50. Saito to Hirota, 4 March 1938, Red Machine, no. 1490. Wakasugi, Japanese Consul in New York, to Hirota, 20 April 1938, ibid., no. 1808.

19. *NYT*, 10 February 1938, p. 12. Tenth Army's Legal Department, "Dai-10-gun (Yanagawa Heidan) Homubu Jinchu Nisshi" [10th Army (Yanagawa Army Group) Legal Department Record], in *Zoku Gendaishi Shiryo* [Source Materials of Modern History: Second Series], vol. 6, *Gunji Keisatsu* [Military Police], pp. 35, 47, 60, 62, 65, 68, 76, 82, 85, 90. CCAA Military Court, "Chu-Shina Homen-gun Gunpo Kaigi Jinchu Nisshi" [CCAA Court-martial Record], in ibid., pp. 137, 147–48, 163, 181. According to the regulations of the CCAA military court, the legal sections of the SEF and the Tenth Army were in charge of cases in the Nanking and Hangchou areas, respectively, while the CCAA court could judge any cases it deemed appropriate. Ibid., p. 128. The "special service unit," *tokumubu* in Japanese, was a miniature-size *tokumu kikan* [special service], which undertook nonmilitary and covert activities.

20. Rabe to Allison, 19 February 1938, in *DNSZ*, no. 69, p. 166. Matsui Diary, 19 February 1938, in *NSS*2, p. 178. Headquarters, United States Army Troops in China, Office of the Intelligence Officer, "G-2 Digest of Information, Sino-Japanese Situation 12–18 March 1938," p. 4, M1513-50. Smythe, *War Damage in the Nanking Area*, p. ii.

21. George R. Merrell, U.S. Consul in Harbin, to the Secretary of State, "Interviews of Two Americans with Japanese Military Officials," 16 February 1938, 793.94/12859, M976–52.

22. International Prosecution Section (IPS), Interrogation of Ishikawa Tatsuzo, 11 May

1946, pp. 7–8, case 439, file 6, RG331, M1683: Numerical Case Files Relating to Particular Incidents and Suspected War Criminals, International Prosecution Section, 1945–47, NA2 (henceforth M1683), reel 68. Ishikawa's book was published after the war. Ishikawa Tatsuzo, *Ikiteiru Heitai* [Living Soldiers] (Tokyo: Kawade Shobo, 1945). As for the films of atrocities, John G. Magee took these films, which George A. Fitch, director of the Nanking chapter of the Young Men's Christian Association, brought first to Shanghai and then to the United States. A British woman named Murial Lester approached Fitch in Shanghai and proposed to show them to Japanese Christians. George A. Fitch, *My Eighty Years in China* (Taipei, Taiwan: Mei Ya Publications, 1967), pp. 105–06.

23. Samuel Sokobin, U.S. Consul in Tsingtao, to Nelson T. Johnson, U.S. Ambassador to China, quoting Frank A. Brown, American Presbyterian Mission at Hsuchou, 1 August 1938, 793.94/13868, M976-56. Frank P. Lockhart, U.S. Consul General in Shanghai, to the Secretary of State, 29 July 1938, 793.94/13752, M976-56.

24. Eleventh Army Command, "Gun Sanbo-cho no Chui Jiko" [Directive from Army Staff Chief] accompanying Chu-shi Sakumei [CCAA Operation Order] no. 125, in "Dai-11-gun Kimitsu Sakusen Nisshi" [Eleventh Army Confidential Operation Diary], quoted in Kojima, *Nitchu Senso* [Sino-Japanese War], vol. 5, pp. 151–52.

25. P. R. Josselyn, U.S. Consul General in Hankow, to the Secretary of State, 27 October 1938, 793.94/14025, 28 October 1938, 793.94/14229, M976-57; 8 November 1938, 793.94/14322, M976-58.

26. David D. Barrett, Assistant Military Attaché, China, G-2 Report, Situation Report 13 October–8 November 1938," no. 9694, M1444-10.

27. Josselyn to the Secretary of State, 28 October 1938, 793.94/14229, M976-57; 8 November 1938, 793.94/14322, 10 November 1938, 793.94/14346, M976-58. G. L. Heath, Lieutenant, the U.S. Navy, "Intelligence Report," 26 November 1938, no. 45–19, file 808–300, M1513-41. Irving N. Linnell, U.S. Consul General in Canton, to the Secretary of State, 26 October 1938, 793.94/14213, 28 October 1938, 793.94/14230, M976-57.

28. CCAA Military Police, "Gunji Keisatsu Kinmu Kyotei" [Military Police Manual], 1 July 1943, quoted in Hata, *Nankin Jiken* [Nanking Incident], p. 239. John Davies, American Vice Consul, Hankow, "Memorandum: Conditions in Rural Areas near Wuhan," 29 March 1939, pp. 2–3, M1513-42. Linnell to the Secretary of State, 26 October 1938, 793.94/14213, M976-57. U.S. Embassy, Peiping, "Japanese Atrocities," 25 May 1938, Radiogram no. 318, M1513-42.

29. Lockhart, "Regarding Increasing Cruelty of the Japanese Military," in an untitled report, p. 8, 18 February 1938, 793.94/12705, M976-52. Laurence E. Salisbury, First Secretary of U.S. Embassy, to N. T. Johnson, "Destruction by Japanese Military in Shansi, Shantung, and Hopei Provinces," 13 July 1938, 793.94/13658, M976-55. Joseph W. Stilwell, Colonel, Infantry, Military Attaché to China, "General Notes on the Character of the War," ca. 25 September 1938, M1513-38. A. A. McFadyen to U.S. Consulate in Shanghai, n.d., enclosure no. 1 to Lockhart to the Secretary of State, 29 July 1938, 793.94/13752, M976-56. Carl C. Hawthorne, U.S. Vice Consul in Tsinan, to Willys R. Peck, U.S. Charge D'Affaires ad interim in Peiping, 17 February 1939, 793.94/14805, M976-60. George E. James, Second Lieutenant, "Wrecking of Chinese Area which Sheltered General Doolittle's Men: Interview with Father George Yager," 14 June 1943, M1513-42.

30. N. T. Johnson to the Secretary of State, 29 December 1938, 793.94/11888, M976-48. The Chinese army's losses were heavy especially among the best trained troops under Chiang Kai-shek's direct command. Michael Richard Gibson, "Chiang Kai-shek's Central Army, 1924–1938" (Ph. D. Diss. George Washington University, 1985), pp. 388–91.

31. Headquarters, United States Army Troops in China, Office of the Intelligence Officer, G-2 Report, 15 June 1938, M1513-39.

32. Kojima, *Nitchu Senso* [Sino-Japanese War], vol. 5, p. 136.

33. Hollington K. Tong, *China and the World Press* (Nanking: n.p., 1948), p. 54. *Hankow Chung-hsi-pao* [Hankow Midwestern Times], 23 December 1937, in *HP*, p. 167. Kuo-min Cheng-fu T'e-kung Jen-yuan [Special agent of the Nationalist Government], Kuo-min Cheng-fu T'e-kung Jen-yuan Chiu Jih-chun Ta-t'u-sha Shih Kei K'ung Ling-k'an Te Chi-lu" [Intelligence Sent by the Special Agent of the Nationalist Government to K'ung Ling-k'an Concerning Japanese Aggressor Troops' Massacre], 7 March 1938, in *TA*, p. 51. Mayling Soong Chiang [Madame Chiang Kai-shek] to Miriam H. Clark, 5 January 1938, 793.94/12294, M976-49.

34. *Hsin-hua Jih-pao* [New China Daily], 23 January 1938, p. 2; 16 February 1938, p. 2; 11 March 1938, p. 4.

35. *China Weekly Review*, 13 August 1938, p. 348. *Hsin-hua Jih-pao* [New China Daily], 5 March 1938, p. 2; 30 May 1938, p. 2. Headquarters, United States Army Troops in China, Office of the Intelligence Officer, "G-2 Digest of Information: Sino-Japanese Situation 12–18 March 1938," p. 4, M1513-50.

36. *Hsin-hua Jih-pao* [New China Daily], 24 January 1938, p. 2. This English translation is the one found in Hirota to Saito, 17 January 1938, Red Machine, no. 1263. Parenthesis in the original. Some recent works incorrectly cited this "Red Machine" document as a proof that a top Japanese leader personally admitted to the massacre of 300,000. See *RNFH*, pp. 103–04, Shi Young and James Yin, *The Rape of Nanking: An Undeniable History in Photographs* (Chicago: Innovative Publishing Group, 1997), pp. 276–78. For more details, see Conclusion.

37. Hirota to Saito, 19 January 1938, Red Machine, no. 1257. *Manchester Guardian*, 20 January 1938, p. 11. *Hsin-hua Jih-pao* [New China Daily], 30 May 1938, p. 2.

38. Timperly, ed., *Japanese Terror in China*, p. 71.

39. Headquarters, United States Army Troops in China, Office of the Intelligence Officer, "G-2 Digest of Information: Sino-Japanese Situation, 4–10 June 1938," p. 5, M1513–50.

40. Chinese Ministry of Information, comp., *China Handbook 1937–1943: A Comprehensive Survey of Major Developments in China in Six Years of War* (New York: Macmillan, 1943), pp. iii, 831. The list of "national holidays, anniversaries and memorial days" includes "July 7: War anniversary (1937)," "August 13: Outbreak of war in Shanghai (1937)," and "September 18: Mukden outrage anniversary (1931)." As for the review of the media reporting by the Chinese Communist Party, see Inoue Hisashi, "Nankin Jiken to Chugoku Kyosanto" [Nanking Incident and the Chinese Communist Party], in *NJK*, pp. 166–80.

41. Kuo-min Cheng-fu [Nationalist Government], "1943–1944 nien Kuo-min Cheng-fu Ti-jen Tsui-hsing Tiao-ch'a Wei-yuan-hui Te Tiao-ch'a" [Nationalist Government Investigation of the Enemy's Criminal Acts in 1943–44], in *HP*, pp. 371–77. *NYT*, 26 October 1944, p. 3.

42. Thomas W. Lamont to N. T. Johnson, 26 February 1938, Papers of Nelson Trusler Johnson, the Manuscript Division, LC, container 35 (henceforth PNTJ-container number).

43. *NYT*, 23 September 1937, p. 19.

44. *Times* (London), 22 September 1937, p. 12.

45. Editorial, *NYT*, 24 September 1937, p. 20. James W. Garner to the editor of the *NYT*, 27 September 1937; *NYT*, 3 October 1937, p. 8. Joseph Clark Grew, *Ten Years in Japan: A Contemporary Record Drawn from the Diaries and Private and Official Papers of Joseph C. Grew, United States Ambassador to Japan 1932–1942* (New York: Simon and Schuster, 1944), pp. 218–19. *NYT*, 29 April 1937, p. 4.

46. *NYT*, 27 September 1937, p. 20. The quotation is from Pearl S. Buck, "Western Weapons in the Hands of the Reckless East," *Asia*, October 1937, p. 673.

47. According to Hamilton Darby Perry, *The Panay Incident: Prelude to Pearl Harbor* (Toronto: MacMillan, 1969), accounts provided by the naval pilots who actually bombed the *Panay* ruled out any possibility of deliberate planning by the Japanese (pp. 69–76). So did the explanation by a Japanese admiral who commanded the air group that included the squadron responsible for the bombing (pp. 279–83). To the contrary, the U.S. sources, especially the Navy's 37-point "Finding of Facts," suggested that the Japanese bombed the *Panay*, at least knowing its nationality (p. 214).

48. Grew, *Ten Years in Japan*, pp. 233–35. *CDN*, 13 December 1937, p. 1. One of the eleven incidents mentioned by the *CDN* was a strafing of the British ambassador's vehicle by a Japanese fighter plane on August 29. Hirota to Saito, 29 August 1937, Red Machine, no. 620.

49. *NYT*, 19 December 1937, p. 8 (E).

50. *CDN*, 17 December 1937, p. 26.

51. *Washington Post*, 17 December 1937, p. 15. *Los Angeles Times*, 17 December 1937, part I, p. 3. *Chicago Daily Tribune*, 17 December 1937, p. 4; 18 December 1937, p. 8.

52. Allison to the Secretary of State, 8 January 1938, 793.94/12021, M976-48. Grew to the Secretary of State, 21 January 1938, 793.94/12345, M976-50, enclosures nos. 15, 20–22, 25, 29. Among the newspapers that carried the AP dispatch about Allison's protest were the *Seattle Post Intelligence*, 15 January 1938, p. 2; *Washington Post*, 15 January 1938, p. 2; *Los Angeles Times*, 15 January 1938, p. 2, 20 January 1938, p. 11; *Atlanta Journal*, 19 January 1938, p. 5.

53. *NYT*, 25 January 1938, p. 1; 29 January 1938, p. 1. *Los Angeles Times*, 25 January 1938, part I, p. 1; 26 January 1938, part II, p. 4.

54. One can see the front-page coverage of the Allison Incident in the *Seattle Post Intelligence*, 28 January 1938, p. 1; *Washington Post*, 28 January 1938, p. 1; *Los Angeles Times*, 28 January 1938, p. 1; *Chicago Daily Tribune*, 28 January 1938, p. 1; *Atlanta Journal*, 28 January 1938, p. 1.

55. *Los Angeles Times*, 29 January 1938, part II, p. 4.

56. Grew to Secretary of State, "Recommendations Made and Steps Taken by the American Embassy and Steps Taken by the British and French Embassies in Tokyo with Respect to the Sino-Japanese Conflict," 3 February 1938, enclosure no. 1: "Recommendations Made and Steps Taken by the American Embassy in Tokyo with Respect to the Sino-Japanese Conflict from January 19 to February 1, 1938," 793.94/12478, M976-50.

57. Wendel P. Barker to the editor of the *NYT*, *NYT*, 24 December 1937, p. 16.

58. D. R. Johnson, Chairman of Missouri Peace Action Committee, to the Secretary of State, 15 December 1937, 793.94/11968, M976-48.

59. *NYT*, 9 January 1938, p. 8(E).

60. *Washington Post*, 16 January 1938, part III, p. 1. Also, See Manny T. Koginos, *The Panay Incident: Prelude to War* (Lafayette, IN: Purdue University Studies, 1967), pp. 31–35, for more information about the poll at the time.

61. Gregory S. Prince, Jr., "The American Foreign Service in China, 1935–1941: A Case Study of Political Reporting" (Ph.D. Diss. Yale University, 1973), p. 33. This interpretation—that the Rape of Nanking was overshadowed by the *Panay* Incident—is more plausible than the contention that "the *Panay* incident was dwarfed by the fall of Nanjing the following day, December 13, 1937, and the subsequent 'rape of Nanjing' carried out by the Japanese army" in Edwin P. Hoyt, *The Rise of the Chinese Republic: From the Last Emperor to Deng Xiaoping* (New York: McGraw-Hill, 1989), p. 176.

62. The phrases that negatively characterized Japanese are from the *Chicago Daily Tribune*, 3 February 1938, p. 10; N. T. Johnson to Roy W. Howard, quoting a remark made by Lillie Abegg, a German news correspondent, 6 September 1938, PNTJ-34; N. T. Johnson to Stanley K. Hornbeck, 14 January 1938, PNTJ-66; and Grew to the Secretary of State, "Japanese Prospects after One Year's Fighting in China," 11 July 1938, 793.94/13585, M976-55. John Cole McKim defended the Japanese in his letter to the *NYT* editor, 11 January 1938, *NYT*, 16 January 1938, p. 9. F. H. Charity wrote to the editor of the *Washington Post*, quoting the Bible. *Washington Post*, 12 January 1938, p. 8. Charity quoted the following from Psalm 55:20.21: "He hath put forth his hands against such as be at peace with him; he hath broken his covenant. The words of his mouth were smoother than butter, but war was in his heart; his words were softer than oil; yet they were drawn swords." The articles that compared Japanese conduct to that of Western powers were J. O. Knott to the editor of the *Washington Post*, 2 January 1938, Kelly Miller to the editor of the *Washington Post*, 3 January 1938; *Washington Post*, 6 January 1938, p. 10. John A. Zimmerman defended the Japanese sentry who had slapped Allison in his letter to the editor of the *Chicago Daily Tribune*, *Chicago Daily Tribune*, 31 January 1938, p. 10.

63. N. T. Johnson to Bill Hard, 3 April 1938; N. T. Johnson to Gage Brownell, 28 April 1938, PNTJ-34. Ashley Clarke, first secretary at the British embassy in Tokyo, to Edward S. Crocker, second secretary at the U.S. embassy in Tokyo, 18 January 1938, enclosure no. 25 to Grew to the Secretary of State, 21 January 1938, 793.94/12345, M976-50. N. T. Johnson to the Secretary of State, 11 January 1938, 793.94/12049, M976-48. *NYT*, 25 January 1938, p. 1. Gauss to the Secretary of State, 3 February 1938, 793.94/12303, M976-49. *North China Daily News*, 25 December 1937, no page number, quoted in Gauss to the Secretary of State, "Editorials from local English Language Newspapers during December 1937," 7 February 1938, M976-51, 793.94/12679. Wakasugi, Japanese Consul in New York to Saito, 2 July 1938, Red Machine no. 2307, quoting Thomas Lamont of Morgan and Company. *NYT*, 25 January 1938, p. 1. *Manchester Guardian*, 7 February 1938, p. 10. *Washington Post*, 26 February 1938, p. 6. AP dispatch from Shanghai, 19 February 1938, *Chicago Daily Tribune*, 20 February 1938, p. 6.

64. Saito to Hirota, 20 September 1937, Red Machine, no. 666, quoting conversations between Saito and the Assistant Secretary of State on September 20, 1937. N. T. Johnson to Roger S. Green, 17 January 1938, PNTJ-34. For Johnson's similar remarks, see N. T. Johnson to Roy W. Howard, 6 September 1938, ibid.; N. T. Johnson to Thomas W. Lamont, 8 February 1938, PNTJ-35; and N. T. Johnson to Sir Miles Lampson, 24 January 1938, ibid. M. S. Bates to W. Reginald Wheeler, "Notes on German Atrocities in Belgium," 21 March 1938, enclosed in Wheeler to Stanley K. Hornbeck, 28 May 1938, 793.94/13177, M976-54.

65. N. T. Johnson to Hornbeck, 14 January 1938, PNTJ-66. Grew to the Secretary of State, "Japanese Prospects after One Year's Fighting in China," 11 July 1938, 793.94/13585, M976-55. *Chicago Daily Tribune*, 3 February 1938, p. 10.

66. All of the following letters were forwarded to the State Department with an instruction like "not for publication": H. L. Sone, Methodist mission in Nanking, to Arthur J. Bowen, 11 January 1938, 793.94/12489, M976-51; M. S. Bates, George A. Fitch, and Sone to Frank W. Price, enclosed in Frank W. Price to Maxwell M. Hamilton, Chief of the Division of Far Eastern Affairs, the Department of State, 17 February 1938, 793.94/12548, M976-51; Ernest H. Forster to Irving U. Townsend, n.d., enclosed in Townsend to Hamilton, 8 March 1938, 793.94/12636, M976-51; Bates to unidentified addressees, enclosed with N. T. Johnson to the Secretary of State, 10 January 1938, 793.94/12728, M976-52; Forster to Townsend, enclosed with Townsend to Hamilton, 29 March 1938, 793.94/12749, M976-52; and a letter by anonymous writer quoted in Mary M. Wilbur to the Secretary of State, 8 November 1938, 793.94/14408, M976-58.

67. *Los Angeles Times*, 18 March 1938, part I, p. 11. Fitch, *My Eighty Years in China*, p. 108. Clyde F. Gould to Senator Prentiss M. Brown, 24 May 1938, 793.94/13100, M976-54. W. E. MacDonald, professor of mathematics at Lingnan University, Canton, to F. R. Moulton of the American Association for the Advancement of Science, 15 June 1938, p. 3, quoted in Moulton to Stanley K. Hornbeck, 20 July 1938, 793.94/13646, M976-55. A part of Magee's film is reproduced in Peter Wang, *Magee's Testament* (Alliance in Memory of Victims of Nanjing Massacre, 1991).

68. *Life*, 10 January 1938, pp. 50–51.

69. *Look*, 22 November 1938, pp. 54–55. Frank P. Lockhart, U.S. Consul General in Shanghai, to the Secretary of State, "Photographs of Executions by Japanese Armed Forces," 16 September 1938, 793.94/14040, M976-57.

70. *Look*, 17 January 1939, p. 49.

71. W. A. Farmer to the editors of *Look* magazine, n.d., *Look*, 22 November 1938, p. 54.

72. Fitch to Frank W. Price, enclosed in Frank W. Price to Maxwell M. Hamilton, 17 February 1938, 793.94/12548, M976-51. Edward James of the Nanking Theological Seminary wrote a poem entitled "The Japanese Sack of Nanking," enclosed in Helen M. Loomis, Secretary, China Information Service, to Cordell Hull, Secretary of State, 23 May 1938, 793.94/13073, M976-53. Hallett Edward Abend, *Chaos in Asia* (New York: Ives Washburn, 1939), pp. 191, 221, 287. Examples of publications that used the phrase, "rape of Nanking," include Frank Oliver, "Three Years of the China War," *Amerasia*, July 1940, p. 208. Harold S. Quigley, *Far Eastern War 1937–41* (Boston: World Peace Foundation, 1942), p. 74.

73. "The Horrors of War: 240 True Stories of Modern Warfare Issued by Gum Inc., in Philadelphia in 1938," prepared by George Maull, a Sunday school teacher and the firm's advertising counsel. Some of these cards are now on display at the National Museum of American History in Washington, D.C. *International Golden Rule Fellowship*, vol. 7, no. 5, p. 10.

74. Snow, *The Battle for Asia*, p. 57. Herrymon Maurer presented a similar account in his work. "In roughly one month they [the Japanese] had covered the almost two-hundred-mile distance between Nanking and Shanghai, leaving behind hundreds of thousands of murdered civilians. Even before the fall of Nanking civilian casualties probably equalled casualties among soldiers." Herrymon Maurer, *The End Is Not Yet: China at War* (New York: National Travel Club, 1941), p. 24. Bates' report said that the civilian

victims in Nanking after the occupation was estimated to be "about 12,000 . . . not to mention 25,000 to 30,000 unarmed and passive remnants of the Chinese defense forces, killed within or near the walled city after the occupation." Bates, "Notes on German Atrocities in Belgium," 21 March 1938, enclosed to W. Reginald Wheeler to Stanley K. Hornbeck, 28 May 1938, 793.94/13177, M976-54. Bates most likely quoted the figure of 12,000 civilian victims from Smythe's report. Smythe, *War Damage in the Nanking Area*, p. 8n.

75. Saito to Hirota, 27 August 1937, Red Machine, no. 567A. Saito to Hirota, 9 October 1938, ibid., no. 759A. Masutani, Japanese Consul in Chicago, to Hirota, 18 December 1937, ibid., no. 1149A. Willys R. Peck to N. T. Johnson, 30 May 1938, PNTJ-35. *NYT*, 19 December 1937, p. 37. *North China Daily News*, 21 January 1938, no page number; and *Shanghai Evening Post and Mercury*, 21 February 1938, no page number; both in Gauss to the Secretary of State, "Summary of Editorial Comments in English Language Newspapers of Shanghai during the Month of January 1938." 1 March 1938, 793.94/12750, M976-52. *NYT*, 27 June 1939, p. 22.

76. Robert W. Barnett, *China—America's Ally* (New York: American Council Institute of Pacific Relations, 1942): Far Eastern Pamphlet, no. 5, p. 9.

77. Michael Evans, "The Facts on Jap Atrocities," *Coronet*, September 1942, p. 39.

78. Ibid.

79. Hallett Edward Abend, *Ramparts of the Pacific* (Garden City, NY: Doubleday, 1942), p. 308.

80. Idem, *My Life in China 1926–1941* (New York: Harcourt, 1943), p. 274.

81. Agnes Smedley, *Battle Hymn of China* (New York: Alfred A. Knopf, 1943), p. 213.

82. For brief accounts of this news coverage, see John W. Dower, *War without Mercy: Race and Power in the Pacific War* (New York: Pantheon Books, 1986), pp. 48–52.

83. *Washington Post*, 23 April 1943, p. 10. The editorial of the *Seattle Post Intelligence* was more emphatic in a race war stance in its sensational sentence, "The war in the Pacific is the World War, the war of Oriental races against Occidental races for the domination of the world." *Seattle Post Intelligence*, 23 April 1943, p. 1. Examples of reports about atrocities against the Chinese who shielded the Doolittle airmen were AP dispatch from San Francisco, 28 April 1942, quoting Treasury Secretary Henry Morgenthau, *Los Angeles Times*, 29 April 1943, p. 1, and *Chicago Daily Tribune*, 29 April 1943, p. 1. AP dispatch by Spencer Moosa from Chungch'ing, 29 April 1943, *Los Angeles Times*, 30 April 1943, p. 3.

84. *Chicago Tribune*, 6 October 1943, p. 1.

85. *Chicago Tribune*, 7 October 1943, p. 18.

86. *Seattle Post Intelligence*, 17 October 1943, pp. 1, 13.

87. *Washington Post*, 29 January 1944, p. 10; 30 January 1944, p. 6B. *NYT*, 31 January 1944, p. 9.

88. *Los Angeles Times*, 12 October 1943, part II, p. 4. *NYT*, 13 May 1945, part VI, p. 35.

89. *NYT*, 27 August 1945, p. 18; 27 June 1939, p. 22.

6

War Crimes Trials

CHINESE PREPARATIONS FOR WAR CRIMES TRIALS

The collection of eyewitness accounts and other documentary evidence by Nanking municipal government organizations, the district attorneys' office, and the Nationalist Government started in late September 1945 and continued through July of the following year.[1] Since the incident had taken place in China, the information available from the population there was considered to be reliable and would have considerable impact on the expected war crimes trials. In reality, however, it was mainly the evidence originating from China that became a source of controversy later. Although Chinese investigators collected a sizable amount of evidence, quite a few pieces of information were of questionable quality, while the interpretation and analysis of the collected evidence did not show much professional quality from either a legal or a scholarly standpoint. One can enumerate several aspects of and reasons for this flawed interpretation and analysis.

First, eyewitness accounts were initially hard to obtain. When Chiang Kai-shek visited Nanking in December 1945, the Nationalist government's Committee for the Disposition of War Criminals collected only fifty-three testimonies about the Rape of Nanking. A Western observer attributed the lack of response to the indifference of ordinary people, fear of retribution from the Japanese underground they still believed to be in existence, and the lack of education among the populace. The Chinese authorities also cited several factors such as the lapse of time, death of victims, and the dilution of the grudge against the Japanese.[2]

Second, such scarcity of information might have caused a certain degree of disinformation, either willfully or unwillfully, in the process of collecting evidence. Some of the eyewitness accounts submitted to the authorities contained controversial, and often questionable, information sometimes contradicting each other or stories based on rumors or hearsay. For example, two reports filed on October 1, 1945, said that the Japanese massacred about 50,000 disarmed men in a place called Yentzuchi near the Mufu Mountain. Then, about two months later a person named Lu Su said that the Japanese massacred the retreating soldiers of the army as well as men and women of all ages totaling 57,418 at a place called Ts'aohsiehhsiah near the same mountain. Chinese authorities thereafter adopted the latter explanation and figure as an official account of atrocities near the Mufu Mountain with no apparent effort to reconcile the difference between the two accounts. Judging from the locations mentioned in these documents, they told about the execution of Chinese POWs by the Japanese 65th Regiment on December 16–17, 1937.[3]

In yet another example of dubious eyewitness accounts, former policeman Wu Chang-te, apparently in reference to the Japanese troops' search, arrest, and execution of plainclothes soldiers in the Safety Zone, described the rounding up of about 2,000 people at the Justice Ministry building and claimed that it had happened on December 15, 1937. An ICNSZ document, however, clearly stated that the Japanese troops did not search the Justice Ministry building on that specific date. This discrepancy might well have been attributable to Wu's memory error. However, one can detect a more obvious flaw: not only Wu but also several other witnesses who described Japanese troops' activities in the Safety Zone identified the responsible Japanese troops as the "Nakajima Unit," which apparently refers to Lieutenant General Nakajima's 16th Division. In particular, one document mentions a big white flag reading "Burning Killing Squad of Great Japanese Nakajima Unit" spearheading the troops. In reality, however, the unit that engaged in the mopping-up operations within the Safety Zone was Colonel Isa Kazuo's 7th Regiment under the 9th Division commanded by Lieutenant General Yoshizumi Ryosuke. Chinese historians today seem to attribute this confusion to the 16th Division's notoriety, which made most Chinese residents in Nanking identify the Japanese troops responsible for atrocities in Nanking as the Nakajima Unit. A report by the Nanking District Attorney's Office underlined this reasoning to a certain extent by attributing 263,845 out of a total of 294,911 reported victims of collective massacre as well as 369 out of 403 individually murdered persons to the conduct of the Nakajima unit. This reasoning, however, does not fit well with some witness accounts, which claimed to have seen insignia of the Nakajima unit during the time of atrocities. Since Japanese military men were unlikely to wear any insignia showing their commander's name, at least that portion of these accounts lacks credibility. Although the insertion of such an unrealistic episode does not entirely nullify the credibility of these accounts as a whole, it nevertheless suggests strongly that witnesses who submitted such stories based a part of their stories on rumors or official accounts circulated among the populace at the time.[4]

Third, those who filed eyewitness accounts with the authorities sometimes provided unbelievably accurate figures regarding the number of victims. In addition to the 57,418 victims who, according to Lu Su, were killed near the Mufu

Mountain, a police report computed the number of those killed at a coal port on the Yangtze River at 3,281 while one person said that the Japanese had massacred 28,730 people in the area called Shanghsinhe. Very often, official reports adopted these figures without any supporting evidence or data.[5]

Fourth, some documents were of questionable authenticity. By far the most controversial document was the burial record of Ch'ung-shan-t'ang. According to the table showing the number of bodies buried by this organization, it dealt with 7,549 corpses in a four-month period from December 1937 through April 4, 1938, whereas it buried 104,718 from April 7 through May 1, 1938—about fourteen times as many in a quarter of the time period. In addition to this unrealistic data, its origin is also obscure. Among the list of fourteen government and private organizations the Nanking District Attorneys' Office invited to form a committee to investigate Japanese war crimes on November 7, 1945, one can find the Red Swastika Society, but not Ch'ung-shan-t'ang. It would have been quite unnatural if Chinese legal authorities in Nanking had not been aware of this organization that, according to its document, had conducted a much larger scale of burial activities than the Red Swastika. This document likely surfaced some time between this date and January 26 of the following year from a private source in Nanking, since a report compiled by the Nanking municipal government on the latter date was the first to mention this organization. The Nanking District Attorney's Office was the next to adopt this document as evidence in its report the following month. There was, however, an indication that even some Chinese investigators had serious doubts about the authenticity and reliability of this document. The investigation committee's report in June 1946, for example, did not mention this material as evidence, although it did refer to the burial records of the Red Swastika.[6]

Fifth, judging from the way the Chinese authorities handled the collected evidence, their subsequent compilation of reports proceeded apparently without careful examination and cross references of these materials. It seems that one of the origins of the oft-claimed 300,000 victims was the demographic statistics compiled by the Nanking municipal government after the war. In its report on May 4, 1946, the municipal government said that the number of people dead or wounded up to April 10 of the same year totaled 295,608. The impression is that Chinese investigators thereafter were merely trying to obtain a figure close to this total by manipulating the data available to them. There was obviously no effort to analyze or compare each of the available data for the purpose of finding out which part of the burial statistics represented the victims of which massacre. Instead, Chinese authorities almost always computed the total number of victims by accumulating the figures from various sources without considering the possibility of overlap or duplication among these data. A report compiled by the Nanking District Attorneys' Office, for example, determined the total number of victims in Nanking at 250,800 by accumulating all the figures from various sources, among which was the Red Swastika document. Although one could easily detect in the Red Swastika statistics its extensive burial activities

Chart 6.1
Chinese Statistics of Rape of Nanking Victims and Its Analysis

Source	Number of deaths	Note and comment	Actual number (estimate)
Ch'ung-shan-t'ang	112,266	Highly likely a fabrication.	0
Red Swastika Society	43,071	Very credible, but likely to include military casualties.	43,071
Hsiak'uan Area	26,100	Part of the Red Swastika statistics, which recorded extensive burial activities in this area.	0
Wu Chang-te's statement	2,000	Wu's testimony contradicts a part of truth; likely to be included in the Red Swastika statistics.	0
Lu Su's statement	57,400	Actually, execution of POWs on Dec. 16-17 near the Mufu Mountain, resulting in the death of at best one-fourth of this figure.	4,000-15,000
Statement by Jui, Chang, and Yang	7,000	They said 2,000 of these were military men; judging from their statement, their work was possibly included in the burial of the Red Cross, which may constitute a part of the Red Swastika.	unknown
Tomb of unknown victims	3,000	Its location and source are unclear; possibly included in the Red Swastika statistics.	unknown
Total	About 260,000 atrocity victims		45,000-65,000, including military casualties

Source: Shou-tu Ti-fang Fa-yuan Chien-ch'a-ch'u Pian Nanking Tz'u-shan Chich'uan Chi Jen-min
Lu Su Teng Pao-kao Ti-jen Ta-t'u-sha Kai-k'uang T'ung-chi-piao [Capital District Attorney's
Office comp., Statistical Data Based on the Reports by Charity Organizations in Nanking and
Citizen Lu Su about the Massacre], *HP*, p. 411. Also, see *RNFH*, p. 102.

in the Hsiak'uan area, the report separately listed 26,100 victims in the same
area by quoting from other sources. So did the table created by the Nanking
District Attorneys' Office. In another instance, the Nationalist Government's
Justice Ministry treated the alleged massacre of 50,000 people in Yentzuchi as
a separate incident from the killing of 57,418 people of both sexes and all ages
near the Mufu Mountain as was alleged by Lu Su.[7]

The initial Chinese investigation of atrocities in Nanking was thus characterized by serious defects, especially in its computation and analytical methods
(Chart 6.1). Without critical analysis, the investigators accepted as evidence
some questionable data as well as partially unreliable private testimonies, which
were likely dependent on rumor or hearsay. They accumulated the figures appearing in these materials without considering any possibility of overlap or duplication, whether intentionally or unintentionally. A positive side of the Chinese
effort was that the information they collected drew a rough outline of atrocities.

The locations of the alleged massacre and burial sites—such as Hsiak'uan, Shanghsinhe, and the Mufu Mountain—did correspond to places where more reliable sources indicate that major incidents occurred, whether they were formal military engagements or unlawful killing.

TRIAL OF TANI HISAO

The indictment as a war criminal of Lieutenant General Tani Hisao, commander of the 6th Division at the time of the Nanking campaign, in late December 1946 was seemingly an improvised decision by Chinese authorities. According to Japanese and Chinese personnel who had access to the information relevant to the allies' preliminary investigation of war crimes, the Chinese were eager to make Tani stand at the Chinese court since Matsui was to remain in Tokyo as a Class A war criminal while Nakajima—a much more notorious Japanese general in Nanking—was already dead.[8] On the Japanese side, some former officers of the Imperial Japanese Army were reportedly trying to have Tani incriminated to spare Prince Asaka—an imperial family member and then SEF commander—from prosecution as a war criminal. The Allied Powers arrested Tani on February 2, 1946, and interrogated him on February 23 at the Sugamo Prison in Tokyo. Tani said that his division had not committed atrocities in Nanking, and added that he had not heard any atrocity stories. Nevertheless, Tani was sent to China in August of the same year for trial.[9]

The Chinese investigation of Tani's case, however, started very late for unknown reasons, and the authorities did not issue a public notice to call for information until October 28, 1946. The prosecution's indictment merely two months later on December 31 set the tone for subsequent war crimes trials. The prosecution charged that Tani was responsible for having killed "several hundred thousands victims" for the purpose of "crushing our nation's [China's] will to resist." The prosecution then claimed that Tani's unit had committed massacres and rape in multiple locations outside the Chunghua Gate and added that the incident was a "blot on the history of modern civilization." In a document attached to the indictment, the prosecution enumerated 122 cases of shooting that resulted in the deaths of 334 people; fourteen cases of stabbing causing the deaths of 195 people; fifteen cases of group massacre that claimed the lives of ninety-five people; sixty-nine deaths for other reasons; fifteen cases of rape involving fourty-three women; and three cases of property damages suffered by seventeen people.[10]

Tani pleaded not guilty. In a statement submitted to the tribunal on January 15, 1947, he denied any knowledge about the alleged atrocities and added that the atrocities made known to him were the events that happened in the operation theater of the Nakajima Unit. Tani's contention was valid to a large extent in view of the 16th Division's extensive military activities and POW execution in the Hsiak'uan area. Nevertheless, Tani might have given a negative impression of himself to the Chinese military tribunal by blaming an already dead Nakajima and subsequently trying to make himself look better than Nakajima in terms of both personal character and the conduct of subordinate troops. Actually, Tani possibly had a questionable idea regarding military discipline. When he gave a lecture at the naval staff college as a guest instructor in the 1920s, he reportedly said that robbery, looting, and rape committed by a victorious army or by the troops in pursuit of the enemy would help boost soldiers' morale. He also seemingly overstated the disciplinary conduct of his division if one considers a remark made by a ranking general of the Japanese army about the problematic behavior of the 6th Division at the time of the Nanking campaign.[11]

Still, the Chinese tribunal deliberated on Tani's case in a questionable manner from a legal standpoint. One can detect an obvious influence of the tribunal on the eyewitness accounts adduced to the court. For example, one may see a remarkable contrast between testimony produced in early 1946 about the alleged massacre in Shanghsinhe and another testimony about the same incident submitted to the court during the trial in 1947. Although the former did not mention Tani's division as a responsible Japanese military unit, the latter called the defendant "Murdering Devil Tani Hisao." Then, a public prosecution on February 8 enumerated almost all alleged massacres in Nanking—many of which were said to have happened outside the operation area of Tani's 6th Division—and declared the total number of victims as 400,000. This accusation contrasts starkly with the preceding year's Nanking District Attorneys' Office report, which did not mention Tani's division as the Japanese unit responsible for atrocities. To strengthen its claim, the prosecution even had the location of alleged massacres excavated and obtained a report on about 1,000 exhumed corpses, which, however, included only three female bodies. Besides such procedural issues, the highly emotional atmosphere surrounding the trial undoubtedly helped the prosecution. One day, the prosecution invited to the court about fifty witnesses who were missing an arm or leg or had conspicuous bullet or sword wounds. While about 2,000 to 3,000 people surrounded the court building and constantly jeered, some of the audience inside the courtroom cried out, "Kill them [Tani and his attorney] immediately!"[12]

The death sentence handed down to Tani on March 10 was a foregone conclusion. The court again enumerated almost all large-scale massacres alleged to have taken place in Nanking both in its verdict and its appendix before delving into the details about the cases related to the accused Tani. Among the major incidents attributable to Tani's unit were an alleged massacre of 28,730 military men in Shanghsinhe, the killing of 400 to 500 civilians in a refugee shelter in Sanyuhe, and the slaughter of about 5,000 refugees and 2,000 military personnel outside the Chunghua Gate. In addition, there were 487 cases of alleged individual murder, twenty-five cases of rape, nine cases of robbery, and ninety cases of arson. These figures represented a considerable increase compared with the number of victims and cases enumerated in the original indictment. This verdict was thus extraordinary from the standpoint of criminal justice because it found the defendant responsible for more than what the prosecution had charged. As for the defense's contention of disclaiming Tani's responsibility for the crimes committed by other troop units including Nakajima's, the tribunal recognized a "conspiracy" among the Japanese military leaders in Nanking and charged Tani with "collective responsibility" for the crimes.[13]

Chiang Kai-shek finalized the death sentence for Tani on April 25, 1947, and Tani was executed the following day. Compared with Class A war criminals of Tokyo War Crime Trials, Tani died a relatively honorable death as a military man by standing in front of an execution squad. Nevertheless, he did not die with a peaceful mind. He stated in his will, "To the end, I spent all my energy denying the allegation of war crimes by providing the truth. Nevertheless, the one-sided decision by the Chinese court disregarded my claim and sentenced me to death."[14]

TRIAL OF THREE OFFICERS—MUKAI, NODA, AND TANAKA

Despite all the allegations of mass execution, murder, and other criminal acts committed by the Japanese soldiers, the Chinese court tried and convicted only three Japanese officers for their alleged acts of brutality in the field. One of the three was Captain Tanaka Gunkichi, a company commander of the 6th Division's 45th Regiment in 1937. A Japanese publication in 1940 hailed him as an officer who single-handedly killed 300 enemy soldiers with his sword. The other two, Mukai Toshiaki and Noda Tsuyoshi, were both lieutenants of the 9th Regiment under the SEF's 16th Division at the time of the Nanking campaign. Mukai was a commander of the artillery platoon within that infantry regiment, and Noda was an adjutant of the same regiment's 3rd Battalion. It was a Japanese newspaper that first reported their story shortly before the capture of Nanking in 1937. The November 30 issue of the *Tokyo Nichinichi Shinbun* [Tokyo Nichinichi Newspaper] said that the two lieutenants were in the midst of a sword combat race, in which each aimed to be first to slash to death 100 soldiers, and that Mukai and Noda had so far killed fifty-six and twenty-five, respectively. According to follow-up reports in the December 4 and 6 issues of the same paper, Noda and Mukai extended their respective scores to eighty-six and sixty-five by December 3, then eighty-nine and seventy-eight two days later. When the two lieutenants met face to face with each other on the foot of the Tzuchin Mountain in the suburb of Nanking on December 10, the final report said, they found that each had increased their scores to 106 and 105. Since they could not determine which one had reached the goal of 100 first, they agreed to renew the competition by setting a new target of 150.[15]

Westerners first learned about this story when the *Japan Advertiser*, an English newspaper issued in Tokyo, carried English translations of these articles on December 7 and 14 of the same year. Chinese news sources picked up this story and reported it as an atrocity rather late. The *New China Daily*, quoting a Central News dispatch, carried an article about the "Killing Competition in

Nanking's Tzuchin Mountain" in its January 25, 1938, issue.[16] Thereafter, almost the entire world forgot about this story until the end of World War II.

Judging from the circumstances of their indictment, one may conclude that these men were named as war criminals more for their initial fame in Japan and notoriety abroad than for their actual conduct as reported by eyewitnesses. In its report in February 1946, the Nanking District Attorney's Office, which had greater access to local information than other legal authorities, did not include Tanaka, Mukai, and Noda among the fourteen lower-ranking Japanese military men allegedly responsible for atrocities. Nor did the United Nations War Crime Commission in August 1946 list their names among 127 prospective war criminals. It was the Justice Ministry of the Chinese Nationalist Government that included the two lieutenants in the list of fifty-nine prospective defendants among such celebrity defendants like Matsui, Nakajima, and Tani. Apparently, the Justice Ministry obtained the information about them only from the newspaper articles in 1937–38 because the ministry entered Noda's first name incorrectly in a way that reflected the misprint in the original Japanese newspaper article on December 13, 1937.[17]

The International Prosecution Section (IPS) first interrogated two newspaper correspondents who had written the articles about Mukai and Noda. The two correspondents, Asami Kazuo and Suzuki Jiro, stated in July 1946 that they had written the truth in the articles. One can find, however, a discrepancy between the description in the articles and their statement. Although both Asami and Suzuki signed the articles in question, giving the impression that they were constantly with the unit the two lieutenants belonged to, Asami stated in the interrogation that he was frequently transferred among various units and that he was not with the said unit when he entered Nanking.[18]

Still, the IPS issued a search warrant for the three. Fortunately or unfortunately, all three officers survived the war. Among them, Mukai was living in western Japan when the Japanese police visited his home in the spring of 1947 and informed him that the American military police were looking for him. Although the Japanese police implicitly advised Mukai to conceal his identity and not to report to the IPS, Mukai volunteered to turn himself in, saying, "I did nothing wrong. I will report to the prosecution's office. . . . It will be quite an experience to witness what I can rarely see. Moreover, I might be of help to those who are in trouble in some way or the other. Do not worry. The Allied powers will provide a fair trial."[19] When his wife warned him about the possibility of being indicted for the reported killing contest, Mukai answered, "That was a fake story." His wife responded, "Oh, then, you lied to me!" Apparently, the wartime news report about the killing competition had provided Mukai a chance to meet his wife and marry her. Mukai then told his wife in a serious tone, "Never mind. The Imperial Military Headquarters was the biggest liar of all." Mukai then went to Tokyo, leaving behind his wife and children, and never returned.[20]

The Chinese mission in Japan requested custody of Tanaka on April 19, 1947, and took him to China in the following month. They also seized the sword he had allegedly used to kill 300 Chinese as well as photos showing him beheading a Chinese person sitting on the ground. Likewise, the Chinese mission asked for Mukai and Noda on July 11, 1947, and escorted them to Nanking in October.[21]

The Chinese military court indicted Mukai and Noda on December 4, 1947, for the killing of "89 by Mukai and 78 by Noda at the time of their entry to the Kuyung Hsien on December 5 of the republic's 26th year [1937]" and for the slaughter of "106 by Mukai and 105 by Noda on the foot of the Tzuchin Mountain on December 11 the same year." Again, judging from these numbers, the Chinese prosecution apparently relied only on the articles of the *Tokyo Nichinichi* ten years before. An attorney for Mukai submitted a report to prove his innocence. The report said Mukai had an alibi because he had been injured on December 2, 1937, and had been either carried on a stretcher or in hospital until December 15; and that the said newspaper article was a complete fabrication to satisfy the needs of the parties involved, for the news correspondents to write an exciting story and for the two lieutenants to become famous in order to facilitate their search for prospective brides.[22]

Stories that surfaced several decades later partially pointed to their guilt. A cameraman who took their photo on their way to Nanking said in a magazine article in the 1970s that he took the photos of Mukai and Noda on a day when Mukai was supposed to be carried on a stretcher after his injury.[23] In another magazine a man who had listened to Noda's speech following his return to Japan noted what Noda had said: "Newspapers have acclaimed me as a hometown hero or the very person who accomplished the one-hundred-man slashing. . . . The truth is, however, that I killed only four or five soldiers in real engagements. . . . If I called on the Chinese soldiers who had surrendered their outposts, foolish Chinese soldiers moved out and approached us. I ordered them to stand in rank and slashed one soldier after another. . . . Most of what is known as one-hundred-man killing now was done in this manner."[24]

Nevertheless, several factors suggest that the story about the two lieutenants might be false. First, the truthfulness of Noda's account is doubtful for the simple reason that it was extremely difficult to keep a slender Japanese sword usable if one tried to slash so many people. Second, the cameraman's account contains another story that is inconsistent with what the newspaper articles in the 1930s said. According to the cameraman's recollection, when he was told about the story of the sword contest, he asked the two how they would verify each man's score. The answer was that the two lieutenants would exchange their adjutant soldiers to count the number of enemies they killed. If they had truly made such an arrangement, they should have known which one had reached the goal first and would not have had to renew their competition as the final report by the *Tokyo Nichinichi* claimed. Third and most important, their respective posts—a commander of artillery platoon and a battalion adjutant—were unlikely to give them opportunities for such an independent competition. Thus, their story was likely to be wartime propaganda. In a similar way, the story of Major Tanaka having killed 300 soldiers single-handedly was probably an account fabricated to inspire the people during the war.[25]

The trial, however, came to a speedy conclusion on December 18 after only two weeks of deliberation. The Chinese tribunal sentenced all three to death. Regarding the credibility of evidence, the verdict determined the content of newspaper articles about Mukai and Noda to be credible by referring to the Japanese military authorities' strict censorship of media reporting. Rather than dismissing Mukai's story about a "prospective bride search," the judges used it to emphasize the heinous nature of the alleged crime. The judges said that the defendants who had committed brutality to make themselves attractive to women displayed an attitude "unheard of in the modern history of mankind." As for Tanaka, the tribunal accepted all the evidence the prosecution submitted. Although Tanaka argued that the alleged photographic evidence showed him wearing summer clothes, an unlikely circumstance in the Nanking campaign that took place in the winter, the verdict reasoned that it was natural for him to take off his winter clothing while he was engaging in a severe and exhausting sword fight. One may conclude that, overall, the trial and conviction of the three former Japanese officers revolved around circumstantial evidence as in the trial of Tani Hisao.[26]

Chiang Kai-shek confirmed their death sentences on January 26, 1948. All three were put to death two days later.[27] In his last will, Mukai said, "In the names of deities of heaven and earth, I swear that I never murdered POWs or civilians. I am completely innocent of the alleged charges in connection with the Rape of Nanking. I consider my death as heaven's mandate and dedicate my body to the soil of China. But my soul will return to the home land."[28]

It appeared, however, that Mukai, still in his thirties, agonized much more than did the old soldier Tani. In a memoir he wrote in his prison cell, Mukai said, "It is making less and less sense for me that I am going to be killed. Why was I convicted of murder even though I have never killed any person in my life? Those who will kill me will indeed deserve a murder charge. How thoughtlessly I came to Nanking! I am disgusted at my foolishness. I was wrong in my trust, but even such a remark testifies to my foolishness."[29] Although Mukai did not explain what his trust was, most likely he alluded to what he told his wife: "the Allied powers would give a fair trial."

TOKYO WAR CRIMES TRIAL

The Prosecution's Case

CCAA commander Matsui Iwane was named a Class A war criminal at the Tokyo War Crimes Trial. The prosecution indicted Matsui on twenty-nine counts.[30] Among the counts concerning the alleged Nanking atrocities was Count 44, which charged all the defendants with having participated in a plan or conspiracy to "procure and permit the murder on a wholesale scale of prisoners of war, members of the armed forces of countries opposed to Japan who might lay down their arms, and civilians, who might be in the power of Japan."[31] Count 45, created solely to indict those involved in the Nanking incident, charged twelve defendants including Matsui with having unlawfully ordered their subordinates to attack Nanking and "to slaughter the inhabitants contrary to international law" and, as a result, "unlawfully killed and murdered many thousands of civilians and disarmed soldiers of the Republic of China, whose names and number are at present unknown."[32]

This count was thus to prosecute defendants for large-scale war crimes comparable to Nazi atrocities. Matsui was also indicted under Counts 53, 54, and 55—conventional war crimes and crimes against humanity.[33] Count 53 charged several defendants with having authorized and permitted their subordinates "to commit the breaches of the Laws and Customs of War, as contained in and proved by the Conventions, assurances and practices . . . against the armed forces of the countries hereinafter named [which include China] and against many thousands of prisoners of war and civilians."[34]

Count 54 accused the defendants of having "ordered, authorized and permitted the same persons as mentioned in Count 53 to commit the offenses therein mentioned and thereby violated the laws of War," and Count 55 held Matsui and others responsible for having "deliberately and recklessly disregarded their legal duty to take adequate steps to secure the observance and prevent breaches" of the conventions of warfare "and thereby violated the laws of war."[35]

Matsui pleaded not guilty on May 6, 1946. Starting on June 4, the prosecution relentlessly indicted Japanese wartime conduct in China. Quoting a report compiled by the Army Information Section of the Japanese Imperial Headquarters, the prosecution claimed that more than two million Chinese civilians were killed in the four-year period starting in July 1937, while Chinese military losses amounted to 3.8 million.[36] Regarding the atrocities in Nanking, in his opening statement Chinese prosecutor Hsiang Che-chun presented the Chinese version of the Nanking incident, an interpretation that Chinese authorities and almost all Chinese and Western scholars continue to endorse:

After all resistance on the part of the Chinese military forces had ceased, and the city was entirely in control of the Japanese Army under command of the defendant General Matsui, an orgy of violence and crimes began and continued unabated for more than forty days. *The Japanese soldiers, with full knowledge and assent of their commanding officers and of the High Command in Tokyo sought by means of these atrocities to crush forever all will to resist on the part of the Chinese people.* The details of these crimes (which have come historically to be known collectively as "The Rape of Nanking") will be shown by the evidence. . . .

It will be shown that the conduct of the Japanese soldiers at Nanking was no isolated instance. It was typical of the numerous incidents of this character, the judicial agencies of Chinese have officially reported more than 95,000 separate cases perpetrated during the period from 1937 to 1945 and in every province in occupied China. Knowledge of these continuing atrocities by Japanese soldiers in China was brought home to the Japanese High Command in Tokyo. Notwithstanding frequent notification and protest, the atrocities continued. *This was the Japanese pattern for warfare.* [Italics added.][37]

As this statement shows, the prosecution was seemingly convinced that the atrocities in Nanking were conducted under the official sanction of Japan's military leaders and thus were comparable to the large-scale atrocities the Nazis inflicted on civilians in Europe. Further indication of the prosecution's firm conviction in this theory is that any IPS analyses of documentary evidence treated the documents relating to the Rape of Nanking as evidence against "the defendants indicated in Count 45," that is, the unlawful ordering of the slaughter of civilians and disarmed soldiers in Nanking.[38]

The IPS interrogation of suspects and Japanese witnesses, however, did not necessarily turn up information corroborating the prosecution's theory. The interrogations occasionally revealed that the Japanese military lacked a POW policy, but most of the accounts did not amount to confessing to the execution of POWs.[39] Regarding the atrocities against civilians, quite a few witnesses admitted that a small number of soldiers had misbehaved, but denied the occurrence of large-scale massacres.[40] Even some witnesses who were assumed by the prosecution to be friendly witnesses did not necessarily give accounts favorable to the prosecution's case. Ishikawa Tatsuzo, a writer who had been convicted by the Japanese authorities during the war for his novel based on the Nanking campaign, only said that he had neither personally witnessed the atrocities nor heard soldiers telling about their own atrocious deed. Ishikawa made a further intriguing comment, which could have been useful to categorize different kinds of atrocities but went apparently unheeded by the prosecution: "My own opinion would be that the murder of one or two people could be done by privates by their own will but in the case of 10, 20, or 30 some authorization from the Chief of the Battalion or Brigade would be needed."[41]

Even Tanaka Ryukichi, a former Japanese general who had agreed to testify for the prosecution in exchange for immunity, told only about the killing of POWs and denied that he had ever heard about the large-scale slaughter of ordinary civilians. Moreover, former Japanese military leaders reacted with total surprise to the prosecutor's reference to mass slaughter, saying that they had never heard such a story or that they heard it for the first time from the interrogator. One might argue that they faked surprise to cover up the truth. This reasoning might be true, judging from some of their statements that contradicted the known facts. Then SEF staff chief Iinuma explicitly told an interrogator that he did not know of the large-scale killing of Chinese POWs despite the clear descriptions about such incidents in his diary. Matsui said that a U.S. air raid destroyed his personal records about the incident, including his diary, which is, however, available in some publications today. Still, there was an indication that their surprise was genuine. In a letter from prison addressed to an acquaintance in October 1946, Matsui seemed disgusted to see the stories of the Rape of

Nanking exaggerated, and even asked that person to contact the Chinese judge at the trial to clarify the truth.[42]

A major reason why defendants expressed such surprise was that the two sides, Japanese suspects and witnesses on the one hand and the prosecution on the other, had two different perceptions with respect to the nature of atrocities in Nanking. The Japanese side understood the events at Nanking as incidents attributable to discipline problems. To the contrary, even before interrogating defendants and witnesses, the prosecution had seemingly solidified its own image of the Rape of Nanking as a series of events in which Japanese troops had followed a deliberate plan in massacring innocent civilians and military men indiscriminately and had left the streets of Nanking strewn with their corpses for weeks.

One can infer this view held by the prosecution from the way it handled some evidence. Interrogators not only relied on what looks like questionable evidence, but they also misused it to discredit the information that contradicted their own interpretation of the incident. In the interrogation of Prince Asaka, for example, the prosecution referred to a Chinese claim that there were 160,000 bodies of civilians, including some soldiers who were buried as unknown from the streets of Nanking between December 13 and the latter part of March. The same interrogator told Fukui Kiyoshi, acting Consul General in Nanking at the time of the incident, that "there were over a hundred thousand people whose bodies were found on the streets." Likewise, in the interrogation of Nakasawa Mitsuo, 16th Division staff chief in 1937–38, another interrogator tried to impress Nakasawa with the number of dead buried in Nanking—about 112,000 people, apparently in reference to the Ch'ung-shan-t'ang record. Here, the interrogators first drew on the questionable Ch'ung-shan-t'ang statistics to present their own theory of mass massacre in Nanking. On top of that, they either intentionally applied that evidence for their own benefit or carelessly misread it. Although the interrogators inferred that as many as 112,000 bodies were found on the streets of Nanking within the walls and were subsequently buried between December 15, 1937, and March 1938, the Ch'ung-shan-t'ang statistics said that the burial parties found and buried over 100,000 corpses in the *suburbs* of Nanking, not on the streets within the wall and mostly in April 1938, much later than the interrogators insisted. When Prince Asaka expressed his disbelief at that figure of 160,000, which represented most likely the sum total of Red Swastika and Ch'ung-shan-t'ang data, and he cited an estimated population of 200,000 at the time of Nanking's fall, the interrogator quickly changed the topic. In a similar way, when Nakasawa argued that the killing of so many people would have depopulated Nanking entirely, the prosecution only said, "Almost," switched the subject, and did not delve into it again.[43]

One can find another instance that illuminates the prosecution's mindset in its handling of Matsui's testimony. When Matsui told an interrogator that he had heard of "many outrages" committed by the Japanese soldiers, most likely he had in mind the cases of misconduct. After that interrogation, however, the prosecution triumphantly filed a report entitled "Admission by Subject against Himself," and later referred to it as Matsui's admission about the occurrence of large-scale massacres when it interrogated other Japanese witnesses. In the interrogation of Nakasawa, a prosecutor said that an American witness had narrated to him an account of the massacre of about 1,300 people. When Nakasawa discounted that story, the prosecutor said, "But it is a verified incident. Do you know that General Matsui admits these atrocities and blames his divisional commanders?" The prosecution made little effort to establish precisely the events to which General Matsui referred as "many outrages" or to attempt to distinguish between a deliberate policy of massacre and loss of control over their troops by Japanese commanders in Nanking. Nor did it attempt to establish the credibility of Chinese burial records by comparing those records with the size of the population in Nanking at the time.[44]

There is no indication that in court the prosecutors modified their theory about the Rape of Nanking. They seemingly presented most of their evidence, whether from Chinese, Japanese, or Western sources, without evaluating the credibility of each witness. In general, Western witnesses provided analytical accounts more or less consonant with the stories originating from 1937–38, although these accounts, as the defense later charged, frequently rested on hearsay. Spearheading the series of sworn witnesses, Robert O. Wilson, an associate in surgery at the university hospital in Nanking in 1937–38, described how he had treated a number of people who narrowly escaped mass execution by Japanese troops. Wilson's account sounds more or less credible, although one can also detect some unreliable stories. According to Wilson, he saw a man with a bullet wound, and that man was "the *only survivor* of a large group of men who were taken to the river bank of the Yangtze River and individually shot." Wilson then claimed that policeman Wu Chang-te, who was "the *only survivor* of a large group taken outside the city wall," came to the hospital. He also told about another man who was admitted to the hospital with a very severe burn and claimed to be "the *only survivor* of a large group who had been bound together, had gasoline sprayed over them, and were set afire" [italics added]. It is striking that each of the three persons Wilson mentioned in his testimony claimed to be the *only survivor* of a massacre. On the one hand, this account of so many only survivors gives some indication of the clumsy and inefficient way the Japanese army executed prisoners. A Japanese first-class private at the time recorded in his diary a story that a machine gun company in charge of an execution was surrounded by Chinese soldiers who had pretended to be dead, a circumstance that makes it likely that there were many survivors of the massacre. On the other hand, the presence of as many as three *only survivors* in Wilson's short account raises the possibility that the Chinese eyewitnesses may have inflated their stories to obtain preferential treatment at the hospital.[45]

M. S. Bates, a University of Nanking Professor and an ICNSZ member, in his testimony, attributed such massacres to the Japanese army's activities in hunting down former Chinese soldiers:

the Japanese officers expected to find within the city a very large number of Chinese soldiers. When they did not discover the soldiers, they insisted that they were in hiding within the zone and that we were responsible for concealing them. . . . It was their common practice to require all able-bodied men in a certain section of the zone, or in a certain refugee camp, to line up for inspection and then to be seized if they had callouses upon their hands or the marks of wearing a hat showing on the skin of the forehead.

. . . It was undoubtedly true that there were some soldiers—former soldiers among these refugees, men who had thrown away their arms and uniforms and secured civilian clothes. . . . The men so accused of having been soldiers were seized, taken away, and, in most cases, shot immediately in large groups at the edges of the city.[46]

Other affidavits submitted to the court provided similar accounts. George A. Fitch, a secretary of the international committee of the YMCA in Nanking and the ICNSZ director at the time of the incident, said, quoting from his diary, that he had seen "approximately 1,300 men, all in civilian clothes, just taken" from a camp in the Safety Zone on December 15, 1937. James H. McCallum, who was in Nanking at the time, also quoted his own diary in a separate affidavit and described the butchering of many who "gave themselves up to the mercy of the Japanese when they were promised their lives would be spared."[47]

John G. Magee, an Episcopal missionary in Nanking and ICNSZ member, was a star witness for the prosecution. Magee said that, "there was organized killing of great bodies of men." He narrated several stories of group massacre:

On December 14, our school cook's boy was taken off with a hundred other men down, outside the city walls near the railroad tracks. . . . they were divided into two groups of about fifty each, their hands were bound in front of them, and they began killing them in front.

On the same evening or the next evening . . . I passed two long columns of Chinese all tied up with their hands in front of them, four by four. . . . I do not remember seeing a single Chinese soldier in the group. At least, they were all in civilian clothes.

On December 16, they [the Japanese soldiers] came to a refugee camp . . . and took out fourteen men. . . . Four days later, one member of that fourteen, a coolie, came back to tell us the fate of the others. They had been gathered together with about a thousand men and marched to the bank of the Yangtze River and there mowed down with cross-fire machine guns from either end.[48]

Referring to the individual Japanese soldiers' misconduct, Magee told a story of a Buddhist nun, herself wounded by a bullet, who claimed to have seen her colleagues and superiors killed by the Japanese. Magee also described an incident he personally witnessed, in which he and his colleague chased away two Japanese soldiers raping a girl from a Chinese household.[49]

Western sources also described plundering and arson. Fitch's diary contained a description about "many Japanese trucks being loaded with the loot" and Japanese soldiers setting fire to a building after they had looted it. Also according to Fitch, he saw from the window of his residence fourteen fires in the city on the night of December 20 alone.[50]

By far the most damaging evidence against Matsui came from Western diplomatic sources, which were considered more reliable than private accounts. Among such documents was a secret report contained in a message sent by then German ambassador to China Oskar Trautmann to the German Foreign Office in Berlin. It referred to the Japanese army's conduct in Nanking as "organized thieving and plundering" and defined the entire event as "the lack of discipline, atrocities, and criminal acts not of an individual but of an entire" Japanese army. The prosecution also read U.S. Vice Consul James Espy's report branding the Japanese troops as "an invading army whose members seemed to have set upon the prize to commit unlimited depredations and violence."[51]

The testimonies, especially from Westerners, included abundant numerical data drawn from more or less reliable sources although much of it was based on speculation or estimates from the late 1930s. Bates quoted ICNSZ chairman John H. D. Rabe's report as saying "not less than 20,000 cases of rape had occurred" during the first month of the occupation while Bates himself gave a more conservative estimate of 8,000 cases. McCallum's diary said that there were "at least 1,000 cases of rape a night." As for the number of Chinese who lost their lives, Trautmann's report to Berlin said that "the Japanese shot dead at least 5,000 men, mostly at the river" while McCallum said that the soldiers rounded up and executed approached "the 10,000 mark."[52]

Although these Western testimonies and data were usually in agreement with earlier sources produced in the 1930s, at least one account was introduced to the court in a form slightly modified from its original state. In his testimony, Bates estimated that "twelve thousand civilians, men, women, and children" lost their lives inside the walls alone, while he also claimed that the international committee buried 30,000 Chinese soldiers. Here, Bates either intentionally or mistakenly altered the original finding in Smythe's report, which had said that 12,000 civilians were killed "in the city and in areas adjacent to the walls." Although the wording was only slightly different, the implication was drastically different. Smythe's report suggested that the 12,000 represented the upper limit of the number of civilian victims whereas Bates's testimony implied that the same figure marked the bottom limit.[53]

Of the Chinese evidence introduced to the court, individual testimonies had a relatively high degree of credibility although they still contained some questionable information. A Nanking resident, Shang Teh-yi, for example, recounted an execution of about 1,000 men on December 16, 1937, in Hsiak'uan, a likely event judging from the timing and location, although he said that the soldiers responsible for the killing were "presumably of the Nakashima [sic] Unit," which was actually not in charge of the mopping-up operation in the Safety Zone. Lee Tih-sung, then a grocery merchant, said that two Japanese officers came to a refugee camp around December 23 to encourage ex-Chinese soldiers to step forward, and that about fifty to sixty persons responded, only to be shot to death on the shore of a pond nearby. This story depicted almost the same scene as the one found in a memoir written by Bates in December 1937.[54]

The prosecution adduced to the court the affidavits of more than ten other Chinese witnesses, most of whom gave more or less reliable testimonies of misconduct the Japanese soldiers committed individually. Shui Fang-tseng, director of dormitories of Ginling College, for example, spoke about the plight of about 10,000 women and children who took refuge in college facilities. Starting on December 17, when the Japanese carried off eleven girls, the Japanese soldiers successively entered the school compounds for four to five weeks to look for girls despite frantic efforts by Shui and an American woman identified as Minnie Vautrin to keep them out. One can find Vautrin's name on the State Department's list of American nationals remaining in Nanking. Again, one may conclude that testimony and documents from Western sources as well as private accounts by atrocity survivors and witnesses were reliable in general, despite occasional insertions of questionable information.[55]

For unknown reasons, the Chinese included the statement by Lu Su, a document about the alleged massacre of over 50,000 near the Mufu Mountain, in the report of the Nanking District Court instead of presenting it as a separate affidavit. It was mainly those Chinese official documents, which the Chinese brought to the tribunal without further analysis or reexamination, that contained some numerical data and other information that painted quite a different picture of the Rape of Nanking from the one based on earlier accounts. The Chinese prosecution presented the report of the Nanking District Attorneys' Office, which estimated the number of victims at approximately 260,000, with its attached documents including the burial records of two organizations, Ch'ung-shan-t'ang and the Red Swastika. Also introduced was the Report on the Investigations of Japanese War Crimes Committee in Nanking prepared by the procurator of the Nanking district court. It claimed that over 300,000 victims were reported, and it is believed that over 200,000 more were yet to be confirmed. As a basis for these figures, the report charged that there were two major massacres in and near Nanking immediately after the occupation: one allegedly took place in the vicinity of Mufu Mountain in the suburb of Nanking and resulted in the deaths of 50,000 to 60,000 persons; and the biggest slaughter occurred in the refugee district and caused the death of 200,000 people. At the end of the report, the figures became more precise as the number of killed stood at 278,586 and the total number of bodies buried by the two organizations, Ch'ung-shan-t'ang and the Red Swastika, amounted to 155,300.[56]

In addition to the adoption of a small amount of such questionable evidence, a major problem in the prosecution's treatment of evidence was that it did not carefully evaluate each piece of evidence in such a way as to relate it to specific crimes described in each count. There were several counts in the indictment for different kinds of atrocities, that is, Counts 45 and 54 for atrocities caused by a deliberate plan and authorization on the one hand and Count 55 for atrocities as a result of disregard of duty on the other. The prosecution apparently made no effort to classify the evidence in accordance with such criteria. One can recognize the prosecution's rough and primitive handling of evidence in its disregard of a hint found in testimony provided by one of its witnesses. Magee said, "We couldn't do anything about keeping them [Japanese soldiers] from taking off men, but we could prevent them from raping these women."[57] The implication is that the "taking off" of Chinese men on the one hand referred to the search for former Chinese soldiers, which the Japanese carried out under orders, wherever the source of such orders. It was therefore an act to be indicted under Count 45 or 54. On the other hand, rape was an atrocity committed by the Japanese soldiers out of the control of supervising officers and thus should have been indicted as a crime covered by Count 55. It seems, however, that the prosecution did not care at all about such classifications, due probably to its preconceived notion of the Rape of Nanking, that is, a large-scale massacre orchestrated by the military leadership.

Yet what looks like a serious problem from the standpoint of a historian was probably not so serious from a legal standpoint. The prosecution merely followed the principle of collecting as much incriminating evidence as possible to substantiate the most serious of the charges lodged against the defendants. Moreover, judging from the verdict, the prosecution's failure to analyze evidence by relating it to different crimes in multiple counts did not negatively affect its case, probably because of the prevailing sentiment immediately after the war: people were ready to listen to and believe anything critical of a former enemy as a result of wartime propaganda.[58] In addition, the prosecution's method of presenting evidence from various sources in a lump sum was probably effective in making what appeared to be less reliable evidence look more credible, and thus served the prosecution's needs.

The Case for the Defense

The defense counsels' initial tactics in the cross examination of prosecution witnesses were to point out contradictions and inconsistencies in the witness testimony. Apparently, however, they were not very successful. For example, Counsel Kiyose Ichiro questioned the truthfulness of witness Wilson's story of having treated a rape victim who was in the second stage of syphilis two months after the rape had taken place. Kiyose quoted from a medical book he had read and claimed that the second stage of syphilis does not manifest itself until more than three months have passed. Counsel Ito Kiyoshi pounced on minor inconsistencies in witness Hsu Chuan-ying's remarks: that Hsu initially testified that the Russian embassy building was totally burned down but later said that he did not know whether it had been completely burned, and that Hsu described the identities of victims he had witnessed in several different ways such as "they were all civilians," "most of them were civilians," and "these people were civilians." In the cross-examination of witness Magee, Captain Alfred W. Brooks, one of the defense counsels from the United States, tried to show how similar the Japanese and Chinese soldiers looked, suggesting that the witness might have mistaken one for the other. Brooks also referred to Magee's statement that Magee had taken to Japanese authorities a Japanese bayonet left on the scene of a rape as evidence of the crime, but had not examined an identification number on the bayonet. Although Brooks apparently tried to illustrate how difficult it was for Japanese crime investigators in Nanking to identify the real criminals, his tactics backfired. The president of the court, Sir William Flood Webb of Australia, cautioned Brooks not to delve into too much detail, saying that the "identity of the particular Japanese [soldier] or the unit to which he belonged is quite insignificant," and even advised him to carry out the cross-examination more profitably for the defense. Although the defense merely employed the tactics commonly used in criminal trials, the effects of such tactics at the IMTFE were questionable. Even at the final stage of the trial, when the defense again tried to disprove the prosecution's evidence in a document entitled "Appendix: Concerning the Alleged Nanking Atrocities," it could refute the stories of prosecution witnesses only in passive ways. The defense argued that many witnesses did not appear in the court; that only their affidavits had been presented; and that many of their statements were based on hearsay and not eyewitness accounts.[59]

The defense did deal what looked like some effective counterblows. When Captain Brooks asked witness Magee how many cases of murder he had actually witnessed in Nanking, Magee answered, "I only personally witnessed the killing of one man," illustrating the defense's contention that much of the witness testimony was based on hearsay. In another instance, Brooks and his colleague Major George A. Furness interrupted the prosecution's reading of witness McCallum's diary notes several times and pointed out that the prosecution intentionally skipped some portions that could work favorably for the defense, that is, the descriptions of some well-behaving Japanese and misbehaving Chinese. Although President Webb did not approve the defense's request that the prosecution should also read such portions, he allowed the defense to read these portions later during the presentation of its own case. Brooks scored another point when the prosecution was reading the report compiled by the Nanking district court. He apparently noticed how unrealistic the number of victims, 300,000, cited on the report was and drew it to the attention of his colleague Michael Levin. Levin soon reminded President Webb that other affidavits presented by the prosecution said that the population of Nanking at the time was about 200,000 people. The president again refused to listen to this claim, simply saying, "you cannot get it in at this stage." This was because the judges decided "not to allow the defense to wedge its case into the prosecution's case" and only allowed the defense to use a part of the prosecution's evidence in the later presentation of its own case.[60]

Although the defense tried to counter every piece of evidence introduced by the prosecution, it focused its attention especially on some Chinese evidence. The defense allocated a considerable portion of its "Appendix: Concerning the

Alleged Nanking Atrocities" to a numerical analysis of the prosecution's evidence, especially Chinese burial records. In contrast with the clumsy method of refuting individual testimony at the court, the defense criticism of these documents was logical, elaborate, and persuasive. The defense pointed out that those data appeared for the first time in 1946, ten years after the incident, and concluded that they were "all based on assumption or guesswork." It also made it clear that there were severe military engagements in and around Nanking and suggested that not all the corpses buried were those massacred unlawfully by the Japanese. Finally, the defense declared some figures in the burial records to be "fraud[ulent] and incredible" by citing several unrealistic figures in the tables.[61] Scholars who deny the fact or discount the extent of the Rape of Nanking today still employ the same analysis the defense made at this occasion. For example, the defense maintained that

the 'Ch'ung' Burial Party buried 404 corpses during its work from 26th to the 28th of December 1937, that is to say, it has buried 130 corpses a day, on the average, but the said party buried 21,612 of them in the vast area of the Army Arsenal and Yuhua Tai from the 9th to the 18th of April 1938 and the average of its work amounted to 2,600 corpses a day. If you compare the above-mentioned amount of work in December 1937 with that in April 1938, you find the exaggeration of statement and the unreliability of the figures. There could not have been so many corpses five months after the battle, in the area of Yuhua Tai already cleared up by our troops. . . .

Concerning the number of corpses buried by the 'Red Fylfot' [Red Swastika] Party, it dealt with 672 corpses in a day and 996 in another day, while they were estimated at 4,685 on the 9th of February and 5,805 on the 21st of the same month. However changed the number of workers might have been, there cannot have been such a large difference.

. . . on observing this table as a report of the scheduled burial work, the "Red Fylfot" [Red Swastika] Party worked continuously at the Mine Unit Wharf at Hsia Kuan [Hsiak'uan], from the 19th to the 22nd of February, and though the party dealt with 5,226 corpses on the 21st, on the 19th and 20th it dealt with only 524 and 197 corpses respectively. It is contrary to reason that on the first day of work the figure should be large, but that it should gradually decrease day by day.[62]

As a previous chapter has shown, even though these contentions were valid and reasonable, one may infer at least the authenticity of the Red Swastika statistics from the existence of other supporting evidence. To the contrary, there is a good reason to doubt the authenticity of the Ch'ung-shan-t'ang data.

While trying to discredit the prosecution's evidence, the defense made efforts to establish its own case to exonerate the defendants of charges lodged against them. In a desperate but ineffective effort to better the image of the defendants and the Japanese troops in general, the defense referred to some of the prosecution's evidence and picked up some passages containing the descriptions of some well-behaved Japanese soldiers. For example, the defense pointed to the following excerpts from McCallum's diary:

We have had some very pleasant Japanese who have treated us with courtesy and respect. Others have been very fierce and threatened us, striking or slapping some. Mr. Riggs had suffered most at their hands. Occasionally have I seen a Japanese helping some Chinese, or picking up a Chinese baby to play with it.

Recently several very nice Japanese have visited the hospital. We told them of our lack of food supplies for the patients. Today they brought in 100 shing of beans along with some beef. We have had no meat at the hospital for a month and these gifts were mighty welcome. They asked what else we would like to have.[63]

Even such a strategy sometimes turned out to be countereffective. For instance, quite a few defense witnesses claimed in their affidavits that the city of Nanking was spared from battle fire and remained undamaged. Their statements did more harm than good for the defense because the prosecution's witnesses had also told the same story to show how severe the effect of incendiarism by the Japanese was after their entry into Nanking.[64]

Accordingly, the main focus of the defense turned into absolving Matsui of responsibility for any wrongdoing in Nanking, regardless of what had actually happened in the city. This strategy became apparent when the defense presented a motion on January 28, 1948, to dismiss charges against all the defendants, including Matsui, for lack of sufficient evidence. Counsel Floyd J. Mattice did not discuss whether the atrocities actually happened. Instead, Mattice simply maintained that there was no evidence that "the accused Matsui had any culpable part in any killing or murder of civilians or disarmed soldiers in China" because (1) Matsui commanded the attack on Nanking by order of superior authorities in Tokyo; (2) his command post was far from Nanking when the alleged atrocities occurred; and (3) Matsui took sufficient and appropriate measures to discipline and punish the offenders. After the court turned down the motion and the defense started presenting its own case, Counsel Kiyose deliberated on the "atrocities perpetrated by some Japanese troops in several parts of China," including Nanking, and confirmed their occurrence by saying that they were "admittedly most regrettable." Kiyose, however, soon added that they were "believed to be unduly magnified and in some degree fabricated" and that the persons in command at the time took sufficient measures to prevent such incidents and punish the offenders.[65]

The defense, however, faced an uphill battle for several reasons. First, the defendants themselves admitted to the occurrence of some wrongdoing on the part of the Japanese troops in their pre-trial interrogations and thus confessed to their knowledge of atrocities. Besides Matsui's admission, General Muto Akira, who had served as CCAA deputy staff chief under Matsui at the time, told an interrogator that he had been informed by his superior of the "incidents of stealing, killing, assault and rape" by Japanese soldiers and added that Matsui had become "quite enraged" to learn about them. Regarding the cause of such misconduct, in a tacit admission of the leadership's responsibility, Muto said that too many troops had been allowed into Nanking. Second, the defendants and witnesses exhibited the tendency of the Japanese military to make the source of responsibility obscure. Although the defense might be able to disguise this attitude as a court strategy, such an attitude was likely to paint a negative image of the defendant in the eyes of judges at the same time.[66]

The first line of defense was to claim that all the atrocities that had happened in Nanking were the result of military action and therefore not illegal. Matsui's defense counsel emphasized this point at the beginning of Matsui's individual case, and defense witnesses testified along this line.[67] The second way to clear Matsui of criminal responsibility was to blame the Chinese for the atrocities either directly or indirectly. The defense argued that the Chinese were responsible for similar outrages and that they must have perpetrated some of the misdeeds allegedly committed by the Japanese. It quoted the following portion from U.S. diplomatic correspondence previously presented by the prosecution:

the Chinese themselves are not altogether exonerated of depredations, at least to some extent, before the entry of the Japanese. During the last few days some violations of people and property were undoubtedly committed by them. Chinese soldiers in their mad rush to discard their military uniforms and put on civilian clothes, in a number of incidents, killed civilians to obtain clothing. Retreating soldiers and also civilians were known to have carried on sporadic looting during that period of disorder.[68]

The defense also tried to prove that there were certain circumstances, which the Chinese created, that made some atrocities inevitable. Hidaka Shinrokuro, then Consul General in Shanghai, testified as the first witness for the defense and described some of these circumstances. Hidaka did not elaborate on what happened in Nanking, dismissing the reports of atrocities as "based on hearsay." Instead, he pointed to the Chinese scorched-earth policy and the anti-Japanese propaganda as major factors that fostered "a feeling of hostility and an attitude of suspicious watchfulness" among the Japanese soldiers, and he suggested that such hostile activities among the Chinese civilians compelled the Japanese army to resort to robbery-like requisition and other violent acts. He also maintained that the responsibility for the lawlessness in Nanking rested primarily on the Nationalist government, which left the city without any civil administration, as well as on the Chinese soldiers who changed into civilian clothing and mingled with the civilians in the Safety Zone. Nevertheless, Hidaka's testimony confirmed an important fact, that is, that Matsui did learn about the atrocities and thus was aware of them. According to Hidaka, when he met Matsui on January 1, 1938, Matsui was "sincerely grieved to find for the first time that some of his subordinates had done wrong." The prosecution did not cross-examine Hidaka because, according to the prosecution, the witness turned out to present not only "certain admissions valuable to the prosecution" but also statements so completely at variance with the mass of the prosecution witnesses' oral testimony, alluding most likely to Hidaka's statement about Matsui's knowledge of atrocities. Again, the prosecution did not pay much attention to what kinds of atrocities Matsui had learned about. Instead, they focused on whether Matsui had been aware of the atrocities.[69]

Most of the former army officers who had served under Matsui and stood at the court as witnesses testified in a similar manner. Both Nakayama Yasuto, CCAA staff then, and then SEF chief of staff Iinuma said that quite a few first-line troops entered Nanking by defying an initial order that only designated troops were to march inside the walls. The two former officers, however, maintained that the Chinese scorched-earth policy made that measure inevitable because the Chinese had burned down almost all the buildings where Japanese soldiers could have been quartered. Another witness, then 16th Division staff chief Nakasawa, pointed to the absence of Chinese civil administration in Nanking and implicitly blamed the lawlessness in the city on the Chinese. These three witnesses did admit to having heard reports concerning the looting and other misconduct committed by Japanese soldiers. Nakasawa's observation was that the cases of looting and rape had been sporadic and limited and that the Chinese might have committed some of them since such acts were common on the battlefield in China. At the same time, the three disclaimed Matsui's responsibility. Nakayama emphasized how the organizational arrangement made it difficult for the CCAA to extend effective command over the subordinate units with respect to policing and disciplinary matters. He also stated that until the end of December 1937 the CCAA lacked a legal affairs department, which the SEF and the Tenth Army had, because the CCAA was only designed to coordinate the military operations of the two armies, and thus was unable to prosecute or punish criminals within those armies. Iinuma mentioned Matsui's repeated instructions that his subordinate officers should "do their best to prevent the occurrence of misdeed" as well as his insistence "on a severe punishment on lawlessness." It is beyond doubt that these witnesses made their statements in order to exonerate Matsui of criminal responsibility. Yet they did harm to Matsui to a certain extent. Although Nakayama's statement relating to the organizational problem of the CCAA was certainly true, at the same time it attested to the lack of clarity regarding where legal responsibility lay in the Japanese army—hence the "command irresponsibility." This was a weakness the prosecution later exploited aggressively. In addition, although Iinuma discussed Matsui's repeated instructions for the prevention of misdeeds, this gave another tool to the prosecution: it could point to an apparent inconsistency between Matsui's capacity to issue such instructions and the alleged lack of legal authority in the CCAA.[70]

Since the three witnesses were present in Nanking with Matsui, the prosecution was eager to press them. The prosecution's cross-examination of Nakayama turned out to be useful in categorizing the atrocities for later historians. The prosecution asked him whether he had seen any large-scale execution of civilians, and Nakayama's answer was an absolute "no." Nakayama did say that the Japanese troops had executed some Chinese POWs, but added that the story had been exaggerated. He did not deny the occurrence of misconduct by Japanese soldiers and recalled that Matsui had started receiving reports about unlawful acts by Japanese soldiers immediately after entry into Nanking from various sources such as the military police, his subordinates, and Japanese diplomats. Nakasawa mostly concurred with Nakayama's statement. Nakasawa said that he had seen the bodies of only soldiers, denied seeing any women or children among the dead bodies, and admitted that some cases of plundering and rape had occurred.[71]

The defendants maintained this line of argument consistently, that is, the Japanese army committed some individual criminal acts such as robbery, rape, and murder, but did not conduct a large-scale massacre. Muto stated in his pretrial testimony that he had been aware of ten to twenty reports of such crimes, but could not "believe or imagine that there were incidents numbering into thousands." Matsui was equally firm in denying the mass execution of civilians, saying, "That is absolutely untrue. There was no, absolutely no, grounds for such accusations. This I can state upon my honor."[72]

Witness Nakasawa, however, made quite an intriguing remark regarding the fate of Chinese POWs. In the discussion of the registration of civilians in the Safety Zone for the purpose of separating out plainclothes Chinese soldiers late in December 1937, he said that, "Those who were determined to be stragglers by these means were turned over to the Headquarters of the Shanghai Expeditionary Force. Accordingly, it is indeed not true that they were slaughtered."[73] President Webb, however, subjected Nakasawa's last statement to a relentless scrutiny by questioning him on behalf of the judges. When Webb asked Nakasawa whether the prisoners had been tried for any offense, Nakasawa simply answered, "That is a matter for superior headquarters. I do not know what happened later."[74]

Most likely, this statement by Nakasawa not only left a serious doubt in the minds of judges regarding the fate of Chinese war prisoners, it also made them aware of the tendency of Japanese military commanders to evade responsibility by transferring it to others. Although Nakasawa apparently tried to shift it upward, Iinuma seems to have done so in the opposite direction by mentioning the "chain of command." The following exchange between Iinuma and the prosecution during the cross-examination exemplifies such an attitude:

Q: Who told General Matsui [about the misbehavior]?

A: I believe it must have been the military police.

Q: Did you tell him?

A: No.

Q: Did the Japanese Consul General tell him?

A: That I do not know.

Q: Do you know whether his divisional commanders told him?

A: I don't think that was possible.

Q: Why not?

A: The chain of command is different.

Q: How is it different?

A: Well, the system—if a divisional commander wanted to report something, either the commander of the division or his Chief of Staff would report it to the Chief of Staff, to General Matsui, or . . . would report it to the Chief of Staff of the Army or to Prince Asaka, and from there it would go to General Matsui.[75]

It seems that in the last statement Iinuma tried to show that someone in this "chain of command" was responsible for the soldiers' misbehavior, but not Matsui. Predictably, the prosecution narrowed down the question to who in that "chain of command" should be held responsible for alleged atrocities. When two key defendants—Matsui and Muto—finally testified at the court, both refused to accept any responsibility for the enforcement of military discipline among troops under their command. Muto said,

The functions of Assistant Chief of Staff (which are provided for in the Higher Headquarters Service Regulations) were to assist the Chief of Staff and chiefly to act as an intermediary to coordinate work of other organs, etc. in replacement of personnel, supplies or provisions, arms and ammunition, etc., so that these matters might be carried out smoothly. The Assistant Chief of Staff was partial assistant for the Chief of Staff and had no power to make a decision at all. Moreover, the duties were not to maintain military discipline and morale.[76]

As for Matsui, he again emphasized the limited authority he had as CCAA commander and said, "my relation with the officers and men in the field in regard to the command and supervision was entirely indirect." He also emphasized his geographical separation from the site of the alleged atrocities: he had been "sick in bed at Soochow, some 140 miles away" at the time Nanking was captured and heard rumors of atrocities for the first time "after entering Nanking on 17 December." Besides, Matsui added that he had done everything in his power as the CCAA commander to "prevent the occurrence of such unfortunate incidents" and "to give severe punishment to the guilty."[77]

In its cross-examination, the prosecution soon pointed to what looked like an apparent inconsistency in his statement, that is, his disclaiming of responsibility for the military discipline of his soldiers on the one hand and the fact of his having taken some measures to enforce such discipline on the other. When Brigadier H. G. Nolan, cross-examining Matsui on behalf of the prosecution, asked Matsui if he had the authority to enforce discipline on the troops under his command, Matsui made a distinction between the operational authority, which he had, and the authority to handle the discipline, which he did not have. In answer to Nolan's question about what enabled Matsui to take necessary measures to prevent misbehavior and punish the offenders immediately after his entry into Nanking, Matsui defined it as "obligation rather than authority."[78]

This explanation did not satisfy Nolan. Exchanges between the two ensued and ended inconclusively with more ambiguous statements from Matsui:

Q: Well, then, how do you explain your efforts to show that you ordered severe punishment meted out to the guilty for the outrages in Nanking, and that you did everything in your power as Commander of the Central China Area Army to give severe punishment to the guilty?

A: I had no authority except to express my desires as overall Commander-in-Chief to the commander of the army under my command and the divisional commanders thereunder.

Q: And I suppose a general officer commanding expresses his desires to those subordinates to him in the form of orders?

A: No, that would be difficult in the light of law.

Q: Well, when you want those who serve under you to do something, General Matsui, what do you do about it?

A: The authority that was vested in me was to command—was the overall operational command of the two armies under me. That was all. Hence it would be a very difficult matter to determine my legal responsibilitys [*sic*] with regard to my—to the question of discipline and morals and I cannot make any statement, any definite statement, on that at the present time. I cannot make any definite statement on that here.[79]

Nolan finally asked Matsui straightforwardly who the high command in Tokyo would hold responsible if they were dissatisfied with the conduct of Matsui's army. Matsui again avoided a direct answer, seemingly trying to absolve himself by referring only to his past record of having received no reprimand regarding the Nanking operation. His explanation was so ambiguous that Nolan seems to have become quite irritated. Moreover, it is possible that even Matsui himself did not know clearly what he was trying to say.[80]

The judges apparently wished to ask the same question and requested Matsui to clarify his authority over disciplinary matters as the CCAA commander. Matsui's answer was slightly different from the one he had given the prosecution, but it retained its ambiguity. According to him, he "could not say that the maintenance of military discipline had no connection with military strategy" and thus thought that he "did have the power to interfere in matters relating to military discipline." Nevertheless, he finished with the statement that "in the strict legal sense I did not conceive myself as having the power to give specific orders . . . with regard to the maintenance of military discipline."[81]

It is possible to interpret Matsui's ambiguous statement as a court tactic employed by the defense, and one historian has criticized it as a major cause of Matsui's ultimate fate.[82] One may, however, also consider it an example of a typical problem haunting Japanese military personnel at the time, that is, "command irresponsibility" or the tendency to shift responsibility either up or down the command chain. Maruyama Masao, a Japanese political scientist, quoted this exchange between Matsui and Nolan in his book and said,

This common stand of the defendants can certainly not be dismissed as a ruse thought up on the spur of the moment to wriggle out of responsibility. Most of the men in the dock had actually been officials in the Imperial Government and, however politically they may have behaved, the "bureaucratic spirit" (Max Weber's *Beamtengeist*) invariably lurked in the back of their minds. Accordingly when things went badly, they could always represent themselves as having been "specialist officials" (*Fachbeamte*), who could function only within the professional limits laid down by the rules and regulations.[83]

Matsui and Muto, one of Matsui's CCAA staff officers, demonstrated this *Beamtengeist* in their mutually contradictory statements regarding where the legal responsibility lay in the Japanese army. Both in his pre-trial interrogation as well as in his court testimony, Matsui hinted that divisional commanders should be in charge of discipline. His stance showed a clear contrast with Muto's defense, in which his counsel explicitly stated that it was "the duty of the Shanghai Expeditionary Force and the Tenth Army . . . to maintain discipline and morality among the troops." Since both Matsui and Muto tried to shift the legal responsibility outside the CCAA, their difference was not very significant for their court defense. As for which opinion was actually correct, both told the truth in a sense: the division, which was a military unit existent both in peace and wartimes, had legal responsibility at least in peacetime, whereas corps and armies, which were created in wartime to group together divisions, were also vested with an overlapping authority, as shown in the court-martial records of the CCAA and the Tenth Army. It was possibly this lack of clarity that enabled Matsui and Muto to make statements contradictory to each other. Yet that even an army commander and his subordinate staff officer could contradict each other regarding an important issue such as who was chiefly responsible for the enforcement of military discipline attests to the "command irresponsibility" that pervaded the Japanese Army.[84]

There was yet another factor that forced Matsui to hold divisional commanders accountable for the enforcement of discipline. Matsui seemingly pointed to divisional command in an apparent effort to spare Prince Asaka, who had been the SEF commander at the time of the Nanking campaign, from blame. Thus, one can see how Prince Asaka, who was not indicted as a war criminal, affected the course of the trial just as his presence in Nanking had been a major impetus to atrocities: it was mainly the SEF that executed a large number of Chinese POWs prior to the victory parade on December 17, 1937, most likely to guarantee the safety of the prince.[85]

Thus, the defense tried to resolve the question of who was supposed to assume responsibility for the alleged atrocities by shifting it to almost no one or at best someone outside the courtroom. Compared with the prosecution's strong case, this tactic was obviously weak and destined to fail.

When the trial entered its final stages of summation by the two sides, the defense was still fighting a losing battle, but not without a minor success. In its individual summation, the prosecution still contended that Matsui was guilty under Count 45. Yet by this time the prosecution clearly made little effort to convince the judges that Matsui was guilty of that count, that is, guilty of playing an active role in the Nanking incident. Judging from the particular pains they took to show that Matsui was fully aware of the atrocities, their main focus shifted to proving Matsui's guilt for failing to execute his duties as commander despite his knowledge of atrocities. Nevertheless, the prosecution did not alter its finding about the Rape of Nanking. They apparently did not try to resolve a question that many scholars and journalists today dare not attempt to solve either: how the mere negligence of the commander resulted in such a large-scale massacre—most typically symbolized by the huge number of victims. Reflecting this ambiguity, it seems that the prosecution had less confidence in the numerical data contained in its evidence. In the overall summation of the incident, the prosecution cautiously said, "It is impossible definitely to determine the total number of" victims, and simply enumerated four data provided by the Chinese side, that is, the burial record of the Red Swastika (43,071), that of the Ch'ung-shan-t'ang (112,266), the report of the Chief Prosecutor of the District Court of Nanking (260,000), and the report on the investigations of Japanese war crimes committed in Nanking (300,000). The prosecution left the question regarding the number of victims to the judges. As for the defense, it did not focus on this issue. Although it did point in an appendix to an apparent inconsistency in the numerical data—300,000 people alleged by the prosecution to have been killed in a city with a population of 200,000—it did not read the appendix in court.[86]

Historian Hata Ikuhiko attributes Matsui's ultimate fate to the poor court tactics employed by the defense. He said that the defense should have admitted to some atrocities in Nanking, instead of denying them outright, and then contested the credibility of each case. This judgment is too harsh because the defense team had some handicaps. First, conflicts of interests among the defendants made an effective defense almost impossible. A notable example is the different opinions among the defendants regarding where the responsibility for military discipline should lie in the Japanese army. Second, the absence of a chief defense counsel, who could have coordinated or reconciled the defense strategies among defendants, hampered the defense and worsened that situation. A notable example of failure accruing from such handicaps occurred when a former Japanese diplomat testified for the defense. Ishii Itaro, chief of the Foreign Ministry's East Asian Affairs Bureau at the time of the Rape of Nanking, appeared in the court as a defense witness for then Foreign Minister Hirota. Ishii explicitly stated that there had been numerous reports of atrocities filed by third countries and received by Japanese government ministries. In an effort to clear Hirota of any responsibility for the Japanese military's action, however, he emphasized that Hirota had done his best "to suppress such disgraceful deeds." He also said that "the atrocities in Nanking were stopped" for the first time after the army dispatched a special envoy led by general Honma. In a move reminiscent of the serious discord between the diplomatic service and the military before and during the war, the counsel for Matsui examined Ishii, who was a defense witness, in a manner resembling a cross-examination and asked questions about some minor points such as the meaning of "atrocities" in Japanese and the purpose of the Honma mission to Nanking. Overall, Ishii proved to be a more useful witness for the prosecution than for the defense. When the prosecution cross-examined him, Ishii went all the way to state, "The only impression that I still retain in my mind is that the atrocities were very severe."[87]

Still, the biggest handicap imposed on the defense was the same factor that benefited the prosecution, that is, the prevailing hostile environment toward the former enemy immediately after the war. By the time the court deliberation ended in Tokyo, the Chinese Nationalist government had already convicted and executed Lieutenant General Tani and three Japanese officers in Nanking. Also, the trials of other Japanese military leaders such as Honma Masaharu and Yamashita Tomoyuki, who were held responsible for the Bataan Death March and atrocities in the Philippines in 1944–45, respectively, ended with death sentences for both. Yamashita's case not only helped the prosecution in deepening the prevailing atmosphere surrounding the court, but also provided a precedent for Matsui's case—one in which a military commander was held responsible for his failure to prevent atrocities committed by his soldiers. Faced with overwhelming odds, in what looked like a desperate attempt to offset the grim picture of the Rape of Nanking, the defense in its summation made reference to the atomic bombing and the Tokyo air raid as a more savage form of atrocities.[88]

Last and most important, the same legal mindset that affected the prosecution was also present among the defense counsels and influenced their manner of defense. In an effort to refute a substantial part of the prosecution's evidence, the defense often only questioned the probative value of documents such as affidavits presented by unsworn witnesses and based on hearsay.[89] Here, like the prosecution, the defense counsels proved themselves to be legal professionals and definitely not historians in their manner of treating the evidence. Whereas the prosecution tried to make all evidence look credible to create an image of the Rape of Nanking as a horrible bloodbath, the defense was inclined to disprove almost everything to create a more or less peaceful image of events at Nanking except for some cases of soldiers' misbehavior. This strategy backfired the first time a defendant or witness said something that even slightly contradicted that image—for example, an ambiguous statement about the fate of Chinese POWs. Moreover, the defendants' ambiguous statements about who was responsible for discipline problems, as well as their tendency to shift responsibility to people who were not present in the court, either because they were dead or not indicted, most likely gave the judges a negative image of the defendants. Therefore, although their defense strategy was understandable and completely acceptable as a legal strategy, it was destined to fail. From a scholarly viewpoint, neither the defense strategy nor the prosecution's line of argument was useful in clarifying the truth about the Rape of Nanking.

The Verdict

After a recess of nearly seven months, the court reconvened on November 11, 1948, to read the majority opinion and announce the verdict on each defendant. Before rendering judgment, the majority of the court, seven of eleven judges, threw out some counts alleged by the prosecution. The judges decided that the crimes described in Count 45—the one specifically created for defendants connected with the Nanking incident—were "cumulative with charges in Counts 54 and 55," that is, the participation in a "plan or conspiracy to order, authorize and permit" the subordinate military personnel to mistreat the allies' military service men or civilians (Count 54) and the reckless and deliberate disregard of "their legal duty to take adequate steps" to avoid such a mistreatment (Count 55). Judging from the wording of each count, one may conclude that Count 54 absorbed the charges of Count 45, which accused several defendants of having intentionally ordered the slaughter of the POWs and of the civilian population.[90]

The majority opinion contained its own version of the "Rape of Nanking" by accepting a part of the prosecution's argument. According to its finding, the Japanese army killed over 30,000 POWs within seventy-two hours after their surrender as well as more than 20,000 Chinese men of military age on a pretext of separating plainclothes soldiers from ordinary civilians. In addition, the majority judges adopted in their verdict a story provided by a Chinese witness that the Japanese interned about 57,000 civilians in Nanking's suburb and killed most of them. By incorporating the misquotation of Smythe's original finding by the prosecution witness Bates, these judges concluded that about 12,000 noncombatants, including women and children, met their death in the first two or three days. To support these claims, the majority opinion cited the burial records of the two Chinese organizations and determined the number of total victims to be about 155,000. Thus, the majority judges treated the numerical data originating from Chinese private or public sources slightly differently from the way the Chinese authorities and the prosecution had done, that is, the judges seemingly collected the victims' figures in various witness accounts to make the combined total of these come somewhat close to the number of corpses reportedly buried by the two organizations. In this respect, the majority ruling was superior to many of the Chinese legal documents and reports that simply accumulated the available figures without considering the possibility of overlap. Still, it failed to resolve the question of a numerical gap between the small number of people reportedly remaining in the city and the larger number of those alleged to have been killed. Without determining the size of Nanking's population at the time of the fall, the majority opinion simply said that "over one-half of its one million inhabitants" fled from Nanking.[91]

Of the three dissenting judges, only Judge Radhabinod M. Pal of India found all the defendants, including Matsui, innocent. Although Pal did not deny the "devilish and fiendish character of the alleged atrocities," he questioned the value of evidence presented by "excited or prejudiced observers" and concluded that such evidence could not be accepted by the world without some suspicion of exaggeration. To exemplify his point, Pal referred to one of the Chinese witnesses, Chen Fu-pao, who claimed to have witnessed a massacre of thirty-seven men, one case of murder, one case of arson, and two cases of rape. Pal sarcastically called him "a somewhat strange witness" because, according to Pal, the Japanese seem to have taken such a special fancy of him as to take him to various places to witness their various misdeeds and yet spare him unharmed.[92]

The court did not read Pal's and other dissenting opinions as well as Webb's separate opinion despite the protest filed by the defense.

The sentencing of each defendant followed the reading of the majority opinion. Matsui was absolved of twenty-eight out of twenty-nine counts in the original indictment, including Count 54, which had apparently absorbed Count 45, judging from the opinion of the majority judges. In a sense, this was a victory for the defense because the judges concluded that Matsui had not taken an active role in the atrocities in Nanking as Count 45 or 54 charged. In the end, however, it was a devastating defeat for Matsui and his defense counsels. The majority ruling said,

Wholesale massacres, individual murders, rape, looting and arson were committed by Japanese soldiers. Although the extent of the atrocities was denied by Japanese witnesses the contrary evidence of neutral witnesses of different nationalities and undoubted responsibility is overwhelming. . . . In this period of six or seven weeks thousands of women were raped, upwards of 100,000 people were killed and untold property was stolen and burned. . . . From his own observations and from the reports of his staff he must have been aware of what was happening. . . . He did nothing, or nothing effective to abate these horrors. . . . He was in command of the Army responsible for these happenings. He knew of them. He had the power, as he had the duty, to control his troops and to protect the unfortunate citizens of Nanking. He must be held criminally responsible for his failure to discharge this duty.[93]

Thus, the tribunal found Matsui "guilty under Count 55," that is, guilty for having "deliberately and recklessly disregarded [his] legal duty to take adequate steps to secure the observance and prevent breaches" of the conventions of warfare. Then, the tribunal sentenced Matsui to death by hanging. Among the seven defendants who were sentenced to death at the IMTFE, only Matsui was guilty under a single count while some other defendants escaped the death penalty despite being found guilty of multiple counts, including Count 55.[94]

As for the other defendants accused in connection with the Rape of Nanking, former Foreign Minister Hirota was found guilty under the same count. The judges decided that Hirota was "derelict in his duty" because he failed to insist before the cabinet on immediate actions to terminate the atrocities and that "his inaction amounted to criminal negligence." His sentence was also death by hanging. Since Hirota was found guilty under two other counts as well, one cannot determine whether the judges weighed his responsibility for the Nanking atrocities most heavily in this sentencing. As for Muto, he was exonerated of any charge relating to the Rape of Nanking due to his subordinate position at the time, although he was found guilty under Counts 54 and 55 for his responsibility for atrocities in the Philippines and was sentenced to death.[95]

The death sentence for Matsui was likely to have been a close vote. In a petition filed to MacArthur, Matsui's defense counsels argued that not more than six or seven judges voted for Matsui's death sentence.[96] One can verify only three of the four or five judges who voted against Matsui's death penalty. Pal doubted even the validity of Count 55 itself—the one for negative criminality—pointing to the indictments of the Nuremberg Trial where such a count was nonexistent. In addition, Pal maintained that Matsui had taken steps to rectify the situation, however inadequate they were, and thus could not be found insincere enough in his actions to be convicted for "deliberate and reckless disregard of legal duty." He further argued that punishing those who have misbehaved is not the function or duty of a commander-in-chief because he was "entitled to rely on the efficient functioning of the machinery supplied for the purpose of enforcing discipline in the army." According to Pal, Matsui did what he was supposed to do when he received reports from subordinate commands regarding soldiers' misconduct and expressed his disapproval of such conduct. Pal further said that such an expression of disapproval was expected to prompt the subordinate commands to start "the efficient functioning of the machinery . . . for the purpose of enforcing discipline."[97] President Webb, Bernard V. A. Roeling of the Netherlands, and Henri Bernard of France, did not contest the idea that neglect of duty constitutes a crime in some cases. Nevertheless, Webb implicitly opposed death sentences to some defendants charged with conventional war crimes. He defined the purpose of punishing war criminals as a deterrent to others and said that imprisonment for life should be a more suitable deterrent against such crimes than the death penalty. Webb also said that it might be "revolting to hang or shoot" some defendants who were of advanced age.[98] Although Bernard did not explicitly discuss Matsui's case, he was likely to have had in his mind an acquittal or a lighter penalty for Matsui in view of his statement that "the failings from their professional duty or from their moral obligations could not be considered as an element of the crime of complicity by negligence, imprudence, or omission unless the crimes committed were the direct result of this negligence, imprudence or omission, or could only have been committed because of this negligence, imprudence or omission."[99]

As for another dissenting judge, Roeling, despite his caution about the careless application of the criminal responsibility for omission, he clearly stated that he agreed with the majority about the death penalty handed down to Matsui. His major contention was that military men should chiefly be held responsible for crimes of omission on the field rather than placing the blame on every member of the government whose civilian members were not directly connected with conduct on the field. Arguing along this line, he found Hirota, then foreign minister indicted under several counts including Count 55, innocent.[100]

The counsels for all defendants appealed to MacArthur on November 21 to request a review of the verdicts based on the Charter of the International Military Tribunal for the Far East Article 17, which allowed the Supreme Commander for the Allied Powers to "reduce or otherwise alter the sentence except to increase its severity." MacArthur, however, confirmed the convictions after consulting with the diplomatic representatives of the Far Eastern Commission on November 24. The defense then lodged an appeal with the Supreme Court of the United States for writs of habeas corpus. Although Supreme Court justices met to hear the preliminary argument, they in the end turned down the appeal, citing the lack of jurisdiction on December 20. The Supreme Court decision sealed the fate of Matsui and the other six defendants on death row.[101]

Matsui calmly accepted his fate. To a Buddhist chaplain attached to the Sugamo Prison, he said, "The Nanking Incident was a terrible disgrace. . . . I, at least, should have ended this way, in the sense that it may serve to urge self-reflection on many more members of the military of that time."[102] Still, his mind was not completely at peace prior to the execution. Just as he told the chaplain, he said in his last letter to his wife Fumiko that "a part of allegations about the Nanking atrocities was true" and that he was ready to give himself up to pay for the disgrace in place of many of his subordinates at the time. In the same letter, however, he also said that the prosecution made up the story of a large-scale massacre by distorting the facts.[103]

Matsui and the other six Class A war criminals were hanged at midnight on December 23, 1948. Lieutenant General Walton H. Walker was in charge of the actual execution and had the seven bodies cremated and their remains scattered at an unknown location.[104]

The Origins of Controversy

The first source of controversy about the Rape of Nanking was a problem peculiar to war crimes trials. As early as 1943, an American scholar issued the following warning: "[A war crimes trial based on the assumption that] the victors bear no original responsibility for the war or the manner in which it was conducted . . . is not essentially an inquiry into facts, but a collective expression of sentiment—in this case of retribution and aggressive sentiment."[105] The court deliberation on the Rape of Nanking substantiated this theory. The prosecution on the one hand analyzed their evidence based on their own preconception about the Rape of Nanking and introduced some questionable evidence. As a consequence, the prosecution broadened, or even distorted, the nature of atrocities in Nanking and made the Rape of Nanking look like an incident comparable to the Nazi atrocities. As the next chapter will show, the effect of this comparison lingers today: some scholars and journalists from time to time try to establish a parallel between the Rape of Nanking and the Jewish Holocaust. One may, however, say that the prosecutors did not commit these errors willfully and that they carried out their legal duties faithfully as legal professionals. The defense on the other hand tried to discredit every allegation about the atrocities, including what had really happened, such as the execution of many POWs. As a consequence, the defense defined the nature and extent of the Rape of Nanking too narrowly and focused only on the limited issue of the soldiers' misconduct. Yet, like the prosecution, the defense counsels, as legal experts, adopted such an approach out of a sincere effort to exonerate the defendants of the prosecution's charges. Although the two sides pursued completely opposite objectives, both faced the evidence in the same manner, that is, treating the whole set of evidence as an entity instead of analyzing individual pieces separately. Since they were legal experts and not historians, no one involved in the tribunal's deliberation was to blame for such an attitude. The real problem started when historians and journalists accepted the evidence and approach employed by these legal professionals with few modifications. As the next chapter will show, those who have participated in the Rape of Nanking controversy presented their arguments very much like lawyers not only in their style of analysis but also in the way they criticized the other side.

The second source of the controversy rested in the imbalance between the verdict and the sentence. In a sense, the majority verdict of the Tokyo War Crimes Trial was correct in finding Matsui guilty only of negligence or responsibility for omission. Even though the execution of POWs was deliberate crime of commission, evidence available then and now suggests that Matsui did not play a direct role in it. As regards the nature of the atrocities, President Webb in his separate opinion implicitly ruled out the existence of genocidal intent in the Japanese conduct in his remark that the "crimes of the German accused were far more heinous, varied and extensive than those of the Japanese accused." Nevertheless, the tribunal handed down a death sentence to Matsui. This gross imbalance between the verdict, guilty only for negligence, and the penalty imposed, death by hanging, reflected the failure on the part of the judges to determine exactly what had happened in Nanking and how it had happened. Symbolically, the majority opinion entered two separate figures regarding the number of victims. In the discussion of the Rape of Nanking in general, they determined that the number of killed amounted to 155,000 people, which was apparently the sum total of disposed bodies recorded by the Red Swastika and Ch'ung-shan-t'ang. Later, in the sentencing of Matsui, however, they said that "upwards of 100,000 people were killed."[106]

Thereafter, the verdict and the sentence were reflected in the spectrum of views about the Rape of Nanking controversy. Those who focus on the verdict may contend that disregard of duty could not have resulted in such a large-scale massacre, whereas those who pay attention mainly to the death sentence may say that the magnitude of the penalty reflected the scale of atrocities.

NOTES

1. One of the first of such reports was filed with the Nanking municipal government on September 20, 1945. Chi Teng-chin, "Chi Teng-chin Pan Ch'i Mu Pei Jih-chun Sha-hai Chih Nanking-shih Cheng-fu Ch'eng-wen" [Chi Teng-chin's Report to the Nanking Municipal Government on Japanese Aggressor Troops' Murder of His Mother], 20 September 1945, in *TA*, p. 157. Lung Yu-chih, "Lung Yu-chih Pei Jih-chun Ch'ung-sha Te Chi-lu" [Finding Report on Lung Yu-chih's Murder by Japanese Aggressor Troops], comp. Ting Ch'ao, 31 July 1946, in ibid., p. 254, was one of the last ones.

2. Chan-fan Ch'u-li Wei-yuan-hui [Committee for the Disposition of War Criminals], "Chan-fan Ch'u-li Wei-yuan-hui Kuan-yu Sou-chi Nanking Ta-t'u-sha An Tzu-liao Tian Ti-12-tz'u Ch'ang-hui Chi-lu Chai-yao" [Extracts from the Minutes of the Twelfth Meeting of the Committee for the Disposition of War Criminals], 29 January 1946, in *TA*, p. 523. *NYT*, 1 April 1946, p. 11. Nanking-shih Lin-shih Ts'an-i-hui [Nanking Municipal Interim Council], "Nanking-shih Lin-shih Ts'an-i-hui Kuan-yu Pu-chu Tiao-ch'a Nanking Ta-t'u-sha An Ching-kuo Kai-shu" [Nanking Municipal Interim Council's Brief Account about Its Investigation of the Nanking Massacre], November 1946, in *TA*, p. 555.

3. Ch'en Wan-lu, "Ch'en Wan-lu Te Chieh-wen" [Ch'en Wan-lu's Statement], comp. Li Lung-fei, 1 October 1945, *HP*, pp. 611–12. Li Lung-fei, "Jih-chun Tsai Yen-tzuchi Chi-t'i T'u-sha Te Ch'ung-sha-piao Chi-lu" [Finding Report on Japanese Aggressor Troops' Massacre at Yentzuchi], 1 October 1945, in *TA*, p. 102. Lu Su, "Lu Su Ch'en-shu Jih-chun Tsai Ts'aohsiehhsia Chi-t'i T'u-sha Te Chieh-wen" [Lu Su's Statement on Japanese Aggressor Troops' Massacre at Ts'aohsiehhsia], comp. Chen Kuang-ching, 7 December 1945, in ibid., p. 55.

4. Wu Chang-te, "Wu Chang-te Ch'en-shu Jih-chun Tsai Hanchung-men Chi-t'i T'u-sha Te Chieh-wen" [Wu Chang-te's Statement on the Massacre at Hanchung Gate], 1 November 1945, in ibid., p. 62. Smythe, "Memorandum on Incident at the Ministry of Justice," 18 December 1937, no. 11, *DNSZ*, p. 24. "Nanking-shih Lin-shih Ts'an-i-hui Chiao Chung K'e Ch'en-shu Jih-chun Tsai Hanhsi-men Chi-t'i T'u-sha Ch'eng-wen Chih Nei-cheng-pu Han" [Message from the Nanking Municipal Interim Council to the Ministry of Interior Containing Chung K'e's Statement on Japanese Aggressor Troops' Massacre at Hanhsi Gate], 2 November 1946, in *TA*, pp. 66–67. *TA*, p. 98n. Nanking Shou-tu Ti-fang Fa-yuan [Capital City District Attorneys' Office], "Ti-jen Tsui-hsing Tiao-ch'a T'ung-chi-piao" [Statistical Table about Enemy's Criminal Acts], February 1946, in *HP*, pp. 408–09. For examples of Chinese eyewitnesses claiming to have seen the Nakajima Unit's insignia, see Hsu Chia-lu, "Hsu Chia-lu Pan Jih-chun Tsai Ta-fanghsiang Kuang-yang Ta-t'u-sha Shih Chih Nanking-shih Cheng-fu Ch'eng-wen" [Hsu Chia-lu's Report to the Nanking Municipal Government on the Massacre at the Ta-fanghsiang Square], 14 October 1945, in *TA*, p. 85, and Yu Chung-to and Yu Chu-shih, "Yu Chung-to Yu Chu-shih Pan Ch'i Tzu Tsai Tafanghsiang Pei Chi-t'i T'u-sha Chih Shou-tu Ti-fang Fa-yuan Ch'eng-wen" [Report by Yu Chung-to and Yu Chu-shih to the Nanking Local Court on Their Son's Murder at Tafanghsiang by Japanese Aggressor Troops], 29 March 1946, in ibid., p. 87.

5. Hsiak'uan Ching-ch'a-chu [Hsiak'uan Police Station], "Hsiak'uan Ching-ch'a-chu Tiao-ch'a Jih-chun Yuleiying Chi-t'i T'u-sha Chun-min Chih Shou-tu Ti-fang Fa-yuan Chien-ch'a-ch'u Kung-han" [Hsiak'uan Police Station's Official Letter to the

Nanking Local Court Prosecution's Office Concerning the Investigation of Japanese Aggressor Troops' Massacre at Yuleiying], 8 January 1946, in *TA*, p. 108. Sheng Shih-cheng et al., "Sheng Shih-cheng Teng Jih-chun Tsai Shanghsinhe Ti-ch'u Ta-t'u-sha Chih Nanking-shih K'ang-chan Sun-shih Tiao-ch'a Wei-yuan-hui Ch'eng-wen" [Sheng Shih-cheng et al.'s Report to the Nanking Committee for the Investigation of War Damages on Japanese Aggressor Troops' Massacre in the Shanghsinhe Area], 9 January 1946, in ibid., p. 100.

6. Ch'ung-shan-t'ang, "Nanking-shih Ch'ung-shan-t'ang Yen-mai Kung-tso I-lan-piao" [Working List of the Nanking Ch'ung-shan-t'ang's Burying Team], in *TA*, pp. 423–24. See Appendix C for its English version. Nanking Shou-tu Ti-fang Fa-yuan [Capital City District Attorneys' Office], "Nanking Shou-tu Ti-fang Fa-yuan Chien-ch'a-ch'u Feng-ling Tiao-ch'a Ti-jen Tsui-hsing Pao-kao-shu" [Report by the Capital City District Attorney's Office of Nanking about the Enemy's Criminal Activities], February 1946, in *HP*, pp. 404–10. Nanking-shih Cheng-fu [Nanking Municipal Government], ed., "Ti-jen Tui Yu Nanking Hui-huai Chi Ch'i Pao-hsing I-pan" [A Glimpse into Enemy's Destructive and Violent Activities in Nanking], 26 January 1946, in ibid., p. 461. Nanking Ta-t'u-sha An Ti-jen Tsui-hsing Tiao-ch'a Wei-yuan-hui [Committee for the Investigation of the Nanking Massacre], "Nanking Ta-t'u-sha An Ti-jen Tsui-hsing Tiao-ch'a Wei-yuan-hui Ti-1-tz'u Hui-i Chi-lu" [Minutes of the First Meeting of the Committee for the Investigation of the Nanking Massacre], 23 June 1946, in *TA*, pp. 534–35.

7. Nanking-shih Cheng-fu [Nanking Municipal Government], "Nanking-shih Cheng-fu Kuan-yu Jen-k'ou Shang-wang Shu-tzu Chih Nei-cheng-pu K'ang-chan Sun-shih Tiao-ch'a Wei-yuan-hui Tai-tien Kao" [Dispatch of the Nanking Municipal Government to the Committee for the Investigation of War Damages of the Ministry of Interior Concerning the Figures of Nanking Massacre Victims], 4 May 1946, in *TA*, pp. 523–34. Nanking Shou-tu Ti-fang Fa-yuan [Capital City District Attorneys' Office], "Nanking Tz'u-shan Chi-ch'uan Chi Jen-min Lu Su Teng Pao-kao Ti-jen Ta-t'u-sha Kai-k'uang T'ung-chi-piao" [Statistical Data Based on Reports by Charity Organizations in Nanking and Citizen Lu Su about the Massacre], n.d., in ibid., p. 553. Kuo-min Cheng-fu [Nationalist Government], "Kuo-min Cheng-fu Szu-fa Hsing-cheng-pu Kuan-yu Jih-chun Tsai Nanking Ta-t'u-sha Te Chan-tsui Shen-ch'a-piao" [Investigation Report by Nationalist Government's Justice Ministry Concerning Japanese Troops' War Crimes Relating to the Rape of Nanking], n.d. 1946, in *HP*, p. 545. It seems that the total of 26,100 victims in Hsiak'uan as reported by the Nanking District Attorneys' Office also entailed a certain degree of duplication. The police in the Hsiak'uan area first calculated the total victims in the area as 9,796, some of whom were buried. (Hsiak'uan Ching-ch'a-chu [Hsiak'uan Police Station], "Hsiak'uan Ching-ch'a-chu Tiao-ch'a Jih-chun Tsai Yen-chiang-pian I-t'i Chi-t'i T'u-sha Chun-min Kei Shou-tu Ti-fang Chien-ch'a-ch'u Te Kung-han" [Hsiak'uan Police Station's Official Letter Concerning Japanese Aggressor Troops' Massacre of Military and Civilian Personnel on the River Shore to Nanking District Attorney's Office], 8 January 1946, in *HP*, p. 403.) Then, the chief of the ward that includes the area obtained the figure of 15,991 by quoting a portion of Red Swastika statistics. (Wu Chia-kan, "Nanking-shih Ti-7-ch'u Ch'u-ch'ang Wu Chia-kan Chih Nanking-shih Cheng-fu Ch'eng-wen" [Statement Submitted to the Nanking Municipal Government by Nanking 7th Ward Chief Wu Chia-kan], 20 May 1946, in ibid., pp. 470–74.) The sum total of these two figures is 25,787. Although there is a discrepancy of about 300 between this figure and 26,100, it is reasonable to assume that the report used these two sources to compute the number of victims in the said area.

8. Remark made by Lieutenant Colonel Taketomi Shigefumi, then—1945–46—staff member of the Demobilization Bureau, quoted in Shimono, *Nankin Sakusen no Shinso* [Truth of Nanking Campaign], p. 100. Nakajima died of illness on October 19, 1945. He reportedly gasped his last breath when American military policemen knocked on the door of his hospital room to arrest him. Kimura, *Nakajima Kesago*, p. 267. Nanking-shih Lin-shih Ts'an-i-hui [Nanking Municipal Interim Council], "Nanking-shih Lin-shih Ts'an-i-hui Kuan-yu Pu-chu Tiao-ch'a Nanking Ta-t'u-sha An Ching-kuo Kai-shu" [Nanking Municipal Interim Council's Brief Account about Its Investigation of the Nanking Massacre], November 1946, in *TA*, p. 557, n. 2.

9. Hiramatsu Takashi, *Kyodo Butai Funsenshi* [Battle Records of Hometown Units] (Oita: Oita Godo Shinbunsha [Oita Godo Newspaper], 1983), p. 213. IPS, Interrogation of Tani Hisao, 23 February 1946, p. 3, case 375, M1683-63.

10. Kuo-fang-pu [Defense Ministry], "Kuo-fang-pu Shen-p'an Chan-fan Chun-shih Fa-t'ing Kuan-yu Tiao-ch'a Chan-fan Tani Hisao Tsui-cheng Te Pu-gao" [Public Notice Issued by the Military Tribunal for the War Criminals of the Ministry of National Defense Concerning the Investigation of Tani Hisao's Crimes], 28 October 1946, in *TA*, p. 550. Kuo-fang-pu [Defense Ministry], "Kuo-fang-pu Shen-p'an Chan-fan Chun-shih Fa-t'ing Chien-ch'a-kuan Chiu Tui Chan-fan Tani Hisao Te Ch'i-su-chuang" [The Prosecution's indictment against Tani Hisao at the Military Tribunal for War Criminals], 31 December 1946, in *HP*, p. 718. Kuo-fang-pu [Defense Ministry], "Tani Hisao Chan-fan An-chien Ch'i-su-chuang Chih Fu-chien" [Appendix to Indictment of War Criminal Tani Hisao], in ibid., pp. 722–42.

11. Tani Hisao, "Tani Hisao Chujo no Shinbensho" [Statement by Lieutenant General Tani Hisao], 15 January 1947, quoted in Suzuki Akira, *"Nankin Daigyakusatsu" no Maboroshi* [Illusion of the Rape of Nanking"] (Tokyo: Bungeishunju, 1973), pp. 130, 139. Takagi Sokichi, *Jidenteki Nihon Kaigun Shimatsuki* [Autobiographical Chronicle of the Imperial Japanese Navy] (Tokyo: Kojinsha, 1979), p. 65. *Okamura Neiji Taisho Shiryo* [Materials Concerning General Okamura Neiji], vol. 1 (Tokyo: Hara Shobo, 1970) quoted in Hata, *Nankin Jiken* [Nanking Incident], p. 239.

12. Sheng Shih-cheng et al., "Sheng Shih-cheng Teng Jih-chun Tsai Shanghsinhe Ti-ch'u Ta-t'u-sha Chih Nanking-shih K'ang-chan Sun-shih Tiao-ch'a Wei-yuan-hui Ch'eng-wen" [Sheng Shih-cheng et al.'s Report to the Nanking Committee for the Investigation of War Damages on Japanese Aggressor Troops' Massacre in the Shanghsinhe area], 9 January 1946, in *TA*, p. 100. Ch'en Che-wen, "Ch'en Che-wen Pan Jih-chun Shanghsinhe Chi-t'i T'u-sha Chih Shih Mei-yu Ch'eng-wen" [Chen Che-wen's Report to Shih Mei-yu on Japanese Aggressor Troops' Massacre in the Shanghsinhe Area], 11 February 1946 [*sic*], in ibid., p. 101. (Although *TA* listed this document with the date of 11 February 1946, this was highly likely to be the testimony submitted during the trial, that is, early 1947, judging from its content.) Kuo-fang-pu [Defense Ministry], "Shen-p'an Chan-fan Chun-shih Fa-t'ing Chien-ch'a-kuan Ch'en Kuang-yu Tui Chan-fan Tani Hisao Kung-su-tz'u" [Public Prosecution Statement by Ch'en Kuang-yu of Tani Hisao at the Military Tribunal for War Criminals], 8 February 1947, in *HP*, p. 743. Nanking Shou-tu Ti-fang Fa-yuan [Capital City District Attorneys' Office], "Nanking Shou-tu Ti-fang Fa-yuan Chien-ch'a-ch'u Feng-ling Tiao-ch'a Ti-jen Tsui-hsing Pao-kao-shu" [Report by the Capital City District Attorneys' Office of Nanking about the Enemy's Criminal Acts], February 1946, in *HP*, p. 407. (Among the Japanese units named in this report, the Hasegawa Unit allegedly responsible for the group massacre of 1,600 seems to mean then Tani's 6th Division's 47th Regiment commanded by then Colonel Hase-

gawa Masanori. Ibid., p. 408.) Nanking Shou-tu Ti-fang Fa-yuan [Capital City District Attorneys' Office], "Shou-tu Ti-fang Fa-yuan Chien-ch'a-ch'u Wei-sung Tani An-nei Pei-hai-jen I-hai Chien-ting-shu Chih Kuo-fang-pu Shen-p'an Chan-fan Chun-shih Fa-t'ing Kung-han" [Official Letter from the Nanking Local Court Prosecutorate to the Military Tribunal for War Criminals Presenting the Identification of Murder Victims' Bodies], 5 February 1947, in *TA*, pp. 599–600. Ogasawara Kiyoshi, special attorney representing Tani Hisao, "Ima koso Akasu 'Nankin Daigyakusatsu' no Shinso" [Truth of "Nanking Massacre" Revealed Today] *Shukan Sankei* [Sankei Weekly], 16 August 1971, p. 51.

13. Kuo-fang-pu [Defense Ministry], "Kuo-fang-pu Shen-p'an Chan-fan Chun-shih Fa-t'ing Kuan-yu Tui Chan-fan Tani Hisao Te P'an-chueh" [Judgement of the Defense Ministry's Military Tribunal for War Criminals on Tani Hisao], 10 March 1947, in *HP*, pp. 744–48; idem, "Tani Hisao Chan-fan An P'an-chueh-chuang Fu-chien Kuan-yu Chi-t'i T'u-sha Pu-fen T'ung-chi Chi-lu" [Record of Massacres Attached to the Verdict on Tani Hisao's Case at the Military Tribunal], 1947, in ibid., pp. 753–56. (Only at the end of the appendix did the verdict clarify briefly that eight of the twenty-eight incidents listed in the list were attributable to Tani's troops. Ibid., p. 756.) Kuo-fang-pu [Defense Ministry], "Tani Hisao Chan-fan An P'an-chueh-shu Fu-chien T'ung-chi Chi-lu" [Statistical Records Attached to Verdict on War Criminal Tani Hisao], 1947, in ibid., pp. 757–827. Kuo-fang-pu, "Shen-p'an Chan-fan Chun-shih Fa-t'ing Kuan-yu Tui Chan-fan Tani Hisao Te Pan-chueh" [Judgement of the Defense Ministry's Military Tribunal for War Criminals on Tani Hisao], in ibid., p. 749.

14. Quoted in Shimono, *Nankin Sakusen no Shinso* [Truth of Nanking Campaign], p. 101.

15. Hata, *Nankin Jiken* [Nanking Incident], p. 49. *Tokyo Nichinichi Shinbun* [Tokyo Nichinichi Newspaper], 30 November 1937; 4, 6, 13 December 1937, quoted in Kuroda Hidetoshi, *Nankin, Hiroshima, Aushubittsu* [Nanking, Hiroshima, and Auschwitz] (Tokyo: Taihei Shuppansha, 1974), pp. 80–83. The book that mentioned Tanaka was Yamanaka Minetaro, ed., *Kohei* [His Majesty's Soldiers] published in 1940.

16. *Hsin-hua Jih-pao* [New China Daily], 25 January 1938, p. 2.

17. Nanking Shou-tu Ti-fang Fa-yuan [Capital City District Attorneys' Office], "Nanking Shou-tu Ti-fang Fa-yuan Chien-ch'a-ch'u Feng-ling Tiao-ch'a Ti-jen Tsui-hsing Pao-kao-shu" [Report by Nanking District Attorney's Office about the Enemy's Criminal Acts], February 1946, in *HP*, p. 407. United Nations War Crimes Commission, Far Eastern and Pacific Sub-Commission, "List of War Criminals and Material Witnesses," no. 1, August 1946, M1683-48. Kuo-min Cheng-fu [Nationalist Government], "Kuo-ming Cheng-fu Szu-fa Hsing-cheng-pu Kuan-yu Jih-chun Tsai Nanking Ta-t'u-sha Te Chan-tsui Shen-ch'a-piao" [Investigative Report by the Nationalist Government Justice Department Regarding the Japanese Army's War Crimes in Nanking], 1946, in *HP*, pp. 535–37. *Tokyo Nichinichi*'s article on December 13, 1937, misprinted Noda's first name 毅, which reads "Tsuyoshi," as 嚴 reading "Iwao." *Tokyo Nichinichi*, 13 December 1937, quoted in Kuroda, *Nankin, Hiroshima Aushubittsu* [Nanking, Hiroshima, and Auschwitz], p. 83. The Chinese Nationalist government's document, which listed the names of Japanese personalities in the Asian way of surname first, reversed Noda's surname and first name and gave his first name as 岩 尾, which one could pronounce "Iwao." Kuo-min Cheng-fu [Nationalist Government], "Kuo-min Cheng-fu Szu-fa Hsing-cheng-pu Kuan-yu Jih-chun Tsai Nanking Ta-t'u-sha Te Chan-tsui Shen-ch'a-piao" [Investigative Report by the Nationalist Government Justice Department Regarding the Japanese Army's War Crimes in Nanking], 1946, in *HP*, p. 535.

18. IPS, Interrogation of Suzuki Jiro and Asami Kazuo, case 444, pp. 5–7, M1683–69. An Affidavit signed by Asami and Suzuki, 15 June 1946, IPS no. 1,920, RG331, M1690: Numerical Evidentiary Documents Assembled as Evidence by the Prosecution for Use before the International Military Tribunal for the Far East 1945–1947 (henceforth M1690), NA2, reel 272.

19. Testimony of Kitaoka Chieko, widow of Mukai Toshiaki, quoted in Suzuki Akira, *"Nankin Daigyakusatsu" no Maboroshi* [Illusion of the "Rape of Nanking"], p. 66.

20. Ibid., p. 67.

21. Headquarters Sugamo Prison, records regarding the release of inmates, 15 May 1947, File 99B; 26 August and 8 September 1947, File 99B, M1683–29; Sugamo Prison Records 1945–1952, RG338: Records of U.S. Army Commands 1942-: Records of the U.S. Eighth Army, Box 40, File 7 and Box 34, File 27. Chung-kuo Chu-jih Tai-piao-t'uan [Chinese Delegation in Japan], "Chung-kuo Chu-jih Tai-piao-t'uan Kuan-yu Chan-fan Tanaka Gunkichi Tai-pu Ching-kuo Chih Kuo-fang-pu 2-ting Tai-tien" [Dispatch from the Chinese Delegation in Japan to the Ministry of National Defense Second Department Concerning the Arrest of Tanaka Gunkichi], 9 June 1947, in *TA*, pp. 614–15.

22. Kuo-fang-pu [Defense Ministry], "Kuo-fang-pu Shen-p'an Chan-fan Chun-shih Fa-t'ing Chien-ch'a-kuan Tui Chan-fan Mukai Toshiaki Teng-jen Te Ch'i-su-chuang" [Indictment of the Prosecutor of the Military Tribunal for War Criminals to Mukai Toshiaki et al.], 4 December 1947, in *TA*, p. 615. Attorney of Mukai, "Joshinsho" [report to authorities] to the Chinese military court, original possessed by Kitaoka Chieko, printed on Suzuki, *"Nankin Daigyakusatsu" no Maboroshi* [Illusion of the "Rape of Nanking"], pp. 60–62.

23. Kuroda, *Nankin, Hiroshima, Aushubittsu* [Nanking, Hiroshima, and Auschwitz], p. 84, quoting *Shukan Shincho* [Weekly Shincho], 29 July 1972.

24. Kuroda, p. 88, quoting *Chugoku* [China], December 1971. The cameraman named Sato Shinju gives a more detailed account of his own experience in the Shanghai-Nanking battles, including his encounter with the two officers, in "Jugun to wa Aruku Koto" [War Correspondent Must Walk], in *NSS*2, pp. 495–641.

25. Yamamoto Shichihei, *Watashi no Naka no Nihongun* [Japanese Army within Myself], vol. 1, pp. 179–80; vol. 2, pp. 78, 158–60, 232–33. When the author of this book was in the Philippines during World War II, he chopped off the wrist of a comrade killed in action. He did so to remove the thumb to preserve the thumb bone for his kins. He severed the wrist with a Japanese sword, but in the process the pin connecting the sword grip to the blade was dislocated. As a result, his sword became almost useless. Sato, "Jugun to wa Aruku Koto" [War Correspondent Must Walk], in *NSS*2, p. 574.

26. Kuo-fang-pu [Defense Ministry], "Kuo-fang-pu Shen-p'an Chan-fan Chun-shih Fa-t'ing Chien-ch'a-kuan Tui Chan-fan Mukai Toshiaki Teng-jen Te P'an-chueh-chuang" [Judgement of the Military Tribunal for War Criminals on Mukai Toshiaki et al.], 18 December 1947, in *TA*, pp. 618–20.

27. Chiang Kai-shek, "Chiang Kai-shek P'i-chun P'an-ch'u Chan-fan Mukai Toshiaki Teng-jen Szu-hsing Chih Kuo-fang-pu Shen-p'an Chan-fan Chun-shi Fa-t'ing T'ing-ch'ang Shih Mei-yu Tien" [Chiang Kai-shek's Telegram to Shi Mei-yu Approving the Judgement to Sentence Mukai Toshiaki et al. to Death], 26 January 1948, in *TA*, p. 621.

28. Mukai's remarks quoted in Suzuki, *"Nankin Daigyakusatsu" no Maboroshi* [Illusion of the "Rape of Nanking"], p. 77.

29. Ibid., p. 86.

30. Article 5 of the tribunal's charter classified the crimes under the court's jurisdiction into three groups, that is, (a) crimes against peace, (b) conventional war crimes and (c) crimes against humanity. There were fifty-five counts, of which the first thirty-six charged "crimes against peace"; Counts 37 through 52 were concerned with "murder, and conspiracy to murder" related to all three previously mentioned categories; and the remaining three covered "other conventional war crimes and crimes against humanity" under categories b and c. Charter of the International Military Tribunal for the Far East, in *Trial of Japanese War Criminals*, Department State Publication 2613, Far Eastern Series 12 (Washington, D.C.: U.S. Government Printing Office, 1946), p. 40. IMTFE, pp. 33–71. For detailed discussion of the legal issues concerning the war crimes trials, especially the International Military Tribunal for the Far East, one should refer to Solis Horwitz, "The Tokyo Trial," *International Conciliation* 465 (November 1950): pp. 474–584; Joseph B. Keenan and Brendan Francis Brown, *Crimes against International Law* (Washington, D.C.: Public Affairs Press, 1950); Arnold C. Brackman, *The Other Nuremberg: The Untold Story of the Tokyo War Crimes Trials* (New York: Williams Morrow, 1987); Richard H. Minear, *Victors' Justice: The Tokyo War Crimes Trial* (Princeton, NJ: Princeton University Press, 1971); and Philip R. Piccigalo, *The Japanese on Trial: Allied War Crimes Operations in the East, 1945–1951* (Austin: University of Texas Press, 1979).

31. IMTFE, pp. 59–60.

32. Ibid., p. 60. Other defendants indicted under the same count were Araki Sadao (member of the Cabinet Advisory Council on China as of December 1937), Hashimoto Kingoro (Commander, the 13th Field Artillery Regiment, 10th Army), Hata Shunroku (Army's Superintendent of Education), Hiranuma Kiichiro (President of Privy Council), Hirota Koki (Foreign Minister), Itagaki Seishiro (attached to the Army's General Staff), Kaya Okinobu (Finance Minister), Kido Koichi (Education Minister), Muto Akira (Deputy Staff Chief, CCAA), Suzuki Teiichi (commander, 14th Regiment), and Umezu Yoshijiro (Deputy Minister of Army).

33. Each of the three counts distinguishes those involved in the Pacific War from those allegedly responsible for the Manchurian Incident and the Sino-Japanese War. In addition to Matsui, the following defendants were indicted under the latter charge: Araki, Hashimoto, Hiranuma, Hirota, Matsuoka Yosuke (President of South Manchurian Railway as of December 1937), and Minami Jiro (Governor-General of Korea).

34. IMTFE, pp. 68–69.

35. IMTFE, pp. 70–71. Other counts applied to Matsui were Counts 1, 2, 3, 4, and 5 (conspiracy to wage war); 6, 7, and 18 (planning and preparation of war); 19, 25, 26, 27, 28, 29, 30, 31, 32, 34, 35, and 36 (initiation and waging of war); 46 and 47 (atrocities in Canton and Hankow); 51 and 52 (aggression against Mongolia and the Soviet Union).

36. Ibid., p. 465.

37. IMTFE, pp. 3,887–88.

38. IPS Analysis of Documentary Evidence, Document no. 1724, analyzed on 24 May 1946; nos. 1,718–19, 1,722 analyzed on 25 May 1946; nos. 1,728–31, 1,733–39, analyzed on 28 May; no. 1,741, analyzed on 29 May 1946; M1683-48, Case 239.

39. IPS, Interrogation of Fukuda Tokuyasu, 25 April 1946, case 61 file 78, p. 13, M1683-22; Interrogation of Iinuma Mamoru, 3 May 1946, case 439 file 3, pp. 3, 11, M1683-68; Interrogation of Nakasawa Mitsuo, 30 April 1946, case 61, p. 7, M1683-22.

40. IPS, Interrogation of Asaka Yasuhiko, 1 May 1946, case 61, p. 3, M1683-22; Interrogation of Fujita Susumu, 2 May 1946, case 439, file 2, p. 13, M1683-68; Inter-

rogation of Fukui Kiyoshi, 27 April 1946, case 61, file 79, pp. 9–10, M1683-22; Interrogation of Ishikawa Tatsuzo, 11 May 1946, p. 9, M1683-68; Interrogation of Nakasawa Mitsuo, 30 April 1946, case 61, p. 11, M1683-22.

41. IPS, Interrogation of Ishikawa Tatsuzo, 11 May 1946, p. 11, M1683-68.

42. IPS, Interrogation of Tanaka Ryukichi, 24 May 1946, case 438, file 9, p. 11, M1683-68. IPS, Interrogation of Matsui, 8 March 1946, case 61, file 27, p. 9, M1683-22. Civil Censorship Detachment, summary of content of letter from Matsui to Kayano Nagatomo, 22 September 1946, 10 October 1946, file 99F, M1683-30. For the surprise expressed by the former Japanese military leaders, see IPS, Interrogation of Iinuma Mamoru, 3 May 1946, p. 5, M1683-68; Interrogation of Matsui Iwane, 7 March 1946, case 61, file 25, p. 2, M1683-22; Interrogation of Muto Akira, 22 April 1946, case 319, p. 3, M1683-58; Interrogation of Tada Hayao, 26 April 1946, case 53, file 29, p. 5, M1683-17. For Iinuma's inconsistent statement, see IPS, Interrogation of Iinuma, p. 3, M1683-68, and Iinuma Diary, 21, 26 December 1937, in *NSS*1, pp. 222, 227.

43. IPS, Interrogation of Asaka Yasuhiko, 1 May 1946, p. 4; Interrogation of Fukui Kiyoshi, 27 April 1946, p. 12; Interrogation of Nakasawa Mitsuo, pp. 14–15, M1683-22.

44. IPS, Interrogation of Matsui, 8 March 1946, case 61, p. 1; Interrogation of Nakasawa, 30 April 1946, p. 11, M1683-22. IPS, "Admission by Subject against Himself, Subject: Matsui Iwane," case 61, no. 42, M1683-22.

45. IMTFE, pp. 2,536-38. Mizutani Diary, 17 December 1937, in *NSS*1, p. 502.

46. IMTFE, pp. 2,631-32.

47. IPS 1,947, Court Exhibit (CE) 307, Ibid., pp. 4,461–62. IPS 2,466, CE 309, ibid., p. 4,470.

48. IMTFE, pp. 3,894, 3,897–98.

49. IMTFE, pp. 3,914-16.

50. IPS 1,947, CE 307; IMTFE, p. 4,462.

51. IPS 4,039, CE 329; IMTFE. pp. 4,600, 4,604. IPS 1,906; CE 328, ibid., p. 4,563. Originally, James Espy, "The Conditions at Nanking: January 1938," p. 2, 25 January 1938, 793.94/12674, M976-51.

52. IMTFE, pp. 2,633-34. IPS 2,466, CE 209; ibid., p. 4,467. IPS 4,039, CE 329; ibid. p. 4,601. IPS 2,466, CE 309; ibid., p. 4,471.

53. IMTFE, pp. 2,630, 2,632. Smythe, *War Damage in the Nanking Area*, p. 8n.

54. IPS 1,735, CE 206; IMTFE, pp. 2,599–2,602. IPS 1,729, CE 311; ibid., pp. 4,486–87. Bates, "Memorandum on Aftermath of Registration of Refugees at Nanking University," 26 December 1937, in *DNSZ*, pp. 100–07. IMTFE, p. 4,487.

55. IPS 1,736, CE 308; IMTFE, pp. 4,464–65. Grew to the Japanese Ministry of Foreign Affairs, 10 December 1937, enclosure no. 20 to Grew to the Secretary of State, 10 December 1937, 793.94/11840, M976-47. For Vautrin's personal history and activities in Nanking, see *RNFH*, pp. 129–38, 186–87.

56. IPS 1,702; CE 324, IMTFE, p. 4,538. IPS 1,702, CE 324; Ibid. p. 4,537. (The original of the document of the Nanking District Attorney's office was Nanking Shou-tu Ti-fang Fa-yuan [Capital City District Attorney's office], "Nanking Tz'u-shan Chi-ch'uan Chi Jen-min Lu Su Teng Pao-kao Ti-jen Ta-t'u-sha Kai-k'uang T'ung-chi-piao" [Statistical Data Based on Reports by Charity Organizations in Nanking and Citizen Lu Su about the Massacre], n.d., in *TA*, p. 553.) IPS 1,706, CE 327; ibid., pp. 4,541–42. (The original of the document from the investigating committee was Nanking Shou-tu Ti-fang Fa-yuan [Capital City District Attorneys' Office], "Nanking Shou-tu Ti-fang Fa-

yuan Chien-ch'a-ch'u Feng-ling Tiao-ch'a Ti-jen Tsui-hsing Pao-kao-shu" [Report by the Capital City District Attorneys' Office of Nanking about the Enemy's Criminal Acts], in *HP*, pp. 404–07.) Ibid., pp. 4,542–43, 4,547–48.

57. IMTFE, p. 3,906.

58. Douglas MacArthur said, "The choice . . . was not between fair trials or flawed trials but between show trials or no trials." Geoffrey Perret, *Old Soldiers Never Die: The Life of Douglas MacArthur* (New York: Random House, 1996), p. 510. Also, then Chief Justice Harlan Fiske Stone privately criticized the war crimes trial in Nuremberg as "the high-grade lynching party." Stone to Sterling Carr, 4 December 1945, Fiske Stone Papers, Manuscript Division, LC, quoted in ibid.

59. IMTFE, pp. 2,554, 2,588, 2,612, 3,937–41, 47,265–68.

60. IMTFE, p. 3,929, 4,473, 4,551, 4,480–81, 4,589–90. Neither Brooks nor Levin stated which affidavit mentioned that figure of 200,000 as the size of the population of Nanking at the time of its fall. It was likely to be either the IPS 4,039, CE 329 (Trautmann's message to the German Foreign Office), which said, "Thus far our Committee has been able to feed the 200,000 inhabitants of the city who have crowded into our zone." Ibid. p. 4,594, or the IPS 1,906, CE 328 (U.S. Vice Consul James Espy's report to the State Department), which included a statement, "In the neighborhood of four-fifths of the population had fled from the city." Ibid., p. 4,469. The defense reiterated this point in its final summation as well. Ibid., p. 47,271.

61. IMTFE, pp. 47,269–71.

62. IMTFE, pp. 47,271–73.

63. IPS 2,466, CE 309; IMTFE, p. 21,470.

64. For the statements about how the Japanese army spared the city from military fire, see the affidavits of Osugi Hiroshi, Defense Document (DD) 2,238, CE 3,398, IMTFE, p. 32,590; Ouchi Yoshihide, DD 2,668, CE 3,394, ibid., p. 32,601; Nishijima Takeshi, DD 2714, CE 3396, ibid., p. 32,612; and Iinuma Mamoru, DD 2,626, CE 3,399, ibid., p. 32,651. For the statements arguing about the devastation caused by Japanese soldiers after the occupation, see the testimony of Bates, ibid., p. 2,636; McCallum, IPS 2,466, CE 309, ibid., p. 4,469; and the report of then U.S. Vice Consul in Nanking Espy, included in IPS 1,906, CE 328; ibid., p. 4,568.

65. IMTFE, pp. 16,447, 16,450–51, 17,078–79.

66. Ibid., pp. 3,553–54.

67. Matsui's defense counsel said, "All our evidence will prove that no atrocities were carried out with the understanding and consent of Matsui, as referred in the statement of Prosecutor Hsiang. Our witnesses, who were actually on the job of guarding Nanking, will clarify the condition of guarding and the activities of the Japanese Army and the fact that there were, besides the casualties caused by fighting, no acts of atrocity as claimed by the prosecution." Ibid., p. 32,584.

68. IPS 1,906, CE 328; Ibid., p. 21,473. Originally from James Espy, U.S. Vice Consul, "The Conditions at Nanking: January 1938," p. 5, 25 January 1938, 793.94/ 12674, M976-51.

69. IMTFE, pp. 21,448, 21,453, 21,455–58, 21,460, 21,465.

70. Ibid., pp. 21,890–91, 21,899–900, 21,904–05, 21,912, 32,624, 32,650, 32,626–27, 32,651.

71. Ibid., pp. 21,923–25, 21,940–44, 32,639–42.

72. Ibid., pp. 3,463, 3,558.

73. Ibid., p. 32,625.

74. Ibid., p. 32,644.

75. Ibid., pp. 32,657–58.

76. Ibid., p. 33,090.

77. DD 2,738, CE 3,498; IMTFE, p. 33,820. Ibid., pp. 33,822, 33,825.

78. Ibid., pp. 33,873–74.

79. Ibid., pp. 33,875–76.

80. Ibid., p. 33,876.

81. Ibid., p. 33,883.

82. Hata, *Nankin Jiken* [Nanking Incident], p. 42.

83. Maruyama, *Thought and Behavior in Modern Japanese Politics*, p. 118.

84. IMTFE, pp. 3,461, 33,871, 44,915.

85. In his answer to a question regarding Prince Asaka's responsibility, Matsui said, "Prince Asaka had joined the army only about ten days before its entry into Nanking and in view of the short time he was connected with this army I do not think he can be held responsible. I would say that the Division Commanders are the responsible parties." IMTFE, p. 3,461. He repeated the last part of this statement again in the cross-examination: "Ordinarily discipline and morale within an army was the responsibility of the Division Commander." Ibid, p. 33,871.

86. IMTFE, pp. 40,147–56, 41,270, 41,274, 47,271.

87. Hata, *Nankin Jiken* [Nanking Incident], pp. 43–44. Horwitz, "The Tokyo Trial," p. 492. IMTFE, pp. 29,970–75, 29,985.

88. IMTFE, pp. 41,385, 47,226.

89. For example, see IMTFE, pp. 47,261–67.

90. IMTFE, pp. 48,452–53. The seven majority judges were Lord Patrick (Britain), Myron H. Cramer (U.S.A.), Mei Ju-ao (China), I. M. Zaryanov (U.S.S.R.), Edward Stuart McDougall (Canada), Erima Harvey Northcroft (New Zealand), and Delfin Jaranilla (the Philippines). Among them, Jaranilla of the Philippines presented a separate concurrent opinion demanding stiffer penalty for all the defendants. President of the tribunal, Sir William Flood Webb of Australia, agreed with the majority, but wrote a separate opinion to express his disagreement over legal and procedural matters, including his opposition to the death penalty. Three other judges, Radhabinod M. Pal of India, Bernard V. A. Roeling of the Netherlands, and Henri Bernard of France, dissented from the majority.

91. IMTFE, pp. 49,604–07.

92. Radhabinod M. Pal, "Judgement of the Honorable Justice Pal, Member from India," pp. 1,061, 1,064, 1,089, in *TWCT*, vol. 21. IPS 1,742, CE 208; IMTFE, pp. 2,608–10.

93. IMTFE, pp. 49,815–16.

94. Several scholars pointed to inconsistencies in sentencing. Minear, for example, said, "Koiso [Kuniaki, former prime minister], guilty of the conspiracy, of four counts of aggression, and of "reckless disregard of legal duty," received life imprisonment. Matsui, guilty *only* of "reckless disregard," was sentenced to death. Shigemitsu [Mamoru, former foreign minister], guilty of five counts of aggression and of "reckless disregard," received seven years' imprisonment. Minear, *Victors' Justice*, p. 210. (Italic by Minear.) Also, see Piccigallo, *The Japanese on Trial*, p. 28. Brackman, *The Other Nuremberg*, p. 382.

95. IMTFE, pp. 49,791, 49,820.

96. Ito Kiyoshi, Jodai Takayoshi, and Floyd J. Mattice to General Douglas MacArthur, Supreme Commander of the Allied Powers, "Petition for Review of Conviction and Sentence on Behalf of Matsui Iwane," p. 3, in *TWCT*, vol. 22.

97. Pal's Opinion, pp. 1,050, 1,117, in *TWCT*, vol. 21.

98. William Flood Webb, "Separate Opinion of the President, the International Military Tribunal for the Far East," 1 November 1948, pp. 17–18, in ibid.

99. Henri Bernard, "Dissenting Judgment of the Member from France of the International Military Tribunal for the Far East," 12 November 1948, pp. 16–17, in ibid.

100. Bernard Victor A. Roeling, "The Dissenting Judgment of the Member from the Netherlands," p. 178, 203–10, in ibid.

101. Charter of the International Military Tribunal for the Far East, in *Trial of Japanese War Criminals*, p. 44. Horwitz, "The Tokyo Trial," p. 573.

102. Hanayama, *Eien e no Michi: Waga 80-nen no Shogai* [Path to Eternity: My 80-Year Life], p. 220. Idem, *The Way of Deliverance*, pp. 185–86.

103. Matsui Iwane to Matsui Fumiko, 15 December 1948, *Nihon Shuho* [Japan Weekly], 25 February 1957, p. 10.

104. Three years later, Walker was commanding the U.S. Eighth Army in Korea. At midnight on December 23, 1951—about the time when Matsui and six other Class A war criminals were hanged three years earlier—a traffic accident killed Walker, and the cause of death was a broken neck. An adjutant of Walker was so mystified at this coincidence that he paid homage to a monument built in memory of the executed Class A war criminals in Japan in the following year. Tanaka, *Matsui Iwane Taisho no Jinchu Nisshi* [Field Diary of General Matsui Iwane], pp. 313–14.

105. C. Arnold Anderson, "The Utility of the Proposed Trial and Punishment of Enemy Leaders," *American Political Science Review* 37–6 (December 1943): p. 1,090.

106. Webb's Separate Opinion, p. 15, in *TWCT*, vol. 21. IMTFE, pp. 49,607, 49,815.

7

Sounds of Controversy

There was scarcely a debate about the Rape of Nanking until the establishment of formal diplomatic ties between Japan and the People's Republic of China in 1972. The lack of new information and original research allowed a rough consensus to form about the issue. The Chinese and the Westerners accepted the IMTFE indictment or ruling as their version of the Rape of Nanking, leaving no room for further discussion. A glimpse into some publications at the time indicates that not only the Communists on the mainland but also the Nationalists on Taiwan were still dependent on the IMTFE materials, especially its majority ruling, for their own account of the Rape of Nanking. Nationalist military sources usually mentioned the Rape of Nanking very briefly in their discussion of the Nanking campaign and estimated the number of victims at "more than 100,000 civilians" or "over 200,000 military and civilian personnel."[1]

The Japanese, at least in public, did not challenge this account of the Rape of Nanking until the early 1970s because the extremely negative image of pre-World War II Japan painted at the IMTFE had such a strong influence, even on the academic world, that few people voiced opposition to the IMTFE version of the Rape of Nanking. Among the few publications relating to the Rape of Nanking in Japan were magazine articles written by former newspaper correspondents who had accompanied the Japanese troops in China. Imai Masatake, a former correspondent of the *Tokyo Asahi Shinbun* [Tokyo Asahi Newspaper], said that he had witnessed Japanese soldiers shooting to death 400 to 500 Chinese men near the newspaper company's branch office in Nanking and that he had narrowly saved two men he knew. Another former correspondent, Hata Kensuke, who had not been in Nanking at the time, told a story of 20,000 POWs executed by Japanese soldiers. Hata apparently referred to the incident at the Mufu Mountain because he identified the commander of the responsible unit as Colonel Morozumi. His article was, however, full of factual errors: he referred to the unit Morozumi commanded as the 29th Regiment under the 2nd Division, although Morozumi was actually the commander of the 13th Division's 65th Regiment; he said that the incident had taken place on December 15, one day prior to the actual dates of December 16–17; according to Hata, the regiment escorted the POWs all the way inside the Nanking walls—a statement contradicting the stories of many eyewitnesses who testified to the executions near the Mufu Mountain.[2]

Such contradictions in his story, which appeared well before the start of the controversy, foreshadowed what was to come.

START AND RENEWAL OF CONTROVERSY

In the History Channel's program entitled "The Rape of Nanking" in its "History Undercover" series on August 22, 1999, one of the themes presented was an alleged cover-up of the Rape of Nanking for half a century by the Japanese.[3] But the heated controversy and debate about the incident in Japan, as I am about to describe, is more than enough to prove that there was no cover-up. Instead, many Japanese scholars and journalists have discussed this issue openly and tried to obtain the truth. Although quite a few of them disagree with the prevailing opinion in the United States, it is obvious that the expression of disagreement is not necessarily an act of cover-up.

Honda Katsuichi, a correspondent for the *Asahi Shinbun* [Asahi Newspaper], undoubtedly is the best known among the group commonly called *gyakusatsu-ha* [massacre school] in the Rape of Nanking controversy in Japan. As this chapter will show, one can recognize the emergence of subtle differences of opinions within this group with the passing of time. Therefore, it might not be advisable to categorize all the people close to Honda in a single group. Nevertheless, while recognizing differences, for convenience, this school will be called the "traditionalists" here.

Honda's reporting about the Japanese troops' wartime atrocities in China started shortly before Japan and Communist China normalized their diplomatic relations in 1972. His original version of the Rape of Nanking was an exact recounting of the stories from the Chinese side. In his *Chugoku no Tabi* [Trip to China], Honda said, quoting a Chinese witness,

the eyewitness accounts I obtained from [Rape of Nanking] survivors far surpassed the image I had constructed by reading the records available to me in Japan. . . . the Japanese troops that approached Nanking first occupied Yuhuatai to the south of the walls. They had already killed an enormous number of civilians. . . . Chiang Kai-shek's Nationalist forces had more than 100,000 soldiers. They might have been able to repel the attack with a determined resistance. But they betrayed the people and sold them off to the invading troops. . . . the Japanese army showered upon civilians and disorganized soldiers machine-gun bullets and rifle fire as well as hand grenades. They even unleased hungry dogs to let them eat the flesh of Chinese people. The two main streets . . . filled with corpses and blood became like a hell. . . . The Japanese troops marched on to the outside of the walls and moved along the Yangtze downstream (to the northeast) while massacring people in Hsiak'uan, the coal port, Paot'ach'iao and Ts'aohsiehhsia. In Yentzuchi, about seven kilometers from the Nanking walls, they cornered as many as 100,000 civilians to the river shore and slaughtered them with machine-guns. By this time, about 200,000 are estimated to have been killed including those massacred within the walls. . . . In the Tzuchin Mountain, they buried alive 2,000 people. The historically unprecedented tragedies like these continued through to early February the following year, resulting in the loss of 300,000 lives.[4]

The details in this account are almost identical with those found in the Chinese evidence presented to the IMTFE. It is thus appropriate to conclude that the traditionalists agreed with the mainland Chinese, who adopted the IMTFE prosecution's case as their official story and maintained it through to the early 1970s. Honda and other traditionalists might argue that he merely quoted the Chinese side of the story and that this account does not necessarily reflect the view of the Japanese traditionalists.[5] Judging from the wording in the previous quotation—especially Honda's comment that "the eyewitness accounts . . . surpassed the image I had constructed"—one cannot help having an impression that Honda, at least at this point, accepted this story as the truth.

In 1973, Suzuki Akira, a journalist, wrote a controversial book entitled *"Nankin Daigyakusatsu" no Maboroshi* [Illusion of the "Rape of Nanking"]. Suzuki focused on the two lieutenants, Mukai Toshiaki and Noda Tsuyoshi, who had been reported by a Japanese newspaper to have engaged in the sword contest to slash 100 enemies and were subsequently executed by the Chinese Nationalist government for this alleged killing competition. He more or less convincingly proved their innocence based on his extensive interviews with the families, relatives, and acquaintances of these two officers. Regarding the overall situation in Nanking, he presented the following "speculation" of his own by drawing on his interviews with some former journalists who had been in Nanking at the time:

immediately following the occupation, probably starting with the morning of [December] 14, mopping-up operations progressed within the walls and affected a considerable number of those who are presumed to have been ordinary civilian males. Occasionally, it [execution] was conducted in front of the eyes of Nanking residents. . . . A rumor was widely circulated among both the Japanese and the Chinese that those who looked like plainclothes soldiers were shot to death in Hsiak'uan. One can also speculate that the shooting of POWs secretly took place around the Hanhsi Gate prior to the victory parade.[6]

Despite the sensational title, Suzuki did not deny the occurrence of atrocities. Regarding that title, he noted in the book's postscript that he did "not mean to say that the Rape of Nanking was an illusion" and that he only intended to criticize the reluctance of journalists both in the 1930s and in the 1970s to report the truth, an attitude that, according to Suzuki, helped obscure the truth of the incident and turned it into an "illusion." In the end, he did not make a definite judgment about the Rape of Nanking and concluded his book with the following passage: "Although several tens of thousands of Chinese military men and civilians are estimated to have been killed at the time, the reporting of the incident was so politically motivated even from the beginning that its exact truth is unknown to anyone even today."[7] Thus, his work did not deny the incident, but rather raised a question. Nevertheless, *maboroshi* [illusion]—a part of the provocative book title—became a rallying call for those who wished to disprove the traditionalists' claim. At the same time, Suzuki was seen as one of the leading personalities of the school known as *maboroshi-ha* or the illusion school. Like the traditionalists, the people in the illusion school do not speak with one voice. Moreover, as subsequent sections of this chapter will show, continued research has led some individuals to shift their initial positions. Yet, again for convenience, this school will be called the "revisionists" here.[8]

Among several other people who espoused a traditionalist view in this first round of the Rape of Nanking controversy was Hora Tomio, then a professor of history at Waseda University. Hora, in *Nankin Jiken* [Nanking Incident] in 1972, quoted journalist Hata Kensuke's article about the massacre allegedly conducted by Colonel Morozumi's regiment and accepted the story as the truth despite a few reservations about small details. Suzuki, who criticized Hora's work, argued for the unreliability of both Hata himself as a journalist and the content of his article, and presented his own theory based on his interviews with some former Japanese military men. According to Suzuki, the Japanese troops fired on the Chinese POWs in self-defense when their effort to release the POWs across the Yangtze River failed. Suzuki argued that the Japanese troops had to open fire at the POWs who were getting out of control after firing from the other shore of the Yangtze by an unidentified party caused a panic among the POWs. This set off a long debate about the incident near the Mufu Mountain and the Rape of Nanking as a whole.[9]

On the revisionist side, Yamamoto Shichihei, an essayist, joined Suzuki in questioning the truthfulness of the story about the sword contest between the two lieutenants. In his persuasive criticism Yamamoto explained how wartime journalism made the two lieutenants media heroes. He concluded that the writers of the newspaper article were responsible for the deaths of the lieutenants not only by their reporting of a false "sword contest" story during the war but also by their refusal to confess that the story was false at the postwar war crimes trial. He, however, had a very poor knowledge of the Nanking campaign. Yamamoto, for example, speculated that the Chinese troops in Nanking retreated from the city in a calm and orderly manner contrary to the truth.[10]

As the quality of these works suggests, researchers, scholars, and journalists were still groping their way in the darkness in the early 1970s and were still dependent on second-hand information. For instance, except for Suzuki's interview with some former military men, there was almost no effort to look for primary materials such as diaries of former soldiers. Also, as Suzuki implied in his conclusion, political or ideological bias pertinent to the contemporary political events was already behind this phase of the debate, especially on the side of the traditionalists. For example, Honda's book, entitled *Chugoku no Nihongun* [Japanese Military in China], in its discussion of Japanese atrocities in China, drew numerous parallels between Japan's war against China and the U.S. involvement in Vietnam.[11] In addition to the Vietnam War, a pro-Communist China mood in the wake of Japan's establishment of formal diplomatic ties with the People's Republic had a strong effect on the controversy. Although Honda said that he reserved his judgment about China's current conditions, the captions he attached to the photos were full of what looks like blind praise of Communist China.[12] At the same time, the diplomatic development between the People's Republic of China and Japan had such a considerable impact that, according to Suzuki, some Japanese eyewitnesses he interviewed hesitated to provide their own accounts out of concern about negative impact on the fledgling ties between the two countries.[13]

Up to this point, the debate had taken place mostly within Japan and had not received the same amount of attention in foreign countries. Yet there was one notable attitude among the Chinese analysts outside Taiwan and the mainland, who tended to adopt a more gruesome interpretation resembling, or superseding, the Chinese prosecution's description at the IMTFE. For example, an article in the July 1978 issue of *Eastern Horizon*, a Hong Kong magazine, declared the figure of 300,000 people allegedly killed in Nanking to be "grossly underestimated" and projected the number of victims at "over 430,000." Contrary to the heroic resistance by the Nanking defenders as implied in the Nationalist publications, the article was critical of Chiang Kai-shek and Nationalist military leaders who allegedly "commandeered all vehicles to carry away their personal belongings and furniture."[14] Thus, one can see a strange twist on the Chinese side: the Nationalists, who had participated in the Nanking campaign and thus were likely to have more information, adopted a less gruesome image of the Rape of Nanking than did the non-Nationalist Chinese, who had not been involved in the incident.

The next round of debates about the Rape of Nanking started in the summer of 1982 when Japanese news media reported that the Education Ministry had directed writers of Japanese high school history textbooks to revise or modify the descriptions of modern historical events, including the Rape of Nanking. According to the initial Japanese news reports, among the revisions advised by the ministry regarding the Sino-Japanese conflict of 1937–45 was the change from "invasion" of China into "advance" to China. Although it became known later that there was no instance of such a change urged on any textbook, the news soon spread to other countries. Moreover, there were indeed other revisions suggested by the ministry, including one concerning descriptions of the Rape of Nanking, with more emphasis on the provocation by the Chinese side as well as the deletion of the specific number of victims. The governments of Asian countries that had been subjected to Japan's aggression before and during World War II filed immediate protests with the Japanese government. The Chinese authorities on the mainland in particular charged that the textbook revision reflected the desire shared by some Japanese "to revive Japan's wartime military empire." The news also attracted the attention of Westerners. Even then U.S. President Ronald Reagan commented on the issue. The Rape of Nanking thus became an international topic again for the first time since the Tokyo War Crimes Trial.[15]

It took nearly two months before the Chinese and other governments accepted the settlement proposed by Japanese authorities in September 1982. The Japanese government announced that it would add another criterion to the guidelines concerning the textbook screening process, that is, "to pay due consideration to diplomatic relations with neighboring countries." This settlement, however, did not put an end to the Rape of Nanking controversy. Since this solution mandated another rewriting of Japanese high school history textbooks in favor of the traditionalists, some scholars with revisionist inclinations formed an association named *Nihon o mamoru kokumin kaigi* [National Association for Defense of Japan] and wrote a history textbook entitled *Shinpen Nihonshi* [Newly Compiled Japanese History] in 1986 to present Japanese history from their standpoint. This time the Education Ministry advised the authors to alter some descriptions of historical events to make them more agreeable to the interpretations of foreign countries. Regarding the Rape of Nanking, the ministry initially urged the authors to delete the following passage in that textbook: "The people of this country [Japan] learned about this incident [the Rape of Nanking] for the first time after World War II. Thereafter, various forms of studies such as archival research and interview with witnesses have continued to determine its truth." For a reason not explained even to the writers, the ministry retracted this advice soon afterward. The Education Ministry approved this textbook later in the same year after the writers had agreed on numerous other revisions advised by the ministry's textbook inspectors.

Even prior to the compilation of this textbook, some other revisionists had started their counterattack by printing their own opinions in publications other than textbooks. Therefore, far from terminating the controversy, the diplomatic settlement of the textbook issue renewed the debate and added fuel to it. The ensuing "fight"—a fitting word in view of some emotional exchanges of words between the traditionalists and the revisionists, some of which sounded like slander—compelled each side to clarify its stance more distinctly while also causing divisions within each group. Simultaneously, thanks to the continuing international news coverage, Chinese and Western intellectuals started paying more attention to the issue.[16]

CRITICAL REVIEW AND ANALYSIS OF REVISIONIST VIEWS

It was principally former military personnel of the Imperial Japanese Army who took critical note of the textbook issue and tried to refute the Chinese and traditionalist version of the Rape of Nanking. Notably, *Kaikosha*, an association of Imperial Japanese Army veterans, collected eyewitness accounts from its members to support a series of articles about the Nanking campaign in its monthly periodical *Kaiko* from April 1984 to March 1985. Although Japanese traditionalists and Chinese media sources condemned such a move as an attempt to revive militarism, most of these ex-military men, who were of quite advanced age, seemingly pursued that project only to refute what looked like excessive and unfair criticism of the Imperial Japanese Army. Their primary concern was the number of victims, an issue that they apparently determined to be a serious topic related to the character of atrocities. One can detect such motives in the statements some *Kaiko* members voiced prior to the start of the article series:

today, the Japanese people accept the "Rape of Nanking" as a historical fact without any doubt. This is highly disgraceful not only for me—a participant in the campaign—but also for the Imperial Japanese Army of the Showa era.

We cannot tolerate the theory of "the massacre of 200,000 to 300,000" as was proclaimed during the textbook dispute last year [1982] since it is a fictionally based slander inflicted not only upon the Army of the Showa era but also upon the Japanese race.

We must establish a solid fact about this issue [the Rape of Nanking] while we are still alive.

Since the participants who know the truth of this issue are steadily passing away, we will definitely have no opportunity to clarify the truth unless we investigate it now.

. . . the participants in the campaign cannot tolerate a too exorbitant figure [of Rape of Nanking victims] to be accepted as a historical truth.[17]

Yet one cannot deny that a certain degree of bias dictated the course of their research. Some of them undoubtedly extended to the Imperial Japanese Army what one may call the "presumption of innocence." For example, an article calling for eyewitness accounts contained the following passage: "not only what you saw or what you heard from somebody but also . . . that *you saw or heard nothing* is useful information" [italics written in bold letters in the original]. One of the prominent *Kaikosha* members who approached the Rape of Nanking issues under the "presumption of innocence" was Unemoto Masami, a former Imperial Japanese Army officer and veteran of the Nanking battle. After *Kaiko* concluded the article series, Unemoto confessed that he had conducted his investigation hoping to prove that nothing atrocious had happened in Nanking or at least that there were only some "gray" areas—some actions that one might call either atrocity or legitimate military activity, depending on one's point of view—in the stories of the Nanking campaign.[18]

From the beginning, however, some people within the circle of former Japanese military men did not believe in the complete exoneration of the Japanese army and thus disagreed with Unemoto's presumption. The editorial staff of *Kaiko*, for example, said in its call for eyewitness accounts, "Truly regrettably, we cannot possibly argue for absolving ourselves from all charges."[19] Likewise, another officer said before *Kaiko*'s article series started, "No more cover-up of facts out of concern about such a thing as the reputation of His Majesty's army. . . . We should admit to the misdeeds the Japanese troops committed in Nanking. Based on such repentant admission of that fact, should we not try to refute the numerical fiction, that is, the massacre of 300,000?"[20] Therefore, even prior to the beginning of the *Kaiko* project, there was a split within the former Japanese military men's group. One may label Unemoto's group as the "extreme revisionists"—although Unemoto at the end of the article series seemingly moderated his stance by admitting to some unlawful killing and thus switched to the other side—and those represented by the opinion quoted above as the "moderate revisionists." In the conclusion of the series, the *Kaiko* frankly admitted to the rift between these two groups. One of the editors wrote in the final article of the series:

I was a student of the Army's staff college when this [Nanking] incident took place 48 years ago. Already at the time, that some "illegal acts" had been committed in the Nanking front reached my ears. . . . Accordingly, from the beginning I did not hold a view that the Japanese troops were entirely "innocent."

Mr. Unemoto tended to collect as many stories pointing to "innocence" as possible to refute the widely accepted exorbitant number of victims. . . . To the contrary, we tried to be as open-minded as possible and examine even the evidence pointing to "guilt."[21]

Although the writer of these passages added that both approaches shared the same goal of countering the "slanderous charge of 'grandiose guilt,' " the disagreement was evident. The same article went so far in support of the moderate revisionist position as to criticize the army leadership for its unclear policy regarding the handling of POWs while emphasizing the widespread lack of discipline among the troops—a phenomenon unattributable to only a handful of outlaws. It also quoted Unemoto's estimate of 3,000 to 6,000 victims resulting from unlawful conduct, such as the POW execution, and then said that "Even with all discussion of what the face of the battle was or how the battle psychology worked, there is no excuse for this unlawful killing of a large number. As a person connected with the former Imperial Japanese Army, I have nothing but a word of profound apology to the people of China. I am sorry. We committed horrible atrocities."[22]

Naturally, there was a barrage of protests to this line of argument from those who supported the extreme revisionist stance. Again, much of their criticism came from men concerned about their own and the Imperial Japanese Army's reputations. One letter, for example, condemned the above quoted words of apology as a statement that "spoils the effort to preserve the glorious history of His Majesty's Army," and expressed a belief that "all former military commanders who fought in the front and lost many of their brave men are equally enraged" to read it. The same person also presented a justification typical of the extreme revisionist argument, that is, to draw on instances of atrocities perpetrated by other peoples while claiming that the entire story of the Japanese army's atrocities was a fabrication. He said, "Why do we have to be this servile merely because we lost a war? . . . Why do the Japanese *alone* have to apologize for an incident which is very much suspected of having been fabricated?" [Italics added.][23] Yet there was also a considerable level of support for the moderate revisionist position. Although *Kaiko* did not print any letters in support of the moderate revisionist stance, it noted that there had been many phone calls that praised the decision to apologize.[24]

A similar split happened in the revisionist camp outside the group of ex-army men. Among the prominent revisionist researchers was Tanaka Masaaki, who had been a secretary of Matsui Iwane before Matsui returned to the active service in 1937 to assume the post of SEF commander. Tanaka is best known for his 1984 publication entitled *"Nankin Gyakusatsu" no Kyoko* ["Rape of Nanking" as a Fiction]. In this book, Tanaka did not deny the licentious nature of the Japanese troops' conduct in Nanking due to the lack or loosening of discipline. He, however, did try to justify all executions of Chinese POWs as an extension of legitimate military action. Because of this attempt to define the atrocities in Nanking as narrowly as possible, one may call Tanaka the most vocal proponent of the extreme revisionist position.[25]

Another prominent personality on the revisionist side was Itakura Yoshiaki, a factory owner and part-time researcher of Rape of Nanking issues. Itakura initially acted in concert with Tanaka, and both cooperated with the *Kaiko* staff in drafting its article series. Tanaka acknowledged Itakura as one of the contributors to his book and the two persons chaired roundtable talks with some veterans of the Nanking battle—all of them contributing their stories to the *Kaiko* series—to write an article for a more popular magazine. According to Itakura's later remarks, however, he started distancing himself from Tanaka after the roundtable meeting at which Tanaka appeared "so emphatic in denying the Rape of Nanking that he often spoke as if nothing atrocious had happened."[26]

A decisive break between the two came in late 1985 when Tanaka was found to have committed a major academic blunder. In his second Rape of Nanking-related publication entitled *Matsui Iwane Taisho no Jinchu Nisshi* [Field Diary of General Matsui Iwane], he reprinted a part of Matsui's diary along with his comments in an apparent attempt to refute the traditionalist theory. After reading the book, a person close to Itakura found that Tanaka had tampered with the diary and altered its content in over 900 locations. Although Tanaka later attributed these errors to his own transcription of many illegible handwritten letters of Matsui into a modern writing style for the convenience of modern readers, this justification does not explain some changes.[27] For example, Matsui's diary contains the passage in the December 20, 1937, entry: "I was told that our soldiers committed a few cases of robbery (they mainly stole art pieces) and rape for a certain time period. It was inevitable for a certain number of those crimes to happen in view of the situation."[28] In Tanaka's version, the extra words "but highly regrettable" are added at the end.[29] In another instance, one can read in the diary Matsui's speech to his subordinates about how they should conduct pacification activities in the occupied areas: "all we have to do is to make them [the Chinese people] attached to us, treat them with affection and take pity on them."[30] The impression here is that Matsui told his men that they could pacify the Chinese civilians only by assuming, or even pretending, an amicable attitude whatever they really thought in their minds. Tanaka altered this portion a little so that it conveyed a slightly different implication: "we have to treat them tenderly, make them attached to us, and take pity on them. All we have to do [to accomplish this] is to have a sense of mercy."[31] In this altered version, Matsui seemingly emphasized the importance of what they must really have in their minds.

Itakura criticized Tanaka's tampering of the historical record as an "unbelievable ethical violation." At the same time, he also contended that the disclosure of even the untampered Matsui diary would not help authenticate the traditionalist theory of the Rape of Nanking. His assailing of the two positions— the extreme revisionist position of Tanaka and the traditionalist view—symbolizes his stance. Itakura classified the atrocities in Nanking into three categories: (1) violation of foreign interests including the *Panay* Incident, (2) violence committed against Chinese civilians, and (3) the execution of POWs on a large scale. He found the third category was a major component of the atrocities, blamed it on the Japanese army's lack of a POW policy—a defect that Itakura condemned as the Japanese army's "significant blind spot and gigantic blot"— and estimated the number of victims at 10,000 to 20,000. This admission of large-scale unlawful slaughter entitled him to claim a position as a leading "moderate revisionist" or, as a later section will discuss, even a "centrist" in the Rape of Nanking debate.[32]

As for Tanaka, he strengthened his extreme revisionist stance even further after his break with Itakura and other moderate revisionists. Tanaka tried to exploit any mistake committed by the traditionalists to support his own claims. A typical method was to question the origin of various atrocity photos or point to some minor inconsistencies in primary sources such as diaries and eyewitness testimonies. Although he had assisted the *Kaiko* article series, he later tried to block the *Kaikosha*'s plan to turn it into a single volume by actively speaking against the plan to former army generals as well as leaders of local ex-army officers' associations. Because of such pressure, it was not until 1989—well over four years after *Kaiko*'s article series ended—that a book entitled *Nankin Senshi* [Nanking Campaign Chronicle] went into print. Naturally, it did not include Tanaka's name in the list of contributors, but retained a trace of the pressure exerted by the extreme revisionists that he represented. Although one section of the book contained detailed analyses of POW executions in multiple locations, it said, "we decided not to discuss the legality or illegality of execution" for several reasons such as the ambiguity of the situation in which each case took place and the lack of information about the POWs in the Chinese sources. This noncommittal attitude of keeping the issue of such a large-scale killing ambivalent without any discussion of its legality is seemingly a typical position of the moderate revisionists at present.[33]

A compact description of the two revisionist groups would define the extreme revisionist stance as a movement oriented toward the preservation of the Imperial Japanese Army's honor, and the moderate revisionist stance as a more academic effort to analyze the incidents in Nanking under the pressure exerted by the extreme revisionists.

Although Tanaka, an extreme revisionist, committed a shameful blunder as a scholar, he did provide some valid and useful theses for later research. The foremost among them was that he distinguished the unlawful acts committed by undisciplined Japanese soldiers—atrocities to which he admitted the occurrence—from the alleged indiscriminate massacre of POWs and civilians—the story he denounced as a fiction. Such a distinction undoubtedly has helped other researchers classify the atrocities, which had thus far been known under a single name, the "Rape of Nanking," in a variety of ways. In his third publication, *Nankin Jiken no Sokatsu* [Nanking Incident Summed Up], for example, Tanaka criticized Hata Ikuhiko—a historian of the "centrist school," with which a later section will deal—for his contention that Matsui's testimony at the IMTFE was full of contradictions and ambiguity because Matsui, according to Hata, alternated between denial and admission when he was interrogated about his knowledge of atrocities. Tanaka pointed out that Hata incorrectly linked Matsui's admission of the atrocities resulting from the lack of discipline to the alleged massacres on a large scale, which Matsui actually denied. In view of the surprise Matsui and other Japanese military leaders expressed at the allegation of large-scale atrocities lodged at the IMTFE pre-trial interrogations, one may conclude that Tanaka's criticism has validity. Another intriguing thesis Tanaka put forward was his analysis of how the Chinese coined the word *Nanking Ta-t'u-sha*—the Chinese equivalent of the "Rape of Nanking." Tanaka theorized that the word *t'u-sha*, meaning massacre, is closely related to *t'u-cheng*, which refers to a time-old Chinese military custom, that is, the massacre of inhabitants in forcibly captured cities. According to Tanaka, Chinese historical records are rich with atrocity stories connected with the storming of cities such as indiscriminate massacre of inhabitants, mutilation of their bodies, and cannibalism by conquerors. He reasoned that the Chinese account of the Rape of Nanking has its origin in such stories found in their own history.[34]

Although such an interpretation is seemingly persuasive and valid to a certain extent, one can detect several problems in his analysis. First, he lacked a perspective of the military history of other geographical areas and appeared to conclude that massacres accompanying the storming of a city were unique to Chinese history. As a result, Tanaka hardly considered some factors that were likely to cause atrocities almost universally. His second problem was that he either refuted the story of POW executions completely or defined the atrocities too narrowly even in light of contemporary international law and excluded the execution of POWs from the category of atrocities. For example, he adopted a twisted, or acrobatic, interpretation of the controversial passage in 16th Division chief Nakajima's diary reading, "our policy is not to take prisoners." Quoting from a remark by a former SEF staff member, Tanaka concluded that Nakajima merely intended to release Chinese POWs instead of killing them. One would need quite a leap of imagination to accept this interpretation if one reads the rest of the diary passage—a portion Tanaka did not quote either intentionally or unintentionally: "we made a point of disposing of one prisoner after another." In another instance, Tanaka mentioned the fate of 328 straggling soldiers captured by a company of the 20th Regiment. Although the company clearly shot them to death after it had taken them into its custody, Tanaka treated this event as a lawful execution, again by altering a part of a primary document. He not only defined these Chinese soldiers as straggling soldiers but also called them "plainclothes soldiers" in parentheses—the latter being a term that never appeared in the corresponding section of the company's official battle report.[35]

The moderate revisionists were not as explicit as the extreme revisionists in their justification of such group massacres. Nevertheless, the impression is that they attempt to minimize the Japanese army's responsibility either by interpreting primary sources for their own convenience or treating the execution of POWs as a "gray" area that one cannot determine to be either "white" (justifiable) or "black" (unlawful) under the contemporary international legal provisions. *Nankin Senshi* [Nanking Campaign Chronicle], for example, shows an obvious tendency to play down the number of Chinese victims in its analyses of Smythe's *War Damage in the Nanking Area*, in passages like the following: "among the 4,200 reported to have been taken away by the Japanese troops, there might have been some who later came back or remained alive elsewhere."[36] The same book also quoted from some pre-World War II legal scholars and concluded,

if the captors are not able to accommodate or feed the captives and can expect the captives to break their oath and fight against them after their release, the captors cannot be prevented from killing them under the regulation of military conduct.[37]

one cannot rule out the possibility of refusing to accept surrender depending on the military necessity arising in the course of military action.[38]

plainclothes soldiers are defined as those who engage in conduct harmful to the opponent without qualifications as legal combatants, hence violators of the regulation of military conduct. Since those who are caught in the course of that act are comparable to bandits, they can either be killed on the spot or charged with the violation of combat regulation.[39]

Although these legal theories and interpretations were applicable to some events in Nanking, the writers of *Nankin Senshi* [Nanking Campaign Chronicle] avoided any attempt to examine the applicability in specific cases. This is the weakness of the moderate revisionists. Naturally, those who examined the incident from the standpoint of the victims assailed such an attitude.

CRITICAL REVIEW AND ANALYSIS OF TRADITIONALIST VIEWS

The same familiar faces as well as new personalities were active on the traditionalist side in the 1980s. Although they still maintained what looked like a "traditionalist monolith," one can detect a schism similar to that in the revisionist camp.

Asahi Shinbun [Asahi Newspaper] correspondent Honda made trips to China again in 1983–84 and wrote a series of articles for the magazine *Asahi Journal*. The articles were about not only the Rape of Nanking but also the Japanese atrocities committed in the area stretching from Shanghai to Nanking. Like his earlier work, he drew heavily on his interviews with eyewitnesses and survivors of atrocities. The article series later became a book entitled *Nankin e no Michi* [Road to Nanking]. Most of the accounts Honda quoted in his book are stories of atrocities perpetrated by Japanese soldiers individually, such as a woman living in the Shanghai area who had her husband murdered and was herself injured and raped by six Japanese soldiers; eight Japanese soldiers who murdered twelve out of thirteen members of a family; one Japanese soldier who attempted to rape a woman and then, having failed to do so, out of frustration set ablaze the house where she lived; and two Japanese soldiers who raped Chinese girls in an occupied town for several days. A notable, and controversial, aspect of his work was Honda's expansion of the framework of the Rape of Nanking in terms of both time and space. He said,

the atrocities such as massacre, violence, and rape perpetrated against ordinary people and POWs did not take place abruptly in Nanking. They started happening immediately following the landing at the Hangchou Bay. . . . Some of the people who discuss the atrocities known as the "Rape of Nanking" limit the time frame of the incident to the five-day period from the Japanese Army's complete occupation of Nanking on December 13 to their victory parade on December 17. . . . One can understand how meaningless it is to discuss only the massacre, violence, and rape in these five days or only in the city area of Nanking. It is impossible to draw a boundary. The incident in Nanking was merely one phase of the "Nanking Campaign." . . . one may reasonably set the beginning of the time frame at the time of the landing operation at Hangchou (in early November).[40]

For the revisionists, this statement is Honda's partial admission of his defeat. In their eyes, Honda had to expand the time and space limits of atrocities because he had realized the impossibility of massacring 300,000 people in a period of five days. Tanaka, an extreme revisionist, called it a "bogus theory unheard of even at the IMTFE."[41]

Although Tanaka's criticism might have been an overstatement, Honda undoubtedly modified his opinion regarding some aspects of the Rape of Nanking. At the same time, in a departure from his previous practice of copying the Chinese version of events, Honda made an apparent effort to formulate his own version of the incident. For example, as he had done in the 1970s, he again uncritically quoted one Chinese person as saying, "In my impression, the figure of 300,000 is too small. There were more victims." Yet, unlike his previous practice, he did not forget to attach his own comments about the number of victims in an apparent effort to undercut anticipated criticism of the lack of his own view. Honda's own opinion was, however, evasive. While quoting another traditionalist's estimate of more than 100,000 victims, Honda again blurred the time frame and geographical boundary issue and simply said, "It is undeniable that a massacre in the six-digit range took place."[42]

In terms of political and ideological background, the traditionalists basically inherited Honda's stance in the 1970s. The traditionalists often criticize the revisionists for their political bias. Inoue Hisashi, one of the traditionalist scholars, for example, maintained that a political conclusion dictated, or even precluded, the careful evidentiary analysis in the revisionist interpretation of the Rape of Nanking. According to Yoshida Yutaka, another scholar of the same group, what motivated the revisionist camp was the growing confidence of the Japanese nationalists who were becoming increasingly hostile to the criticism directed against Japan from other Asian nations—something seen in the textbook crisis of the early 1980s. Takasaki Ryuji, another traditionalist, also juxtaposed the revisionist stance with what he called the "return to the pre-war period" and "inclination to the rightist tendency."[43]

As far as political ideology is concerned, however, the traditionalists are much more expressive in the manifestation of their underlying concepts than are the revisionists. In contrast with the revisionists, who view the incident mainly from the standpoint of regular soldiers and examine the incident in the light of the legal and moral standards of the 1930s, the traditionalists clearly approach the issue from the standpoint of the Chinese, who in their eyes were more or less like insurgents as contrasted with regular soldiers, and apply the standards of today—an aspect that will be subject to critical analysis later in this section. The following quotes from these traditionalists' works exemplify how they approach the issue:

the international legal provisions at the time reflected the interests of colonial powers and were defective in various ways in terms of humanitarian international law, an example being the insufficient protection of insurgents.[44]

[those who justify the execution of plainclothes soldiers in Nanking] uphold tightly the traditional international legal system, which supported colonialism. Today, we are required to interpret such a legal system itself in the context of historical development and understand correctly its historical limitation.[45]

As a natural consequence, they define the scope of the alleged massacre as broadly as possible. For example, they very often describe the Chinese soldiers who lost their lives in Nanking as straggling soldiers "who completely lost their organizational cohesion and fighting morale," and then include among the massacre victims many of those who were killed during the Japanese army's military operations.[46]

The traditionalist camp has held to these contentions almost unanimously. Recently, however, one can discern a slight difference of opinion emerging within this group over some questions. In criticizing the revisionists' smaller estimate of the number of victims, most traditionalists simply argue that the number does not matter since a massacre was a massacre however many, or few, people were killed. Others, however, take this issue more seriously. It is noteworthy that one of the traditionalists wondered whether so many people had really lost their lives in the city. Quoting a Japanese military policeman's poem containing the phrase, "80,000 dead bodies left behind," Takasaki Ryuji said on the one hand that this surely tells the truth, but on the other hand he made a somewhat contradictory remark: "That as many as "80,000" dead bodies were left behind as a result of a three-day ordinary military engagement had been unprecedented in world history. This number is exorbitant for a battle casualty tally—an unlikely figure unless the Japanese had dropped an atomic bomb in Nanking."[47] Another scholar maintained that numerical analysis is important since one would have to reach a different interpretation of the incident, depending on the number of victims.[48] Although the division between these two groups was much less distinct compared with the split among the revisionists, one may tentatively call the group who discounts the number issues as the "extreme traditionalists" and the other group as the "moderate traditionalists."

The two traditionalist groups, although again in a very subtle manner, also take different approaches to a controversial piece of Rape of Nanking evidence, that is, the burial record of the Ch'ung-shan-t'ang. The extreme traditionalists on the one hand remain firm in their belief in the reliability of this document by pointing to the testimonies of eyewitnesses who claimed to have participated in the burials conducted by this organization. The moderate traditionalists on the other hand cast a certain degree of doubt on its reliability and authenticity, although, unlike the revisionists, they do not dismiss it as fake evidence. Thus, the moderate traditionalists leave the issue concerning the Ch'ung-shan-t'ang ambiguous in the same way as the moderate revisionists leave the legality issue of POW execution unanswered.[49]

Another issue that divides the traditionalist group is in the way they treat the alleged killing contest between the two lieutenants. Honda in his *Nankin e no Michi* [Road to Nanking] still made an effort to convince readers of the truthfulness of this story by referring to similar stories he obtained from Chinese eyewitnesses, although none of these stories is about the killing contest in question. Thus, the extreme traditionalists still hold on to the original interpretation.

To the contrary, the moderate traditionalists are beginning to exclude this story from the Rape of Nanking debate, although they do not dismiss it entirely as a fiction. In roundtable talks with other scholars and researchers, Hora, without discussing whether or not the story was true, explicitly stated that one cannot include the alleged killing contest in the atrocities in Nanking.[50]

One can summarize the gradually emerging but not yet distinctly established distinction between the extreme and moderate traditionalists as a difference between the journalistic, or possibly propaganda, approach and the scholarly approach as was seen within the revisionist side.

The most distinguished contribution of the traditionalists to the Rape of Nanking debate was the discovery of various primary sources, soldiers' diaries in particular, pursued most likely out of an inclination to disprove the revisionist argument. In this regard, Honda is undoubtedly the most outstanding among the researchers of both the traditionalist and revisionist camps. Nevertheless, there are several problems with the traditionalists' theses.

First, the traditionalist effort to overestimate or inflate the number of massacre victims is as intense as the revisionist effort to do the opposite. Honda, for example, concluded that one Chinese division had about 16,000 men *apart from* those assigned to rear duties, drawing on an account provided by a former brigade commander of the Chinese Nationalist Army. This figure contradicts data presented in another article in the same book quoting from the same witness. The latter article said that one Chinese division had two brigades, each of which was composed of 5,000 combatants and 2,000 in charge of rear duties, hence 14,000 in all for one division. In another instance, Honda, either intentionally or unintentionally, misquoted an eyewitness account to set the estimate of massacre victims higher. The *Mainichi Shinbun* [Mainichi Newspaper] in August 1984 quoted a former corporal of the 65th Regiment as saying that the Japanese army inflicted 75,000 *casualties* on the Chinese in Nanking. In his *Nankin e no Michi* [Road to Nanking], Honda said that the same former corporal estimated the number of *executed POWs* at 75,000 (emphasis added).[51]

Second, the traditionalists tend to define the atrocities so broadly that they include in the victims of massacre even those who appear to have been combat casualties. The logic they often employ is that most of the Chinese soldiers killed by the Japanese in the course of the mopping-up operations were merely straggling soldiers who had already lost any means or intention to fight. They then condemn the Japanese military action immediately before the fall of Nanking as "one-sided slaughter."[52] Their argument, however, appears to be equally one-sided in their disregard of the problems facing the Japanese troops, such as how alert the Japanese soldiers were to the danger posed by plainclothes Chinese soldiers prior to and during the Nanking campaign; whether the Chinese soldiers' loss of combat capability was known, or could have been known, to the Japanese military leadership in the course of the hot pursuit of the enemy; what measures Japanese military leaders could have taken if they had known of such a state. The traditionalists' neglect to analyze such factors is comparable to the extreme revisionists' refusal to recognize any element of unlawfulness in the execution of prisoners.

The third problem lies in their ideological paradigm, which allowed them to adopt such a broad definition of massacre. As the following passage quoted from a traditionalist scholar's article shows, they clearly try to apply today's moral and legal standards to the past event:

guerrilla warfare has become one of the most dominant forms of warfare after World War II, and international law has been showing a tendency to accord the warriors engaging in people's liberation conflicts the same protection as has been extended to regular soldiers. At present, with such a trend setting in, one can clearly understand how outdated and inhumane an effort it is to dismiss the allegation of the Rape of Nanking on the pretext of the execution of plain-clothed soldiers.[53]

The traditionalists' attack on the revisionists' reliance on outdated moral and legal standards might sound valid from a humanitarian standpoint. Yet the applicability of such logic is very questionable from a legal as well as historical standpoint, and definitely refutable from the standpoint of criminal justice, which prohibits *ex post facto* legislation. In terms of historical interpretation, their logic contains one possible weakness, or even a self-destructive element. By transferring today's standards onto past events, they conjure up the possibility that their own position might be subject to similar criticism in the future. To the contrary, the revisionists are unlikely to face such a problem since their interpretation rests on the standards of the 1930s. In determining the legal and moral standard on the battlefield in the 1930s when the incident happened, one may note that even the Chinese prosecutor at the IMTFE indicted only the Japanese conduct following the occupation of the city and did not discuss any issues related to Japanese military activities during the battle.[54]

Finally, despite their repeated criticisms of the revisionists' lower estimates of the number of victims, the traditionalists, whether they are moderate or extreme, have made almost no serious attempt to compute the final death toll in Nanking in a manner persuasive enough to refute the revisionist claims. Even the moderate traditionalists simply say, "the number of massacre victims far exceeded 100,000" and avoid setting any upper ceiling. One of the few exceptions is Hora Tomio's estimate of about 200,000 dead, including combat casualties. That they have refrained from determining the number of victims is likely to be attributable to their unwillingness to antagonize the Chinese side by providing any numerical analysis contradicting the Chinese official statistics of 300,000 or more. The estimate of "over 100,000" is seemingly very convenient for the traditionalists since arithmetically it includes 300,000.[55]

One can observe a good example of this tendency—to avoid any reference that might conflict with the Chinese account—in a debate between Hora and another traditionalist scholar on the one hand and revisionist researcher Itakura on the other. In this debate concerning the exact location of the 65th Regiment's mass execution of POWs near the Mufu Mountain, Itakura, referring to Honda's article dealing with this incident, charged that Honda had deliberately pinpointed a place different from the actual location to make the event look like a separate incident from the 100,000-men slaughter near the Mufu Mountain as was alleged by the Chinese. After careful documentary and on-the-spot investigations, Hora and his colleague more or less convincingly showed that the massacre location was where they claimed it to be. These traditionalists, however, did not address a crucial aspect of the Chinese story, that is, whether the alleged slaughter of 100,000 people was actually the 65th Regiment's execution of POWs, the number of which proved to be much smaller than 100,000, even according to the traditionalists' estimate. They skillfully avoided giving a definite answer to this question by saying merely that Honda himself did not say anything like a massacre of 100,000 and that such a story appears only in the Chinese version—a statement not entirely true, judging from Honda's uncritical quotation of the Chinese side of the story in his earlier work *Chugoku no Tabi* [Trip to China].[56]

Thus, their deference to the Chinese side—or at least their unwillingness to present any thesis contradicting the Chinese version of the Rape of Nanking—is the biggest weakness of the traditionalists, although this factor has at the same time also served to maintain what appears to be the "traditionalist monolith" despite some subtle differences of opinions. This "China syndrome" might be comparable to the pressure of the extreme revisionists on the moderate revisionists since both forms of pressure seem to inhibit more objective research.

THE EMERGENCE OF CENTRIST VIEWS AND THE BALANCE SHEET OF THE DEBATE

Although the term "centrist" is very ambiguous, one may define the "centrist" school—*chukan-ha* in Japanese—of the Rape of Nanking debate simply as those who criticize, or are criticized by, both the revisionists and the traditionalists. Basically, the centrists oppose the all-or-nothing or, more fittingly, "guilty-or-not-guilty" approach reminiscent of the IMTFE deliberations of both extremes.

The most prominent of the "centrists" is Hata Ikuhiko, a historian who specializes in Japan's modern history. Hata's work *Nankin Jiken* [Nanking Incident] is very critical of the Japanese army's inefficient and ineffective ways of military planning and execution. It also discusses specific cases of POW execution as well as the atrocities committed by individual soldiers. Hata's negative view concerning the Japanese military and Japan's policy in China in general is apparent in the following remark in the book's postscript:

It is a firmly established historical fact that Japan's invasion of China lasted over a decade starting with the Manchurian Incident and that it caused an enormous pain and damage to the Chinese people. Nevertheless, the Chinese did not retaliate against the Japanese soldiers and residents after Japan's defeat in World War II and allowed them to go home.

They did not press any reparation demand, which the Japanese side had anticipated, at the time of the restoration of formal diplomatic relations between Japan and China in 1972.[57]

Hata is critical of the revisionists who try to disclaim the figure of 300,000—the number Hata called a "symbolic figure"—and "persist in the denial of the Rape of Nanking even by tampering with primary material"—an apparent reference to Tanaka Masaaki, the extreme revisionist who rewrote Matsui's diary in the course of editing. What makes him different from the traditionalists is that by effectively rejecting the controversial Ch'ung-shan-t'ang document he estimated the number of atrocity victims at about 38,000 to 42,000. He also holds a cynical opinion about the traditionalists who, according to him, epitomize what he calls "intellectual masochism"—a self-incriminating trend among some Japanese scholars and journalists who, in their study of modern Japanese history, are under the heavy influence of the mentality created at the IMTFE.[58]

It is natural that Hata, who was critical of both the traditionalists and the revisionists, became the target of attack by both sides. On the revisionist side, Tanaka Masaaki accused Hata of still being spellbound by what Tanaka called the "IMTFE syndrome" despite Hata's thesis of the IMTFE being the source of "intellectual masochism" affecting the minds of the traditionalists. As for the traditionalists, they regarded Hata as a revisionist like Tanaka merely because Hata's estimate of the number of victims was much lower than the Chinese official claim or because Hata excluded from the victims those who were killed in the near-one-sided slaughter in the Nanking battle. They made such a criticism in an apparent disregard of Hata's repentant remarks about the Japanese conduct in China in his postscript.[59]

As a previous section has shown, Itakura Yoshiaki, who initially did research on the Rape of Nanking issues in concert with the revisionists, later broke with the extreme revisionists. Itakura might be distinct even from the moderate revisionists in his more candid admission of the Japanese troops' misconduct and unlawful killings. Because of this stance, one may include him in the "centrists." Yet the traditionalists still see him as a leading revisionist and point to his relativism expressed in the following passage in one of his articles: "In the madness of war, an army of every country commits evil. So did His Majesty's Army. Nevertheless, no Japanese national is entitled to say aloud that His Majesty's, or the Japanese, army alone was a group of savage soldiers rarely seen in the world."[60]

This relativist stance contrasts with Hata's more open admission of Japan's war responsibility and somewhat sympathetic attitude toward the Chinese interpretation of the Rape of Nanking. Accordingly, Itakura deserves to be called a "revisionist centrist" while Hata might be appropriately called a "traditionalist centrist."

A major dividing line between the "revisionist centrists" and the "traditionalist centrists" is their different attitudes toward Japan's war responsibility. As Hata's remark suggests, the traditionalist centrists accept such a responsibility uncon-ditionally in the same way the traditionalists do. For them, the repentant ad-mission of war responsibility should precede the probe into the facts, although, as Hata's criticism of "intellectual masochism" suggests, such a repentant feeling must not affect the investigation into the historical truth. In contrast, the revi-sionist centrists profess to accept the responsibility based on what the Japanese troops actually did. Thus, the establishment of fact must precede acceptance of the responsibility to determine how and to what extent the Japanese were re-sponsible. Such a difference is manifest in their treatment of the IMTFE evi-dence, especially the evidence originating from Chinese sources. Itakura professed to criticize both the traditionalists and the revisionists by defining the two approaches as "a vain effort to reduce the estimated number [of victims] to as close as zero and another vain effort to boost it to as close as 300,000." Yet it is obvious that Itakura, who rejects most IMTFE evidence from official Chi-nese sources, is more critical of the traditionalists. Compared with Itakura, Hata shows a certain degree of understanding of Chinese claims. Despite his critical remarks about the negative effect of the IMTFE on postwar Japan, he does not appear very critical of the Chinese evidence introduced to the IMTFE. Touching on the Chinese estimate of 300,000 victims, he seems to trace its origin to an honest mistake by the Chinese. He said that there seems to have been no inten-tional inflation of numerical data and attributed some exorbitant figures provided by survivors of atrocities to "exaggeration ascribable to victim's psychology." In addition, Hata, who estimated the number of Rape of Nanking victims at about 40,000 in his book, said in its postscript, "This figure is a tentative esti-mate, which should be revised *upward* pending discovery of new evidence" [italics added]. One can infer his inclination toward the traditionalist position from his mentioning only a possible "upward" revision in disregard of the pres-ence of some scholars who have estimates lower than his 40,000.[61]

Common denominators that separate the two centrist groups from both the traditionalists and the revisionists are their smaller estimate of massacre victims and their explicit admission of unlawful killing in Nanking (Chart 7.1). It is appropriate to divide the centrists further into two groups, the revisionist cen-trists and the traditionalist centrists, because of their different attitude toward war responsibility and resulting inclination toward either the revisionists or the traditionalists.

The emergence of such centrist positions clearly demonstrates that neither the traditionalists nor the revisionists have won an overwhelming victory in the Rape of Nanking controversy. One can discern the symptoms of this deadlock in increasingly similar tones and arguments adopted by both sides—especially by those on the extreme positions—despite their completely opposite conclusions.

For example, both sides claim an overwhelming victory over the other. On the traditionalist side, Honda, summing up the Rape of Nanking debate, em-phasized how victorious the traditionalists are: "Among the various public de-bates since the end of World War II, none of them showed a winner and a loser

Chart 7.1
Rape of Nanking Controversy in Japan: Schools and Their Opinions

	Soldiers' Misbehavior	Execution of POWs	Massacre of Civilians	Adoption of Burial Data	Number of Victims	Personalities
Extreme Traditionalists	It happened, and it was illegal.	It happened, and it was illegal.	It happened.	Red Swastika Society, Ch'ung-shan-t'ang, and others.	300,000 or more	Honda Katsuichi, Fujiwara Akira
Moderate Traditionalists	It happened, and it was illegal.	It happened, and it was illegal.	It happened.	Red Swastika Society; a little reservation about Ch'ung-shan-t'ang.	150,000-300,000	Hora Tomio
Traditionalist Centrists	It happened, and it was illegal.	It happened, and it was illegal.	It did not happen.	Red Swastika Society.	38,000-42,000	Hata Ikuhiko
Revisionist Centrists	It happened, and it was illegal.	It happened, and it was illegal.	It did not happen.	Red Swastika Society, but claims it includes military casualties.	10,000-20,000	Itakura Yoshiaki
Moderate Revisionists	It happened, and it was illegal.	It happened. No comment about its legality.	It did not happen.	Red Swastika Society, but claims it includes military casualties and disputes a part of it.	50-7,000	Editors of *Kaiko* series
Extreme Revisionists	It happened, and it was illegal.	It happened, but it was legal.	It did not happen.	Red Swastika Society, but claims it includes military casualties and disputes a part of it.	50	Tanaka Masaaki

more clearly [than the Rape of Nanking debate]."[62] On the revisionist side, in a postscript to one of his works, Tanaka remarked with equal self-complacency about his own achievement of the downplaying of the Rape of Nanking: "I would like to state that we were able to secure clearly and confidently in our hands solid evidence to disprove the 'great massacre.' "[63] Both comments, reminiscent of wartime propaganda for the purpose of covering up defeat, seem to symbolize the stalemate in the Rape of Nanking debate rather than showing a clear victory for either side.

Second, the two sides have attacked each other's ideological motives in a similar manner. Traditionalist scholar Fujiwara Akira, on the one hand, pointed to the Japanese government's increasingly active military build-up policy in the

1970s through the 1980s and the alleged revival of militarism as a driving force behind the Rape of Nanking revisionism. Tanaka, on the other hand, identified the objective of the traditionalists with that of the Japanese Communist Party, that is, to charge the emperor with his war responsibility and eventually to abolish the imperial family.[64]

Third, the traditionalists and the revisionists have used similar logic in criticizing their opponents' research and analytical methods. Yamamoto Shichihei, in his analysis of the media coverage of the alleged killing contest, pointed to many descriptions that strongly suggest fabrications by news reporters in the 1930s but were not detected by contemporary readers. Here, Yamamoto, in a criticism of such a writing technique, charged that not only the writer of the original article but also Honda, who continued to believe in the truthfulness of this story, used what he called "Hitler's law," that is, that "a big lie, if supported by some truths in minute details, can be accepted by a million." On the traditionalist side, Hora criticized the revisionists' handling of this case as an attempt to deny the whole—the Rape of Nanking—by denying a part—the killing contest.[65]

As the exchange of criticisms escalated, both sides began to use slanderous expressions that were highly unsuitable for an academic debate. A former officer of the Japanese army called traditionalist scholar Hora a "hypocritical historian" and taunted him by his name "Hora," one homonym of which could mean "demagogy" in Japanese. Revisionist centrist Itakura attached a title reading "Stealing cookies while being carried on a parent's back: foolish remarks made by a kid who knows nothing about war" to a book review of traditionalist Yoshida Yutaka's book. The traditionalists were equally intense in their use of emotional language. In his criticism of the revisionist thesis, Honda said that he would keep himself away from any debate with these "noise-making 'intellectual bouncers' " and spend the limited amount of time in his life for works that he thought more important. Hora quoted this remark by Honda in one of his books. Several pages later in the same book, however, Hora criticized revisionist Suzuki for his "failure to respond to [traditionalists'] criticism while criticizing others one-sidedly." Here, Hora adopted an obvious double standard by praising his colleague's attitude on the one hand and speaking ill of the same attitude by a revisionist on the other. On another occasion, Honda taunted some revisionists and centrists in a childish manner. When quoting from former Japanese soldiers' diaries, Honda often uses aliases for the ostensible purpose of keeping the writers anonymous so that they can avoid verbal and other forms of abuses by revisionists. In some of such cases, he used as aliases "Itakura," "Unemoto," and "Tanaka"—names of those who represent the opposing side in the Rape of Nanking debate.[66]

Finally, both sides have perpetrated similar blunders in their handling of evidence. The discovery of Matsui's diary, for example, appeared first to benefit the revisionists. The tide, however, soon turned when Tanaka's tampering with the diary became known. Although, as centrist Itakura said, the contents of

Matsui's diary, even in its original untampered version, do not necessarily corroborate the traditionalist theory, it was a setback for the revisionist side. Similar upturns and downturns have also struck the traditionalists. They seemed to be gaining the upper hand with each successive publication of former Japanese soldiers' diaries or memoirs that contained numerous self-incriminating descriptions about their own atrocious deeds. Their advantage was, however, nullified to a certain extent when some of these supposedly primary sources were found to be forgeries or at least to be questionable in their authenticity. In one such instance, a man who identified himself as a former corporal and squad commander of an infantry unit wrote several books to confess various cases of atrocities he allegedly had either witnessed or committed. Later, however, it was found that he had actually been a first-year private in a logistics column and that all atrocities he claimed to have seen or perpetrated as a corporal were fabrications. In another instance, a former private of the 16th Division described a brutal atrocity scene in his memoir. He said that a fellow soldier forcibly pushed an innocent Chinese civilian into a big postal bag, set the bag ablaze after soaking it with gasoline, and finally threw it into a pond with some hand grenades attached to it. That former fellow soldier, whose identity one could infer from the content of that memoir, filed a libel suit against the writer in 1993. In a judgment handed down in 1996, the Tokyo District Court ruled in favor of the plaintiff and ordered the writer to pay compensatory damages. Although numerous other pieces of evidence, especially those originating from the West, prove the existence of atrocities in Nanking, such cases of what looked like fabrications undoubtedly encouraged the revisionist side to deny at least a part of the atrocities and thus further compounded the controversy.[67]

Although both sides have experienced similar ups and downs, one may conclude that the balance sheet slightly favors the revisionist side.

The first reason for this conclusion is that the traditionalist definition of the revisionist position is a little misleading. As a previous section shows, almost all revisionists from the beginning admitted that Japanese troops had committed some atrocious deeds. Nevertheless, the traditionalists have often claimed that they have completely disproved the revisionist argument that nothing atrocious happened in Nanking.[68] It seems that they misused, or were misguided by, the word *maboroshi-ha*—a Japanese phrase meaning "illusion school" and a term for the Rape of Nanking revisionists—and may have believed that there was a group of people who tried to deny any form of atrocity in Nanking. Centrist historian Hata correctly said that such a way of labeling was a source of confusion in the debate.[69] Thus, it is appropriate to conclude that the existence of the "illusion school," as the traditionalists say, is itself an illusion and that what the traditionalists claimed to be an overwhelming victory against it was also an illusory victory against a nonexistent foe.

Second, in the debate about the number of victims—an issue that inevitably connects with the character of atrocities—the traditionalists have been less vigorous than the revisionists in their effort to determine even an approximate figure. One may regard their attempts to trivialize this issue as their unwilling-ness to debate this question or even as their implicit concession. That some traditionalists have adopted a broader definition of the Rape of Nanking in terms of both time and space also seems to signify the same underlying attitude.

Finally, the traditionalists initially saw the atrocities in Nanking as an event caused by a single factor instead of an incident composed of multiple kinds of atrocities. Subsequently, they lagged behind the revisionists' more elaborate analysis of atrocities. One can find a typical example in the traditionalist Yo-shida's work. In his *Tenno no Guntai to Nankin Jiken* [Emperor's Military and Nanking Incident], Yoshida first said that "the Japanese troops committed group massacres of ordinary Chinese people and POWs as well as robbery, arson, and rape on a large scale . . . they conducted many of them systematically while maintaining their basic organizational structure as an army."[70] The implication here is that the Japanese troops committed all these atrocities while maintaining their discipline. Then, later in the same book, he said, "The fact that the serious decline of military discipline had already manifested itself is an important key to analyze the Japanese army's violence at the time of the Nanking campaign."[71]

Inconsistency in his logic is obvious, that is, he at one point attributed the atrocities to the military's systematic conduct committed under disciplined con-trol and then later pointed to a factor accruing from the breakdown of that control as a cause of the same atrocities. In an article written several years later—after some revisionist and centrist works had made extensive efforts to categorize the atrocities—he seemingly treated the cases of individually com-mitted violence such as robbery and rape as incidents that the military leadership had overlooked or tolerated and seemingly distinguished them from the POW executions.[72] Conclusions that ultimately ascribe everything to the leadership might be suitable for a prosecutorial purpose, as when the IMTFE ruled that Matsui's crime was a "deliberate and reckless disregard of military duty." For the historical analysis of the atrocities, however, the revisionist and centrist approach, which draws on distinctions among various kinds of victims, is ob-viously superior. Such a method of analysis will help determine what circum-stances caused each category of atrocities, and then analyze who should assume what kind of responsibility—for example, responsibility for omission or com-mission.

Thus, the debate is tipped slightly in favor of the revisionists, but not over-whelmingly so, as the emergence of the centrist positions shows. Of the centrists, the traditionalist centrist position still demonstrates some degree of emotional inclination toward the Chinese stance, like Hata's treatment of the claim of 300,000 victims as a "symbolic figure." This is where the traditionalist centrist position becomes very ambiguous. In reference to a political dispute concerning this figure, Hata said in an article, "In my impression, it is impossible for the Japanese to present a figure which can refute the [Chinese] estimate of 300,000 victims although this is a figure based on their improvised investigation im-mediately after World War II."[73] Then, in the very next paragraph in the same article, he said, "Academic research and discussion must, however, be conducted separately," and mentioned his own estimate of about 40,000.[74] In what looks like two mutually contradictory statements, it seems that Hata tried to detach academic discussion of the Rape of Nanking from political and diplomatic disputes relating to the war responsibility issue and proposes to discuss the number and other related issues only in academic circles. Yet as the following sections will show, some Chinese and Western scholars seemingly use this figure to make what looks like a very political statement. Moreover, they often attempt to investigate crucial issues in the academic debate such as the nature and scale of the atrocities based on this estimate. Therefore, in the discussion of the Rape of Nanking, the analysis of this figure is indispensable whether one accepts or refutes it. The ambivalent stance assumed by Hata on this number issue is thus a weakness of the "traditionalist centrist" position. Compared with this position, the revisionist centrist position is more clear-cut: it tries to determine the scale and nature of the atrocities by critically analyzing documentary and numerical data for the purpose of establishing how and to what extent the Japanese were responsible for the atrocities. Since such an approach is more beneficial for objective historical analysis, the centrist revisionist position is the one the author has determined to be the most persuasive.

RECENT CHINESE AND WESTERN VIEWS

There has been scarcely any difference of opinions about the Rape of Nanking in China or in the West simply because there have been almost no revisionists among Chinese scholars and only a few among Westerners. It seems that the wartime empathy the two parties fostered as victims of the same Japanese atrocities has survived through the years. One can see the most notable effect of that empathy nurtured by the wartime propaganda in the treatment of the alleged atrocity photographs. Only a photographic magazine carried such photographs in the 1930s, and it received mostly skeptical reactions from its readers. In addition, at the time, people who believed in their authenticity treated them as photographs that depicted atrocities that occurred well after the Rape of Nanking by pointing to the summer uniforms worn by the Japanese soldiers in the photographs. Today, published books often carry these photos as evidence of Japanese atrocities in Nanking. Moreover, writers in these publications seemingly make no effort to explain why Japanese soldiers in summer uniforms should be seen as evidence of the Rape of Nanking, which took place in the winter.[75]

Most of Chinese and Western journalists and scholars have maintained consistently that the Rape of Nanking was an indiscriminate massacre of men, women, and children totaling as many as 300,000 victims. Communist China seems to have solidified its opinion regarding the number issue since the Memorial Hall of the Victims in the Nanjing Massacre, which opened in 1985, has "Victims 300,000" engraved on the wall of its main entrance. In addition, Tuan Yueh-p'ing, a Chinese scholar specializing in the Rape of Nanking issue, recently adopted 340,000 as the number of POWs and civilians killed, and computed an average of 8,095 per day over the six-week period. By comparing this figure with the daily average of 879 people gassed at Auschwitz—one and a half million executed over fifty-six months from June 1940 to January 1945—she declared the level of killing involved in the Rape of Nanking to be "an extremely rare event in human history." This scholar's analysis shows that the Chinese side does not treat the figure of 300,000 victims or more only symbolically, contrary to the traditionalist centrist Hata's claim. Unlike the Japanese "traditionalists," however, this Chinese historian maintained the time frame of the atrocities as was adopted at the IMTFE, that is, the six-week period from immediately after Nanking's fall on December 13, 1937, until early February 1938. Treatment of other individual atrocity stories has been unchanged since the end of World War II. Chinese sources still discuss the story of the killing contest as a fact constituting an important aspect of the Rape of Nanking. Thus, one may conclude that the Chinese version of the Rape of Nanking has been very consistent.[76]

There are other long-term tendencies in the ways the Chinese have handled the Rape of Nanking stories. First, they have often rekindled this issue more in reaction to outside news reports, specifically by Japanese news media, than as a result of their own investigation—just as they began their initial reporting of the incident in the 1930s by following up the Western media reports. Second, they have linked the Rape of Nanking question to the alleged revival of Japanese militarism just as the American news media had treated the Rape of Nanking as the symbol and precursor of Japanese brutalities expressed against their own countrymen during World War II.

Besides the Japanese high school textbook crisis in the early 1980s, the most recent such incident occurred in the spring of 1994. In an interview with a Japanese newspaper early in May of that year, Nagano Shigeto, the newly appointed Japanese justice minister in the cabinet of prime minister Hata Tsutomu, made a remark that seemingly denied the Rape of Nanking. Nagano, who as a young army officer had visited Nanking shortly after the Japanese army's occupation, said that he did not believe the "massacre as usually reported" had happened. To support his opinion, Nagano said he had not felt "antipathy among the [Chinese] people"—an atmosphere he could have felt if Japanese troops had committed such "an awful thing." Although he quickly added that one could not deny the occurrence of some violent acts typical in warfare, the content of Nagano's remark quickly spread overseas and precipitated angry reactions everywhere. Taiwan's *Central Daily News* quoted Nagano as saying that the Rape of Nanking was a fabrication, while a commentator for the paper accused Nagano of representing Japanese rightists in support of a resurgent militarism and a cover-up of past criminal acts. The Communists' *People's Daily*, in a rare alliance with the Taiwanese, criticized the presence of a Japanese cabinet member who "openly distorts history, denies the fact, and justifies the aggression by the Japanese militarists." Under bombardment by such criticisms not only from

Taiwan and mainland China but also from other Asian nations such as South Korea, the Philippines, and Vietnam, Nagano retracted his remark and resigned from his ministerial post on May 7. Although most of these Asian nations were satisfied to see Nagano's resignation, some continued to blast what to them appeared to be the "revival of militarism in Japan." This event showcased how a diplomatic crisis concerning the Rape of Nanking issues unfolds: starting with a media report about a remark or policy decision made by the Japanese government circle, it precipitated protests from other countries, and ended with an apology from the Japanese government.[77]

Since the Chinese have consistently adhered to the position first displayed in the IMTFE proceedings, there have been almost no stories of evidence tampering by scholars or journalists. Nevertheless, the Chinese are not completely innocent of intellectual dishonesty. They sometimes seem to create dummy witnesses. In what looks like one of those instances, a Japanese historian who visited the Chinese mainland in the mid-1970s met a self-described survivor of the Rape of Nanking. Since that witness looked very young for a person who had witnessed the fall of Nanking in 1937, the cautious Japanese historian asked when he had been born. The answer was in 1938, one year after the incident happened. In Taiwan, two Japanese journalists separately interviewed an individual who identified himself as Shih Mei-yu, one of the judges who presided at the trial of the two Japanese lieutenants accused of the alleged killing contest. Although they supposedly met with the same person, each of them obtained testimony that was quite different from the other. Suzuki Akira, author of *"Nankin Daigyakusatsu" no Maboroshi* [Illusion of the "Rape of Nanking"], said that the strong Shanghai dialect of Shih made his interview very difficult even with an interpreter. According to Suzuki, who managed to summarize Shih's remarks by listening to the taped interview over and over later, Shih did not express his personal opinion about the guilt or innocence of the two accused and only praised the attitude of Mukai Toshiaki, one of the executed lieutenants, as a military man. At the same time, Suzuki quoted Shih as saying that there was a certain degree of pressure exerted from Chiang Kai-shek and other Chinese Nationalist leaders on the military court's decision. Shortly afterward, another journalist named Watada Susumu met Shih, who according to Watada spoke clear Chinese understandable to his interpreter. Watada's interview quoted Shih as saying that there was solid incriminating evidence against the two lieutenants. The former judge also added an episode, which had reportedly been revealed during the trial, that the two lieutenants bet a bottle of brandy on the killing contest. When one looks at these two interviews, one cannot but suspect that Suzuki and Watada met with two different individuals. It is possible that one of them interviewed was a stand-in for Shih. Or, it is even possible that neither of them met with the right person because, although the two interviews shared one story, ironically the story common in both contradicts the truth. Both interviews quoted Shih as saying that a Japanese publication during the war

establish any parallel between the Nazi persecution of Jews in Germany and the Japanese atrocities in China. Her choice of that word was merely to emphasize the carnage suffered by the Chinese population in wartime.

It was the Japanese traditionalist group that in the 1970s first juxtaposed the Rape of Nanking with the Jewish Holocaust. Its main intent was, however, more to make a political or ideological statement to criticize what it termed as imperialist aggression against the small powers by the great powers, most likely in reference to the Vietnam War, than to find qualitative similarities between the two events. A typical work was Kuroda Hidetoshi's *Nankin, Hiroshima, Aushubittsu* [Nanking, Hiroshima, and Auschwitz], which discussed the Rape of Nanking, the atomic bombing of Hiroshima, and the Jewish extermination in World War II Europe from the standpoint of the victims. Kuroda said that the common denominators in these three cases were (1) the sense of racial superiority existent on the part of aggressors, and (2) the role of a military that, according to him, did not represent the people unlike some other supposedly people's armies, with typical examples being the People's Liberation Army in China or the Vietcong. Another consideration behind some traditionalists' effort to link the Rape of Nanking to the Holocaust is to illuminate how Japanese political leaders have neglected to assume Japan's responsibility in World War II as compared with German leaders. Traditionalist scholar Yoshida's book about the Rape of Nanking, for example, starts with a quote from a speech of West German Chancellor Richard von Weitzsaecker in 1985, a speech in which the chancellor expressed regret for Germany's conduct during World War II.[88]

Apart from such symbolic and ideological parallels, however, the Japanese involved in the Rape of Nanking debate have mostly denied the existence of common elements between Nanking and the Holocaust. The Rape of Nanking revisionists, for example, have countered the traditionalists' Nanking–Holocaust parallels by distinguishing the Japanese military from the Nazis. Typically, Tanaka severely criticized the underlying logic of the IMTFE, that is, its attempt to indict Japan as a Far Eastern counterpart of Nazi Germany. He correctly pointed out numerous divisions and internal dissention within the Japanese leadership to contrast it with the Nazi dictatorship, in which Hitler's command had a predominant effect on policy decisions. More significantly, unlike the Holocaust deniers who tend to play down the nature and magnitude of the Jewish Holocaust, Tanaka accepted the basic facts about the Jewish Holocaust such as the extermination of six million European Jews, and spent much of his energy emphasizing how the Japanese were different from the Nazis. His only questionable argument in denying a Nazi–Japanese parallel was that he went so far as to claim that Japan had a "well functioning parliament and sound form of constitutional government" that was unlike Nazi Germany.[89]

As for the centrist historian Hata, he pointed to the substantially different backgrounds of the Nazi Holocaust and of the Rape of Nanking. The Rape of Nanking was, according to Hata, an atrocity caused by inefficient military leadership and a lack of discipline, whereas the Nazi Holocaust was a planned and state-orchestrated genocide. Later in the same book, however, Hata also suggested that both the Japanese and Nazi atrocities were the products of fascist military systems and could be terminated only with the abolition of their war machines. These two seemingly mutually contradictory statements symbolize Hata's position as a "traditionalist centrist." Yet Hata's latter remark is on a par with that of the previously mentioned traditionalist Kuroda's—that is, that both the Nazi atrocities and the Japanese atrocities were caused by the military without the support of the people. It is appropriate to conclude that Hata did not try to establish a parallel between Nanking and the Holocaust.[90]

There have been only a few cases of what looks like Holocaust–Nanking revisionist parallelism in Japan. First, Kobori Keiichiro, a University of Tokyo professor of literature, wrote a foreword for the extreme revisionist Tanaka's book *Nankin Jiken no Sokatsu* [Nanking Incident Summed up] while he later wrote for a Japanese newspaper to praise the work of the Institute for Historical Review—a California-based organization known for its denial of the Holocaust. Second, in 1994 another Japanese professor disclaimed the existence of gas chambers at German concentration camps in an article printed in *Marco Polo*, a monthly English-language magazine published in Japan by Bungeishunju. This publishing house is noted for its inclination toward the revisionist stance on the Rape of Nanking issues. Except for these somewhat indirect links, so far there have been no known Japanese scholars who discuss Nanking and the Holocaust at the same time and deny both.[91]

It is the Western Holocaust deniers who have become increasingly interested in the Rape of Nanking issue, although their probe into this question has not yet been extensive. It is probable that the Western Holocaust deniers in the near future will approach the Japanese revisionists in a bid to form a united revisionist front. Symptomatically, a web site connected with prominent Holocaust denier Ernst Zuendel referred to a revisionist movement against the "false atrocity story of the rape of Nanking" as one of the "promising developments." In addition, Zuendel's newsletter dated on May 2, 1997, mentioned Fujioka Nobukatsu—a University of Tokyo professor known for his revisionist stance on modern historical issues, including the Rape of Nanking—as a possible ally. Yet another web site created by the Committee for Open Discussion of the Holocaust Story—another Holocaust denial organization—carried a brief article describing the "strange fauna and flora" in the IMTFE proceedings such as questionable evidence and witness testimonies related to the Rape of Nanking.[92]

What makes the Holocaust deniers feel close to the Rape of Nanking revisionists, however, seems to be mostly superficial similarities, namely the logic both employ. First, both groups have focused extensively on the number of victims—the Holocaust's six million and the Rape of Nanking's 300,000. The former Japanese army men's association *Kaiko* emphatically proclaimed the purpose of its article series about the Nanking campaign as the "refutation of the commonly accepted figure of 200,000 to 300,000 victims." On the Holocaust denial side, one can see in book titles such as *The Six Million Swindle* and *Did*

Six Million Really Die? a parallel interest in reducing the alleged death toll. Second, both groups question the reliability of some evidence, photographic evidence in particular. Revisionists Suzuki Akira and Tanaka Masaaki in their respective books disputed the authenticity of several photos that allegedly captured scenes of Japanese atrocities. In the same way, a booklet published by Historical Review Press carried an allegedly fake photo showing concentration camp inmates. Third, both groups admitted to some atrocious conduct by the Japanese or the Germans. As a previous section shows, even extreme revisionist Tanaka said that Japanese soldiers in Nanking committed a substantial number of criminal acts. As for the Holocaust deniers, they did admit that the condition of the concentration camps deteriorated toward the end of the war and caused a substantial number of deaths in the camps, but blamed them on the allies' bombing and the resulting food shortage. Fourth, both groups resort to relativism by mentioning allies' military actions that resulted in high death tolls such as the bombing of Dresden and the atomic bombing of Hiroshima.[93]

It is possible that the increasingly extensive communications using computer technology worldwide will further enhance the contact between Western Holocaust deniers and Eastern revisionists. Yet some fundamental differences between the two are likely to inhibit their concerted effort at a certain point in the future just as the Japan–German Axis alliance led to little meaningful cooperation in the 1940s due to the substantially different objectives they intended to achieve through the alliance.

The foremost difference is the lineup of each group—a factor that reflects the ideological or political backgrounds of each. The Holocaust deniers encompass various racial and national groups, some of them former concentration camp inmates and even Jews. Paul Rassinier, who disclaimed the existence of gas chambers in the Buchenwald camp in his *Le Mensonge d'Ulysse* [The Lies of Odysseus] and went on to deny the entire Holocaust story, had been a French socialist interned in that camp during the war. Other prominent Holocaust deniers include David Irving of England as well as Harry Elmer Barnes, Austin J. App, and Arthur R. Butz of the United States. As for the denial group's Jewish connection, one of the guests on the Montel Williams television talk show on the discussion of Holocaust denial on April 30, 1992, was David Cole, a Jewish member of the Committee for the Open Debate of the Holocaust. The presence of people with such a broad range of national and ethnic backgrounds in support of Holocaust denial reflects the deep-rooted issues behind the debate, such as anti-Semitism and individual human rights, especially the right that the Holocaust deniers claim in order to deny the Holocaust. The Holocaust deniers on the one hand often elaborate on what they call the long-standing disruptive activities of Jews in the Western world to justify some anti-Jewish policies adopted by the Nazis, and they criticize any attack on their own position as a violation of their freedom of speech. The Holocaust scholars on the other hand point to the deniers' affiliation with right-wing or anti-Semitic organizations and identify Holocaust denial with anti-Semitism. In contrast with the inclusion of a wide range of nationalities and political groups among the Holocaust deniers, the Rape of Nanking revisionists have so far been almost exclusively Japanese nationals who in many cases represent a conservative political force. Although the traditionalists' concern about the revival of Japanese militarism seems to be on a par with the Holocaust scholars' fear of growing anti-Semitism, the former appears to be a much less potent force due to its limited range of acceptance within a single nation.[94]

The second fundamental difference is the way each group has changed its thesis in the eyes of its respective opponent. According to Deborah E. Lipstadt, a Holocaust scholar, those who in the early post-World War II years justified the Nazi conduct did not deny the Holocaust itself, but only tried to minimize its death toll or adopt a relativist interpretation by pointing to allied atrocities. The Holocaust deniers changed their tactics in the 1970s, Lipstadt said, "when they finally began to recognize the futility of trying to justify Nazi antisemitism." Therefore, Holocaust denial moved from partial denial or relativism to total denial. To the contrary, according to some traditionalist criticisms, the Rape of Nanking revisionists followed a completely reverse course, that is, from total denial to partial denial. As a previous section has shown, however, this inter-pretation also seems fraudulent because almost no revisionists have ever resorted to total denial in the Rape of Nanking controversy. One may contend that the Rape of Nanking revisionist opinion has been relatively consistent in its admis-sion of POW execution and individual soldiers' irregular behavior. Moreover, as a previous section suggests, it is rather the traditionalists who have changed their thesis in the course of the debate by expanding the definition of massacre and trying to count even those killed in combat action as victims.[95]

Finally, the ways the deniers and revisionists in the West and the East treated the defendants' testimonies at war crimes trials show a stark contrast. Holocaust deniers discounted the affidavits and court testimonies of Nazi officials as in-formation extorted by threat or torture. They conclude that these confessions are unreliable. To the contrary, the Rape of Nanking revisionists have never advo-cated such an extortion theory in their discussion of the IMTFE affidavits and court testimonies. Instead, they have criticized the way the court handled the evidence that was introduced. They say that the court adopted too much pros-ecution evidence and rejected too much defense evidence. This final point relates not only to historiographical differences but also to historical differences be-tween the Holocaust and Nanking as atrocities. An implication here is that the Rape of Nanking revisionists do not have to resort to, or concoct, an extortion theory because no Japanese defendants or witnesses admitted to the occurrence of a massacre along the prosecution's line of argument. They do not have to refute the theory of state-orchestrated atrocities, either, because even the IMTFE majority ruling found Matsui guilty only of having "deliberately and recklessly disregarded his legal duty." As for the Holocaust deniers, they have to resort to these tactics to deny the Nazi war criminals' confessions because these court documents clearly establish the existence of deliberate extermination planning among the Nazi leaders. In view of all these differences, it is inappropriate to treat Eastern revisionists and Western deniers in entirely the same light. It is worth noting that Holocaust historians today tend to distinguish "revisionism," which they regard as a legitimate form of historical research, from "denial," which they denounce as an unacceptable attack on historical truth. One may characterize those who oppose the traditionalist interpretation of the Rape of Nanking as revisionists rather than deniers.[96]

Now, the question is how Holocaust scholars and Rape of Nanking researchers relate to each other. For comparison purposes, some Holocaust scholars have discussed other cases of incidents involving mass murder such as the Turkish massacre of Armenians, the atomic bombing of Hiroshima and Nagasaki, and the massacre at My Lai village during the Vietnam War. Nevertheless, they have so far not included the Rape of Nanking among the incidents they use to illustrate the history of massacre. Moreover, they have been almost unanimous in their efforts to establish the Holocaust as a unique historical event in which every member of a certain racial group became the target of extermination. For example, Lucy S. Dawidowicz drew a clear demarcation line between ordinary war atrocities and the Jewish Holocaust in her article:

Auschwitz . . . was neither conceived nor constructed as a theater of atrocity to play out Everyman's capacity for evil, to satisfy a universal lust for killing. Auschwitz was the direct consequence of a specific and particular history of anti-Semitism.

America's decision to use the atomic bomb against Japan was not motivated by a wish to wipe out the Japanese people. . . . The more persuasive evidence indicated that the killings [in My Lai village in Vietnam] were prompted by fear that the civilians were in fact members of the Viet Cong. . . . the argument that America committed crimes as monumental as those of the Nazis can justify a reverse claim: since the United States committed crimes as evil as those of Nazi Germany, then Nazi Germany committed no worse crimes than other states and was not unique among nations as a perpetrator of evil deed.[97]

Given their emphasis on the unique nature of the Holocaust in human history as well as their fear that the Holocaust might be seen as a parallel event with other cases of war atrocities, it is too presumptuous to conclude that Holocaust scholars are the Western counterparts of the Rape of Nanking traditionalists. The two groups apparently differ also in the way they conduct their respective research. Holocaust scholars, for example, have made, and are still making, extensive endeavors to refute theories of a much smaller number of Jewish victims, which deniers formulated by manipulating demographic and other data. Despite an emotional enmity they surely have toward the deniers, they counter these claims in a scholarly manner.[98] Such an effort enabled one Holocaust scholar to say confidently, "For scholars, the chore of trying to pin down the actual number of Jews and others killed by the Nazis continues."[99] This attitude shows a stark contrast with Chinese and Western Rape of Nanking commentators who assume very ambivalent attitudes regarding the number issue. On the one hand, their writings on the incident emphasize the magnitude of the Rape of Nanking by insisting on the figure—300,000 or more—and contrasting this alleged killing with other historical incidents.

The Japanese outdid the Romans at Carthage (only 150,000 died in that slaughter), the Christian armies during the Spanish Inquisition, and even some of the monstrosities of Timur Lenk, who killed 100,000 prisoners at Delhi in 1398 and built two towers of skulls in Syria in 1400 and 1401.[100]

Japanese soldiers murdered tens of thousands of surrendered Chinese soldiers, and almost certainly more than 300,000 noncombatants. (Civilian deaths at Hiroshima and Nagasaki totaled 210,000. Britain and France suffered a combined total of 169,000 civilian deaths from 1939 to 1945.)[101]

On the other hand, some scholars say, "the debate over numbers has become unnecessarily politicized and indeed distracting."[102] Adoption of such a double standard makes their argument less persuasive than the Holocaust scholars'.

Despite the involvement of the Simon Wiesenthal Center in the Rape of Nanking controversy in the wake of the publication of Iris Chang's *The Rape of Nanking*, one can find only a weak Holocaust–Nanking connection in Holocaust-related literature so far. Lipstadt made a reference to a recent Japanese attempt to distort the "historical reality of the Japanese 'Rape of Nanking,' calling it the 'Nanking Incident,' " as one of the trends supporting the calls for Holocaust denial in Japan, although Holocaust denial in Japan is apparently much smaller in scale than in the West.[103] She, however, did not make any attempt to compare the Rape of Nanking to the Jewish Holocaust.

Ethnic Chinese, Chinese-American scholars in particular, have been the most active in trying to establish the Nanking–Holocaust parallel. It seems, however, that the motive behind this movement has been political rather than strictly for historical analysis. Various ethnic Chinese organizations are concerned with Rape of Nanking issues, including the Hong Kong-based Chinese Alliance for the Commemoration of the Sino-Japanese War Victims, the Northern California-based Alliance for Preserving the Truth of Sino-Japanese War, the Global Alliance for Preserving the History of World War II in Cupertino, California, and the Alliance in Memory of Victims of the Nanjing Massacre in New Jersey. They proclaim a multitude of objectives, but the one shared almost unanimously by all groups is the effort to seek an indemnity from the Japanese government.[104] At the same time, they focus on the lack of an official apology from the Japanese government after World War II, contrasting the Japanese attitude with quite the opposite stance assumed by the German government.[105] It is a logical conclusion that once the Rape of Nanking is found to have been a genocidal atrocity comparable to the Holocaust, the Japanese government will be obliged to pay an indemnity to Rape of Nanking victims in the same way the German government has done for Holocaust victims. Although this reasoning is pure speculation, the recently popular Nanking–Holocaust parallel seems to have its origin in such a political motivation. Their claim for redress is justifiable to a certain extent since there were undoubtedly atrocity victims. Nevertheless, it appears that the Nanking–Holocaust parallel is less a theory based on the solid analysis of historical facts than an argument helpful in enhancing their specific objective.

One could deduce the plausibility of this line of reasoning from statements made by some ethnic Chinese in the wake of a recent publication about the Rape of Nanking. Iris Chang, a Chinese-American author, discovered the diary of John H. Rabe, a German ICNSZ member in Nanking, and wrote a book entitled *The Rape of Nanking: The Forgotten Holocaust*. In a strange twist, Rabe was a Nazi party member at the time. Rabe was, however, enough of a humanitarian to try to stop the rampage caused by the Japanese soldiers and to shield some Chinese who sought his help. In a symbolic statement reflecting the approach explicit in the title of her work, Chang called Rabe "Oskar Schindler in China." Commenting on this publication in the *New York Times*, David W. Chen said that publishing the book would "bolster the efforts" of ethnic Chinese organizations, one of which is to extract compensation from the Japanese government.[106]

One may attribute the existence of the variety of attitudes about the Nanking–Holocaust parallel to the political or ideological background of four groups: Chinese-American Rape of Nanking researchers, Holocaust deniers, Holocaust scholars, and Rape of Nanking revisionists. The Chinese-American scholars regard both events as the most extreme form of atrocity, that is, genocide or an atrocity as intense as genocide. They attempt to establish such a parallel because it will obviously enhance their cause, that is, to seek compensation from the Japanese government. Ironically, some Holocaust revisionists are eager to adopt a similar approach, although their objective is exactly the opposite. For the Holocaust revisionists, the Rape of Nanking could be a useful tool to deny or downplay the image of the Holocaust by drawing on similarities between the two and pointing to many controversial stories in the Rape of Nanking. For them, both events were no more than tragedies that are common in time of war. On the other side of the debate, two groups that also have completely different motives—Western Holocaust scholars and Japanese revisionists—are unlikely allies bent on disproving any similarity between the two events. Holocaust scholars emphasize the unique nature of the Holocaust, that is, a state-orchestrated attempt to erase one entire ethnic group, whereas the Japanese revisionists wish to contrast the Japanese military with the Nazi army to show that the Imperial Japanese Army was completely different from Nazi *Einsatzgruppen* in charge of exterminating Jews in the German occupied area. An implicit agreement between the two is that the Holocaust far surpassed the Rape of Nanking in terms of the scale and nature of atrocities.

SUMMARY OF THE RAPE OF NANKING DEBATE:
ANALOGY WITH A COURT OF LAW

Historian Hata Ikuhiko said that there is "something devilish which upsets people's minds" in the Rape of Nanking debate.[107] One obvious reason is the political and ideological motivation that compels many people involved in the debate to make strong statements. Another reason is the lingering influence of the IMTFE on various opinions about the Rape of Nanking. Although the revisionists have criticized the traditionalists for their continuing acceptance of the IMTFE verdict, or what they called the "IMTFE syndrome," the revisionists are also under the spell of the IMTFE by presenting arguments similar to those adopted by the defense at the war crimes trial. Another major problem haunting both the traditionalists and the revisionists is that they still present their arguments in a way similar to lawyers in a criminal case in which a verdict must be guilty or not guilty. On the one hand, the traditionalists refuse to depart even a little from their own view based on the IMTFE or Chinese version of the Rape of Nanking in the same way that a criminal prosecutor persists in convicting a defendant in accordance with the original indictment. The revisionists, on the other hand, refuse to admit that atrocities happened, except for criminal acts attributable to the lack of discipline, in the same way a defense attorney in a criminal trial attempts to prove the innocence of the defendant. Both the traditionalists and the revisionists must assume such a rigid stance because of outside pressure. The traditionalists have always been careful not to contradict the Chinese version of the Rape of Nanking, while the revisionists refuse to accept any historical finding that might dishonor the Imperial Japanese Army. The debate has continued so long also because there have been, and still are, no judges who preside at the "court of debate."

Chinese and Western scholars see the IMTFE ruling as an uncontestable final judgment and behave like supporters of the Japanese traditionalists outside the court. Their attitude is more rigid than that of the Japanese traditionalists, who make an obvious effort to counter the revisionists' claim. Since probing into the details of the atrocities, which is comparable to the fact-finding phase in a criminal case, is already a finished business for these groups, they are mainly concerned with other questions. The ethnic Chinese groups, for example, are interested in a matter comparable to a civil lawsuit in their attempt to extract compensation from the Japanese government. Besides, they tend to focus on moral issues based on the judgment they deem correct. Here, they speak as if they were in the penalty phase of a criminal trial. Commenting on the issue of how many people were killed in Nanking, for example, one of the organizers of Princeton University's event commemorating the 60th anniversary of the Rape of Nanking said, "Would the Japanese Imperial Army be redeemed if they merely killed 80,000 people for example?"[108] Here, he sounds like a prosecutor who tries to justify a severe penalty that he seeks to impose on a defendant by referring to the heinous nature of crime the defendant committed.

Likewise, Western scholars often do not seem to see the Rape of Nanking debate as an academic discussion. Instead, they view it as a contest between good and evil. In their eyes the revisionists are like a condemned criminal unrepentantly seeking a retrial, whereas the traditionalists are like champions of justice fighting that criminal. Referring to the Rape of Nanking traditionalists in Japan, for example, Carol Gluck, an American scholar, said, "For twenty-five years, progressive Japanese intellectuals have fought, with little success, for *honesty* in school textbooks and public memory" [italics added]. The underlying implication is that the traditionalists represent honesty, thus the truth, as opposed to the dishonesty and falsehood of the revisionists. She also said, "The crucial historical question remains the moral one: how could ordinary Japanese have done what they did? Numerological arguments about the death count and distinctions of comparative atrocities do not address this point. And the attempts to explain why Japanese soldiers behaved as they did in Nanking—they were tired, hungry, untrained, oppressed, and so on—fall far short of persuasion."[109] Here, this scholar only demands from the Japanese an explanation for "what they did" based on the traditionalist view without questioning whether "what they did," according to the traditionalists, is correct.

A major weakness of the Western and Chinese scholars' arguments relating to Japanese responsibility is their failure to define that responsibility clearly. One Chinese-American scholar, for example, argues that "Without first acknowledging Japan's responsibility for these war atrocities . . . obsession with historical particularities can appear to be excuses for Japanese behavior."[110] In this statement, it is not clear whether he refers to the responsibility for the alleged massacre of 300,000 people as the Chinese and many Western scholars have argued, or for the atrocities according to the Japanese revisionist version, that is, the execution of prisoners numbering much less than 300,000 and individually committed crimes attributable to the lack of discipline. In view of such ambiguity, one may make a reverse claim by rephrasing this passage: without first establishing the historical particularities of these war atrocities, obsession with Japan's responsibility can appear to be excuses for Chinese and Western lack of historical investigation. In the discussion of Japanese responsibility, a distinction between the two cases is crucial because the Japanese would have to accept quite a different type of responsibility depending on which one is the case. If the first case were true, the Japanese should be charged with responsibility for a massacre of a genocidal nature, whereas, if the second case were found to be more valid, the responsibility of the Japanese should be different—for example, guilty of "deliberate or reckless disregard of legal duty" as the IMTFE verdict said. A majority of the Japanese, including even some revisionists, admit that the Japanese army committed some forms of atrocities in Nanking, whatever their scale. Thus, they pleaded guilty. Yet many of them feel, quite rightly, that they should not, and need not, accept the responsibility for the alleged massacre of 300,000, a figure that would make the historical interpretation of the event completely different from that of the revisionists. This difference is so crucial as to be comparable to the difference in criminal charges between first-degree murder and involuntary manslaughter. In view of such a concern shared by the Japanese, the recently emerging Nanking-Holocaust parallel will make it more difficult for the Japanese to accept the ambiguously defined responsibility. Consequently, the extraction of compensation from the Japanese government, which various ethnic Chinese groups aim to achieve, will become more difficult as well.

It is imperative to determine how and to what extent the Japanese were responsible. If one uses an analogy from criminal justice, the fact-finding phase is not yet over, or there should be a retrial. To determine the extent and nature of the responsibility, the "numerological arguments about the death count and distinctions of comparative atrocities," which the previously quoted American scholar termed as irrelevant to the moral question, are essential. Only after firmly establishing "historical particularities" can one clearly define Japan's responsibility. And based on a clear definition of the responsibility there can be an answer to the "moral" question. Also, one can measure for the first time how appropriate the moral and compensatory claims set forth by the Western and Chinese scholars are when one has answered various historical questions: what really happened; in what way were the Japanese responsible; and how grave were the consequences.

NOTES

1. Chen Cheng, ed., *Chung-kuo 8-nien K'ang-chan Ching-kuo Kai-yao* [Summary of Eight Years of Resistance War in China] (Taipei, 1946), p. 11; Kuo-fang-pu Shih-cheng Chu [History Section, Defense Department, Republic of China], ed., *K'ang-chan Chien-shih* [Short History of Resistance War], p. 52; idem, ed., *Chung-jih Chan-chen-shih Lueh* [Brief History of War between China and Japan] (Taipei: History Section of the Defense Department, 1962), p. 198. Chiang Wei-kuo, *Kuo-min Ke-ming Chan-shih Ti-3-pu K'ang-jih Yu-wu* [History of Nationalist Revolutionary War, part 3, Resistance War against Japan], p. 75.

2. Imai Masatake, "Nankin Jonai no Tairyo Satsujin" [Mass Murder within Nanking Walls], *Tokushu Bungeishunju* [Special Edition of Bungeishunju], December 1956, pp. 156–57. Hata Kensuke, "Horyo no Chi ni Mamireta Byakko Butai: Nankin Gyakusatsu Jiken no Jisso" [White Tiger Unit Stained with Blood of Prisoners of War: Truth of Nanking Massacre], *Nihon Shuho* [Japan Weekly], 25 February 1957, pp. 13–15.

3. "History Undercover" on the History Channel, 22 August 1999.

4. Honda Katsuichi, *Chugoku no Tabi* [Trip to China] (Tokyo: Asahi Shinbun [Asahi Newspaper], 1972; Suzusawa Shoten, 1977), pp. 290–92.

5. For example, see Hora Tomio and Watada Susumu, "Kaizan Shita no wa Dare ka: Itakura-shi Hihan" [Who Tampered with Evidence?: Rebuttal to Mr. Itakura's Theory] in *NDG*, pp. 126, 155.

6. Suzuki, *"Nankin Daigyakusatsu" no Maboroshi* [Illusion of the "Rape of Nanking"], p. 230.

7. Ibid., pp. 268, 271–72. As for Suzuki's intent with respect to the use of the word

"illusion," see idem, "Haikei 'Jinmin Nippo' Henshu-cho-dono" [Dear Editor-in-Chief of "People's Daily"], *Bungeishunju*, October 1982, p. 98.

8. This naming of "revisionists" is only for identifying purpose and is by no means to suggest any parallel with or similarity to the revisionists in other controversial subjects such as Pearl Harbor, and the origins of the Cold War.

9. Hora Tomio, *Nankin Jiken* [Nanking Incident] (Tokyo: Shin Jinbutsu Oraisha, 1972), quoted in Suzuki, *"Nankin Daigyakusatsu" no Maboroshi* [Illusion of the "Rape of Nanking"], pp. 186–87. Ibid., pp. 186–200.

10. Yamamoto Shichihei, *Watashi no naka no Nihongun* [Japanese Military within Myself], vol. 2, p. 306.

11. In the section dealing with the Rape of Nanking, he said, "the exact number of [Rape of Nanking] victims cannot be known. But the number is not the core of the issue. The essence is that indiscriminate massacre and large-scale violence took place. When such a charge is made, the same old trick aggressors emphatically employ in the face of such an allegation is to demand an exact 'figure' or 'visible evidence' . . . and in the end resort to a sophistry in which they conclude 'Such was not the fact'. . . . The U.S. government is constantly pursuing the same policy right now in its war in Vietnam." Honda, *Chugoku no Nihongun* [Japanese Military in China] (Tokyo: Sojusha, 1972), pp. 94–95. Also, see pp. 9, 14, 182–83, 238–39, 247 of the same book.

12. Honda, who observed a Chinese school, said, "the [Chinese] education which emphasizes the importance of serving populace is remarkable. . . . In a [mathematics] class, for example, students were asked to compute the rate of price hike in Taiwan, which is under the oppressive rule of the United States and Chiang Kai-shek, and contrast it with the rate of price cut in the mainland where the government policy for the benefit of the people is contributing to price reduction." Ibid., p. 272.

13. Suzuki, *"Nankin Daigyakusatsu" no Maboroshi* [Illusion of the Rape of Nanking"], pp. 190, 222.

14. "Chinese Revolution: 1919–1949, Two Battlefields in the War against Japan," *Eastern Horizon*, vol. 17, no. 7 (July 1978), p. 40. Overall, the information contained in this article is not accurate. For example, it said that Chiang Kai-shek ordered the Nanking garrison force to retreat from the city "by one single route" contrary to what the official military sources said, that is, that the garrison troops tried to escape from Nanking through several routes. Ibid.

15. *NYT*, 14 August 1982, p. 4. AP dispatch from Peking, 28 August 1982, *NYT*, 29 August 1982, p. 20. *NYT*, 29 August 1982, p. 4(E).

16. Hayashi Kentaro, "Kyokasho Mondai o Kangaeru" [Comment on Textbook Issue], *Bungeishunju*, October 1986, p. 100. Kabashima Yuzo, " 'Shinpen Nihon-shi o Osotta Gaiatsu to Naiatsu." [Foreign and Domestic Pressure Exerted on 'Newly Compiled Japanese History'], *Bungeishunju*, September 1986, pp. 150, 152.

17. Tsuchiya Masaharu, "Mokka Shite Yoi no ka Nankin Daigyakusatsu no Hodo" [Can We Overlook Reporting of the Rape of Nanking?], *Kaiko*, March 1983, p. 3. Unemoto Masami, " 'Nankin Daigyakusatsu' no Shinso wa?: Senjo no Taikendan o Motomu" [What Is the Truth of the Rape of Nanking?: Call for Eyewitness Accounts on the Field], *Kaiko*, May 1983, p. 5. Kobayashi Yuichi, Nankin Mondai ni tsuite Kinkyu Onegai" [Emergency Proposition Regarding the Nanking Issue], *Kaiko*, October 1983, p. 43. *Kaiko* Henshubu [Editing Staff of *Kaiko* Magazine], "Iwayuru 'Nankin Jiken' ni Kansuru Joho Teikyo no Onegai" [Call for Information about the So-Called "Nanking Incident"], *Kaiko*, November 1983, p. 35. Katogawa Kotaro, "Shogen ni yoru Nankin Senshi: Sono

Sokatsuteki Kosatsu" [Nanking Campaign Chronology Based on Eyewitness Accounts: Concluding Remark] *Kaiko*, March 1985, p. 10.

18. *Kaiko* Henshubu [Editing Staff of *Kaiko* Magazine], "Iwayuru 'Nankin Jiken' ni Kansuru Joho Teikyo no Onegai" [Call for Information about the So-Called "Nanking Incident"], *Kaiko*, November 1983, p. 37. Unemoto, " 'Shogen ni yoru Nankin Senshi' Shushi Sagyo o Oete" [Postscript to "Nanking Campaign Chronology Based on Eyewitness Accounts"] in "SNS" extra, *Kaiko*, May 1985, p. 8.

19. *Kaiko* Henshubu [Editing Staff of *Kaiko* Magazine], "Iwayuru 'Nankin Jiken' ni Kansuru Joho Teikyo no Onegai" [Call for Information about the So-Called "Nanking Incident"], *Kaiko*, November 1983, p. 35.

20. Article by Tsuchiya Masaharu, *Kaiko*, April 1983, quoted in "SNS" extra, *Kaiko*, July 1985, p. 9.

21. Katogawa, "Shogen ni yoru Nankin Senshi: Sono Sokatsuteki Kosatsu" [Nanking Campaign Chronology Based on Eyewitness Accounts: Concluding Remark] *Kaiko*, March 1985, pp. 9, 11.

22. Ibid., pp. 15–16, 18.

23. Morio Taku to Katogawa Kotaro, 6 April 1985, *Kaiko*, May 1985, pp. 6–7.

24. Takahashi Toshiro, "Nankin Senshi no Sokatsuteki Kosatsu ni Hantai Sareta Kata e no Okotae" [Response to Those Who Disagreed to the Summation of Nanking Campaign Chronology Series], *Kaiko*, May 1985, p. 11.

25. Tanaka Masaaki, *"Nankin Gyakusatsu" no Kyoko* ["Rape of Nanking" as a Fiction] (Tokyo: Nihon Kyobunsha, 1984), pp. 29, 189–90.

26. Tanaka Masaaki, *"Nankin Gyakusatsu" no Kyoko* ["Rape of Nanking" as a Fiction], p. 356. Itakura Yoshiaki and Tanaka Masaaki, " 'Nankin Gyakusatsu' Sansen-sha no Shogen" [Testimonies of Participants in the Nanking Campaign] *Bungeishunju*, December 1984, pp. 214–36. Itakura Yoshiaki, "Matsui Iwane Nikki no Kaizan ni Tsuite" [Regarding the Tampering of Matsui Iwane's Diary] *Bungeishunju*, January 1986, p. 187.

27. Tanaka, *Nankin Jiken no Sokatsu* [Nanking Incident Summed Up], pp. 340–41.

28. Matsui Diary, 20 December 1937, in *NSS*1, p. 22.

29. Tanaka, *Matsui Iwane Taisho no Jinchu Nisshi* [Field Diary of General Matsui Iwane] (Tokyo: Fuyo Shobo, 1985), p. 135.

30. Matsui Diary, 8 February 1938, in *NSS*1, p. 40.

31. Tanaka, *Matsui Iwane Taisho no Jinchu Nisshi* [Field Diary of General Matsui Iwane] p. 166. Tanaka not only emphasized this altered portion by sidelining the sentences with dots (Japanese sentences are usually written from top to bottom), but also attached his own comment in a separate note of editor: "This is what Matsui genuinely thought. This passage exemplifies Matsui's attitude toward the Chinese people very well."

32. Itakura, "Matsui Iwane Nikki no Kaizan ni Tsuite" [Regarding the Tampering of Matsui Iwane's Diary], pp. 186, 190–91.

33. Hata Ikuhiko, "Ronsoshi kara Mita Nankin Jiken" [Rape of Nanking Historiography] in idem, *Showashi no Nazo o Ou* [In Pursuit of History Mysteries of the Showa Era], vol. 1 (Tokyo: Bungeishunju, 1993), p. 134. *NS*, p. 336.

34. Hata, *Nankin Jiken* [Nanking Incident], pp. 37–38. Tanaka, *Nankin Jiken no Sokatsu* [Nanking Incident Summed Up], pp. 51, 240–49.

35. Nakajima Diary, 13 December 1937, in *NSS*1, p. 326. Tanaka, *Nankin Jiken no Sokatsu* [Nanking Incident Summed Up], p. 231, quoting an interview by Ara Ken'ichi

with Onishi Hajime in "Nihonjin no Mita Nankin Kanraku" [Fall of Nanking in the Eyes of Japanese Witnesses], *Seiron* [Sound Argument], May 1986. Ibid., p. 277.

36. *NS*, p. 374.

37. Ibid., p. 313, quoting Nobuyu Atsuo, *Senji Kokusaiho Kogi* [Discourse on Belligerent Law], vol. 2 (n.p.: n.d.), pp. 113–14.

38. *NS*, p. 314, quoting Taoka Ryoichi, *Zoho: Kokusai Hogaku Taiko* [Outline of International Law: Enlarged Edition], vol. 2 (Tokyo: Tokyo Ganshodo, n.d.), p. 225.

39. *NS*, p. 317, quoting Nobuyu, *Senji Kokusaiho Kogi* [Discourse on Belligerent Law], pp. 112–13.

40. *NEM*, pp. 33–34, 48–51, 73–74, 146, 173–74.

41. Tanaka, *"Nankin Gyakusatsu" no Kyoko* ["Rape of Nanking" as a Fiction], pp. 19–20.

42. *NEM*, pp. 346, 378.

43. Inoue Hisashi, "Nankin Jiken to Chugoku Kyosanto" [Rape of Nanking and the Chinese Communist Party] in *NJK*, p. 166. Yoshida Yutaka, "15-nen Sensoshi Kenkyu to Senso Sekinin Mondai: Nankin Jiken o Chushin ni" [Academic and War Responsibility Issues Concerning 15-Year War, Nanking Incident in Particular], in ibid., p. 73. Takasaki Ryuji, "Kabushiki Gaisha Bungeishunju no Sensochu to Genzai to o Kangaeru" [Critical Review of Bungeishunju Corporation's Wartime and Today's Activities], in ibid., p. 201.

44. Yoshida, "15-nen Sensoshi Kenkyu to Senso Sekinin Mondai: Nankin Jiken o Chushin ni" [Academic and War Responsibility Issues Concerning 15-Year War, Nanking Incident in Particular], in *NJK*, pp. 83–84.

45. Idem, *Tenno no Guntai to Nankin Jiken* [Emperor's Military and the Nanking Incident], p. 134.

46. Yoshida, "15-nen Sensoshi Kenkyu to Senso Sekinin Mondai: Nankin Jiken o Chushin ni" [Academic and War Responsibility Issues Concerning 15-Year War, Nanking Incident in Particular], in *NJK*, p. 84. Idem, *Tenno no Guntai to Nankin Jiken* [Emperor's Military and the Nanking Incident], p. 134. Kasahara Tokushi, "Nankin Boeigun no Hokai kara Gyakusatsu made" [From the Collapse of Nanking Garrison to Massacre], in *NDG*, p. 104. Idem, "Nankin Boeisen to Chugokugun" [Nanking Siege and Chinese Force], in ibid., pp. 262, 286, 315.

47. Takasaki Ryuji, "Kabushiki Gaisha Bungeishunju no Sensochu to Genzai to o Kangaeru" [Critical Review of Bungeishunju Corporation's Wartime and Today's Activities], in *NJK*, p. 206.

48. Ishijima Noriyuki, "Nankin Jiken o Meguru Aratana Ronsoten" [New Topics of the Rape of Nanking Controversy], in *NJK*, p. 124.

49. Examples of extreme traditionalist stance on the credibility of the Ch'ung-shan-t'ang data are Fujiwara Akira, "Ima Naze Nankin Jiken na no ka" [Why the Rape of Nanking Is an Issue Now], in *NDG*, p. 25; and Idem, "Nankin Daigyakusatsu to Kyokasho-Kyoiku Mondai" [Rape of Nanking and Textbook/Education Problems], in *NJK*, p. 27. Moderate traditionalist opinion is expressed in Inoue Hisashi, "Itai Maiso kara Mita Nankin Jiken Giseishasu" [Number of Rape of Nanking Victims Based on Burial Records], in *NDG*, p. 61; idem, "Nankin Jiken to Itai Maiso Mondai" [Rape of Nanking and Questions Regarding Burial Activities], in *NJK*, p. 102; and Ishijima, "Nankin Jiken o Meguru Aratana Ronsoten" [New Topics of the Rape of Nanking Controversy] in ibid., p. 136.

50. *NEM*, pp. 160–70. " 'Nankin Daigyakusatsu' no Kakushin" [Heart of the "Rape of Nanking" Controversy], an article summarizing a roundtable discussion chaired by

Hando Kazutoshi for Hora Tomio, Hata Ikuhiko, Suzuki Akira, and Tanaka Masaaki, *Shokun!* [Comrades!], April 1985, p. 73.

51. Honda, "Gonin no Taikenshi" [Accounts by Five Survivors], in *NDG*, p. 234. Kasahara, "Nankin Boeigun no Hokai kara Gyakusatsu made" [From the Collapse of Nanking Garrison to Massacre], in ibid., p. 83. *Mainichi Shinbun* [Mainichi Newspaper], 7 August 1984. *NEM*, p. 318.

52. For example, see Yoshida, *Tenno no Guntai to Nankin Jiken* [Emperor's Military and the Nanking Incident], pp. 107–10; Ishijima, "Nankin Jiken o Meguru Aratana Ronsoten" [New Topics of the Rape of Nanking Controversy], in *NJK*, p. 132; Kasahara Tokushi, "Nankin Boeigun no Hokai kara Gyakusatsu made" [From the Collapse of Nanking Garrison to Massacre], in *NDG*, pp. 104, 107.

53. Ishijima, "Nankin Jiken o Meguru Aratana Ronsoten" [New Topics of the Rape of Nanking Controversy], in *NJK*, p. 131.

54. IMTFE, p. 3,887.

55. Ishijima, "Nankin Jiken o Meguru Aratana Ronsoten" [New Topics of the Rape of Nanking Controversy], in *NJK*, p. 136. Hora Tomio, *Ketteiban: Nankin Daigyakusatsu* [Nanking Massacre: Definitive Version] (Tokyo: Gendaishi Shuppan-kai, 1982), pp. 149–52. Hata, "Ronsoshi kara Mita Nankin Jiken" [Rape of Nanking Historiography] in idem, *Showashi no Nazo o Ou* [In Pursuit of History Mysteries of Showa Era], vol. 1, pp. 124–25. The Chinese inscribed this figure on the outer wall of the Rape of Nanking memorial museum, which opened in the city in 1985.

56. Itakura, "Matsui Iwane Nikki no Kaizan ni Tsuite" [Regarding the Tampering of Matsui Iwane's Diary], *Bungeishunju*, January 1986, p. 193, referring to Honda's article in *Asahi Journal*, 7 September 1985. Hora and Watada Susumu, "Kaizan Shita no wa Dare ka: Itakura-shi Hihan" [Who Tampered with Evidence: Rebuttal to Mr. Itakura's Theory], in *NDG*, pp. 118–56. Idem, "Bakufu-yama no Horyo Shokei ni Kansuru 'Shinsetsu' Hihan: Sayonara Itakura-shi" [Criticism of "New Theory" Regarding POW Execution at Mufu Mountain: Farewell to Mr. Itakura], in *NDK*, pp. 150–96.

57. Hata, *Nankin Jiken* [Nanking Incident], p. 244.

58. Hata, *Nankin Jiken* [Nanking Incident], pp. 25–27, 214. In one of his articles, Hata called the tone of argument in traditionalist Honda's writings as being "masochistic." Idem, "Ronsoshi kara Mita Nankin Jiken" [Rape of Nanking Historiography], p. 126.

59. Tanaka, *Nankin Jiken no Sokatsu* [Nanking Incident Summed Up], pp. 51–55. Shimosato Masaki, "Nankin Koryaku to Kakyu Heishi" [Capture of Nanking and Enlisted Soldiers], in *KS*, p. 479. Fujiwara Akira, "Ima Naze Nankin Jiken na no ka" [Why the Rape of Nanking Is an Issue Now], in *NDG*, p. 18. Kasahara Tokushi, "Nankin Boeigun no Hokai kara Gyakusatsu made" [From the Collapse of Nanking Garrison to Massacre], in ibid., p. 78.

60. *Getsuyo Hyoron* [Monday Commentary], no. 785, 1986, quoted in Yoshida, "Nankin Jiken o meguru Ronso no Soten" [Focal Points of the Rape of Nanking Debate], in *NDG*, p. 46.

61. Itakura, "Matsui Iwane Nikki no Kaizan ni Tsuite" [Regarding the Tampering of Matsui Iwane's Diary], p. 194. Itakura defined the IMTFE as a "trial for the purpose of retaliation" and said, "It is no exaggeration to say that the image of the Rape of Nanking was created at the IMTFE." Itakura, "Nanking Jiken: Gyakusatsu no Sekininron" [The Nanking Massacre and the Issue of Responsibility], *Gunji Shigaku* [Journal of Military

History, Japan] 33 (December 1997): p. 182. Hata, *Nankin Jiken* [Nanking Incident], p. 214.

62. *NEM*, p. 386.

63. Tanaka, *"Nankin Gyakusatsu" no Kyoko* ["Rape of Nanking" as a Fiction], p. 357.

64. Fujiwara, "Nankin Daigyakusatsu to Kyokasho/Kyoiku Mondai" [Rape of Nanking and Textbook/Education Issues], in *NJK*, p. 13. Hora, *Ketteiban: Nankin Daigyakusatsu* [Nanking Massacre: Definitive Version], p. 307. Tanaka, *Nankin Jiken no Sokatsu* [Nanking Incident Summed Up], p. 281.

65. According to Yamamoto, the article did not explicitly state that one of the lieutenants was a battalion adjutant and made him look like an infantry platoon commander. Yamamoto, *Watashi no naka no Nihongun* [Japanese Military within Myself], vol 1, pp. 228–31. Ibid., vol. 2, p. 271. Hora, *Ketteiban: Nankin Daigyakusatsu* [Nanking Massacre: Definitive Version], p. 204, quoting an article from *Shukan Asahi* [Weekly Asahi], 4 May 1973, and Oda Makoto's remark in *Gunzo* [Group of Statues], August 1973.

66. Nomura Toshinori, "Watashi no Nankin-sen" [Battle of Nanking I Witnessed], *Kaiko*, May 1983, p. 5. Itakura's article in *Getsuyo Hyoron* [Monday Commentary], no. 785, 1986, quoted in Yoshida, *Tenno no Guntai to Nankin Jiken* [Emperor's Military and Nanking Incident], p. 46. Hora, *Ketteiban: Nankin Daigyakusatsu* [Nanking Massacre: Definitive Version], pp. 201, 210. Honda, Nitchu no Futari no Ikishonin" [Two Live Witnesses from Japan and China], in *NJK*, pp. 37, 43. *NEM*, p. 307.

67. Itakura, "Matsui Iwane Nikki no Kaizan ni Tsuite" [Regarding the Tampering of Matsui Iwane's Diary], p. 190. *Getsuyo Hyoron* [Monday Commentary], no, 1281, 15 May 1996, pp. 2–3. Three books written by the self-claimed Rape of Nanking eyewitness, Sone Kazuo, are: Sone Kazuo, *Shiki Nankin Gyakusatsu* [Rape of Nanking: Private Account] (Tokyo: Sairyusha, 1984); idem, *Zoku Shiki Nankin Gyakusatsu* [Rape of Nanking: Private Account, part 2] (Tokyo: Sairyusha, 1984); and idem, *Nankin Gyakusatsu to Senso* [Rape of Nanking and War] (Tokyo: Tairyusha, 1988). A part of his first works is translated into Chinese in *HP*, pp. 979–96. For the contradictions and falsification in these works, see Itakura Yoshiaki, " 'Nankin Gyakusatsu' no Zange-ya 'Sone Kazuo' no Shotai" [True Face of Sone Kazuo, Professional Penitent of "Rape of Nanking"], *Shokun!* [Comrades!], December 1988, pp. 126–46. The murder of a Chinese civilian is described in Azuma Memoir, *KS*, p. 305. The Chinese version of this portion is available in *HP*, pp. 973–74.

68. For example, see Fujiwara Akira, "Ima Naze Nankin Jiken na no ka" [Why the Rape of Nanking Is an Issue Now], in *NDG*, pp. 15–17; idem, "Nankin Daigyakusatsu: Senso Bika ni Tsujiru Gyakusatsu Shosuron" [Rape of Nanking: Lower Estimate of Number of Victims Encourages Glorification of War], *Bijinesu Interijensu* [Business Intelligence], August 1994, p. 20; and Yoshida, "Nankin Jiken o meguru Ronso no Soten" [Focal Points of Rape of Nanking Debate], in *NDG*, p. 33.

69. Hata, *Nankin Jiken* [Nanking Incident], pp. 184–85.

70. Yoshida, *Tenno no Guntai to Nankin Jiken* [His Majesty's Military and Nanking Incident], p. 6.

71. Ibid., p. 38.

72. Idem, "Nankin Jiken o meguru Ronso no Soten" [Focal Points of Rape of Nanking Debate], in *NDG*, pp. 41–44. For the categorization of atrocities, see, for example, Hata, *Nankin Jiken* [Nanking Incident], pp. 188–204.

73. He referred to an incident at the time of the opening of the Rape of Nanking

memorial museum in Nanking in 1985: one former Japanese cabinet minister tried to pressure the foreign ministry to file a formal protest with the Chinese government so that "300,000 victims" engraved on the wall of the museum be erased. Hata, "Ronsoshi kara Mita Nankin Jiken" [Rape of Nanking Historiography], pp. 138–39.

74. Ibid.

75. See, for example, *HP*, the fifth page in the opening photo section; Honda Katsuichi, *Chugoku no Nihongun* [Japanese Troops in China] (Tokyo: Sojusha, 1972), pp. 109, 115–16; Louis Wheeler Snow, *Edgar Snow's China: A Personal Account of the Chinese Revolution Compiled from the Writings of Edgar Snow* (New York: Random House, 1981), p. 166; and *RNFH*, photo section between, p. 146 and p. 147.

76. Li Haibo, "Unforgivable Atrocity," *Beijing Review*, 14–20 August 1995, pp. 16–17, 19–20. The *Chung-yang Jih-pao* [Central Daily News], 6 May 1994, p. 2. Reuter's dispatch from Beijing, 13 December 1937, in *NYT*, 14 December 1987, p. 14.

77. *Asahi Shinbun* [Asahi Newspaper], 5 May 1994, p. 2, quoting *Mainichi Shinbun* [Mainichi Newspaper], 4 May 1994. *Japan Times*, 7 May 1994, p. 1. *Chung-yang Jih-pao* [Central Daily News], 6 May 1994, p. 2. *Jen-min Jih-pao* [People's Daily], overseas edition, 5 May 1994, p. 1. *Free China Journal*, 13 May 1994, p. 2.

78. Kojima, *Nitchu Senso* [Sino-Japanese War], vol. 5, p. 420. Suzuki, *"Nankin Daigyakusatsu" no Maboroshi* [Illusion of the "Rape of Nanking"], p. 106. Watada Susumu, "Coverage of Suzuki Akira's 'Coverage'," in *NJK*, pp. 195–96.

79. *Newsweek*, 9 August 1982, p. 29. *Chung-yang Jih-pao* [Central Daily News], 9 May 1994, p. 2. Li, "Unforgivable Atrocity," *Beijing Review*, 14–20 August 1995, pp. 16–17.

80. Michael Montgomery, *Imperialist Japan: The Yen to Dominate* (London: Christopher Helm, 1987), p. 397. John Whitney Hall, *Japan: From Prehistory to Modern Times* (New York: Delacorte Press, 1970), p. 340. Michael Richard Gibson, "Chiang Kai-shek's Central Army, 1924–1938" (Ph.D. Diss., George Washington University, 1985), p. 391.

81. Harries, *Soldiers of the Sun*, pp. 227–29. Sources that adopted the death toll of 20,000 POWs and 12,000 noncombatants are Hall, *Japan: From Prehistory to Modern Times*, p. 340; and Jonathan D. Spence, *The Search for Modern China* (New York: W. W. Norton, 1990), p. 448. Those that opt for 40,000 to 42,000 are Lloyd E. Eastman, "Nationalist China during the Sino-Japanese War 1937–1945," in *The Cambridge History of China*, vol. 13, *Republican China 1912–1949* part 2, ed. John K. Fairbank and Albert Feurewerker (Cambridge: Cambridge University Press, 1986), p. 552; and Arthur Zich, *The Rising Sun* (Alexandria, VA: Time-Life Books, 1977), p. 23. One source that estimates the death toll at 100,000 is Dick Wilson, *When Tigers Fight: The Story of the Sino-Japanese War, 1937–1945* (New York: Viking Press, 1982), p. 82. Some examples of those that accept 200,000 as the total number of victims are Agnes Smedley, *The Great Road: The Life and Times of Chu Teh* (New York: Monthly Review Press, 1956), p. 358; Mikiso Hane, *Modern Japan: Historical Survey* (Boulder: Westview Press, 1992), p. 278; Dower, *War without Mercy*, pp. 43, 326, n26; Rudolph J. Rummel, *China's Bloody Century: Genocide and Mass Murder since 1900* (New Brunswick, NJ: Transaction Publishers, 1991), p. 146; Leonard Mosley, *Hirohito: Emperor of Japan* (Englewood Cliffs, NJ: Prentice-Hall, 1966), p. 177; and Edwin P. Hoyt, *Japan's War: The Great Pacific Conflict 1853–1952* (New York: McGraw-Hill, 1986), p. 174. Those that choose the highest number are; Montgomery, *Imperialist Japan*, p. 397; Edward L. Dreyer, *China at War, 1901–1949* (New York: Longman, 1995), p. 219; David Berga-

mini, *Japan's Imperial Conspiracy* (New York: William Morrow and Co., 1971), p. 44; and Frank Dorn, *The Sino-Japanese War, 1937–41: From Marco Polo Bridge to Pearl Harbor* (New York: Macmillan, 1974), p. 93.

82. Ian Johnson, "Breaking Silence: Beijing Permits Screening of Nanjing Massacre Film," *Far Eastern Economic Review*, 24 August 1995, p. 40.

83. Spence, *The Search for Modern China*, p. 448.

84. A letter posted by Victor Hancock of the United States, 3 September 1995, in *Tokyo Kalaidoscoop*, "The Decision of dropping the A-bomb in 1945 was right?" http: www.smn.co.jp/square/bomb.html.

85. A letter posted by Joseph Edward Nemec, Massachusetts, the United States, 8 September 1995, in ibid.

86. Quoted in Kevin Ulrich, "The Other Holocaust," *Los Angeles Readers*, 1 July 1994, quoted in *Basic Facts on the Nanking Massacre and the Tokyo War Crimes Trial*, http://www.cnd.org:8006/mirror/nanjing/.

87. Madame Chiang's speech, 20 March 1938, printed on the *New York Herald*, PNTJ-34.

88. Kuroda, *Nankin, Hiroshima, Aushubittsu* [Nanking, Hiroshima, and Auschwitz], pp. 227–28. Yoshida, *Tenno no Guntai to Nankin Jiken* [Emperor's Military and the Nanking Incident], pp. 3–4.

89. Tanaka, *"Nankin Gyakusatsu" no Kyoko* ["Rape of Nanking" as a Fiction], pp. 294, 296. Idem, *Nankin Jiken no Sokatsu* [Nanking Incident Summed Up], pp. 12–13.

90. Hata, *Nankin Jiken* [Nanking Incident], pp. 187, 232–35.

91. Tanaka, *Nankin Jiken no Sokatsu* [Nanking Incident Summed up], foreword. Kenneth S. Stern, *Holocaust Denial* (New York: American Jewish Committee, 1993), p. 48. The Israeli government and the Simon Wiesenthal Center immediately filed protests. Bungeishunju ultimately shut down the *Marco Polo*. "The IHR Denounces Campaign against Japanese Publishing Company" in *Greg Raven's Web Site for Revisionist Materials from the Institute for Historical Review (and elsewhere)*. http://www.kaiwan.com/ ~ihrgreg/ihr/jhr/v15/v15np-9__Weber.html.

92. "Power Letter—August 1995 (Ernst Zuendel: Personal Opinions of the Author) in *The Zuendel Site: "Did Six Million Really Die"*. http://www.codoh.com/zundel/ english/pow1995/pow9508.html. Zgram, 2 May 1997, http:www.webcom.com/ ~ezundel/ english/zgrams/zg1997/zg9705/970502.html, in ibid. Carlos Whitlock Porter, "Rape of Nanking: Very Sorry or, How I Got My Rocks off in Old China Town" in *Home Page of the Committee for Open Discussion of the Holocaust Story*. http:www. codoh.com/ trials/trijapan.html.

93. Takahashi Toshiro, "Nankin Senshi no Sokatsuteki Kosatsu ni Hantai Sareta Kata e no Okotae" [Response to Those Who Disagreed to the Summation of Nanking Campaign Chronology Series], *Kaiko*, May 1985, p. 9. Suzuki, *"Nankin Daigyakusatsu" no Maboroshi* [Illusion of the Rape of Nanking"], pp. 263–66. Tanaka, *Nankin Jiken no Sokatsu* [Nanking Incident Summed up], pp. 323–38. Richard E. Harwood [Richard Verrall], *Did Six Million Really Die, Historical Fact No. 1* (Sussex, England: Historical Review Press, n.d.), pp. 22–24. Austin A. App, *The Six Million Swindle: Blackmailing the German People for Hard Marks with Fabricated Corpses* (Takoma Park, MD: Boniface Press, 1973), p. 18. Arthur R. Butz, *The Hoax of the Twentieth Century* (Torrance, CA: Institute for Historical Review, 1976), pp. 34, 203. Ishihara, Shintaro. "Nihon o Otoshiireta Joho Kukan no Kai." [Mysterious Information Vacuum That Has Haunted Japan] *Bungeishunju*, September 1991, pp. 96–97.

94. Stern, *Holocaust Denial*, p. 30. Dawidowicz, "Lies About the Holocaust," p. 34. For Rassinier's profile, see Lucy S. Dawidowicz, "Lies about the Holocaust," *Commentary*, December 1988, p. 33. No author (presumed to be David L. Hoggan), *The Myth of the Six Million*. 2nd edition (Los Angeles: Noontide Press, 1974), pp. 78–79. The whole transcript of the conversations in the Montel Williams Show is in Stern, *Holocaust Denial*, pp. 113–34. Regarding the alleged Jewish conspiracy, Austin J. App, for example, said, "Long before there was a Third Reich, the Jews in Germany defamed Germany the way American Jews and liberals defamed America and our armed forces during the Vietnam War!" App, *The Six Million Swindle*, p. 14.

95. Deborah E. Lipstadt, *Denying the Holocaust: The Growing Assault on Truth and Memory* (New York: Free Press, 1993), pp. 47, 52. Fujiwara, "Nankin Daigyakusatsu to Kyokasho/Kyoiku Mondai" [Rape of Nanking and Textbook/ Education Issues], in *NJK*, pp. 17–21; Kimishima Kazuhiko, " 'Nankin Jiken' no Kotei to 'Nankin Daigyakusatsu' no Hitei" [Admission to "Nanking Incident" and Denial of "Rape of Nanking"], in *NJK*, pp. 105–20; Fujiwara, Ima Naze Nankin Jiken na no ka" [Why the Rape of Nanking Is an Issue Now], in *NDG*, pp. 13–22.

96. App, *The Six Million Swindle*, pp. 21–22. Butz, *The Hoax of the Twentieth Century*, p. 23. Harwood, *Did Six Million Really Die?*, pp. 10–13. Tanaka, *"Nankin Gyakusatsu" no Kyoko* ["Rape of Nanking" as a Fiction], pp. 299–303. Idem, *Nankin Jiken no Sokatsu* [Nanking Incident Summed Up], pp. 31–33. For a distinction between revisionism and denial, see Lipstadt, *Denying the Holocaust*, pp. 20–21, and Stern, *Holocaust Denial*, p. 2.

97. Quotes are from Dawidowicz, "Thinking about the Six Million: Facts, Figures, Perspective," pp. 61, 64. Also, see Yehuda Bauer, "The Place of the Holocaust in Contemporary History," in *Holocaust: Religious and Philosophical Implications*, ed. John K. Roth and Michael Berenbaum (New York: Paragon House, 1989), pp. 16–18; and Michael R. Marrus, *The Holocaust in History* (Hanover, NH: University Press of New England, 1987), pp. 23–24.

98. The following is a quote from Stern, *Holocaust Denial*, p. 66: "In 'Auschwitz: Truth or Lie,' by Thies Christophersen, the number of Jews in 1938 is given as 15,688,259—source, the American Jewish Committee; and 18,700,000 in 1948—source, a *New York Times* article. The contention is that if there were three million more Jews after the war than before, how could six million have been killed. The 1938 American Jewish *Year Book*—where the American Jewish committee publishes these data when available—had no precise data for 1938. However, the 1939 *Year Book* gave the world Jewish population as 16,633,675. The 1948 *Year Book* listed world Jewry at 11,373,350. That, of course, was not mentioned by Christophersen."

99. Stern, *Holocaust Denial*, p. 67.

100. *RNFH*, p. 5.

101. George F. Will, "Breaking a Sinister Silence," *Washington Post*, 19 February 1998, p. A17.

102. One of the organizers of Princeton University's Rape of Nanking 60th anniversary commemorative event to Masahiro Yamamoto, 14 October 1997, re: conference on Nanking Massacre, through e-mail. To prove the correctness of their contention regarding the number issue, recent writers of the Rape of Nanking referred to a Chinese census record and pointed to a vast gap between the sizes of Nanking's population before and after the occupation of the city. They claim that about 500,000 to 600,000 people remained in the city when the Japanese occupied it. *RNFH*, p. 100. Yin and Young, *The*

Rape of Nanking, pp. 275–76. Yet, some crucial questions remain unanswered about their source and conclusion such as (1) why Chinese authorities did not present such an important record to the IMTFE; (2) whether the alleged massacre alone contributed to that numerical gap even if the census record were accurate; (3) how one should interpret the Western government and media reports in November–December 1937, which effectively contradict these writers' theory by referring to a more drastic reduction in the city's population from about one million to merely 200,000 even before the Japanese occupation. See Chapter 2 for more details.

103. Lipstadt, *Denying the Holocaust*, pp. 13–14.

104. For example, see the following web sites: Ignatius Ding, "A Declaration to the Japanese Government and the Japanese People," issued by the Global Alliance for Preserving the History of World War II in Asia," 25 June 1995, in *Basic Facts on the Nanking Massacre and the Tokyo War Crimes Trial*, http://www.cnd.org:8006/mirror/nanjing/NMDing2.html; "Q. And A. On CAMAJ," *The Chinese Alliance for Memorial and Justice* http://www.hk.super.net/~csjwv/CAMAJ-QA.html; and "About the Chinese Alliance for Commemoration of the Sino-Japanese War Victims," *The Chinese Alliance for Commemoration of the Sino-Japanese War Victims*, http://hk.super.net/~csjwv.html.

105. For example, see the following web sites: "Introduction," *Basic Facts on the Nanking Massacre and the Tokyo War Crimes Trial*. http://www.cnd.org.8006/mirror/nanjing/. Ding, "A Declaration to the Japanese Government and the Japanese People," in *Basic Facts on the Nanking Massacre and the Tokyo War Crimes Trial*, http://www.cnd.org:8006/mirror/nanjing/NMDing2.html; and "Historical Background," *Alliance for Preserving the Truth of Sino-Japanese War*, http://www.cnd.org:8008/NJMassacre/aptsjw.htm.

106. *RNFH*, p. 109. *NYT*, 12 December 1997, p. A3.

107. Hata, "Ronsoshi kara Mita Nankin Jiken" [Rape of Nanking Historiography], p. 129.

108. One of the organizers of Princeton University's Rape of Nanking 60th anniversary commemorative event to Masahiro Yamamoto, 14 October 1997, re: conference on Nanking Massacre, through e-mail.

109. Carol Gluck, "The Rape of Nanking: How 'the Nazi Buddha' Resisted the Japanese," *Times Literary Supplement*, 27 June 1997, p. 10.

110. Daqing Yang, "Pondering the Meaning of the Nanjing Massacre," in Association for Asian Studies, *Abstracts of the 1997 Annual Meeting, March 13–16, 1997* (Ann Arbor, MI: Association for Asian Studies, 1997), p. 267.

Conclusion

The historical analysis of the Rape of Nanking shows that the Japanese conduct in Nanking resembled the Nazi atrocities at least in one aspect: "The Axis atrocities against many of those who were directly under their control—whether Jews, prisoners of war, or inhabitants of occupied territories—formed the one really strong ground for conviction"[1] and this concerns the "treatment of largely defenseless people in the hands of the adversary."[2] Therefore, the demand for an apology and redress from the Japanese is certainly justifiable and correct to a certain extent. In terms of scale, length of time, and nature, however, the two cases did not resemble each other. The Rape of Nanking lasted six weeks and claimed the lives of 15,000 to 50,000 people, a vast majority of whom were adult men, whereas the Nazi Holocaust raged through all of Europe for a substantial period of World War II, resulting in the deaths of six million Jews and at least six million non-Jews regardless of sex and age. More important, the Japanese atrocities were attributable to the lack of discipline and the negligence of military commands, whereas the Nazis conducted their killing under the systematic planning of the political leadership.

It is appropriate to conclude that multiple factors, both long-term and short-term, caused this incident. The context of the Sino-Japanese War, which had increasingly assumed the character of guerrilla warfare, was a crucial factor common in other 20th-century wars. That the Nanking battle was like a siege was also a circumstance one cannot overlook, since a similar large-scale massacre did not happen thereafter in China. At the same time, one should also focus on an important phenomenon on the Japanese side: the "command irresponsibility" or a tendency among Japanese military commanders to transfer their responsibility either upward or downward in the chain of command. All these factors point to the conclusion that the incident should be viewed as an atrocity of conventional war crimes that were on a par with some events in the previous history of warfare rather than with the Nazi genocide. Accordingly, one should define the Japanese responsibility in a different manner, hence the manner and extent of the apology and redress.

Actually, despite their frequent use of the word "Holocaust" and allusion to parallels between Nazi and Japanese militarism, recent publications about the Rape of Nanking implicitly admit the differences between the two:

The Rape of Nanking should be perceived as a cautionary tale—an illustration of how easily human beings can be encouraged to allow their teenagers to be molded into efficient killing machines able to suppress their better natures.[3]

By contrast [with the Nazi atrocities], Japan's bloodletting in Nanking was largely retail, with individual soldiers and units freed by their superiors to murder at will.[4]

Thus, for all the accusations that the Rape of Nanking was an atrocity on an unprecedented scale comparable to the Nazi Holocaust, these authors stopped short of exploring what was unique in this incident.

Again, it is based on this recognition—that the Rape of Nanking was an atrocity of conventional war crimes—that one should consider the claim that the Japanese government should compensate the victims of atrocities. Since the atrocity is not comparable to the Nazi Holocaust, it is not appropriate to demand that the Japanese compensate the victims in the same way as the Germans have done. To such logic, one could almost hear an immediate moral outcry that the plight of victims was identical whatever the type of atrocity. But the problem here is a legal one.

Recently, some Japanese worked out a scheme that might be applicable to this problem as well. In the early 1990s, the issue of Asian women whom the Japanese army allegedly used as prostitutes during World War II became a serious political issue. Some of these women, with the support of several scholars including Japanese, sued the Japanese government. In response, some Japanese statesmen created a fund and called for monetary contributions from Japanese citizens for this fund to compensate these women. At the same time, it was decided that each recipient of the monetary compensation would also receive some medical benefit through the fund as well as a letter of apology from the Japanese government. According to one scholar who participated in this scheme, this was the most desirable choice for the benefit of these women of advanced age because any legislation at the parliament, treaty negotiations between Japan and other countries, or lawsuit in a court would likely consume a long period of time.[5] Also, questions still remain unsolved about this issue, such as whether the government was directly responsible for the prostitution in the Japanese military and whether all prostitutes were forcibly impressed into the military. The creation of such a fund not only dispensed with time-consuming bureaucratic processes that would be necessary for a legislative, executive, or judicial settlement, but also separated the highly political compensation issue from the academic discussion. In view of the considerable difficulty in securing donations to the fund for the former "comfort women," further discussion will be needed to implement this program for other cases. Nevertheless, a similar scheme would be the first step for the "healing process" as suggested by the Princeton University group I quoted in the introduction.

Having commented on historical and compensation issues, it is time to turn to historiographical questions. In conclusion, it is appropriate to answer the question I posed in the introduction: whether Western researchers so far have subjected the prevailing interpretation of this incident to the same level of scrutiny as some professional scholars have done to James Bacque's *Other Losses*, which charged that some 800,000 to one million German POWs had died in the Allies' camps immediately after World War II; or to the same author's *Crimes and Mercies*, which accused the Allies of having caused the death of over nine million German civilians around the same period. The answer is negative. The reviewers of Bacque's books subjected them to rigorous scholarly scrutiny *before* they determined Bacque's claims to be unsubstantiated or at least not proven sufficiently. In contrast, many scholars who have discussed the Rape of Nanking have overlooked serious flaws in recent publications about the incident and rendered their own judgment without subjecting these books to the same level of academic scrutiny. Careful investigation would lead to a conclusion that the same praise and criticism that Western historians applied to Bacque's book are valid with these works.

Stephen E. Ambrose said that the stories about the mistreatment of German POWs as advanced by Bacque "must be confronted, and it is to Mr. Bacque's credit that he forces us to do so," although he dismissed many of Bacque's claims as being unfounded.[6] Also, David Stafford, a reviewer of Bacque's *Crimes and Mercies* said, "That human rights were violated and millions suffered tragically in the aftermath of Hitler's war is true. That they were Germans makes it no less important . . . James Bacque is right to make the general point, but the specific of his indictment and his allegations about Allied intent and the numbers involved remain distinctly not proven."[7]

The publications that have dealt with the Rape of Nanking deserve the same praise and criticism. Stories of cruelty exacted by Japanese soldiers on POWs and civilians are compelling enough. This truth must be confronted. Yet one may argue that many "specifics" of "allegations" about the Japanese Army's "intent and the numbers involved remain distinctly not proven." The absence of solid historical study has so far reduced all the discussion about the Rape of Nanking to a simple moral outcry, resulting in less clarification of the truth. Without such clarification, there will be no way to determine in what way the Japanese should confront this issue or how and to what extent the Japanese should be held responsible—whether the Japanese should be quarantined internationally because they are barbaric enough to commit a Nazi-scale genocide-type atrocity even without the benefit of gas chambers and special killing squads or if they should be obliged to redress the wrongs of their conventional war crimes in some way or another.

Unfortunately, recent publications about the Rape of Nanking did not present a thesis to answer these questions because of many flaws found in Bacque's works. Ambrose concluded that Bacque's book is "flawed in the most fundamental aspects" and said that "Mr. Bacque misuses documents, he misreads documents, he ignores contrary evidence, his statistical methodology is hopelessly compromised, he makes no attempt to see the evidence he gathered in its relationship to the broader situation, he makes no attempt to look at comparative contexts, he puts words into the mouth of his principal source, he ignores a readily available and absolutely critical source that decisively deals with his central accusation."[8] One can find almost all of these defects in recent Rape of Nanking publications. The foremost example of misuse or misreading of documents is the treatment of a document found in the "Red Machine," a collection of Japanese diplomatic messages decoded and translated by U.S. military intelligence in the late 1930s. One of these documents, now preserved at the National Archives and Records Administration in College Park, Maryland, is a message from then Japanese foreign minister Hirota Koki to the Japanese embassy in Washington, D.C. The document, carrying a serial number 1263 by a translator, contains a passage reading, "(Not) less than three hundred thousand Chinese civilians slaughtered, many cases (in) cold blood."[9] One author cited this document as "compelling evidence" of the massacre of 300,000 people in Nanking because, according to that author, "the Japanese themselves believed at the time" that about 300,000 people had been killed. Apparently, that author disregarded or overlooked a passage below the main text: "This message was sent in enciphered English and is the one referred to in S.I.S. #1257." Although it is not clear what "S.I.S." stands for, it is obvious that "#1257" refers to the serial number of another document in the same series. The corresponding document, sent and received by the same parties and translated as no. 1257, starts with the following passage: "The night of the [January] 16th, Teinpare [H. J. Timperly], special correspondent of the Manchester Guardian, was discovered by our censors as he was about to send a communication as given in separate message #176."[10] Turning back to no. 1263, one can find at the top what appears to be the cable serial number entered by the Japanese foreign ministry: "Received from Shanghai as #176." It is therefore obvious that no. 1263 of Red Machine does not carry Hirota's own opinion or observation. Instead, it is what Timperly said and was subsequently censored by Japanese military authorities. The Japanese foreign ministry sent it to Washington merely as information pertinent to the main correspondence, which was no. 1257. As a logical consequence, regardless of whether or not the massacre of 300,000 truly happened, claiming this document as proof of the Japanese admission of the massacre of 300,000 is a distorted interpretation.[11]

Although Smythe's *War Damage in the Nanking Area* is "a readily available and absolutely critical source that decisively deals with" central issues such as the extent of human losses in Nanking, the authors who assert the massacre of 300,000 people seldom quote from this source, most likely because Smythe's estimate of civilian abductees and victims of violence combined in the Nanking city proper amounted to less than 7,000. They thus "ignored contrary evidence."[12]

Discovery of Rabe's diary was an admirable undertaking by Iris Chang as a journalist. Yet the content of the diary as quoted even by her contradicts rather than supports her statement that Rabe was "Oskar Schindler in China." Of course, as people who acted courageously in the midst of atrocities, the bravery of both of them should be merited equally. Comparison between Schindler and Rabe, however, reveals more contrasts than similarities, and illustrates the different situations that faced the two personalities, hence the fundamental difference between the Holocaust and the Rape of Nanking as atrocities. As Chang said in her book quoting the diary, Japanese soldiers respected Rabe and often ran away if Rabe showed his swastika armband to them. No one would doubt that Rabe's effort to restrain the Japanese soldiers' misbehavior was courageous and that he sometimes risked his own life. Nevertheless, the implication is that Rabe could chase away these soldiers because their conduct was not condoned by Japanese military authorities. Thus, he could behave like an enforcer of law. If Japanese soldiers had killed Rabe, Japanese authorities would have had to make an apology and compensation. On the contrary, what Schindler did was a possible violation of rules set by his state authority, which was the enforcer of law. By shielding Jews in his factory and giving food to them, Schindler and his family were always running a risk of arrest and even execution. Nazi authorities could have killed Schindler legally at any time. Failure to illustrate such differences is an instance of making "no attempt to see the evidence . . . gathered in its relationship to the broader context."[13] Regarding "statistical methodology," the same author said, "Japanese treatment of their POWs surpassed in brutality even that of the Nazis. Only one in twenty-five American POWs died under Nazi captivity, in contrast to one in three under the Japanese."[14] Here, for unknown reasons, this author not only failed to mention the Nazi racial policy that accorded a preferential treatment to Anglo-Saxon POWs, but also neglected to discuss the high death rate of over 60 percent for 5.7 million Russian POWs—compared with only about 90,000 American POWs—in the hands of the Nazis.[15]

Finally, one can observe a tendency to "put words into the mouth of principal sources." Some recent Rape of Nanking publications quoted testimony given by then Major Ota Toshio during his internment until 1956 in a Chinese prison for war criminals. According to that document, Ota confessed to disposing of more than 100,000 dead bodies when he was in Nanking as a member of the 2nd Port Authorities Headquarters. Lack, or absence, of textual critique is obvious because they quoted this document without any consideration of the environment in which Ota wrote it: he made this confession during his nearly ten-year captivity as a war criminal. The testimony contained a trace of Ota's flattering attitude toward Chinese authorities. At the end of the document, Ota said, "It is needless to say today that the Japanese army committed inhumane acts at the time of the capture of Nanking . . . I am naturally responsible even for the crimes committed by my subordinates beyond my supervision, and thus these were the crimes I committed"[16] Moreover, a diary written by Ota's subordinate at the time of the Nanking campaign contradicts the content of Ota's testimony. Although Ota said that his unit was busy disposing of more than 100,000 dead bodies on December 14–18, a cavalry sergeant of the same unit recorded the dumping of dead bodies into the Yangtze River only on December 22.[17]

Another alleged eyewitness account that caught the attention of Western writers was a remark by Sumi Yoshiharu, adjutant of General Matsui at the time of the Nanking campaign. In response to the call for eyewitness accounts by *Kaiko* magazine, Sumi provided what he described as his recollection, including the following:

On the morning of December 18, the 6th Division called the [CCAA] information section. The 6th Division said, "How should we do with about 120,000 to 130,000 Chinese people in Hsiak'uan?" Lieutenant Colonel Cho [Isamu], information section chief, simply said, "Finish them off!" over the phone. . . . When I inspected the Hsiak'uan area on December 19, dead bodies filled from about 50 meters off the shore of Hsiak'uan over two kilometers downstream. They were estimated to number 120,000 to 130,000. . . . On December 20, [the vehicle carrying Matsui] drove over dead bodies lying on the river shore road for about two kilometers."[18]

Overlooking the advanced age of Sumi when he made this confession and the possibility of his memory confusion, the writer who referred to this statement did not pay attention to some important facts that contradict Sumi's statement: that the 6th Division did not operate in the Hsiak'uan area; and that the number of dead bodies estimated by Sumi in that area contradicts even the estimate in a source quoted by that very writer.[19]

It seems that confusion among the research is attributable not to the scarcity of primary materials but to the researchers' failure to analyze these materials in an academic manner. Such failure results because Western scholars today still inherit the confusion in the IMTFE majority ruling on Matsui, that is, imbalance between the verdict—guilty for a crime of omission—and the sentence, death by hanging. It is also because a less-than-scholarly consideration is existent. Here, it is worth quoting the same passage from the introduction. In a book review of Iris Chang's *The Rape of Nanking*, one American writer mentioned Chang's estimate of at least 260,000 victims in Nanking and compared it with 323,000 American military service men who lost their lives on all fronts in World War II as well as an average 350,000 people gassed to death in Auschwitz every two months. Based on this comparison he said,

The Japanese killed roughly the same number in a few months without the benefit of the technology of mass murder available to the Nazis and without the advantage of concentration camps. What's more, the Japanese troops weren't "specialized": nothing comparable to the *Einsatzgruppen* existed in their military. These were the boys next door. . . . The Rape of Nanking reminds us how recently Japan emerged from its medieval age: a scant 140 years ago, less than 100 at the time of the Rape. What European armies did during the Thirty Years War . . . the soldiers of Hirohito did at Nanking.[20]

The writer of these passages correctly analyzed the character of the Japanese troops, who lacked the means of carrying out mass murder comparable to the Jewish Holocaust. In this sense, he viewed the Rape of Nanking from the standpoint of the IMTFE verdict. Yet his agreement to the larger estimate of the number of victims made him accept the magnitude of the atrocities as presented by the traditionalists and caused him to interpret the Rape of Nanking from the standpoint supporting Matsui's death sentence. Such a way of reasoning prevented him from conducting further analysis of the incident—notably, how the Japanese troops "without the benefit of the technology of mass murder available to the Nazis" killed so many people in such a short time. In other words, those who accepted the alleged death toll of 300,000 or more in the Rape of Nanking apparently did not ask themselves a question—a reasonable question that reviewers and critics of James Bacque's works most likely asked: Could such a historically unprecedented massacre have been possible without the use of efficient mechanisms such as gas chambers or special killing units? It seems that they even did not consider making a cautionary statement as David Stafford, a reviewer of Bacque's *Crimes and Mercies*, did: the specific of allegations about the Japanese intent and the numbers involved remain distinctly not proven.

What prevents them from thinking about such a question is most likely a lingering prejudice against the Japanese as a national group. Attempts to establish a parallel between the Nazi Holocaust and the Rape of Nanking mark a culmination of such a trend. Today, it is the Japanese who are subjected to criticism—partly justified, but partly based on unwarranted prejudice—in connection with the Rape of Nanking. No one can predict which national group will be under the same prejudicial verbal attack in the future if this way of denouncing a nation continues to be accepted unconditionally in this country.

The Rape of Nanking itself is certainly a "cautionary tale" about how cruel human beings could become. At the same time, its historiography tells us another cautionary tale: how the discussion of history may serve less than academic interests, whether soundly or unsoundly.

Although this book has reached its own conclusions regarding some crucial issues, it is by no means the end of the debate about the incident. The estimated number of Rape of Nanking victims, for example, might have to be revised either upward or downward depending on future research. Yet it is hoped that this study will at least clear some of the clouds of politics and emotion that surround the debate so that researchers will conduct more scholarly investigations in the future.

NOTES

1. Adam Roberts, "Land Warfare: From Hague to Nuremberg," in *The Laws of War*, ed. Howard et al., p. 135.

2. Ibid.

3. *RNFH*, p. 220.

4. Young and Yin, *The Rape of Nanking*, p. 276.

5. Takasaki Soji, "Moto Ianfu ni Tsugunai-kin o Tewatasu no Ki" [A Report on Extending Compensation to Ex-Comfort Women], *Bungeishunju*, March 1997, pp. 382–88.

6. Stephen E. Ambrose, "Ike and Disappearing Atrocities," *New York Times Book Review*, 24 February 1991, p. 35.

7. David Stafford, "Case Not Proven," *Times Literary Supplement*, 10 July 1998, p. 29.

8. Stephen E. Ambrose, "Ike and Disappearing Atrocities," *New York Times Book Review*, 24 February 1991, p. 35.

9. Hirota to Saito, 17 January 1938, Red Machine, no. 1263. Parentheses in the original.

10. Hirota to Saito, 19 January 1938, Red Machine, no. 1257.

11. *RNFH*, pp. 103–04. Young and Yin, *The Rape of Nanking*, pp. 262, 276–78.

12. Smythe, *War Damage in the Nanking Area*, Table 4. Also, see Appendix D, Table 1.

13. *RNFH*, pp. 109, 120–21. Emile Schindler, *Where Light and Shadow Meet*, trans. from Spanish by Delores M. Koch (New York: W. W. Norton & Co., 1996), pp. 84, 88. Actually, the police arrested Schindler several times and interrogated him about the embezzlement of materials, some of which were used to feed the Jews. Thomas Keneally, *Schindler's List* (New York: Simon and Schuster, 1982), pp. 296–316.

14. *RNFH*, p. 173.

15. Of over 5.7 million Russian POWs captured by the Germans during World War II, only about two million were recorded as having been released from camps or survived as POWs. Alexander Dallin, *German Rule in Russia 1941–1945: A Study of Occupation Policies* (London: Macmillan & Co., 1957), p. 427. *RNFH* said only in a separate end note and in parentheses that the data excludes the Russian POWs. *RNFH*, p. 274.

16. "Ota Toshio Pi-kung" [Written Confession of Ota Toshio], 3 August 1954, *HP*, p. 863. Reference to this document was made in *RNFH*, pp. 101–02; Young and Yin, *The Rape of Nanking*, pp. 86–97, 260–61.

17. Kajiya Takeo, Diary of Kajiya Takeo, 22 December 1937, in *NSS2*, p. 436. One must, however, note that Kajiya's diary does contain come descriptions of atrocities such as the shooting of a woman in a rice paddy on December 9 and the machine gunning of about two thousand Chinese POWs in Hsiak'uan on each day of 16–17 December. Ibid., pp. 434–35.

18. Katogawa Kotaro, "Shogen ni yoru Nankin Senshi: Sono Sokatsuteki Kosatsu" [Nanking Campaign Chronology Based on Eyewitness Accounts: Concluding Remark] *Kaiko*, March 1985, p. 14.

19. *NSS1*, pp. 758–60. *RNFH*, pp. 102, 212–13. Another source worthy of reference is Matsui's diary. Matsui did not mention such a drive over corpses in his diary entry on December 20. Matsui Diary, 20 December 1937, *NSS1*, p. 22.

20. Russell Jenkins, "The Japanese Holocaust," *National Review*, 10 November 1997, p. 58.

Appendix A: Japanese and Chinese Forces in Nanking

JAPANESE ARMY UNITS IN NANKING

Central China Area Army [Matsui Iwane]

Shanghai Expeditionary Force [Prince Asaka Yasuhiko]

    Yamada Detachment

        103rd Brigade [Yamada Senji]

            65th Regiment [Morozumi Gyosaku]

    16th Division [Nakajima Kesago]

        19th Brigade [Kusaba Tatsumi]

            9th Regiment [Katagiri Goro]
            20th Regiment [Ono Noriaki]

        30th Brigade [Sasaki Toichi]

            33rd Regiment [Noda Kengo]
            38th Regiment [Sukekawa Seiji]

    9th Division [Yoshizumi Ryosuke]

        6th Brigade [Akiyama Yoshimitsu]

            7th Regiment [Isa Kazuo]
            35th Regiment [Fujii Suekichi]

        18th Brigade [Ide Senji]

            19th Regiment [Hitomi Shuzo]
            36th Regiment [Wakizaka Jiro]

3rd Division

    68th Regiment [Takamori Takashi]

Tenth Army [Yanagawa Heisuke]

    114th Division [Suematsu Shigeharu]

        127th Brigade [Akiyama Jusaburo]

            102nd Regiment [Chiba Kotaro]
            66th Regiment [Yamada Jota]

        128th Brigade [Oku Yasuo]

            115th Regiment [Yagasaki Setsuzo]
            150th Regiment [Yamamoto Shigemi]

    6th Division [Tani Hisao]

        11th Brigade [Sakai Tokutaro]

            13th Regiment [Okamoto Yasuyuki]
            47th Regiment [Hasegawa Masanori]

        36th Brigade [Ushijima Mitsuru]

            23rd Regiment [Okamoto Shizuomi]
            45th Regiment [Takeshita Yoshiharu]

    Kunisaki Detachment

        9th Brigade [Kunisaki Noboru]

        Regiment [Yamada Tetsujiro]

CHINESE ARMY UNITS IN NANKING

Nanking Garrison Force [T'ang Sheng-chih (Wade-Giles)/ Tang Shengzhi (Pinyin)]

Second Army Group [Hsu Yuen-ch'uan/Xu Yuanquan]

    41st Division [T'ing Chih-p'an/Ding Zhipan]
    48th Division [Hsu Chi-wu/Xu Jiwu]

66th Army [Yeh Chao/Ye Zhao]

    159th Division [T'an Sui/Tan Sui]
    160th Division [Yeh Chao/Ye Zhao]

71st Army [Wang Ching-Chiu/Wang Jingjiu]

    87th Division [Shen Fa-tsao/Shen Fazao]

72nd Army [Sun Yuan-liang/Sun Yuanliang]

    88th Division [Sun Yuan-liang/Sun Yuanliang]

    74th Army [Yu Chi-Shih/Yu Jishi]

    51st Division [Wang Yao-wu/Wang Yaowu]
    58th Division [Feng Sheng-fa/Feng Shengfa]

78th Army [Sung Hsi-lien/Song Xilian]

    36th Division [Sung Hsi-lien/Song Xilian]

83rd Army [Teng Lung-kuang/Deng Longguang]

    154th Division [Wu Chian-hsiung/Wu Gianxiong]
    156th Division [Li Ch'iang/Li Qiang]

Training Units [Kui Yung-ch'ing/Gui Yongqiong]

Military Police Units [Su Shan-ling/Su Shanling]

Chiangning/Jiangning Fort Garrison [Shao Pai-ch'ang/Shao Baichang]

Other Independent Units

    103rd Division [He Chih-chung/He Zhizhong]
    112th Division [Huo Shou-yi/Huo Shouyi]

Appendix B: Burial Statistics of Red Swastika Society in Nanking

Table B.1
Burial Statistics of Red Swastika Society in Nanking: within Walls

Date	Corpses found at	Men	Women	Children	Total
22 Dec. 37	around Shouping Bridge	129	---	---	129
26 Jan. 38	around Hsich'iaot'ang	124	1	---	125
2 Feb.	around Hanchung Rd.	17	2	---	19
6 Feb.	around Lungp'anli	49	---	---	49
7 Feb.	around Hsits'an	147	---	2	149
11 Feb.	around Shanghai Rd.	16	---	4	20
14 Feb.	around Kulin Temple	107	2	---	109
19 Feb.	all over northern city	650	2	20	672
20 Feb.	Lungch'ihhan	154	---	---	154
22 Feb.	all over northern city	29	1	---	30
27 Feb.	all over northern city	337	---	---	337
Total (within walls)		1,759	8	26	1,793

Table B.2
Burial Statistics of Red Swastika Society in Nanking: Suburbs

Date	Corpses found at	Men	Women	Children	Total
22 Dec. 37	all over the city	100	9	---	109
22 Dec.	all over the city	250	11	---	261
22 Dec.	all over the city	280	---	---	280
28 Dec.	all over the city	6,468	---	---	6,468
10 Jan. 38	Shanghsinhe	996	2	---	998
23 Jan.	all over the city	407	21	3	431
7 Feb.	outside Shuihsi Gate	843	---	---	843
8 Feb.	Tayangkung	457	---	---	457
9 Feb.	around Shuihsi Gate	124	1	---	125
9 Feb.	Erhkeng, Shanghsinhe	850	---	---	850
9 Feb.	around Chiangtung Bridge	1,850	---	---	1,850
9 Feb.	Mienhuati, Shang-hsinghe	1,860	---	---	1,860
11 Feb.	outside Hanhsi Gate	271	1	---	272
11 Feb.	outside Shuihsi Gate	34	---	---	34
12 Feb.	Tukuli, Hsiak'uan	1,191	---	---	1,191
14 Feb.	around Central Athletic Field	82	---	---	82
14 Feb.	in the Central Prison	328	---	---	328
15 Feb.	Kuanyinan, Shang-hsinghe	81	---	---	81
16 Feb.	around Hsichieh	244	---	---	244
18 Feb.	around river bank	1,123	---	---	1,123
18 Feb.	Peihsink'ou, Shanghsinhe	380	---	---	380
18 Feb.	riverside, Hsiak'uan	480	---	---	480
18 Feb.	Torpedo Barracks, Hsiak'uan	524	---	---	524
20 Feb.	wharf, Torpedo Barracks	197	---	---	197
21 Feb.	wharf, Torpedo Barracks	226	---	---	226
21 Feb.	wharf, Torpedo Barracks	5,000	---	---	5,000
21 Feb.	Mufu Hill	147	---	---	147
21 Feb.	Ts'aohsiehcha	115	---	---	115
21 Feb.	Wufu, Shanghsinhe	217	---	---	217
22 Feb.	wharf, Torpedo Barracks	151	---	---	151
22 Feb.	wharf, Torpedo Barracks	300	---	---	300
23 Feb.	all over the city	106	---	---	106
25 Feb.	all around Hsiak'uan	85	---	---	85
26 Feb.	Mufu Hill	1,902	---	---	1,902

Date	Corpses found at	Men	Women	Children	Total
26 Feb.	wharf, Coal Harbor, Hsiak'uan	194	---	---	194
27 Feb.	inside Shangyuan Gate	591	---	---	591
28 Feb.	all over northern city	87	---	---	87
1 Mar.	Mufu Hill	1,346	---	---	1,346
1 Mar.	S.W. Of Sanch'ahsin	998	---	---	998
2 Mar.	Tawotzu	1,409	---	---	1,409
3 Mar.	Mufu Hill	786	---	---	786
6 Mar.	riverside, Coal Harbor	1,772	---	---	1,772
14 Mar.	near Navy Hospital, Hsiak'uan	87	---	---	87
15 Mar.	Sanch'iahsin	29	---	---	29
15 Mar.	near Kanlou Temple, Shanghsinhe	83	---	---	83
19 Mar.	around Ante Gate	100	---	---	100
23 Mar.	near Kanlou Temple	354	---	---	354
24 Mar.	Shanghsinhe	133	---	---	133
25 Mar.	all over the city	799	---	---	799
27 Mar.	wallside, outside Taiping Gate	500	---	---	500
14 Apr.	northern & southern city	1,177	---	---	1,177
16 Apr.	Shanghsinhe	700	---	---	700
19 Apr.	Sanch'ahsin	282	---	---	282
27 Apr.	river bank & river	385	---	---	385
29 Apr.	river bank	102	---	---	102
30 Apr.	arsenal & in the city	486	---	---	486
1 May	river bank	518	---	---	518
15 May	river bank	94	---	---	94
18 May	river bank & river	65	---	---	65
20 May	river bank, Shanghsinhe	57	---	---	57
26 May	all over the city	216	---	---	216
31 May	river bank	74	---	---	74
30 Jun.	all over the city	26	---	---	26
31 Jul.	all over the city	29	5	1	35
31 Aug.	all over the city	14	4	---	18
30 Sep.	all over the city	31	8	9	48
30 Oct.	all over the city	42	13	7	62
Total (in suburbs)		41,208	75	20	41,303

Table B.3
Burial Statistics of Red Swastika Society in Nanking, 1938: Month-by-Month Cumulative Total

Time Period	Location	Men	Women	Children	Total	percent
Through January	within walls	253	1	- - -	254	14.2
	suburbs	8,501	43	3	8,547	20.7
	total	8,754	44	3	8,801	20.4
Through February	within walls	1,759	8	26	1,793	100
	suburbs	28,541	45	3	28,589	69.2
	total	30,300	53	29	30,382	70.5
Through March	within walls	1,759	8	26	1,793	100
	suburbs	36,937	45	3	36,985	89.5
	total	38,696	53	29	38,778	89.9
Through April	within walls	1,759	8	26	1,793	100
	suburbs	40,069	45	3	40,117	97.1
	total	41,828	53	29	41,910	97.2
Through May	within walls	1,759	8	26	1,793	100
	suburbs	41,093	45	3	41,141	99.5
	total	42,852	53	29	42,934	99.6
Through October	within walls	1,759	8	26	1,793	100
	suburbs	41,235	75	20	41,330	100
	total	42,994	83	46	43,123	100

Source: Shih-chieh Hung-wan-tsu-hui Nanking Fen-hui Chiu-chi-tui Yen-mai-tsu Yen-mai Shih-t'i Chu-shu T'ung-chi-piao [Statistics Regarding Bodies Buried by the Burying Group of the Nanking Office of the Red Swastika Society], in *TA*, pp. 431–35.

Appendix C: Burial Records of Ch'ung-shan-t'ang

Table C1
Burial Records of Ch'ung-shan-t'ang

Date	Corpses found at	Men	Women	Children	Total
	between Fuhsi Gate and Kuilang	96	22	6	124
26-28 Dec. 1937 (3 days)	east of Yehchiang Gate	342	38	12	392
	south of Hsinchiehk'ou	83	7	1	91
	east of Chunghua Gate	352	34	18	404
	Total for the period	873	101	37	1,011
Average per day					337
	between N. Gate Bridge and Ch'angchinglou	272	29	9	310
	between Hsinchung Gate and Hsiaotung Gate	350	51	22	423
3 Jan.- 4 Feb. 1938 (33 days)	between Laowangfu and Lucheng P'ailou	284	46	4	334
	between Hsiaoyingfu and Liantzuying	432	31	25	488
	Total for the period	1,338	157	60	1,555
Average per day					47

Date	Corpses found at	Men	Women	Children	Total
	between Kulou and Tashih Bridge	354	13	8	375
	between Yushihlang and Kaoch'iao Gate	587	28	7	622
4 Feb.- 6 Mar. (30 days)	between Huap'ailou and Hungwu Gate	529	24	15	568
	between Changle Rd. And Panshanyuan	878	36	28	942
	Total for the period	2,348	101	58	2,507
Average per day					84
	between Taiping Gate and Fukueishan	610	22	16	648
	between Tashuch'eng and Lanchiachuang	472	39	17	528
7 Mar.- 8 Apr. (31 days)	between Shihpan Bridge and Shangshuchieh	715	48	62	825
	eastern half of Ch'ing-ch'ach'eng	385	54	35	474
	Total for the period	2,182	163	130	2,475
Average per day					80

Date	Corpses found at	Men	Women	Children	Total
9-18 Apr.	outside Chunghua Gate, yard of the Arsenal, Yuhuatai to Huashenmiao	25,752	567	293	26,612
9-23 Apr.	between Shuihsi Gate and Shanghsinhe	18,429	336	23	18,788
9 Apr.- 1 May	between Chungshan Gate and Machung	33,601	191	36	33,828
7-20 Apr. (24 days)	between T'ungchi Gate and Fangshan	24,839	475	176	25,490
	Total for the period	102,621	1,569	528	104,718
Average per day					4,363
	Grand Total	109,362	2,091	813	112,266

Source: Nanking-shih Ch'ung-shan-t'ang Yen-mai Kung-tso Yi-lan-piao [Working List of the Nanking Ch'ung-shan-t'ang's Burying Team], in *TA*, pp. 423–24.

Table C.2
Burial Statistics of Ch'ung-shan-t'ang: Period-by-Period Cumulative Total and Comparison with Red Swastika Data

Time Period		corpses	percent	comparative percent rate in Red Swastika Data
Through Dec. 28, 1937	Men	873	0.9	
	Women	101	4.8	
	Children	37	4.6	
	Total	1,011	0.9	
Through Feb. 4 1938	Men	2,211	2.0	
	Women	258	12.3	
	Children	97	11.9	
	Total	2,566	2.3	20.4 (end-Jan. 1938)
Through Mar. 6 1938	Men	4,559	4.2	
	Women	359	17.2	
	Children	155	19.1	
	Total	5,073	4.5	70.5 (end-Feb. 1938)
Through Apr. 7	Men	7,255	6.6	
	Women	522	25.0	
	Children	285	35.1	
	Total	8,062	7.2	89.9 (end-Mar. 1938)
Through May 1	Men	109,362	100	
	Women	2,091	100	
	Children	813	100	
	Total	112,266	100	97.2 (end-Apr. 1938)

Appendix D: Civilian Losses Based on Smythe's Data

Table D.1
Number and Cause of Civilian Deaths in Nanking

Date (1937-38)	Deaths by Military operations	Deaths by Soldiers' violence	Taken away	Total
Before Dec. 12	600	---	---	600
Dec. 12-13	50	250	200	600
Dec. 14-Jan. 13	---	2,000	3,700	3,900
Jan. 14-Mar. 15	---	---	250	250
Date unknown	200	150	50	400
Total	850	2,400	4,200	7,450

Source: Lewis S. C. Smythe, *War Damage in the Nanking Area December 1937 to March 1938: Urban and Rural Survey* (Shanghai: Mercury Press, 1938), Table 4.

Table D.2
Sex and Age of Civilian Deaths and of Persons Taken Away in Nanking:
Shown in Percentage

| Age group | Males by | | Females by | | Taken away |
	Soldiers' violence	Others	Soldiers' violence	Others	(males only)
5-14	6	8	8	---	- - -
15-29	25	25	23	---	55
30-44	22	8	15	14	36
45-59	19	42	15	57	9
60 and over	28	17	39	29	- - -
Total	100	100	100	100	100

Source: Lewis S. C. Smythe, *War Damage in the Nanking Area December 1937 to March 1938: Urban and Rural Survey* (Shanghai: Mercury Press, 1938), Table 5.

Table D.3
Sex and Age of Civilian Deaths in Kiangning Hsien

Age group	Death by violence		Sickness	All deaths
	Males	Females		
Total deaths	7,170	1,990	1,590	10.750
Under 5 years	3	- - -	- - -	2 (percent)
5-14	9	6	14	9
15-29	35	11	9	30
30-44	24	- - -	22	21
45-59	21	44	41	26
60 and above	8	39	14	12
Total	100	100	100	100 (percent)

Source: Lewis S. C. Smythe, *War Damage in the Nanking Area December 1937 to March 1938: Urban and Rural Survey* (Shanghai: Mercury Press, 1938), Table 24–25.

Bibliography

PUBLISHED COLLECTIONS OF PRIMARY MATERIALS

Chung-kuo Ti-2 Li-shih Tang-an Kuan [The Second Historical Archives of China], Nanking-shih Tang-an Kuan [Nanking Municipal Archives] and Nanking Ta-t'u-sha Shih-liao Pien-chi Wen-yuan-hui [Rape of Nanking Source Materials Collection Compilation Committee], ed. *Ch'in-hua Jih-chun Nanking Ta-t'u-sha Tang-an* [Archival Documents Relating to the Massacre Committed by the Japanese Troops in Nanking]. Chiangsu Province: Chiangsu Ku-chi Ch'u-pan-she [Chiangsu Classics Publishing], 1987.

———— ed., *K'ang-jih Chan-cheng Cheng-mian Chan-ch'ang* [Resistance War against Japan: Regular Warfare Front]. Chiangsu Province: Chiangsu Ku-chi Ch'u-pan-she [Chiangsu Classics Publishing], 1987.

Chung-yung Tang-an Kuan [Central Archives], Chung-kuo Ti-2 Li-shih Tang-an Kuan [The Second Historical Archives of China], and Chilin-sheng She-hui Ke-hsueh-yuen [Chilin Province Social Science Academy], ed. *Jih-pen Ti-kuo Chui Ch'in-hua Tang-an Hsuan-pien*. Vol. 12, *Nanking Ta-t'u-sha* [Selected Archival Documents Relating to Japan's Imperialistic Aggression of China. Vol. 12, The Rape of Nanking]. Peking: Chung-hua Shu-chu [China Publishing], 1995.

Hsu, Shuhsi, ed. *Documents of the Nanking Safety Zone*. Shanghai: Kelly and Walsh, 1939.

Iguchi, Waki, Kisaka Jun-ichiro, and Shimosato Masaki, ed., *Nankin Jiken: Kyoto Shidan Kankei Shiryoshu* [Rape of Nanking: Materials Relating to the Kyoto Division]. Tokyo: Aoki Shoten, 1989.

Kaikosha, ed., *Nankin Senshi Shiryo-shu* [Nankin Campaign Chronology Primary Source Collections]. Vol. 1 and 2. Tokyo: Kaikosha, 1989.

Ono, Kenji, Fujiwara Akira, and Honda Katsuichi, ed. *Nankin Daigyakusatsu o Kiro-kushita Kogun Heishitachi* [Imperial Japanese Army's Soldiers Who Recorded the Rape of Nanking]. Tokyo: Otsuki Shoten, 1996.

Pritchard, R. John and Sonia Magbanua Zaide, comp. and ed. *The Tokyo War Crimes Trial: The Complete Transcripts of the Proceedings of the International Military*

Tribunal for the Far East in Twenty-Two Volumes. Vol. 21, *Separate Opinions*; Vol. 22, *Review of the Judgment Proceedings in Chambers.* New York: Garland Publishing, 1981.

T'ang, Te-hsin, ed. *Yuan Kuo-min-tang Chiang-ling Chan-cheng K'ang-jih Chan-chen Ch'in-li-shih: Nanking Pao-wei-chan* [Personal Experiences of Former Nationalist Party Generals in Resistance War against Japan: Defense of Nanking]. Peking: Chung-kuo Wen-hsueh Ch'u-pan-she [China Historical Publishing], 1987.

U.S. Department of State. *Foreign Relations of the United States: Diplomatic Papers*, 1937. Vols. 3–4. Washington, D.C.: U.S. Government Printing Office, 1954.

UNPUBLISHED COLLECTIONS OF PRIMARY MATERIALS

Correspondence of the Military Intelligence Division Relating to General, Political, Economic and Military Conditions in China 1918–1941. Record Group 165. Microfilm M1444. NA1.

Court Exhibits in English and Japanese, International Prosecution Section, 1945–1947. Record Group 331. Microfilm M1688. NA2.

Department of State. Department of State File 793.94: China-Japan Relations. Microfilm M976. NA2.

Exhibits of the Prosecution and the Defense, Introduced as Evidence before the International Military Tribunal for the Far East, 1945–47. Record Group 331, Microfilm M1686. NA2.

Iketani, Hanjiro, comp. Dai-10-gun Sakusen Shido ni Kansuru Sanko Shiryo [Reference Materials Concerning the 10th Army's Operation Planning]. Vol. 1–3. MHD.

International Military Tribunal for the Far East. Record of the Proceedings of the International Military Tribunal for Far East, 1946–1948. Microfilm.

International Prosecution Section Documents Relating to Witnesses for the Prosecution and the Defense, 1946–47. Record Group 331. Microfilm M1684. NA2.

Military Intelligence Division Regional File Relating to China. Record Group 165. Microfilm M1513. NA2.

Nakasawa, Mitsuo, comp. Dai-16-shidan Kankei Shiryo-tsuzuri [Materials Concerning the 16th Division]. MHD.

Numerical Case Files Relating to Particular Incidents and Suspected War Criminals, International Prosecution Section, 1945–47. Record Group 331. Microfilm M1683. NA2.

Numerical Evidentiary Documents Assembled as Evidence by the Prosecution for Use before the International Military Tribunal for the Far East. Record Group 331. Microfilm M1690. NA2.

Papers of Nelson Trusler Johnson, the Manuscript Division, LC.

Red Machine: Translation of Japanese Diplomatic Messages, 1934–1938. Record Group 457. NA2.

Rikugunsho [Japanese Ministry of Army]. Rikushi Mitsu Dainikki [Army's Secret Diary about China Campaign], Vols. 2, 7, 15, 16, and 29, 1938; Vols. 65 and 90, 1939. MHD.

The Horrors of War: 240 True Stories of Modern Warfare Issued by Gum Inc., in Philadelphia in 1938. Prepared by George Maull. National Museum of American History.

ARCHIVAL MATERIALS IN ENGLISH (1): CORRESPONDENCE AND REPORTS

Allison, John M., Third Secretary of the U.S. Embassy to China. To the Secretary of State. 8 January 1938. 793.94/12021. M976-48.

————. To the Secretary of State. Losses Suffered in Nanking by Chinese as a Result of Present Hostilities. 28 April 1938. M1513-42.

Atcheson, George, Second Secretary of the U.S. Embassy to China, Nanking. To the Secretary of State. 22 November 1937. 793.94/11231. M976-45.

————. To the Secretary of State. 23 November 1937. 793.94/11247. M976-45.

————. To the Secretary of State. 27 November 1937. 793.94/11318. M976-45.

————. To the Secretary of State. 28 November 1937. 793.94/11330. M976-45.

————. To the Secretary of State. 29 November 1937. 793.94/11358. M976-46.

————. To the Secretary of State. 4 December 1937. No serial number. M976-46.

————. To the Secretary of State. 4 December 1937. 793.94/11465. M976-46.

————. To the Secretary of State. 6 December 1937. 793.94/11491. M976-46.

————. To the Secretary of State. 7 December 1937. 793.94/11504. M976-46.

————. To the Secretary of State. 8 December 1937. 793.94/11535. M976-46.

————. To the Secretary of State. 8 December 1937. 793.94/11536. M976-46.

————. To the Secretary of State. 9 December 1937. 793.94/11549. In *Foreign Relations of the United States, 1937*. Vol. 3, *The Far East*, pp. 781–82.

————. To the Secretary of State. 11 December 1937. 793.94/11582. M976-46.

————. To the Secretary of State. 10 December 1937. 793.94/11564. M976-46.

Barrett, David D., Major, Infantry, Assistant Military Attaché to China. G-2 Report: Situation Report 13 October–8 November 1938. Report no. 9694. M1444-10.

Bates, M. S. "Memorandum on Aftermath of Registration of Refugees at Nanking University." 26 December 1937. In *DNSZ*, No. 50, pp. 100–07.

————. To unidentified addresses. 10 January 1938. Enclosed to Nelson T. Johnson to the Secretary of State. 11 February 1938. 793.94/12728, M976-52.

————. To W. Reginald Wheeler. "Notes on the Present Situation." 21 March 1938. Enclosed in W. Reginald Wheeler to Stanley K. Hornbeck. 28 May 1938. 793.94/13177. M976-54.

————. To W. Reginald Wheeler. "Notes on German Atrocities in Belgium." 21 March 1938. Enclosed in W. Reginald Wheeler to Stanley K. Hornbeck. 28 May 1938. 793.94/13177. M976-54.

————. To Frank W. Price. Enclosed in Frank W. Price to Maxwell M. Hamilton, Chief of the Division of Far Eastern Affairs, the Department of State. 17 February 1938. 793.94/12548. M976-51.

Chiang, Mayling Soong [Madame Chiang Kai-shek] to Miriam H. Clark. 5 January, 1938. 793.94/12294. M976-49.

Clarke, Ashley, First Secretary at the British Embassy in Tokyo. To Edward S. Crocker, Second secretary at the U.S. Embassy in Tokyo. 18 January 1938. Enclosure no. 25 to Grew to Secretary of State. 21 January 1938. 793.94/12345. M976-50.

Commander in Chief of Asian Fleet (CINCAF). "Information to the U.S. Embassy in China." 7 December 1937. 793.94/11515. M976-46.

————. "Information to the U.S. Embassy et al." 12 December 1937. 793.94/11587. M976-45.

Commander of the Yangtze Patrol. Information to the U.S. Embassy et al. 17 November
     1937. 793.94/11165. M976-45.

Creswell, Harry I. T. Major, Acting Military Attaché to China. "Observations in Shanghai
     Area." In G-2 Report. 17 December 1937. M1513-39.

Davies, John, American Vice Consul, Hankow. "Memorandum: Conditions in Rural Ar-
     eas near Wuhan." 29 March 1939. M1513-42.

Espy, James. "The Conditions at Nanking: January 1938." 25 January 1938. 793.94/
     12674. M976-51.

Fitch, George A. et al. "Finding Regarding Burning of Nanking City." 21 December
     1937. In *DNSZ*, No. 22, pp. 50–52.

―――. To Frank W. Price. Enclosed in Frank W. Price to Maxwell M. Hamilton.
     17 February 1938. 793.94/12548. M976-51.

Foreign Community of Nanking to Japanese Embassy. Signed by 22 foreigners. 21 De-
     cember 1937. In *DNSZ*, No. 20, pp. 48–49.

Forster, Ernest H., American church mission in Nanking. To Irving U. Townsend, n.d.
     Enclosed in Townsend to Maxwell M. Hamilton. 8 March 1938. 793.94/12636.
     M976-51.

―――. To Irving U. Townsend. Enclosed in Townsend to Maxwell M. Hamilton.
     29 March 1938. 793.94/12749. M976-52.

Gauss, Clarence E., Consul General at Shanghai. To the Secretary of State. 4 December
     1937. 793.94/11456. In *Foreign Relations of the United States, 1937*. Vol. 3, *The
     Far East*, pp. 757–58.

―――. To the Secretary of State. 20 December 1937. 793.94/11739. M976-47.

―――. To the Secretary of State. 3 February 1938. 793.94/12303. M976-49.

―――. "Report on Japanese Military Operations during the Month of February 1938."
     10 March 1938. 793.94/12832. M976-52.

Gould, Clyde F. to Senator Prentiss M. Brown. 24 May 1938. 793.94/13100. M976-54.

Grew, Joseph Clark, U.S. Ambassador to Japan. To the Japanese Ministry of Foreign
     Affairs. 10 December 1937. Enclosure No. 20 to Grew to the Secretary of State.
     10 December 1937. 793.94/11840. M976-47.

―――. To the Secretary of State. 21 January 1938. 793.94/12345. Enclosures Nos. 15,
     20–22, 25, 29. M976-50.

―――. To the Secretary of State. "Recommendations Made and Steps Taken by the
     American Embassy and Steps Taken by the British and French Embassies in
     Tokyo with Respect to the Sino-Japanese Conflict." 3 February 1938. Enclosure
     No. 1: "Recommendations Made and Steps Taken by the American Embassy in
     Tokyo with Respect to the Sino-Japanese Conflict from January 19 to February
     1, 1938." 793.94/12478. M976-50.

―――. To the Secretary of State. 23 February 1938. 793.94/12496. M976-51.

―――. "Japanese Prospects after One Year's Fighting in China." 11 July 1938. 793.94/
     13585, M976-55.

Hawthorne, Carl C., U.S. Vice Consul in Tsinan. To Willys R. Peck, U.S., Charge
     D'Affaires ad interim in Peiping. 17 February 1939. 793.94/14805. M976-60.

Headquarters, United States Army Troops in China, Office of the Intelligence Officer.
     "Intelligence Summary 15–31 December 1937." Report No. 26. M1513-39.

―――. G-2 Report. 13 June 1938. M1513-39.

―――. G-2 Report. 15 June 1938. M1513-39.

———. G-2 Digest of Information: "Sino-Japanese Situation 23–29 January 1938." 793.94/12401. M976-50.

———. G-2 Digest of Information: "Sino-Japanese Situation 12–18 March 1938." M1513-50.

———. Untitled document. 15 June 1938. M1513-39.

———. G-2 Digest of Information: "Sino-Japanese Situation 4–10 June 1938." M1513-50.

———. "Medical Services in the Chinese Army." 28 November 1941. M1513–50.

Heath, G. L., Lieutenant, the U.S. Navy. Intelligence Report. 26 November 1938. No. 45–19. File 808-300. M1513-41.

Hirota, Koki, Foreign Minister of Japan. To Saito Hiroshi, Japanese Ambassador to the United States in Washington, D.C. 14 August 1937. Red Machine. No. 570A.

———. To Saito. 29 August 1937. Red Machine. No. 620.

———. To Saito. 8 September 1937. Red Machine. No. 665C.

———. To Saito. 23 December 1937. Red Machine. No. 1185.

———. To Saito. 26 December 1937. Red Machine. No. 1171.

———. To Saito. 26 December 1937. Red Machine. No. 1162.

———. To Saito. 3 January 1938. Red Machine. No. 1193B.

———. To Saito. 19 January 1938. Red Machine. No. 1257.

———. To Saito. 17 January 1938. Red Machine. No. 1263.

———. To Grew. 15 February 1938. Quoted in Grew to the Secretary of State. 16 February 1938. 793.94.393.1115, M976-50.

Hsiao, Tsun-cheng. "The War at Shanghai." In G-2 Report. 25 April 1939. M1513-40.

Ishii, Itaro, Director, East Asian Affairs Bureau, Japanese Foreign Ministry. Conversation with E. H. Dooman, Counselor of the U.S. Embassy to Japan. 15 January 1938. Enclosure No. 15 to Grew to Secretary of State. 21 January 1938. 793.94/12345. M976-50.

James, Edward, Nanking Theological Seminary. "The Japanese Sack of Nanking." Enclosed in Helen M. Loomis, Secretary, China Information Service, to the Secretary of State. 23 May 1938. 793.94/13073. M976-53.

James, George E., Second Lieutenant. "Wrecking of Chinese Area Which Sheltered General Doolittle's Men: Interview with Father George Yager." 14 June 1943. M1513-42.

Johnson, D. R., Chairman of Missouri Peace Action Committee. To Secretary of State. 15 December 1937. 793.94/11968. M976-48.

Johnson, Nelson Trusler. U.S. Ambassador to China, Hankow. To the Secretary of State. 10 December 1937. 793.94/11556, In *Foreign Relations of the United States, 1937*. Vol. 3, *The Far East*, p. 784.

———. To the Secretary of State. 25 December 1937. 793.94/11804. In *Foreign Relations of the United States, 1937*. Vol. 4, *The Far East*, pp. 414–15.

———. To the Secretary of State. 29 December 1938. 793.94/11888. M976-48.

———. To the Secretary of State. 11 January 1938. 793.94/12049. M976-48.

———. To Stanley K. Hornbeck. 14 January 1938. PNTJ-66.

———. To Roger S. Green. 17 January 1938. PNTJ-34.

———. To Sir Miles Lampson. 24 January 1938. PNTJ-35.

———. To Thomas W. Lamont. 8 February 1938. PNTJ-35.

———. To Bill Hard. 3 April 1938. PNTJ-34.

———. To Gage Brownell. 28 April 1938. PNTJ-34.

———. To Roy W. Howard. 6 September 1938. PNTJ-34.

Josselyn, P. R., U.S. Consul General in Hankow. To the Secretary of State, 27 October 1938, 793.94/14025, M976-57.

———. To the Secretary of State. 28 October 1938. 793.94/14229. M976-57.

———. To the Secretary of State. 8 November 1938. 793.94/14322. M976-58.

———. To the Secretary of State. 10 November 1938. 793.94/14346. M976-58.

Kagan, K. G., Major, U.S. Marine Corps, Assistant Naval Attaché. "Resume of the Political-Military Situation: Shanghai-Nanking-Hangchow Area, 11–20 January 1938." M976-52.

Lamont, Thomas W. to N. T. Johnson. 26 February 1938. PNTJ-35.

Linnell, Irving N., U.S. Consul General in Canton. To Secretary of State, 26 October 1938. 793.94/14213. M976-57.

———. To the Secretary of State. 28 October 1938. 793.94/14230. M976-57.

Lockhart, Frank P., Nanking. To the Secretary of State. 8 November 1937. 793.94/11021. M976-43.

———. "Regarding Increasing Cruelty of the Japanese Military." In an untitled report. 18 February 1938. 793.94/12705. M976-52.

———. To Secretary of State. 29 July 1938. 793.94/13752. M976-56.

———. "Photographs of Executions by Japanese Armed Forces." 16 September 1938. 793.94/14040. M976-57.

MacDonald, W. E., professor of mathematics at Lingnan University, Canton. To F. R. Moulton of the American Association for the Advancement of Science. 15 June 1938. Enclosed in Moulton to Stanley K. Hornbeck. 20 July 1938. 793.94/13646. M976-55.

McFadyen, A. A., an American medical missionary. To U.S. Consulate in Shanghai. n.d. Enclosure No. 1 to Lockhart to the Secretary of State. 29 July 1938. 793.94/13752. M976-56.

Masutani, Japanese Consul in Chicago, to Hirota. 18 December 1937. Red Machine. No. 1149A.

Merrell, George R. U.S. Consul in Harbin. To the Secretary of State. "Interviews of Two Americans with Japanese Military Officials." 16 February 1938. 793.94/12859. M976-52.

Nanking Commander of Military Police of the Japanese Army. "Proclamation by Nanking Commander of Military Police of the Japanese Army." 22 December 1937. Translation from Japanese. In *DNSZ*, No. 23, p. 53.

Peck, Willys R. To N. T. Johnson 30 May 1938. PNTJ-35.

Rabe, John H. D. To Fukuda Tokuyasu, Attaché to the Japanese Embassy in Nanking. 15 December 1937. In *DNSZ*, No. 4, pp. 4–5.

———. To Japanese Embassy. 17 December 1937. In *DNSZ*, No. 9, pp. 12–18.

———. To Japanese Embassy. 18 December 1937. In *DNSZ*, No. 10, pp. 18–23.

———. To Japanese Embassy. "Cases of Disorder by Japanese Soldiers in Safety Zone." Filed 20 December 1937. In *DNSZ*, No. 17, pp. 39–44.

———. To Japanese Embassy. 27 December 1937. In *DNSZ*, No. 26, pp. 56–58.

———. Rabe to Japanese Embassy. "Cases of Disorder by Japanese Soldiers in the Safety Zone." Filed 4 January 1938. In *DNSZ*, No. 32, pp. 64–66.

———. To Fukuda. 14 January 1938. In *DNSZ*, No. 41, pp. 82–85.

———. To Japanese Embassy. 17 January 1938. In *DNSZ*, No. 43, pp. 86–87.

———. To Allison. 19 February 1938. In *DNSZ*, No. 69, pp. 166–67.

Saito, Hiroshi, Japanese Ambassador to the United States. To Hirota. 27 August 1937. Red Machine. No. 567A.

———. To Hirota. 20 September 1937. Red Machine. No. 666.

———. To Hirota. 9 October 1937. Red Machine. No. 759A.

———. To Hirota. 4 March 1938. Red Machine. No. 1490.

Salisbury, Laurence E., First Secretary of U.S. Embassy. To N. T. Johnson. "Destruction by Japanese Military in Shansi, Shantung, and Hopei Provinces." 13 July 1938. 793.94/13658. M976-55.

Smythe, Lewis S. C., ICNSZ Secretary. To Fukuda. 16 December 1937. In *DNSZ*, No. 7, pp. 7–9.

———. To Fukuda. "Cases of Disorder by Japanese Soldiers in the Safety Zone." Filed 16 December 1937. In *DNSZ*, No. 8, pp. 9–11.

———. "Memorandum on Incident at the Ministry of Justice." 18 December 1938. In *DNSZ*, No. 11, pp. 23–24.

———. To Japanese Embassy. "Cases of Disorder by Japanese Soldiers in the Safety Zone." Filed 19 December 1937. In *DNSZ*, No. 15, pp. 27–38.

———. To Japanese Embassy. "Cases of Disorder by Japanese Soldiers in the Safety Zone." Filed 21 December 1937. In *DNSZ*, No. 19, pp. 45–48.

———. To Japanese Embassy. "Cases of Disorder by Japanese Soldiers in the Safety Zone." Filed 26 December 1937. In *DNSZ*, No. 25, pp. 54–56.

———. "Memorandum of Interview Regarding Wang Hsing-lung Case." 31 December 1937. In *DNSZ*, No. 28, pp. 59–60.

———. "Memorandum on Relief Problems." 10 February 1938. In *DNSZ*, No. 68, pp. 163–66.

———. "Notes on Present Situation." 22 January 1938. In *DNSZ*, No. 48, pp. 94–95.

Sokobin, Samuel, U.S. Consul in Tsingtao. To Nelson T. Johnson. 1 August 1938, 793.94/13868. M976-56.

Sone, H. L., methodist mission in Nanking, to Arthur J. Bowen. 11 January 1938. 793.94/12489. M976-51.

———. To Frank W. Price. Enclosed in Frank W. Price to Maxwell M. Hamilton. 17 February 1938. 793.94/12548. M976-51.

Stilwell, Joseph W., Colonel, Infantry, Military Attaché to China. G-2 Report. No. 9582. 5 August 1937. M1444-17.

———. "General Notes on the Character of the War." ca. 25 September 1938. M1513-38.

Tsitsashan Temple. "Memorandum by Tsitsashan Temple." In *DNSZ*, No. 60, pp. 135–37.

U.S. Embassy, Peiping. "Japanese Atrocities." 25 May 1938. Radiogram No. 318. M1513-42.

Wakasugi, Japanese Consul in New York. To Hirota. 20 April 1938. Red Machine. No. 1808.

———. To Tokyo. 2 July 1938. Red Machine. No. 2307.

Wilbur, Mary M. To the Secretary of State. 8 November 1938. 793.94/14408. M976-58.

Yoshida, Shigeru, Japanese Ambassador to Britain. To Hirota. 11 November 1937. Red Machine. No. 889C.

ARCHIVAL MATERIALS IN ENGLISH (2): IMTFE DOCUMENTS

Bernard, Henri. "Dissenting Judgment of the Member from France of the International Military Tribunal for the Far East." 12 November 1948. In *TWCT*, Vol. 21.

Civil Censorship Detachment. "Summary of Content of Letter from Matsui Iwane to Kayano Nagatomo 22 September 1946." 10 October 1946. File 99F. M1683-30.

Headquarters Sugamo Prison. Records Regarding the Release of Inmates. 15 May, 26 August, 8 September 1947. File 99B. M1683-29.

————. Sugamo Prison Records 1945–1952. RG338: Records of U.S. Army Commands 1942–: Records of the U.S. Eighth Army. Box 40, File 7. Box 34, File 27.

International Military Tribunal for the Far East. "Charter of the International Military Tribunal for the Far East." In *Trial of Japanese War Criminals*, Department of State Publication 2613. Far Eastern Series 12, pp. 39–44. Washington: United States Government Printing Office, 1946.

International Prosecution Section. Interrogation Records:

Asaka, Yasuhiko. 1 May 1946. Case 61. M1683-22.

Fujita, Susumu. 2 May 1946. Case 439. File 2. M1683-68.

Fukuda, Tokuyasu. 25 April 1946. Case 61. File 78. M1683-22.

Fukui, Kiyoshi. 27 April 1946. Case 61. File 79. M1683-22.

Iinuma, Mamoru. 3 May 1946. Case 439. File 3. M1683-68.

Ishikawa, Tatsuzo. 11 May 1946. Case 439. File 6. M1683-68.

Matsui, Iwane. 7–8 March 1946. Case 61. Files 25, 27. M1683-22.

Muto, Akira. 20, 22 April 1946. Case 319. M1683-58.

Nakasawa, Mitsuo. 30 April 1946. Case 61. M1683-22.

Suzuki, Jiro and Asami Kazuo. Case 444. M-1683-69.

Tada, Hayao. 26 April 1946. Case 53. File 29. M1683-17.

Tanaka, Ryukichi. 24 May 1946. Case 438. File 9. M1683-68.

Tani, Hisao. 23 February 1946. Case 375. M1683-63.0

————. "Admission by Subject against Himself. Subject: Matsui Iwane." Case 61. No. 42. M1683-22.

————Affidavit Signed by Asami and Suzuki. 15 June 1946. IPS no. 1920. M1690-272

Ito, Kiyoshi, Jodai Takayoshi and Floyd J. Mattice to Douglas MacArthur, Supreme Commander of the Allied Powers. "Petition for Review of Conviction and Sentence on Behalf of Matsui Iwane." In *TWCT*, Vol. 22.

Pal, Radhabinod M. "Judgement of the Honorable Justice Pal, Member from India." In *TWCT*. Vol. 21.

Roeling, Bernard Victor A. "Dissenting Judgment of the Member from the Netherlands." In *TWCT*, Vol. 21.

United Nations War Crimes Commission, Far Eastern and Pacific Sub-Commission. List of War Criminals and Material Witnesses. No. 1. August 1946. M1683-48.

Webb, William Flood. "Separate Opinion of the President, the International Military Tribunal for the Far East." 1 November 1948. In *TWCT*, Vol. 21.

ARCHIVAL MATERIALS IN JAPANESE (1): DIPLOMATIC RECORDS

Consul General for the Netherlands in Shanghai to the Japanese Foreign Ministry. "Value of Losses: House Mr. [F. J. M.] Bourdrez, Shanghai Road 86, Nanking, 24 February 1938." Accompanied with Dutch Ministry in Tokyo to Japanese Foreign Minister Ugaki Kazushige. "Nankin Zaiju Orandajin Tonan Jiken ni kansuru 9-gatsu Itsuka zuke Zaikyo Oranda Koshi Hatsu Ugaki Daijin ate Shokan" [A letter addressed to (Foreign) Minister Ugaki from the Dutch Ministry in Tokyo dated September 5 regarding the looting committed against a Dutch man living in Nanking]. 5 September 1938. In "Shina Jihen: Dai-san-koku-jin Kankei Jiko oyobi Higai Kankei (Hakengun Kodo ni yoru Jiko o Fukumu)" [China Incident: Materials Relating to Incidents Involving Third Countries' Nationals and Damages Suffered by Them (including the incidents caused by the actions of Expeditionary Forces)]. Gaimusho Kiroku [Foreign Ministry Record (GK)] A110-30-11. GS.

Deutsche Botschaft nach das Kaiserlich Japanische Ministerium der Auswaertigen Angelegenheiten [German Embassy to the Imperial Japanese Ministry of Foreign Affairs]. "Verbalnote" [verbal note]. 22 June 1938. In "Higai Kiroku" [Damage Records] Doitsujin Kankei (2) [Cases Concerning German Nationals (2)]. GK A110-30-11. GS.

Higai Chosashitsu [Damage Assessment Team]. "Shina Jihen ni yoru Daisankokujin Higai Anken Kaiketsuhyo" [Charts Regarding Solutions to Damages Suffered by Third Countries' Nationals during the Sino-Japanese War]. July 1941. In "Higai Kiroku" [Damage Reports]. GK A110-30-11. GS.

Inoue, chief of the Japanese Foreign Ministry's European and Asian Affairs Department. "Nankin Dokujin Kaoku Higai Mondai tou ni kanshi Zaikyo Doku Taishikan 'Neeberu' Sanjikan Inoue O-a Kyokucho Raidan Yoshi." [Summary of Conversations between Counsel Nebel of the German Embassy in Tokyo and European and Asian Department Chief Inoue about the German Residents' Houses Damaged in Nanking]. 25 January 1938. In "Higai Kiroku" [Damage Records] Doitsujin Kankei (1) [Cases Concerning German Nationals (1)]. GK A110-30-11. GS.

Japanese Foreign Ministry. "A Guideline Regarding Damage Claim Filed by Third-Country Nationals in the Course of the Sino-Japanese War." 22 November 1937. Quoted in "Zai-shi Doitsu-jin Higai Baisho Seikyu ni taisuru Oshu-furi ni Kansuru Ken" [Regarding the Response toward the Compensation Demand for Damages by German Nationals in China]. 7 September 1938. In "Higai Kiroku" [Damage Reports] Doitsujin Kankei (1) [Cases Concerning German Nationals (1)]. GK A110-30-11, GS.

———. "Zaikyo Doitsu Taishikan nite Sakusei-seru Zaishi Doitsujin Higaihyo: Nankin ni okeru Higai Jiken" [Table compiled by the German Embassy in Tokyo to List the German Individuals Who Suffered Damages in China: Data Concerning Nanking]. In "Higai Kiroku" [Damage Reports] Doitsujin Kankei (1) [Cases Concerning German Nationals (1)]. GK A110-30-11, GS.

ARCHIVAL MATERIALS IN JAPANESE (2): MILITARY RECORDS [IN THE ORDER OF COMMAND SUPERIORITY]

General Staff, Imperial Japanese Army. Rin-san-mei [General Staff Special Order] No. 73. 15 August 1937. In *NSS*1, p. 533.

————. Rin-san-mei [General Staff Special Order] No. 138. 7 November 1937. In *NSS*1, p. 533.

————. Rin-mei [Army Special Order] No. 600. 7 November 1937. In *NSS*1, p. 534.

————. Dai-riku-den [Army's Telegraph] No. 19. 24 November 1937. In DSKS, Vol. 2. MHD.

————. Dai-riku-mei [Army Special Order] No. 8. 1 December 1937. In *NSS*1, pp. 534–35.

Tada, Hayao, Deputy Chief of the General Staff. To Tanabe Moritake, Tenth Army Chief of Staff. "Dai-10-gun Sanbo-cho ni Atauru Heitan ni Kansuru Chui-jiko" [Directive to Tenth Army Chief of Staff Concerning Logistics]. 20 October 1937. In DSKS, Vol. 1. MHD.

————. To Matsui Iwane, CCAA Commander. 20 November 1937, DSKS, Vol. 2, MHD.

Yamashita, Tomoyuki, Staff Chief of Hoku Shina Homen-gun [North China Area Army]. To Yamawaki Masataka, Deputy Minister of Army. "Nankin ni okeru Beikokujin no Songai Ichiranhyo Sofu no Ken" [Concerning the list Showing Material Losses Suffered by Americans in Nanking]. 21 June 1939. RMD, 1939, Vol. 65, No. 104. MHD.

Army's Infantry School. "Tai-Shina-Gun Sento-ho no Kenkyu" [How to Fight Chinese Military]. 1933. Quoted in Yoshida Yutaka. *Tenno no Guntai to Nankin Jiken* [Emperor's Military and the Nanking Incident], p. 45. Tokyo: Aoki Shoten, 1986.

Deputy Minister of the Army to CCAA et al. "Shina Jihen Chi yori Kikansuru Guntai oyobi Gunjin no Gunki Fuki oyobi Keiko Bukken no Torishimari ni Kansuru Ken" [Report about the Morale/Discipline of Troops and Soldiers Returning from China and about the Inspection of Items They Are Carrying to Homeland]. 8 April 1938. RMD, 1939, Vol. 90, No. 267. MHD.

————. "Senchi Kikan Shohei Fusei Keiko Bukken (Taizoku Kamotsu o Fukumu) Ichiran-hyo" [List of Illegal Items Carried by Soldiers Returning from Battlefield (including those transported as baggage of military units)] 28 December 1937 to 15 March 1938. Appendix to RMD, 1939, Vol. 90, No. 267. MHD.

Kan'in, Kotohito to CCAA Commander. Chu-ho-san Dai-19-go [Telegram no. 19 to CCAA]. "Gunki Fuki ni Kansuru Sanbo-socho Yobo [Directive from Chief of Staff Concerning Military Discipline and Ethics]. 4 January 1938. RMD. In *NSS*1, pp. 564–65.

Military Affairs Division of the Ministry of Army. To CCAA staff chief et al. "Nihonhei no Nankin Beikoku Taishikan Shinnyu ni Kansuru Ken" [Concerning Japanese Soldiers' Intrusion into the U.S. Embassy in Nanking]. In Rikushi Mitsuden [Army's Secret Telegram to China] No. 753. 28 December 1937. RMD, 1938, Vol. 7, No. 114. MHD.

Inada, Masazumi. "Shina Jihen Senso Shido Kankei Shiryo" [Reflection on Strategic Planning during the China Incident]. MHD.

CCAA Command. Chu-ho-san-den [CCAA to General Staff] No. 167. "Chu-shina Homen Kongo no Sakusen ni Kansuru Iken Gushin" [Proposal Regarding Future Military Campaign in Central China]. 22 November 1937. In *NSS*1, p. 537.

————. "Nankinjo no Koryaku oyobi Nyujo ni Kansuru Chui Jiko" [Directive concerning the Military Operation in and Entry to Nanking]. n.d. DSKS, Vol. 3; and in *NSS*1, p. 540.

————. "Chu-shina Homen-gun Dai-2-ki Sakusen no Taiko" [Guideline of CCAA's 2nd Phase of Operation]. 24 November 1937. In DSKS, Vol. 2, and *NSS*1, p. 538.

————. "Nankinjo Koryaku Yoryo" [Instruction Concerning Capture of Nanking]. 7 December 1937. In *NSS*1, p. 539.

————. "Chu Shina Hakengun Kenpeitai Fukumukitei" [CCAA Military Police Regulations]. In "Chu-Shina Haken Kenpeitai no Hensei Haichi oyobi Fukumu ni Kansuru Ken Hokoku" [Report Concerning the Formation, Disposition and Jurisdiction of CCAA Military Police]. 12 January 1938. RMD, 1938, Vol. 2, No. 97. MHD.

CCAA Military Court. Chu-Shina Homen-gun Gunpo Kaigi Jinchu Nisshi [CCAA Court-martial Record] 4 January–6 February 1938. In *Zoku Gendaishi Shiryo* [Source Materials of Modern History: Second Series]. Vol. 6, *Gunji Keisatsu* [Military Police], ed. Takahashi Masae, pp. 123–218. Tokyo: Misuzu Shobo, 1982.

CCAA Military Police. "Gunji Keisatsu Kinmu Kyotei" [Military Police Textbook]. 1 July 1943. Quoted in Hata Ikuhiko. *Nankin Jiken* [Nanking Incident], p. 239. Tokyo: Chuo Koron, 1986.

Tsukada, Osamu, CCAA Staff Chief. To Umezu Yoshijiro, Deputy Army Minister. "Chu Shina Haken Kenpeitai no Hensei Haichi oyobi Fukumu ni Kansuru Ken Hokoku" [Report Concerning the Formation, Disposition and Jurisdiction of CCAA Military Police]. 12 January 1938. RMD, 1938, Vol. 2, No. 97. MHD.

————. To Deputy Army Minister and Deputy Chief of General Staff. "Shoshu Kenpei Kashikanhei no Kyuyo ni Kansuru Ken" [Regarding the Payment to Enlisted Noncommissioned Military Police Officers]. 31 January 1938. RMD, 1938, Vol. 11, No. 33. MHD.

Tenth Army Command. "Dai-2-ki Sakusen Shido Yoryo" [Operation Guideline for the 2nd Phase of Campaign]. 2 November 1937. DSKS, Vol. 2. MHD.

————. Teishu Sakumei Gogai [Tenth Army Operation Order extra]. 15 December 1937. DSKS, Vol. 3. MHD.

————. "Kunji" [Directive (to Tenth Army Soldiers)] by Yanagawa Heisuke, Commander of the Tenth Army. 17 November 1937. In DSKS, Vol. 2. MHD.

————. Tei-shu-saku-mei [Tenth Army Operation Order] No. 31. 7 A.M. 19 November 1937. In *NSS*1, p. 552.

————. To Chief of General Staff and Commander of CCAA. "Nankin Tsuigeki Mondai" [Regarding the Advance toward Nanking]. 22 November 1937. In *NSS*1, p. 651.

————. "Nankin Koryaku ni Kansuru Iken" [Proposal for Capturing of Nanking]. 30 November 1937. In DSKS, Vol. 2. MHD.

————. Tei-shudan Shireibu Joho Kiroku [Tenth Army Information Record] No. 30. 3 December 1937. Gokuhi, Shimitsu 5037-7 [Top Secret, Secret Report from China no. 5037-7]. RMD, 1938, Vol. 29, No. 4. MHD.

————. "Gun Sanbo-cho Chui-jiko" [Directive by (Tenth) Army's Chief of Staff]. n.d. In DSKS, Vol. 1. MHD.

————. Tei-shu Sakumei Kou Gogai: Tei-Shudan Meirei [Tenth Army Operation Order Extra: Tenth Army Order]. 13 December 1937. In *NSS*1, pp. 554–55.

Tenth Army's Legal Department. "Dai-10-gun (Yanagawa Heidan) Homubu Jinchu Nisshi" [10th Army (Yanagawa Army Group) Legal Department Record] 12 October 1937–23 February 1938. In *Zoku Gendaishi Shiryo* [Source Materials of Modern History: Second Series]. Vol. 6, *Gunji Keisatsu* [Military Police], pp. 3–119.

Tanabe (Tenth Army Chief of Staff). To 18th and 101st Division Chiefs, et al. "Koshu Senryo ni Tomonau Chitsujo Iji oyobi Haishuku tou ni Kansuru Ken" [About the Maintenance of Order and Arranging of Accommodation Following the Occupation of Hangchou]. 20 December 1937. DSKS, Vol. 3. MHD.

Terada, Masao. "Dai-10-gun Sakusen Shido ni Kansuru Kosatsu" [Commentary on the Tenth Army's Operation Planning]. MHD.

Eleventh Army Command. "Gun Sanbo-cho no Chui Jiko" [Directive from Army Staff Chief]. Accompanying Chu-shi Sakumei [CCAA Operation Order] No. 125. In "Dai-11-gun Kimitsu Sakusen Nisshi" [Eleventh Army Confidential Operation Diary]. Quoted in Kojima Noboru. *Nitchu Senso* [Sino-Japanese War], Vol. 5, pp. 151–52. Tokyo: Bungeishunju, 1988.

6th Division, "Senji Junpo" [Wartime Report] Nos. 13–14, No. 15 Appendix. In *NSS*1, pp. 689–99.

————. 6-Shi Sakumei Kou [6th Division Operation Order] No. 84. 11:30 A.M., 14 December 1937. In *NSS*1, p. 558.

9th Division. "Dai-9-Shidan Sento Keika no Gaiyo: Shanhai-fukin no Sento yori Nankin Koryaku ni Itaru" [Outline of 9th Division's Military Operation: From Battles in Shanghai Area to Attack on Nanking]. n.d. MHD.

————. 9-Shi Sakumei Kou [9th Division's Operation Order] No. 131. Noon, 13 December 1937. In *NSS*1, p. 547.

16th Division. "Jokyo Hokoku" [Report of Situation]. 24 December 1937. In *NSS*1, pp. 577–78.

————. "Dai-16-shidan Sakusen Keika no Gaiyo" [Outline of 16th Division's Operation]. 10 January 1938. In *NSS*1, pp. 578–80.

Nakasawa, Mitsuo. "Sanbo-cho no Shiji" [Directive by (Divisional) Chief of Staff]. n.d. In Dai-16-Shidan Kankei Shiryo Tsuzuri [Collection of Source Materials Relating to 16th Division], MHD.

————. "Nankin Kogeki-ji no Dai-16-Shidan Taisei" [16th Division's Deployment at the Time of Nanking Operation], a map prepared by Colonel Nakasawa Mitsuo, then staff chief of the 16th Division. n.d. In Dai-16-Shidan Kankei Shiryo Tsuzuri [Collection of Source Materials Relating to 16th Division].

————. "Nankin ni okeru Moshiokuri Yoten" [Important Information Given at the Time of Transfer of Command in Nanking]. n.d. In *NSS*1, p. 581.

114th Division. "Dai-114-shidan Sakusen Keika no Gaiyo" [Outline of 114th Division's Operation]. 7 November–14 December 1937. In *NSS*1, pp. 653–54.

————. 114-Sakumei Kou [114th Division's Operation Order] No. 62. 9:30 A.M., 13 December 1937. In *NSS*1, p. 556.

Kunisaki Detachment Command. "Kunisaki Shitai Sento Shoho" [Battle Report of Kunisaki Detachment] No. 10. 3–16 December 1937. In *NSS*1, pp. 701–7.

6th Infantry Brigade. 6-Ryo Sakumei Kou [6th Brigade Operation Order] No. 138. 4:30 P.M., 13 December 1937. In *NSS*1, pp. 550–51.

————. "Soto Jisshi ni Kansuru Chui" [Instructions Regarding Mopping-up Operation]

In 6-Ryo Sakumei Kou [6th Brigade operation order] No. 138. 4:30 P.M., 13 December 1937. In *NSS*1, pp. 550–51.

30th Infantry Brigade. Hohei Dai-30-Ryodan Meirei [30th Infantry Brigade Order]. 4:50 A.M., 14 December 1937. In *NSS*1, p. 545.

7th Infantry Regiment. "Hohei Dai-7-Rentai Sento Shoho." [Battle Report of 7th Infantry Regiment]. 7–24 December 1937. In *NSS*1, pp. 618–30.

———. Ho-7 Sakumei Kou [7th Infantry Regiment's Operation Order] No. 107. 1:40 P.M., 14 December 1937. In *NSS*1, p. 621.

———. Ho-7 Sakumei Kou [7th Infantry Regiment's Operation Order] No. 109. 10 P.M., 14 December 1937. In *NSS*1, p. 621.

———. Ho-7 Sakumei Kou [7th Infantry Regiment's Operation Order] No. 111. 8:30 P.M., 15 December 1937. In *NSS*1, p. 622.

33rd Infantry Regiment. "Nankin-fukin no Sento Shoho" [Report of Battles in Nanking Area] 10–14 December 1937. MHD.

———. "33-Rentai Sento Shoho" [33rd Regiment's Battle Report]. n.d. MHD.

38th Infantry Regiment. "Hohei Dai-38-Rentai Sento Shoho" [Battle Report of 38th Infantry Regiment] No. 11. 12–13 December 1937. MHD.

———. "Nankin Jonai Sento Shoho" [Report of Battle within Nanking Walls]. MHD.

65th Infantry Regiment. "Hohei Dai-65-Rentai Sento Shoho" [Battle Report of 65th Infantry Regiment]. Quoted in a memoir by Sugano Yoshio, private first class of 65th Regiment's Artillery Company. In *NDKK*, pp. 298–305.

150th Infantry Regiment. "Sento Shoho" [Battle Report] No. 6. 10–13 December 1937. In *NSS*1, pp. 679–88.

1st Battalion of the 66th Infantry Regiment. "Sento Shoho" [Battle Report] 10–13 December 1937. MHD; In *NSS*1, pp. 666–78.

———. Daitai Meirei [Battalion Order]. 2:30 P.M., 12 December 1937. Quoted in "Sento Shoho" [Battle Report]. In *NSS*1, pp. 666–67.

1st Battalion of the 68th Infantry Regiment. "Sento Shoho" [Battle Report]. 28 November–13 December 1937. In *NSS*1, pp. 633–39.

3rd Battalion of the 68th Infantry Regiment. "Sento Shoho" [Battle Report]. 27 November–13 December 1937. In *NSS*1, p. 640–47.

———. "Jinchu Nisshi" [Field Diary]. 16 December 1937. In *NSS*1, pp. 648–49.

2nd Independent Siege Heavy Artillery Battalion. "Sento Shoho" [Battle Report]. No. 9 Appendix. In *NSS*1, p. 650.

4th Company of the 20th Infantry Regiment. "Jinchu Nisshi" [Field Diary]. No. 5. 1–31 December 1937. In *KS*, pp. 370–413.

12th Company of the 41st Infantry Regiment. "Koyosu Haizanhei Soto ni Kansuru Sento Shoho" [Battle Report about Mopping-up Operation of Straggling Soldiers on Chianghsingchou]. 14 December 1937. In *NSS*1, pp. 709–10.

1st Company of the 1st Tank Battalion. "Kodo Kiroku" [Campaign Record]. 14 December 1937. In *NSS*2, pp. 404–19.

3rd Field Chemical Weapon Experimenting Unit. "Ho-gun 3-ya-ka-ho dai-14-go: Kagaku-sen ni Kansuru Chosa Hokoku" [Area Army's Field Chemical Unit's Report No. 14]. 25 February 1938. RMD, 1938, No. 15. MHD.

Nanking Special Service. "Nankin-han Dai-2-ji Hokoku (2-gatsu Jokyo)" [Second Report by Nanking Team (Situation in February)]. Chinese translation. In *HP*, pp. 335–53.

————. Nankin-han Dai-3-ji Hokoku (3-gatsu Jokyo) [Third Report by Nanking Team (Situation in March)]. Chinese Translation. In *HP*, pp. 353–60.

ARCHIVAL MATERIALS IN CHINESE (1):
MILITARY RECORDS

Chiang, Kai-shek. To Ku Chu-tung, Liu Hsiang, and T'ang Sheng-chih. 30 November 1937. In *KCCC*, p. 400.

General Headquarters, Chinese Armed Forces. "Kuo-chun Tso-chan Chih-tao Chi-hua" [Directive for National Army's Operation Planning]. 20 August 1937. In *KCCC*, p. 5.

Hsu, Yuan-chuan to Chiang Kai-shek, 23 December 1937, in *KCCC*, p. 418.

Nanking Garrison Command. "Nanking Pao-wei-chan Chan-tou Hsiang-pao" [Battle Report about the Defense of Nanking]. In *KCCC*, pp. 405–16.

Sung, Hsi-lien. "Lu-chun Ti-78-chun Nanking Chih Yi Chan-tou Hsiang-pao" [Chinese 78th Army's Report on Battle of Nanking]. January 1938. In *KCCC*, pp. 419–26.

Wang, Yao-wu. "Ti-51-shih Chan-tou Hsiang-pao" [Battle Report of 51st Division]. In *KCCC*, pp. 426–29.

Yue, Chao. "Lu-chun Ti-66-chun Nanking T'u-wei Chan-tou Hsiang-pao" [66th Army's Battle Report on Its Escape from Nanking]. 4 July 1938. In *KCCC*, p. 436.

Yue, Chen-chung. "Lu-chun Ti-160-Shih Hsich'eng Nanking Liang-yi Chan-tou Hsiang-pao" [160th Division's Report on the Battles in Hsich'eng and Nanking]. April 1938. In *KCCC*, pp. 436–46.

ARCHIVAL MATERIALS IN CHINESE (2):
WAR CRIMES TRIALS

Chan-fan Ch'u-li Wei-yuan-hui [Committee for the Disposition of War Criminals]. "Chan-fan Ch'u-li Wei-yuan-hui Kuan-yu Sou-chi Nanking Ta-t'u-sha An Tzu-liao Tian Ti-12-tz'u Ch'ang-hui Chi-lu Chai-yao" [Extracts from the Minutes of the Twelfth Meeting of the Committee for the Disposition of War Criminals]. 29 January 1946. In *TA*, p. 523.

Ch'en, Che-wen. "Ch'en Che-wen Pan Jih-chun Shanghsinhe Chi-t'i T'u-sha Chih Shih Mei-yu Ch'eng-wen" [Ch'en Che-wen's Report to Shih Mei-yu on Japanese Aggressor Troops' Massacre in the Shanghsinhe Area]. 11 February 1947. In *TA*, p. 101.

Ch'en, Wan-lu. "Ch'en Wan-lu Te Chieh-wen" [Ch'en Wan-lu's Statement]. Compiled by Li Lung-fei. 1 October 1945. In *HP*, pp. 611–12.

Chi, Teng-chin. "Chi Teng-chin Pan Ch'i Mu Pei Jih-chun Sha-hai Chih Nanking-shih Cheng-fu Ch'eng-wen" [Chi Teng-jin's Report to the Nanking Municipal Government on Japanese Aggressor Troops' Murder of His Mother]. 20 September 1945. In *TA*, p. 157.

Chiang, Kai-shek. "Chiang Kai-shek P'i-chun P'an-ch'u Chan-fan Mukai Toshiaki Teng-jen Szu-hsing Chih Kuo-fang-pu Shen-p'an Chan-fan Chun-shi Fa-t'ing T'ing-ch'ang Shih Mei-yu Tien [Chiang Kai-shek's Telegram to Shi Mei-yu Approving printed the episode about the two lieutenants. There was, however, no publication about the two lieutenants until Suzuki wrote his book in the early 1970s to disprove their alleged crime. It seems that Shih, or a person who claimed to be Shih, confused the story of the two lieutenants with that of Tanaka Gunkichi, a Japanese army captain who was also tried and executed with the two lieutenants for the alleged slashing of 300 people—the story that did go into print in 1940. Memory error might have caused such confusion in his story, but it was also likely that this interviewee was actually not the former judge.[78]

Although the presence of those who seem to be dummy witnesses does not—or should not—affect the scholarly endeavor to seek the truth of the Rape of Nanking, it nevertheless is likely to compound the debate by reducing the credibility of evidence available from similar sources.

Westerners, Americans in particular, were the first to report the incident in the 1930s. Their research into this historical event since the end of World War II, however, has seen much less progress than that of the Japanese or even the Chinese. In the wake of the textbook crisis in 1982, *Newsweek* referred to the Rape of Nanking as atrocities characterized by the "slaughter of 200,000 to 300,000 Chinese *civilians* and raping, looting and arson by Japanese troops" [italics added]. That this account is quite primitive and does not describe the truth is obvious if one compares it even with Chinese versions. A Nationalist news source, quoting the IMTFE ruling, estimated the combined total of *both civilians and POWs* at no less than 200,000. Likewise, a communist source mentions 340,000 Chinese *POWs and civilians*. The Western media coverage thus tends to paint a more grisly image of the Rape of Nanking than even the Chinese do.[79]

Scholarly works have been more accurate, but have lacked original investigations into the question. Their explanations of the cause of the incident, for example, do not go beyond the theses presented in the 1930s, such as "a cold-calculated attempt to intimidate the Chinese into surrender," "punishment for the 'anti-Japanese,' " and the Japanese venting of their anger after the Chinese defense at Shanghai and Nanking.[80] Although a multitude of publications have offered varying estimates of the death toll, they all depend on earlier works to reach their conclusions, such as 20,000 POWs and 12,000 noncombatants from Smythe's report, 40,000 to 42,000 as reported by Bates and later adopted by Snow, the initial official Chinese Nationalist estimate of 100,000, a total of 200,000 civilians and POWs from the IMTFE evidence or traditionalist scholar Hora's publication, and 200,000 to 300,000 victims from either IMTFE, or secondary Japanese or Chinese sources. One of the few exceptions to such uncritical dependence on earlier works was Meirion and Susie Harries' *Soldiers of the Sun*. Relying partially on Smythe's statistics, the Harries concluded that 31,000 Chinese POWs and men of military age lost their lives, including 22,000 in the city area. The Harries also proposed a new theory regarding the cause of the Rape of Nanking. Quoting unidentified "analysts," they said that it was a part of Japan's deliberate policy to devastate and impoverish the Yangtze area so that the Japanese-controlled northern China area would supersede that area economically.[81]

The few Westerners who have paid attention to the Japanese revisionist and centrist positions have refused to accept them. In one instance of their inattention to the revisionist and centrist theses, Ian Johnson, an American writer, in a complete disregard of Hata's critical notes about the Japanese military and the revisionist stance, referred to Hata as a "right-wing Japanese historian."[82] As a result of their heavy reliance on Chinese and Japanese traditionalist publications, an overwhelming majority has come to view the Rape of Nanking as an atrocity of unprecedented scale. Consequently, some Westerners are simply overwhelmed by the stories and are unable to find a plausible explanation. The result is either to abandon any effort to analyze the incident or to find a similar event in modern history for explanatory purposes. An example of the first case is a remark made by Jonathan D. Spence: "There is no obvious explanation for this grim event nor perhaps can one be found."[83] Those who choose to adopt the second method are most likely to compare the Rape of Nanking to the Nazi Holocaust and try to establish a parallel between Nazism and Japanese militarism. Such reasoning compels some Westerners to search for a deliberate Japanese plan behind the Rape of Nanking. At an Internet web site, one can find the following remarks posted by American citizens:

Why did the Japanese kill over 300,000 Chinese during a six week period Dec. 1937 to January 1938? Certainly, their leaders must have discussed alternatives.[84]

The Japanese killed millions of Chinese for racial purification. . . . The Japanese fought a war of aggression, based on theories of racial and ethnic purity.[85]

This recent tendency is strongest in the Chinese-American community. Wu Tienwei, a professor emeritus at Southern Illinois University, said, "In terms of measures and cruelty of the genocide, its duration and large numbers of people killed, neither the Hiroshima atomic bombing nor the Jewish Holocaust can rival the Nanking Massacre."[86] It is against such a background that the titles of some recent journal articles and publications about the Rape of Nanking include "Holocaust."

NANKING AND THE HOLOCAUST: HISTORIOGRAPHICAL ANALYSIS

One of the first uses of the word "holocaust" to describe the Japanese military conduct in China was in Madame Chiang's speech in Wuchang on March 20, 1938, in which she used the phrase "holocaust in China."[87] Judging from this date—well before the "crystal night" later in the same year in Germany—and the uncapitalized first letter in "holocaust," it is apparent that she did not try to the Judgement to Sentence Mukai Toshiaki et al. to Death]. 26 January 1948. In *TA*, p. 621.

Chou, Yi-yu. "Ch'ung-shan-t'ang Tang-chang Chou Yi-yu Ch'ing-ch'iu Pu-chu Ching-fei Chih Jih-Chiang-su-sheng Chen-wu Wei-yuan-hui Ch'eng-wen Chi- lu" [Chou Yi-yu's Report to the Chiangsu Relief Commission, Reformed Government Requesting Subsidy]. 6 December 1938. In *TA*, p. 426.

Chung-kuo Chu-jih Tai-piao-t'uan [Chinese Delegation in Japan]. "Chung-kuo Chu-jih Tai-piao-t'uan Kuan-yu Chan-fan Tanaka Gunkichi Tai-pu Ching-kuo Chih Kuo-fang-pu 2-ting Tai-tien" [Dispatch from the Chinese Delegation in Japan to the Ministry of National Defense Second Department Concerning the Arrest of Tanaka Gunkichi]. 9 June 1947. In *TA*, pp. 614–15.

Chung-kuo Hung-shih-tzu-hui Nanking Fen-hui [Chinese Red Cross, Nanking Office]. "Chung-kuo Hung-shih-tzu-hui Nanking Fen-hui Yen-mai-tui Ti-1-tui An-yueh T'ung-chi-piao" [Monthly Statistics Regarding the Burial Activities Undertaken by the First Burial Team of the Nanking Office of the Chinese Red Cross]. January–May 1938. In *TA*, pp. 440–45.

————. "Chung-kuo Hung-shih-tzu-hui Nanking Fen-hui Yen-mai-tui Ti-2-tui An-yueh T'ung-chi-piao" [Monthly Statistics Regarding the Burial Activities Undertaken by the Second Burial Team of the Nanking Office of the Chinese Red Cross]. January–May 1938. In *TA*, pp. 446–49.

Ch'ung-shan-t'ang. "Nanking-shih Ch'ung-shan-t'ang Yen-mai Kung-tso Yi-lan-piao" [Working List of the Nanking Ch'ung-shan-t'ang's Burying Team]. In *TA*, pp. 423–25.

Hsiak'uan Ching-ch'a-chu [Hsiak'uan Police Station]. "Hsiak'uan Ching-ch'a-chu Tiao-ch'a Jih-chun Yuleiying Chi-t'i T'u-sha Chun-min Chih Shou-tu Ti- fang Fa-yuan Chien-ch'a-ch'u Kung-han" [Hsiak'uan Police Station's Official Letter to the Nanking Local Court Prosecution's Office Concerning the Investigation of Japanese Aggressor Troops' Massacre at Yuleiying]. 8 January 1946. In *TA*, pp. 108–09.

————. "Hsiak'uan Ching-ch'a-chu Tiao-ch'a Jih-chun Tsai Yen-chiang-pian I-t'i Chi-t'i T'u-sha Chun-min Kei Shou-tu Ti-fang Chien-ch'a-ch'u Te Kung-han" [Hsiak'uan Police Station's Official Letter Concerning Japanese Aggressor Troops' Massacre of Military and Civilian Personnel on the River Shore to Nanking District Attorney's Office]. 8 January 1946. In *HP*, p. 403.

Hsu, Chia-lu. "Hsu Chia-lu Pan Jih-chun Tsai Tafanghsiang Kuang-yang Ta-t'u-sha Shih Chih Nanking-shih Cheng-fu Ch'eng-wen" [Hsu Chia-lu's Report to the Nanking Municipal Government on the Massacre at the Tafanghsiang Square]. 14 October 1945. In *TA*, pp. 85–86.

Kuo-fang-pu [Defense Ministry]. "Kuo-fang-pu Shen-p'an Chan-fan Chun-shih Fa-t'ing Kuan-yu Tiao-ch'a Chan-fan Tani Hisao Tsui-cheng Te Pu-gao [Public Notice Issued by the Military Tribunal for the War Criminals of the Ministry of National Defense Concerning the Investigation of Tani Hisao's Crimes]. 28 October 1946. In *TA*, p. 550.

————. "Kuo-fang-pu Shen-p'an Chan-fan Chun-shih Fa-t'ing Chien-ch'a-kuan Chiu Tui Chan-fan Tani Hisao Te Ch'i-su-chuang" [The Prosecution's indictment against Tani Hisao at the Military Tribunal for War Criminals]. 31 December 1946. In *HP*, pp. 717–22.

————. "Tani Hisao Chan-fan An-chien Ch'i-su-chuang Chih Fu-chien" [Appendix to

Indictment of War Criminal Tani Hisao]. 31 December 1946. In *HP*, pp. 722–42.

———."Shen-p'an Chan-fan Chun-shih Fa-t'ing Chien-ch'a-kuan Ch'en Kuang-yu Tui Chan-fan Tani Hisao Kung-su-tz'u" [Public Prosecution Statement by Ch'en Kuang-yu of Tani Hisao at the Military Tribunal for War Criminals]. 8 February 1947. In *HP*, p. 743.

———."Kuo-fang-pu Shen-p'an Chan-fan Chun-shih Fa-t'ing Kuan-yu Tui Chan-fan Tani Hisao Te P'an-chueh" [Judgement of the Defense Ministry's Military Tribunal for War Criminals on Tani Hisao]. 10 March 1947. In *HP*, pp. 744–53.

———."Tani Hisao Chan-fan An P'an-chueh-chuang Fu-chien Kuan-yu Chi-t'I T'u- sha Pu-fen T'ung-chi Chi-lu" [Record of Massacres Attached to the Verdict on Tani Hisao's Case at the Military Tribunal]. n.d. 1947. In *HP*, pp. 753–56.

———. "Tani Hisao Chan-fan An P'an-chueh-shu Fu-chien T'ung-chi Chi-lu" [Statistical Records Attached to Verdict on War Criminal Tani Hisao]. n.d. 1947. In *HP*, pp. 757–827.

———. "Kuo-fang-pu Shen-p'an Chan-fan Chun-shih Fa-t'ing Chien-ch'a-kuan Tui Chan-fan Mukai Toshiaki Teng-jen Te Ch'i-su-chuang" [Indictment of the Prosecutor of the Military Tribunal for War Criminals to Mukai Toshiaki et al.]. 4 December 1947. In *TA*, pp. 615–16.

———. "Kuo-fang-pu Shen-p'an Chan-fan Chun-shih Fa-t'ing Chien-ch'a-kuan Tui Chanfan Mukai Toshiaki Tengjen Te P'anchuehchuang" [Judgement of the Military Tribunal for War Criminals on Mukai Toshiaki et al.]. 18 December 1947. In *TA*, pp. 617–21.

Kuo-min Cheng-fu [Nationalist Government]. "Nanking Ta-t'u-sha Shi-chien Pei-hai Jen-min Hsiang-piao" [Table of Rape of Nanking Individual Victims]. In "Kuo-min Cheng-fu Chu-hsi Hsiang-yuan Mi-shu-ch'u Chih Szu-fa Hsing-cheng-pu Han" [Correspondence from the Secretary's office of the National Government's General Secretary to the Ministry of Justice]. 17 January 1946. In *HP*, pp. 485–507.

———. "1943–1944 nien Kuo-min Cheng-fu Ti-jen Tsui-hsing Tiao-ch'a Wei-yuan-hui Te Tiao-ch'a" [Nationalist Government Investigation of the Enemy's Criminal Acts in 1943–44]. In *HP*, pp. 371–77.

———. "Kuo-min Cheng-fu Szu-fa Hsing-cheng-pu Kuan-yu Jih-chun Tsai Nanking Ta-t'u-sha Ti Chan-tsui Shen-ch'a-piao" [Investigation Report by Nationalist Government's Justice Ministry Concerning Japanese Troops' War Crimes Relating to the Rape of Nanking]. n.d. 1946. In *HP*, pp. 534–49.

Kuo-min Cheng-fu Chun-shih Wei-yuan-hui Chun-shih Pien-tsuan Wei-yuan-hui [Military History Compilation Committee, Nationalist Government's Military Affairs Committee], ed. *Sunghu K'ang-chan* [Resistance War in Sunghu: Siege Battle of Nanking]. n.p., 1938. In *HP*, pp. 41–61.

Kuo-min Cheng-fu T'e-kung Jen-yuan [Special agent of the Nationalist Government]. "Kuo-min Cheng-fu T'e-kung Jen-yuan Chiu Jih-chun Ta-t'u-sha Shih Kei K'ung Ling-k'an Te Chi-lu" [Intelligence Sent by the Special Agent of the Nationalist Government to K'ung Ling-k'an Concerning Japanese Aggressor Troops' Massacre]. 7 March 1938. In *TA*, p. 51.

Li, Lung-fei. "Jih-chun Tsai Yentzuchi Chi-t'i T'u-sha Te Ch'ung-sha-piao Chi-lu [Finding Report on Japanese Aggressor Troops' Massacre at Yentzuchi]. 1 October 1945. In *TA*, p. 102.

Lu, Su. "Lu Su Ch'en-shu Jih-chun Tsai Ts'ao-hsieh-hsia Chi-t'i T'u-sha Te Chieh-wen"

[Lu Su's Statement on Japanese Aggressor Troops' Massacre at Ts'ao-hsieh-hsia]. Compiled by Chen Kuang-ching. 7 December 1945. In *TA*, p. 55.

Lung, Yu-chih. "Lung Yu-chih Pei Jih-chun Ch'ung-sha Te Chi-lu" [Finding Report on Lung Yu-chih's Murder by Japanese Aggressor Troops]. Compiled by Ting Ch'ao. 31 July 1946. In *TA*, pp. 254–55.

Nanking-shih Cheng-fu [Nanking Municipal Government], ed. "Ti-jen Tui Yu Nanking Hui-huai Chi Ch'i Pao-hsing I-pan" [A Glimpse at Enemy's Destructive and Violent Activities in Nanking]. 26 January 1946. In *HP*, pp. 460–63.

———. "Nanking-shih Cheng-fu Kuan-yu Jen-k'ou Shang-wang Shu-tzu Chih Nei-cheng-pu K'ang-chan Sun-shih Tiao-ch'a Wei-yuan-hui Tai-tien Kao" [Dispatch of the Nanking Municipal Government to the Committee for the Investigation of War Damages of the Ministry of Interior Concerning the Figures of Nanking Massacre Victims]. 4 May 1946. In *TA*, pp. 523–34.

Nanking-shih Lin-shih Ts'an-i-hui [Nanking Municipal Interim Council]. "Nanking-shih Lin-shih Ts'an-i-hui Kuan-yu Pu-chu Tiao-ch'a Nanking Ta-t'u-sha An Chingkuo Kai-shu" [Nanking Municipal Interim Council's Brief Account about Its Investigation of the Nanking Massacre]. November 1946. In *TA*, p. 555.

———. "Nanking-shih Lin-shih Ts'an-i-hui Chiao Chung K'e Ch'en-shu Jih-chun Tsai Hanhsi-men Chi-t'i T'u-sha Ch'eng-wen Chih Nei-cheng-pu Han [Message from the Nanking Municipal Interim Council to the Ministry of Interior Containing Chung K'e's Statement on Japanese Aggressor Troops' Massacre at Hanhsi Gate]. 2 November 1946. In *TA*, pp. 66–70.

Nanking Shou-tu Ti-fang Fa-yuan [Capital City District Attorneys' Office]. "Nanking Shou-tu Ti-fang Fa-yuan Chien-ch'a-ch'u Feng-ling Tiao-ch'a Ti-jen Tsui- hsing Pao-kao-shu [Report by the Capital City District Attorneys' Office of Nanking about the Enemy's Criminal Acts]. February 1946. In *HP*, pp. 404–10.

———. Ti-jen Tsui-hsing Tiao-ch'a T'ung-chi-piao [Statistical Table about Enemy's Criminal Acts]. February 1946. In *HP*, pp. 408–09.

———. "Nanking Tz'u-shan Chi-ch'uan Chi Jen-min Lu Su Teng Pao-kao Ti-jen Ta-t'u-sha Kai-k'uang T'ung-chi-piao" [Statistical Data Based on Reports by Charity Organizations in Nanking and Citizen Lu Su about the Massacre]. n.d. In *TA*, p. 553.

———. "Shou-tu Ti-fang Fa-yuan Chien-ch'a-ch'u Wei-sung Tani An-nei Pei-hai-jen I-hai Chien-ting-shu Chih Kuo-fang-pu Shen-p'an Chan-fan Chun-shih Fa-t'ing Kung-han" [Official Letter from the Nanking Local Court Prosecutorate to the Military Tribunal for War Criminals Presenting the Identification of Murder Victims]. 5 February 1947. In *TA*, pp. 599–601.

Nanking Ta-t'u-sha An Ti-jen Tsui-hsing Tiao-ch'a Wei-yuan-hui [Committee for the Investigation of the Nanking Massacre]. "Nanking Ta-t'u-sha An Ti-jen Tsui-hsing Tiao-ch'a Wei-yuan-hui Ti-1-tz'u Hui-i Chil-u" [Minutes of the First Meeting of the Committee for the Investigation of the Nanking Massacre]. 23 June 1946. In *TA*, pp. 534–36.

Ota, Toshio. Ota Toshio Pi-kung [Written Confession of Ota Toshio]. 3 August 1954. In *HP*, pp. 855–68.

Sheng, Shih-cheng et al. "Sheng Shih-cheng Teng Jih-chun Tsai Shang-hsin-he Ti-ch'u Ta-t'u-sha Chih Nanking-shih K'ang-chan Sun-shih Tiao-ch'a Wei-yuan-hui Ch'eng-wen [Sheng Shih-cheng et al.'s Report to the Nanking Committee for the

Investigation of War Damages on Japanese Aggressor Troops Massacre in the Shanghsinhe Area]. 9 January 1946. In *TA*, pp. 100–01.

Shih-chieh Hung-wan-tzu-hui Nanking Fen-hui [Red Swastika Society]. "Shih-chieh Hung-wan-tzu-hui Nanking Fen-hui Chiu-chi-tui Yen-mai-tsu Yen-mai Shih-t'i Chu-shu T'ung-chi-piao" [Statistics Regarding Bodies Buried by the Burying Group of the Nanking Office of the Red Swastika Society]. In *TA*, pp. 431–35.

———. "Shih-chieh Hung-wan-tzu-hui Nanking Fen-hui Ch'ing-ch'iu Yuan-k'uan Yuan-ch'e Yun-shih Chih Jih-Nanking-shih Tzu-chih Wei-yuan-hui Han" [Message from the Nanking Office of the World Red Swastika Society to the Nanking Self-Government Committee Requesting Appropriation of Funds and Cars for the Transportation of Bodies]. 4 April 1938. In *TA*, p. 436.

———. "Shih-chieh Hung-wan-tzu-hui Nanking Fen-hui Ch'ing-ch'iu Yuan-chu Chen-k'uan Chih Jih-Hsing-cheng-yuan Ch'eng-wen" [Report of the Nanking Office of the World Red Swastika Society to the Executive Yuan, Nanking Reformed Government, Requesting Appropriation of Relief Funds]. 14 October 1938. In *TA*, pp. 437–38.

Shu, Teng-fu. "Chang-sheng Tz'u-shan-hui Chu-hsi Shu Teng-fu Ch'ing-ch'iu Yuan-k'uan Pu-chu Chih Tu-pan Nanking Shih-cheng Kung-shu Ch'eng-wen" [Shu Teng-fu's Report to the Nanking Municipality Administration Requesting Relief Funds]. 21 January 1939. In *TA*, p. 457.

Wu, Chang-te. "Wu Chang-te Ch'en-shu Jih-chun Tsai Hanchung-men Chi-t'i T'u-sha Te Chieh-wen" [Wu Chang-te's Statement on the Massacre at Hanchung Gate]. 1 November 1945. In *TA*, p. 62.

Wu, Chia-kan. "Nanking-shih Ti-7-ch'u Ch'u-ch'ang Wu Chia-kan Chih Nanking-shih Cheng-fu Ch'eng-wen [Statement Submitted to the Nanking Municipal Government by Nanking 7th Ward Chief Wu Chia-kan]. 20 May 1946. In *HP*, pp. 470–74.

Yu, Chung-to and Yu Chu-shih. "Yu Chung-to Yu Chu-shih Pan Ch'i Tzu Tsai Tafanghsiang Pei Chi-t'i T'u-sha Chih Shou-tu Ti-fang Fa-yuan Ch'eng-wen" [Report by Yu Chung-to and Yu Chu-shih to the Nanking Local Court on Their Son's Murder at Tafanghsiang by Japanese Aggressor Troops]. 29 March 1946. In *TA*, pp. 87–88.

DIARIES AND PRIVATE TESTIMONIES

Anami, Korechika, Commander, 11th Army. Quoted in Katogawa Kotaro, "Shogen ni yoru Nankin Senshi: Sono Sokatsuteki Kosatsu" [Nanking Campaign Chronology Based on Eyewitness Accounts: Concluding Remark], *Kaiko*, March 1985, p. 13.

Aratsuma, Tomio, Private Upper Class, 65th Regiment, 7th Company. In *NDKK*, pp. 178–81.

Araumi, Kiyoe, Private Upper Class, 65th Regiment. In *NSS2*, pp. 342–46.

Azuma, Shiro, Private Upper Class, 20th Regiment. In *KS*, pp. 173–316.

Chao, Shih-fa, Private Second Class, Chinese 88th Division. In *NEM*, pp. 223–28.

Endo, Jutaro, Private, 65th Regiment, 1st Battalion. In *NDKK*, pp. 88–95.

Endo, Takaaki, Sublieutenant, 65th Regiment, 8th Company. In *NDKK*, pp. 212–29.

Fitch, George A., Secretary of the Nanking chapter of the Young Men's Christian Association. Diary enclosed in Frank W. Price to Maxwell M. Hamilton. 17 February

1938. 793.94/12548. M976-51. George A. Fitch. *My Eighty Years in China*, pp. 430–52. Taipei: Mei Ya Publications, 1967.

Fujita, Kiyoshi, Sergeant, Independent Second Light Armored Vehicle Company. In "Shogen ni yoru 'Nankin Senshi' " ["Nanking Campaign Chronology" Based on Eyewitness Accounts] ("SNS") (2), *Kaiko*, May 1984, p. 14.

Fukumoto, Tsuzumi, Private Upper Class, 45th Regiment. In *NSS*2, pp. 385–86.

Hashimoto, Mochiyuki, Lieutenant, Imperial Japanese Navy. In "SNS" (10), *Kaiko*, January 1985, p. 30.

Hatayama, Hiromichi, Colonel, Navy's Medical Unit. "Shanhai-sen Jugun Nisshi" [Diary of Shanghai Battle]. In *NSS*1, pp. 525–32.

Hata, Shunroku, Army's Superintendant of Education. *Zoku Gendaishi-shiryo* [Source Materials of Modern History: Second Series]. Vol. 4, *Rikugun* [Army], ed. Ito Takashi, pp. 120–27. Tokyo: Misuzu Shobo, 1983.

Hayashi, Masaaki, Corporal, 20th Regiment. *NSS*1, pp. 516–20.

Hirai, Akio, Commander, 33rd Regiment's Communication Unit. In "SNS" (9), *Kaiko*, December 1984, p. 6.

Honma, Masakatsu, Private Second Class, 65th Regiment, 9th Company. In *NDKK*, pp. 232–44.

Horikoshi, Fumio, Corporal, 65th Regiment. In *NDKK*, pp. 58–85.

Iinuma, Mamoru, Major General, SEF Staff Chief. In *NSS*1, pp. 64–252.

Inoie, Mataichi, Private Upper Class, 7th Regiment. In *NSS*1, pp. 471–81.

Inoue Unit (the 12th Company, the 3rd Battalion under the 20th Regiment), comp. "Ichu ni Saishi Jugo ni Kotau" [Response to Home Front on the Occasion of Transfer and Homecoming]. 1 July 1939. In *KS*, pp. 421–39.

Isa, Kazuo, Colonel, 7th Regiment Commander. *NSS*1, pp. 439–42.

Ishii, Itaro, Director, European and Asian Affairs Bureau, Foreign Ministry. Ishii Itaro. *Ishii Itaro Nikki* [Diary of Ishii Itaro]. Edited by Ito Takashi. Tokyo: Chuo Koronsha, 1993.

Ishimatsu, Masatoshi, Adjutant of the 2nd Field Anti-Aircraft Artillery Unit. In "SNS" (11) *Kaiko*, February 1985, pp. 9–10.

Ito, Kihachi, Private Upper Class, 65th Regiment. In *NDKK*, pp. 98–111.

Kajiya, Takeo, Sergeant, Second Port Authorities Headquarters. In *NSS*2, pp. 428–38.

Kanemaru, Yoshio, Sergeant, 16th Division. In *NSS*1, pp. 361–65.

Kawabe, Torashiro, "Kawabe Torashiro Shosho Otoroku" [Interview with Major-General Kawabe Torashiro]. Interview by Prince Takeda Tsunenori (Tokyo, 1940). In *Gendaishi Shiryo* [Source Materials of Modern History]. Vol. 12, *Nitchu-Senso* [Sino-Japanese War]. Part 4, ed. Kobayashi Tatsuo, pp. 401–56. Tokyo: Misuzu-shobo, 1965.

Kisaki, Hisashi, Lieutenant Colonel, 16th Division Staff. In *NSS*1, pp. 415–35.

Kitaoka, Chieko, widow of Mukai Toshiaki. Quoted in Suzuki Akira. *Nankin Daigyaku-satsu no Maboroshi* [Illusion of the Rape of Nanking], p. 66. Tokyo: Bunge-ishunju, 1973.

Kitayama, Atau, Private, 20th Regiment. In *KS*, pp. 41–80.

Kondo, Eishiro, Corporal, 19th Mountain Artillery Regiment. In *NDKK*, pp. 312–33.

Kurosu, Tadanobu, Private Upper Class, 19th Mountain Artillery Regiment, 3rd Battalion. In *NDKK*, pp. 336–58.

Liu, Szu-hai, Private Second Class, Chinese 87th Division. In *NEM*, pp. 220–22.

Maeda, Yoshihiko, Sublieutenant, 45th Regiment. In *NSS*1, pp. 453–68.

Makihara, Nobuo, Private Upper Class, 20th Regiment. In *KS*, pp. 89–165.

Masuda, Rokusuke, Corporal, 20th Regiment. In *NSS*1, pp. 521–22; *KS*, pp. 5–12.

Matsui, Iwane, General, SEF Commander, later CCAA Commander. In *NSS*2, pp. 3–182.

———. "Seinan Yuki" [Record of Travel to Southwest]. 2 February to 20 March 1936. In Tanaka, ed. *Matsui Iwane Taisho no Jinchu Nisshi* [Field Diary of General Matsui Iwane], pp. 219–57.

Matsukawa, Seisaku, Private Upper Class, 1st Railway Regiment. In "SNS" (11), *Kaiko*, February 1985, p. 10.

Meguro, Tomiharu, Corporal, 19th Mountain Artillery Regiment, 3rd Battalion. In *NDKK*, pp. 360–74.

Miyamoto, Shiro, Lieutenant Colonel, Adjutant, 16th Division. In "SNS" (8), *Kaiko*, November 1984, p. 8.

Miyamoto, Shogo, Sublieutenant, 65th Regiment, 4th Company. In *NDKK*, pp. 124–40.

Mizutani, So, Private First Class, 7th Regiment. "Senjin" [Battle Dust]. In *NSS*1, pp. 499–505.

Mori, Hideo, Lieutenant, 3rd Company, 20th Regiment. In "SNS" (8), *Kaiko*, November 1984, p. 5.

Morozumi, Gyosaku, Colonel, 65th Regiment Commander. In *NSS*2, pp. 339–41.

N.Y. (Anonymous), Private First Class, 7th Regiment. "Shonenhei no Shuki: Shoen no Aima nite" [Memoirs of First-Year Soldier: In the Interval of Gun Smokes]. In *NSS*1, pp. 485–97.

Nakajima, Kesago, Lieutenant General, 16th Division Commander. In *NSS*1, pp. 306–57.

Nakano, Masao, Private Upper Class, 65th Regiment. In *NDKK*, pp. 114–21.

Naritomo, Fujio, Lieutenant Colonel, Commander, 2nd Battalion, 45th Regiment. In "SNS" (6), *Kaiko*, September 1984, p. 8.

Oda, Mamoru, Sublieutenant, 23rd Regiment. In *NSS*1, pp. 447–49.

Odera, Takashi, Private Upper Class, 65th Regiment. In *NSS*2, pp. 347–51.

Onishi, Hajime, Major, SEF Staff Officer. In "SNS" (8), *Kaiko*, November 1984, p. 9.

Orikono, Suetaro, Major, 23rd Regiment. In *NSS*1, pp. 443–46.

Rabe, John H.D. *Nankin no Shinjitsu* [The Truth of Nanking]: *The Diary of John Rabe.* Edited by Erwin Wickert. Translated into Japanese by Hirano Kyoko. Tokyo: Kodansha, 1997.

Saito, Jiro, Private, 65th Regiment. In *NDKK*, pp. 4–55.

Sakakibara, Kazue, Lieutenant Colonel, Accounting Staff, SEF. In "SNS" (11) *Kaiko*, February 1985, p. 8.

Sasaki, Toichi, Major General, 30th Brigade Commander. In *NSS*1, pp. 371–82.

———. Interview by Suzuki Akira, n.d. In Suzuki Akira. *Nankin Daigyakusatsu no Maboroshi* [Illusion of the Rape of Nanking], pp. 190–97. Tokyo: Bungeishunju, 1973.

Sawada, Masahisa, Lieutenant, Commander, Observation Unit, 1st Company, Independent Second Siege Heavy Artillery Battalion. In "SNS" (5), *Kaiko*, August 1984, p. 7.

Seki, Hiroshi, Private, Independent 9th Machine Gun Battalion. Owned by Seki Naohiro.

Shen, Hsi-en, Resident in Nanking. In *NEM*, pp. 322–30.

Shimada, Katsumi, Major, Machine-gun Company, 33rd Regiment. In "SNS" (9) *Kaiko*, December 1984, p. 5.

Sugano, Yoshio, Private First Class, 65th Regiment, Artillery Company. In *NDKK*, pp. 298–310.

Sugawara, Shigetoshi, Sublieutenant, 36th Regiment. In *NSS2*, pp. 355–77.

Sumita, Masao, Platoon Commander, 38th Regiment. In "SNS" (5), *Kaiko*, August 1984, p. 6.

Takahashi, Mitsuo, Private Upper Class, 65th Regiment, 11th Company. In *NDKK*, pp. 282–96.

Takahashi, Yoshihiko, Lieutenant attached to the command of the Japanese Independent 2nd Mountain Artillery Regiment. In "SNS" (6), *Kaiko*, September 1984, p. 10.

T'ang, Kung-pu, errand boy, Chinese Training Unit. In *NEM*, pp. 284–94.

———. Testimony made in March 1984. In *HP*, pp. 902–04.

Tani, Hisao. "Tani Hisao Chujo no Shinbensho" [Statement by Lieutenant General Tani Hisao]. 15 January 1947. Quoted in Suzuki Akira. *Nankin Daigyakusatsu no Maboroshi* [Illusion of the Rape of Nanking], pp. 130–341. Tokyo: Bungeishunju, 1973.

Tsuchiya, Masaharu, Lieutenant, Commander 4th Company, 19th Regiment. In "SNS" (7), *Kaiko*, October 1984, p. 6.

Tsutsumi, Chisato, Sublieutenant, Adjutant, 2nd Battalion, 33rd Regiment. In "SNS" (9), *Kaiko*, December 1984, p. 6.

Ueba, Buichiro, Medic, 16th Division. In *KS*, pp. 17–35.

Uemura, Toshimichi, Colonel, SEF Deputy Staff Chief. In *NSS1*, pp. 263–301.

Wu, Chang-te, policeman, Nanking. In *NEM*, pp. 276–84.

Yaginuma, Kazuya, Private Upper Class, 65th Regiment, 7th Company. In *NDKK*, pp. 154–76.

Yamada, Senji, Major General, Commander, 103rd Brigade. In *NSS2*, pp. 285–338.

———. Interview by Suzuki Akira. Suzuki Akira. *Nankin Daigyakusatsu no Maboroshi* [Illusion of the Rape of Nanking], pp. 190–97. Tokyo: Bungeishunju, 1973.

Yamazaki, Masao, Lieutenant Colonel, 10th Army Staff. In *NSS1*, pp. 385–412.

SECONDARY SOURCES: (A) ENGLISH

Abend, Hallett Edward. *Chaos in Asia*. New York: Ives Washburn, 1939.

———. *Ramparts of the Pacific*. Garden City, NY: Doubleday, Doran & Co., 1942.

———. *My Life in China 1926–1941*. New York: Harcourt, Brace & Co., 1943.

Adair, John. "The Court Martial Papers of Sir William Waller's Army, 1644." *Journal of the Society for Army Historical Research* 44 (1966): pp. 205–26.

Allmand, C. T. "The War and the Non-combatant." In *The Hundred Years War*, ed. Kenneth Alan Fowler, pp. 163–83. London: MacMillan, 1971.

Ambrose, Stephen E. "Ike and Disappearing Atrocities." *New York Times Book Review*, 24 February 1991, pp. 1, 35–37.

Anderson, C. Arnold. "The Utility of the Proposed Trial and Punishment of Enemy Leaders." *American Political Science Review* (37–6) December 1943: pp. 1,081–100.

Anderson, Flavia Gifford. *The Rebel Emperor*. London: Victor Gollancz, 1958.

App, Austin J. *The Six Million Swindle: Blackmailing the German People for Hard Marks with Fabricated Corpses*. Takoma Park, MD: Boniface Press, 1973.

Bacque, James. *Other losses: An Investigation into the Mass Deaths of German Prisoners at the Hands of the French and Americans after World War II*. Toronto: Stoddart, 1989.

————. *Crimes and Mercies: The Fate of German Civilians under Allied Occupation, 1944–1950*. Toronto: Little, Brown, 1997.

Baker, Kevin. "The Rape of Nanking." *Contemporary Review* (September 1995): pp. 124–28.

Barnett, Robert W. *China—America's Ally*. Far Eastern Pamphlet No. 5. New York: American Council Institute of Pacific Relations, 1942.

Bauer, Yehuda. "The Place of the Holocaust in Contemporary History." In *Holocaust: Religious and Philosophical Implications*, ed. John K. Roth and Michael Berenbaum, pp. 16–42. New York: Paragon House, 1989.

Becker, George J., ed. and trans. *Paris under Siege, 1870–1871: From the Goncourt Journal*. Ithaca: Cornell University Press, 1969.

Bergamini, David. *Japan's Imperial Conspiracy*. New York: William Morrow and Co., 1971.

Berkov, Robert. *Strong Man of China: The Story of Chiang Kai-shek*. Boston: Houghton Mifflin, 1938.

Best, Geoffrey. *Humanity in Warfare*. New York: Columbia University Press, 1980.

Blewett, George F. "Victor's Injustice: The Tokyo War Crimes Trial." *American Perspective*, Summer 1955: pp. 282–92.

Borg, Dorothy. *The United States and the Far Eastern Crisis of 1933–1938: From the Manchurian Incident through the Initial Stage of the Undeclared Sino-Japan War*. Cambridge, MA: Harvard University Press, 1964.

Borg, Dorothy and Okamoto Shumpei, ed. *Pearl Harbor as History: Japanese-American Relations 1931–1941*. New York: Columbia University Press, 1973.

Borton, Hugh. *Japan's Modern Century*. New York: Ronald Press, 1955.

Brackman, Arnold C. *The Other Nuremberg: The Untold Story of the Tokyo War Crimes Trials*. New York: William Morrow, 1987.

Brodie, Bernard and Fawn M. Brodie. *From Crossbow to H-Bomb*. Bloomington: Indiana University Press, 1973.

Brownlee, Richard S. *Gray Ghosts of the Confederacy: Guerrilla Warfare in the West, 1861–1865*. Baton Rouge: Louisiana State University Press, 1984.

Buchan, John. *A History of the Great War*. Vol. 2. Boston: Houghton Mifflin, 1923.

Buck, Pearl S. "Western Weapons in the Hands of the Reckless East." *Asia* (October 1937): pp. 672–73.

Burke, James. "The New Model Army and the Problems of Siege Warfare, 1648–51." *Irish Historical Studies* 105 (May 1990): pp. 1–29.

Butow, Robert J. C. *Tojo and the Coming of the War*. Stanford: Stanford University Press, 1961.

Butz, Arthur R. *The Hoax of the Twentieth Century*. Torrance, CA: Institute for Historical Review, 1976.

Carlson, Evans Fordyce. *The Chinese Army: Its Organization and Military Efficiency*. New York: Institute of Pacific Relations, 1940.

Castel, Albert. *A Frontier State at War: Kansas, 1861–1865*. Westport, CT: Greenwood Press, 1979.

Cecil, Hugh and Peter H. Liddle, ed. *Facing Armageddon: The First World War Experienced*. London: Leo Cooper, 1996.

Chang, Iris. *The Rape of Nanking: The Forgotten Holocaust of World War II*. New York: BasicBooks, 1997.

———. "Exposing the Rape of Nanking." *Newsweek*, 1 December 1997, pp. 55–57.

Ch'i, Hsi-Sheng. *Nationalist China at War: Military Defeats and Political Collapse, 1937–45*. Ann Arbor: University of Michigan Press, 1982.

Chiang, Kai-shek. *Resistance and Reconstruction: Messages during China's Six Years of War 1937–1943*. New York: Harper & Brothers, 1943.

Chinese Ministry of Information, comp. *China Handbook 1937–1943: A Comprehensive Survey of Major Developments in China in Six Years of War*. New York: Macmillan, 1943.

Clark, Ian. *Waging War: A Philosophical Introduction*. Oxford: Clarendon Press, 1988.

Coble, Parks M. *Facing Japan: Chinese Politics and Japanese Imperialism, 1931–1937*. Cambridge, MA: Council on East Asian Studies, Harvard University, 1991.

Creveld, Martin van. *Supplying War: Logistics from Wallenstein to Patton*. Cambridge: Cambridge University Press, 1977.

Crowley, James B. *Japan's Quest for Autonomy: National Security and Foreign Policy, 1930–1938*. Princeton, NJ: Princeton University Press, 1966.

Czech, Danuta. *Auschwitz Chronicle 1939–1945*. New York: Henry Holt, 1990.

Dadrian, Vahakn N. *The History of the Armenian Genocide: Ethnic Conflict from the Balkans to Anatolia to the Caucasus*. Providence, RI: Berghahn Books, 1995.

Dallin, Alexander. *German Rule in Russia 1941–1945: A Study of Occupation Policies*. London: Macmillan & Co., 1957.

Dawidowicz, Lucy S. "Lies about the Holocaust." *Commentary* (December 1980): pp. 31–37.

———. "Thinking about the Six Million: Facts, Figures, Perspective." In *Holocaust: Religious and Philosophical Implications*, ed. John K. Roth and Michael Berenbaum, pp. 51–68. New York: Paragon House, 1989.

Derez, Mark. "The Flames of Louvain: The War Experience of an Academic Community." In *Facing Armageddon: The First World War Experienced*, ed. Hugh Cecil and Peter H. Liddle, pp. 617–29. London: Leo Cooper, 1996.

Dorn, Frank. *The Sino-Japanese War, 1937–41: From Marco Polo Bridge to Pearl Harbor*. New York: Macmillan, 1974.

Dower, John W. *War without Mercy: Race and Power in the Pacific War*. New York: Pantheon Books, 1986.

Dreyer, Edward L. *China at War, 1901–1949*. New York: Longman, 1995.

Duffy, Christopher. *Siege Warfare: The Fortress in the Early Modern World 1494–1660*. London: Routledge & Kegan Paul, 1979.

Eastman, Lloyd E. *Seeds of Destruction: Nationalist China in War and Revolution 1937–1949*. Stanford: Stanford University Press, 1984.

———. "Nationalist China during the Sino-Japanese War 1937–1945" In *The Cambridge History of China*. Vol. 13, *Republican China 1912–1949*. Part 2, ed. John K. Fairbank and Albert Feuerwerker, pp, 547–608. New York: Cambridge University Press, 1986.

Edelheit, Abraham J. And Hershel Edelheit. *Bibliography on Holocaust Literature*. Boulder: Westview Press, 1990.

Edwards, Stewart. *The Paris Commune 1871*. New York: Quadrangle Books, 1971.

Emin, Ahmed. *Turkey in the World War*. New Haven: Yale University Press, 1930.

Esthus, Raymond A. *Double Eagle and Rising Sun: The Russians and Japanese at Portsmouth in 1905*. Durham: Duke University Press, 1988.

Evans, Michael. "The Facts of Jap Atrocities." *Coronet* (September 1942): pp. 39–43.

Fitch, George A. *My Eighty Years in China*. Taipei, Taiwan: Meiya Publications, 1967.

Franke, Herbert. "Siege and Defense of Towns in Medieval China." In *Chinese Ways in Warfare*, ed. Frank A. Kierman, Jr. and John K. Fairbank, pp. 151–201. Cambridge, MA: Harvard University Press, 1974.

Fuller, J. F. C. *Military History of the Western World*. Vol. 1, *From the Earliest Times to the Battle of Lepanto*. New York: Da Capo Press, 1954.

———. *The Conduct of War 1789–1961: A Study of the Impact of the French, Industrial, and Russian Revolutions on War and Its Conduct*. Westport, CT: Greenwood Press, 1961.

Furuya, Kenji, *Chiang Kai-shek: His Life and Times*, abridged English edition ed. by Chun-ming Chang. New York: St. John's University, 1981.

Gardiner, Samuel Rawson. *The Thirty Years' War, 1618–1648*. London: Longmans, Green, & Co., 1912.

Gibson, Michael Richard. "Chiang Kai-shek's Central Army, 1924–1938." Ph.D. Diss. George Washington University, 1985.

Gilbert, Martin. *The First World War: A Complete History*. New York: Henry Holt, 1994.

Gilbert, Rodney. "The War in China Continues." *Foreign Affairs* (January 1939): pp. 321–35.

Gluck, Carol. "The Rape of Nanking: How 'the Nazi Buddha' Resisted the Japanese." *Times Literary Supplement* (27 June 1997): pp. 9–10.

Goodrich, Thomas. *Bloody Dawn: The Story of the Lawrence Massacre*. Kent, OH: Kent State University Press, 1991.

Gray, Jack. *Rebellions and Revolution: China from the 1800s to the 1980s*. New York: Oxford University Press, 1990.

Grew, Joseph Clark. *Report from Tokyo: A Message to the American People*. New York: Simon and Schuster, 1942.

———. *Ten Years in Japan: A Contemporary Record Drawn from the Diaries and Private and Official Papers of Joseph C. Grew, United States Ambassador to Japan 1932–1942*. New York: Simon and Schuster, 1944.

Haines, C. Groves and Ross J. S. Hoffman. *The Origins and Background of the Second World War*. New York: Oxford University Press, 1943.

Hall, John Whitney. *Japan: From Prehistory to Modern Times*. New York: Delacorte Press, 1970.

Hamilton, V. Lee and Joseph Sanders. *Everyday Justice: Responsibility and the Individual in Japan and the United States*. New Haven: Yale University Press, 1992.

Hanayama, Shinsho. *The Way of Deliverance: Three Years with the Condemned Japanese War Criminals*. Translated by Suzuki Hideo, Noda Eiichi, and James K. Sasaki. New York: Charles Scribner's Sons, 1950.

Hane, Mikiso. *Modern Japan: Historical Survey*. Boulder: Westview Press, 1992.

Harries, Meirion and Susie Harries. *Soldiers of the Sun: The Rise and Fall of the Imperial Japanese Army*. New York: Random House, 1991.

Harwood, Richard E. [Richard Verrall]. *Did Six Million Really Die?: The Truth at Last*. Sussex, England: Historical Review Press, n.d.

Hata, Ikuhiko. "Continental Expansion, 1905–1941." Translated by Alvin D. Coox. In

The Cambridge History of Japan. Vol. 6, *The Twentieth Century*, ed. Peter Duus, pp. 271–314. Cambridge: Cambridge University Press, 1988.

Headquarters, Military Division of the Mississippi. Special Field Order No. 120. In the Field, Kingston, Georgia. 9 November 1864. Quoted in Edgar L. McCormick, Edward G. McGehee, and May Strahl, ed. *Sherman in Georgia: Selected Source Materials for College Research Paper*, p. 65. Boston: D. C. Heath, 1961.

Hill, Rosalind, ed. *Gesta Francorum et aliorum Hierosolimitanorum* [The Deeds of the Franks and the Other pilgrims to Jerusalem]. New York: Thomas Nelson and Sons, 1962.

Hoggan, David L. *The Myth of the Six Million*. 2nd edition. Los Angeles: Noontide Press, 1974.

Holt, Edgar. *The Opium War in China*. Chester Springs, PA: Dufour Editions, 1964.

Horne, Alistair. *The Fall of Paris: The Siege and the Commune 1870–71*. New York: St. Martin's Press, 1965.

Horne, John and Alan Kramer. "German 'Atrocities' and Franco-German Opinion, 1914: The Evidence of German Soldiers' Diaries," *Journal of Modern History*. Vol. 66, No. 1 (March 1994): pp. 1–33.

Horwitz, Solis. "The Tokyo Trial" *International Conciliation* (465) November 1950: pp. 473–584.

Hoyt, Edwin P. *Japan's War: The Great Pacific Conflict 1853 to 1952*. New York: McGraw-Hill Book, 1986.

———. *The Rise of the Chinese Republic: From the Last Emperor to Deng Xiaoping*. New York: McGraw-Hill, 1989.

Hsiung, James C. and Steven I. Levine, ed. *China's Bitter Victory: The War with Japan*. New York: M. E. Sharpe, 1992.

Hunter, MacLean. "Were the Allies Genocidal? Most Historians Dismiss Claims That 9.3 Million Germans Starved to Death." *MacLean's*, 3 November 1997, p. 74.

Jansen, Marius B. *Sakamoto Ryoma and the Meiji Restoration*. Stanford: Stanford University Press, 1971.

Johnson, Ian. "Breaking Silence: Beijing Permits Screening of Nanjing Massacre Film." *Far Eastern Economic Review* (24 August 1995): pp. 40–41.

Kawakami, K. K. *Manchoukuo* [sic]: *Child of Conflict*. New York: Macmillan, 1933.

Keen, Maurice H. *The Laws of War in the Late Middle Ages*. London: Routledge and Kegan Paul, 1965.

Keenan, Joseph B. and Brendan Francis Brown. *Crimes against International Law*. Washington: Public Affairs Press, 1950.

Keneally, Thomas. *Schindler's List*. New York: Simon and Schuster, 1982.

Koginos, Manny T. *The Panay Incident: Prelude to War*. Lafayette, IN: Purdue University Studies, 1967.

Lauer, Thomas L. "German Attempts at Mediation of the Sino-Japanese War, 1937–1938." Ph.D. Diss., Stanford University, 1973.

Legge, James, ed. *The Chinese Classics*. Vol. 1, *Confucian Analects, The Great Learning, The Doctrine of the Mean*. Taipei: SMC Publishing, 1991.

Li, Haibo. "Unforgivable Atrocity." *Beijing Review* (14–20 August 1995): pp. 14–22.

———. "Unforgettable Aggression." *Beijing Review* (21–27 August 1995): pp. 8–15.

Liddell-Hart, Basil. *The Revolution in Warfare*. New Haven: Yale University Press, 1947.

Linderman, Gerald F. *Embattled Courage: The Experience of Combat in the American Civil War*. New York: Macmillan, 1987.

Lipstadt, Deborah E. *Denying the Holocaust: The Growing Assault on Truth and Memory*. New York: Free Press, 1993.

Liu, Frederick Fu. *A Military History of Modern China 1929–1949*. Princeton, NJ: Princeton University Press, 1956; reprint, Westport, CT: Greenwood Press, 1981.

Liu, James T. C. "The Tokyo Trial." *China Monthly*, July 1947: pp. 242–47.

Lone, Steward. *Japan's First Modern War: Army and Society in the Conflict with China 1894–95*. New York: St. Martin, 1994.

Lory, Hillis. *Japan's Military Masters: The Army in Japanese Life*. Westport, CT: Greenwood Press, 1943.

MacKinnon, Stephen R. and Oris Friesen. *China Reporting: An Oral History of American Journalism in the 1930s and 1940s*. Berkeley: University of California Press, 1987.

Malozemoff, Andrew. *Russian Far Eastern Policy, 1881–1904, with Special Emphasis on the Causes of the Russo-Japanese War*. Berkeley: University of California Press, 1958.

March, Francis A. *History of the World War: An Authentic Narrative of the World's Greatest War*. Philadelphia: United Publishers of the United States and Canada, 1919.

Marrus, Michael R. *The Holocaust in History*. Hanover, NH: University Press of New England, 1987.

Maruyama, Masao. *Thought and Behavior in Modern Japanese Politics*, ed. Ivan Morris. New York: Oxford University Press, 1969.

Maurer, Herrymon. *The End Is Not Yet: China at War*. New York: National Travel Club, 1941.

Michael, Franz. *The Taiping Rebellion: History and Documents*. Vol. 1, *History*. Seattle: University of Washington Press, 1966.

———, ed. *The Taiping Rebellion: History and Documents*. Vol. 3, *Documents*. Seattle: University of Washington Press, 1966.

Minear, Richard H. *Victors' Justice: The Tokyo War Crimes Trial*. Princeton, NJ: Princeton University Press, 1971.

Montgomery, Michael. *Imperialist Japan: The Yen to Dominate*. London: Christopher Helm, 1987.

Mosley, Leonard. *Hirohito: Emperor of Japan*. Englewood Cliffs, NJ: Prentice-Hall, 1966.

Mote, Frederick W. "The T'u-mu Incident of 1449." In *Chinese Ways in Warfare*, ed. Kierman and Fairbank, pp. 243–72.

Motley, John Lothrop. *The Rise of the Dutch Republic: A History*. Vol. 2. New York: Harper & Brothers, 1871.

Nevins, Allan. *Ordeal of the Union*. Vol. 8. New York: Scribner's, 1971. Quoted in Thomas Goodrich. *Bloody Dawn: The Story of the Lawrence Massacre*, p. 23. Kent, OH: Kent State University Press, 1991.

Ogata, N. Sadako. *Defiance in Manchuria: The Making of Japanese Foreign Policy, 1931–1932*. Berkeley: University of California Press, 1964.

Okamoto, Shumpei. *The Japanese Oligarchy and the Russo-Japanese War*. New York, Columbia University Press, 1970.

Oliver, Frank. "Three Years of the China War." *Amerasia* 17 (July 1940): pp. 205–12.

Olmstead, A. T. *History of Assyria*. Chicago: University of Chicago Press, 1968.

Parker, Geoffrey. "Early Modern Europe." In *The Laws of War: Constraints on Warfare in the Western World*, ed. Michael Howard, George J. Andreopopulos, and Mark R. Shulman, pp. 40–58. New Haven: Yale University Press, 1994.

Peattie, Mark P. *Ishiwara Kanji and Japan's Confrontation with the West*. Princeton: Princeton University Press, 1975.

Perret, Geoffrey. *Old Soldiers Never Die: The Life of Douglas MacArthur*. New York: Random House, 1996.

Perry, Hamilton Darby. *The Panay Incident: Prelude to Pearl Harbor*. Toronto: Macmillan, 1969.

Peterson, Charles A. "Regional Defense against the Central Power: The Huai-hsi Campaign, 815–817." In *Chinese Ways in Warfare*, ed. Kierman and Fairbank, pp. 123–50.

Piccigalo, Philip R. *The Japanese on Trial: Allied War Crimes Operations in the East, 1945–1951*. Austin: University of Texas Press, 1979.

Prince, Gregory S., Jr. "The American Foreign Service in China, 1935–1941: A Case Study of Political Reporting." Ph.D. Diss., Yale University, 1973.

Quigley, Harold S. *Far Eastern War 1937–41*. Boston: World Peace Foundation, 1942.

Roberts, Adam and Richard Guelff, ed. *Documents on the Laws of War*. 2nd Edition. Oxford: Clarendon Press, 1989.

———. "Land Warfare: From Hague to Nuremberg." In *The Laws of War*, ed. Howard et al, pp. 116–39.

Robinson, John J. *Dungeon, Fire and Sword: The Knights Templar in the Crusades*. New York: M. Evans & Co., 1991.

Rummel, Rudolph J. *China's Bloody Century: Genocide and Mass Murder since 1900*. New Brunswick, NJ: Transaction Publishers, 1991.

Runciman, Steven. *A History of the Crusades*. Vol. 1, *The First Crusade and the Foundation of the Kingdom of Jerusalem*. Cambridge: Cambridge University Press, 1951.

———. *A History of the Crusades*. Vol. 2, *The Kingdom of Jerusalem and the Frankish East 1100–1187*. Cambridge: Cambridge University Press, 1952.

———. *The Fall of Constantinople*. Cambridge: Cambridge University Press, 1965.

Schindler, Emile. *Where Light and Shadow Meet*. Translated from Spanish by Delores M. Koch. New York: W. W. Norton & Co., 1996.

Scott, James Brown, ed. *The Hague Conventions and Declarations of 1899 and 1907*. 3rd Edition. New York: Oxford University Press, 1918.

Scott, Robert N., comp. and ed. *The War of the Rebellion: A Compilation of the Official Records of the Union and Confederate Armies*. Series 1. Vol. 8. Washington, D.C.: U.S. Government Printing Office, 1883.

Seps, Jerry Bernard. "German Military Advisers and Chiang Kai-Shek, 1927–1938." Ph.D. Diss., University of California, Berkeley, 1972.

Shaw, Stanford J. and Ezel Kural Shaw. *History of the Ottoman Empire and Modern Turkey*. Vol. 2, *Reform, Revolution, and Republic: The Rise of Modern Turkey 1808–1975*. Cambridge: Cambridge University Press, 1977.

Simonds, Frank H. *History of the World War*. Vol. 2. New York: Doubleday Page, 1919.

Smedley, Agnes. *Battle Hymn of China*. New York: Random House, 1941.

———. *The Great Road: The Life and Times of Chu Teh*. New York: Monthly Review Press, 1956.

Smythe, Lewis S. C. *War Damage in the Nanking Area December 1937 to March 1938: Urban and Rural Survey*. Shanghai: Mercury Press, 1938.

Snow, Edgar. *The Battle for Asia.* New York: Random House, 1941.

Snow, Lois Wheeler. *Edgar Snow's China: A Personal Account of the Chinese Revolution Compiled from the Writings of Edgar Snow.* New York: Random House, 1981.

Spence, Jonathan D. *The Search for Modern China.* New York: W. W. Norton, 1990.

Stacey, Robert C. "The Age of Chivalry." In *The Laws of War,* ed. Howard et al., pp. 27–39.

Stafford, David. "Case Not Proven." *Times Literary Supplement,* 10 July 1998, p. 29.

Stern, Kenneth S. *Holocaust Denial.* New York: American Jewish Committee, 1993.

Strachan, Hew. "The Morale of the German Army, 1917–18." In *Facing Armageddon: The First World War Experienced,* ed. Hugh Cecil and Peter H. Liddle, pp. 383–98. London: Leo Cooper, 1996.

Sun, Tzu. *The Art of War.* Translated by Thomas Cleary. Boston: Shambhala Publications, 1988.

Sun, Youli. *China and the Origins of the Pacific War, 1931–1941.* New York: St. Martin's Press, 1993.

Timperly, H. J., ed. *Japanese Terror in China.* New York: Modern Age Books, 1938.

Tong, Hollington K. *China and the World Press.* Nanking: n.p., 1948.

Tsei, W. C. "Six Years of China's Resistance to Japanese Aggression." *Free World* (September 1943): pp. 228–31.

Tuchman, Barbara W. "American Experience in China 1911–45, Japan Strikes: 1937." *American Heritage* 22 (December 1970): pp. 5–10, 79–90.

Ulrich, Kevin. "The Other Holocaust." *Los Angeles Readers.* 1 July 1994. Quoted in *Basic Facts on the Nanking Massacre and the Tokyo War Crimes Trial.* http://www.cnd.org:8006/mirror/nanjing/.

Villiers, Frederic. "The Truth about Port Arthur." *North American Review* (March 1895): pp. 325–30.

Webster, Graham. *The Roman Imperial Army of the First and Second Centuries A.D.* Totowa, NJ: Barnes & Noble Books, 1985.

Wedgewood, C. V. *The Thirty Years War.* New Haven: Yale University Press, 1939.

Westwood, J. N. *Russia against Japan, 1904–05: A New Look at the Russo-Japanese War.* Albany: State University of New York Press, 1986.

White, Trumbull. *The War in the East: Japan, China and Corea* [*sic*]. Philadelphia: P. W. Ziegler, 1895.

Willmore, J. Selden. *The Great Crime and Its Moral.* New York: George H. Doran, 1917.

Wilson, Dick. *When Tigers Fight: The Story of the Sino-Japanese War 1937–1945.* New York: The Viking Press, 1982.

Winter, Jay and Blaine Baggett. *The Great War and the Shaping of the 20th Century.* New York: Penguin Studio, 1996.

Yang, Daqing. "Pondering the Meaning of the Nanjing Massacre" In *Abstracts of the 1997 Annual Meeting, March 13–16, 1997,* ed. Association for Asian Studies, pp. 266–67. Ann Arbor, MI: Association for Asian Studies, 1997.

Young, Arthur Morgan. *Imperial Japan, 1926–1938.* Westport, CT.: Greenwood Press, 1974.

Young, Shi and James Yin. *The Rape of Nanking: An Undeniable History in Photographs.* Chicago: Innovative Publishing Group, 1997.

Zich, Arthur. *The Rising Sun.* Alexandria, VA: Time-Life Books, 1977.

————. "Chinese Revolution: 1919–1949, Two Battlefields in the War against Japan." *Eastern Horizon*. Vol. 17, no. 7 (July 1978): pp. 38–43.

SECONDARY SOURCES: (B) FOREIGN LANGUAGES

Abegg, Lilie. "Wie Wir aus Nanking Fluechteten." [How We Escaped from Nanking]. In *Frankfurter Zeitung und Handelsblatt*, 19 December 1937, pp. 1–2. Translated by Suga Hiroo into Japanese: "Nankin Dasshutsu-ki: Shuto Nankin Saigo no Hi" [Escape from Nanking: Last Day of Capital City Nanking]. *Bungeishunju* (February 1938): pp. 250–53.

Ara, Ken'ichi. "Kaku Datta Nankin Daigyakusatsu no Shoko: Nazo no 'Suzendo' to Sono Jittai" [Proven Fictionality of Rape of Nanking Evidence: Mysterious "Ch'ung-shan-t'ang" and Its True Outlook]. *Seiron* [Sound Argument] (October 1985): pp. 166–78.

Boeicho Boei Kenshujo Senshishitsu [Military History Section, Defense Study Institute, Defense Agency], ed. *Senshi Sosho: Shina-Jihen Rikugun Sakusen* [Military History Series: Army's Plannings and Campaigns in the Sino-Japanese War]. Vol. 1. Tokyo: Choun Shinbunsha, 1975.

Chen, Cheng, ed. *Chung-kuo 8-nien K'ang-chan Ching-kuo Kai-yao* [Summary of Eight Years of Resistance War in China]. Taipei, 1946.

Ch'en, I-ting, "Ti-87-shih tsai Nanking Pao-wei-chan Chung" [87th Division in the Defense of Nanking]. In *NP*, pp. 152–58.

Chiang, Kung-yi, "Hsian-ching San-yueh-chi" [Three Months in Fallen Capital]. In *Ch'in-hua Jih-chun Nanking Ta-t'u-sha Shih-liao* [Source Materials Relating to the Horrible Massacre Committed by the Japanese Troops in Nanking in December 1937], ed. "Nanking Ta-t'u-sha" Shih-liao Pian-chi Wei-yuan-hui ["Rape of Nanking" Historical Sources Compilation Committee] and Nanking T'u-shu-kuan [Nanking Library], pp. 60–100. Nanking: Chiangsu Ku-chi Chu-pan-she [Chiangsu Classics Publishing], 1985.

Chiang, Wei-kuo. *Kuo-min Ke-ming Chan-shih Ti-3-pu K'ang-jih Yu-wu* [History of the Chinese Revolutionary War. Part 3. Resistance against Japan]. Vol. 4. Taipei: Li Ming Culture Enterprise, 1978.

Chiangsu Sheng Li-shih Hsueh-hui [Chiangsu Province Historical Society], ed. *K'ang-jih Chan-cheng-shih Shih-so* [Essays on Resistance War against Japan]. Shanghai: Shanghai Ke-hsueh-yuen Ch'u-pan-she [Shanghai Science Academy Publisher]. 1988.

Chou, Chen-ch'ien. "Chiao-tao Chung-tui tsai Nanking Pao-wei-chan Chung" [Training Unit in the Defense of Nanking]. In *NP*, pp. 166–69.

Chou, Erh-fu. *Nanking te Hsian-lo* [Fall of Nanking]. Peking: Jen-min Pan-hsueh-she, 1987.

Dai Ajia Kyokai Soritsu Iin [Founding members of the Great Asian Society]. "Dai Ajia Kyokai Soritsu Shuisho" [Statement of Purpose for the Founding of the Great Asian Society]. In *Matsui Iwane Taisho no Jinchu Nisshi* [Field Diary of General Matsui Iwane], ed. Tanaka Masaaki, pp. 260–63. Tokyo: Fuyo Shobo, 1985.

Fujimura, Michio. *Nisshin Senso* [Sino-Japanese War]. Tokyo: Iwanami Shinsho, 1973.

Fujiwara, Akira. "Nankin Daigyakusatsu to Kyokasho/Kyoiku Mondai" [Rape of Nanking and Textbook/Education Issues]. In *Nankin Jiken o Kangaeru* [Analyses of

Nanking Incident], ed. Hora Tomio, Fujiwara Akira, and Honda Katsuichi, pp. 12–34. Tokyo: Otsuki Shoten, 1987. *(NJK)*

———. "Ima Naze Nankin Jiken na no ka" [Why Rape of Nanking Is an Issue Now]. In *Nankin Daigyakusatsu no Genba e* [Visit to Rape of Nanking Locations], ed. Hora Tomio, Fujiwara Akira, and Honda Katsuichi, pp. 10–31. Tokyo: Asahi Shinbunsha [Asahi Newspaper], 1988. *(NDG)*

———. "Nankin Daigyakusatsu: Senso Bika ni Tsujiru Gyakusatsu Shosuron" [Rape of Nanking: Lower Estimate of Number of Victims Encourages Glorification of War]. *Bijinesu Interijensu* [Business Intelligence] (August 1994): pp. 20–23.

Fujiwara, Shin'ya, ed. *Minna ga Shitteiru: Hyakuman Shina Hakengun ni yoru Chugoku Fujoshi no Junan* [Everybody Knows: Ordeals Suffered by Chinese Women and Children by One-Million Expedition Force to China]. Tokyo: Shun'yodo, 1957, pp. 31–32. Quoted in Honda Katsuichi, *Nankin e no Michi* [Road to Nanking], p. 232. Tokyo: Asahi Shinbunsha [Asahi Newspaper], 1989.

Fukushima Min'yu Shinbunsha [Fukushima Min'yu Newspaper]. *Kyodo-butai Funsen-ki* [Battle Records of Hometown Unit]. Fukushima: Fukushima Min'yu Newspaper, 1964.

Hanayama, Shinsho. *Eien e no Michi: Waga 80-nen no Shogai* [Path to Eternity: My 80-Year Life]. Tokyo: Nihon Kogyo Shinbunsha, 1982.

Hanekura, Shoro. "Watashi no Mita Nankin Kanraku Zengo" [Nanking I Witnessed before and after Its Fall]. *Kaiko* (June 1983): p. 19.

Hara, Takeshi. "Nisshin Senso ni okeru Hondo Boei" [Japanese Defense Plans of the Homeland during the Sino-Japanese War]. *Gunji Shigaku* [Journal of Military History, Japan]. Vol. 20, No. 3 (December 1994): pp. 35–46.

Hasegawa, Shin. *Nihon Horyo-shi* [Prisoner of War History of Japanese People]. Tokyo: Chuo Koron-sha, 1979.

Hata, Ikuhiko. *Nankin Jiken* [Nanking Incident]. Tokyo: Chuo Koron, 1986.

———. "Ronsoshi kara Mita Nankin Jiken" [Rape of Nanking Historiography]. Chap. in *Showashi no Nazo o Ou* [In Pursuit of History Mysteries of Showa Era]. Vol. 1. Tokyo: Bungeishunju, 1993.

———. "Nihon-gun ni okeru Horyo Kan-nen no Keisei" [The Ideas of POWs in the Making: The Case of the Imperial Japanese Army]. *Gunji Shigaku* [Journal of Military History, Japan] 28 (September 1992): pp. 4–23.

Hata, Kensuke. "Horyo no Chi ni Mamireta Byakko Butai" [White Tiger Unit Stained with Blood of POWs]. *Nihon Shuho* [Japan Weekly], 25 February 1957, pp. 13–15.

Hayashi, Kentaro. "Kyokasho Mondai o Kangaeru" [Comment on Textbook Issue]. *Bungeishunju* (October 1986): pp. 94–109.

Hiramatsu, Takashi. *Kyodo Butai Funsenshi* [Battle Records of Hometown Units]. Oita: Oita Godo Shinbunsha [Oita Godo Newspaper], 1983.

Ho, Ying-ch'in. *Chung-kuo Hsian-tai-shih Tzu-liao Ts'ung-shu: Tui-jih K'ang-chan* [China's Modern Historical Materials Series: War against Japan]. Taipei: Wen-hsing Shutien, 1948. Quoted in Tanaka Masaaki. *Nankin Jiken no Sokatsu* [Nanking Incident Summed Up], pp. 204–05. Tokyo: Kenkosha, 1987.

Honda, Katsuichi. *Chugoku no Tabi* [Trip to China]. Tokyo: Asahi Shinbun [Asahi Newspaper], 1972; Suzusawa Shoten, 1977.

———. *Chugoku no Nihongun* [Japanese Military in China]. Tokyo: Sojusha, 1972.

———. *Nankin e no Michi* [Road to Nanking]. Tokyo: Asahi Shinbunsha, 1989.

————. "Nitchu no Futari no Ikishonin" [Two Live Witnesses from Japan and China]. In *NJK*, pp. 35–54.

Honda, Katsuichi and Ono Kenji. "Bakufuyama no Horyo Shudan Gyakusatsu" [Mass Murder of POWs at the Mufu Mountain]. In *Nankin Daigyakusatsu no Kenkyu* [Study of Great Nanking Massacre], ed. Hora Tomio, Fujiwara Akira, and Honda Katsuichi, pp. 128–49. Tokyo: Bansuisha, 1992. *(NDK)*

Hora, Tomio. *Ketteiban: Nankin Daigyakusatsu* [Nanking Massacre: Definitive Version]. Tokyo: Gendaishi Shuppan-kai, 1982.

Hora, Tomio and Watada Susumu. "Kaizan Shita no wa Dare ka: Itakura-shi Hihan" [Who Tampered with Evidence?: Rebuttal to Mr. Itakura's Theory]. In *NDG*, pp. 118–56.

————. "Bakufu-yama no Horyo Shokei ni Kansuru 'Shinsetsu' Hihan: Sayonara Itakura-shi" [Criticism of 'New Theory' Regarding POW Execution at the Mufu Mountain: Farewell to Mr. Itakura]. In *NDK*, pp. 150–96.

Imai, Masatake. "Nankin Jonai no Tairyo Satsujin" [Mass Murder within Nanking Walls]. *Bungeishunju* (December 1956): pp. 154–59.

Imoto, Kumao. *Sakusen Nisshi de Tsuzuru Shina Jihen* [China Incident Chronicled by Operation Diaries]. Tokyo: Fuyo Shobo, 1978.

Inoue, Hisashi. "Itai Maiso kara Mita Nankin Jiken Giseishasu" [Computation of Rape of Nanking Victims Based on Burial Records]. In *NDG*, pp. 50–76.

————. "Nankin Jiken to Chugoku Kyosanto" [Nanking Incident and the Chinese Communist Party]. In *NJK*, pp. 166–80.

Ishihara, Shintaro. "Nihon o Otoshiireta Joho Kukan no Kai" [Mysterious Information Vacuum That Has Haunted Japan]. *Bungeishunju* (September 1991): pp. 94–110.

Ishijima, Noriyuki. "Nankin Jiken o Meguru Aratana Ronsoten" [New Topics in Rape of Nanking Controversy]. In *NJK*, pp. 121–39.

Ishikawa, Tatsuzo. *Ikiteiru Heitai* [Living Soldiers]. Tokyo: Kawade Shobo, 1945.

Itakura, Yoshiaki. "Matsui Iwane Nikki no Kaizan ni Tsuite" [Regarding the Tampering of Matsui Iwane's Diary]. *Bungeishunju* (January 1986): pp. 186–94.

————. "Koo Shite Tsukurareta 'Nankin Daigyakusatsu': Shimosato Masaki cho 'Kakusareta Rentai-shi' Hihan" [How "Rape of Nanking" was fabricated: Critical Review of Shimosato Masaki, *Hidden Regimental History*]. *Seiron* [Sound Argument]. (April 1988): pp. 194–205.

————. " 'Nankin Gyakusatsu' no Zange-ya 'Sone Kazuo' no Shotai" [True Face of Sone Kazuo, Professional Penitent of the 'Rape of Nanking']. *Shokun!* [Comrades!]. (December 1988): pp. 126–46.

————. "Nankin Daigyakusatsu: Gyakusatsu wa seizei 1–2 man-nin" [The Rape of Nanking: Number of Victims Totals 10,000 to 20,000 at Largest]. *Bijinesu Interijensu* [Business Intelligence] (August 1994): pp. 16–19.

————. "Nanking Jiken: Gyakusatsu no Sekininron" [The Nanking Massacre and the Issue of Responsibility]. *Gunji Shigaku* [Journal of Military History, Japan] 33 (December 1997): pp. 182–96.

Itakura, Yoshiaki and Tanaka Masaaki. "Nankin Gyakusatsu Sansen-sha no Shogen" [Testimonies by Participants in the Nanking Campaign]. *Bungeishunju* (December 1984): pp. 214–36.

Kabashima, Yuzo. "'Shinpen Nihon-shi o Osotta Gaiatsu to Naiatsu" [Foreign and Domestic Pressure Exerted on 'Newly Compiled Japanese History']. *Bungeishunju* (September 1986): pp. 148–61.

Kaiko Henshubu [Editing Staff of *Kaiko* Magazine]. "Iwayuru 'Nankin Jiken' ni Kansuru Joho Teikyo no Onegai" [Call for Information about So-Called 'Nanking Incident']. *Kaiko* (November 1983): pp. 35–37.

Kaikosha, ed. *Nankin Senshi* [Nanking Campaign Chronology]. Tokyo: Kaikosha, 1989.

Kasahara, Tokushi, "Nankin Boeigun no Hokai kara Gyakusatsu made" [From the Collapse of Nanking Garrison to Massacre]. In *NDG*, pp. 77–117.

———. "Nankin Boeisen to Chugokugun." [Nanking Siege and Chinese Force]. In *NDK*, pp. 214–328.

Katogawa, Kotaro. "Shogen ni yoru Nankin Senshi: Sono Sokatsuteki Kosatsu" [Nanking Campaign Chronology Based on Eyewitness Accounts: Concluding Remark]. *Kaiko* (March 1985): pp. 9–18.

Kimura, Kuninori. *Koseiha Shogun Nakajima Kesago* [Nakajima Kesago: A General of Unique Personality]. Tokyo: Kojinsha, 1987.

Kobayashi, Masao, ed. *Sakigake: Kyodo Butai Senki* [Harbingers: Records of Hometown Units]. Ise: Ise Shinbunsha, 1984.

Kojima, Noboru. *Oyama Iwao* [Biography of Oyama Iwao]. Vols 3–4. Tokyo: Bungeishunju, 1985.

———. *Nitchu Senso* [Sino-Japanese War]. Vols. 2–5. Tokyo: Bungeishunju, 1988.

Komori, Yoshihisa. "Nanki Jiken o Sekai ni Shiraseta Otoko" [A Man Who Reported the Nanking Atrocities to the World]. *Bungeishunju* (October 1989): pp. 174–82.

Kumamoto Heidan Senshi Hensan Iinkai [Compilation Committee of Kumamoto Division's Battle Record], ed. *Kumamoto Heidan Senshi* [History of Kumamoto Division]. Kumamoto: Kumamoto Nichinichi Shinbunsha, 1965. Quoted in *NS*, pp. 134–35.

Kuo-fang-pu Shih-cheng Chu [History Section, Defense Department, Republic of China], ed. *K'ang-chan Chien-shih* [Short History of Resistance War]. Taipei: Defense Department's History Section, 1952.

———. *Chung-jih Chan-chen-shih Lueh* [Brief History of War between China and Japan]. Taipei: Defense Department's History Section, 1962.

Kuroda, Hidetoshi. *Nankin, Hiroshima, Aushubittsu* [Nanking, Hiroshima, and Auschwitz]. Tokyo: Taihei Shuppansha, 1974.

Li, Hsi-k'ai. "Tzuchin-shan Chan-tou" [Battle of Tzuchin Mountain]. In *NP*, pp. 170–75.

Li, Tsun-jen and Te-kong Tong. *The Memoirs of Li Tsung-jen*. Boulder, CO: Westview Press, 1979.

Liu, Fei. "K'ang-chan Ch'u-ch'i te Nanking Pao-wei-chan" [Defense of Nanking in the Early Phase of Resistance of War]. In *NP*, pp. 6–13.

Lu, Wei-san. "Ti-88-shih E-shou Yuhuatai Chunghua-men P'ian-tuan" [An Episode in 88th Division's Defense in Yuhuatai and Chunghua-men]. In *NP*, pp. 164–65.

Long, A. *Nanking Tung-k'u* [Nanking Wails]. Translated by Sekine Ken into Japanese. Tokyo: Satsuki Shobo, 1994.

Maeda, Yuji. "Shanhai-sen kara Nankin Koryaku e" [Battle of Shanghai through Capture of Nanking]. In *Showa no Senso: Jaanarisuto no Shogen* [Wars in Showa Era: Accounts by Journalists], ed. Matsumoto Shigeharu. Vol. 1, *Nitchu Senso* [Sino-Japanese War], pp. 95–125. Tokyo: Kodansha, 1986.

Matsuda, Kuro; Kamei Shizuka, and Hiranuma Takeo. "Chugoku ni Namerarete Tamaruka" [We Will Not Be Humiliated by China]. *Bungeishunju* (September 1987): pp. 124–34.

Matsumoto, Shigeharu. *Shanhai Jidai* [Shanghai Era]. Vol. 3. Tokyo: Chuko Shinsho, 1974.

Min'yu-sha. *Nisshin Gunki* [Soldiers' Stories of Sino-Japanese War]. Vol. 1. Tokyo: Min'yu-sha, 1894. Quoted in Otani Tadashi. "Ryojun Gyakusatsu Jiken no Ichi Kosatsu" [An Analysis of Port Arthur Massacre], pp. 266–67. *Senshu Hogaku Ronshu* [Journal of Senshu University Law School] 45 (March 1987): pp. 215–96.

Miyabe, Kazumi. *Fuu-un Nankinjo* [Battle of Nanking Walls]. Tokyo: Sobunsha, 1983.

Miyakonojo Hohei Dai-23-rentai Senki Henshu Iinkai [Compilation Committee of Miyakonojo 23rd Infantry Regiment's Battle Record]. *Miyakonojo Hohei Dai-23rentai Senki* [Battle Record of Miyakonojo 23rd Infantry Regiment]. Miyazaki: Miyakonojo Hohei Dai-23-rentai Senki Henshu Iinkai [Compilation Committee of Miyakonojo 23rd Infantry Regiment's Battle Record], 1978.

Noguchi, Toshio *Nara Rentai Senki* [Battle Stories of Nara (38th) Regiment]. Nara: Yamato Times, 1963.

Nomura, Toshinori. "Watashi no Nankin-Sen" [Nanking Campaign I Took Part in]. *Kaiko* (May 1983): pp. 4–5.

Ochiai, Nobuhiko. *Mezamenu Hitsuji-tachi* [Unawakened Sheep]. Tokyo: Shogakkan, 1995.

Ogasawara, Kiyoshi. "Ima koso Akasu 'Nankin Daigyakusatsu' no Shinso" [Truth of Nanking Massacre Revealed Today]. *Shukan Sankei* [Sankei Weekly] (16 August 1971): pp. 49–63.

Okabe, Makio, comp. "Ichi Heishi no Mita Nisshin Senso: Kubota Chuzo no Jugun Nikki" [Sino-Japanese War Witnessed by A Soldier: Field Diary of Kubota Chuzo]. *Sobun* 126 (November 1974). Quoted in Okamoto Shumpei. *Impressions of the Front: Woodcuts of the Sino-Japanese War, 1894–95*, p. 37. Philadelphia: Philadelphia Museum of Art, 1983.

Okuno, Seisuke. " 'Shinryaku Hatsugen' Doko ga Warui!?" [What is Wrong about My Remark about 'Invasion'!?]. *Bungeishunju* (July 1988): pp. 112–26.

Onishi, Hajime. "Nankin Daigyakusatsu no Shinso" [Truth about Great Nanking Massacre]. *Kaiko* (February 1983): pp. 3–4.

Otani Tadashi. "Ryojun Gyakusatsu Jiken no Ichi Kosatsu" [An Analysis of Port Arthur Massacre]. *Senshu Daigaku Hogaku Ronshu* [Journal of the Senshu University Law School] 45 (March 1987): pp. 215–96.

P'eng, Yueh-hsiang. "Ts'ung Chian-shou Chen-ti tao Pei-ch'e Ch'ang-chiang" [From Defense of Fort till Retreat to North across Yangtze]. In *NP*, pp. 176–79.

Roeling, Bernard and Kojima Noboru. "Tokyo Saiban wa Nani o Sabaita ka" [Reflection on the Judgement at the Tokyo War Crimes Trials]. *Bungeishunju* (July 1983): pp. 164–173.

Sakamoto, Chikashi. "Iwayuru Nankin Daigyakusatsu ni Tsuite" [Comment on So-called Great Nanking Massacre]. *Kaiko* (December 1982): pp. 3–4.

Sankei Shimbun Shizuoka Shikyoku [Sankei Newspaper Shizuoka Branch], ed. *Aa Shizuoka 34-rentai: Fusa dake no Gunki to Tomoni* [34th Regiment in Shizoka: With Regimental Color of Only Tassel]. Shizuoka: Fuji Pr Pro, 1963.

Sasaki, Motokatsu. *Yasen Yubin-ki* [Memoirs of Field Post Office Chief]. Vol. 1. Tokyo: Gendaishi Shiryo Sentaa Shuppankai [Modern History Source Material Publishing Center], 1973.

Sato, Shinju. "Jugun to wa Aruku Koto" [War Correspondent Must Walk]. In *NSS*2, pp. 495–641.

Shimono, Ikkaku. *Nankin Sakusen no Shinso: Kumamoto Dai-6-shidan Senki* [Truth of Nanking Campaign: Battle Record of Kumamoto 6th Division]. Tokyo: Tokyo Johosha, 1966.

Sumitani, Iwane. "Memoir of Sumitani Iwane." Originally printed in *Togo* (December 1983). Quoted in "SNS" (10), *Kaiko* (January 1985), pp. 31–32.

Sung, Hsi-lian, "Nanking Shou-ch'eng-chan" [Siege Defense of Nanking], in *NP*, pp. 228–39.

Sun, Chai-wei, "Nanking Pao-wei-chan Shuang-fang Ping-li te Yen-chiu" [Estimated Force Strength of Two Sides in Nanking Battle]. In *K'ang-jih Chan-cheng-shih Shih-so* [Essays on Resistance War against Japan], ed. Chiangsu Sheng Li-shih Hsueh-hui [Chiangsu Province Historical Society], pp. 115–28. Shanghai: Shanghai Ke-hsueh-yuen Ch'u-pan-she [Shanghai Science Academy Publisher], 1988.

Suzuki, Akira. *"Nankin Daigyakusatsu" no Maboroshi* [Illusion of the "Rape of Nanking"]. Tokyo: Bungeishunju, 1973.

———. "Haikei 'Jinmin Nippo' Henshu-cho-dono." [Dear Editor-in-Chief of 'People's Daily']. *Bungeishunju* (October 1982): pp. 94–101.

Takada, Norifumi. "Watashi no Mita Nakajima Kenpei Shireikan" [Military Police Chief Nakajima in My Eyes]. Quoted in Kimura Kuninori, *Koseiha Shogun Nakajima Kesago* [Nakajima Kesago: A General of Unique Personality], pp. 183–84. Tokyo: Kojinsha, 1987.

Takagi, Sokichi. *Jidenteki Nihon Kaigun Shimatsuki* [Autobiographical Chronicle of the Imperial Japanese Navy]. Tokyo: Kojinsha, 1979.

Takasaki, Ryuji. "Kabushiki Gaisha Bungeishunju no Sensochu to Genzai to o Kangaeru" [Critical Review of Bungeishunju Corporation's Wartime and Today's Activities]. In *NJK*, pp. 201–23.

Takahashi, Toshiro. "Nankin Senshi no Sokatsuteki Kosatsu ni Hantai Sareta Kata e no Okotae" [Response to Those Who Disagreed to the Summation of Nanking Campaign Chronology Series]. *Kaiko* (May 1985): pp. 9–11.

T'an, Tao-p'ing. "Nanking Wei-shu-chan" [Garrison War at Nanking]. In *NP*, pp. 14–32.

Tanaka, Masaaki. *Nankin Gyakusatsu no Kyoko* [Rape of Nanking as a Fiction]. Tokyo: Nihon Kyobun-sha, 1984.

———. "Asahi Shinbun ni Kyohi-sareta Go-tsu no Hanron" [Five Rebuttal Opinions the Asahi Newspaper Refused to Print]. *Bungeishunju* (October 1984): pp. 286–306.

——— ed. *Matsui Iwane Taisho no Jinchu Nisshi* [Field Diary of General Matsui Iwane]. Tokyo: Fuyo Shobo, 1985.

———. *Nankin Jiken no Sokatsu* [Nanking Incident Summed Up]. Tokyo: Kenko-sha, 1987.

T'ang, Sheng-chih. "Wei-shu Nanking Chih Ching-wei" [How Nanking was Defended]. In *NP*, pp. 1–5.

Terasaki, Hidenari, ed. "Showa Tenno no Dokuhaku 8-jikan: Taiheiyo Senso no Zenbo o Kataru" [Emperor Hirohito's 8-Hour Monologue about Japan's War in the Pacific]. *Bungeishunju* (December 1990): pp. 96–145.

Tsuchiya, Masaharu. "Mokka Shite Yoi no ka Nankin Daigyakusatsu no Hodo" [Can We Overlook the Reporting of the Rape of Nanking?]. *Kaiko* (March 1983): pp. 3–4.

Ukai, Toshisada. "Asahi Shinbun 'Dokugasu Shashin' Goyo-jiken" [Photo Miscaptioned by Asahi Newspaper as Japanese Army's Poisonous Gas Operation]. *Bungeishunju* (February 1985): pp. 180–93.

Unemoto, Masami. " 'Nankin Daigyakusatsu' no Shinso wa?: Senjo no Taikendan o Motomu" [What is the Truth of Rape of Nanking?: Call for Eyewitness Accounts on the Field]. *Kaiko* (May 1983): p. 5.

———. ed. "Shogen ni yoru 'Nankin Senshi' " ["Nanking Campaign Chronology" Based on Eyewitness Accounts] (1)–(12), extra. *Kaiko* (April 1984–March 1985, May 1985).

Wang, Yao-wu. "Ti-74-chun Ts'an-chia Nanking Pao-wei-chan Ching-kuo" [Story of the 74th Army in the Defense of Nanking]. In *NP*, pp. 141–47.

Wei, Shih-ch'en. "Hu-wei T'uan-ch'i T'ui-ch'u Nanking" [Retreat from Nanking with Regimental Color]. In *NP*, pp. 159–63.

Yamamoto, Isamu. *Nankin, Joshu, Bukan-sanchin: Omoide no Shingun* [Nanking, Hsuchou, Wuhan-san-chen: March in My Memory]. Gifu: San-9 Sen'yukai Ji-musho [Ninth Artillery Regiment Veteran's Association], 1973.

Yamamoto, Shichihei. *Watashi no Naka no Nihongun* [Japanese Military within Myself]. Vols. 1 and 2. Tokyo: Bungeishunju, 1983.

Yoshida, Yutaka. *Tenno no Guntai to Nankin Jiken: Moo Hitotsu no Nitchu Sensoshi* [Emperor's Military and the Nanking Incident: Another History of Sino-Japanese War]. Tokyo: Aoki Shoten, 1986.

———. "15-nen Sensoshi Kenkyu to Senso Sekinin Mondai: Nankin Jiken o Chushin ni" [Academic and War Responsibility Issues Concerning 15-Year War, Nanking Incident in Particular]. In *NJK*, pp. 69–94.

———. "Nankin Jiken to Kokusaiho" [Nanking Incident and International Law]. In *NDK*, pp. 95–125.

"An-non naru Goke Seikatsu Kan-yo Nari: Fumiko Fujin e no Isho" [Live Quiet Life of Widow: Matsui's Will to His Wife Fumiko]. *Nihon Shuho* [Japan Weekly], 25 February 1957, pp. 10–12.

" 'Nankin Daigyakusatsu' no Kakushin" [Heart of 'Rape of Nanking' Controversy]. An article summarizing a roundtable discussion chaired by Hando Kazutoshi among Hora Tomio, Hata Ikuhiko, Suzuki Akira, and Tanaka Masaaki. *Shokun!* [Comrades!] (April 1985): pp. 68–87.

NEWSPAPERS AND MAGAZINES

Asahi Shinbun [Asahi Newspaper]
Atlanta Journal
Chicago Daily News
Chicago Daily Tribune
China Weekly Review
Chung-yang Jih-pao [Central Daily News]
Frankfurter Zeitung und Handelsblatt
Free China Journal
Getsuyo Hyoron [Monday Commentary]
Hsin-hua Jih-pao [New China Daily]
Hankow Chung-hsi-pao [Hankow Midwestern Times]. In *HP*, p. 167.

International Golden Rule Fellowship
Japan Times
Japan Times Weekly
Jen-min Rih-pao [People's Daily]
Life
Look
Los Angeles Times
Mainichi Shinbun [Mainichi Newspaper]
Manchester Guardian
New York Times
New York World
Newsweek
North China Daily News. Quoted in Gauss to the Secretary of State. "Editorials from local English Language Newspapers during December 1937." 7 February 1938. M976–51. 793.94/12679. In Gauss to the Secretary of State. "Summary of Editorial Comments in English Language Newspapers of Shanghai during the month of January 1938." 1 March 1938. 793.94/12750. M976–52.
Seattle Post Intelligence.
Shanghai Evening Post and Mercury. Quoted in Gauss to the Secretary of State. "Summary of Editorial Comments in English Language Newspapers of Shanghai during the Month of January 1938." 1 March 1938. 793.94/12750. M976–52.
Time
Times (London)
Tokyo Nichinichi Shinbun [Tokyo Nichinichi Newspaper]. Quoted in Otani Tadashi, "Ryojun Gyakusatsu Jiken no Ichi Kosatsu" [An Analysis of Port Arthur Massacre], p. 270. Quoted in Kuroda Hidetoshi, *Nankin, Hiroshima, Aushubittsu* [Nanking, Hiroshima, and Auschwitz] (Tokyo: Taihei Shuppansha, 1974), pp. 80–81.
Washington Post

VIDEOS, INTERNET WEB SITES, AND OTHER SOURCES (ALL WEB PAGE ADDRESSES ARE THOSE AVAILABLE AT THE TIME OF RESEARCH)

One of the organizers of Princeton University's Rape of Nanking 60th anniversary commemorative event to Yamamoto Masahiro, 14 October 1997. E-mail transmission. Re: conference on Nanking Massacre.

Wang, Peter. *Magee's Testament*. Alliance in Memory of Victims of Nanjing Massacre, 1991.

Alliance for Preserving the Truth of Sino-Japanese War. http://www.cnd.org:8008/NJMassacre/aptsjw.htm.

Basic Facts on the Nanking Massacre and the Tokyo War Crimes Trial. http://www.cnd.org:8006/mirror/nanjing/.

"History Undercover: The Rape of Nanking." The History Channel. 22 August 1999.

Commemorating the 60th Anniversary of the Nanking Massacre. http://www.princeton.edu./~nanking.

Greg Raven's Web Site for Revisionist Materials from the Institute for Historical Review (and elsewhere). http://www.kaiwan.com/~ihrgreg/ihr/jhr/.

Home Page of the Committee for Open Discussion of the Holocaust Story. http:www. codoh.com/trials/trijapan.html.

The Chinese Alliance for Commemoration of the Sino-Japanese War Victims. http:// hk.super.net/~csjwv.html.

The Chinese Alliance for Memorial and Justice. http://www.hk.super.net/~csjwv/ CAMAJ-QA.html

The Zundelsite: "Did Six Million Really Die?" http://www.webcom.com/ezundel/.

Tokyo Kalaidoscoop. "The Decision of dropping the A-bomb in 1945 was right?" http:// www.smn.co.jp/square/bomb.html.

Index

About the Author

MASAHIRO YAMAMOTO is currently a Visiting Assistant Professor of Asian Studies at Randolph-Macon College in Ashland, Virginia. His specialty is military and naval history as well as Japanese History. He also teaches Japanese language.